ARCHIVES O

EDITED BY BARBARA HARL... ...D MIA CARTER

ARCHIVES OF EMPIRE
VOLUME II · THE SCRAMBLE
FOR AFRICA

EDITED BY BARBARA HARLOW WITH MIA CARTER

Duke University Press   *Durham and London*   2003

©2003 Duke University Press   All rights reserved
Printed in the United States of America on acid-free paper ∞
Designed by Mary Mendell
Typeset in Caslon by Keystone Typesetting, Inc.
Library of Congress Cataloging-in-Publication Data
appear on the last printed page of this book.

FOR E3W COMRADES AND COLLEAGUES

AND

EDWARD W. SAID

IN MEMORIAM

CONTENTS

II. THE BODY POLITIC: RATIONALIZING RACE

III. THE POLITICAL CORPS

ACKNOWLEDGMENTS

ANY PEOPLE AT THE University of Texas at Austin, in other universities across the country, and on at least two additional continents have expressed ongoing interest in and support for *Archives of Empire.* We have spent several years collecting material and sharing presentations of the work-in-progress. The earlier, one-volume edition, *Imperialism and Orientalism: A Documentary Sourcebook,* was published by Blackwell in 1999, having been first envisioned by Blackwell's then-editor Simon Prosser, then produced with the support of Simon Eckley and the talented assistance of our copy editor, Helen Rappaport.

We presently have Ken Wissoker of Duke University Press to thank for supporting and contracting an even larger and more ambitious project than that Blackwell reader. Ken's daring is something to marvel at, and we thank him vociferously for his commitment and support. Some of the materials presented herein were literally disintegrating on the library shelves, but the General Libraries of the University of Texas at Austin and their unfailingly collaborative staff continue to make possible preservation and innovation, all in the interest of the libraries, their resources, and—no less important—their patrons. Their work enables all of us. Thank you, also, to the production staff of Duke University Press. We well know what kind of effort it takes to make a mountain of xeroxed material into an attractive and user-friendly product. Thank you for hanging in there with this one! We would also like to thank Duke's outside reviewers who, somehow, managed to work through and read enthusiastically a very massive package of materials. We thank each of you for the time and energy you contributed to this project; your thoughtful remarks and suggestions were highly appreciated.

Finally, and perhaps most important of all, we would like to thank the students in the University of Texas's ethnic and third-world literatures concentration in the department of English. *Archives of Empire* has been a shared labor. Thank you for being creative and critical historiographers, wonderful cheerleaders, and partners in collecting. Mia would especially like to thank her research assistant and friend, Miriam Murtuza: Miriam, you amaze me. Thank you for constantly replenishing energy, meticulous work, critical acumen, generosity, and good company. It has been, as always, an honor to work with you. And Barbara salutes the unflagging contributions of Eve Dunbar, her research assistant, who saw new ideas in old materials, even as she sorted through the reams and realms of documentary histories and paper trails of race and empire. Bravo! The talented cartographer Maria Lane created our maps. Thank you, Maria, for sharing your gifts. And thanks to Terry Gregston and Alan Smith of u.t.'s Photographic Services Center (cookies and brownies represent a mere morsel of our gratitude). Mia would also like to thank her family for being zany, life-affirming, unceasingly supportive, and kind. And Mia thanks Barbara too, for being a comrade, a mentor, family member, and true friend. Additionally, Barbara acknowledges gratefully the support of Louann and Larry Temple whose generous endowments to the study of English literature made much of our effort possible. And then there's Mia: what can Barbara say, except that this project—and so much else— couldn't have been done without you. So there! Finally, Mia and Barbara want to thank the talented, patient, and especially generous production team at Duke; they inherited a hulking, unruly leviathan and transformed it into an elegant volume. Thanks to Fiona Morgan, Leigh Anne Couch, the typesetters, designer Mary Mendell, and special thanks to our amazing copy-editor, Patricia Mickelberry.

GENERAL INTRODUCTION
Readings in Imperialism and Orientalism
BARBARA HARLOW AND MIA CARTER

ARCHIVES OF EMPIRE is a four-volume collection of original documents and primary source materials relating to the varied processes and various procedures of the colonial project. Ranging from East India Company charters to Cecil Rhodes's "last will and testament," and including such disparate but historically related artifacts as Salvation Army hymns, missionary tracts, parliamentary debates, adventurers' accounts, administrators' account books, satirical cartoons, popular appeals, and legislative records, the four volumes both provide critical research and teaching resources for students of empire and propose new directions for current inquiries into late-twentieth-century consequences of nineteenth-century imperialism.

Each volume of *Archives of Empire* emphasizes a particular period and its place in the history of British imperialism: *Volume 1: From the Company to the Canal; Volume 2: The Scramble for Africa; Volume 3: The Great Game;* and *Volume 4: Jubilee. From the Company to the Canal* covers the first half of the nineteenth century and British engagements in the Indian subcontinent and in Egypt, from the East India Company's exploits, to its handover to the Crown following the Sepoy Uprising in 1857–1858, to the opening of the Suez Canal in 1869. The opening of the Suez Canal radically altered British relations with its colonial reaches; by shortening the distance—for transportation, commerce, and communication—between England and its representatives in India, the canal significantly transformed British interests along the coast of Africa, in particular in southern Africa. *The Scramble for Africa* concentrates on the European contest over that continent, its peoples, and its resources, particularly following the Berlin Conference of 1885 and the ensuing crises in Khartoum, in the Congo, and during the Anglo-Boer War. India, in its turn, was both the "jewel in the crown" of Victoria and a part of the board on which the "great game"—or the struggle over central Asia—was to be played out. *The Great Game* focuses on that game, its rules, its players, and the larger gameboard from the Crimea to and through the Afghan passes. *Jubilee* examines the beginnings, means, and ends of empire as these conjunctures were staged "at home," in Queen Victoria's England, by schoolboys and scouts, by suffragettes, in the streets, and in the reviews and popular periodicals as well as in parliamentary debates.

Rather than celebrating the riches of empire, however, *Archives of Empire* instead emphasizes, through its sampling of imperialism's documentary history, the richness of the substantial critical resources and the substantive grounds for the critique of imperialism. The volumes thus suggest as well that the imperial project was by no means an uncontested or unargued enterprise, but a much-debated one, even among its putative participants and apparent adherents—between Jonesian orientalists and Macauleyan anglicists, between "patriots" and "pro-Boers." Those sympathetic to the independence-oriented causes of Tipu Sultan in Mysore or Arabi in Egypt argued with strict upholders of imperial law and order. Figures like Florence Nightingale battled against the generals in the Crimea, and Emily Hobhouse passionately called her audience's attention to the dreadful conditions of concentration camps in South Africa. Rescue missions and reforms also highlighted fractures and divisions: Should "Chinese" Gordon be rescued in the Sudan? Could the Indian civil service be revised and reorganized? How to halt atrocities and reform King Leopold's Congo?

In order to draw out such controversies, the four volumes of *Archives of Empire* follow several themes, in particular political economy, parliamentary debate, and popular culture. The issue of political economy, for example, can be traced through the history of charter companies, from the East India Company to the Suez Canal and British South African companies, and through disputes over free trade between jingoists and "little Englanders." Such debates were heard in the houses of Parliament, recorded in Hansard's and in Blue Books, disputed in journals such as the *Pall Mall Gazette* or the *Review of Reviews,* and caricatured in periodicals such as *Punch.* Missionaries supported imperial designs and protested them, explorers traversed and mapped imperial territories and encouraged others to follow in their footsteps, while bureaucrats and businessmen pursued their own interests; such observations, memoirs, and narratives also appear in these volumes. The writers of that time lived in the present moment and observed, by practice, by accident or, increasingly, by means of graphic and photographic representation, the cultural, political, and social changes that expansionism effected at home and abroad. Literary authors like Charles Dickens and Jules Verne, popular authors like G. A. Henty (writer of boys' adventure novels), and everyday citizens like Flora Annie Steel (wife of a British civil servant stationed in India) recorded the changing times and allowed their imaginations to be inspired or inflamed by travel accounts, news of sensational "discoveries" or spectacular colonial crises. The literatures of that time reflect these firsthand experiences or secondhand representational encounters with "native" peoples and lands. The culture of imperialism and colonialism were widespread and all encompassing. Sciences, political and governmental theories, and entertainment cultures were equally influenced by colonial trade, imperial exploration, and the material exploitation of foreign lands. Nineteenth-century forms of entertainment included the popular lecture circuit, with travelers like Henry M. Stanley and Mary Kingsley able to fill the house. Architectural innovations were designed to display colonial goods, both human and material; for example, the Crystal Palace was designed to showcase the products, collections, and inventions of both industry and empire. Indian-style bungalows were soon incorporated into the British landscape, and British fashion and cuisine were forever altered by colonial spices and fabrics. Among empire's principal practitioners were men such as Robert Clive, Frederick Lugard, Cecil Rhodes, Benjamin Disraeli, and Gladstone, who envisioned the details. What were their shared interests? What were their dramatic differences?

While designed according to the historical specificities and the archival resources of the period, each volume of *Archives of Empire* attempts to address and highlight specific conflicts and crises so as to be useful in its own right but also to complement the other volumes in order to display the continuities, consistencies, and discordances of imperialism. Each individual volume is introduced by an editorial preface that lays out the features of the period, its major personnel, and the debates that accompanied the pursuit of empire there and then. Each volume is then organized into sections that are amply illustrated and preceded by brief introductions, with bibliographies, filmographies, maps, and chronologies included where appropriate, in order to enhance the pedagogical usefulness of the volumes and to offer suggestions for further investigation and research projects.

Archives of Empire builds on the single-volume documentary sourcebook *Imperialism and Orientalism* (Blackwell, 1999) but is significantly different, both in its expansion of the material bases of the archival register of the resources and in its organization into four distinct volumes. While coherent as a series, these volumes are also individually useful for pedagogical and scholarly use according to time and place: the early nineteenth century, the latter half of the nineteenth century, the Indian subcontinent, the African continent, and Great Britain itself. We hope that, as a set and each volume in turn, *Archives of Empire* will be of considerable interest and continuing usefulness to students, teachers, researchers, and readers of the imperial narrative.

ARCHIVES OF EMPIRE

VOLUME INTRODUCTION
The Scramble for Africa
BARBARA HARLOW

FROM THE CAPE TO CAIRO/FROM THE CAPE TO CALCUTTA

CONVENED IN LATE 1884 and concluded in February of the following year, the Berlin Conference, which had been summoned by Germany's Prince Bismarck, sought to color in the map of what was commonly known as the "dark continent." According to the General Act of the Berlin Conference, Africa was to be partitioned among five primary European national contestants—Britain, France, Germany, Portugal, and Italy—and King Leopold II of Belgium. The project to partition the continent and portion it out nonetheless did little more than sanction the ongoing "scramble for Africa." According to Sir Frederick Lugard, writing in 1922, "When, however, the 'scramble for Africa' followed the Berlin Act of 1885, the popular demand that Britain, as the foremost colonizing Power, should not be backward in claiming her share was irresistible, and it was due to this popular demand to 'peg out claims for futurity'—however little their value was understood at the time—that we owe our African Empire of today. It was, moreover, felt that whatever value our existing tropical possessions might have, would be lost if other nations with exclusive tariffs appropriated their hinterlands" (*Dual Mandate*, 12). Joseph Conrad's Marlow had also noted in 1898 those European hues swatched across the map of Africa in a company office's anteroom in Brussels: "There was a vast amount of red," Marlow observed, "good to see at any time, because one knows that some real work is done there, a deuce of a lot of blue, a little green, smears of orange, and, on the East Coast, a purple patch, to show where the jolly pioneers drink the jolly lager-beer" (*Heart of Darkness*, 13).

Although the cape at the southern tip of Africa had lost much of its significance for Britain's route to the Indian subcontinent with the opening of the Suez Canal in 1869, it found renewed importance with the discovery of diamonds in 1867 in Kimberley and gold in 1884 on the Witwatersrand. Meanwhile, East Africa loomed larger as a strategic holding to secure the transit of vessels through the canal and into the Red Sea. It was, however, Cecil John Rhodes, the British mining magnate and eventual scholarship endower who had made his personal fortune from the gold and diamonds dug from the ground of southern Africa, who dreamed of coloring the continent entirely in red, the red of British imperial ambition, which was, according to Rhodes's expansionist vision, to extend from the "Cape to Cairo" and secure the passages and thoroughfares across the empire's reaches—from the "Cape to Calcutta."

The scramble for Africa enacted as unseemly and motley a set of conflicts as the numbered paragraphs and articles of the Berlin Act attempted to draft a decorous and stately document, curtailing the concupiscence and spoilage of the European rivals for the continent and its resources. The British vied with the French over Egypt and other portions of sub-Saharan Africa and with the Germans over east and South-West Africa, and all three nations eventually challenged King Leopold's autocratic dominion in his Congo Free State. Each of the European powers, meanwhile, had to face resistance from the Africans themselves as well as the recalcitrance of their critics at home. Mottled as the scramble was, it was also fought in white and black. The Anglo-Zulu Wars in 1879, for example, saw the eventual defeat of the Zulu warriors by British troops, and the Arabi nationalist uprising in Egypt was contained in 1882 and its leader exiled to Ceylon. But the British would in 1899 fight the last of their colonial wars—a "white man's war," according to Boy Scout founder Robert Baden-Powell—against the Boer settlers in southern Africa, Horatio Kitchener having routed the Sudanese Mahdist forces at Omdurman the year before. In other words, Africa was won for and by Europe not only through David Livingstone's "3 Cs"—commerce, Christianity, and civilization—but by a fourth C as well: conquest.

Each of these colonizing proceedings, however, was the subject of vociferous debate in the metropolis as well, from the antislavery movement at the beginning of the century to that movement's continuation in the Aborigines Protection Society to the antiwar/pro-Boer protestations at century's end. Meanwhile the free traders confronted the protectionists—the "little Englanders"—over competing commercial interests, while entrepreneurs lobbied Parliament for royal charters for their companies and missionaries sought to represent the spiritual needs of the converts from the heart of the "dark continent" as well as their own more worldly claims for material support and local autonomy. Dark indeed have been the deeds that distinguished the European competitors in the scramble for Africa.

ROSTERS, REGIMENS, REGIMES, REGISTERS

The perpetrators of those hallowed and harrowing deeds were all profes-
sionals of sorts, drawn from the ranks and the rank and file of the military—
the Tom Browns and the Tommy Atkinses—from the corridors of political
power, from the lobbies of the missionary organizations, from the halls of
royal geographic and ethnographic societies, from the boardrooms of trading
companies, from the classrooms of public schools, from the editorial offices of
major newspapers and journals, and indeed from other far-flung parts of the
empire itself.

David Livingstone, for example, combined a missionary's propagandizing
zeal with the intrepid adventurism of the explorer of "unknown" lands and
peoples. An emissary from the London Missionary Society, he arrived in
Africa in 1841, and died there in 1873. In the course of those three decades, he
had "discovered" Lake Ngami, Victoria Falls, the central Zambezi Valley,
Lake Nyasa, and Lualaba. And in 1871 he had been "found" by Henry M.
Stanley, an enterprising journalist from the *New York Herald* who would later
"rescue" Emin Pasha in equatorial Africa and consort with King Leopold in
consolidating his Congo holdings in Central Africa. Bishop John Colenso,
whose evangelical work took him to Natal in South Africa, explored instead
the language and customs of his native parishioners and, with the help of his
assistant William Ngidi, translated into Zulu the books of the Pentateuch,
only to face the ire of Matthew Arnold, that ardent overseer of English
civilization and its culture against the threats of anarchy.

The adherents of Christianity and civilization, two of Livingstone's Cs,
were inveterately assisted, albeit just as often confronted, by the advocates of
the third C, commerce. Charter companies proliferated, extending the two-
centuries-old tradition established by the East India Company. There was the
Suez Canal Company, for example, over which Britain contended with
France, the German East Africa Company, the Royal Niger Company, and
perhaps the most notorious of all, Cecil Rhodes's British South Africa Company. Rhodes, like many other of his compatriots, had gone to South Africa
for his health and remained there—with intermittent visits home to England,
long enough to acquire an Oxford degree and secure a royal charter for his
company—until his death in 1902. According to his wishes, he was buried
atop the Matopos, in the territory named after him: Rhodesia. His career on
the continent saw him as governor of the Cape Colony; mining magnate, or
"randlord"; and incorrigible schemer who envisioned railroads and telegraphs
connecting the reaches of the continent with each other and London. Like
Rhodes, Frederick Lugard combined administrative ambition in West Africa

British Trade with Tropical Africa before and after the Partition (in £1000s as annual average)

	Total Exports	Exports to Tropical Africa	Total Imports	Imports from Tropical Africa
1877–1879	194,427	1,249	375,394	1,805
1898–1901	267,266	3,062	500,161	2,572

From W. Scholet, *British Overseas Trade from 1700 to 1830.* Quoted in Robinson and Gallagher, *Africa and the Victorians,* 51.

with commercial interests in George Goldie's Royal Niger Company. Following World War I, he became a member of the League of Nations Permanent Mandates Commission, administering a second scramble for colonies in the early part of the twentieth century.

Such investors in the "commercialization, Christianization, and civilization" of the African continent were just as ably aided and abetted by their colleagues in conquest: the politicians and the military officers; fighting men like General "Chinese" Gordon and General Horatio Kitchener, who had conducted military campaigns across the empire, in Southeast Asia, in South Asia, and eventually in Africa; and governors-general like Lord Milner, whose oversight of southern Africa involved enlisting the ranks of recent public-school graduates, a group of young men who were later to be known—not always flatteringly—as Milner's "kindergarten." According to Milner in his 1908 discussion of "preferential trade" before the House of Lords, "Sometimes when thinking of Africa as a whole, Egypt, Tunis, and Morocco, of the Soudan, and of Abyssinia, of the Congo and of the Zambesi, of the many fruitless attempts made by many nations to discover, conquer, and civilize, of the many hopes which have been raised and dashed, of the many expectations which have been formed and falsified, it occurs to me that there must be upon this great continent some awful curse, some withering blight, and that to delude and to mock at the explorer, the gold-hunter, the merchant, the speculator, and even at ministers and monarchs, is its dark fortune and its desperate fate" (*The Nation and the Empire*, 273–74).

And then there were the radical reformers: women like Emily Hobhouse, who organized relief for the Boer women and children in the British concentration camps in South Africa, and like Olive Schreiner, who insisted on the importance of the "native question" in her challenge to the impresario aggrandizations of a Cecil Rhodes. There were men, too, agitators like Roger Casement, whose 1903 Congo Report to Parliament exposed the abuses and atrocities being perpetrated in Leopold's Congo Free State, and who with E. D. Morel formed the Congo Reform Association to challenge the com-

plicity of the signatories to the Berlin Act and their share in Leopold's liabilities. Casement was executed ignominiously for his participation in the
Irish Easter Uprising in 1916, but Morel continued to represent African concerns in the prelude to the Versailles Peace Conference that concluded World
War I. In his pamphlet, *Africa and the Peace of Europe* (1917), Morel argued,
however problematically,

> To the ordinary working man and his family the very name of Africa's
> rivers and mountains would be unknown; to the average politician its
> existence would be little more than an abstraction. But from its primeval
> forests, from its mysterious swamps, from its fertile plains and barren
> deserts would emanate vapours poisoning the diplomatic atmosphere of
> Europe. From intrigues and rivalries for their possession would spring
> conflicts filling Europe with turmoil, and with the hum of great factories
> turning out weapons for human slaughter. From this selfish lust of mod-
> ern industrial exploitation would arise disturbance and unrest, base and
> sordid manoeuvres, murdering Europe's peace. From wrongs inflicted
> upon Africa's helpless peoples would be generated evils corroding the
> relations between European Governments and, by a fatal and inevitable
> sequence, reacting upon the whole character of European statesman-
> ship. Upon the secular quarrels of Europe, quarrels of dynasties, of racial
> distribution and the adjustment of political forces, would be grafted a
> new cause for diplomatic friction, to wit, the partition and exploitation
> of a Continent rich in natural resources, more easily accessible than
> China, not barred from European interference like Southern and Cen-
> tral America by the fiat of a great nation, and inhabited races incapable,
> in the main, of offering organized resistance to injustice, invasion and
> oppression. (5–6)

ORGANIZATION OF THE VOLUME

In Conrad's *Heart of Darkness* narrator Marlow describes his adventure to his
shipmates aboard the *Nellie* in such a way as to contrast—and confuse—the
contradictions between the "civilizing mission" of empire-builders and the
culture of Africa that they discovered. "'Going up that river,'" says Marlow,
"'was like travelling back to the earliest beginnings of the world, when vegetation rioted on the earth and the big trees were kings.'" He concludes with
doubt: "'truth is hidden—luckily, luckily. But I felt it all the same; I felt often
its mysterious stillness watching me at my monkey tricks, just as it watches
you fellows performing on your respective tight-ropes for—what is it? half a

crown a tumble.'" His audience is indignant at the very suggestion: "'Try to be civil, Marlow,' growled a voice." But as Marlow says, "'What saves us is efficiency—the devotion to efficiency. . . . The conquest of the earth, which mostly means the taking it away from those who have a different complexion or slightly flatter noses than ourselves, is not a pretty thing when you look into it too much. What redeems it is the idea only'" (35–36).

The Scramble for Africa attempts to "look into it," to describe some of the efforts at "efficiency," to expose the putatively redemptive "idea," and to document just why it might turn out to have been not such a very "pretty thing" after all. Part 1, "The Berlin Conference 1885," presents materials related to the consequential meeting of European powers in Berlin that partitioned the continent, including the Berlin Act, along with commentaries that the meeting elicited and cartoons that caricatured it. In the early part of the nineteenth century Hegel maintained that Africa had yet to enter the annals of historical narrative, but by the century's turn Europe had largely grabbed Africa for its own purposes. The documentary evidence herein composes a picture of the various processes that characterized Europe's colonization: conferences, scrambles, incidents—from international rivalry to national statecraft.

In part 2, "The Body Politic: Rationalizing Race," texts that trace emergent theories of race through the course of the nineteenth century are presented as part of the prospectus of imperialism, its ratification, rationalization, and even its unreasonableness, from the antislavery campaigners to the social Darwinists. Part 3, "The Political Corps," turns to the various personnel who prosecuted the imperial project, that is, the "political corps," from missionaries and explorers like Livingstone and Bishop John William Colenso, to administrators like Lugard and Rhodes. Finally, in part 4, "Crises of Empire," the materials highlight the fissures in the "civilizing mission," the debates at home, the debacles on the continent—in Khartoum, South Africa, and the Congo—and the emergent critical voices—proto–human-rights activists and antiwar protesters—that would continue to challenge imperial maneuvers throughout the subsequent century and mark the history of decolonization at its end. As Marlow's journey "up that river" reveals to him, "'It was the stillness of an implacable force brooding over an inscrutable intention. It looked at you with a vengeful aspect. I got used to it afterwards. I did not see it any more. I had not time'" (36). But time would tell. . . .

FROM THE "SCRAMBLE FOR AFRICA" TO THE "SCRAMBLE FOR CONTRACTS"

In her book-length study, *South West Africa*, Ruth First, the South African historian and anti-apartheid activist, maintains that "barmen, commercial travellers, and lawyers briefed in diamond cases, tell the best diamond stories, part of the folk-lore of a territory still steeped in the excitement of prospecting, ore-rushes and the lucky finds of unexpected wealth" (156). By 1990, with the release of Nelson Mandela from South African prison and the beginning of the negotiations between the African National Congress (ANC) and the ruling National Party, the decolonization of Africa was well-nigh complete. Yet the lines drawn across the map of Africa more than a century before in Berlin remain much the same. To be sure, some of the names have changed: Rhodesia shed its reference to Cecil Rhodes in becoming Zimbabwe, South-West Africa is now Namibia, but the Congo is once again the Congo (or rather the Democratic Republic of the Congo [DRC]) after a quarter of a century as Zaire, and Eritrea is now a state in its own right, rather than an Ethiopian province. However, the territorial boundaries are still virtually indelible, albeit bloodied and disputed, now among the new and not-so-new, resource-rich, highly indebted, and deeply impoverished African states, the former imperial powers, and the multinational corporations and Bretton Woods institutions that continue to manage the legacy of wealth.

Where once Cecil Rhodes dreamed of a continent washed in red, the red of British imperialism, and leftist struggles for national liberation and decolonization came to envision an altogether different shade of red, it is as if Africa, at the turn-of-the-twentieth-century march toward globalization, had instead been "redlined," ruled off-limits for further and/or future investment. According to the geographer Neil Smith, in the "mid-1980s, when 'third world debt' led the list of economic crises in the 'Western' press, the utter silence concerning sub-Saharan debt revealed loudly that this region was too poor even to have the luxury of Latin American-level indebtedness. In the 1980s, the fourteen countries of sub-Saharan Africa (excluding West Africa and South Africa) amassed a mere $4.8 billion in debt to the United States. (By way of comparison, New York State had a budget deficit of nearly $5 billion in its 1995–1996 budget, and Harvard University has an endowment of $5.2 billion)" ("Satanic Geographies," 180–81). The debate waged at the end of the nineteenth century over the political and economic priorities of imperialism, its human and humanitarian costs, and the sociocultural consequences of empire continues unabated at the millennial transition. Lenin argued in 1916 that imperialism was the "highest stage of capitalism," and his contemporary,

J. A. Hobson, had mused in 1902 that imperialism's emissaries, "missionaries, travellers, sportsmen, scientists, traders," had been "actuated by private personal motives" (*Imperialism,* 357), and that imperialism itself was a "depraved choice of national life, imposed by self-seeking interests which appeal to the lusts of quantitative acquisitiveness and of forceful domination surviving in a nation from early centuries of animal struggle for existence" (368).

Conrad's "idea only" continues in any case to be subject to renewed scrutiny in the work of late-twentieth-century anti-imperialists and opponents of globalization, along with postcolonialism's critics, like the historian of Africa Basil Davidson, who sees the "black man's burden" as the "curse of the nation-state," or like Ugandan social scientist, Mahmood Mamdani, whose *Citizen and Subject* (1996) and *When Victims Become Killers* (2001) challenge many of the shibboleths of the story of "contemporary Africa and the legacy of late colonialism." But the scramble in and over Africa persists, even if the model of a "distinct rupture with the predatory economies of the nineteenth century and its prolongation into the colonial period, generally in the guise of concessionary companies and forced labour regimes" has yielded to a new version of the "criminalization of the state in Africa" (Bayart, Ellis, and Hibou). Gold, diamonds, and oil provided the grounds for resource war, civil war, and genocide.

From the scramble for Africa to the scramble for contracts—"not a pretty thing," perhaps, "when you look into it too much." But its nineteenth-century documentary history remains a critical part of the twentieth and twenty-first centuries' current events, cultural studies, political scientific constructions, national budgets, and literary ledgers.

BIBLIOGRAPHY

Bayart, Jean Francois, Stephen Ellis, and Beatrice Hibou. *The Criminalization of the State in Africa.* Bloomington: Indiana University Press, 1999.

Brantlinger, Patrick. *Rule of Darkness: British Literature and Imperialism 1830–1914.* Ithaca, N.Y.: Cornell University Press, 1988.

Conrad, Joseph. *Heart of Darkness.* 3rd ed. Edited by Robert Kimbrough. New York: W. W. Norton, 1988.

Davidson, Basil. *The Black Man's Burden: Africa and the Curse of the Nation-State.* New York: Random House, 1992.

Hobson, J. A. *Imperialism.* London: George Allen and Unwin, 1902.

Lenin, V. I. *Imperialism: The Highest Stage of Capitalism.* 1916. London: Pluto Press, 1996.

Mamdani, Mahmood. *Citizen and Subject: Contemporary Africa and the Legacy of Late Colonialism.* Princeton, N.J.: Princeton University Press, 1996.

—. *When Victims Become Killers: Colonialism, Nativism, and the Genocide in Rwanda.* Princeton, N.J.: Princeton University Press, 2001.

Milner, Lord Alfred. *The Nation and the Empire.* London: Constable and Company, 1913.

Pakenham, Thomas. *The Scramble for Africa: White Man's Conquest of the Dark Continent from 1876 to 1912.* New York: Random House, 1991.

Robinson, Ronald, and John Gallagher. *Africa and the Victorians: The Climax of Imperialism.* New York: St. Martin's Press, 1961.

Smith, Neil. "Satanic Geographies." *Public Culture* 10, no. 1 (1998): 169–89.

I

THE BERLIN CONFERENCE 1885:

MAKING/MAPPING

HISTORY

It was in 1868, when nine years old or thereabouts, that while looking at a map of Africa of the time and putting my finger on the blank space then representing the unsolved mystery of that continent, I said to myself with absolute assurance and an amazing audacity which are no longer in my character now:

"When I grow up I shall go *there.*"—Joseph Conrad, *A Personal Record,* 1913

Deal table in the middle, plain chairs all around the walls, on one end a large shining map, marked with all the colours of a rainbow. There was a vast amount of red—good to see at any time, because one knows that some real work is done there, a deuce of a lot of blue, a little green, smears of orange, and, on the East Coast, a purple patch, to show where the jolly pioneers of progress drink the jolly lager-beer.—Joseph Conrad, *Heart of Darkness,* 1898/99

INTRODUCTION
The Scramble for Africa: From the Conference at Berlin to the Incident at Fashoda
BARBARA HARLOW

ARLOW WAS MEETING with representatives of the Company in Brussels, engaging to pursue their enterprises in Africa, when he observed the colors of that map, colors that had redesigned the map's "blank space," which had been identified by his author in his own childhood. Red marked the spaces claimed by England, blue those of the French, orange those of the Portuguese, and purple those of the Germans. Much of this kaleidoscopic design had been drawn by the European participants in the Berlin Conference convened by Bismarck in November 1884 and concluded in February 1885. But the scramble for Africa was not only a variegated collage; it was also a struggle between black and white.

Early in the century, Hegel's *Philosophy of History* had excluded the African continent from all existing historical processes: "Africa proper, as far as History goes back," he wrote in the introduction, "has remained—for all purposes of connection with the rest of the World—shut up; it is the Gold-land compressed within itself—the land of childhood, which lying beyond the day of self-conscious history, is enveloped in the dark mantle of Night" (91). The German philosopher concludes his abbreviated discussion of Africa: "What we properly understand by Africa, is the Unhistorical, Undeveloped Spirit, still involved in the conditions of mere nature, and which had to be presented here only as on the threshold of the World's History" (94). Hegel's displacement of Africa from the world-historical map draws on hues for its outlines and contours to be sure, but imposes on the diagrammatic sketch three other paradigms as well—child/adult, nature/culture, night/day—and instantiates the cultural grounds for a narrative of development that would significantly overdetermine Europe's imperial and imperious relations, as well as the rationales for its territorial claims, with Africa for the next two centuries.

"Civilization, Christianity, and Commerce," according to the legendary missionary David Livingstone, were the bases for the European "mission" across Africa. And each of those agendas had its respective, if not always respectable, proponents: precipitous explorers, zealous missionaries, and opportunistic traders cum administrators. The English occasionally referred to their empire as a "civilizing mission," which the French in turn translated as "la mission civilisatrice": Africa and its African inhabitants had to be taught to "grow up," to enter "history," but on European terms. Race then provided an important additional legitimization to that mission, from the scientific theories of Darwin to their revisions into social Darwinism. The imperial project was, in that regard, a white and black one; the other colors on Marlow's map came from the political and economic competitions among the European powers themselves for control over the resources of the continent. It was, as Conrad maintained, "not a pretty thing when you look[ed] into it too much." For Conrad, and his spokesperson in the very heart of darkness, "What redeems it is the idea only."

The "idea," however, was not necessarily any more coherent—or pretty or redemptive—than the mottled maps: Germans competing with Portuguese, Italians with Belgians, the French against the English, and each against the other—and the African peoples. From the Suez Canal to the Cape of Good Hope, from the Congo River to the Nile, administrators like Rhodes and Lugard, adventurers such as Stanley and Leopold II, soldiers like Gordon and Kitchener, competed in the interests of their national governments in claiming personal status and states' rights. The General Act of the Conference of Berlin, signed on 26 February 1885, was written to adjudicate such disputes of trade, territory, spheres of influence, and the use of "spirituous liquors," but the persistent altercations and tendentious ambitions would be fought out repeatedly in the last decades of the imperial century: at Khartoum, at Omdurman, along the Congo River, in the Transvaal. Crises were continuous, but the statesmanly "conference" of Berlin among the European nations might be said to have culminated in the "incident at Fashoda" and the fateful meeting between French career diplomat Jean-Baptiste Marchand and the British General Sir Herbert Horatio Kitchener. It had been Marchand's plan to proceed east across Africa to confront the British as they moved south from Egypt through the Sudan. If the British, in Rhodes's formulation, designed to map Africa along the Cape-to-Cairo axis, the French would redraw the lines from the Congo to the Nile, from the Atlantic Ocean to the Red Sea. But it didn't happen that way. And the incident at Fashoda, on 19 September 1898, concluded in a capitulation of French claims to British demands. A century later, however, the map of Africa, albeit colored differently following decolonization, remains drawn along much the same (disputed) lines as those determined at the Berlin Conference of 1885.

BIBLIOGRAPHY

Apter, Andrew. "Africa, Empire, and Anthropology: A Philological Exploration of Anthropology's Heart of Darkness." *Annual Review of Anthropology* 28 (1999): 577–98.

Boahen, A. Adu, ed. *General History of Africa, Volume 7: Africa under Colonial Domination.* London: James Currey, 1990.

Bull, Bartle. *Safari: A Chronicle of Adventure.* London: Penguin, 1988.

Davidson, Basil. *The Black Man's Burden: Africa and the Curse of the Nation State.* New York: Times Books, 1992.

—. *The Search for Africa: History, Culture, Politics.* New York: Times Books, 1994.

Desai, Gaurav. *Subject to Colonialism: African Self-Fashioning and the Colonial Library.* Durham, N.C.: Duke University Press, 2001.

Hegel, G. W. F. *The Philosophy of History.* Translated by J. Sibree. New York: Dover, 1956.

Hertslet, Sir E. *The Map of Africa by Treaty.* 3 vols. London: Harrison and Sous, 1909.

Lewis, David Levering. *The Race to Fashoda: European Colonialism and African Resistance in the Scramble for Africa.* New York: Weidenfield and Nicolson, 1987.

National Portrait Gallery. *David Livingstone and the Victorian Encounter with Africa.* London: National Portrait Gallery, 1996.

Pakenham, Thomas. *The Scramble for Africa: White Man's Conquest of the Dark Continent from 1876 to 1912.* New York: Avon Books, 1991.

Robinson, Ronald, and John Gallagher, with Alice Denny. *Africa and the Victorians: The Climax of Imperialism.* 1961. Reprint, New York: Doubleday, 1968.

Chronology of Events

1807		Slave trade abolished throughout the British Empire
1810		Saartje Bartmann ("The Hottentot Venus") on exhibit in Europe
1834		Slavery abolished throughout the British Empire
1848		Slavery abolished throughout the French colonies
1849–1850		David Livingstone's first expedition
1870–1871		Diamond rush to Kimberley
1871		Charles Darwin publishes *The Descent of Man*
1874	18 April	David Livingstone buried in Westminster Abbey
1876		Stanley travels down the Congo River
1883		Stanley plants the Belgian flag over Stanley Falls
1884–1885		Berlin Conference
1885		H. Rider Haggard publishes *King Solomon's Mines*
1885		Relief expedition to Gordon in Khartoum
1886		Gold rush to the Witwatersrand
1898	1 September	Kitchener defeats Mahdist forces at Omdurman
1898	19 September	Incident at Fashoda
1898		*Heart of Darkness* published in *Blackwood* magazine
1889–1902		Anglo-Boer War
1902		Death of Cecil Rhodes
1904		Creation of the Congo Reform Association

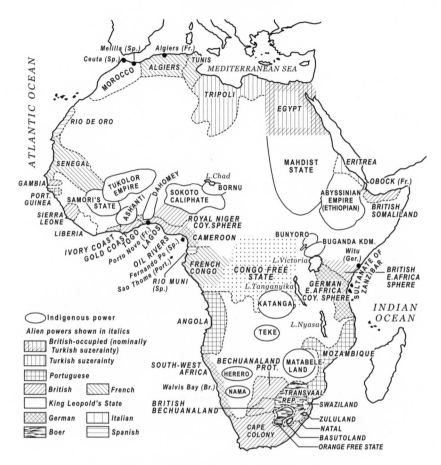

ATLANTIC OCEAN

Melilla (Sp.)
Ceuta (Sp.)
Algiers (Fr.)
MOROCCO
ALGIERS
TUNIS
MEDITERRANEAN SEA
TRIPOLI
EGYPT
RIO DE ORO
MAHDIST STATE
ERITREA
OBOCK (Fr.)
SENEGAL
GAMBIA
PORT. GUINEA
TUKOLOR EMPIRE
L.Chad
BORNU
SOKOTO CALIPHATE
ABYSSINIAN EMPIRE (ETHIOPIAN)
BRITISH SOMALILAND
SAMORI'S STATE
SIERRA LEONE
LIBERIA
ASHANTI
DAHOMEY
ROYAL NIGER COY. SPHERE
IVORY COAST
GOLD COAST
TOGO
Porto Novo (Fr.)
LAGOS
OIL RIVERS
CAMEROON
BUNYORO
BUGANDA KDM.
Witu (Ger.)
Fernando Po (Sp.)
Sao Thome (Port.)
RIO MUNI (Sp.)
FRENCH CONGO
CONGO FREE STATE
L.Victoria
L.Tanganyika
GERMAN E.AFRICA COY. SPHERE
SULTANATE OF ZANZIBAR
BRITISH E.AFRICA SPHERE
KATANGA
TEKE
ANGOLA
L.Nyasa
INDIAN OCEAN
SOUTH-WEST AFRICA
BECHUANALAND PROT.
MATABELE LAND
MOZAMBIQUE
HERERO
Walvis Bay (Br.)
NAMA
BRITISH BECHUANALAND
TRANSVAAL REP.
SWAZILAND
ZULULAND
NATAL
BASUTOLAND
ORANGE FREE STATE
CAPE COLONY

Indigenous power
Alien powers shown in italics
British-occupied (nominally Turkish suzerainty)
Turkish suzerainty
Portuguese
British
French
King Leopold's State
German
Italian
Boer
Spanish

Africa in 1886: The Scramble Half Complete

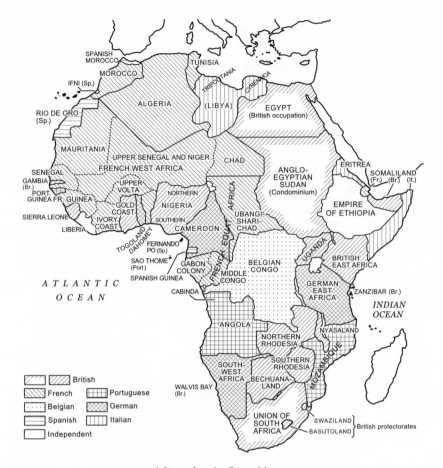

SPANISH
MOROCCO
MOROCCO
IFNI (Sp.)
RIO DE ORO
(Sp.)
MAURITANIA
SENEGAL
GAMBIA
(Br.)
PORT.
GUINEA FR. GUINEA
SIERRA LEONE
LIBERIA
ALGERIA
TUNISIA
TRIPOLITANIA
CYRENAICA
(LIBYA)
EGYPT
(British occupation)
UPPER SENEGAL AND NIGER
FRENCH WEST AFRICA
CHAD
ANGLO-
EGYPTIAN
SUDAN
(Condominium)
ERITREA
SOMALILAND
(Fr.) (Br.) (It.)
UPPER
VOLTA
NORTHERN
GOLD
COAST
IVORY
COAST
NIGERIA
SOUTHERN
TOGOLAND
DAHOMEY
CAMEROON
UBANGI-
SHARI-
CHAD
EMPIRE
OF ETHIOPIA
FERNANDO
PO (Sp.)
SAO THOME
(Port.)
GABON
COLONY
SPANISH GUINEA
FRENCH EQUATORIAL AFRICA
MIDDLE
CONGO
CABINDA
BELGIAN
CONGO
UGANDA
BRITISH
EAST AFRICA
GERMAN
EAST
AFRICA
ZANZIBAR (Br.)

ATLANTIC
OCEAN

INDIAN
OCEAN

ANGOLA
NORTHERN
RHODESIA
NYASALAND
MOZAMBIQUE

British
French   Portuguese
Belgian   German
Spanish   Italian
Independent

SOUTH-
WEST
AFRICA
WALVIS BAY
(Br.)
SOUTHERN
RHODESIA
BECHUANA-
LAND

UNION OF
SOUTH
AFRICA
SWAZILAND
BASUTOLAND
British protectorates

Africa after the Scramble, 1912

Africa 1898. Showing territories controlled by the "charter companies."

SOURCE: Margery Perham, *Lugard: The Years of Adventure 1858–1898*
(London: Collins, 1956).

Excerpts from *Heart of Darkness*

JOSEPH CONRAD

[*Heart of Darkness* has become a classic of both the modern British novel and, more recently, of narratives of the scramble for Africa. Conrad (1857–1924) had visited the Congo in 1890 in the service of the Société Anonyme Belge pour le Commerce du Haut-Congo. His seafaring ended in 1894 when he settled in England and continued his career as a novelist.]

What saves us is efficiency—the devotion to efficiency. . . . The conquest of the earth, which mostly means the taking it away from those who have a different complexion or slightly flatter noses than ourselves, is not a pretty thing when you look into it too much. What redeems it is the idea only.

JOURNEY UP THE RIVER

"Going up that river was like travelling back to the earliest beginnings of the world, when vegetation rioted on the earth and the big trees were kings. An empty stream, a great silence, an impenetrable forest. The air was warm, thick, heavy, sluggish. There was no joy in the brilliance of sunshine. The long stretches of the waterway ran on, deserted, into the gloom of overshadowed distances. On silvery sandbanks hippos and alligators sunned themselves side by side. The broadening waters flowed through a mob of wooded islands. You lost your way on that river as you would in a desert and butted all day long against shoals trying to find the channel till you thought yourself bewitched and cut off for ever from everything you had known once—somewhere—far away—in another existence perhaps. There were moments when one's past came back to one, as it will sometimes when you have not a moment to spare to yourself; but it came in the shape of an unrestful and noisy dream remembered with wonder amongst the overwhelming realities of this strange world of plants and water and silence. And this stillness of life did not in the least resemble a peace. It was the stillness of an implacable force brooding over an inscrutable intention. It looked at you with a vengeful aspect. I got used to it afterwards. I did not see it any more. I had no time. I had to keep guessing at the channel; I had to discern, mostly by inspiration, the signs of hidden banks; I watched for sunken stones; I was learning to clap my teeth smartly before my heart flew out when I shaved by a fluke some infernal sly old snag that would have ripped the life out of the tin-pot steam-boat and drowned all the pilgrims; I had to keep a look-out for the signs of dead wood we could cut up in the night for next day's steaming. When you have to attend to things of that sort, to the mere incidents of the surface, the reality—the reality I tell you—fades. The inner truth is hidden—luckily, luckily. But I felt it all the same; I felt often its mysterious stillness watching me at my monkey tricks, just as it watches you fellows performing on your respective tight-ropes for—what is it? half a crown a tumble. . . ."

"Try to be civil, Marlow," growled a voice, and I knew there was at least one listener awake besides myself.

SOURCE: Joseph Conrad, *Heart of Darkness* (1898/99), 3rd ed., ed. Robert Kimbrough (New York: W.W. Norton, 1988), 10, 35–36.

Africa

G. W. F. HEGEL

In accordance with these data we may now consider the three portions of the globe with which History is concerned, and here the three characteristic principles manifest themselves in a more or less striking manner: Africa has for its leading classical feature the Upland, Asia the contrast of river regions with the Upland, Europe the mingling of these several elements.

Africa must be divided into three parts: one is that which lies south of the desert of Sahara—Africa proper—the Upland almost entirely unknown to us, with narrow coast-tracts along the sea; the second is that to the north of the desert—European Africa (if we may so call it)—a coastland; the third is the river region of the Nile, the only valley-land of Africa, and which is in connection with Asia.

Africa proper, as far as History goes back, has remained—for all purposes of connection with the rest of the World—shut up; it is the Gold-land compressed within itself—the land of childhood, which lying beyond the day of self-conscious history, is enveloped in the dark mantle of Night. Its isolated character originates, not merely in its tropical nature, but essentially in its geographical condition. The triangle which it forms (if we take the West Coast—which in the Gulf of Guinea makes a strongly indented angle—for one side, and in the same way the East Coast to Cape Gardafu for another) is on two sides so constituted for the most part, as to have a very narrow Coast Tract, habitable only in a few isolated spots. Next to this towards the interior, follows to almost the same extent, a girdle of marsh land with the most luxuriant vegetation, the especial home of ravenous beasts, snakes of all kinds—a border tract whose atmosphere is poisonous to Europeans. This border constitutes the base of a cincture of high mountains, which are only at distant intervals traversed by streams, and where they are so, in such a way as to form no means of union with the interior; for the interruption occurs but seldom below the upper part of the mountain ranges, and only in individual narrow channels, where are frequently found innavigable waterfalls and torrents crossing each other in wild confusion. During the three or three and a half centuries that the Europeans have known this border-land and have taken places in it into their possession, they have only here and there (and that but for a short time) passed these mountains, and have nowhere settled down beyond them. The land surrounded by these mountains is an unknown Upland, from which on the other hand the Negroes have seldom made their way through. In the sixteenth century occurred at many very distant points, outbreaks of terrible hordes which rushed down upon the more peaceful inhabitants of the declivities. Whether any internal movement had taken place, or if so, of what character, we do not know. What we do know of these hordes, is the contrast between their conduct in their wars and forays themselves—which exhibited the most reckless inhumanity and disgusting barbarism—and the fact that afterwards, when their rage was spent, in the calm time of peace, they showed themselves mild and well disposed towards the Europeans, when they became acquainted with them. This holds good of the Fullahs and of the Mandingo tribes, who inhabit the mountain terraces of the Senegal and Gambia. The second portion of Africa is the river district of the Nile—Egypt; which was adapted to become a mighty centre of independent civilization, and therefore is as isolated and singular in Africa as Africa itself appears in relation to the other parts of the world. The northern part of Africa, which may be specially called that of the *coast-territory* (for Egypt has been frequently driven back on itself, by the Mediterranean) lies on the Mediterranean and the Atlantic; a magnificent territory, on which Carthage once lay—the site of the modern Morocco, Algiers, Tunis, and Tripoli. This part was to be—*must* be attached to Europe: the French have lately made a successful effort in this direction: like Hither-Asia, it looks Europe-wards.

Here in their turn have Carthaginians, Romans, and Byzantines, Mussulmans, Arabians, had their abode, and the interests of Europe have always striven to get a footing in it.

The peculiarly African character is difficult to comprehend, for the very reason that in reference to it, we must quite give up the principle which naturally accompanies all *our* ideas—the category of Universality. In Negro life the characteristic point is the fact that consciousness has not yet attained to the realization of any substantial objective existence—as for example, God, or Law—in which the interest of man's volition is involved and in which he realizes his own being. This distinction between himself as an individual and the universality of his essential being, the African in the uniform, undeveloped oneness of his existence has not yet attained; so that the Knowledge of an absolute Being, an Other and a Higher than his individual self, is entirely wanting. The Negro, as already observed, exhibits the natural man in his completely wild and untamed state. We must lay aside all thought of reverence and morality—all that we call feeling—if we would rightly comprehend him; there is nothing harmonious with humanity to be found in this type of character. The copious and circumstantial accounts of Missionaries completely confirm this, and Mahommedanism appears to be the only thing which in any way brings the Negroes within the range of culture. The Mahommedans too understand better than the Europeans, how to penetrate into the interior of the country. The grade of culture which the Negroes occupy may be more nearly appreciated by considering the aspect which *Religion* presents among them. That which forms the basis of religious conceptions is the consciousness on the part of man of a Higher Power—even though this is conceived only as a *vis naturæ*—in relation to which he feels himself a weaker, humbler being. Religion begins with the consciousness that there is something higher than man. But even Herodotus called the Negroes sorcerers:— now in *Sorcery* we have not the idea of a God, of a moral faith; it exhibits man as the highest power, regarding him as alone occupying a position of command over the power of Nature. We have here therefore nothing to do with a spiritual adoration of God, nor with an empire of Right. God thunders, but is not on that account recognized as God. For the soul of man, God must be more than a thunderer, whereas among the Negroes this is not the case. Although they are necessarily conscious of dependence upon nature—for they need the beneficial influence of storm, rain, cessation of the rainy period, and so on—yet this does not conduct them to the consciousness of a Higher Power: it is they who command the elements, and this they call "magic." The Kings have a class of ministers through whom they command elemental changes, and every place possesses such magicians, who perform special ceremonies, with all sorts of gesticulations, dances, uproar, and shouting, and in the midst of this confusion commence their incantations. The second element in their religion, consists in their giving an outward form to this supernatural power—projecting their hidden might into the world of phenomena by means of images. What they conceive of as the power in question, is therefore nothing really objective, having a substantial being and different from themselves, but the first thing that comes in their way. This, taken quite indiscriminately, they exalt to the dignity of a "Genius"; it may be an animal, a tree, a stone, or a wooden figure. This is their *Fetich*—a word to which the Portuguese gave currency, and which is derived from *feitizo,* magic. Here, in the Fetich, a kind of objective independence as contrasted with the arbitrary fancy of the individual seems to manifest itself; but as the objectivity is nothing other than the fancy of the individual projecting itself into space, the human individuality remains master of the image it has adopted. If any mischance occurs which the Fetich has not averted, if rain is suspended, if there is a failure in the crops, they bind and beat or destroy the Fetich and so get rid of it, making another immediately, and thus holding it in their own power. Such a Fetich has no independence as an object of religious worship; still less has it æsthetic independence as a work of art; it is merely a creation that expresses the arbitrary choice of its maker, and which always remains in his hands. In short there is no relation of dependence in this religion. There is however one feature that points to something beyond;—the *Worship of the Dead*—in which their deceased forefathers and ancestors are regarded by them as a power influencing the living. Their idea in the matter is that these ancestors exercise vengeance and inflict upon man various injuries—exactly in the sense in which this was supposed of witches in the Middle Ages. Yet the power of the dead is not held superior to that of the living, for the Negroes command the dead and lay spells upon them. Thus the power in question remains substantially always in bondage to the living subject. Death itself is looked upon by the Negroes as no universal natural law; even this, they think, proceeds from evil-disposed magicians. In this doctrine is certainly involved the elevation of man over Nature; to such a degree that the chance volition of man is superior to the merely natural—that he looks upon this as an instrument to which he does not pay the compliment of treating it in a way conditioned by itself, but which he commands.

But from the fact that man is regarded as the Highest, it follows that he has no respect for himself; for only with the consciousness of a Higher Being does he reach a point of view which inspires him with real reverence. For if arbitrary choice is the absolute, the only substantial objectivity that is realized, the mind cannot in such be conscious of any Universality. The Negroes indulge, therefore, that perfect *contempt* for humanity, which in its bearing on Justice and Morality is the fundamental characteristic of the race. They have more-over no knowledge of the immortality of the soul, although spectres are supposed to appear. The undervaluing of humanity among them reaches an incredible degree of intensity. Tyranny is regarded as no wrong, and cannibal-ism is looked upon as quite customary and proper. Among us instinct deters from it, if we can speak of instinct at all as appertaining to man. But with the Negro this is not the case, and the devouring of human flesh is altogether consonant with the general principles of the African race; to the sensual Negro, human flesh is but an object of sense—mere flesh. At the death of a King hundreds are killed and eaten; prisoners are butchered and their flesh sold in the markets; the victor is accustomed to eat the heart of his slain foe. When magical rites are performed, it frequently happens that the sorcerer kills the first that comes in his way and divides his body among the by-standers. Another characteristic fact in reference to the Negroes is Slavery. Negroes are enslaved by Europeans and sold to America. Bad as this may be, their lot in their own land is even worse, since there a slavery quite as absolute exists; for it is the essential principle of slavery, that man has not yet attained a consciousness of his freedom, and consequently sinks down to a mere Thing—an object of no value. Among the Negroes moral sentiments are quite weak, or more strictly speaking, non-existent. Parents sell their children, and conversely children their parents, as either has the opportunity. Through the pervading influence of slavery all those bonds of moral regard which we cherish towards each other disappear, and it does not occur to the Negro mind to expect from others what we are enabled to claim. The polygamy of the Negroes has frequently for its object the having many children, to be sold, every one of them, into slavery; and very often naïve complaints on this score are heard, as for instance in the case of a Negro in London, who lamented that he was now quite a poor man because he had already sold all his relations. In the contempt of humanity displayed by the Negroes, it is not so much a despising of death as a want of regard for life that forms the characteristic feature. To this want of regard for life must be ascribed the great courage, supported by enormous bodily strength, exhibited by the Negroes, who allow themselves to be shot down by thousands in war with Europeans. Life has a value only when it has something valuable as its object.

Turning our attention in the next place to the category of *political constitu-tion*, we shall see that the entire nature of this race is such as to preclude the existence of any such arrangement. The standpoint of humanity at this grade is mere sensuous volition with energy of will; since universal spiritual laws (for example, that of the morality of the Family) cannot be recognized here.

Universality exists only as arbitrary subjective choice. The political bond can therefore not possess such a character as that free laws should unite the community. There is absolutely no bond, no restraint upon that arbitrary volition. Nothing but external force can hold the State together for a moment. A ruler stands at the head, for sensuous barbarism can only be restrained by despotic power. But since the subjects are of equally violent temper with their master, they keep him on the other hand within limits. Under the chief there are many other chiefs with whom the former, whom we will call the King, takes counsel, and whose consent he must seek to gain, if he wishes to undertake a war or impose a tax. In this relation he can exercise more or less authority, and by fraud or force can on occasion put this or that chieftain out of the way. Besides this the Kings have other specified prerogatives. Among the Ashantees the King inherits all the property left by his subjects at their death. In other places all unmarried women belong to the King, and whoever wishes a wife, must buy her from him. If the Negroes are discontented with their King they depose and kill him. In Dahomey, when they are thus displeased, the custom is to send parrots' eggs to the King, as a sign of dissatisfaction with his government. Sometimes also a deputation is sent, which intimates to him, that the burden of government must have been very troublesome to him, and that he had better rest a little. The King then thanks his subjects, goes into his apartments, and has himself strangled by the women. Tradition alleges that in former times a state composed of women made itself famous by its conquests: it was a state at whose head was a woman. She is said to have pounded her own son in a mortar, to have besmeared herself with the blood, and to have had the blood of pounded children constantly at hand. She is said to have driven away or put to death all the males, and commanded the death of all male children. These furies destroyed everything in the neighborhood, and were driven to constant plunderings, because they did not cultivate the land. Captives in war were taken as husbands: pregnant women had to betake themselves outside the encampment; and if they had born a son, put him out of the way. This infamous state, the report goes on to say, subsequently disappeared. Accompanying the King we constantly find in Negro States, the executioner, whose office is regarded as of the highest consideration, and by whose hands the King, though he makes use of him for putting suspected persons to death, may himself suffer death, if the grandees desire it. Fanaticism, which, notwithstanding the yielding disposition of the Negro in other respects, can be excited, surpasses, when roused, all belief. An English traveller states that when a war is determined on in Ashantee, solemn ceremonies precede it: among other things the bones of the King's mother are laved with human blood. As a prelude to the war, the King ordains an onslaught upon his own metropolis, as if to excite the due degree of frenzy. The King sent word to the English Hutchinson: "Christian, take care, and watch well over your family. The messenger of death has drawn his sword and will strike the neck of many Ashantees; when the drum sounds it is the death signal for multitudes. Come to the King, if you can, and fear nothing for yourself." The drum beat, and a terrible carnage was begun; all who came in the way of the frenzied Negroes in the streets were stabbed. On such occasions the King has all whom he suspects killed, and the deed then assumes the character of a sacred act. Every idea thrown into the mind of the Negro is caught up and realized with the whole energy of his will; but this realization involves a wholesale destruction. These people continue long at rest, but suddenly their passions ferment, and then they are quite beside themselves. The destruction which is the consequence of their excitement, is caused by the fact that it is no positive idea, no thought which produces these commotions;—a physical rather than a spiritual enthusiasm. In Dahomey, when the King dies, the bonds of society are loosed; in his palace begins indiscriminate havoc and disorganization. All the wives of the King (in Dahomey their number is exactly 3,333) are massacred, and through the whole town plunder and carnage run riot. The wives of the King regard this their death as a necessity; they go richly attired to meet it. The authorities have to hasten to proclaim the new governor, simply to put a stop to massacre.

From these various traits it is manifest that want of self-control distinguishes the character of the Negroes. This condition is capable of no development or culture, and as we see them at this day, such have they always been. The only essential connection that has existed and continued between the Negroes and the Europeans is that of slavery. In this the Negroes see nothing unbecoming them, and the English who have done most for abolishing the slave-trade and slavery, are treated by the Negroes themselves as enemies. For it is a point of first importance with the Kings to sell their captured enemies, or even their own subjects; and viewed in the light of such facts, we may conclude *slavery* to have been the occasion of the increase of human feeling among the Negroes. The doctrine which we deduce from this condition of slavery among the Negroes, and which constitutes the only side of the question that has an interest for our inquiry, is that which we deduce from the Idea: viz. that the "Natural condition" itself is one of absolute and thorough injustice—contravention of the Right and Just. Every intermediate grade between this and the realization of a rational State retains—as might be expected—elements and aspects of injustice; therefore we find slavery even in the Greek and Roman States, as we do serfdom down to the latest times. But thus existing in a State, slavery is itself a phase of advance from the merely isolated sensual existence—a phase of education—a mode of becoming participant in a higher morality and the culture connected with it. Slavery is in and for itself *injustice,* for the essence of humanity is *Freedom;* but for this man must be matured. The gradual abolition of slavery is therefore wiser and more equitable than its sudden removal.

At this point we leave Africa, not to mention it again. For it is no historical part of the World; it has no movement or development to exhibit. Historical movements in it—that is in its northern part—belong to the Asiatic or European World. Carthage displayed there an important transitionary phase of civilization; but, as a Phœnician colony, it belongs to Asia. Egypt will be considered in reference to the passage of the human mind from its Eastern to its Western phase, but it does not belong to the African Spirit. What we properly understand by Africa, is the Unhistorical, Undeveloped Spirit, still involved in the conditions of mere nature, and which had to be presented here only as on the threshold of the World's History.

SOURCE: In G. W. F. Hegel, *The Philosophy of History* (1822), trans. J. Sibree (New York: Dover, 1956), 91–99.

<hr>

General Act of the Conference of Berlin

I. GENERAL ACT OF THE CONFERENCE OF BERLIN, SIGNED FEBRUARY 26, 1885

Chapter I.—Declaration relative to Freedom of Trade in the Basin of the Congo, its Mouths and circumjacent Regions, with other Provisions connected therewith.

Article 1

The trade of all nations shall enjoy complete freedom—

1. In all the regions forming the basin of the Congo and its outlets. This basin is bounded by the watersheds (or mountain ridges) of the adjacent basins, namely, in particular, those of the Niari, the Ogowé, the Sohari, and the Nile, on the north; by the eastern watershed line of the affluents of Lake Tanganyika on the east; and by the watersheds of the basins of the Zambesi and the Logé on the south. It therefore comprises all the regions watered by the Congo and its affluents, including Lake Tanganyika, with its eastern tributaries.

2. In the maritime zone extending along the Atlantic Ocean from the parallel situated in 2° 30′ of south latitude to the mouth of the Logé.

The Black Baby. Mr. Bull. "What, another!!!—Well, I suppose
I must take it in!!!" SOURCE: *Punch* 106 (21 April 1894): 187.

The northern boundary will follow the parallel situated in 2° 30′ from the coast to the point where it meets the geographical basin of the Congo, avoiding the basin of the Ogowé, to which the provisions of the present Act do not apply.

The southern boundary will follow the course of the Logé to its source, and thence pass eastwards till it joins the geographical basin of the Congo.

3. In the zone stretching eastwards from the Congo Basin as above defined, to the Indian Ocean from 5 degrees of north latitude to the mouth of the Zambesi in the south, from which point the line of demarcation will ascend the Zambesi to 5 miles above its confluence with the Shiré, and then follow the watershed between the affluents of Lake Nyassa and those of the Zambesi, till at last it reaches the watershed between the waters of the Zambesi and the Congo.

It is expressly recognized that in extending the principle of free trade to this eastern zone, the Conference Powers only undertake engagements for themselves, and that in the territories belonging to an independent Sovereign State this principle shall only be applicable in so far as it is approved by such State. But the Powers agree to use their good offices with the Governments established on the African shore of the Indian Ocean for the purpose of obtaining such approval, and in any case of securing the most favourable conditions to the transit (traffic) of all nations.

Article 2

All flags, without distinction of nationality, shall have free access to the whole of the coast-line of the territories above enumerated, to the rivers there running into the sea, to all the waters of the Congo and its affluents, including the lakes, to all the ports situate on the banks of these waters, as well as to all canals which may in future be constructed with intent to unite the watercourses or lakes within the entire area of the territories described in Article 1. Those trading under such flags may engage in all sorts of transport, and carry on the coasting trade by sea and river, as well as boat traffic, on the same footing as if they were subjects.

Article 3

Wares, of whatever origin, imported into these regions, under whatsoever flag, by sea or river, or overland, shall be subject to no other taxes than such as may be levied as fair compensation for expenditure in the interests of trade, and which for this reason must be equally borne by the subjects themselves and by foreigners of all nationalities. All differential dues on vessels, as well as on merchandize, are forbidden.

Article 4

Merchandize imported into these regions shall remain free from import and transit dues.

The Powers reserve to themselves to determine after the lapse of twenty years whether this freedom of import shall be retained or not.

Article 5

No Power which exercises or shall exercise sovereign rights in the above-mentioned regions shall be allowed to grant therein a monopoly or favour of any kind in matters of trade.

Foreigners, without distinction, shall enjoy protection of their persons and property, as well as the right of acquiring and transferring movable and immovable possessions; and national rights and treatment in the exercise of their professions.

Article 6   Provisions relative to Protection of the Natives, of Missionaries and Travellers, as well as relative to Religious Liberty

All the Powers exercising sovereign rights or influence in the aforesaid territories bind themselves to watch over the preservation of the native tribes, and to care for the improvement of the conditions of their moral and material well-being, and to help in suppressing slavery, and especially the Slave Trade. They shall, without distinction of creed or nation, protect and favour all religious, scientific, or charitable institutions, and undertakings created and organized for the above ends, or which aim at instructing the natives and bringing home to them the blessings of civilization.

Christian missionaries, scientists, and explorers, with their followers, property, and collections, shall likewise be the objects of especial protection.

Freedom of conscience and religious toleration are expressly guaranteed to the natives, no less than to subjects and to foreigners. The free and public exercise of all forms of Divine worship, and the right to build edifices for religious purposes, and to organize religious Missions belonging to all creeds, shall not be limited or fettered in any way whatsoever.

Article 7   Postal Régime

The Convention of the Universal Postal Union, as revised at Paris the 1st June, 1878, shall be applied to the Conventional basin of the Congo.

The Powers who therein do or shall exercise rights of sovereignty or Protectorate engage, as soon as circumstances permit them, to take the measures necessary for the carrying out of the preceding provision.

*Article 8   Right of Surveillance vested in the International
Navigation Commission of the Congo*

In all parts of the territory had in view by the present Declaration, where no Power shall exercise rights of sovereignty or Protectorate, the International Navigation Commission of the Congo, instituted in virtue of Article 17, shall be charged with supervising the application of the principles proclaimed and perpetuated ('consacrés') by this Declaration.

In all cases of difference arising relative to the application of the principles established by the present Declaration, the Governments concerned may agree to appeal to the good offices of the International Commission, by submitting to it an examination of the facts which shall have occasioned these differences.

Chapter II.—Declaration relative to the Slave Trade

Article 9

Seeing that trading in slaves is forbidden in conformity with the principles of international law as recognized by the Signatory Powers, and seeing also that the operations, which, by sea or land, furnish slaves to trade, ought likewise to be regarded as forbidden, the Powers which do or shall exercise sovereign rights or influence in the territories forming the Conventional basin of the Congo, declare that these territories may not serve as a market or means of transit for the trade in slaves, of whatever race they may be. Each of the Powers binds itself to employ all the means at its disposal for putting an end to this trade and for punishing those who engage in it.

*Chapter III.—Declaration relative to the Neutrality of the Territories
comprised in the Conventional Basin of the Congo*

Article 10

In order to give a new guarantee of security to trade and industry, and to encourage, by the maintenance of peace, the development of civilization in the countries mentioned in Article 1, and placed under the free trade system, the High Signatory Parties to the present Act, and those who shall hereafter adopt it, bind themselves to respect the neutrality of the territories, or portions of territories, belonging to the said countries, comprising therein the territorial waters, so long as the Powers which exercise or shall exercise the rights of sovereignty or Protectorate over those territories, using their option of proclaiming themselves neutral, shall fulfil the duties which neutrality requires.

Article 11

In case a Power exercising rights of sovereignty or Protectorate in the countries mentioned in Article 1, and placed under the free trade system, shall be involved in a war, then the High Signatory Parties to the present Act, and those who shall hereafter adopt it, bind themselves to lend their good offices in order that the territories belonging to this Power and comprised in the Conventional free trade zone shall, by the common consent of this Power and of the other belligerent or belligerents, be placed during the war under the rule of neutrality, and considered as belonging to a non-belligerent State, the belligerents thenceforth abstaining from extending hostilities to the territories thus neutralized, and from using them as a base for warlike operations.

Article 12

In case a serious disagreement originating on the subject of, or in the limits of, the territories mentioned in Article 1 and placed under the free trade system, shall arise between any Signatory Powers of the present Act, or the Powers which may become parties to it, these Powers bind themselves, before appealing to arms, to have recourse to the mediation of one or more of the friendly Powers.

In a similar case, the same Powers reserve to themselves the option of having recourse to arbitration.

Chapter IV.—Act of Navigation for the Congo

Article 13

The navigation of the Congo, without excepting any of its branches or outlets, is, and shall remain, free for the merchant-ships of all nations equally, whether carrying cargo or ballast, for the transport of goods or passengers. It shall be regulated by the provisions of this Act of Navigation, and by the Rules to be made in pursuance thereof.

In the exercise of this navigation the subjects and flags of all nations shall in all respects be treated on a footing of perfect equality, not only for the direct navigation from the open sea to the inland ports of the Congo and *vice versa*, but also for the great and small coasting trade, and for boat traffic on the course of the river.

Consequently, on all the course and mouths of the Congo there will be no distinction made between the subjects of Riverain States and those of non-Riverain States, and no exclusive privilege of navigation will be conceded to Companies, Corporations, or private persons whatsoever.

These provisions are recognized by the Signatory Powers as becoming henceforth a part of international law.

Article 14

The navigation of the Congo shall not be subject to any restriction or obligation which is not expressly stipulated by the present Act. It shall not be exposed to any landing dues, to any station or depot tax, or to any charge for breaking bulk, or for compulsory entry into port.

In all the extent of the Congo the ships and goods in process of transit on the river shall be submitted to no transit dues, whatever their starting-place or destination.

There shall be levied no maritime or river toll based on the mere fact of navigation, nor any tax on goods aboard of ships. There shall only be levied taxes or duties having the character of an equivalent for services rendered to navigation itself, to wit:—

1. Harbour dues on certain local establishments, such as wharves, ware-houses, &c., if actually used.

The Tariff of such dues shall be framed according to the cost of constructing and maintaining the said local establishments; and it will be applied without regard to whence vessels come or what they are loaded with.

2. Pilot dues for those stretches of the river where it may be necessary to establish properly-qualified pilots.

The Tariff of these dues shall be fixed and calculated in proportion to the service rendered.

3. Charges raised to cover technical and administrative expenses incurred in the general interest of navigation, including lighthouse, beacon, and buoy duties.

The last-mentioned dues shall be based on the tonnage of vessels as shown by the ship's papers, and in accordance with the Rules adopted on the Lower Danube.

The Tariffs by which the various dues and taxes enumerated in the three preceding paragraphs shall be levied, shall not involve any differential treatment, and shall be officially published at each port.

The Powers reserve to themselves to consider, after the lapse of five years, whether it may be necessary to revise, by common accord, the above-mentioned Tariffs.

Article 15

The affluents of the Congo shall in all respects be subject to the same Rules as the river of which they are tributaries.

And the same Rules shall apply to the streams and rivers as well as the lakes and canals in the territories defined in paragraphs 2 and 3 of Article 1.

At the same time the powers of the International Commission of the Congo will not extend to the said rivers, streams, lakes, and canals, unless with the assent of the States under whose sovereignty they are placed. It is well understood, also, that with regard to the territories mentioned in paragraph 8 of Article 1, the consent of the Sovereign States owning these territories is reserved.

Article 16

The roads, railways, or lateral canals which may be constructed with the special object of obviating the innavigability or correcting the imperfection of the river route on certain sections of the course of the Congo, its affluents, and other water-ways placed under a similar system, as laid down in Article 15, shall be considered in their quality of means of communication as dependencies of this river, and as equally open to the traffic of all nations.

And, as on the river itself, so there shall be collected on these roads, railways, and canals only tolls calculated on the cost of construction, maintenance, and management, and on the profits due to the promoters.

As regards the Tariff of these tolls, strangers and the natives of the respective territories shall be treated on a footing of perfect equality.

Article 17

There is instituted an International Commission, charged with the execution of the provisions of the present Act of Navigation.

The Signatory Powers of this Act, as well as those who may subsequently adhere to it, may always be represented on the said Commission, each by one Delegate. But no Delegate shall have more than one vote at his disposal, even in the case of his representing several Governments.

This Delegate will be directly paid by his Government. As for the various agents and employés of the International Commission, their remuneration shall be charged to the amount of the dues collected in conformity with paragraphs 2 and 3 or Article 14.

The particulars of the said remuneration, as well as the number, grade, and powers of the agents and employés, shall be entered in the returns to be sent yearly to the Government represented on the International Commission.

Article 18

The members of the International Commission, as well as its appointed agents, are invested with the privilege of inviolability in the exercise of their functions. The same guarantee shall apply to the offices and archives of the Commission.

Article 19

The International Commission for the Navigation of the Congo shall be constituted as soon as five of the Signatory Powers of the present General Act shall have appointed their Delegates. And pending the constitution of the Commission the nomination of these Delegates shall be notified to the Imperial Government of Germany, which will see to it that the necessary steps are taken to summon the meeting of the Commission.

The Commission will at once draw up navigation, river police, pilot, and quarantine Rules.

These Rules, as well as the Tariffs to be framed by the Commission, shall, before coming into force, be submitted for approval to the Powers represented on the Commission. The Powers interested will have to communicate their views with as little delay as possible.

Any infringements of these Rules will be checked by the agents of the International Commission wherever it exercises direct authority, and elsewhere by the Riverain Power.

In the case of an abuse of power, or of an act of injustice, on the part of any agent or employé of the International Commission, the individual who considers himself to be aggrieved in his person or rights may apply to the Consular Agent of his country. The latter will examine his complaint, and if he finds it *prima facie* reasonable, he will then be entitled to bring it before the Commission. At his instance then, the Commission, represented by at least three of its members, shall, in conjunction with him, inquire into the conduct of its agent or employé. Should the Consular Agent look upon the decision of the Commission as raising questions of law ('objections de droit'), he will report on the subject to his Government, which may then have recourse to the Powers represented on the Commission, and invite them to agree as to the instructions to be given to the Commission.

Article 20

The International Commission of the Congo, charged in terms of Article 17 with the execution of the present Act of Navigation, shall in particular have power—

1. To decide what works are necessary to assure the navigability of the Congo in accordance with the needs of international trade.

On those sections of the river where no Power exercises sovereign rights, the International Commission will itself take the necessary measures for assuring the navigability of the river.

On those sections of the river held by a Sovereign Power the International Commission will concert its action ('s'entendra') with the riparian authorities.

2. To fix the pilot tariff and that of the general navigation dues as provided for by paragraphs 2 and 3 of Article 14.

The Tariffs mentioned in the first paragraph of Article 14 shall be framed by the territorial authorities within the limits prescribed in the said Article.

The levying of the various dues shall be seen to by the international or territorial authorities on whose behalf they are established.

3. To administer the revenue arising from the application of the preceding paragraph (2).

4. To superintend the quarantine establishment created in virtue of Article 24.

5. To appoint officials for the general service of navigation, and also its own proper employés.

It will be for the territorial authorities to appoint Sub-Inspectors on sections of the river occupied by a Power, and for the International Commission to do so on the other sections.

The Riverain Power will notify to the International Commission the appointment of Sub-Inspectors, and this Power will undertake the payment of their salaries.

In the exercise of its functions, as above defined and limited, the International Commission will be independent of the territorial authorities.

Article 21

In the accomplishment of its task the International Commission may, if need be, have recourse to the war-vessels of the Signatory Powers of this Act, and of those who may in future accede to it, under reserve, however, of the instructions which may be given to the Commanders of these vessels by their respective Governments.

Article 22

The war-vessels of the Signatory Powers of this Act that may enter the Congo are exempt from payment of the navigation dues provided for in paragraph 8 of Article 14; but unless their intervention has been called for by the International Commission or its agents, in terms of the preceding Article, they shall be liable to the payment of the pilot or harbour dues which may eventually be established.

Article 23

With the view of providing for the technical and administrative expenses which it may incur, the International Commission created by Article 17 may, in its own name, negotiate loans to be exclusively guaranteed by the revenues raised by the said Commission.

The decisions of the Commission dealing with the conclusion of a loan must be come to by a majority of two-thirds. It is understood that the Governments represented on the Commission shall not in any case be held as assuming any guarantee, or as contracting any engagement or joint liability ('solidarité') with respect to the said loans, unless under special Conventions concluded by them to this effect.

The revenue yielded by the dues specified in paragraph 8 of Article 14 shall bear, as a first charge, the payment of the interest and sinking fund of the said loans, according to agreement with the lenders.

Article 24

At the mouth of the Congo there shall be founded, either on the initiative of the Riverain Powers, or by the intervention of the International Commission, a quarantine establishment for the control of vessels passing out of as well as into the river.

Later on the Powers will decide whether and on what conditions a sanitary control shall be exercised over vessels engaged in the navigation of the river itself.

Article 25

The provisions of the present Act of Navigation shall remain in force in time of war. Consequently all nations, whether neutral or belligerent, shall be always free, for the purposes of trade, to navigate the Congo, its branches, affluents, and mouths, as well as the territorial waters fronting the embouchure of the river.

Traffic will similarly remain free, despite a state of war, on the roads, railways, lakes, and canals mentioned in Articles 15 and 16.

There will be no exception to this principle, except in so far as concerns the transport of articles intended for a belligerent, and in virtue of the law of nations regarded as contraband of war.

All the works and establishments created in pursuance of the present Act, especially the tax-collecting offices and their treasuries, as well as the permanent service staff of these establishments, shall enjoy the benefits of neutrality ('placés sous le régime de la neutralité'), and shall, therefore, be respected and protected by belligerents.

Chapter V.—Act of Navigation for the Niger.

Article 26

The navigation of the Niger, without excepting any of its branches and outlets, is and shall remain entirely free for the merchant-ships of all nations equally, whether with cargo or ballast, for the transportation of goods and passengers. It shall be regulated by the provisions of this Act of Navigation, and by the rules to be made in pursuance of this Act.

In the exercise of this navigation the subjects and flags of all nations shall be treated, in all circumstances, on a footing of perfect equality, not only for the direct navigation from the open sea to the inland ports of the Niger, and *vice versa*, but for the great and small coasting trade, and for boat trade on the course of the river.

Consequently, on all the course and mouths of the Niger there will be no distinction made between the subjects of the Riverain States and those of non-Riverain States; and no exclusive privilege of navigation will be conceded to Companies, Corporations, or private persons.

These provisions are recognized by the Signatory Powers as forming henceforth a part of international law.

Article 27

The navigation of the Niger shall not be subject to any restriction or obligation based merely on the fact of navigation.

It shall not be exposed to any obligation in regard to landing-station or depot, or for breaking bulk, or for compulsory entry into port.

In all the extent of the Niger the ships and goods in process of transit on the river shall be submitted to no transit dues, whatever their starting-place or destination.

No maritime or river toll shall be levied based on the sole fact of navigation, nor any tax on goods on board of ships. There shall only be collected taxes or duties which shall be an equivalent for services rendered to navigation itself. The Tariff of these taxes or duties shall not warrant any differential treatment.

Article 28

The affluents of the Niger shall be in all respects subject to the same rules as the river of which they are tributaries.

Article 29

The roads, railways, or lateral canals which may be constructed with the special object of obviating the innavigability or correcting the imperfections of the river route on certain sections of the course of the Niger, its affluents, branches, and outlets, shall be considered, in their quality of means of communication, as dependencies of this river, and as equally open to the traffic of all nations.

And, as on the river itself, so there shall be collected on these roads, railways, and canals only tolls calculated on the cost of construction, maintenance, and management, and on the profits due to the promoters.

As regards the Tariff of these tolls, strangers and the natives of the respective territories shall be treated on a footing of perfect equality.

Article 30

Great Britain undertakes to apply the principles of freedom of navigation enunciated in Articles 26, 27, 28, and 29 on so much of the waters of the Niger, its affluents, branches, and outlets, as are or may be under her sovereignty or protection.

The rules which she may establish for the safety and control of navigation shall be drawn up in a way to facilitate, as far as possible, the circulation of merchant-ships.

It is understood that nothing in these obligations shall be interpreted as hindering Great Britain from making any rules of navigation whatever which shall not be contrary to the spirit of these engagements.

Great Britain undertakes to protect foreign merchants and all the trading nationalities on all those portions of the Niger which are or may be under her sovereignty or protection as if they were her own subjects, provided always that such merchants conform to the rules which are or shall be made in virtue of the foregoing.

Article 31

France accepts, under the same reservations, and in identical terms, the obligations undertaken in the preceding Articles in respect of so much of the waters of the Niger, its affluents, branches, and outlets, as are or may be under her sovereignty or protection.

Article 32

Each of the other Signatory Powers binds itself in the same way in case it should ever exercise in the future rights of sovereignty or protection over any portion of the waters of the Niger, its affluents, branches, or outlets.

Article 33

The arrangements of the present Act of Navigation will remain in force in time of war. Consequently, the navigation of all neutral or belligerent nations will be in all time free for the usages of commerce on the Niger, its branches, its affluents, its mouths, and outlets, as well as on the territorial waters opposite the mouths and outlets of that river.

The traffic will remain equally free in spite of a state of war on the roads, railways, and canals mentioned in Article 29.

There will be an exception to this principle only in that which relates to the transport of articles destined for a belligerent, and considered, in virtue of the law of nations, as articles of contraband of war.

Chapter VI.—Declaration relative to the essential Conditions to be observed in order that new Occupations on the Coasts of the African Continent may be held to be effective.

Article 34

Any Power which henceforth takes possession of a tract of land on the coasts of the African Continent outside of its present possessions, or which, being hitherto without such possessions, shall acquire them, as well as the Power which assumes a Protectorate there, shall accompany the respective act with a notification thereof, addressed to the other Signatory Powers of the present Act, in order to enable them, if need be, to make good any claims of their own.

Article 35

The Signatory Powers of the present Act recognize the obligation to insure the establishment of authority in the regions occupied by them on the coasts of the African Continent sufficient to protect existing rights, and, as the case may be, freedom of trade and of transit under the conditions agreed upon.

Chapter VII.—General Dispositions.

Article 36

The Signatory Powers of the present General Act reserve to themselves to introduce into it subsequently, and by common accord, such modifications and improvements as experience may show to be expedient.

Article 37

The Powers who have not signed the present General Act shall be free to adhere to its provisions by a separate instrument.

The adhesion of each Power shall be notified in diplomatic form to the Government of the German Empire, and by it in turn to all the other Signatory or adhering Powers.

Such adhesion shall carry with it full acceptance of all the obligations as well as admission to all the advantages stipulated by the present General Act.

Article 38

The present General Act shall be ratified with as little delay as possible, the same in no case to exceed a year.

It will come into force for each Power from the date of its ratification by that Power.

Meanwhile, the Signatory Powers of the present General Act bind themselves not to take any steps contrary to its provisions.

Each Power will address its ratification to the Government of the German Empire, by which notice of the fact will be given to all the other Signatory Powers of the present Act.

The ratifications of all the Powers will be deposited in the archives of the Government of the German Empire. When all the ratifications shall have been sent in, there will be drawn up a Deposit Act, in the shape of a Protocol, to be signed by the Representatives of all the Powers which have taken part in the Conference of Berlin, and of which a certified copy will be sent to each of those Powers.

II. CHAPTER VI OF THE GENERAL ACT OF THE BRUSSELS CONFERENCE, SIGNED AT BRUSSELS, JULY 2, 1890.

Chapter VI.—Restrictive Measures concerning the Traffic in Spirituous Liquors.

Article XC

Justly anxious about the moral and material consequences which the abuse of spirituous liquors entails on the native populations, the Signatory Powers have agreed to apply the provisions of Articles XCI, XCII, and XCIII within a zone extending from the 20th degree north latitude to the 22nd degree south latitude, and bounded by the Atlantic Ocean on the west and by the Indian

Ocean on the east, with its dependencies, comprising the islands adjacent to the mainland, up to 100 sea miles from the shore.

Article XCI

In the districts of this zone where it shall be ascertained that, either on account of religious belief or from other motives, the use of distilled liquors does not exist or has not been developed, the Powers shall prohibit their importation. The manufacture of distilled liquors there shall be equally prohibited.

Each Power shall determine the limits of the zone of prohibition of alcoholic liquors in its possessions or Protectorates, and shall be bound to notify the limits thereof to the other Powers within the space of six months. The above prohibition can only be suspended in the case of limited quantities destined for the consumption of the non-native population and imported under the régime and conditions determined by each Government.

Article XCII

The Powers having possessions or exercising protectorates in the region of the zone which are not placed under the action of the prohibition, and into which alcoholic liquors are at present either freely imported or pay an import duty of less than 15 fr. per hectolitre at 50 degrees Centigrade, undertake to levy on these alcoholic liquors an import duty of 15 fr. per hectolitre at 50 degrees Centigrade for three years after the present General Act comes into force. At the expiration of this period the duty may be increased to 25 fr. during a fresh period of three years. At the end of the sixth year it shall be submitted to revision, taking as a basis the average results produced by these Tariffs, for the purpose of then fixing, if possible, a minimum duty throughout the whole extent of the zone where the prohibition referred to in Article XCI is not in force.

The Powers have the right of maintaining and increasing the duties beyond the minimum fixed by the present Article in those regions where they already possess that right.

Article XCIII

The distilled liquors manufactured in the regions referred to in Article XCII, and intended for inland consumption, shall be subject to an excise duty.

This excise duty, the collection of which the Powers undertake to insure as far as possible, shall not be lower than the minimum import duty fixed by Article XCII.

Article XCIV

Signatory Powers having in Africa possessions contiguous to the zone specified in Article XC undertake to adopt the necessary measures for preventing the introduction of spirituous liquors within the territories of the said zone by their inland frontiers.

Article XCV

The Powers shall communicate to each other, through the Office at Brussels, and according to the terms of Chapter V, information relating to the traffic in alcoholic liquors within their respective territories.

III. DECLARATION ANNEXED TO THE GENERAL ACT OF THE BRUSSELS CONFERENCE, SIGNED JULY 2, 1890.

The Powers assembled in Conference at Brussels, who have ratified the General Act of Berlin of the 26th February, 1885, or who have acceded thereto,

After having drawn up and signed in concert, in the General Act of this day, a collection of measures intended to put an end to the Slave Traffic by land as well as by sea, and to improve the moral and material conditions of existence of native races,

Taking into consideration that the execution of the provisions which they have adopted with this object imposes on some of them who have possessions or Protectorates in the conventional basin of the Congo, obligations which absolutely demand new resources to meet them,

Have agreed to make the following Declaration:—

The Signatories or acceding Powers who have possessions or Protectorates in the said Conventional basin of the Congo shall be able, so far as authority is required to this end, to establish duties upon imported goods, the scale of which shall not exceed a rate equivalent to 10 per cent. *ad valorem* at the port of entry, always excepting spirituous liquors, which are regulated by the provisions of Chapter VI of the General Act of this day.

After the signing of the said General Act, negotiations shall be opened between the Powers who have ratified the General Act of Berlin or who have acceded to it, in order to draw up, within a maximum limit of the 10 per cent. *ad valorem,* the system of Customs Regulations to be established in the conventional basin of the Congo.

Nevertheless it is understood:—

1. That no differential treatment or transit duty shall be established;

2. That in applying the Customs Regulations which are to be agreed upon,

each Power will undertake to simplify formalities as much as possible, and to facilitate trade operations;

3. That the arrangement resulting from the proposed negotiations shall remain in force for fifteen years from the signing of the present Declaration.

At the expiration of this term, and failing a fresh Agreement, the Contracting Powers will return to the conditions provided for by Article IV of the General Act of Berlin, retaining the power of imposing duties up to a maximum of 10 per cent. upon goods imported into the conventional basin of the Congo.

The ratifications of the present Declaration shall be exchanged at the same time as those of the General Act of this day.

IV. CONVENTION RESPECTING LIQUORS IN AFRICA, SIGNED AT BRUSSELS, NOVEMBER 3, 1906.

Article I

From the coming into force of the present Convention, the import duties on spirituous liquors shall be raised, throughout the zone where there does not exist the system of total prohibition provided by Article XCI of the General Act of Brussels to the rate of 100 fr. the hectolitre at 50 degrees Centigrade.

It is understood, however, as far as Erythrea is concerned, that this duty may be at the rate of 70 fr. only the hectolitre at 50 degrees Centigrade, the surplus being represented in a general and permanent manner by the total of the other duties of that Colony.

The import duty shall be augmented proportionally for each degree above 50 degrees Centigrade. It may be diminished proportionally for each degree below 50 degrees Centigrade.

The Powers retain the right of maintaining and increasing the duty beyond the minimum fixed by the present Article in the regions in which they now possess that right.

Article II

In accordance with Article XCIII of the General Act of Brussels, distilled drinks made in the districts mentioned in Article XCII of the said General Act, and intended for consumption, shall pay an excise duty.

This excise duty, the collection of which the Powers undertake to ensure as far as is possible, shall not be lower than the minimum import duty fixed by Article I of the present Convention.

It is understood, however, as far as Angola is concerned, that the Portuguese Government shall be able, with a view to effecting the gradual and complete transformation of the distilleries into sugar factories, to deduct from the money raised by the duty of 100 fr. a sum of 30 fr., which shall be given to the producers on condition that they effect such transformation under Government control.

If the Portuguese Government make use of this facility, the number of distilleries working and the capacity for production of each one of them must not exceed the number and capacity certified on the 81st October, 1906.

Article III

The provisions of the present Convention are to hold good for a period of ten years.

At the end of this period, the import duty fixed in Article I shall be submitted to revision, taking as a basis the results produced by the preceding rate.

Each of the Contracting Powers shall, however, have the option of calling for such a revision at the end of the eighth year.

Such Powers as shall make use of this option must notify their intention six months before the date of expiry to the other Powers through the intermediary of the Belgian Government, who shall undertake to convoke the Conference within the six months above mentioned.

Article IV

It is understood that the Powers who signed the General Act of Brussels or who have acceded to it, and who are not represented at the present Conference, preserve the right of acceding to the present Convention.

Article V

The present Convention shall be ratified, and the ratifications shall be deposited at the Ministry for Foreign Affairs at Brussels within the shortest possible period, and such period shall not in any case exceed one year.

A certified copy of the *procès-verbal* of deposit shall be addressed by the Belgian Government to all the Powers interested.

Article VI

The present Convention shall come into force in all the possessions of the Contracting Powers situated in the zone defined by Article XC of the General Act of Brussels on the 30th day after the date of the termination of the *procès-verbal* of deposit mentioned in the preceding Article.

From that date, the Convention regulating the question of spirituous liquors in Africa, signed at Brussels on the 8th June, 1899, shall cease to have effect.

V. DECLARATION MODIFYING PARAGRAPH 5 OF THE DECLARATION ANNEXED TO THE GENERAL ACT, SIGNED AT BRUSSELS JULY 2, 1890, SIGNED AT BRUSSELS JUNE 15, 1910

The Powers which have ratified or acceded to the Berlin General Act of the 26th February, 1885, have agreed to make the following Declaration:—

In modification of paragraph 5 of the Declaration annexed to the Brussels General Act of the 2nd July, 1890, the Powers which signed that Act or acceded thereto, and which have possessions or protectorates in the Conventional Basin of the Congo, are authorised, so far as such authorisation is necessary, to impose therein upon imported arms and munitions duties exceeding the maximum limit of 10 per cent. of the value at the port of importation fixed by the aforesaid Declaration.

The present Declaration shall be ratified and the Ratifications shall be deposited at the Ministry for Foreign Affairs at Brussels within a period of one year or sooner if possible.

It shall come into force on thirty days after the date on which the Protocol recording such deposit shall have been closed.[1]

SOURCE: Appendix in Henry Wellington Wade, *The Story of the Congo Free State* (New York: G. P. Putnam's Sons, 1905), 302–22. Wade was a member of the New York Bar.

———

International Rivalry and the Berlin Conference
ARTHUR BERRIEDALE KEITH

[Arthur Berriedale Keith (1879–1944) was a distinguished commentator on British politics and foreign policy, as well as constitutional issues.]

On November 7, 1880, when Stanley was in the thick of the struggle to establish the route to Stanley Pool, he was surprised to receive near Ndambi Mbongo a visit from a French naval officer, who presented himself as Le

1. This took place on December 31, 1911 (Cd. 6037, p. 112).

Comte Savorgnan de Brazza, Enseigne de Vaisseau.[1] In the friendly conversations which followed this meeting no hint of rivalry seems to have been breathed by his guest, and Stanley appears not to have entertained any suspicion that his guest was other than the explorer and agent of the French Committee of the International Association he claimed to be. If Stanley's lack of suspicion were real, it must have been a painful surprise to him to find on emerging at the end of his wearisome journey on the north bank of Stanley Pool that he had been anticipated in the selection of the natural site for the terminus of his road. On his arrival on July 27, 1881, at the village Bwabwa Njali, he was met by the Senegalese Sergeant Malamine, the faithful and able servant of de Brazza, who produced a treaty purporting to grant to de Brazza as the representative of France the territory from the Gordon Bennet river, flowing into the Congo about forty yards below the first dangerous rapid, and Impila on the north bank of Stanley Pool. Malamine explained that he was instructed merely to show this document to all Europeans who might approach the Pool.[2]

De Brazza had in fact stolen a march on Stanley, and had outwitted the International Association by means which are subject to the same imputation of dubious morality[3] as the actions of the Association itself. De Brazza, of Italian origin, had entered the French naval service in 1870, and had been employed in the revival of French colonizing enterprise which followed the defeats of 1870–71 in exploration of the once-despised colony of the Gaboon. In company with Dr. Ballay and M. Marche he was engaged from 1875–8 in the exploration of the Ogoué river, which, it was hoped, would prove an effective mode of access to the interior. This belief was proved false by the discovery of cataracts, and de Brazza passed beyond the head-waters of the Ogoué and reached the Alima, flowing eastwards to the Congo. De Brazza, however, had not then heard of Stanley's famous journey, and instead of following, as would else have been the case, the Alima to its junction with that stream, returned, shattered in health, to Europe. There he became aware of the discoveries of his rival, and determined to secure the profits of them for France. To effect this aim, while obtaining the countenance of the French Government, which commissioned him to establish a legal priority of occupation on the navigable Congo at the spot nearest to the Atlantic, he applied for aid to the French Committee of the International Association, and his expedition was financed from that source. Further, to disarm suspi-

1. Stanley, *The Congo*, i. 231–4. Yet Stanley had heard of the French aims by February 6, 1880 (*ibid.* i. 159).
2. Stanley, *The Congo*, i. 292 sq.
3. Masoin, *Histoire*, i. 341.

cion, it was announced[4] at a meeting of the Paris Geographical Society that his mission had the eminently laudable but innocuous purpose of exploring the country between the Gaboon and Lake Chad. Though he only left Europe on December 27, 1879, the route which he chose to gain the Congo proved fairly easy for his small party. After founding a station, Franceville on the Ogoué, June 1880, he followed the Léfini to the Congo, and there, on September 10, 1880, concluded the treaty which Malamine presented to Stanley.

The position of Stanley was decidedly difficult: even had he been inclined to ignore the emphatic notification of de Brazza that the territory had been acquired in sovereignty on behalf of France, he would have been unable to obtain the permission of the natives to establish a station either on the spot claimed by de Brazza or in its vicinity, for de Brazza had succeeded by his great charm of personality and energy of character in convincing the natives that it was to their interest to hamper the access of other white men to their territories, and earlier in the year, in February, Messrs. Crudgington and Bentley had been foiled in their efforts to establish a mission station on the Pool by the hostility of the natives at Kinshasa to the south and Mfwa to the north of the Pool alike.[5] He determined, therefore, to try his fortune to the south of the Pool, and by a mixture of menace and cajolery secured authority from the chief who claimed control of the land and from Ngalyema, who *de facto* had occupied the territory, to establish a station near Kintamo, to which the name of Leopoldville was given.[6] Over four months were spent in the foundation of Leopoldville, and on April 19, 1882, the first expedition for the Upper Congo left the new base. Lake Leopold II was circumnavigated in May, but the expedition terminated with the serious illness of Stanley, who had to return to Vivi, where he found a German explorer, Dr. Peschuel-Loesche, who bore a sealed commission from the President of the International Association of the Congo, which had superseded the Comité d'Êtudes, appointing him commander of the expedition in the event of Stanley's disablement. Leaving him in charge, Stanley proceeded with a light heart on July 15 *via* Loanda to Europe. De Brazza in the meantime had not been idle. After his flying visit to Stanley in November, 1880, he proceeded to the Gaboon, where to his disappointment he found that the help which he had expected was not available. He set himself to remedy this defect, and under his direction the existing stations were reprovisioned and a road made to the

4. Scott Keltie, *Partition of Africa*, p. 137.

5. Stanley, *The Congo*, i. 250, 261. Malamine saved them from injury at Mfwa, but secured their departure.

6. Stanley, *The Congo*, i. 303 sq.

Alima, on which a new station was founded, in the hope that a steamer could be transported thither and then launched on the stream. At the beginning of 1882 all was in readiness for his return to the coast, and he proceeded thither exploring *en route* part of the Niari-Kwilu river, which he hoped to use as a means of access to the Congo by connecting the point, to which it proved navigable from the coast, with Stanley Pool, by a short railway. The hostility of the natives prevented his accomplishing in full degree his aims, and compelled him to proceed direct to the coast, arriving in Europe in June, when he set about to secure the ratification by France of the treaty which he had procured from the Makoko of Mbe.[7]

The body to which Stanley made in October the full report of his transactions was the Comité de l'Association internationale du Congo, which had replaced, as has been seen, the Comité d'Études in circumstances of which no more information has been vouchsafed than that the change was made when the International African Association took over responsibility for the actions of the Comité d'Études.[8] In effect, at any rate, the new Association was, as before, the mere instrument of the King of the Belgians, by whose liberality the ever-increasing cost of the expedition was defrayed. Stanley's advice[9] to the Association was simple: nothing could be secured without obtaining from the chiefs in the Congo basin the cession of whatever rights of government they possessed, and it was essential to construct a railway in substitution for the road, which was clearly a hopeless obstacle to effective trade. These proposals would require large additions of staff, and involve heavy expenditure, but the Committee were ready for this, and Stanley was pressed to resume control of the expedition and to superintend personally the carrying out of the policy which he advised. Stanley consented to return to the Congo and complete the establishment of the stations as far as Stanley Falls, provided that within a reasonable period an efficient assistant chief were dispatched to administer the establishments on the Lower Congo during his absence on the Upper Congo, so clearly had experience convinced him that it was impossible to leave the principal base of operations in the hands of youthful and inexperienced officers. This condition was accepted by the Committee of the Association, and Stanley left Cadiz on November 23, 1882, reaching Vivi on December 20. He immediately set about expeditions to secure for the Association control over the Niari-Kwilu district south of the

7. In addition to the treaty shown to Stanley, de Brazza had secured another ceding territory between the Ogoué, Alima, and Congo (Masoin *Histoire*, i. 344); cf. P. Gaffarel, *Notre Expansion coloniale*, pp. 211 sq.

8. *The Congo*, i. 51, 462.

9. *Ibid.* i. 462 sq.

Gaboon, which had not yet been declared French territory, in order to provide what was then expected to prove a simpler and more effective route to the
Upper Congo. One party, under Captain J. G. Elliott, was dispatched on
January 13, 1883, to found a set of stations along the lower course of the Niari,
starting from the point on that river nearest to the Congo station of Isangila;
while on February 5 Lieutenant Van de Velde was dispatched by sea to ascend
the Kwilu and to acquire territory on either bank. Finally, Captain Hanssens
was sent from Manyanga for the upper course of the Niari, with instructions
to establish connexion between Manyanga and the river and to join hands
with Captain Elliott's expedition. All three missions were successfully carried
out by April, and treaties ceding sovereign right acquired on both banks of the
river, thus ensuring connexion with the Upper Congo. Stanley himself, after
securing treaties with the chiefs of Vivi and its neighbourhood, proceeded to
advance to Stanley Falls, which he reached on December 1, finding on the
latter stages of his journey melancholy proof of the savagery of the Arab
slave-traders, who had followed in his footsteps and had ravaged what was
formerly a thickly populated district. After establishing at the Falls a station
under the control of a Scottish engineer, he returned to Leopoldville and
Vivi, taking steps *en route* to secure treaties of cession of sovereignty from the
natives, either directly or by the action of his officers. So successful were his
efforts that on April 23, 1884, he was able to report[10] that from Boma to the
Lubamba river on the right bank of the Congo, and thence north to the
Niari-Kwilu a solid block of territory had been acquired for the Association,
while on the south bank treaties had been made, or were about to be made,
covering the whole way from Noki to Stanley Falls. Stanley had accomplished in the fullest measure the mission which he had undertaken, and he
was, it is clear, temperamentally unfitted for work too long continued, but his
anxiety to return to Europe was restrained by the fact that the Committee had
not kept their promise to provide him with an effective successor, who could
administer the affairs of the Lower Congo during his absence. Sir Frederick
Goldsmid was, indeed, nominated Commissioner—in what relation to Stanley is not altogether clear—by the King in July, 1883, but though he paid a visit
to the Congo and restored for a period order in the troubled affairs of Leopoldville, he had returned to Europe by January, 1884,[11] and the King
had chosen—again with no clear indication of his relationship to Stanley—
General Gordon to take his place.[12] To Gordon, as is clear from the letter

10. *The Congo*, ii. 225.
11. *Ibid.* ii. 187. Dr. Peschuel-Loesche had thrown up his commission in November, 1882; *ibid.* i.
469.
12. *Ibid.* ii. 226; *Autobiography*, p. 338.

which he addressed to Stanley on January 6, the interest of the proposed appointment lay merely in the opportunity which it would afford to attack the slave-traders in their haunts, doubtless the Nile basin, and it is not remarkable that Stanley should have demurred to a plan which seemed to him to be equivalent to the abandonment of the fundamental business of the consolidation of the position in the Congo. Gordon, however, was diverted from this project by receiving the opportunity to go to the Sudan under British auspices, and the Committee at last provided Stanley with the substitute whom he needed in the person of Colonel Sir Francis de Winton, a man of proved competence. De Winton's arrival in May made it possible for Stanley to leave the Congo on June 10. No one recognized more clearly than he did that the time had come when the position of the Congo could not be determined by treaties with ignorant negroes, but by the arbitrament of the Great Powers in conference.

De Brazza in the meantime had showed much activity, but less happily directed than that of his rival.[13] The French Parliament on November 21, 1882, approved his treaty with the Makoko, and voted in December 275,000 fr. for an expedition to confirm the result which he had obtained; but unluckily for France's claims de Brazza was slow in proceeding to West Africa, sailing only on March 21, 1882, and when he arrived the activity of Stanley's agents had already secured the territory on the Niari-Kwilu which would have served his purpose of securing an effective route to the Upper Congo. But de Brazza claimed, and the French Government accepted his view, that the treaty—or treaties—which he had obtained gave him a footing on the south bank of the river, a claim which the Association strenuously denied. The question, indeed, permits of no dispute if Stanley's version of the facts is to be accepted, for it would then appear that the cession was merely of a strip of land, of indefinite extension inland, but running some nine miles along the right bank of Stanley Pool.[14] On the other hand, it appears clear from Stanley's own narrative[15] that Malamine had much influence on the southern bank, and that there was great conflict of evidence among the natives as to what chief had power over the territory. The evidence, however, on the whole tells in favour of the contention of the Association: the French hold, if any, on the south bank was always weak compared to their unquestioned rights on the north bank, and, while they continued to hold a station on the latter, they

13. Masoin, *Histoire,* i. 347 sq.
14. *The Congo,* i. 293.
15. *Ibid.* i. 299.

early abandoned whatever settlement they might have effected on the south bank, though they maintained obstinately their theoretic claim.

Apart, however, from the rival claims of France, which, if made good, would clearly jeopardize the hold of the Association on the river, the legal position of that body was open to grave doubt. It might be true that the Association had concluded treaties with 450 independent chiefs[16]—or over 400 treaties with more than 2,000 native chiefs[17]—but it would be absurd to suppose that Stanley of all men believed what he wrote when he said[18] that the rights of these chiefs 'would be conceded by all to have been indisputable, since they held their lands by undisturbed occupation, by long ages of succession, by real divine right'. It is a minor point that the treaties published[19] show a distressing confusion between the International African Association and the International Congo Association, but that the terms of these documents were really intelligible to the natives who affixed their marks can scarcely be credible,[20] and it is still more doubtful—as Stanley's own investigations in the case of de Brazza's cession show—whether the signatories had the right to undertake the obligations which they did. Admitting, however, that Stanley had obtained what was possible in the state of anarchy and barbarism of the country, it still remained to be seen whether the Powers would accept the validity of the claim to sovereign rights by the Association. It was not enough to contend[21] that the precedents of the English Puritans of the *Mayflower* in 1620, of the New Hampshire colonists in 1639, of the East India Company, Sarawak, Liberia, and Borneo favoured the right of individuals to accept cessions of territory and found sovereign states. Apart from the technical inaccuracy of part of the argument, it remained true that it was entirely for the Great Powers to decide under what conditions, if any, they would recognize a new sovereignty, and that precedents of recognition were of no substantial importance.

In the meantime Portugal had been engaged in a determined effort to defeat the plans of the International Association by securing from England that recognition of her claims on the Congo which had been withheld during

16. *The Congo*, ii. 379.

17. *Ibid.* i. 18.

18. *Ibid.* ii. 379.

19. *Ibid.* ii. 195–206.

20. The case of Pallaballa, where a new treaty of April 19, 1884, was required to explain the first treaty of January 8, 1883, is a clear proof of this; *ibid.* ii. 205.

21. Cf. the Report of the Committee of Foreign Relations to the 48th Congress of the United States, *ibid.* ii. 380, 381; Sir Travers Twiss, *An International Protectorate of the Congo River* (1883).

the earlier part of the century. The visit of Cameron had been followed on January 24, 1876, by another appeal to the British Government to reconsider the question, but Lord Derby on February 8 curtly responded with a reminder that the British determination to prevent by force any violation of the *status quo* still prevailed,[22] and though a series of shocking crimes committed against slaves by Portuguese subjects, with the aid of a British subject named John Scott, in 1877, strengthened the Portuguese claim[23] that effective jurisdiction should be established, the British Government maintained its attitude of reserve. The action of de Brazza, however, in special seems to have quickened the fears of Portugal, which in 1881 took steps to render closer its relations with San Salvador, and on November 22, 1882,[24] an earnest appeal was made to the British Government to recognize Portuguese sovereignty in exchange for assurances of commercial freedom and effective action against the slave trade. On December 15, 1882,[25] Lord Granville was able to intimate that, whilst the British Government declined absolutely to consider the historic claims of Portugal as having any validity, they were prepared to consider favourably an arrangement which would further the freedom of commerce of all nations, and the civilization of Africa by the suppression of the slave trade. The conditions of acceptance of the Portuguese claim were specified as the free navigation of the Congo and the Zambezi and their affluents; the adoption of a low maximum tariff in all the Portuguese African dominions, with the guarantee to Great Britain of most favoured nation treatment; the concession to British subjects in the Congo district of the same rights as were granted to Portuguese subjects as regards purchase or lease of lands, missionary operations, or taxation; the suppression of the slave trade and of slavery; and the precise definition of the extent of the Portuguese possessions in Africa, together with the transfer to Britain of any Portuguese rights in West Africa between 5° W. long. and 5° E. long. Not unnaturally the proposal thus to recognize the position of Portugal caused uneasiness to the International Association, and on March 15, 1883,[26] Lord Granville made it clear that, in delimiting the internal boundary of the lands over which it was proposed to recognize Portuguese sovereignty, care must be taken to exclude the possibility of extending Portuguese control over Stanley Pool. Generous as were these terms, Portugal with singular fatuity persisted in fighting them item by

---

22. C. 3531, pp. 70 sq.
23. *Ibid.*, p. 86.
24. C. 3885, pp. 1–6.
25. *Ibid.*, pp. 6, 7; Fitzmaurice, *Lord Granville*, ii. 344 sq.
26. C. 3885, pp. 12–15.

item, and the final agreement was delayed to February 26, 1884.[27] The treaty showed at every point concessions to Portuguese obstinacy: the sovereignty of Portugal over the coast from 5° 12′ S. lat. to 8° S. lat. was conceded, the inland limit on the Congo to be Noki, and on the rest of the coast to be the boundaries of the existing possessions of the coast and riparian tribes, the delimitation being entrusted to Portugal, but to be approved by the United Kingdom. All foreigners were to receive equal treatment with Portuguese subjects in all matters in the territory recognized as subject to Portuguese sovereignty; there was to be complete freedom of trade and of navigation on the Congo and its affluents; complete religious equality was to be established, and the régime of freedom of navigation was to apply to the Zambezi. The customs tariff in the territory was not for ten years to exceed the Mozambique tariff of 1877, and only to be altered thereafter by agreement. A British and Portuguese Commission was to supervise the measures taken to secure free navigation of the Congo, Portugal declining absolutely to permit the establishment of the international control for which Britain pressed. No cession of territory was made by Portugal, but she admitted that her rights on the Shiré did not extend beyond the confluence of the Ruo with that river, gave a right of pre-emption over her West African possessions between 5° E. long. and 5° W. long., forbade the raising of the customs tariffs in her African possessions for ten years, and gave British subjects most favoured nation treatment in all these possessions. Portugal also undertook to suppress the slave trade and slavery in her new territory.

The motives of the British Government in arranging this treaty have been much canvassed. Sir H. Johnston,[28] who praises its terms, censures the British Parliament for failing to ratify it, an accusation which is open to the technical objection that it does not rest with Parliament, save when expressly so provided, to ratify a treaty concluded by the Crown. On the other hand, Dr. Scott Keltie[29] finds it necessary to defend Lord Granville's action by the assumption that he and Stanley himself acted in the belief that on completing the organization of an administration on the Congo the King of the Belgians would hand over the territory to Britain, which would then have no reason to regret that the mouth of the river was in Portuguese hands. It must be remembered that at this time it was still doubtful whether French claims would not prevail, and that, in any event, as the United Kingdom did not desire itself

27. C. 3886.
28. *J. A. S.* iii. 459, 460; *Journ. Soc. Comp. Leg.* xviii. 30, 31; Fitzmaurice, *Lord Granville,* ii. 345, 346.
29. *Partition of Africa,* p. 145. This theory is not favoured by what we now know of Lord Granville's views (Fitzmaurice, ii. 355, 356).

to take possession, it may have seemed well to settle the matter by allotting power to the one claimant which had some show of historic right. Moreover, the advantages to be gained by the treaty were not negligible, and criticism of its terms is possible only if it could be established that the British might have secured the control for themselves.

In England itself the treaty was the reverse of popular: it was denounced by the Manchester Chamber of Commerce[30] on the ground that Portugal would as elsewhere in her possessions hamper British trade, and by the Anti-Slavery Society[31] on the ground that, whatever her promises, Portugal would never deal effectively with the slave trade. These arguments could be answered, but Lord Granville from the first had dealt with the matter on the basis that Portugal must obtain the assent of the Great Powers to the proposed assertion of her sovereignty, and it was soon obvious that this assent would not be forthcoming. The King of the Belgians recognized in the treaty a grave menace to his plans, and he found ready support both in France and Germany. France still entertained hopes of obtaining the Congo, and on March 13[32] definitely informed Portugal of her refusal to acknowledge her rights. Germany had no immediate prospect of acquiring the Congo, though as early as 1875 annexation had been suggested, and since then Pogge had travelled in the western basis of the Congo and Böhm and Reichardt in the south.[33] But her merchants had the strongest possible objection to Portuguese sovereignty. Prince Bismarck was only too glad to favour France at the expense of England, and still more to support a project which would place the Congo in the hands of a weak power in lieu of France. On April 17 Prince Bismarck seems to have sounded France as to the desirability of an international discussion of the question, and on the following day he delivered to Portugal and Britain alike a characteristically peremptory refusal to accept the treaty.[34] On April 22 the Association was further strengthened by the formal accord of recognition of its flag as that of a friendly government by the Government of the United States.[35] This—the first recognition of its territorial sovereignty—was the work of General Sanford, who had taken the deepest interest in the undertaking, and by representing the King as embued with the ideals of the founders of Liberia had won the Senate on April 10 to approve recognition by the execu-

30. C. 4023, pp. 17, 30.

31. *Ibid.*, pp. 40, 44.

32. Masoin, *Histoire,* i. 36. The British Government were very imperfectly informed at the time of these proceedings; see C. 4205.

33. Johnston, *George Grenfell,* i. 83.

34. Masoin, *loc. cit.*

35. C. 4361, p. 262; Stanley, *The Congo,* ii. 382–3.

tive power. On the following day the King brought to fruition his prolonged dealings with France by the signature of an agreement, under which the Association pledged itself not to cede without previous consultation with France any of the free stations and territories which it had established on the Congo and the Niari-Kwilu, and 'wishing to afford a new proof of its friendly feeling towards France, pledges itself to give her the right of preference, if through any unforeseen circumstances the Association were one day led to realize its possession'.[36] It can hardly be doubted that this agreement appeared to France little more than a prelude to the formal transfer of the territory to her control.

The trend of international opinion resulted in a volte-face on the part of Portugal, which decided to see if, since the United Kingdom could not secure the carrying out of the treaty, it were not possible to obtain at least the substance of her aims by recourse to Germany and France. Subsequent events make it clear that the basis of the *rapprochement* that was then effected between Portugal and the Powers, which had refused to recognize her territorial claims in terms the reverse of complimentary, was their promise, implemented in 1886, to recognize by treaty her preposterous claims to the territory lying between her possessions in Angola and Mozambique, whose union would have shut the United Kingdom out from Central Africa.[37] Great Britain[38] made an effort to save the treaty by suggesting wholesale modification especially in the direction of entrusting the control of navigation to an International Commission as originally proposed, but from June on it became clear that only an International Conference could dispose of the issue. The formal proposal was credited to Portugal,[39] and Germany secured the assent of France to it, by recognizing on September 13, in a note from Prince Bismarck to Baron de Courcel, the validity of the agreement of April 23 giving France the right of pre-emption.[40] On October 8,[41] therefore, Germany in concert with France issued formal invitations to the leading Powers to take part in an international conference to discuss (1) freedom of commerce in the basin and mouths of the Congo; (2) the application to the Congo and the Niger of the principles adopted by the Congress of Vienna with a view to

36. Stanley, *The Congo*, ii. 388.
37. Scott Keltie, *Partition of Africa*, pp. 440–1; Franco-Portuguese treaty of May 12, 1886, Article IV; German-Portuguese treaty of December 30, 1886, Article VII. These claims were for ever settled by the Anglo-Portuguese treaty of June 11, 1891.
38. C. 4205, pp. 1 sq.
39. C. 4205, p. 2.
40. Stanley, *The Congo*, ii. 388.
41. C. 4205, p. 5.

preserving freedom of navigation on certain international rivers, principles applied later on to the Danube; and (3) a definition of the formalities necessary to be observed so that new occupations on the African coast should be deemed effective. The British Government took no exception in principle to the Conference, though the hostile temper of its promoters was obvious, but insisted—finally with success—on obtaining from Prince Bismarck assurances as to the nature of the topics which were to form the subject of discussion.[42]

In any estimate of the attitude of the British Government during this period, whether as regards the Congo or other African questions, including that of Angra Pequena, then at its height, or as regards New Guinea, on which Germany was about to establish a hold, it is imperative to take into account the actual position of general European politics. It is easy, if this essential consideration is disregarded, as it normally is by critics of Lord Granville's action in Africa and Oceania alike, to represent the period as one of foolish surrenders of territory made without any justification at the expense of the interest of British communities in South Africa and Australasia. Yet nothing can possibly be more unfair or less worthy of a historian than this attitude. The facts of the case are simple: France was under the ministry of M. Jules Ferry,[43] 'whose self-imposed mission it had been to stir up trouble in every part of the world against Great Britain and to be a useful instrument for Prince Bismarck'. Prince Bismarck[44] was engaged in an energetic and unscrupulous campaign to secure for Germany colonies, an aim in itself, however, not illegitimate unless the United Kingdom was to maintain a monopoly of oversea possessions and to demand that the progress of civilization should wait until she had time to annex all unoccupied Africa and administer it, a task far beyond her powers. Russia[45] was pursuing a steady advance upon India, which on March 29, 1885, was to culminate after a long record of broken promises in the incident of Panjdeh, which almost resulted in war. From 1882 the question of Egypt involved with increasing emphasis the strength of the United Kingdom, and presented her with the alternative of maintaining her position there at the cost of sacrifices elsewhere to Germany or being forced to abandon Egypt. Following upon an angry dispatch from Prince Bismarck of June 10,[46] 1884, Count Münster in June informed Lord Granville verbally[47] 'that the German Government could not maintain a

---

42. C. 4205, pp. 11 sq.; C. 4360.
43. Fitzmaurice, *Lord Granville*, ii. 429, 439.
44. *Ibid.* ii. 337 sq.; cf. Rouard de Card, *Le Prince de Bismarck* (1918).
45. *Ibid.* ii. 418 sq., 440 sq.
46. *Ibid.* ii. 352; cf. 427 sq.
47. *Ibid.* ii. 354.

The "Irrepressible" Tourist: B-sm-rck. "H'm!—Ha!—Where shall I go next?"
SOURCE: *Punch* 89 (29 August 1885): 103.

friendly attitude on Egyptian matters if Great Britain maintained an unfriendly attitude on colonial questions'. In these circumstances the sacrifice
of Angra Pequena and of part of New Guinea, as well as of the Anglo-
Portuguese Treaty, become acts of prudent and far-seeing statesmanship, for
no sane judgement can possibly compare the value of Egypt to Britain with
that of Angra Pequena and New Guinea, and it may be added that in the
former case the claim of the Cape to part at least of the lost territory was
hopelessly compromised by the inexcusable reluctance of her ministries to
accept the obligation of governing and providing for the territory which they
desired to see annexed.[48]

SOURCE: Chapter 3 in *The Belgian Congo and the Berlin Act* (Oxford: Clarendon Press, 1919),
42–56.

Excerpt from "The Modern Traveller"
HILAIRE BELLOC

[Hilaire Belloc (1870–1953) was born in France and educated in England
at Birmingham and Oxford. He worked as a journalist, became a natural-
ized British subject, and served as a member of Parliament (1906–1910).
Known for his light verse and children's literature as well as his political
essays, Belloc was a follower of the nineteenth-century radical William Cobbett.]

V

Oh! Africa, mysterious Land!
Surrounded by a lot of sand
　　And full of grass and trees,
And elephants and Afrikanders,
And politics and Salamanders,
And Germans seeking to annoy,
And horrible rhinoceroi,
And native rum in little kegs,
And savages called Touaregs
　　(A kind of Soudanese).
And tons of diamonds, and lots

48. *Ibid.* ii. 350, 354.

Of nasty, dirty Hottentots,
And coolies coming from the East;
And serpents, seven yards long at least,
    And lions, that retain
Their vigour, appetites and rage
Intact to an extreme old age,
    And never lose their mane.
Far Land of Ophir! Mined for gold
By lordly Solomon of old,
Who sailing northward to Perim
Took all the gold away with him,
    And left a lot of holes;
Vacuities that bring despair
    To those confiding souls
Who find that they have bought a share
In marvellous horizons, where
The Desert terrible and bare
    Interminably rolls.

Great Island! Made to be the bane
Of Mr Joseph Chamberlain.
Peninsula! Whose smouldering fights
Keep Salisbury awake at nights;
And furnished for a year or so
Such sport to M. Hanotaux.

Vast Continent! Whose cumbrous shape
Runs from Bizerta to the Cape
(Bizerta on the northern shore,
Concerning which, the French, they swore
It never should be fortified,
Wherein that cheerful people lied).

Thou nest of Sultans full of guile,
Embracing Zanzibar the vile
And Egypt, watered by the Nile
(Egypt, which is, as I believe,
The property of the Khedive):
Containing in thy many states
Two independent potentates,
    And one I may not name.

Look carefully at number three,
Not independent quite, but he
Is more than what he used to be.
To thee, dear goal, so long deferred
Like old Æneas—in a word
     To Africa we came.

We beached upon a rising tide
At Sasstown on the western side;
     And as we touched the strand
I thought—I may have been mistook—
I thought the earth in terror shook
     To feel its Conquerors land.

VI

In getting up our Caravan
We met a most obliging man,
The Lord Chief Justice of Liberia,
And Minister of the Interior;
Cain Abolition Beecher Boz,
Worked like a Nigger—which he was—
     And in a single day
Procured us Porters, Guides, and kit,
And would not take a sou for it
     Until we went away.[1]
We wondered how this fellow made
Himself so readily obeyed,
And why the natives were so meek;
Until by chance we heard him speak,
And then we clearly understood
How great a Power for Social Good
     The African can be.
He said with a determined air:
'You are not what your fathers were;
Liberians, you are Free!
Of course, if you refuse to go—'
And here he made a gesture.

1. But when we went away, we found
   A deficit of several pound.

He also gave us good advice
Concerning Labour and its Price.
'In dealing wid de Native Scum,
Yo' cannot pick an' choose;
Yo' hab to promise um a sum
Ob wages, paid in Cloth and Rum.
But, Lordy! that's a ruse!
Yo' get yo' well on de Adventure,
And change de wages to Indenture.'

We did the thing that he projected,
The Caravan grew disaffected,
    And Sin and I consulted;
Blood understood the Native mind,
He said: 'We must be firm but kind.'
    A Mutiny resulted.
I never shall forget the way
That Blood upon this awful day
Preserved us all from death.
He stood upon a little mound,
Cast his lethargic eyes around,
And said beneath his breath:
'Whatever happens we have got
The Maxim Gun, and they have not.'

He marked them in their rude advance,
He hushed their rebel cheers;
With one extremely vulgar glance
He broke the Mutineers.
(I have a picture in my book
Of how he quelled them with a look.)
We shot and hanged a few, and then
The rest became devoted men.
And here I wish to say a word
Upon the way my heart was stirred
    By those pathetic faces.
Surely our simple duty here
Is both imperative and clear;
While they support us, we should lend
Our every effort to defend,
And from a higher point of view

To give the full direction due
 To all the native races.
And I, throughout the expedition,
Insisted upon this position.

VII

Well, after that we toiled away
At drawing maps, and day by day
Blood made an accurate survey
 Of all that seemed to lend
A chance, no matter how remote,
Of letting our financier float
That triumph of Imagination,
'The Libyan Association.'
 In this the 'Negroes' friend,
Was much concerned to show the way
Of making Missionaries pay.

At night our leader and our friend
 Would deal in long discourses
Upon this meritorious end,
And how he would arrange it.
'The present way is an abuse
 Of Economic Forces;
They Preach, but they do not Produce.
Observe how I would change it.
I'd have the Missionary lent,
Upon a plot of land,
A sum at twenty-five per cent;
And (if I understand
The kind of people I should get)
An ever-present risk of debt
Would make them work like horses,
And form the spur, or motive spring,
In what I call "developing
 The Natural resources";
While people who subscribe will find
Profit and Piety combined.'

SOURCE: In *The Modern Traveller* (London: E. Arnold, 1898), 181–86.

The Fashoda Incident

WINSTON CHURCHILL

[Winston Churchill (1874–1965), often described in his last years as the "greatest living Englishman," began his political and literary career in the British military service in the 4th Hussars in 1895. He served under General Kitchener in Omdurman (1898) with the Nile Expeditionary Forces, of which *The River War* is an account. From there he went to South Africa as a London newspaper correspondent during the Anglo-Boer War.]

The long succession of events, of which I have attempted to give some account, has not hitherto affected to any great extent other countries than those which are drained by the Nile. But this chapter demands a wider view, since it must describe an incident which might easily have convulsed Europe, and from which far-reaching consequences have arisen. It is unlikely that the world will ever learn the details of the subtle scheme of which the Marchand Mission was a famous part. We may say with certainty that the French Government did not intend a small expedition, at great peril to itself, to seize and hold an obscure swamp on the Upper Nile. But it is not possible to define the other arrangements. What part the Abyssinians were expected to play, what services had been rendered them and what inducements they were offered, what attitude was to be adopted to the Khalifa, what use was to be made of the local tribes: all this is veiled in the mystery of intrigue. It is well known that for several years France, at some cost to herself and at a greater cost to Italy, had courted the friendship of Abyssinia, and that the weapons by which the Italians were defeated at Adowa had been mainly supplied through French channels. A small quick-firing gun of continental manufacture and of recent make which was found in the possession of the Khalifa seems to point to the existence or contemplation of similar relations with the Dervishes. But how far these operations were designed to assist the Marchand Mission is known only to those who initiated them, and to a few others who have so far kept their own counsel.

The undisputed facts are few. Towards the end of 1896 a French expedition was despatched from the Atlantic into the heart of Africa under the command of Major Marchand. The re-occupation of Dongola was then practically complete, and the British Government were earnestly considering the desirability of a further advance. In the beginning of 1897 a British expedition, under Colonel Macdonald, and comprising a dozen carefully selected officers, set out from England to Uganda, landed at Mombassa, and struck inland. The misfortunes which fell upon this enterprise are beyond the scope of this account, and I shall not dwell upon the local jealousies and disputes which marred it. It is sufficient to observe that Colonel Macdonald was provided with Soudanese troops who were practically in a state of mutiny and actually mutinied two days after he assumed command. The officers were compelled to fight for their lives. Several were killed. A year was consumed in suppressing the mutiny and the revolt which arose out of it. If the object of the expedition was to reach the Upper Nile, it was soon obviously unattainable, and the Government were glad to employ the officers in making geographical surveys.

At the beginning of 1898 it was clear to those who, with the fullest information, directed the foreign policy of Great Britain that no results affecting the situation in the Soudan could be expected from the Macdonald Expedition. The advance to Khartoum and the reconquest of the lost provinces had been irrevocably undertaken. An Anglo-Egyptian force was already concentrating at Berber. Lastly, the Marchand Mission was known to be moving towards the Upper Nile, and it was a probable contingency that it would arrive at its destination within a few months. It was therefore evident that the line of advance of the powerful army moving south from the Mediterranean and of the tiny expedition moving east from the Atlantic must intersect before the end of the year, and that intersection would involve a collision between the Powers of Great Britain and France.

I do not pretend to any special information not hitherto given to the public in this further matter, but the reader may consider for himself whether the conciliatory policy which Lord Salisbury pursued towards Russia in China at this time—a policy which excited hostile criticism in England—was designed to influence the impending conflict on the Upper Nile and make it certain, or at least likely, that when Great Britain and France should be placed in direct opposition, France should find herself alone.

With these introductory reflections we may return to the theatre of the war.

On the 7th of September, five days after the battle and capture of Omdurman, the *Tewfikia*, a small Dervish steamer—one of those formerly used by General Gordon—came drifting and paddling down the river. Her Arab crew soon perceived by the Egyptian flags which were hoisted on the principal buildings, and by the battered condition of the Mahdi's Tomb, that all was not well in the city; and then, drifting a little further, they found themselves surrounded by the white gunboats of the 'Turks,' and so incontinently surrendered. The story they told their captors was a strange one. They had left Omdurman a month earlier, in company with the steamer *Safia*, carrying a force of 500 men, with the Khalifa's orders to go up the White Nile and collect grain. For some time all had been well; but on approaching the old Government station of Fashoda they had been fired on by black troops commanded by white officers under a strange flag—and fired on with such effect that they had lost some forty men killed and wounded. Doubting who these formidable enemies might be, the foraging expedition had turned back, and the Emir in command, having disembarked and formed a camp at a place on the east bank called Reng, had sent the *Tewfikia* back to ask the Khalifa for instructions and reinforcements. The story was carried to the Sirdar and ran like wildfire through the camp. Many officers made their way to the river, where the steamer lay, to test for themselves the truth of the report. The woodwork of the hull was marked with many newly made holes, and cutting into these with their penknives the officers extracted bullets—not the roughly cast leaden balls, the bits of telegraph wire, or old iron which savages use, but the conical nickel-covered bullets of small-bore rifles such as are fired by civilised forces alone. Here was positive proof. A European Power was on the Upper Nile: which? Some said it was the Belgians from the Congo; some that an Italian expedition had arrived; others thought that the strangers were French; others, again, believed in the Foreign Office—it was a British expedition, after all. The Arab crew were cross-examined as to the flag they had seen. Their replies were inconclusive. It had bright colours, they declared; but what those colours were and what their arrangement might be they could not tell; they were poor men, and God was very great.

Curiosity found no comfort but in patience or speculation. The camp for the most part received the news with a shrug. After their easy victory the soldiers walked delicately. They knew that they belonged to the most powerful force that had ever penetrated the heart of Africa. If there was to be more war, the Government had but to give the word, and the Grand Army of the Nile would do by these newcomers as they had done by the Dervishes.

On the 8th the Sirdar started up the White Nile for Fashoda with five steamers, the xith and xiiith Battalions of Soudanese, two companies of the Cameron Highlanders, Peake's battery of artillery, and four Maxim guns. Three days later he arrived at Reng, and there found, as the crew of the *Tewfikia* had declared, some 500 Dervishes encamped on the bank, and the *Safia* steamer moored to it. These stupid fellows had the temerity to open fire on the vessels. Whereat the *Sultan*, steaming towards their *dêm*, replied with a fierce shell fire which soon put them to flight. The *Safia*, being under steam, made some attempt to escape—whither, it is impossible to say—and Commander Keppel by a well-directed shell in her boilers blew her up, much to the disgust of the Sirdar, who wanted to add her to his flotilla.

After this incident the expedition continued its progress up the White Nile. The *sudd* which was met with two days' journey south of Khartoum did not in this part of the Nile offer any obstacle to navigation, as the strong current of the river clears the waterway; but on either side of the channel a belt of the tangled weed, varying from twelve to twelve hundred yards in breadth, very often prevented the steamers from approaching the bank to tie up. The banks themselves depressed the explorers by their melancholy inhospitality. At times the river flowed past miles of long grey grass and swampland, inhabited and habitable only by hippopotami. At times a vast expanse of dreary mud flats stretched as far as the eye could see. At others the forest, dense with an impenetrable undergrowth of thorn-bushes, approached the water, and the active forms of monkeys and even of leopards darted among the trees. But the country—whether forest, mud-flat, or prairie—was always damp and feverish: a wet land steaming under a burning sun and humming with mosquitoes and all kinds of insect life.

Onward and southward toiled the flotilla, splashing the brown water into foam and startling the strange creatures on the banks, until on the 18th of September they approached Fashoda. The gunboats waited, moored to the bank for some hours of the afternoon, to allow a message which had been sent by the Sirdar to the mysterious Europeans, to precede his arrival, and early in the morning of the 19th a small steel rowing-boat was observed coming down stream to meet the expedition. It contained a Senegalese sergeant and two men, with a letter from Major Marchand announcing the arrival of the French troops and their formal occupation of the Soudan. It, moreover, congratulated the Sirdar on his victory, and welcomed him to Fashoda in the name of France.

A few miles' further progress brought the gunboats to their destination, and they made fast to the bank near the old Government buildings of the town. Major Marchand's party consisted of eight French officers or non-commissioned officers, and 120 black soldiers drawn from the Niger district. They possessed three steel boats fitted for sail or oars, and a small steam launch, the *Faidherbe*, which latter had, however, been sent south for reinforcements. They had six months' supplies of provisions for the French officers, and about three months' rations for the men; but they had no artillery, and were in great want of small-arm ammunition. Their position was indeed precarious. The little force was stranded, without communications of any sort, and with no means of either withstanding an attack or of making a retreat. They had fired away most of their cartridges at the Dervish foraging party, and were daily expecting a renewed attack. Indeed, it was with consternation that they had heard of the approach of the flotilla. The natives had carried the news swiftly up the river that the Dervishes were coming back with five steamers, and for three nights the French had been sleeplessly awaiting the assault of a powerful enemy.

Their joy and relief at the arrival of a European force were undisguised. The Sirdar and his officers on their part were thrilled with admiration at the wonderful achievements of this small band of heroic men. Two years had passed since they left the Atlantic coast. For four months they had been absolutely lost from human ken. They had fought with savages; they had struggled with fever; they had climbed mountains and pierced the most gloomy forests. Five days and five nights they had stood up to their necks in swamp and water. A fifth of their number had perished; yet at last they had carried out their mission and, arriving at Fashoda on the 10th of July, had planted the tricolour upon the Upper Nile.

Moved by such reflections the British officers disembarked. Major Marchand, with a guard of honour, came to meet the General. They shook hands warmly. 'I congratulate you,' said the Sirdar, 'on all you have accomplished.' 'No,' replied the Frenchman, pointing to his troops; 'it is not I, but these soldiers who have done it.' And Kitchener, telling the story afterwards, remarked, 'Then I knew he was a gentleman.'

Into the diplomatic discussions that followed, it is not necessary to plunge. The Sirdar politely ignored the French flag, and, without interfering with the Marchand Expedition and the fort it occupied, hoisted the British and Egyptian colours with all due ceremony, amid musical honours and the salutes of the gunboats. A garrison was established at Fashoda, consisting of the XIth Soudanese, four guns of Peake's battery, and two Maxims, the whole under the command of Colonel Jackson, who was appointed military and civil commandant of the Fashoda district.

At three o'clock on the same afternoon the Sirdar and the gunboats resumed their journey to the south, and the next day reached the mouth of the Sobat, sixty-two miles from Fashoda. Here other flags were hoisted and another post formed with a garrison of half the XIIIth Soudanese battalion and the remaining two guns of Peake's battery. The expedition then turned northwards, leaving two gunboats—the *Sultan* and the *Abu Klea*—at the disposal of Colonel Jackson.

I do not attempt to describe the international negotiations and discussions that followed the receipt of the news in Europe, but it is pleasing to remember that a great crisis found England united. The determination of the Government was approved by the loyalty of the Opposition, supported by the calm resolve of the people, and armed with the efficiency of the fleet. At first indeed, while the Sirdar was still steaming southward, wonder and suspense filled all minds; but when suspense ended in the certainty that eight French adventurers were in occupation of Fashoda and claimed a territory twice as large as France, it gave place to a deep and bitter anger. There is no Power in Europe which the average Englishman regards with less animosity than France. Nevertheless, on this matter all were agreed. They should go. They should evacuate Fashoda, or else all the might, majesty, dominion, and power of everything that could by any stretch of the imagination be called 'British' should be employed to make them go.

Those who find it difficult to account for the hot, almost petulant, flush of resolve that stirred the nation must look back over the long history of the Soudan drama. It had always been a duty to reconquer the abandoned territory. When it was found that this might be safely done, the duty became a pleasure. The operations were watched with extravagant attention, and while they progressed the earnestness of the nation increased. As the tides of barbarism were gradually driven back, the old sea-marks came one after another into view. Names of towns that were half forgotten—or remembered only with sadness—re-appeared on the posters, in the gazettes, and in the newspapers. We were going back. 'Dongola,' 'Berber,' 'Metemma'—who had not heard of them before? Now they were associated with triumph. Considerable armies fought on the Indian Frontier. There was war in the South and the East and the West of Africa. But England looked steadfastly towards the Nile and the expedition that crawled forward slowly, steadily, unchecked, apparently irresistible.

When the final triumph, long expected, came in all its completeness it was hailed with a shout of exultation, and the people of Great Britain, moved far beyond their wont, sat themselves down to give thanks to their God, their Government, and their General. Suddenly, on the chorus of their rejoicing there broke a discordant note. They were confronted with the fact that a 'friendly Power' had, unprovoked, endeavoured to rob them of the fruits of their victories. They now realised that while they had been devoting themselves to great military operations, in broad daylight and the eye of the world, and prosecuting an enterprise on which they had set their hearts, other operations—covert and deceitful—had been in progress in the heart of the Dark Continent, designed solely for the mischievous and spiteful object of depriving them of the produce of their labours. And they firmly set their faces against such behaviour.

First of all, Great Britain was determined to have Fashoda or fight; and as soon as this was made clear, the French were willing to give way. Fashoda was a miserable swamp, of no particular value to them. Marchand, Lord Salisbury's 'explorer in difficulties upon the Upper Nile,' was admitted by the

French Minister to be merely an 'emissary of civilisation.' It was not worth their while to embark on the hazards and convulsions of a mighty war for either swamp or emissary. Besides, the plot had failed. Guy Fawkes, true to his oath and his orders, had indeed reached the vault; but the other conspirators were less devoted. The Abyssinians had held aloof. The negro tribes gazed with wonder on the strangers, but had no intention of fighting for them. The pride and barbarism of the Khalifa rejected all overtures and disdained to discriminate between the various breeds of the accursed 'Turks.' Finally, the victory of Omdurman and its forerunner—the Desert Railway— had revolutionised the whole situation in the Nile valley. After some weeks of tension, the French Government consented to withdraw their expedition from the region of the Upper Nile.

Meanwhile events were passing at Fashoda. The town, the site of which had been carefully selected by the old Egyptian Government, is situated on the left bank of the river, on a gentle slope of ground which rises about four feet above the level of the Nile at full flood. During the rainy season, which lasts from the end of June until the end of October, the surrounding country is one vast swamp, and Fashoda itself becomes an island. It is not, however, without its importance; for it is the only spot on the west shore for very many miles where landing from the river is possible. All the roads—mere camel-tracks—from Lower Kordofan meet at the Government post, but are only passable in the dry season. The soil is fertile, and, since there is a superabundance of sun and water, almost any crop or plant can be grown. The French officers, with the adaptive thrift of their nation, had already, in spite of the ravages of the water-rats, created a good vegetable garden, from which they were able to supplement their monotonous fare. The natives, however— aboriginal negroes of the Dinka and Shillook tribes—are unwilling to work, except to provide themselves with the necessaries of life; and since these are easily obtained, there is very little cultivation, and the fertility of the soil may be said to increase the poverty of the country. At all seasons of the year the climate of Fashoda is pestilential, and the malarial fever attacks every European or Egyptian, breaking down the strongest constitutions, and in many cases causing death.[1]

On this dismal island, far from civilisation, health, or comfort, the Marchand Mission and the Egyptian garrison lived in polite antagonism for nearly three months. The French fort stood at the northern end. The Egyptian camp lay outside the ruins of the town. Civilities were constantly ex-

---

1. The place is most unhealthy, and in March 1899 (the driest season of the year) out of a garrison of 317 men only 37 were fit for duty.—*Sir William Garstin's Report: Egypt, No. 5, 1899.*

changed between the forces, and the British officers repaid the welcome gifts of fresh vegetables by newspapers and other conveniences. The Senegalese rifle-men were smart and well-conducted soldiers, and the blacks of the Soudanese battalion soon imitated their officers in reciprocating courtesies. A feeling of mutual respect sprang up between Colonel Jackson and Major Marchand. The dashing commandant of the xith Soudanese, whose Egyptian medals bear no fewer than fourteen clasps, was filled with a generous admiration for the French explorer. Realising the difficulties, he appreciated the magnificence of the achievement; and as he spoke excellent French a good and almost cordial understanding was established, and no serious disagreement occurred. But, notwithstanding the polite relations, the greatest vigilance was exercised by both sides, and whatever civilities were exchanged were of a formal nature.

The Dinkas and Shillooks had on the first arrival of the French made submission, and had supplied them with provisions. They knew that white men were said to be coming, and they did not realise that there were different races among the whites. Marchand was regarded as the advance guard of the Sirdar's army. But when the negroes gradually perceived that these bands of white men were at enmity with each other—were, in fact, of rival tribes—they immediately transferred their allegiance to the stronger force, and, although their dread of the Egyptian flag was at first very marked, boycotted the French entirely.

In the middle of October despatches from France arrived for Marchand by steamer; and that officer, after reading them, determined to proceed to Cairo. Jackson, who was most anxious that no disagreement should arise, begged him to give positive orders to his subordinate to maintain the *status quo,* as had been agreed. Marchand gladly consented, and departed for Omdurman, where he visited the battlefield, and found in the heaps of slain a grim witness of the destruction from which he had been saved, and so on to Cairo, where he was moved to tears and speeches. But in his absence Captain Germain, who succeeded to the command, diverged from his orders. No sooner had Marchand left than Germain, anxious to win distinction, embarked upon a most aggressive policy. He occupied the Dinka country on the right bank of the river, pushed reconnoitring parties into the interior, prevented the Dinka Sheikhs from coming to make their submission at Fashoda, and sent his boats and the *Faidherbe* steam launch, which had returned from the south, beyond the northern limits which the Sirdar had prescribed and Marchand had agreed to recognise.

Colonel Jackson protested again and again. Germain sent haughty replies, and persisted in his provoking policy. At last the British officer was compelled to declare that if any more patrols were sent into the Dinka country, he would not allow them to return to the French post. Whereat Germain rejoined that he would meet force with force. All tempers were worn by fever, heat, discomfort, and monotony. The situation became very difficult, and the tact and patience of Colonel Jackson alone averted a conflict which would have resounded in all parts of the world. He confined his troops strictly to their lines, and moved as far from the French camp as was possible But there was one dark day when the French officers worked in their shirts with their faithful Senegalese to strengthen the entrenchments, and busily prepared for a desperate struggle. On the other side little activity was noticeable. The Egyptian garrison, although under arms, kept out of sight, but a wisp of steam above the funnels of the redoubtable gunboats showed that all was ready.

At length in a fortunate hour Marchand returned, reproved his subordinate, and expressed his regrets to Colonel Jackson. Then it became known that the French Government had ordered the evacuation of Fashoda. Some weeks were spent in making preparations for the journey, but at length the day of departure arrived. At 8.20 on the morning of the 11th of December the French lowered their flag with salute and flourish of bugle. The British officers, who remained in their own camp and did not obtrude themselves, were distant but interested spectators. On the flag ceasing to fly, a *sous-officier* rushed up to the flagstaff and hurled it to the ground, shaking his fists and tearing his hair in a bitterness and vexation from which it is impossible to withhold sympathy, in view of what these men had suffered uselessly and what they had done. The French then embarked, and at 9.30 steamed southward, the *Faidherbe* towing one oblong steel barge and one old steel boat, the other three boats sailing, all full of men. As the little flotilla passed the Egyptian camp a guard of honour of the xith Soudanese saluted them and the band struck up their national anthem. The French acknowledged the compliment by dipping their flag, and in return the British and Egyptian flags were also lowered. The boats then continued their journey until they had rounded the bend of the river, when they came to land, and, honour being duly satisfied, Marchand and his officers returned to breakfast with Colonel Jackson. The meeting was very friendly. Jackson and Germain exchanged most elaborate compliments, and the commandant, in the name of the xith Soudanese, presented the expedition with the banner of the Emir who had attacked them, which had been captured at Reng. Marchand shook hands all round, and the British officers bade their gallant opponents a final farewell.

Once again the eight Frenchmen, who had come so far and accomplished so much, set out upon their travels, to make a safe though tedious journey through Abyssinia to the coast, and thence home to the country they had served faithfully and well, and which was not unmindful of their services.

Let us settle the international aspect of the reconquest of the Soudan while we are in the way with it. The disputes between France and England about the valley of the Upper Nile were terminated, as far as material cause was concerned, by an Agreement, signed in London on the 21st of March, 1899, by Lord Salisbury and M. Cambon. The Declaration limiting the respective spheres of influence of the two Powers took the form of an addition to the ivth Article of the Niger Convention, concluded in the previous year. The actual text, which is so concise that it may be understood from a few minutes' study with a map, will be found among the Appendices to this volume. Its practical effect is to reserve the whole drainage system of the Nile to England and Egypt, and to engage that France shall have a free hand, so far as those Powers are concerned, in the rest of Northern Africa west of the Nile Valley not yet occupied by Europeans. This stupendous partition of half a continent by two European Powers could scarcely be expected to excite the enthusiasm of the rest. Germany was, however, soothed by the promise of the observance of the 'Open Door' policy upon the Upper Nile. Italy, protesting meekly, followed Germany. Russia had no interests in this quarter. France and England were agreed. The rest were not consulted: and the Declaration may thus be said to have been recognised by the world in general.

It is perhaps early to attempt to pronounce with which of the contracting Powers the advantage lies. France has acquired at a single stroke, without any serious military operations, the recognition of rights which may enable her ultimately to annex a vast African territory. At present what she has gained may be described as a recognised 'sphere of aspiration.' The future may convert this into a sphere of influence, and the distant future may witness the entire subjugation of the whole region. There are many difficulties to be overcome. The powerful influence of the Senussi has yet to be overthrown. The independent kingdom of Wadai must be conquered. Many smaller potentates will resist desperately. Altogether France has enough to occupy her in Central Africa for some time to come: and even when the long task is finished, the conquered regions are not likely to be of great value. They include the desert of the Great Sahara and wide expanses of equally profitless scrub or marsh. Only one important river, the Shari, flows through them, and never reaches the sea: and even Lake Chad, into which the Shari flows, appears to be leaking through some subterranean exit, and is rapidly changing from a lake into an immense swamp.

Great Britain and Egypt, upon the other hand, have secured a territory which, though smaller, is nevertheless of enormous extent, more fertile, comparatively easy of access, practically conquered, and containing the waterway of the Nile. France will be able to paint a great deal of the map of Africa blue, and the aspect of the continent upon paper may please the patriotic eye; but it is already possible to predict that before she can develop her property—can convert aspiration into influence, and influence into occupation—she will have to work harder, pay more, and wait longer for a return than will the more modest owners of the Nile Valley. And even when that return is obtained, it is unlikely that it will be of so much value.

It only remains to discuss the settlement made between the conquerors of the Soudan. Great Britain and Egypt had moved hand in hand up the great river, sharing, though unequally, the cost of the war in men and money. The prize belonged to both. The direct annexation of the Soudan by Great Britain would have been an injustice to Egypt. Moreover, the claim of the conquerors to Fashoda and other territories rested solely on the former rights of Egypt. On the other hand, if the Soudan became Egyptian again, it must wear the fetters of that imprisoned country. The Capitulations would apply to the Upper Nile regions, as to the Delta. Mixed Tribunals, Ottoman Suzerainty, and other vexatious burdens would be added to the difficulties of Soudan administration. To free the new country from the curse of internationalism was a paramount object. The Soudan Agreement by Great Britain and Egypt, published on the 7th of March, 1899, achieves this. Like most of the best work done in Egypt by the British Agency, the Agreement was slipped through without attracting much notice. Under its authority a State has been created in the Nile Valley which is neither British nor Ottoman, nor anything else so far known to the law of Europe. International jurists are confronted with an entirely new political status. A diplomatic 'Fourth Dimension' has been discovered. Great Britain and Egypt rule the country together. The allied conquerors have become the joint-possessors. 'What does this Soudan Agreement mean?' the Austrian Consul-General asked Lord Cromer; and the British Agent, whom twenty-two years' acquaintance with Egyptian affairs had accustomed to anomalies, replied, 'It means simply this'; and handed him the inexplicable document, under which the conquered country may some day march to Peace and Plenty.

SOURCE: Chapter 17 in *The River War: An Account of the Reconquest of the Sudan* (London: Eyre and Spottiswoode, 1899), 312–26.

―――――

Geography and Statecraft

LORD ALFRED MILNER

[In 1897, following service in Egypt, Milner (1854–1925) became the high commissioner in southern Africa and governor of the Cape colony. He served there—especially during the crucial years (1899–1902) of the Anglo-Boer War—until 1905, when he returned to England. He participated in the negotiation of the Peace of Vereeniging (1902), after which he encouraged the importation of Chinese laborers for work in the South African mines and sought to encourage British immigration to the region. The assistants who worked under him during his tenure in South Africa were given the soubriquet of "Milner's kindergarten." His writings on South Africa have been collected in two volumes edited by Cecil Headlam, *The Milner Papers: South Africa* (London: Cassell and Company, 1931).]

When the scramble for Africa began in the early eighties, Great Britain, owing to past misunderstandings and mistakes, and to a policy which, among other things, ignored geography, and tried to separate the inseparable, had lost control of the more important—eastern—half of the northward march of European colonisation, and its most advanced posts were no longer on British territory. In 1882–83, the Boer Republic on our right flank had pushed far ahead of the furthest limit of British authority and was some four hundred miles nearer to the centre of Africa. And the fear was that foreign Powers, availing themselves of the split between Boer and Briton, might use the Transvaal to bar the road to the further advance of British influence and civilisation. It was under the impulse of that fear that Rhodes made the great dash, or rather the series of great dashes, to the north, which have resulted in the extraordinary elongation of the British portion of South Africa.

First came the march of the pioneers into Mashonaland in 1890, which interposed a belt of British settlement between the northern Transvaal and the Zambesi. Then followed in 1893 the Matabele War and the subjection of the whole country up to that river. These events gave us the great regions now known as Southern Rhodesia. But Rhodes could not rest content with the boundary of the Zambesi. He was haunted by the thought of the rapidity with which all the vacant spaces of the world were being appropriated by one European Power or another, and he was bent on preserving as large an area as possible for his own countrymen. And so, before his death in 1902, despite failures of his own seeking, and interruptions for which he was not to blame—

Marchez! Marchand! General John Bull (to Major Marchand).
"Come, Professor, you've had a nice little scientific trip! I've smashed the dervishes—
luckily for *you*—and now I recommend you to pack up your flags,
and go home!!" SOURCE: *Punch* 115 (8 October 1898): 162.

despite the Raid and the Rinderpest, the Matabele Rebellion and the great Boer War—he had succeeded in acquiring certain large trading and administrative rights beyond the Zambesi, up to the very confines of the Congo Free State, and in inducing the British Government to throw its aegis over them. These are the countries now known as North-Western and North-Eastern Rhodesia, and, like Southern Rhodesia, virtually incorporated in the British Empire, though no doubt in a much more rudimentary stage in respect of development and administration. It had taken more than two hundred years to carry European authority from Cape Town to Kimberley. It took less than twenty to advance it from Kimberley northwards to a distance twice as great—a colossal achievement, which we owe to the energy, the daring, and the geographical imagination of a single man.

And now, perhaps, enough has been said to enable us to make a fair estimate of this latest stage in the European invasion of Africa from the South, to realise the causes of its feverish haste, the boldness of its conception, and at the same time its inevitable defects. It has been a movement along natural lines, but unduly accelerated by accidental political causes. But for the scramble for Africa, even the restless genius of Rhodes might not have gone so fast or so far. And while it is impossible not to admire the spectacle of this private citizen— for after the end of 1895 he ceased to be even Prime Minister of the Cape— undertaking and financing a great enterprise of State, ensuring the concurrence of a reluctant Government by saving it all expense, and paying his way by a mixed appeal to the speculative instincts and the patriotic ambitions of his countrymen, it is no disparagement to him to say that this is not the best imaginable way in which an empire can be built. He followed the only lines possible under the circumstances. He spent his life in the task. Our gratitude is due to him for the vast opportunities which he created or preserved for us. But Southern and Northern Rhodesia alike will long bear the traces of the strange expedients which had to be adopted in getting them started, and a great many problems will have to be solved before either of them can be satisfactorily fitted into the framework of South Africa or of the Empire.

The system of extending the bounds of Empire by the agency of Chartered Companies is open to many objections. There has been much in the methods of this particular company, especially during its earliest years, which it is impossible to regard with approval. But the British South Africa Company has at least two great claims on our gratitude. It has kept a large and valuable portion of the Dark Continent under the British flag, and it has built up, in a remarkably short space of time, an administration which, if far from perfect, is at least competent, honest, and humane. Government by means of a company is necessarily a transient form of government. But in the case which we have been considering, it is a valuable stop-gap, valuable in maintaining a tolerable condition of affairs and affording time to work out with deliberation, and with a fuller knowledge than we yet possess of all the conditions of one of the least explored of habitable lands, the best permanent arrangements for its welfare.

SOURCE: Inaugural address delivered before the Royal Scottish Geographical Society in Edinburgh, 13 November 1907. In *The Nation and Empire: Being a Collection of Speeches and Addresses* (London: Constable and Company, 1913), 228–29, 230, 233.

Excerpt from *Travels in Africa during the Years 1882–1886*

DR. WILHELM JUNKER

[As Andrew Apter comments, "Junker's sketch adds documentary force to this 'gruesome gift,' ostensibly illustrating African cannibalism and savagery but also implicating the European explorer in the same crimes—framed by exchange relations and modes of accumulation—which remain the hallmark of anthropology's heart of darkness" ("Africa, Empire, and Anthropology: A Philological Exploration of Anthropology's Heart of Darkness," *Annual Review of Anthropology* 28 [1999]: 592).]

During his absence from the station, Zemio was represented by his uncle, Foye, a brother of Tikima's. Foye was still a young man, and much attached to me, carefully providing for all my wants. He was also an excellent shot, and supplied us with more game than I had ever received before, although the tall grass at this season rendered hunting very difficult. I took care to have some jerked-meat prepared for future use, and even made some meat extract, which, taken with abré, always made an excellent dish. I often roasted a fillet of antelope for myself, or else set the meat-mincing machine at work to chop up the tough flesh of old animals, or manipulate the giblets and scraps from poultry. At that time I was even able to fry and bake with real butter, for I had still a small demi-john of Khartum butter in excellent condition. For a second course, or in case of scarcity, there was also rice remaining, which was taken with prunes or other dried fruits.

From Foye I also received the skins of the animals captured by him, and

A Gruesome Gift.

this afforded occupation for the young people, who had to stretch the skins, to detach the adhering tissues, ligatures, and muscles, and remove every scrap of fat by long and careful rubbing with suitable porous stones. I had already taught Dsumbe how to prepare skeletons of mammals, and this work was now again taken in hand. The beginning of fresh collections was made by frequent hunting expeditions, in which Dsumbe would at times spend the whole day.

These collections were now enriched by the gruesome present of a number of human heads. I had merely given a general order to procure bleached skulls, should the occasion present itself. But Zemio's people having once made a raid on some unruly A-Kahle people, those who fell were beheaded, and the heads not eaten, as is customary, but brought to me. I had them for the present buried in a certain place, and after my next journey prepared for the collection.

Amongst my frequent visitors at that time were Yapati and Rabe, two brothers of Foye, besides Nbassani, whose districts lay nearest to Zemio's residence. For Foye I had great projects in view. From this time I decided to let him have my Express rifle on his hunting excursions, in order to bring down large game with the least possible damage to their skins. On November 13th we had some final practice with this gun, as he was to start on an expedition in a few days. But that very day a blow fell suddenly on me, like a bolt in the blue, which caused me most serious loss.

SOURCE: Dr. Wilhelm Junker, *Travels in Africa during the Years 1882–1886*, translated from the German by A. H. Keane, Fellow of the Royal Geographic Society (London: Chapman and Hall, 1892), 160–61.

Africa Shared Out

The continent of Africa is shared out at last—at least on paper. Future genera-tions will smile at the glee with which serious statesmen risked war and the wreck of civilisation in order to increase the area of the African map over which their country's influence is recognised as supreme. For the partition is a mapmaker's partition, about as practical as the famous partition by which a pope, on a map still visible in the museum of the Propaganda at Rome, divided the whole of the New World between Portugal and Spain. That was only four hundred years ago, and to-day neither Portugal nor Spain exercises sovereignty over a single acre of the New World. So it will be with Africa. The geographers who on Afric's downs put elephants instead of 'towns,' were hardly more unprofitably employed than those political geographers who are carefully painting great stretches of African sand or African forest French, British, or German, as the case may be. The agreement happily arrived at between M. Cambon and Lord Salisbury as to the limits of our respective spheres of influence in Northern Africa finally divides up the whole map. Tripoli and Morocco alone remain to be scrambled for. They are the only fragments of the African plum cake yet unappropriated—on the map.

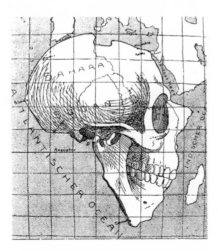

A German Representation of Africa.

SOURCE: In *Review of Reviews* 19 (January–June 1899): 309–10.

II

THE BODY POLITIC:

RATIONALIZING RACE

Human conscience is very gradually developed, and traverses sundry different stages. The value of a conscience therefore is in direct proportion to the advancement of its development. Civilized man who is so energetically conscious of himself is much more man, if I may be permitted to say so, than the savage who is scarcely conscious of his own existence, and whose life is only a small, comparatively valueless phenomenon. This is why the savage sets so little store by life, relinquishes it with such strange unconcern and deprives others of it in mere sport. With him the feeling of individuality has scarcely commenced.—Ernest Renan, *The Future of Science,* 1893

INTRODUCTION
The Body Politic: Rationalizing Race
MIA CARTER AND BARBARA HARLOW

T HE SCIENTIFIC FASCINATION and repulsion articulated by Ernest Renan reflects many nineteenth-century scientists' and philosophers' ambivalent feelings about the discoveries revealed to them by imperialist expansion. Scientific observation unveiled "strange" cultures, "exotic" traditions, and new forms of life—all of which required new descriptive categories and, perhaps, a reorganized understanding of human existence and society. How could one comprehend the density and variety of the earth's living beings? What processes could account for so many differences? The botanists, zoologists, philologists, and ethnologists of the day were preoccupied with two primary scientific issues: one concerned the nature and value of origins, the nature and value of people and things; the other involved an attempt to come to terms with the wealth of the earth's human, plant, and animal organisms. These questions encouraged nineteenth-century thinkers to analyze and theorize the interrelatedness between what frequently appeared to be dramatically different organisms and species. The duty and responsibility of making sense of difference was assumed to belong to the "discoverers." Ordering difference and interpreting the scientific and social reasons for variation became zealous missions; classification became the focus of scientific industry and enterprise.

Scientific naturalism proposed that all phenomena could be explained in terms of natural causes and natural laws, without attributing spiritual, moral, or supernatural significance to what appeared to be the natural order of things. In other words, observation was the key to enlightenment. Science would enable civilized man to locate the secret history of development, the mystery of the world's natural, historical, and social progress. The study of "lowly" forms of life was believed to be central to an understanding of creation and the past, and of progress and the future as well. The rise of the sciences was enthusiastically celebrated in many quarters of secular and academic society; creationist mythology and the Christian belief in divine order and God's immaculate plan were being rigorously challenged. Science, "civilized" culture's beacon of light, would illumine the dark corners of the world and liberate man from superstition and myth. Furthermore, the natural and social sciences would enable scientific observers to understand conflict, and catastrophe, and change. Many scientists included in this section were responding to the era's revolutionary sentiments and social unrest and to natural catastrophes like famine and disease. In a sense, imperial exploration and metropolitan expansion and growth made the century's observers vividly aware of the vast and constantly mutating nature of the living world—the social organism and the body politic.

Charles Darwin's theories of evolution and natural selection suggested that life itself was a struggle for survival: competition existed within a single species and not just between distinct species. This idea, which Herbert Spencer described as "the survival of the fittest," was not unfamiliar to nineteenth-century thinkers. Some of Darwin's predecessors in evolutionary thinking included his grandfather, Erasmus Darwin (*Zoonomia: Or, The Laws of Organic Life*, 1794–1796); J. B. Lamarck (*Zoological Philosophy*, 1809); Robert Chambers (*Vestiges of the Natural History of Creation*, 1844); and Charles Lyell (*Principles of Geology*, 1830–1833). Darwin's theory of evolution was also influenced by Thomas Robert Malthus's *An Essay on the Principle of Population, as it Affects the Future Improvement of Society* (1798). Malthus's essay, which is central to the development of population studies and modern theories of political economy, defined happiness as being dependent on the economic health of the state. The essay critiqued socialized reformers like William Cobbett (*Cottage Economy*, 1822) and William Godwin (*An Inquiry Concerning Political Justice and Its Influence on General Virtue and Happiness*, 1793), and was directed against Liberal reforms (Pitt's Poor Law, 1796). In part, the conflict and survival theories of economy and social organization aimed to reform the Liberal agenda to harbor and protect the labouring classes, the nation's poor. Malthus argued that the health of the state depended on constant and necessary checks on population. A struggle to procure the means of subsistence was one of these natural checks, one that would manage the population of the poor, since the wealthy property owners could control supply and demand. Other checks included delayed marriage for the poor—a pregnancy deterrent—and the expulsion or emigration of the so-called surplus population. The living conditions of the poor would improve, Malthus argued, if their numbers were reduced. These checks were believed to be superior and more economical forms of government and population management than the Liberals' policies of subsidized idleness. Malthus described the poor as nature's expendables and discussed "moral restraint"—a precursor to birth control—and famine and disease as "preventive" and "positive" checks on population growth. Social policy amounted to abnormal expenditure; the state was a vital organism that did not require meticulous and costly tending. The Irish potato famine (1845–1847), for example, was considered a disaster, but one with its own logic and governing principles: lower birth rates, increased mortality, and emigration. These natural discourses were central to Malthus's laissez faire economic theories, and they significantly influenced colonial administration, policy, and governance. If the British and European poor were suitable for sacrifice, the "savage" races were, by extension, neither essential nor valuable.

Victorian capitalists and conservatives believed that a good and effective government should be concerned with the protection and increase of its economy; individuals' fates would be determined by their efforts, by their natural genius or inventiveness and fortitude. A nonproductive individual would have to reform his or her ways to survive. This fiscal pragmatism proved harmful to the metropolitan poor and to colonial subjects, who were often considered obstructions to the state's economic increase. Both would be categorized as belonging to the "lower orders"—those who were born to produce the supplies but who were naturally not in a position to make demands. While Malthus's work influenced Darwin's theory of natural selection, Darwin did not share the political economist's ideological point of view or social pessimism. In Darwin's terms, the struggle for survival was a harsh and brutal process, *and* a creative and progressive one. Natural selection enabled a species to improve itself gradually and systematically; evolution provided another understanding of reform, one that was open to interpretation. Some interpreted evolution as evidence of insurmountable moral, ethical, biological, and intellectual differences. These pessimistic or conservative interpreters of Darwin's theory were polygenists, those who believed that human life consisted of a variety of species, with some species being clearly subordinate to others. In the polygenists' view, the "lowly" could adapt and evolve; however, even the more highly adapted species and races could never completely catch up with the "civilized" (white) ones. As Dudley Kidd stated in *Kafir Socialism* (1908), the African, provided the proper stimuli, might become capable of rising a bit: "He might not be able to become a European, but he can become a Super-Kafir" (265). Monogenists, the polygenists' theoretical adversaries, interpreted the theory in a slightly less deterministic fashion. From their perspective, Darwin's theory of evolution was an indication that the lowly could be uplifted or developed; differences might remain, but progression was emphasized. Despite its variability, the human species consisted of one family; the advantaged races, therefore, had the responsibility to civilize the disadvantaged ones. For scientists of both persuasions, Africans were considered a "sub-species," a popular term adopted in *The Descent of Man* (1871); and for monogenists and polygenists, Africa was the great laboratory, a testing ground for religious and scientific beliefs, a site in which the energies and faculties of civilized society could forcibly shape, refine, and redefine the fecund mass that to them, Africa appeared to be.

One of the most widely assimilated tenets of Darwin's theory of evolution was his understanding of aggressive competition, conflict, and violent struggle as central to the development of a species. The era's numerous social conflicts and revolutions may have made a theory of violent conflict seem familiar and commonsensical; many philosophers, despite all sorts of ideological differences, readily made the tenet central to their understanding of history, philology, physiognomy, biology, and society. In *The Future of Science* (1893), Ernest Renan argues that force itself was the source of civilization, a belief echoed in the works of Arthur Gobineau and Walter Bagehot. "Tyranny," Renan states, "would be legitimate to secure the triumph of the mind." Conquerors were as valuable as scientists and philosophers; conquest was "the violent intrusion of fresh elements which vivified and enlarged the ancient circle of life." The imperialists were, in other words, inventors and artists.

The works included in this section reflect many of the contradictions of the age: the world is ordered by stasis *and* change; a civilized culture is distinguished by its superior values and actions *and* "might makes right"; fidelity to religious values and beliefs is regressive, while a nearly mystical faith in science is progressive. As Andrew Apter and others have recently argued, there is an "imperial palimpsest in Africanist anthropology," a "colonial library" that includes the racialized estimations of African peoples; the pamphlets of the antislavery advocates; the concerns of such polemicists as Thomas Carlyle, whose railery against West Indians in Britain subsumes as well those other islanders, the hungry Irish; and the politicians who had to preserve their hold on prerogatives. At stake were questions scientific, pseudoscientific, and political scientific (Apter 1999). The twentieth-century issues of decolonization, of self-governance and self-determination for the formerly colonized, lay in wait in these high imperial debates in the nineteenth century.

Representations of Africa and Africans, that is, reflect the invention of racial categories and depict the refinement of extremely flexible systems of classification based on questionable forms of evidence. The exemplary standards of beauty, morality, intelligence, and of physical and political strength were fundamentally Aryan; the savage races represented the depths to which humanity, if not racially careful or pure, could sink. Africa, typically described as the Dark Continent, became the absolute measure of scientific, moral, and biological difference. The black body and skin were pointed to as the primary evidence that the African was a thing apart, a "human fossil," an infantile specimen; the frequently parodied African languages and orally based societies were further evidence of the continent's cultural simplicity. The African's blackness became the metaphor for all of the empire's undesirable or unruly subjects: women, the working classes, rebellious Indians, Boers, the Irish, even European colonial competitors were depicted as irrational, unchangeable, impulsive, underdeveloped savages—a designation that frequently rationalized domination and legitimized aggressive and disciplinary scientific, administrative, and legislative regimes.

BIBLIOGRAPHY

Apter, Andrew. "Africa, Empire, and Anthropology: A Philological Exploration of Anthropology's Heart of Darkness." *Annual Review of Anthropology* 28 (1999): 577–98.

Barker, Martin. *The New Racism: Conservatives and the Ideology of the Tribe.* London: Junction Books, 1981.

Beer, Gillian. *Darwin's Plots: Evolutionary Narrative in Darwin, George Eliot, and Nineteenth-Century Fiction.* London: Routledge and Kegan Paul, 1993.

Betzig, Laura L. *Despotism and Differential Reproduction: A Darwinian View of History.* New York: Aldine Publishing, 1986.

Bildiss, Michael D. *Father of Racist Ideology: The Social and Political Thought of Count Gobineau.* New York: Weybright and Talley, 1970.

Bowler, Peter J. *Charles Darwin: The Man and His Influence.* Oxford: Blackwell, 1990.

Brenman, Jan, ed. *Imperial Monkey Business: Racial Supremacy in Social Darwinist Theory and Colonial Practice.* Amsterdam: Vu University Press, 1990.

Bush, Barbara. *Imperialism, Race, and Resistance.* London: Routledge, 1999.

Carroll, Joseph. *Evolution and Literary Theory.* Columbia: University of Missouri Press, 1995.

Cunningham, Suzanne. *Philosophy and the Darwinian Legacy.* Rochester, N.Y.: University of Rochester Press, 1996.

Davis, Mike. *Late Victorian Holocausts: El Niño Famines and the Making of the Third World.* London: Verso, 2001.

Desmond, Adrian, and James R. Moore. *Darwin.* London: Michael Joseph, 1991.

Drayton, Richard. *Nature's Government: Science, Imperial Britain, and the "Improvement of the World."* New Haven, Conn.: Yale University Press, 2000.

Ernst, Waltraud, and Bernard Harris, eds. *Race, Science, and Medicine, 1700–1960.* London: Routledge, 1999.

Eze, Emmanuel Chukwudi. *Race and the Enlightenment: A Reader.* Cambridge, Mass.: Blackwell, 1997.

Goldberg, David Theo, ed. *Anatomy of Racism.* Minneapolis: University of Minnesota Press, 1990.

Greyson, John, dir. *Zero Patience.* Canada, 1993. Film.

Haas, Philip, dir. *Angels and Insects.* United States/United Kingdom, 1995. Film.

Heuman, Gad. *"The Killing Time": The Morant Bay Rebellion in Jamaica*. London: MacMillan, 1994.

Imigoni, David, and Jeffrey Wallace, eds. *Charles Darwin's The Origin of the Species: Interdisciplinary Essays*. Manchester, England: Manchester University Press, 1995.

Kelley, Alfred. *The Descent of Darwin: The Popularization of Darwinism in Germany, 1860–1914*. Chapel Hill, N.C.: University of North Carolina Press, 1981.

Kidd, Dudley. *Kafir Socialism and the Dawn of Individualism: An Introduction to the Study of the Native Problem*. London: A. and C. Black, 1908.

Knox, Robert. *The Races of Men*. Philadelphia: Lea & Blanchard, 1860.

Levine, George Lewis. *Darwin and the Novelists: Patterns of Science in Victorian Fiction*. Cambridge, Mass.: Harvard University Press, 1988.

Mudimbe, V. Y. *The Idea of Africa*. Bloomington, Ind.: Indiana University Press, 1994.

Renan, Ernest. *The Future of Science*. Boston: Roberts Brothers, 1893.

Schaffner, Franklin J., dir. *Planet of the Apes*. United States, 1968. Film.

Stepan, Nancy. *The Idea of Race in Science: Great Britain, 1800–1960*. London: Archon Books, 1982.

Williams, Eric. *British Historians and the West Indies*. Brooklyn, N.Y.: A and B Books, 1994.

SLAVES

The African Slave Trade

WILLIAM WILBERFORCE

[The abolition of the slave trade by England in 1807 and the abolition of slavery throughout the British Empire in 1834 did not come about without debate and controversy. The 1789 speech delivered to the House of Commons by William Wilberforce (1759–1833) suggests both the influence of the revolution in France and the ideals of his own evangelical Christianity. Wilberforce was a leading member of the Society for Effecting the Abolition of the Slave Trade, as well as of the Clapham Sect, and as a member of the House of Commons sponsored much antislavery legislation. William Pitt the Younger (1759–1806) served two nearly continuous terms as prime minister and, as a friend of Wilberforce, was similarly engaged with the issue of abolition. The work of the abolition movement in the late eighteenth and early nineteenth centuries would be continued later in the century by such organizations as the Aborigines Protection Society and other missionary groups.]

William Wilberforce, in the
House of Commons, Pictures the Slave Trade
in All Its Horror [May 12, 1789]

In opening, concerning the nature of the slave trade, I need only observe that it is found by experience to be just such as every man who uses his reason would infallibly conclude it to be. For my own part, so clearly am I convinced of the mischiefs inseparable from it that I should hardly want any further evidence than my own mind would furnish by the most simple deductions. Facts, however, are now laid before the House. A report has been made by his Majesty's privy council, which, I trust, every gentleman has read, and which ascertains the slave trade to be just such in practice as we know, from theory, it must be. What should we suppose must naturally be the consequence of our carrying on a slave trade with Africa? With a country vast in its extent, not utterly barbarous, but civilized in a very small degree? Does anyone suppose a slave trade would help their civilization? Is it not plain that she must suffer from it? That civilization must be checked; that her barbarous manners must be made more barbarous; and that the happiness of her millions of inhabitants must be prejudiced with her intercourse with Britain? Does not everyone see that a slave trade carried on around her coasts must carry violence and desolation to her very center? That in a continent just emerging from barbarism, if a trade in men is established, if her men are all converted into goods, and become commodities that can be bartered, it follows they must be subject to ravage just as goods are; and this, too, at a period of civilization when there is no protecting legislature to defend this their only sort of property in the same manner as the rights of property are maintained by the legislature of every civilized country. We see then, in the nature of things, how easily the practices of Africa are to be accounted for. Her kings are never compelled to war, that we can hear of, by public principles, by national glory, still less by the love of their people. In Europe it is the extension of commerce, the maintenance of national honor, or some great public object that is ever the motive to war with every monarch; but, in Africa, it is the personal avarice and sensuality of their kings; these two vices of avarice and sensuality, the most powerful and predominant in natures thus corrupt, we tempt, we stimulate in all these African princes, and we depend upon these vices for the very maintenance of the slave trade. Does the king of Barbessin want brandy? he has only to send his troops, in the nighttime, to burn and desolate a village; the captives will serve as commodities that may be bartered with the British trader. What a striking view of the wretched state of Africa does the tragedy of Calabar furnish! Two towns, formerly hostile, had settled their differences, and by an intermarriage among their chiefs had each pledged themselves to peace; but the trade in slaves was prejudiced by such pacifications, and it became, therefore, the policy of our traders to renew the hostilities. This, their policy, was soon put in practice, and the scene of carnage which followed was such that it is better, perhaps, to refer gentlemen to the privy council's report than to agitate their minds by dwelling on it.

The slave trade, in its very nature, is the source of such kind of tragedies; nor has there been a single person, almost, before the privy council who does not add something by his testimony to the mass of evidence upon this point. Some, indeed, of these gentlemen, and particularly the delegates from Liverpool, have endeavored to reason down this plain principle: some have palliated it; but there is not one, I believe, who does not more or less admit it. Some, nay most, I believe, have admitted the slave trade to be the chief cause of wars in Africa. . . .

Having now disposed of the first part of this subject, I must speak of the transit of the slaves in the West Indies. This, I confess, in my own opinion, is the most wretched part of the whole subject. So much misery condensed in so little room is more than the human imagination had ever before conceived. I will not accuse the Liverpool merchants; I will allow them, nay, I will believe them, to be men of humanity; and I will therefore believe, if it were not for the multitude of these wretched objects, if it were not for the enormous magnitude and extent of the evil which distracts their attention from individual cases and makes them think generally, and therefore less feelingly, on the subject, they never would have persisted in the trade. I verily believe, therefore, if the wretchedness of any one of the many hundred Negroes stowed in each ship could be brought before their view, and remain within the sight of the African merchant, that there is no one among them whose heart would bear it. Let anyone imagine to himself six or seven hundred of these wretches chained two and two, surrounded with every object that is nauseous and disgusting, diseased, and struggling under every kind of wretchedness! How can we bear to think of such a scene as this? One would think it had been determined to heap on them all the varieties of bodily pain, for the purpose of blunting the feelings of the mind; and yet, in this very point (to show the power of human prejudice), the situation of the slaves has been described by Mr. Norris, one of the Liverpool delegates, in a manner which I am sure will convince the House how interest can draw a film over the eyes so thick that total blindness could do no more; and how it is our duty therefore to trust not to the reasonings of interested men or to their way of coloring a transaction. "Their apartments," says Mr. Norris, "are fitted up as much for their advantage as circumstances will admit. The right ankle of one, indeed, is connected with the left ankle of another by a small iron fetter, and if they are turbulent, by another on their wrists. They have several meals a day; some of their own country provisions, with the best sauces of African cookery; and by the way of variety, another meal of pulse, etc., according to European taste. After breakfast they have water to wash themselves, while their apartments are perfumed with frankincense and lime juice. Before dinner they are amused after the manner of their country. The song and the dance are promoted," and, as if the whole were really a scene of pleasure and dissipation, it is added that games of chance are furnished. "The men play and sing, while the women and girls make fanciful ornaments with beads, which they are plentifully supplied with." Such is the sort of strain in which the Liverpool delegates, and particularly Mr. Norris, gave evidence before the privy council. What will the House think when, by the concurring testimony of other witnesses, the true history is laid open. The slaves, who are sometimes described as rejoicing at their captivity, are so wrung with misery at leaving their country that it is the constant practice to set sail in the night, lest they should be sensible of their departure. The pulse which Mr. Norris talks of are horse beans; and the scantiness of both water and provision was suggested by the very legislature of Jamaica, in the report of their committee, to be a subject that called for the interference of Parliament.

Mr. Norris talks of frankincense and lime juice; when the surgeons tell you the slaves are stowed so close that there is not room to tread among them; and when you have it in evidence from Sir George Younge that even in a ship which wanted two hundred of her complement, the stench was intolerable. The song and the dance are promoted, says Mr. Norris. It had been more fair, perhaps, if he had explained that word "promoted." The truth is that for the sake of exercise these miserable wretches, loaded with chains, oppressed with disease and wretchedness, are forced to dance by the terror of the lash, and sometimes by the actual use of it. "I," says one of the other evidences, "was employed to dance the men, while another person danced the women." Such, then, is the meaning of the word "promoted"; and it may be observed too, with respect to food, that an instrument is sometimes carried out, in order to force them to eat, which is the same sort of proof how much they enjoy themselves in that instance also. As to their singing, what shall we say when we are told that their songs are songs of lamentation upon their departure which, while they sing, are always in tears, insomuch that one captain (more humane as I should conceive him, therefore, than the rest) threatened one of the women with a flogging, because the mournfulness of her song was too painful for his feelings. In order, however, not to trust too much to any sort of description, I will call the attention of the House to one species of evidence which is absolutely infallible. Death, at least, is a sure ground of evidence, and the proportion of deaths will not only confirm, but, if possible, will even aggravate our suspicion of their misery in the transit. It will be found, upon an average of all ships of which evidence has been given at the privy council, that, exclusive of those who perish before they sail, not less than twelve and one half per cent perish in the passage. Besides these, the Jamaica report tells you that not less than four and one half per cent die on shore before the day of sale, which is only a week or two from the time of landing. One third more die in the seasoning, and this in a country exactly like their own, where they are healthy and happy, as some of the evidences would pretend. The diseases, however, which they contract on shipboard, the astringent washes which are to hide their wounds, and the mischievous tricks used to make them up for sale, are, as the Jamaica report says—a most precious and valuable report, which I shall often have to advert to—one principal cause of this mortality.

Upon the whole, however, here is a mortality of about fifty per cent, and this among Negroes who are not bought unless quite healthy at first, and unless (as the phrase is with cattle) they are sound in wind and limb. How then can the House refuse its belief to the multiplied testimonies, before the privy council, of the savage treatment of the Negroes in the middle passage? Nay, indeed, what need is there of any evidence? The number of deaths speaks for itself and makes all such inquiry superfluous. As soon as ever I had arrived thus far in my investigation of the slave trade, I confess to you, sir, so enormous, so dreadful, so irremediable did its wickedness appear that my own mind was completely made up for the abolition. A trade founded in iniquity, and carried on as this was, must be abolished, let the policy be what it might— let the consequences be what they would, I from this time determined that I would never rest till I had effected its abolition. . . .

When we consider the vastness of the continent of Africa; when we reflect how all other countries have for some centuries past been advancing in happiness and civilization; when we think how in this same period all improvement in Africa has been defeated by her intercourse with Britain; when we reflect that it is we ourselves that have degraded them to that wretched brutishness and barbarity which we now plead as the justification of our guilt; how the slave trade has enslaved their minds, blackened their character, and sunk them so low in the scale of animal beings that some think the apes are of a higher class, and fancy the orangutan has given them the go-by. What a mortification must we feel at having so long neglected to think of our guilt, or attempt any reparation! It seems, indeed, as if we had determined to forbear from all interference until the measure of our folly and wickedness was so full and complete; until the impolicy which eventually belongs to vice was become so plain and glaring that not an individual in the country should refuse to join in the abolition; it seems as if we had waited until the persons most interested should be tired out with the folly and nefariousness of the trade, and should unite in petitioning against it.

Let us then make such amends as we can for the mischiefs we have done to the unhappy continent; let us recollect what Europe itself was no longer ago than three or four centuries. What if I should be able to show this House that in a civilized part of Europe, in the time of our Henry VII, there were people who actually sold their own children? What if I should tell them that England itself was that country? What if I should point out to them that the very place where this inhuman traffic was carried on was the city of Bristol? Ireland at that time used to drive a considerable trade in slaves with these neighboring barbarians; but a great plague having infested the country, the Irish were struck with a panic, suspected (I am sure very properly) that the plague was a punishment sent from heaven for the sin of the slave trade, and therefore abolished it. All I ask, therefore, of the people of Bristol is that they would become as civilized now as Irishmen were four hundred years ago. Let us put an end at once to this inhuman traffic—let us stop this effusion of human blood. The true way to virtue is by withdrawing from temptation; let us then withdraw from these wretched Africans those temptations to fraud, violence, cruelty, and injustice which the slave trade furnishes. Wherever the sun shines, let us go round the world with him, diffusing our beneficence; but let us not traffic only that we may set kings against their subjects, subjects against their kings, sowing discord in every village, fear and terror in every family, setting millions of our fellow creatures a-hunting each other for slaves, creating fairs and markets for human flesh through one whole continent of the world, and, under the name of policy, concealing from ourselves all the baseness and iniquity of such a traffic. Why may we not hope, ere long, to see Hanse towns established on the coast of Africa as they were on the Baltic? It is said the Africans are idle, but they are not too idle, at least, to catch one another; seven hundred to one thousand tons of rice are annually bought of them; by the same rule why should we not buy more? At Gambia one thousand of them are seen continually at work; why should not some more thousands be set to work in the same manner? It is the slave trade that causes their idleness and every other mischief. We are told by one witness: "They sell one another as they can"; and while they can get brandy by catching one another, no wonder they are too idle for any regular work.

I have one word more to add upon a most material point; but it is a point so self-evident that I shall be extremely short. It will appear from everything which I have said that it is not regulation, it is not mere palliatives, that can cure this enormous evil. Total abolition is the only possible cure for it. The Jamaica report, indeed, admits much of the evil, but recommends it to us so to regulate the trade that no persons should be kidnaped or made slaves contrary to the custom of Africa. But may they not be made slaves unjustly, and yet by no means contrary to the custom of Africa? I have shown they may; for all the customs of Africa are rendered savage and unjust through the influence of this trade; besides, how can we discriminate between the slaves justly and unjustly made? or, if we could, does any man believe that the British captains can, by any regulation in this country, be prevailed upon to refuse all such slaves as have not been fairly, honestly, and uprightly enslaved? But granting even that they should do this, yet how would the rejected slaves be recompensed? They are brought, as we are told, from three or four thousand miles off, and exchanged like cattle from one hand to another until they reach the coast. We see then that it is the existence of the slave trade that is the spring of all this internal traffic, and that the remedy cannot be applied without abolition. Again, as to the middle passage, the evil is radical there also; the merchant's profit depends upon the number that can be crowded together, and upon the shortness of their allowance. Astringents, escharotics, and all the other arts of making them up for sale are of the very essence of the trade; these arts will be concealed both from the purchaser and the legislature; they are necessary to the owner's profit, and they will be practiced. Again, chains and arbitrary treatment must be used in transporting them; our seamen must be taught to play the tyrant, and that depravation of manners among them (which some very judicious persons have treated of as the very worst part of the business) cannot be hindered, while the trade itself continues. As to the slave merchants, they have already told you that if two slaves to a ton are not permitted, the trade cannot continue; so that the objections are done away by themselves on this quarter; and in the West Indies, I have shown that the abolition is the only possible stimulus whereby a regard to population, and consequently to the happiness of the Negroes, can be effectually excited in those islands.

I trust, therefore, I have shown that upon every ground the total abolition ought to take place. I have urged many things which are not my own leading motives for proposing it, since I have wished to show every description of gentlemen, and particularly the West India planters, who deserve every attention, that the abolition is politic upon their own principles also. Policy, however, sir, is not my principle, and I am not ashamed to say it. There is a principle above everything that is political; and when I reflect on the command which says: "Thou shalt do no murder," believing the authority to be Divine, how can I dare to set up any reasonings of my own against it? And, sir, when we think of eternity, and of the future consequences of all human conduct, what is there in this life that should make any man contradict the dictates of his conscience, the principles of justice, the laws of religion, and of God. Sir, the nature and all the circumstances of this trade are now laid open to us; we can no longer plead ignorance, we cannot evade it, it is now an object placed before us, we cannot pass it; we may spurn it, we may kick it out of our way, but we cannot turn aside so as to avoid seeing it; for it is brought now so directly before our eyes that this House must decide, and must justify to all the world, and to their own consciences, the rectitude of the grounds and principles of their decision. A society has been established for the abolition of this trade, in which Dissenters, Quakers, Churchmen—in which the most conscientious of all persuasions—have all united and made a common cause in this great question. Let not Parliament be the only body that is insensible to the principles of national justice. Let us make reparation to Africa, so far as we can, by establishing a trade upon true commercial principles, and we shall soon find the rectitude of our conduct rewarded by the benefits of a regular and a growing commerce.

SOURCE: Speech in the House of Commons, 19 May 1789 (London: Topographic Press, 1789).

———

William Pitt the Younger Indicts
the Slave Trade and Foresees a Liberated Africa
WILLIAM PITT THE YOUNGER

[April 2, 1792]

The result of all I have said is that there exists no impediment, on the ground of pledged faith, or even on that of national expediency, to the abolition of this trade. On the contrary, all the arguments drawn from those sources plead for it, and they plead much more loudly, and much more strongly in every part of the question, for an immediate than for a gradual abolition. But now, sir, I come to Africa. That is the ground on which I rest, and here it is that I say my right honorable friends do not carry their principles to their full extent. Why ought the slave trade to be abolished? Because it is incurable injustice. How much stronger, then, is the argument for immediate than gradual abolition! By allowing it to continue even for one hour, do not my right honorable friends weaken their own argument of its injustice? If on the ground of injustice it ought to be abolished at last, why ought it not now? Why is injustice to be suffered to remain for a single hour? From what I hear without doors, it is evident that there is a general conviction entertained of its being far from just; and from that very conviction of its injustice, some men have been led, I fear, to the supposition that the slave trade never could have been permitted to begin but from some strong and irresistible necessity: a necessity, however, which if it was fancied to exist at first, I have shown cannot be thought by any man whatever to exist now. This plea of necessity has caused a sort of acquiescence in the continuance of this evil. Men have been led to place it among the rank of those necessary evils which are supposed to be the lot of human creatures, and to be permitted to fall upon some countries or individuals rather than upon others by that Being whose ways are inscrutable to us, and whose dispensations, it is conceived, we ought not to look into. The origin of evil is indeed a subject beyond the reach of human understandings; and the permission of it by the Supreme Being is a subject into which it belongs not to us to inquire. But where the evil in question is a moral evil which a man can scrutinize, and where that moral evil has its origin with ourselves, let us not imagine that we can clear our consciences by this general, not to say irreligious and impious, way of laying aside the question. If we reflect at all on this subject, we must see that every necessary evil supposes that some other and greater evil would be incurred were it removed. I therefore desire to ask, what can be that greater evil which can be stated to overbalance the one in question? I know of no evil that ever has existed, nor can imagine any evil to exist, worse than the tearing of seventy or eighty thousand persons annually from their native land, by a combination of the most civilized nations inhabiting the most enlightened part of the globe, but more especially under the sanction of the laws of that nation which calls herself the most free and the most happy of them all. Even if these miserable beings were proved guilty of every crime before you take them off, ought we to take upon ourselves the office of executioners? And even if we condescend so far, still can we be justified in taking them, unless we have clear proof that they are criminals? But, if we go much further—if we ourselves tempt them to sell their fellow creatures to us—we may rest assured that they will take care to provide by every possible method a supply of victims increasing in proportion to our demand. Can we, then, hesitate in deciding whether the wars in Africa are their wars or ours? It was our arms in the river Cameroon, put into the hands of the trader, that furnished him with the means of pushing his trade; and I have no more doubt that they are British arms, put into the hands of Africans, which promote universal war and desolation than I can doubt their having done so in that individual instance.

I have shown how great is the enormity of this evil, even on the supposition that we take only convicts and prisoners of war. But take the subject in the other way, and how does it stand? Think of 80,000 persons carried out of their native country by we know not what means! for crimes imputed! for light or inconsiderable faults! for debt perhaps! for the crime of witchcraft! or a thousand other weak and scandalous pretexts! Reflect on these 80,000 persons thus annually taken off! There is something in the horror of it that surpasses all the bounds of imagination. Admitting that there exists in Africa something like to courts of justice; yet what an office of humiliation and meanness is it in us, to take upon ourselves to carry into execution the iniquitous sentences of such courts, as if we also were strangers to all religion and to the first principles of justice! But that country, it is said, has been in some degree civilized, and civilized by us. It is said they have gained some knowledge of the principles of justice. Yes, we give them enough of our intercourse to convey to them the means and to initiate them in the study of mutual destruction. We give them just enough of the forms of justice to enable them to add the pretext of legal trials to their other modes of perpetrating the most atrocious iniquity. We give them just enough of European improvements to enable them the more effectually to turn Africa into a ravaged wilderness. Some evidences say that the Africans are addicted to the practice of gambling; that they even sell their wives and children, and ultimately themselves. Are these, then, the legitimate sources of slavery? Shall we pretend that we can thus acquire an honest right to exact the labor of these people? Can we pretend that we have a right to carry away to distant regions men of whom we know nothing by authentic inquiry, and of whom there is every reasonable presumption to think that those who sell them to us have no right to do so? But the evil does not stop here. Do you think nothing of the ruin and the miseries in which so many other individuals, still remaining in Africa, are involved in consequence of carrying off so many myriads of people? Do you think nothing of their families left behind? of the connections broken? of the friendships, attachments, and relationships that are burst asunder? Do you think nothing of the miseries in consequence that are felt from generation to generation? of the privation of that happiness which might be communicated to them by the introduction of civilization, and of mental and moral improvement?—a happiness which you withhold from them so long as you permit the slave trade to continue.

Thus, sir, has the perversion of British commerce carried misery instead of happiness to one whole quarter of the globe. False to the very principles of trade, misguided in our policy, and unmindful of our duty, what astonishing mischief have we brought upon that continent! If, knowing the miseries we have caused, we refused to put a stop to them, how greatly aggravated will be the guilt of this country! Shall we then delay rendering this justice to Africa? I am sure the immediate abolition of the slave trade is the first, the principal, the most indispensable act of policy, of duty, and of justice that the legislature of this country has to take, if it is indeed their wish to secure those important objects to which I have alluded, and which we are bound to pursue by the most solemn obligations. There is, however, one argument set up as a universal answer to everything that can be urged on our side. The slave-trade system, it is supposed, has taken such deep root in Africa that it is absurd to think of its being eradicated; and the abolition of that share of trade carried on by Great Britain is likely to be of very little service. You are not sure, it is said, that other nations will give up the trade if you should renounce it. I answer, if this trade is as criminal as it is asserted to be, God forbid that we should hesitate in relinquishing so iniquitous a traffic; even though it should be retained by other countries! I tremble at the thought of gentlemen indulging themselves in the argument which I am combating. "We are friends," say they, "to humanity. We are second to none of you in our zeal for the good of Africa—but the French will not abolish—the Dutch will not abolish. We wait, therefore, on prudential principles, till they join us or set us an example." How, sir, is this enormous evil ever to be eradicated, if every nation is thus prudentially to wait till the concurrence of all the world shall have been obtained? Let me remark, too, that there is no nation in Europe that has, on the one hand, plunged so deeply into this guilt as Great Britain; or that is so likely, on the other, to be looked up to as an example. But does not this argument apply a thousand times more strongly in a contrary way? How much more justly may other nations point to us, and say, "Why should we abolish the slave trade when Great Britain has not abolished it? Britain, free as she is, just and honorable as she is, and deeply involved as she is in this commerce above all nations, not only has not abolished, but has refused to abolish." This, sir, is the argument with which we furnish the other nations of Europe if we again refuse to put an end to the slave trade. Instead, therefore, of imagining that by choosing to presume on their continuing it, we shall have exempted ourselves from guilt, and have transferred the whole criminality to them; let us rather reflect that on the very principle urged against us we shall henceforth have to answer for their crimes as well as our own.

It has also been urged, that there is something in the disposition and nature of the Africans themselves which renders all prospect of civilization on that continent extremely unpromising. "It has been known," says Mr. Frazer, in his evidence, "that a boy has been put to death who was refused to be purchased as a slave." This single story was deemed by that gentleman a sufficient proof of the barbarity of the Africans, and of the inutility of abolishing the slave trade. My honorable friend, however, has told you that this boy had previously run away from his master three times; that the master had to pay his value, according to the custom of his country, every time he was brought back; and that, partly from anger at the boy for running away so frequently, and partly to prevent a repetition of the same expense, he determined to put him to death. This, sir, is the signal instance that has been dwelt upon of African barbarity. This African, we admit, was unenlightened and altogether barbarous: but let us now ask what would a civilized and enlightened West Indian, or a body of West Indians, have done in any case of a parallel nature? I will quote you, sir, a law passed in the West Indies in 1722; by which law this same crime of running away is, by the legislature of the island, punished with death, in the very first instance. I hope, therefore, we shall hear no more of the moral impossibility of civilizing the Africans, nor have our understandings again insulted by being called upon to sanction the trade until other nations shall have set the example of abolishing it. While we have been deliberating, one nation, Denmark, not by any means remarkable for the boldness of its councils, has determined on a gradual abolition. France, it is said, will take up the trade if we relinquish it. What! Is it supposed that, in the present situation of St. Domingo, an island which used to take three fourths of all the slaves required by the colonies of France, she, of all countries, will think of taking it up? Of the countries which remain, Portugal, Holland, and Spain—let me declare it is my opinion that if they see us renounce the trade, they will not be disposed, even on principles of policy, to rush further into it. But I say more. How are they to furnish the capital necessary for carrying it on? If there is any aggravation of our guilt in this wretched business, it is that we have stooped to be the carriers of these miserable beings from Africa to the West Indies, for all the other powers of Europe. And if we retire from the trade, where is the fund equal to the purchase of 30,000 or 40,000 slaves?—a fund which, if we rate the slaves at £40 or £50 each, cannot require a capital of less than a million and a half, or two millions of money.

Having detained the House so long, all that I will further add shall relate to that important subject, the civilization of Africa. Grieved am I to think that there should be a single person in this country who can look on the present uncivilized state of that continent as a ground for continuing the slave trade—as a ground not only for refusing to attempt the improvement of Africa, but even for intercepting every ray of light which might otherwise break in upon her. Here, as in every other branch of this extensive question, the argument of our adversaries pleads against them; for surely, sir, the present deplorable state of Africa, especially when we reflect that her chief calamities are to be ascribed to us, calls for our generous aid rather than justifies any despair on our part of her recovery, and still less any further repetition of our injuries. I will not much longer fatigue the attention of the House; but this point has impressed itself so deeply on my mind that I must trouble the committee with a few additional observations. Are we justified, I ask, on any one ground of theory, or by any one instance to be found in the history of the world from its very beginning to this day, in forming the supposition which I am now combating? Are we justified in supposing that the particular practice which we encourage in Africa, of men selling each other for slaves, is any symptom of a barbarism that is incurable? Are we justified in supposing that even the practice of offering up human sacrifices proves a total incapacity for civilization? I believe it will be found that both the trade in slaves and the still more savage custom of offering up human sacrifices obtained in former periods throughout many of those nations which now, by the blessings of Providence, and by a long progression of improvements, are advanced the farthest in civilization. I believe that, if we reflect an instant, we shall find that this observation comes directly home to ourselves; and that, on the same ground on which we are now disposed to proscribe Africa forever from all possibility of improvement, we might, in like manner, have been proscribed and forever shut out from all the blessings which we now enjoy. There was a time, sir, when even human sacrifices are said to have been offered in this island. But I would peculiarly observe on this day, for it is a case precisely in point, that the very practice of the slave trade once prevailed among us. Slaves, as we may read in Henry's *History of Great Britain*, were formerly an established article of our exports. "Great numbers," he says, "were exported like cattle, from the British coast, and were to be seen exposed for sale in the Roman market." It does not distinctly appear by what means they were procured; but there is unquestionably no small resemblance, in this particular point, between the case of our ancestors and that of the present wretched natives of Africa; for the historian tells you that "adultery, witchcraft, and debt were probably some of the chief sources of supplying the Roman market with British slaves; that prisoners taken in war were added to the number; and that there might be among them some unfortunate gamesters who, after having lost all their goods, at length staked themselves, their wives, and their children." Every one of these sources of slavery has been stated to be at this hour a source of slavery in Africa. And these circumstances, sir, with a solitary instance or two of human sacrifices, furnish the alleged proofs that Africa labors under a natural incapacity for civilization; that it is enthusiasm and fanaticism to think that she can ever enjoy the knowledge and the morals of Europe; that Providence never intended her to rise above a state of barbarism; that Providence has irrevocably doomed her to be only a nursery for slaves for us free and civilized Europeans. Allow of this principle, as applied to Africa, and I should be glad to know why it might not also have been applied to ancient and uncivilized Britain. Why might not some Roman Senator, reasoning on the principles of some honorable gentlemen, and pointing to British barbarians, have predicted with equal boldness, "There is a people that will never rise to civilization; there is a people destined never to be free; a people without the understanding necessary for the attainment of useful arts; depressed by the hand of nature below the level of the human species; and created to form a supply of slaves for the rest of the world"? Might not this have been said in all respects as fairly and as truly of Britain herself, at that period of her history, as it can now be said by us of the inhabitants of Africa? We, sir, have long since emerged from barbarism; we have almost forgotten that we were once barbarians; we are now raised to a situation which exhibits a striking contrast to every circumstance by which a Roman might have characterized us, and by which we now characterize Africa. There is, indeed, one thing wanting to complete the contrast, and to clear us altogether from the imputation of acting even to this hour as barbarians; for we continue to this hour a barbarous traffic in slaves; we continue it even yet, in spite of all our great and undeniable pretensions to civilization. We were once as obscure among the nations of the earth, as savage in our manners, as debased in our morals, as degraded in our understandings, as these unhappy Africans are at present. But in the lapse of a long series of years, by a progression slow, and for a time almost imperceptible, we have become rich in a variety of acquirements, favored above measure in the gifts of Providence, unrivaled in commerce, pre-eminent in arts, foremost in the pursuits of philosophy and science, and established in all the blessings of civil society: we are in the possession of peace, of happiness, and of liberty; we are under the guidance of a mild and beneficent religion; and we are protected by impartial laws, and the purest administration of justice; we are living under a system of government which our own happy experience leads us to pronounce the best and wisest which has ever yet been framed—a system which has become the admiration of the world. From all these blessings we must forever have been shut out, had there been any truth in those principles which some gentlemen have not hesitated to lay down as applicable to the case of Africa. Had those principles been true, we ourselves had languished to this hour in that miserable state of ignorance, brutality, and degradation in which history proves our ancestors to have been immersed. Had other nations adopted these principles in their conduct towards us; had other nations applied to Great Britain the reasoning which some of the senators of this very island now apply to Africa, ages might have passed without our emerging from barbarism; and we, who are enjoying the blessings of a British civilization, of British laws, and British liberty, might, at this hour, have been little superior, either in morals, in knowledge, or refinement, to the rude inhabitants of the coast of Guinea.

If, then, we feel that this perpetual confinement in the fetters of brutal ignorance would have been the greatest calamity which could have befallen us; if we view with gratitude and exultation the contrast between the peculiar blessings we enjoy and the wretchedness of the ancient inhabitants of Britain; if we shudder to think of the misery which would still have overwhelmed us had Great Britain continued to be the mart for slaves to the more civilized nations of the world, God forbid that we should any longer subject Africa to the same dreadful scourge, and preclude the light of knowledge, which has reached every other quarter of the globe, from having access to her coasts! I trust we shall no longer continue this commerce, to the destruction of every improvement on that wide continent; and shall not consider ourselves as conferring too great a boon in restoring its inhabitants to the rank of human beings. I trust we shall not think ourselves too liberal if, by abolishing the slave trade, we give them the same common chance of civilization with other parts of the world, and that we shall now allow to Africa the opportunity—the hope—the prospect of attaining to the same blessings which we ourselves, through the favorable dispensations of Divine Providence, have been permitted, at a much more early period, to enjoy. If we listen to the voice of reason and duty, and pursue this night the line of conduct which they prescribe, some of us may live to see a reverse of that picture from which we now turn our eyes with shame and regret. We may live to behold the natives of Africa engaged in the calm occupations of industry, in the pursuits of a just and legitimate commerce. We may behold the beams of science and philosophy breaking in upon their land, which, at some happy period in still later times, may blaze with full luster; and, joining their influence to that of pure religion, may illuminate and invigorate the most distant extremities of that immense continent. Then may we hope that even Africa, though last of all the quarters of the globe, shall enjoy at length, in the evening of her days, those blessings which have descended so plentifully upon us in a much earlier period of the world. Then also will Europe, participating in her improvement and prosperity, receive an ample recompense for the tardy kindness (if kindness it can be called) of no longer hindering that continent from extricating herself out of the darkness which, in other more fortunate regions, has been so much more speedily dispelled—

> —*Nos primus equis oriens afflavit anhelis;*
> *Illic sera rubens accendit lumina Vesper.*[1]

Then, sir, may be applied to Africa those words, originally used indeed with a different view—

> *His demum exactis—*
> *Devenere locos lætos, et amœna virecta*
> *Fortunatorum nemorum, sedesque beatas:*
> *Largior hic campos Æther, et lumine vestit*
> *Purpureo.*[2]

---

1. "And when dayspring touches us with his panting horses' breath, there crimson Hesperus kindles his lamp at evenfall."—Virgil, *Georgics*, I. 251 *sq.* (tr. J. W. Mackail)

2. "Now at length, this fully done, they came to the happy place, the green pleasances and blissful seats of the Fortunate Woodlands. Here an ampler air clothes the meadows in lustrous sheen, and they know their own sun and a starlight of their own."—Virgil, *Aeneid*, VI, 637 *sqq.* (tr. J. W. Mackail).

It is in this view, sir—it is as an atonement for our long and cruel injustice towards Africa—that the measure proposed by my honorable friend most forcibly recommends itself to my mind. The great and happy change to be expected in the state of her inhabitants is, of all the various and important benefits of the abolition, in my estimation, incomparably the most extensive and important. I shall vote, sir, against the adjournment; and I shall also oppose to the utmost every proposition which in any way may tend either to prevent or even to postpone for an hour the total abolition of the slave trade; a measure which, on all the various grounds which I have stated, we are bound, by the most pressing and indispensable duty, to adopt.

SOURCE: Speech in the House of Commons, 2 April 1792. In *The Speeches of the Right Honourable William Pitt in the House of Commons*, vol. 12 (London: Longman, Hurst, Rees and Orne, 1806), 50–83.

The Nigger Question
THOMAS CARLYLE

[Thomas Carlyle (1795–1881), the Scottish historian, critic, and sociological writer, was a major contributor to British imperial and domestic debates. His *Sartor Resartus* (1833–1884), for example, looked to questions of appearance as deciding hierarchies; in the *The French Revolution* (1837), Carlyle took issue with the ideas and ideals of democracy that had been raised across the English Channel; and in *Heroes and Hero-Worship* (1858–1865), he looked to other exemplars—from the Prophet Mohammed to Cromwell—for directives. In his essay, "The Nigger Question," Carlyle provides a parodic version of the then current antipathy to the antislavery movement, a parody that nonetheless, a century later, led Trinidadian critic and politician Eric Williams to include Carlyle in his volume *British Historians and the West Indies* (1994), in an essay entitled "The Neo-Fascism of Thomas Carlyle." Exeter Hall, located on the Strand in London, served as the political center of British evangelicalism.]

[Precursor to Latter-day Pamphlets.]
[1849]

OCCASIONAL DISCOURSE ON THE
NIGGER QUESTION

The following Occasional Discourse, delivered by we know not whom, and of date seemingly above a year back, may perhaps be welcome to here and there a speculative reader. It comes to us,—no speaker named, no time or place assigned, no commentary of any sort given,—in the handwriting of the so-called "Doctor," properly "Absconded Reporter," Dr. Phelim M'Quirk, whose singular powers of reporting, and also whose debts, extravagancies and sorrowful insidious finance-operations, now winded-up by a sudden disappearance, to the grief of many poor tradespeople, are making too much noise in the police-offices at present! Of M'Quirk's composition we by no means suppose it to be; but from M'Quirk, as the last traceable source, it comes to us;—offered, in fact, by his respectable unfortunate landlady, desirous to make-up part of her losses in this way.

To absconded reporters who bilk their lodgings, we have of course no account to give; but if the Speaker be of any eminence or substantiality, and feel himself aggrieved by the transaction, let him understand that such, and such only, is our connection with him or his affairs. As the Colonial and Negro Question is still alive, and likely to grow livelier for some time, we have accepted the Article, at a cheap market-rate; and give it publicity, without in the least committing ourselves to the strange doctrines and notions shadowed forth in it. Doctrines and notions which, we rather suspect, are pretty much in a 'minority of one,' in the present era of the world! Here, sure enough, are peculiar views of the Rights of Negroes; involving, it is probable, peculiar ditto of innumerable other rights, duties, expectations, wrongs and disappointments, much argued of, by logic and by grape-shot, in these emancipated epochs of the human mind!—Silence now, however; and let the Speaker himself enter.

My philanthropic friends,—It is my painful duty to address some words to you, this evening, on the Rights of Negroes. Taking, as we hope we do, an extensive survey of social affairs, which we find all in a state of the frightfulest embroilment, and as it were of inextricable final bankruptcy, just at present; and being desirous to adjust ourselves in that huge upbreak, and unutterable welter of tumbling ruins, and to see well that our grand proposed Association of Associations, the Universal Abolition-of-Pain Association, which is meant to be the consummate golden flower and summary of modern Philanthropisms all in one, do *not* issue as a universal "Sluggard-and-Scoundrel Protection Society,"—we have judged that, before constituting ourselves, it would be very proper to commune earnestly with one another, and discourse together on the leading elements of our great Problem, which surely is one of the greatest. With this view the Council has decided, both that the Negro Question, as lying at the bottom, was to be the first handled, and if possible the first settled; and then also, what was of much more questionable wisdom, that—that, in short, I was to be Speaker on the occasion. An honourable duty; yet, as I said, a painful one!—Well, you shall hear what I have to say on the matter; and probably you will not in the least like it.

West-Indian affairs, as we all know, and as some of us know to our cost, are in a rather troublous condition this good while. In regard to West-Indian affairs, however, Lord John Russell is able to comfort us with one fact, indisputable where so many are dubious, That the Negroes are all very happy and doing well. A fact very comfortable indeed. West-Indian Whites, it is admitted, are far enough from happy; West-Indian Colonies not unlike sinking wholly into ruin: at home too, the British Whites are rather badly off; several millions of them hanging on the verge of continual famine; and in single towns, many thousands of them very sore put to it, at this time, not to live "well" or as a man should, in any sense temporal or spiritual, but to live at all:—these, again, are uncomfortable facts; and they are extremely extensive and important ones. But, thank Heaven, our interesting Black population,—equalling almost in number of heads one of the Ridings of Yorkshire, and in *worth* (in quantity of intellect, faculty, docility, energy, and available human valour and value) perhaps one of the streets of Seven Dials,—are all doing remarkably well. "Sweet blighted lilies,"—as the American epitaph on the Nigger child has it,—sweet blighted lilies, they are holding-up their heads again! How pleasant, in the universal bankruptcy abroad, and dim dreary stagnancy at home, as if for England too there remained nothing but to suppress Chartist riots, banish united Irishmen, vote the supplies, and *wait* with arms crossed till black Anarchy and Social Death devoured us also, as it has done the others; how pleasant to have always this fact to fall-back upon: Our beautiful Black darlings are at last happy; with little labour except to the teeth, *which* surely, in those excellent horse-jaws of theirs, will not fail!

Exeter Hall, my philanthropic friends, has had its way in this matter. The Twenty-Millions, a mere trifle despatched with a single dash of the pen, are paid; and far over the sea, we have a few black persons rendered extremely "free" indeed. Sitting yonder with their beautiful muzzles up to the ears in pumpkins, imbibing sweet pulps and juices; the grinder and incisor teeth ready for ever new work, and the pumpkins cheap as grass in those rich climates: while the sugar-crops rot round them uncut, because labour cannot be hired, so cheap are the pumpkins;—and at home we are but required to rasp from the breakfast-loaves of our own English labourers some slight "differential sugar-duties," and lend a poor half-million or a few poor millions now and then, to keep that beautiful state of matters going on. A state of matters lovely to contemplate, in these emancipated epochs of the human mind; which has earned us not only the praises of Exeter Hall, and loud long-eared hallelujahs of laudatory psalmody from the Friends of Freedom everywhere, but lasting favour (it is hoped) from the Heavenly Powers themselves;—and which may, at least, justly appeal to the Heavenly Powers, and ask them, If ever in terrestial procedure they saw the match of it? Certainly in the past history of the human species it has no parallel: nor, one hopes, will it have in the future. [*Some emotion in the audience; which the Chairman suppressed.*]

Sunk in deep froth-oceans of "Benevolence," "Fraternity," "Emancipation-principle," "Christian Philanthropy," and other most amiable-looking, but most baseless, and in the end baleful and all bewildering jargon,—sad product of a sceptical Eighteenth Century, and of poor human hearts left *destitute* of any earnest guidance, and disbelieving that there ever was any, Christian or Heathen, and reduced to believe in rosepink Sentimentalism alone, and to cultivate the same under its Christian, Antichristian, Broad-brimmed, Brutus-headed, and other forms,—has not the human species gone strange roads, during that period? And poor Exeter Hall, cultivating the Broad-brimmed form of Christian Sentimentalism, and long talking and bleating and braying in that strain, has it not worked-out results? Our West-Indian Legislatings, with their spoutings, anti-spoutings, and interminable jangle and babble; our Twenty millions down on the nail for Blacks of our own; Thirty gradual millions more, and many brave British lives to boot, in watching Blacks of other people's; and now at last our ruined sugar-estates, differential sugar-duties, "immigration loan," and beautiful Blacks sitting there up to the ears in pumpkins, and doleful Whites sitting here without potatoes to eat: never till now, I think, did the sun look-down on such a jumble of human nonsenses;—of which, with the two hot nights of the Missing-Despatch Debate,[1] God grant that the measure might now at last be full! But no, it is not yet full; we have a long way to travel back, and terrible flounderings to make, and in fact an immense load of nonsense to dislodge from our poor heads, and manifold cobwebs to rend from our poor eyes, before we get into the road again, and can begin to act as serious men that have work to do in this Universe, and no longer as windy sentimentalists that merely have speeches to deliver

---

1. Does any reader now remember it? A cloudy reminiscence of some such thing, and of noise in the Newspapers upon it, remains with us,—fast hastening to abolition for everybody. (*Note of* 1849.)—This Missing-Despatch Debate, what on earth was it? (*Note of* 1853.)

and despatches to write. O Heaven, in West-Indian matters, and in all manner of matters, it is so with us: the more is the sorrow!—

The West Indies, it appears, are short of labour; as indeed is very conceivable in those circumstances. Where a Black man, by working about half-an-hour a-day (such is the calculation), can supply himself, by aid of sun and soil, with as much pumpkin as will suffice, he is likely to be a little stiff to raise into hard work! Supply and demand, which, science says, should be brought to bear on him, have an uphill task of it with such a man. Strong sun supplies itself gratis, rich soil in those unpeopled or half-peopled regions almost gratis; these are *his* "supply"; and half-an-hour a-day, directed upon these, will produce pumpkin, which is his "demand." The fortunate Black man, very swiftly does he settle *his* account with supply and demand:—not so swiftly the less fortunate White man of those tropical localities. A bad case, his, just now. He himself cannot work; and his black neighbour, rich in pumpkin, is in no haste to help him. Sunk to the ears in pumpkin, imbibing saccharine juices, and much at his ease in the Creation, he can listen to the less fortunate white man's "demand," and take his own time in supplying it. Higher wages, massa; higher, for your cane-crop cannot wait; still higher,—till no conceivable opulence of cane-crop will cover such wages. In Demerara, as I read in the Blue-book of last year, the cane-crop, far and wide, stands rotting; the fortunate black gentlemen, strong in their pumpkins, having all struck till the "demand" rise a little. Sweet blighted lilies, now getting-up their heads again!

Science, however, has a remedy still. Since the demand is so pressing, and the supply so inadequate (equal in fact to *nothing* in some places, as appears), increase the supply; bring more Blacks into the labour-market, then will the rate fall, says science. Not the least surprising part of our West-Indian policy is this recipe of "immigration"; of keeping-down the labour-market in those islands by importing new Africans to labour and live there. If the Africans that are already there could be made to lay-down their pumpkins, and labour for their living, there are already Africans enough. If the new Africans, after labouring a little, take to pumpkins like the others, what remedy is there? To bring-in new and ever new Africans, say you, till pumpkins themselves grow dear; till the country is crowded with Africans; and black men there, like white men here, are forced by hunger to labour for their living? That will be a consummation. To have "emancipated" the West Indies into a *Black Ireland*; "free" indeed, but an Ireland, and Black! The world may yet see prodigies; and reality be stranger than a nightmare dream.

Our own white or sallow Ireland, sluttishly starving from age to age on its act-of-parliament "freedom," was hitherto the flower of mismanagement among the nations: but what will this be to a Negro Ireland, with pumpkins themselves fallen scarce like potatoes! Imagination cannot fathom such an object; the belly of Chaos never held the like. The human mind, in its wide wanderings, has not dreamt yet of such a "freedom" as that will be. Towards that, if Exeter Hall and science of supply-and-demand are to continue our guides in the matter, we are daily travelling, and even struggling, with loans of half-a-million and suchlike, to accelerate ourselves.

Truly, my philanthropic friends, Exeter-Hall Philanthropy is wonderful. And the Social Science,—not a "gay science," but a rueful,—which finds the secret of this Universe in "supply and demand," and reduces the duty of human governors to that of letting men alone, is also wonderful. Not a "gay science," I should say, like some we have heard of; no, a dreary, desolate, and indeed quite abject and distressing one; what we might call, by way of eminence, the *dismal science.* These two, Exeter-Hall Philanthropy and the Dismal Science, led by any sacred cause of Black Emancipation, or the like, to fall in love and make a wedding of it,—will give birth to progenies and prodigies; dark extensive moon-calves, unnamable abortions, wide-coiled monstrosities, such as the world has not seen hitherto! [*Increased emotion, again suppressed by the Chairman.*]

In fact, it will behove us of this English nation to overhaul our West-Indian procedure from top to bottom, and ascertain a little better what it is that Fact and Nature demand of us, and what only Exeter Hall wedded to the Dismal Science demands. To the former set of demands we will endeavour, at our peril,—and, worse peril than our purse's, at our Soul's peril,—to give all obedience. To the latter we will very frequently demur, and try if we cannot stop short where they contradict the former,—and especially *before* arriving at the black throat of ruin, whither they appear to be leading us. Alas, in many other provinces besides the West Indian, that unhappy wedlock of Philanthropic Liberalism and the Dismal Science has engendered such all-enveloping delusions, of the moon-calf sort, and wrought huge woe for us, and for the poor civilised world, in these days! And sore will be the battle with said moon-calves; and terrible the struggle to return out of our delusions, floating rapidly on which, not the West Indies alone, but Europe generally, is nearing the Niagara Falls. [*Here various persons, in an agitated manner, with an air of indignation, left the room; especially one very tall gentleman in white trousers, whose boots creaked much. The President, in a resolved voice, with a look of official rigour, whatever his own private feelings might be, enjoined "Silence, Silence!" The meeting again sat motionless.*]

My philanthropic friends, can you discern no fixed headlands in this wide-weltering deluge, of benevolent twaddle and revolutionary grade-shot, that has burst-forth on us; no sure bearings at all? Fact and Nature, it seems to me, say a few words to us, if happily we have still an ear for Fact and Nature. Let us listen a little and try.

And first, with regard to the West Indies, it may be laid-down as a principle, which no eloquence in Exeter Hall, or Westminster Hall, or elsewhere, can invalidate or hide, except for a short time only, That no Black man who will not work according to what ability the gods have given him for working, has the smallest right to eat pumpkin, or to any fraction of land that will grow pumpkin, however plentiful such land may be; but has an indisputable and perpetual *right* to be compelled, by the real proprietors of said land, to do competent work for his living. This is the everlasting duty of all men, black or white, who are born into this world. To do competent work, to labour honestly according to the ability given them; for that and for no other purpose was each one of us sent into this world; and woe is to every man who, by friend or by foe, is prevented from fulfilling this the end of his being. That is the "unhappy" lot: lot equally unhappy cannot otherwise be provided for man. Whatsoever prohibits or prevents a man from this his sacred appointment to labour while he lives on earth,—that, I say, is the man's deadliest enemy; and all men are called upon to do what is in their power or opportunity towards delivering him from that. If it be his own indolence that prevents and prohibits him, then his own indolence is the enemy he must be delivered from: and the first "right" he had,—poor indolent blockhead, black or white,—is, That every *un*prohibited man, whatsoever wiser, more industrious person may be passing that way, shall endeavour to "emancipate" him from his indolence, and by some wise means, as I said, compel him, since inducing will not serve, to do the work he is fit for. Induce him, if you can: yes, sure enough, by all means try what inducement will do; and indeed every coachman and carman knows that secret, without our preaching, and applies it to his very horses as the true method:—but if your Nigger will not be induced? In that case, it is full certain, he must be compelled; should and must; and the tacit prayer he makes (unconsciously he, poor blockhead), to you, and to me, and to all the world who are wiser than himself, is, "Compel me!" For indeed he *must,* or else do and suffer worse,—he as well as we. It were better the work did come out of him! It was the meaning of the gods with him and with us, that his gift should turn to use in this Creation, and not lie poisoning the thoroughfares, as a rotten mass of idleness, agreeable to neither heaven nor earth. For idleness does, in all cases, inevitably *rot,* and become putrescent;—and I say deliberately, the very Devil is in *it.*

None of you, my friends, have been in Demerara lately, I apprehend? May none of you go till matters mend there a little! Under the sky there are uglier sights than perhaps were seen hitherto! Dead corpses, the rotting body of a brother man, whom fate or unjust men have killed, this is not a pleasant spectacle; but what say you to the dead soul of a man,—in a body which still pretends to be vigorously alive, and can drink rum? An idle White gentleman is not pelasant to me; though I confess the real work for him is not easy to find, in these our epochs; and perhaps he is seeking, poor soul, and may find at last. But what say you to an idle Black gentleman, with his rum-bottle in his hand (for a little additional pumpkin you can have red-herrings and rum, in Demerara),—rum-bottle in his hand, no breeches on his body, pumpkin at discretion, and the fruitfulest region of the earth going back to jungle round him? Such things the sun looks-down upon in our fine times; and I, for one, would rather have no hand in them.

Yes, this is the eternal law of Nature for a man, my beneficent Exeter-Hall friends; this, that he shall be permitted, encouraged, and if need be, compelled to do what work the Maker of him has intended by the making of him for this world! Not that he should eat pumpkin with never such felicity in the West-India Islands is, or can be, the blessedness of our Black friend; but that he should do useful work there, according as the gifts have been bestowed on him for that. And his own happiness, and that of others round him, will alone be possible by his and their getting into such a relation that this can be permitted him, and in case of need, that this can be compelled him. I beg you to understand this; for you seem to have a little forgotten it, and there lie a thousand inferences in it, not quite useless for Exeter Hall, at present. The idle Black man in the West Indies had, not long since, the right, and will again under better form, if it please Heaven, have the right (actually the first "right of man" for an indolent person) to be *compelled* to work as he was fit, and to *do* the Maker's will who had constructed him with such and such capabilities, and prefigurements of capability. And I incessantly pray Heaven, all men, the whitest alike and the blackest, the richest and the poorest, in other regions of the world, had attained precisely the same right, the divine right of being compelled (if "permitted" will not answer) to do what work they are appointed for, and not to go idle another minute, in a life which is so short, and where idleness so soon runs to putrescence! Alas, we had then a perfect world; and the Millennium, and true "Organisation of Labour," and reign of completed blessedness, for all workers and men, had then arrived,—which in these our own poor districts of the Planet, as we all lament to know, it is very far from having yet done. [*More withdrawals; but the rest sitting with increased attention.*]

Do I, then, hate the Negro? No; except when the soul is killed out of him, I decidedly like poor Quashee; and find him a pretty kind of man. With a pennyworth of oil, you can make a handsome glossy thing of Quashee, when

the soul is not killed in him! A swift, supple fellow; a merry-hearted, grin-
ning, dancing, singing, affectionate kind of creature, with a great deal of
melody and amenability in his composition. This certainly is a notable fact:
The black African, alone of wild-men, can live among men civilised. While
all manner of Caribs and others pine into annihilation in presence of the pale
faces, he contrives to continue; does not die of sullen irreconcilable rage, of
rum, of brutish laziness and darkness, and fated incompatibility with his new
place; but lives and multiplies, and evidently means to abide among us, if we
can find the right regulation for him. We shall have to find it; we are now
engaged in the search; and have at least discovered that of two methods, the
old Demerara method, and the new Demerara method, neither will answer.

Alas, my friends, I understand well your rage against the poor Negro's
slavery; what said rage proceeds from; and have a perfect sympathy with it,
and even know it by experience. Can the oppressor of my black fellow-man be
of any use to me in particular? Am I gratified in my mind by the ill-usage of
any two- or four-legged thing; of any horse or any dog? Not so, I assure you.
In me too the natural source of human rage exist more or less, and the
capability of flying out into "fiery wrath against oppression," and of signing
petitions; both of which things can be done very cheap. Good heavens, if
signing petitions would do it, if hopping to Rome on one leg would do it,
think you it were long undone!

Frightful things are continually told us of Negro slavery, of the hardships,
bodily and spiritual, suffered by slaves. Much exaggerated, and mere exceptional cases, say the opponents. Exceptional cases, I answer; yes, and universal
ones! On the whole, hardships, and even oppressions and injustices are not
unknown in this world; I myself have suffered such, and have not you? It is
said, Man, of whatever colour, is born to such, even as the sparks fly upwards.
For in fact labour, and this is properly what we call hardship, misery, etc.
(meaning mere ugly labour not yet done), labour is not joyous but grievous;
and we have a good deal of it to do among us here. We have, simply, to carry
the whole world and its businesses upon our backs, we poor united Human
Species; to carry it, and shove it forward, from day to day, somehow or other,
among us, or else be ground to powder under it, one and all. No light task, let
me tell you, even if each did his part honestly, which each doesn't by any
means. No, only the noble lift willingly with their whole strength, at the
general burden; and in such a crowd, after all your drillings, regulatings, and
attempts at equitable distribution, and compulsion, what deceptions are still
practicable, what errors are inevitable! Many cunning ignoble fellows shirk
the labour altogether; and instead of faithfully lifting at the immeasurable

universal handbarrow with its thousand-million handles, contrive to get on some ledge of it, and be lifted!

What a story we have heard about all that, not from vague rumour since yesterday, but from inspired prophets, speakers and seers, ever since speech began! How the giant willing spirit, among white masters, and in the best-regulated families, is so often not loaded only but overloaded, crushed-down like an Enceladus; and, all his life, has to have armies of pigmies building tabernacles on his chest; marching composedly over his neck, as if it were a highway; and much amazed if, when they run their straw spear into his nostril, he is betrayed into sudden sneezing, and oversets some of them. [*Some laughter, the speaker himself looking terribly serious.*] My friends, I have come to the sad conclusion that SLAVERY, whether established by law, or by law abrogated, existed very extensively in this world, in and out of the West Indies; and, in fact, that you cannot abolish slavery by act of parliament, but can only abolish the *name* of it, which is very little!

In the West Indies itself, if you chance to abolish Slavery to Men, and in return establish Slavery to the Devil (as we see in Demerara), what good is it? To save men's bodies, and fill them with pumpkins and rum, is a poor task for human benevolence, if you have to kill their soul, what soul there was, in the business! Slavery is not so easy to be abolished; it will long continue, in spite of acts of parliament. And shall I tell you which is the one intolerable sort of slavery; the slavery over which the very gods weep? That sort is not rifest in the West Indies; but, with all its sad fruits, prevails in nobler countries. It is the slavery of the strong to the weak; of the great and noble-minded to the small and mean! The slavery of Wisdom to Folly. When Folly all "emanci-pated," and become supreme, armed with ballot-boxes, universal suffrages, and appealing to what Dismal Sciences, Statistics, Constitutional Philoso-phies, and other Fool Gospels it has got devised for itself can say to Wisdom: "Be silent, or thou shalt repent it! Suppress thyself, I advise thee; canst thou not contrive to cease, then?" That also, in some anarchic-constitutional ep-ochs, has been seen. When, of high and noble objects, there remained, in the market-place of human things, at length none; and he that could not make guineas his pursuit, and the applause of flunkies his reward, found himself in such a minority as seldom was before.

Minority, I know, there always was: but there are degrees of it, down to minority of one,—down to suppression of the unfortunate minority, and reducing it to zero, that the flunky-world may have peace from it henceforth. The flunky-world has peace; and descends, manipulating its ballot-boxes, Coppock suffrages, and divine constitutional apparatus; quoting its Dismal

Sciences, Statistics, and other satisfactory Gospels and Talmuds,—into the throat of the Devil; not bothered by the importunate minority on the road. Did you never hear of "Crucify him! Crucify him!" That was a considerable feat in the suppresing of minorities; and is still talked-of on Sundays,—with very little understanding, when I last heard of it. My friends, my friends, I fear we are a stupid people; and stuffed with such delusions, above all with such immense hypocrisies and self-delusions, from our birth upwards, as no people were before; God help us!—Emancipated? Yes, indeed, we are emancipated out of several things, and into several things. No man, wise or foolish, any longer can control you for good or for evil. Foolish Tomkins, foolish Jobson, cannot now singly oppress you: but if the Universal Company of the Tomkinses and Jobsons, as by law established, can more than ever? If, on all highways and byways, that lead to other than a Tomkins-Jobson winning-post, you meet, at the second step, the big, dumb, universal genius of Chaos, and are so placidly yet peremptorily taught, "Halt here!" There is properly but one slavery in the world. One slavery, in which all other slaveries and miseries that afflict the earth are included; compared with which the worst West-Indian, white, or black, or yellow slaveries are a small matter. One slavery over which the very gods weep. Other slaveries, women and children and stump-orators weep over; but this is for men and gods! [*Sensation; some, however, took snuff.*]

If precisely the Wisest Man were at the top of society, and the next-wisest next, and so on till we reached the Demerara Nigger (from whom downwards, through the horse, etc., there is no question hitherto), then were this a perfect world, the extreme *maximum* of wisdom produced in it. That is how you might produce your maximum, would some god assist. And I can tell you also how the *minimum* were producible. Let no man in particular be put at the top; let all men be accounted equally wise and worthy, and the notion get abroad that anybody or nobody will do well enough at the top; that money (to which may be added success in stump-oratory) is the real symbol of wisdom, and supply-and-demand the all-sufficient substitute for command and obedience among two-legged animals of the unfeathered class: accomplish all those remarkable convictions in your thinking department; and then in your practical, as is fit, decide by count of heads, the vote of a Demerara Nigger equal and no more to that of a Chancellor Bacon: this, I perceive, will (so soon as it is fairly under way, and *all* obstructions left behind) give the *minimum* of wisdom in your proceedings. Thus were your minimum producible,—with no God needed to assist, nor any Demon even, except the general Demon of *Ignavia* (Unvalour), lazy Indifference to the production or non-production of such things, which runs in our own blood. Were it beautiful, think you? Folly in such million-fold majority, at length peaceably supreme in this earth. Advancing on you as the huge buffalo-phalanx does in the Western Deserts; or as, on a smaller scale, those bristly creatures did in the Country of the Gadarenes. Rushing, namely, in wild *stampede* (the Devil being in them, some small fly having stung them), boundless,—one wing on that edge of your horizon, the other wing on that, and rearward whole tides and oceans of them:—so could Folly rush; the enlightened public one huge Gadarenes-swinery, tail cocked, snout in air, with joyful animating short squeak; fast and ever faster; down steep places,—to the sea of Tiberias, and the bottomless cloacas of Nature: quenched there, since nowhere sooner. My friends, such sight is *too* sublime, if you are out in it, and are not of it!—

Well, *except* by Mastership and Servantship, there is no conceivable deliverance from Tyranny and Slavery. Cosmos is not chaos, simply by this one quality, That it is governed. Where wisdom, even approximately, can contrive to govern, all is right, or is ever striving to become so; where folly is "emancipated," and gets to govern, as it soon will, all is wrong. That is the sad fact; and in other places than Demerara, and in regard to other interests than those of sugar-making, we sorrowfully experience the same.

I have to complain that, in these days, the relation of master to servant, and of superior to inferior, in all stages of it, is fallen sadly out of joint. As may well be, when the very highest stage and form of it, which should be the summary of all and the keystone of all, is got to such a pass. Kings themselves are grown sham-kings; and their subjects very naturally are sham-subjects; with mere lip-homage, insincere to their sham-kings;—sincere chiefly when they get into the streets (as is now our desperate case generally in Europe) to shoot them down as nuisances. Royalty is terribly gone; and loyalty in consequence has had to go. No man reverences another; at the best, each man slaps the other good-humouredly on the shoulder, with, "Hail, fellow; well met:"— at the worst (which is sure enough to *follow* such unreasonable good-humour, in a world like ours), clutches him by the throat, with "Tyrannous son of perdition, shall I endure thee, then, and thy injustices forever?" We are not yet got to the worst extreme, we here in these Isles; but we are well half-way towards it, I often think.

Certainly, by any ballot-box, Jesus Christ goes just as far as Judas Iscariot; and with reason, according to the New Gospels, Talmuds and Dismal Sciences of these days. Judas looks him in the face; asks proudly, "Am not I as good as thou? Better, perhaps!" slapping his breeches-pocket, in which is audible the cheerful jingle of thirty pieces of silver. "Thirty of them here, thou cowering pauper!" My philanthropic friends, if there be a state of matters under the stars which deserves the name of damnable and damned, this I perceive is it! Alas, I know well whence it came, and how it could not help coming;—and I continually pray the gods its errand were done, and it had begun to go its ways again. Vain hope, at least for a century to come! And there will be such a sediment of Egyptian mud to sweep away, and to fish all human things out of again, once this most sad though salutary deluge is well over, as the human species seldom had before. Patience, patience!—

In fact, without real masters you cannot have servants; and a master is not made by thirty pieces or thirty-million pieces of silver; only a sham-master is so made. The Dismal Science of this epoch defines him to be master good enough; but he is not such: you can see what kind of master he proves, what kind of servants he manages to have. Accordingly, the state of British servant-ship, of American helpship—I confess to you, my friends, if looking out for what was *least* human and heroic, least lovely to the Supreme Powers, I should not go to Carolina at this time; I should sorrowfully stay at home! Austere philosophers, possessed even of cash, have talked to me about the possibility of doing without servants; of trying somehow to serve yourself (boot-cleaning, etc., done by contract), and so escaping from a never-ending welter, dirtier for your mind than boot-cleaning itself. Of which the perpetual *fluctuation,* and change from month to month, is probably the most inhuman element; the fruitful parent of all else that is evil, unendurable and inhuman. A poor Negro overworked on the Cuba sugar-grounds, he is sad to look upon; yet he inspires me with sacred pity, and a kind of human respect is not denied him; him, the hapless brother mortal, performing something useful in his day, and only suffering inhumanity, not doing it or being it. But with what feelings can I look upon an overfed White Flunky, if I know his ways? Disloyal, unheroic, this one; *in*human in his character, and his work, and his position; more so no creature ever was. Pity is not for him, or not a soft kind of it; nor is any remedy visible, except abolition at no distant date! He is the flower of *nomadic* servitude, proceeding by month's warning, and free supply-and-demand; if obedience is not in his heart, if chiefly gluttony and mutiny are in his heart, and he had to be bribed by high feeding to do the shows of obedience,—what can await him, or be prayed for him, among men, except even "abolition"?

The Duke of Trumps, who sometimes does me the honour of a little conversation, owned that the state of his domestic service was by no means satisfactory to the human mind. "Five-and-forty of them," said his Grace; "really, I suppose, the cleverest in the market, for there is no limit to the wages: I often think how many quiet families, all down to the basis of society, I have disturbed, in attracting gradually, by higher and higher offers, that set of fellows to me; and what the use of them is when here! I feed them like aldermen, pay them as if they were sages and heroes:—Samuel Johnson's wages, at the very last and best, as I have heard you say, were 300*l.* or 500*l.* a year; and Jellysnob, my butler, who indeed is clever, gets, I believe, more than the highest of these sums. And, shall I own it to you? In my young days, with one valet, I had more trouble saved me, more help afforded me to live,— actually more of my will accomplished,—than from these forty-five I now get, or ever shall. It is all a serious comedy; what you call a melancholy sham. Most civil, obsequious, and indeed expert fellows these; but bid one of them step-out of his regulated sphere on your behalf! An iron law presses on us all here; on them and on me. In my own house, how much of my will can I have done, dare I propose to have done? Prudence, on my side, is prescribed by a jealous and ridiculous point-of-honour attitude on theirs. They lie here more like a troop of foreign soldiers that had invaded me, than a body of servants I had hired. At free quarters; we have strict laws of war established between us; they make their salutes, and do certain bits of specified work, with many becks and scrapings; but as to *service,* properly so-called—!—I lead the life of a servant, sir; it is I that am a slave; and often I think of packing the whole brotherhood of them out of doors one good day, and retiring to furnished lodgings; but have never done it yet!"—Such was the confession of his Grace.

For, indeed, in the long-run, it is not possible to buy *obedience* with money. You may buy work done with money: from cleaning boots to building houses, and to far higher functions, there is much work bought with money, and got done in a supportable manner. But, mark withal, that is only from a class of supportably wise human creatures: from a huge and ever-increasing insup- portably foolish class of human creatures you cannot buy work in that way; and the attempt in London itself, much more in Demerara, turns out a very "serious comedy" indeed! Who has not heard of the Distressed Needlewo- men in these days? We have thirty-thousand Distressed Needlewomen,—the most of whom cannot sew a reasonable stitch; for they are, in fact, Mutinous Serving-maids, who, instead of learning to work and to obey, learned to give warning: "Then suit yourself, Ma'am!" Hapless enfranchised White Women, who took the "freedom" to serve the Devil with their faculties, instead of serving God or man; hapless souls, they were "enfranchised" to a most high degree, and had not the wisdom for so ticklish a predicament,—"Then suit yourself, Ma'am;"—and so have tumbled from one stage of folly to the other stage; and at last are on the street, with five hungry senses, and no available faculty whatever. Having finger and thumb, they do procure a needle, and call themselves Distressed Needlewomen, but cannot sew at all. I have inquired in the proper places, and find a quite passionate demand for women that can sew,—such being unattainable just now. "As well call them Distressed Astronomers as Distressed Needlewomen!" said a lady to me: "I myself will take three *sewing* Needlewomen, if you can get them for me today." Is not that a sight to set before the curious?

Distressed enough, God knows;—but it will require quite other remedies to get at the bottom of *their* complaint, I am afraid. O Brothers! O Sisters! It is for these White Women that my heart bleeds and my soul is heavy; it is for the sight of such mad notions and such unblessed doings now all-prevalent among mankind,—alas, it is for such life-theories and such life-practices, and ghastly clearstarched life-hypocrisies, playing their part under high Heaven, as render these inevitable and unaidable,—that the world of today looks black and vile to me, and with all its guineas, in the nostril smells badly! It is not to the West Indies that I run first of all; and not thither with "enfranchisement" first of all, when I discern what "enfranchisement" has led to in hopefuler localities. I tell you again and again, he or she that will not work, and in the anger of the gods cannot be compelled to work, shall die! And not he or she only: alas, alas, were it the guilty only!—But as yet we cannot help it; as yet, for a long while, we must be patient, and let the Exeter-Hallery and other tragic Tom-foolery rave itself out. [*Deep silence in the small remnant of audience;—the gentleman in white trousers came in again, his creaking painfully audible in spite of efforts.*]

My friends, it is not good to be without a servant in this world; but to be without master, it appears, is a still fataler predicament for some. Without a master, in certain cases, you become a Distressed Needlewoman, and cannot so much as live. Happy he who has found his master, I will say; if not a good master, then some supportable approximation to a good one; for the worst, it appears, in some cases, is preferable to none!

Happy he who has found a master;—and now, farther I will say, having found, let him well keep him. In all human relations *permanency* is what I advocate; *nomadism,* continual change, is what I perceive to be prohibitory of any good whatsoever. Two men that have to cooperate will do well not to quarrel at the first cause of offence, and throw-up the concern in disgust, hoping to suit themselves better elsewhere. For the most part such hope is fallacious; and they will, on the average, not suit themselves better, but only about as well,—and have to begin again *bare,* which loss often repeated becomes immense, and is finally the loss of everything, and of their joint enterprise itself. For no mutual relation while it continues "bare," is yet a human one, or can bring blessedness, but is only waiting to become such,—mere new-piled crags, which, if you leave them, *will* at last "gather moss," and yield some verdure and pasture. O my friends, what a remedy is this we have fallen upon, for everything that goes wrong between one man and another: "Go, then; I give you a month's warning!" What would you think of a sacrament of marriage constructed on such principles? Marriage by the month,—why this too has been tried, and is still extensively practised in spite of Law and Gospel; but it is not found to do! The legislator, the preacher, all rational mortals, answer, "No, no!" You must marry for longer than a month, and the contract not so easily revocable, even should mistakes occur, as they some-times do.

I am prepared to maintain against all comers, That in every human rela-tion, from that of husband and wife down to that of master and servant, *nomadism* is the bad plan, and continuance the good. A thousand times, since I first had servants, it has occurred to me, How much better had I servants that were bound to me, and to whom I were bound! Doubtless it were not easy; doubtless it is now impossible: but if it could be done! I say, if the Black gentleman is born to be a servant, and, in fact, is useful in God's creation only as a servant, then let him hire not by the month, but by a very much longer term. That he be "hired for life,"—really here is the essence of the position he now holds! Consider that matter. All else is abuse in it, and this only is essence;—and the abuses must be cleared away. They must and shall! Yes; and the thing itself seems to offer (its abuses once cleared away) a possibility of the most precious kind for the Black man and for us. Servants hired for life, or by a contract for a long period, and not easily dissoluble; so and not otherwise would all reasonable mortals, Black and White, wish to hire and to be hired! I invite you to reflect on that; for you will find it true. And if true, it is impor-tant for us, in reference to this Negro Question and some others. The Ger-mans say, "you must empty-out the bathing-tub, but not the baby along with it." Fling-out your dirty water with all zeal, and set it careering down the kennels; but try if you can keep the little child!

How to abolish the abuses of slavery, and save the precious thing in it: alas, I do not pretend that this is easy, that it can be done in a day, or a single generation, or a single century: but I do surmise or perceive that it will, by straight methods or by circuitous, need to be done (not in the West-Indian regions alone); and that the one way of helping the Negro at present (Dis-tressed Needlewomen etc. being quite out of our reach) were, by piously and strenuously beginning it. Begun it must be, I perceive; and carried on in all regions where servants are born and masters; and are *not* prepared to become Distressed Needlewomen, or Demerara Niggers, but to live in some human manner with one another. And truly, my friends, with regard to this world-famous Nigger Question,—which perhaps is louder than it is big, after all,—I would advise you to attack it on that side. Try against the dirty water, with an eye to *save* the baby! That will be a quite new point of attack; where, it seems to me, some real benefit and victory for the poor Negro, might before long be accomplished; and something else than Demerara freedom (with its rum-bottle and no breeches,—'baby' quite *gone* down into the kennels!), or than American stump-oratory, with mutual exasperation fast rising to the desperate pitch, might be possible for philanthropic men and women of the Anglo-Saxon type. Try this; perhaps the very Carolina planter will coöperate with you; he will, if he has any wisdom left in this exasperation! If he do not, he will do worse; and go a strange road with those Niggers of his.

By one means or another these enormities we hear of from the Slave States,—though I think they are hardly so hideous, any of them, as the sight our own Demerara now offers,—must be heard of no more. Men will and must summon "indignation-meetings" about them; and simple persons,—like Wilhelm Meister's Felix flying at the cook's throat for plucking pigeons, yet himself seen shortly after pelting frogs to death with pebbles that lay handy,—will agitate their caucuses, ballot-boxes, dissever the Union, and, in short, play the very devil, if these things are not abated, and do not go on abating more and more towards perfect abolition. *Unjust* master over servant *hired for life* is, once for all, and shall be, unendurable to human souls. To *cut* the tie, and "fling Farmer Hodge's horses quite loose" upon the supply-and-demand principle: that, I will believe, is not the method! But by some method, by hundredfold restrictions, responsibilities, laws, conditions, cunning methods, Hodge must be got to treat his horses *justly,* for we cannot stand it longer. And let Hodge think well of it,—I mean the American two-footed Hodge,—for there is no other salvation for him. And if he would avoid a consummation like our Demerara one, I would advise him to know this secret; which our poor Hodge did not know, or would not practise, and so is come to such a pass!—Here is part of my answer to the Hon. Hickory Buckskin, a senator in those Southern States, and man of really respectable attainments and dimensions, who in his despair appears to be entertaining very violent projects now and then, as to uniting with our West Indies (under a *New Downing Street*), forming a West-Indian empire, etc., etc.

'The *New Downing Street,* I take it, is at a great distance here; and we shall wait yet a while for it, and run good risk of losing all our Colonies before we can discover the way of managing them. On that side do not reckon upon help. At the same time, I can well understand you should "publicly discuss the propriety of severing the Union," and that the resolution should be general, "you will rather die," etc. A man, having certified himself about his trade and post under the sun, is actually called upon to "die" in vindication of it, if needful; in defending the possibilities he has of carrying it on, and eschewing with it the belly of Perdition, when extraneous Insanity is pushing it thither.

All this I pre-suppose of you, of men born of your lineage; and have not a word to say against it.

'Meanwhile suffer me to say this other thing. You will not find Negro Slavery defensible by the mere resolution, never so extensive, to defend it. No, there is another condition wanted: That your relation to the Negroes, in this thing called slavery (with such an emphasis upon the word) be actually fair, just and according to the facts;—fair, I say, not in the sight of New-England platforms, but of God Almighty the Maker of both Negroes and you. That is the one ground on which men can take their stand; in the long-run all human causes, and this cause too, will come to be settled *there*. Forgive me for saying that I do not think you have yet got to that point of perfection with your Negro relations; that there is probably much in them *not* fair, nor agreeable to the Maker of us, and to the eternal laws of fact as written in the Negro's being and in ours.

'The advice of advices, therefore, to men so circumstanced were, With all diligence make them so! Otherwise than *so*, they are doomed by Earth and by Heaven. Demerara may be the maddest remedy, as I think it is a very mad one: but some remedy we must have; or if none, then destruction and annihilation, by the Demerara or a worse method. These things it would behove you of the Southern States, above all men, to be now thinking of. How to make the Negro's position among his White fellow-creatures a just one,—the real and genuine expression of what *commandment* the Maker has given to both of you, by making the one of you thus and the other so, and putting you in juxtaposition on this Earth of His? That you should *cut* the ligature, and say, "He has made us equal," would be saying a palpable falsity, big with hideous ruin for all concerned in it: I hope and believe, you, with our example before you, will say something much better than that. But something, very many things, do not hide from yourselves, will require to be said! And I do not pretend that it will be easy or soon done, to get a proper code of laws (and still more difficult, a proper system of habits, ways of thinking, for a basis to such "code") on the rights of Negroes and Whites. But that also, you may depend upon it, has fallen to White men as a duty;—to you now in the first place, after our sad failure. And unless you can do it, be certain, neither will you be able to keep your Negroes; your portion too will be the Demerara or a worse one. This seems to me indubitable.

'Or perhaps you have already begun? Persist diligently, if so; but at all events, begin! For example, ought there not to be in every Slave State, a fixed legal sum, on paying which, any Black man was entitled to demand his freedom? Settle a fair sum; and let it stand fixed by law. If the poor Black can, by forethought, industry, self-denial, accumulate this sum, has he not proved the actual "freedom" of his soul, to a fair extent: in God's name, why will you keep his body captive? It seems to me a well-considered law of this kind might do you invaluable service:—might it not be a real *safety-valve,* and ever-open *chimney,* for that down-pressed Slave-world with whatever injustices are still in it; whereby all the stronger and really worthier elements would escape peaceably, as they arose, instead of accumulating there, and convulsing you, as now? Or again, look at the Serfs of the Middle Ages: they married and gave in marriage; nay, they could not even be *divorced* from their natal soil; had home, family, and a treatment that was human. Many laws, and gradually a whole code of laws, on this matter could be made! And will have to be made; if you would avoid the ugly Demerara issue, or even uglier which may be in store. I can see no other road for you. This new question has arisen, million-voiced: "What *are* the wages of a Black servant, hired for life by White men?" This question must be answered, in some not insupportably erroneous way: gods and men are warning you that you must answer it, if you would continue there!'—The Hon. Hickory never acknowledged my letter; but I hope he is getting on with the advice I gave him, all the same!

For the rest, I never thought the "rights of Negroes" worth much discussing, nor the rights of men in any form; the grand point, as I once said, is the *mights* of men,—what portion of their "rights" they have a chance of getting sorted out, and realised, in this confused world. We will not go deep into the question here about the Negro's rights. We will give a single glance into it, and see, for one thing, how complex it is.

West-India Islands, still full of waste fertility, produce abundant pumpkins: pumpkins, however, you will observe, are not the sole requisite for human well-being. No; for a pig they are the one thing needful: but for a man they are only the first of several things needful. The first is here; but the second and remaining, how are they to be got? The answer is wide as human society itself. Society at large, as instituted in each country of the world, is the answer such country has been able to give: Here, in this poor country, the rights of man and the mights of man are—such and such! An approximate answer to a question capable only of better and better solutions, never of any perfect, or absolutely good one. Nay, if we inquire, with much narrower scope, as to the right of chief management in cultivating those West-India lands: as to the "right of property" so-called, and of doing what you like with your own? Even this question is abstruse enough. Who it may be that has a right to raise pumpkins and other produce on those Islands, perhaps none can, except temporarily, decide. The Islands are good withal for pepper, for sugar, for sago, arrow-root, for coffee, perhaps for cinnamon and precious spices; things far nobler than pumpkins; and leading towards Commerces,

Arts, Politics and Social Developments, which alone are the noble product, where men (and not pigs with pumpkins) are the parties concerned! Well, all this fruit too, fruit spicy and commercial, fruit spiritual and celestial, so far beyond the merely pumpkinish and grossly terrene, lies in the West-India lands: and the ultimate "proprietorship" of them,—why, I suppose, it will vest in him who can the *best* educe from them whatever of noble produce they were created fit for yielding. He, I compute, it the real "Vicegerent of the Maker" there; in him, better and better chosen, and not in another, is the "property" vested by decree of Heaven's chancery itself!

Up to this time it is the Saxon British mainly; they hitherto have cultivated with some manfulness: and when a manfuler class of cultivators, stronger, worthier to have such land, abler to bring fruit from it, shall make their appearance,—they, doubt it not, by fortune of war, and other confused nego-tiation and vicissitude, will be declared by Nature and Fact to *be* the worthier, and will become proprietors,—perhaps also only for a time. That is the law, I take it; ultimate, supreme, for all lands in all countries under this sky. The one perfect eternal proprietor is the Maker who created them: the temporary better or worse proprietor is he whom the Maker has sent on that mission; he who the best hitherto can educe from said lands the beneficent gifts the Maker endowed them with; or, which is but another definition of the same person, he who leads hitherto the manfulest life on that bit of soil, doing, better than another yet found can do, the Eternal Purpose and Supreme Will there.

And now observe, my friends, it was not Black Quashee, or those he represents, that made those West-India Islands what they are, or can, by any hypothesis, be considered to have the right of growing pumpkins there. For countless ages, since they first mounted oozy, on the back of earthquakes, from their dark bed in the Ocean deeps, and reeking saluted the tropical Sun, and ever onwards till the European white man first saw them some three short centuries ago, those Islands had produced mere jungle, savagery, poison-reptiles and swamp-malaria: till the white European first saw them, they were as if not yet created,—their noble elements of cinnamon, sugar, coffee, pepper black and grey, lying all asleep, waiting the white enchanter who should say to them, Awake! Till the end of human history and the sounding of the Trump of Doom, they might have lain so, had Quashee and the like of him been the only artists in the game. Swamps fever-jungles, man-eating Caribs, rattle-snakes, and reeking waste and putrefaction, this had been the produce of them under the incompetent Caribal (what we call Cannibal) possessors, till that time; and Quashee knows, himself, whether ever he could have introduced an improvement. Him, had he by a miraculous chance been wafted thither, the

Caribals would have eaten, rolling him as a fat morsel under their tongue; for him, till the sounding of the Trump of Doom, the rattlesnakes and savageries would have held-on their way. It was not he, then; it was another than he! Never by art of his could one pumpkin have grown there to solace any human throat; nothing but savagery and reeking putrefaction could have grown there. These plentiful pumpkins, I say therefore, are not his: no, they are another's; they are his only under conditions. Conditions which Exeter Hall, for the present, has forgotten; but which Nature and the Eternal Powers have by no manner of means forgotten, but do at all moments keep in mind; and, at the right moment, will, with the due impressiveness, perhaps in a rather terrible manner, bring again to our mind also!

If Quashee will not honestly aid in bringing-out those sugars, cinnamons and nobler products of the West-Indian Islands, for the benefit of all mankind, then I say neither will the Powers permit Quashee to continue growing pumpkins there for his own lazy benefit; but will shear him out, by and by, like a lazy gourd overshadowing rich ground; him and all that partake with him,—perhaps in a very terrible manner. For, under favour of Exeter Hall, the "terrible manner" is not yet quite extinct with the Destinies in this Universe; nor will it quite cease, I apprehend, for soft sawder or philanthropic stump-oratory now or henceforth. No; the gods wish besides pumpkins, that spices and valuable products be grown in their West Indies; thus much they have declared in so making the West Indies:—infinitely more they wish, that manful industrious men occupy their West Indies, not indolent two-legged cattle, however "happy" over their abundant pumpkins! Both these things, we may be assured, the immortal gods have decided upon, passed their eternal Act of Parliament for: and both of them, though all terrestrial Parliaments and entities oppose it to the death, shall be done. Quashee, if he will not help in bringing-out the spices, will get himself made a slave again (which state will be a little less ugly than his present one), and with beneficent whip, since other methods avail not, will be compelled to work.

Or, alas, let him look across to Haiti, and trace a far sterner prophecy! Let him, by his ugliness, idleness, rebellion, banish all White men from the West Indies, and make it all one Haiti,—with little or no sugar growing, black Peter exterminating black Paul, and where a garden of the Hesperides might be, nothing but a tropical dog-kennel and pestiferous jungle,—does he think that will forever continue pleasant to gods and men? I see men, the rose-pink cant all peeled away from them, land one day on those black coasts; men *sent* by the Laws of this Universe, and inexorable Course of Things; men hungry for gold, remorseless, fierce as the old Buccaneers were;—and a doom for Quashee which I had rather not contemplate! The gods are long-suffering;

but the law from the beginning was, He that will not work shall perish from the earth; and the patience of the gods has limits!

Before the West Indies could grow a pumpkin for any Negro, how much European heroism had to spend itself in obscure battle; to sink, in mortal agony, before the jungles, the putrescences and waste savageries could become arable, and the Devils be in some measure chained there! The West Indies grow pine-apples, and sweet fruits, and spices; we hope they will one day grow beautiful Heroic human Lives too, which is surely the ultimate object they were made for: beautiful souls and brave; sages, poets, what not; making the Earth nobler round them, as their kindred from of old have been doing; true "splinters of the old Harz Rock"; heroic white men, worthy to be called old Saxons, browned with a mahogany tint in those new climates and conditions. But under the soil of Jamaica, before it could even produce spices or any pumpkin, the bones of many thousand British men had to be laid. Brave Colonel Fortescue, brave Colonel Sedgwick, brave Colonel Brayne,—the dust of many thousand strong old English hearts lies there; worn-down swiftly in frightful travail, chaining the Devils, which were manifold. Heroic Blake contributed a bit of his life to that Jamaica. A bit of the great Protector's own life lies there; beneath those pumpkins lies a bit of the life that was Oliver Cromwell's. How the great Protector would have rejoiced to think, that all this was to issue in growing pumpkins to keep Quashee in a comfortably idle condition! No; that is not the ultimate issue; not that.

The West-Indian Whites, so soon as this bewilderment of philanthropic and other jargon abates from them, and their poor eyes get to discern a little what the Facts are and what the Laws are, will strike into another course, I apprehend! I apprehend they will, as a preliminary, resolutely *refuse* to permit the Black man any privilege whatever of pumpkins till he agree for work in return. Not a square inch of soil in those fruitful Isles, purchased by British blood, shall any Black man hold to grow pumpkins for him, except on terms that are fair towards Britain. Fair; see that they be not unfair, not towards ourselves, and still more, not towards him. For injustice is *forever* accursed: and precisely our unfairness towards the enslaved Black man has,—by inevitable revulsion and fated turn of the wheel,—brought about these present confusions.

Fair towards Britain it will be, that Quashee give work for privilege to grow pumpkins. Not a pumpkin, Quashee, not a square yard of soil, till you agree to do the State so many days of service. Annually that soil will grow you pumpkins; but annually also, without fail, shall you, for the owner thereof, do your appointed days of labour. The State has plenty of waste soil; but the State will religiously give you none of it on other terms. The State wants sugar from these Islands, and means to have it; wants virtuous industry in these Islands, and must have it. The State demands of you such service as will bring these results, this latter result which includes all. Not a Black Ireland, by immigration, and boundless black supply for the demand;—not that, may the gods forbid!—but a regulated West Indies, with black working population in adequate numbers; all "happy," if they find it possible; and *not* entirely un-beautiful to gods and men, which latter result they *must* find possible! All "happy," enough; that is to say, all working according to the faculty they have got, making a little more divine this Earth which the gods have given them. Is there any other "happiness,"—if it be not that of pigs fattening daily to the slaughter? So will the State speak by and by.

Any poor idle Black man, any idle White man, rich or poor, is a mere eye-sorrow to the State; a perpetual blister on the skin of the State. The State is taking measures, some of them rather extensive, in Europe at this very time, and already, as in Paris, Berlin and elsewhere, rather tremendous measures, to *get* its rich white men set to work; for alas, they also have long sat Negro-like up to the ears in pumpkin, regardless of 'work,' and of a world all going to waste for their idleness! Extensive measures, I say; and already (as, in all European lands, this scandalous Year of street-barricades and fugitive sham-kings exhibits) *tremendous* measures; for the thing is urgent to be done.

The thing must be done everywhere; *must* is the word. Only it is so terribly difficult to do; and will take generations yet, this of getting our rich European white men 'set to work'! But yours in the West Indies, my obscure Black friends, your work, and the getting of you set to it, is a simple affair; and by diligence, the West-Indian legislatures, and Royal governors, setting their faces fairly to the problem, will get it done. You are not 'slaves' now; nor do I wish, if it can be avoided, to see you slaves again: but decidedly you have to be servants to those that are born *wiser* than you, that are born lords of you; servants to the Whites, if they *are* (as what mortal can doubt they are?) born wiser than you. That, you may depend on it, my obscure Black friends, is and was always the Law of the World, for you and for all men: To *be* servants, the more foolish of us to the more wise; and only sorrow, futility and disappoint-ment will betide both, till both in some approximate degree get to conform to the same. Heaven's laws are not repealable by Earth, however Earth may try,—and it has been trying hard, in some directions, of late! I say, no well-being, and in the end no being at all, will be possible for you or us, if the law of Heaven is not complied with. And if 'slave' mean essentially 'servant hired for life,'—for life, or by a contract of long continuance and not easily dissoluble,—I ask once more, Whether, in all human things, the 'contract of long contin-uance' is not precisely the contract to be desired, were the right terms once found for it? Servant hired for life, were the right terms once found, which I do not pretend they are, seems to me much preferable to servant hired for the month, or by contract dissoluble in a day. What that amounts to, we have known, and our thirty-thousand Distressed Astronomers have known; and we don't want that! [*Some assent in the small remnant of an audience. "Silence!" from the Chair.*]

To state articulately, and put into practical Lawbooks, what on all sides is *fair* from the West-Indian White to the West-Indian Black; what relations the Eternal Maker *has* established between these two creatures of His; what He has written down with intricate but ineffaceable record, legible to candid human insight, in the respective qualities, strengths, necessities and capabilities of each of the two: this, as I told the Hon. Hickory my Carolina correspondent, will be a long problem; only to be solved by continuous human endeavor, and earnest effort gradually perfecting itself as experience successively yields new light to it. This will be to '*find* the right terms'; terms of a contract that will endure, and be sanctioned by Heaven, and obtain prosperity on Earth, between the two. A long problem, terribly neglected hitherto;—whence these West-Indian sorrows, and Exeter-Hall monstrosities, just now! But a problem which must be entered upon, and by degrees be completed. A problem which, I think, the English People also, if they mean to retain human Colonies, and not Black Irelands in addition to the White, cannot begin too soon. What are the true relations between Negro and White, their mutual duties under the sight of the Maker of them both; what human laws will assist both to comply more and more with these? The solution, only to be gained by honest endeavour, and sincere reading of experience, such as have never yet been bestowed on it, is not yet here; the solution is perhaps still distant. But some approximation to it, various real approximations, could be made, and must be made:—this of declaring that Negro and White are *un*related, loose from one another, on a footing of perfect equality, and subject to no law but that of supply-and-demand according to the Dismal Science; this, which contradicts the palpablest facts, is clearly no solution, but a cutting of the knot asunder; and every hour we persist in this is leading us towards *dis*solution instead of solution!

What, then, is practically to be done by us poor English with our Demerara and other blacks? Well, in such a mess as we have made there, it is not easy saying what is first to be done! But all this of perfect equality, of cutting quite loose from one another; all this, with 'immigration loan,' 'happiness of black peasantry,' and the other melancholy stuff that has followed from it, will first of all require to be *un*done, and the ground cleared of it, by way of preliminary to 'doing'! After that there may several things be possible.

Already one hears of Black *Adscripti glebæ;* which seems a promising arrangement, one of the first to suggest itself in such a complicacy. It appears the Dutch Blacks, in Java, are already a kind of *Adscripts,* after the manner of the old European serfs; bound, by royal authority, to give so many days of work a year. Is not this something like a real approximation; the first step towards all manner of such? Wherever, in British territory, there exists a Black man, and needful work to the just extent is not to be got out of him, such a law, in defect of better, should be brought to bear upon said Black man! How many laws of like purport, conceivable some of them, might be brought to bear upon the Black man and the White, with all despatch by way of solution instead of dissolution to their complicated case just now! On the whole, it ought to be rendered possible, ought it not, for White men to live beside Black men, and in some just manner to command Black men, and produce West-Indian fruitfulness by means of them? West-Indian fruitfulness will need to be produced. If the English cannot find the method for that, they may rest assured there will another come (Brother Jonathan or still another) who can. He it is whom the gods will bid continue in the West Indies; bidding us ignominiously, "Depart, ye quack-ridden, incompetent!"—

One other remark, as to the present Trade in Slaves, and to our suppression of the same. If buying of Black war-captives in Africa, and bringing them over to the Sugar Islands for sale again be, as I think it is, a contradiction of the Laws of this Universe, let us heartily pray Heaven to end the practice; let us ourselves help Heaven to end it, wherever the opportunity is given. If it be the most flagrant and alarming contradiction to the said Laws which is now witnessed on this Earth; so flagrant and alarming that a just man cannot exist, and follow his affairs, in the same Planet with it; why, then indeed— — But is it, quite certainly, such? Alas, look at that group of *un*sold, unbought, unmarketable Irish "free" citizens, dying there in the ditch, whither my Lord of Rackrent and the constitutional sheriffs have evicted them; or at those "divine missionaries," of the same free country, now traversing, with rags on back, and child on each arm, the principal thoroughfares of London, to tell men what "freedom" really is;—and admit that there may be doubts on that point! But if it *is,* I say, the most alarming contradiction to the said Laws which is now witnessed on this earth; so flagrant a contradiction that a just man cannot exist, and follow his affairs, in the same Planet with it, then, sure enough, let us, in God's name, fling-aside all our affairs, and hasten out to put an end to it, as the first thing the Heavens want us to do. By all manner of means. This thing done, the Heavens will prosper all other things with us! Not a doubt of it,—provided your premiss be not doubtful.

But now, furthermore, give me leave to ask, Whether the way of doing it is this somewhat surprising one, of trying to blockade the continent of Africa itself, and to watch slave-ships along that extremely extensive and unwholesome coast? The enterprise is very gigantic; and proves hitherto as futile as any enterprise has lately done. Certain wise men once, before this, set about confining the cuckoo by a big circular wall; but they could not manage it!— Watch the coast of Africa? That is a very long Coast; good part of the Coast of the terraqueous Globe! And the living centres of this slave mischief, the live coals that produce all this world-wide smoke, it appears, lie simply in two points, Cuba and Brazil, which *are* perfectly accessible and manageable.

If the Laws of Heaven do authorise you to keep the whole world in a pother about this question; if you really can appeal to the Almighty God upon it, and set common interests, and terrestrial considerations, and common sense, at defiance in behalf of it,—why, in Heaven's name, not go to Cuba and Brazil with a sufficiency of Seventy-fours; and signify to those nefarious countries: "Nefarious countries, your procedure on the Negro Question is too bad; see, of all the solecisms now submitted to on Earth, it is the most alarming and transcendent, and, in fact, is such that a just man cannot follow his affairs any longer in the same Planet with it. You clearly will not, you nefarious populations, for love or fear, watching or entreaty, respect the rights of the Negro enough;—wherefore we here, with our Seventy-fours, are come to be King over you, and will on the spot henceforth see for ourselves that you do it!"

Why not, if Heaven do send us? The thing can be done; easily, if you are sure of that proviso. It can be done: it is the way to "suppress the Slave-trade"; and so far as yet appears, the one way.

Most thinking people,—if hen-stealing prevail to a plainly unendurable extent, will you station police-officers at every hen-roost; and keep them watching and cruising incessantly to and fro over the Parish, in the unwholesome dark, at enormous expense, with almost no effect? Or will you not try rather to discover where the fox's den is, and kill the fox! Which of those two things will you do? Most thinking people, you know the fox and his den; there he is,—kill him, and discharge your cruisers and police-watchers!— [*Laughter.*]

O my friends, I feel there is an immense fund of Human Stupidity circulative among us, and much clogging our affairs for some time past! A certain man has called us, "of all peoples the wisest in action"; but he added, "the stupidest in speech":—and it is a sore thing, in these constitutional times, times mainly of universal Parliamentary and other Eloquence, that the "speakers" have all first to emit, in such tumultuous volumes, their human stupor, as the indispensable preliminary, and everywhere we must first see that and its results *out,* before beginning any business.—(*Explicit MS.*)

SOURCE: In *Fraser's Magazine* (December 1849). Reprinted in *Critical and Miscellaneous Essays,* vol. 4 (London: Chapman and Hall, 1899), 348–83.

———

The Noble Savage

CHARLES DICKENS

[First published in Dickens's weekly, *Household Words,* "The Noble Savage" may have been prompted by the Victorian practice of displaying various non-European cultures—barbarous or noble—for entertainment. Most often touted as ethnographical endeavors, these displays placed non-European bodies in their "natural" habitats for a European public to examine and discuss. The "Hottentot Venus," Saartje Bartmann, tops the list of bodies on display (1810); she is followed by the display of groups ranging from Eskimos to American Indians and Africans at the 1851 Great Exhibition in London. During 1853 alone, such exhibits as "Zulu Kaffirs" housed in St. George's Gallery in Hyde Park and "Aztec Lilliputians" at the Hanover Square Rooms were advertised in the *Illustrated London News.* Though not a direct condemnation of such exhibits, Dicken's essay does disapprove of the application of the title "noble" to the "savages" on display. The essay serves as a marker of Victorian ethnographic and pseudoscientific reliance and obsession with non-European bodies and cultures. (This introduction is by Eve Dunbar.)]

To come to the point at once, I beg to say that I have not the least belief in the Noble Savage. I consider him a prodigious nuisance, and an enormous superstition. His calling rum fire-water, and me a pale face, wholly fail to reconcile me to him. I don't care what he calls me. I call him a savage, and I call a savage a something highly desirable to be civilised off the face of the earth. I think a mere gent (which I take to be the lowest form of civilisation) better than a howling, whistling, clucking, stamping, jumping, tearing savage. It is all one to me, whether he sticks a fish-bone through his visage, or bits of trees through the lobes of his ears, or bird's feathers in his head; whether he flattens his hair between two boards, or spreads his nose over the breadth of his face, or drags his lower lip down by great weights, or blackens his teeth, or knocks them out, or paints one cheek red and the other blue, or tattoos himself, or oils himself, or rubs his body with fat, or crimps it with knives. Yielding to whichsoever of these agreeable eccentricities, he is a savage—cruel, false, thievish, murderous; addicted more or less to grease, entrails, and beastly customs; a wild animal with the questionable gift of boasting; a conceited, tiresome, bloodthirsty, monotonous humbug.

Yet it is extraordinary to observe how some people will talk about him, as they talk about the good old times; how they will regret his disappearance, in the course of this world's development, from such and such lands where his absence is a blessed relief and an indispensable preparation for the sowing of the very first seeds of any influence that can exalt humanity; how, even with the evidence of himself before them, they will either be determined to believe, or will suffer themselves to be persuaded into believing, that he is something which their five senses tell them he is not.

There was Mr. Catlin, some few years ago, with his Ojibbeway Indians. Mr. Catlin was an energetic, earnest man, who had lived among more tribes of Indians than I need reckon up here, and who had written a picturesque and glowing book about them. With his party of Indians squatting and spitting on the table before him, or dancing their miserable jigs after their own dreary manner, he called, in all good faith, upon his civilised audience to take notice of their symmetry and grace, their perfect limbs, and the exquisite expression of their pantomime; and his civilised audience, in all good faith, complied and admired. Whereas, as mere animals, they were wretched creatures, very low in the scale and very poorly formed; and as men and women possessing any power of truthful dramatic expression by means of action, they were no better than the chorus at an Italian Opera in England—and would have been worse if such a thing were possible.

Mine are no new views of the noble savage. The greatest writers on natural history found him out long ago. Buffon knew what he was, and showed why he is the sulky tyrant that he is to his women, and how it happens (Heaven be praised!) that his race is spare in numbers. For evidence of the quality of his moral nature, pass himself for a moment and refer to his "faithful dog." Has he ever improved a dog, or attached a dog, since his nobility first ran wild in woods, and was brought down (at a very long shot) by Pope? Or does the animal that is the friend of man always degenerate in his low society?

It is not the miserable nature of the noble savage that is the new thing; it is the whimpering over him with maudlin admiration, and the affecting to regret him, and the drawing of any comparison of advantage between the blemishes of civilisation and the tenor of his swinish life. There may have been a change now and then in those diseased absurdities, but there is none in him.

Think of the Bushmen. Think of the two men and the two women who have been exhibited about England for some years. Are the majority of persons—who remember the horrid little leader of that party in his festering bundle of hides, with his filth and his antipathy to water, and his straddled legs, and his odious eyes shaded by his brutal hand, and his cry of "Qu-u-u-u-aaa!" (Bosjesman for something desperately insulting, I have no doubt)—conscious of an affectionate yearning towards that noble savage, or is it *idio*syncratic in me to abhor, detest, abominate, and abjure him? I have no reserve on this subject, and will frankly state that, setting aside that stage of the entertainment when he counterfeited the death of some creature he had shot, by laying his head on his hand and shaking his left leg—at which time I think it would have been justifiable homicide to slay him—I have never seen that group sleeping, smoking, and expectorating round their brazier, but I have sincerely desired that something might happen to the charcoal smouldering therein, which would cause the immediate suffocation of the whole of the noble strangers.

There is at present a party of Zulu Kaffirs exhibiting at the St. George's Gallery, Hyde Park Corner, London. These noble savages are represented in a most agreeable manner; they are seen in an elegant theatre, fitted with appropriate scenery of great beauty, and they are described in a very sensible and unpretending lecture, delivered with a modesty which is quite a pattern to all similar exponents. Though extremely ugly, they are much better shaped than such of their predecessors as I have referred to; and they are rather picturesque to the eye, though far from odoriferous to the nose. What a visitor left to his own interpretings and imaginings might suppose these noblemen to be about, when they give vent to that pantomimic expression which is quite settled to be the natural gift of the noble savage, I cannot possibly conceive; for it is so much too luminous for my personal civilisation that it conveys no idea to my mind beyond a general stamping, ramping, and raving, remarkable (as everything in savage life is) for its dire uniformity. But let us—with the interpreter's assistance, of which I for one stand so much in need—see what the noble savage does in Zulu Kaffirland.

The noble savage sets a king to reign over him, to whom he submits his life and limbs without a murmur or question, and whose whole life is passed chin deep in a lake of blood; but who, after killing incessantly, is in his turn killed by his relations and friends, the moment a grey hair appears on his head. All the noble savage's wars with his fellow-savages (and he takes no pleasure in anything else) are wars of extermination—which is the best thing I know of him, and the most comfortable to my mind when I look at him. He has no moral feelings of any kind, sort, or description; and his "mission" may be summed up as simply diabolical.

The ceremonies with which he faintly diversifies his life are, of course, of a kindred nature. If he wants a wife he appears before the kennel of the gentleman whom he has selected for his father-in-law, attended by a party of male friends of a very strong flavour, who screech and whistle and stamp an offer of so many cows for the young lady's hand. The chosen father-in-law—also supported by a high-flavoured party of male friends—screeches, whistles, and yells (being seated on the ground, he can't stamp) that there never was such a daughter in the market as his daughter, and that he must have six more cows. The son-in-law and his select circle of backers screech, whistle, stamp, and yell in reply, that they will give three more cows. The father-in-law (an old deluder, overpaid at the beginning) accepts four, and rises to bind the bargain. The whole party, the young lady included, then falling into epileptic convulsions, and screeching, whistling, stamping, and yelling together—and nobody taking any notice of the young lady (whose charms are not to be thought of without a shudder)—the noble savage is considered married, and his friends make demoniacal leaps at him by way of congratulation.

When the noble savage finds himself a little unwell, and mentions the circumstance to his friends, it is immediately perceived that he is under the influence of witchcraft. A learned personage, called an Imyanger or Witch Doctor, is immediately sent for to Nooker the Umtargartie, or smell out the witch. The male inhabitants of the kraal being seated on the ground, the learned doctor, got up like a grizzly bear, appears, and administers a dance of a most terrific nature, during the exhibition of which remedy he incessantly gnashes his teeth, and howls:—"I am the original physician to Nooker the Umtargartie. Yow yow yow! No connexion with any other establishment. Till till till! All other Umtargarties are feigned Umtargarties, Boroo Boroo! but I perceive here a genuine and real Umtargartie, Hoosh Hoosh Hoosh! in whose blood I, the original Imyanger and Nookerer, Blizzerum Boo! will wash these bear's claws of mine. O yow yow yow!" All this time the learned physician is looking out among the attentive faces for some unfortunate man who owes him a cow, or who has given him any small offence, or against whom, without offence, he has conceived a spite. Him he never fails to Nooker as the Umtargartie, and he is instantly killed. In the absence of such an individual, the usual practice is to Nooker the quietest and most gentlemanly person in company. But the nookering is invariably followed on the spot by the butchering.

Some of the noble savages in whom Mr. Catlin was so strongly interested,

Advertisement. SOURCE: *Illustrated London News*, 9 July 1853.

and the diminution of whose numbers, by rum and small-pox, greatly affected him, had a custom not unlike this, though much more appalling and disgusting in its odious details.

The women being at work in the fields, hoeing the Indian corn, and the noble savage being asleep in the shade, the chief has sometimes the condescension to come forth, and lighten the labour by looking at it. On these occasions, he seats himself in his own savage chair, and is attended by his shield-bearer: who holds over his head a shield of cowhide—in shape like an immense mussel shell—fearfully and wonderfully, after the manner of a theatrical supernumerary. But lest the great man should forget his greatness in the contemplation of the humble works of agriculture, there suddenly rushes in a poet, retained for the purpose, called a Praiser. This literary gentleman wears a leopard's head over his own, and a dress of tigers' tails; he has the appearance of having come express on his hind legs from the Zoological Gardens; and he incontinently strikes up the chief's praises, plunging and tearing all the while. There is a frantic wickedness in this brute's manner of worrying the air, and gnashing out, "O what a delightful chief he is! O what a delicious quantity of blood he sheds! O how majestically he laps it up! O how charmingly cruel he is! O how he tears the flesh of his enemies and crunches the bones! O how like the tiger and the leopard and the wolf and the bear he is! O, row row row row, how fond I am of him!" which might tempt the Society of Friends to charge at a hand-gallop into the Swartz-Kop location and exterminate the whole kraal.

When war is afoot among the noble savages—which is always—the chief holds a council to ascertain whether it is the opinion of his brothers and friends in general that the enemy shall be exterminated. On this occasion, after the performance of an Umsebeuza, or war song,—which is exactly like all the other songs,—the chief makes a speech to his brothers and friends, arranged in single file. No particular order is observed during the delivery of this address, but every gentleman who finds himself excited by the subject, instead of crying "Hear, hear!" as is the custom with us, darts from the rank and tramples out the life, or crushes the skull, or mashes the face, or scoops out the eyes, or breaks the limbs, or performs a whirlwind of atrocities on the body, of an imaginary enemy. Several gentlemen becoming thus excited at once, and pounding away without the least regard to the orator, that illustrious person is rather in the position of an orator in an Irish House of Commons. But several of these scenes of savage life bear a strong generic resemblance to an Irish election, and I think would be extremely well received and understood at Cork.

In all these ceremonies the noble savage holds forth to the utmost possible extent about himself; from which (to turn him to some civilised account) we may learn, I think, that as egotism is one of the most offensive and contemptible littlenesses a civilised man can exhibit, so it is really incompatible with the interchange of ideas; inasmuch as if we all talked about ourselves we should soon have no listeners, and must be all yelling and screeching at once on our own separate accounts: making society hideous. It is my opinion that if we retained in us anything of the noble savage, we could not get rid of it too soon. But the fact is clearly otherwise. Upon the wife and dowry question, substituting coin for cows, we have assuredly nothing of the Zulu Kaffir left. The endurance of despotism is one great distinguishing mark of a savage always. The improving world has quite got the better of that too. In like manner, Paris is a civilised city, and the Théâtre Français a highly civilised theatre; and we shall never hear, and never have heard in these later days (of course) of the Praiser *there*. No, no, civilised poets have better work to do. As to Nookering Umtargarties, there are no pretended Umtargarties in Europe, and no European powers to Nooker them; that would be mere spydom, subordination, small malice, superstition, and false pretence. And as to private Umtargarties, are we not in the year eighteen hundred and fifty-three, with spirits rapping at our doors?

To conclude as I began. My position is, that if we have anything to learn from the Noble Savage, it is what to avoid. His virtues are a fable; his happiness is a delusion; his nobility, nonsense. We have no greater justification for being cruel to the miserable object, than for being cruel to a William Shakespeare or an Isaac Newton; but he passes away before an immeasurably better and higher power than ever ran wild in any earthly woods, and the world will be all the better when his place knows him no more.

SOURCE: In *Household Words* (11 June 1853): 111–17. Reprinted in *Reprinted Pieces* (London: Chapman and Hall, n.d.).

SPECIES

Moral and Intellectual Characteristics of
the Three Great Varieties

COUNT JOSEPH ARTHUR GOBINEAU

[Count Arthur Gobineau (1816–1882) was an aristocrat, novelist, and orientalist. For a brief time, he was employed as the secretary to Alexis de Tocqueville during his term as foreign minister of France (1849). Gobineau's theory of racial determinism was developed, in part, in response to the fervent republicanism and socialism that were influencing French, British, and European politics and culture; his investment in the idea of a strict social, class, and caste hierarchy informed his orientalist interpretations of pseudoscientific racial and anthropological theories. Ironically, this passionate defender of aristocratic order and Aryan privilege was born on Bastille Day. Gobineau's works include the novels *Pléiades* (The Pleiads) (1874) and *Souvenirs de Voyage* (The Crimson Handkerchief) (1872); he is also known for his *Histoire des Perses* (History of the Persians) (1869) and the influential, four-volume *Essai sur l'Inégalité des Races Humaines* (Essay on the inequality of the human races) (1853–1855)—the work that would impress Richard Wagner, Friedrich Nietzsche, Houston Stewart Chamberlain, and Adolf Hitler.]

Impropriety of drawing general conclusions from individual cases—Recapitulatory sketch of the leading features of the Negro, the Yellow, and the White races—Superiority of the latter—Conclusion of volume the first.

In the preceding pages, I have endeavored to show that, though there are both scientific and religious reasons for not believing in a plurality of origins of our species, the various branches of the human family are distinguished by permanent and irradicable differences, both mentally and physically. They are unequal in intellectual capacity,[1] in personal beauty, and in physical strength.

---

1. I do not hesitate to consider as an unmistakable mark of intellectual inferiority, the exaggerated development of instincts that characterizes certain savages. The perfection which some of

Again I repeat, that in coming to this conclusion, I have totally eschewed the method which is, unfortunately for the cause of science, too often resorted to by ethnologists, and which, to say the least of it, is simply ridiculous. The discussion has not rested upon the moral and intellectual worth of isolated individuals.

With regard to moral worth, I have proved that all men, to whatever race they may belong, are capable of receiving the lights of true religion, and of sufficiently appreciating that blessing to work out their own salvation. With regard to intellectual capacity, I emphatically protest against that mode of arguing which consists in saying, "every negro is a dunce;" because, by the same logic, I should be compelled to admit that "every white man is intelligent;" and I shall take good care to commit no such absurdity.

I shall not even wait for the vindicators of the absolute equality of all races, to adduce to me such and such a passage in some missionary's or navigator's journal, wherefrom it appears that some Yolof has become a skilful carpenter, that some Hottentot has made an excellent domestic, that some Caffre plays well on the violin, or that some Bambarra has made very respectable progress in arithmetic.

I am prepared to admit—and to admit without proof—anything of that sort, however remarkable, that may be related of the most degraded savages. I have already denied the excessive stupidity, the incurable idiotcy of even the lowest on the scale of humanity. Nay, I go further than my opponents, and am not in the least disposed to doubt that, among the chiefs of the rude negroes of Africa, there could be found a considerable number of active and vigorous minds, greatly surpassing in fertility of ideas and mental resources, the average of our peasantry, and even of some of our middle classes. But the unfairness of deductions based upon a comparison of the most intelligent blacks and the least intelligent whites, must be obvious to every candid mind.

Once for all, such arguments seem to me unworthy of real science, and I do not wish to place myself upon so narrow and unsafe a ground. If Mungo Park, or the brothers Lander, have given to some negro a certificate of superior intelligence, who will assure us that another traveller, meeting the same individual, would not have arrived at a diametrically opposite conclusion concerning him? Let us leave such puerilities, and compare, not the individuals, but the masses. When we shall have clearly established of what the latter are capable, by what tendencies they are characterized, and by what limits their

_____

their senses acquire, cannot but be at the expense of the reasoning faculties. See, upon this subject, the opinions of Mr. Lesson des Papous, in a memoir inserted in the tenth volume of the *Annales des Sciences Naturelles*.

intellectual activity and development are circumscribed, whether, since the beginning of the historic epoch, they have acted upon, or been acted upon by other groups—when we shall have clearly established these points, we may then descend to details, and, perhaps, one day be able to decide why the greatest minds of one group are inferior to the most brilliant geniuses of another, in what respects the vulgar herds of all types assimilate, and in what others they differ, and why. But this difficult and delicate task cannot be accomplished until the relative position of the whole mass of each race shall have been nicely, and, so to say, mathematically defined. I do not know whether we may hope ever to arrive at results of such incontestable clearness and precision, as to be able to no longer trust solely to general facts, but to embrace the various shades of intelligence in each group, to define and class the inferior strata of every population and their influence on the activity of the whole. Were it possible thus to divide each group into certain strata, and compare these with the corresponding strata of every other: the most gifted of the dominant with the most gifted of the dominated races, and so on downwards, the superiority of some in capacity, energy, and activity would be self-demonstrated.

After having mentioned the facts which prove the inequality of various branches of the human family, and having laid down the method by which that proof should be established, I arrived at the conclusion that the whole of our species is divisible into three great groups, which I call primary varieties, in order to distinguish them from others formed by intermixture. It now remains for me to assign to each of these groups the principal characteristics by which it is distinguished from the others.

The dark races are the lowest on the scale. The shape of the pelvis has a character of animalism, which is imprinted on the individuals of that race ere their birth, and seems to portend their destiny. The circle of intellectual development of that group is more contracted than that of either of the two others.

If the negro's narrow and receding forehead seems to mark him as inferior in reasoning capacity, other portions of his cranium as decidedly point to faculties of an humbler, but not the less powerful character. He has energies of a not despicable order, and which sometimes display themselves with an intensity truly formidable. He is capable of violent passions, and passionate attachments. Some of his senses have an acuteness unknown to the other races: the sense of taste, and that of smell, for instance.

But it is precisely this development of the animal faculties that stamps the negro with the mark of inferiority to other races. I said that his sense of taste was acute; it is by no means fastidious. Every sort of food is welcome to his palate; none disgusts[2] him; there is no flesh nor fowl too vile to find a place in his stomach. So it is with regard to odor. His sense of smell might rather be called greedy than acute. He easily accommodates himself to the most repulsive.

To these traits he joins a childish instability of humor. His feelings are intense, but not enduring. His grief is as transitory as it is poignant, and he rapidly passes from it to extreme gayety. He is seldom vindictive—his anger is violent, but soon appeased. It might almost be said that this variability of sentiments annihilates for him the existence of both virtue and vice. The very ardency to which his sensibilities are aroused, implies a speedy subsidence; the intensity of his desire, a prompt gratification, easily forgotten. He does not cling to life with the tenacity of the whites. But moderately careful of his own, he easily sacrifices that of others, and kills, though not absolutely bloodthirsty, without much provocation or subsequent remorse.[3] Under intense

2. "The negro's sense of smell and of taste is as powerful as it is unselecting. He eats everything, and I have good reasons for asserting, that odors the most disagreeable to us, are positively pleasant to him." (Pruner, *Op. cit.*, vol. i. p. 133.)

Mr. Pruner's assertions would, I think, be corroborated by every one who has lived much among the negroes. It is a notorious fact that the blacks on our southern plantations eat every animal they can lay hold of. I have seen them discuss a piece of fox, or the still more strongly flavored pole-cat, with evident relish. Nay, on one occasion, I have known a party of negroes feast on an alligator for a whole week, during which time they bartered their allowance of meat for trinkets. Upon my expressing surprise at so strange a repast, I was assured that it was by no means uncommon; that it was a favorite viand of the negroes in their native country, and that even here they often killed them with the prospect of a savory roast or stew. I am aware that some persons north of the Mason's & Dixon's line might be disposed to explain this by asserting that *hunger* drove them to such extremities; but I can testify, from my own observation, that this is not the case. In the instances I have mentioned, and in many others which are too repulsive to be committed to paper, the banqueters were well fed, and evidently made such a feast from choice. There are, in the Southern States, many of the poor white population who are neither so well clothed nor so well fed as these negroes were, and yet I never heard of their resorting to such dishes.

In regard to the negro's fondness for odors, I am less qualified to speak from my own observations, but nearly every description of the manners of his native climes that I have read, mentioned the fact of their besmearing themselves with the strong musky fluid secreted by many animals—the alligator, for instance. And I remember having heard woodsmen in the South say, that while the white man shuns the polecat more than he does the rattlesnake, and will make a considerable circuit to get out of its way, the negro is but little afraid of this formidable animal and its nauscous weapon.—II.

3. This is illustrated by many of their practices in their natural state. For instance, the well-known custom of putting to death, at the demise of some prince or great man, a number—corresponding with the rank of the deceased—of his slaves, in order that they may wait upon him in the other world. Hundreds of poor creatures are often thus massacred at the funeral celebrations in honor of some king or ruler. Yet it would be unjust to call the negro ferocious or cruel. It merely proves the slight estimation in which he holds human life.—H.

suffering, he exhibits a moral cowardice which readily seeks refuge in death, or in a sort of monstrous impassivity.[4]

With regard to his moral capacities, it may be stated that he is susceptible, in an eminent degree, of religious emotions; but unless assisted by the light of the Gospel, his religious sentiments are of a decidedly sensual character.

Having demonstrated the little intellectual and strongly sensual[5] character

4. There is a callousness in the negro, which strikingly distinguishes him from the whites, though it is possessed in perhaps an equal degree by other races. I borrow from Mr. Van Amringe's *Nat. Hist. of Man,* a few remarks on this subject by Dr. Mosely, in his *Treatise on Tropical Disease:* "Negroes," says the Doctor, "whatever the cause may be, are devoid of sensibility (physical) to a surprising degree. They are not subject to nervous diseases. They sleep sound in every disease, nor does any mental disturbance ever keep them awake. They bear chirurgical operations much better than white people, and what would be the cause of insupportable pain to a white man, a negro would almost disregard. I have amputated the legs of many negroes, who have held the upper part of the limb themselves." Every southern planter, and every physician of experience in the South, could bear witness to these facts.—II.

5. Thinking that it might not be uninteresting to some of our readers to see the views concerning the negro of another European writer besides Mr. Gobineau, I subjoin the following extract from Mr. Tschudi's *Travels in South America.* Mr. Tschudi is a Swiss naturalist of undoubted reputation, an experienced philosophic observer, and a candid seeker for truth. His opinion is somewhat harsher than would be that of a man who had resided among that class all his life, but it nevertheless contains some valuable truths, and is, at least, curious on account of the source whence it comes.

"In Lima, and, indeed, throughout the whole of Peru, the free negroes are a plague to society. Too indolent to support themselves by laborious industry, they readily fall into any dishonest means of getting money. Almost all the robbers that infest the roads on the coast of Peru are free negroes. Dishonesty seems to be a part of their very nature; and, moreover, all their tastes and inclinations are coarse and sensual. Many warm defenders excuse these qualities by ascribing them to the want of education, the recollection of slavery, the spirit of revenge, etc. But I here speak of free-born negroes, who are admitted into the houses of wealthy families, who, from their early childhood, have received as good an education as falls to the share of many of the white Creoles—who are treated with kindness and liberally remunerated, and yet they do not differ from their half-savage brethren who are shut out from these advantages. If the negro has learned to read and write, and has thereby made some little advance in education, he is transformed into a conceited coxcomb, who, instead of plundering travellers on the highway, finds in city life a sphere for the indulgence of his evil propensities. . . . My opinion is, that the negroes, in respect to capability for mental improvement, are far behind the Europeans; and that, considered in the aggregate, they will not, even with the advantages of careful education, attain a very high degree of cultivation. This is apparent from the structure of the skull, on which depends the development of the brain, and which, in the negro, approximates closely to the animal form. The imitative faculty of the monkey is highly developed in the negro, who readily seizes anything merely mechanical, whilst things demanding intelligence are beyond his reach. Sensuality is the impulse which controls the thoughts, the acts, the whole existence of the negroes. To them, freedom can be only nominal, for if they conduct themselves well, it is because they are com-of the black variety, as the type of which I have taken the negro of Western Africa, I shall now proceed to examine the moral and intellectual characteristics of the second in the scale—the yellow.

This seems to form a complete antithesis to the former. In them, the skull, instead of being thrown backward, projects. The forehead is large, often jutting out, and of respectable height. The facial conformation is somewhat triangular, but neither chin nor nose has the rude, animalish development that characterizes the negro. A tendency to obesity is not precisely a specific feature, but it is more often met with among the yellow races than among any others. In muscular vigor, in intensity of feelings and desires, they are greatly inferior to the black. They are supple and agile, but not strong. They have a decided taste for sensual pleasures, but their sensuality is less violent, and, if I may so call it, more vicious than the negro's, and less quickly appeased. They place a somewhat greater value upon human life than the negro does, but they are more cruel for the sake of cruelty. They are as gluttonous as the negro, but more fastidious in their choice of viands, as is proved by the immoderate attention bestowed on the culinary art among the more civilized of these races. In other words, the yellow races are less impulsive than the black. Their will is characterized by obstinacy rather than energetic violence; their anger is vindictive rather than clamorous; their cruelty more studied than passionate; their sensuality more refinedly vicious than absorbing. They are, therefore, seldom prone to extremes. In morals, as in intellect, they display a mediocrity: they are given to grovelling vices rather than to dark crimes; when virtuous, they are so oftener from a sense of practical usefulness than from exalted sentiments. In regard to intellectual capacity, they easily understand whatever is not very profound, nor very sublime; they have a keen appreciation of the useful and practical, a great love of quiet and order, and even a certain conception of a slight modicum of personal or municipal liberty. The yellow races are practical people in the narrowest sense of the word. They have little scope of imagination, and therefore invent but little: for great inventions, even the most exclusively utilitarian, require a high degree of the imaginative faculty. But they easily understand and adopt whatever is of practical utility. The *summum bonum* of their desires and aspirations is to pass smoothly and quietly through life.

It is apparent from this sketch, that they are superior to the blacks in aptitude and intellectual capacity. A theorist who would form some model society, might wish such a population to form the substratum upon which to

---

pelled, not because they are inclined to do so. Herein lie at once the cause of, and the apology for, their bad character." (*Travels in Peru*, London, 1848, p. 110, *et passim.*)

erect his structure; but a society, composed entirely of such elements, would display neither great stamina nor capacity for anything great and exalted.

We are now arrived at the third and last of the "primary" varieties—the white. Among them we find great physical vigor and capacity of endurance; an intensity of will and desire, but which is balanced and governed by the intellectual faculties. Great things are undertaken, but not blindly, not without a full appreciation of the obstacles to be overcome, and with a systematic effort to overcome them. The utilitarian tendency is strong, but is united with a powerful imaginative faculty, which elevates, ennobles, idealizes it. Hence, the power of invention; while the negro can merely imitate, the Chinese only utilize, to a certain extent, the practical results attained by the white, the latter is continually adding new ones to those already gained. His capacity for combination of ideas leads him perpetually to construct new facts from the fragments of the old; hurries him along through a series of unceasing modifications and changes. He has as keen a sense of order as the man of the yellow race, but not, like him, from love of repose and inertia, but from a desire to protect and preserve his acquisitions. At the same time, he has an ardent love of liberty, which is often carried to an extreme; an instinctive aversion to the trammels of that rigidly formalistic organization under which the Chinese vegetates with luxurious ease; and he as indignantly rejects the haughty despotism which alone proves a sufficient restraint for the black races.

The white man is also characterized by a singular love of life. Perhaps it is because he knows better how to make use of it than other races, that he attaches to it a greater value and spares it more both in himself and in others. In the extreme of his cruelty, he is conscious of his excesses; a sentiment which it may well be doubted whether it exist among the blacks. Yet though he loves life better than other races, he has discovered a number of reasons for sacrificing it or laying it down without murmur. His valor, his bravery, are not brute, unthinking passions, not the result of callousness or impassivity: they spring from exalted, though often erroneous, sentiments, the principal of which is expressed by the word "honor." This feeling, under a variety of names and applications, has formed the mainspring of action of most of the white races since the beginning of historical times. It accommodates itself to every mode of existence, to every walk of life. It is as puissant in the pulpit and at the martyr's stake, as on the field of battle; in the most peaceful and humble pursuits of life as in the highest and most stirring. It were impossible to define all the ideas which this word comprises; they are better felt than expressed. But this feeling—we might call it instinctive—is unknown to the yellow, and unknown to the black races: while in the white it quickens every noble sentiment—the sense of justice, liberty, patriotism, love, religion—it has no name in the language, no place in the hearts, of other races. This I consider as the principal reason of the superiority of our branch of the human family over all others; because even in the lowest, the most debased of our race, we generally find some spark of this redeeming trait, and however misapplied it may often be, and certainly is, it prevents us, even in our deepest errors, from falling so fearfully low as the others. The extent of moral abasement in which we find so many of the yellow and black races is absolutely impossible even to the very refuse of our society. The latter may equal, nay, surpass them in crime; but even they would shudder at that hideous abyss of corrosive vices, which opens before the friend of humanity on a closer study of these races.[6]

Before concluding this picture, I would add that the immense superiority of the white races in all that regards the intellectual faculties, is joined to an inferiority as strikingly marked, in the intensity of sensations. Though his whole structure is more vigorous, the white man is less gifted in regard to the perfection of the senses than either the black or the yellow, and therefore less solicited and less absorbed by animal gratifications.

I have now arrived at the historical portion of my subject. There I shall place the truths enounced in this volume in a clearer light, and furnish irrefragable proofs of the fact, which forms the basis of my theory, that nations degenerate only in consequence and in proportion to their admixture with an inferior race—that a society receives its death-blow when, from the number of diverse ethnical elements which it comprises, a number of diverse modes of thinking and interests contend for predominance; when these modes of thinking, and these interests have arisen in such multiplicity that every effort to harmonize them, to make them subservient to some great purpose, is in vain; when, therefore, the only natural ties that can bind large masses of men, homogeneity of thoughts and feelings, are severed, the only solid foundation of a social structure sapped and rotten.

To furnish the necessary details for this assertion, to remove the possibility of even the slightest doubt, I shall take up separately, every great and independent civilization that the world has seen flourish. I shall trace its first beginnings, its subsequent stages of development, its decadence and final decay. Here, then, is the proper test of my theory; here we can see the laws that govern ethnical relations in full force on a magnificent scale; we can verify their inexorably uniform and rigorous application. The subject is immense,

6. The sickening moral degradation of some of the branches of our species is well known to the student of anthropology, though, for obvious reasons, details of this kind cannot find a place in books destined for the general reader.—H.

the panorama spread before us the grandest and most imposing that the philosopher can contemplate, for its tableaux comprise the scene of action of every instance where man has really worked out his mission "to have dominion over the earth."

The task is great—too great, perhaps, for any one's undertaking. Yet, on a more careful investigation, many of the apparently insuperable difficulties which discouraged the inquirer will vanish; in the gorgeous succession of scenes that meet his glance, he will perceive a uniformity, an intimate relation and connection which, like Ariadne's thread, will enable the undaunted and persevering student to find his way through the mazes of the labyrinth: we shall find that every civilization owes its origin, its development, its splendors, to the agency of the white races. In China and in India, in the vast continent of the West, centuries ere Columbus found it—it was one of the group of white races that gave the impetus, and, so long as it lasted, sustained it. Startling as this assertion may appear to a great number of readers, I hope to demonstrate its correctness by incontrovertible historical testimony. Everywhere the white races have taken the initiative, everywhere they have *brought* civilization to the others—everywhere they have sown the seed: the vigor and beauty of the plant depended on whether the soil it found was congenial or not.

The migrations of the white race, therefore, afford us at once a guide for our historical researches, and a clue to many apparently inexplicable mysteries: we shall learn to understand why, in a vast country, the development of civilization has come to a stand, and been superseded by a retrogressive movement; why, in another, all but feeble traces of a high state of culture has vanished without apparent cause; why people, the lowest in the scale of intellect, are yet found in possession of arts and mechanical processes that would do honor to a highly intellectual race.

Among the group of white races, the noblest, the most highly gifted in intellect and personal beauty, the most active in the cause of civilization, is the Arian[7] race. Its history is intimately associated with almost every effort on the part of man to develop his moral and intellectual powers.

7. As many of the terms of modern ethnography have not yet found their way into the dictionaries, I shall offer a short explanation of the meaning of this word, for the benefit of those readers who have not paid particular attention to that science.

The word "Arian" is derived from *Aryas* or Αριοι, respectively the indigenous and the Greek designation of the ancient Medes, and is applied to a race, or rather a family of races, whose original ethnological area is not as yet accurately defined, but who have gradually spread from the centre of Asia to the mouth of the Ganges, to the British Isles, and the northern extremities of Scandinavia. To this family of races belong, among others, the ancient Medes and Persians, the white conquerers of India (now forming the caste of the Brahmins), *and the Germanic races.* The whole group is often called Indo-European. The affinities between the Greek and the

It now remains for me to trace out the field of inquiry into which I propose to enter in the succeeding volumes. The list of great, independent civilizations is not long. Among all the innumerable nations that "strutted their brief hour on the stage" of the world, ten only have arrived at the state of complete societies, giving birth to distinct modes of intellectual culture. All the others were imitators or dependents; like planets they revolved around, and derived their light from the suns of the systems to which they belonged. At the head of my list I would place:—

1. The Indian civilization. It spread among the islands of the Indian Ocean, towards the north, beyond the Himalaya Mountains, and towards the east, beyond the Brahmapootra. It was originated by a white race of the Arian stock.

2. The Egyptian civilization comes next. As its satellites may be mentioned the less perfect civilizations of the Ethiopians, Nubians, and several other small peoples west of the oasis of Ammon. An Arian colony from India, settled in the upper part of the Nile valley, had established this society.

3. The Assyrians, around whom rallied the Jews, Phenicians, Lydians, Carthaginians, and Hymiarites, were indebted for their social intelligence to the repeated invasions of white populations. The Zoroastrian Iranians, who flourished in Further Asia, under the names of Medes, Persians, and Bactrians, were all branches of the Arian family.

4. The Greeks belonged to the same stock, but were modified by Shemitic elements, which, in course of time, totally transformed their character.

5. China presents the precise counterpart of Egypt. The light of civilization was carried thither by Arian colonies. The substratum of the social structure was composed of elements of the yellow race, but the white civilizers received reinforcements of their blood at various times.

German languages had long been an interesting question to philologists; but Schlegel, I believe, was the first to discover the intimate relations between these two and the Sanscrit, and he applied to the whole three, and their collateral branches, the name of *Indo-Germanic* languages. The discovery attracted the attention both of philologists and ethnographers, and it is now indubitably proved that the civilizers of India, and the subverters of the Roman Empire are descended from the same ethnical stock. It is known that the Sanscrit is as unlike all other Indian languages, as the high-caste Brahmins are unlike the Pariahs and all the other aboriginal races of that country; and Latham has lately come to the conclusion that it has actually been *carried to India from Europe.* It will be seen from this that Mr. Gobineau, in his view of the origin of various civilizations, is supported in at least several of the most important instances.

It is a familiar saying that *civilization travels westward:* if we believe ethnologists, the Arian races have *always migrated in that direction*—from Central Asia to India, to Asia Minor, to Egypt, to Greece, to Western Europe, to the western coasts of the Atlantic, and the same impulse of migration is now carrying them to the Pacific.—II.

6. The ancient civilization of the Italian peninsula (the Etruscan civilization), was developed by a mosaic of populations of the Celtic, Iberian, and Shemitic stock, but cemented by Arian elements. From it emerged the civilization of Rome.

7. Our civilization is indebted for its tone and character to the Germanic conquerors of the fifth century. They were a branch of the Arian family.

8, 9, 10. Under these heads I class the three civilizations of the western continent, the Alleghanian, the Mexican, and the Peruvians.

This is the field I have marked out for my investigations, the results of which will be laid before the reader in the succeeding volumes. The first part of my work is here at an end—the vestibule of the structure I wish to erect is completed.

SOURCE: Chapter 15 in *The Moral and Intellectual Diversity of Races, with Particular Reference to Their Respective Influence in the Civil and Political History of Mankind* (Philadelphia: J. B. Lippincott, 1856), 439–60.

Struggle for Existence
CHARLES DARWIN

[Charles Darwin (1809–1882) was the grandson of the scientist Erasmus Darwin, whose speculative theories of evolution (along with those of Jean-Baptiste Lamarck, Charles Lyell, and others) influenced the young naturalist. After rejecting the medical and theological professions, Darwin accepted employment as an observer to H.M.S. *Beagle* Captain Robert Fitz Roy on his expedition to Patagonia in the Galapagos Islands. Darwin's observations of fossils and the development and transmutation of new species provided the background for his evolutionary theories. Darwin's controversial works led many to assail him with charges of blasphemy, sedition, and heresy. Darwin's theories were central to the rise of modern secular philosophy and thought; his evolutionary theories and their ambiguous racial-biological tenets would be adopted by social Darwinists, like Herbert Spencer, and eugenicists, including his son Leonard. Darwin was made a fellow of the Geological Society in 1836 and elected to the Athenaeum, the exclusive club for artists and scientists, in 1838. The following year he was elected to the Royal Society.]

Its bearing on natural selection—The term used in a wide sense—Geometrical ratio of increase—Rapid increase of naturalised animals and plants—Nature of the checks to increase—Competition universal—Effects of Climate—Protection from

the number of individuals—Complex relations of all animals and plants through-
out nature—Struggle for life most severe between individuals and varieties of the
same species: often severe between species of the same genus—The relation of organ-
ism to organism the most important of all relations.

Before entering on the subject of this chapter, I must make a few preliminary
remarks, to show how the struggle for existence bears on Natural Selection. It
has been seen in the last chapter that amongst organic beings in a state of
nature there is some individual variability: indeed I am not aware that this has
ever been disputed. It is immaterial for us whether a multitude of doubtful
forms be called species or sub-species or varieties; what rank, for instance, the
two or three hundred doubtful forms of British plants are entitled to hold, if
the existence of any well-marked varieties be admitted. But the mere existence of individual variability and of some few well-marked varieties, though
necessary as the foundation for the work, helps us but little in understanding
how species arise in nature. How have all those exquisite adaptations of one
part of the organisation to another part, and to the conditions of life, and of
one organic being to another being, been perfected? We see these beautiful
co-adaptations most plainly in the woodpecker and the mistletoe; and only a
little less plainly in the humblest parasite which clings to the hairs of a
quadruped or feathers of a bird; in the structure of the beetle which dives
through the water; in the plumed seed which is wafted by the gentlest breeze;
in short, we see beautiful adaptations everywhere and in every part of the
organic world.

Again, it may be asked, how is it that varieties, which I have called incip-
ient species, become ultimately converted into good and distinct species
which in most cases obviously differ from each other far more than do the
varieties of the same species? How do those groups of species, which constitute what are called distinct genera, and which differ from each other more
than do the species of the same genus, arise? All these results, as we shall more
fully see in the next chapter, follow from the struggle for life. Owing to this
struggle, variations, however slight and from whatever cause proceeding, if
they be in any degree profitable to the individuals of a species, in their infinitely complex relations to other organic beings and to their physical conditions of life, will tend to the preservation of such individuals, and will generally be inherited by the offspring. The offspring, also, will thus have a better
chance of surviving, for, of the many individuals of any species which are
periodically born, but a small number can survive. I have called this principle,
by which each slight variation, if useful, is preserved, by the term Natural
Selection, in order to mark its relation to man's power of selection. But the

expression often used by Mr. Herbert Spencer of the Survival of the Fittest is more accurate, and is sometimes equally convenient. We have seen that man by selection can certainly produce great results, and can adapt organic beings to his own uses, through the accumulation of slight but useful variations, given to him by the hand of Nature. But Natural Selection, as we shall hereafter see, is a power incessantly ready for action, and is as immeasurably superior to man's feeble efforts, as the works of Nature are to those of Art.

We will now discuss in a little more detail the struggle for existence. In my future work this subject will be treated, as it well deserves, at greater length. The elder De Candolle and Lyell have largely and philosophically shown that all organic beings are exposed to severe competition. In regard to plants, no one has treated this subject with more spirit and ability than W. Herbert, Dean of Manchester, evidently the result of his great horticultural knowledge. Nothing is easier than to admit in words the truth of the universal struggle for life, or more difficult—at least I have found it so—than constantly to bear this conclusion in mind. Yet unless it be thoroughly engrained in the mind, the whole economy of nature, with every fact on distribution, rarity, abundance, extinction, and variation, will be dimly seen or quite misunderstood. We behold the face of nature bright with gladness, we often see superabundance of food; we do not see or we forget, that the birds which are idly singing round us mostly live on insects or seeds, and are thus constantly destroying life; or we forget how largely these songsters, or their eggs, or their nestlings, are destroyed by birds and beasts of prey; we do not always bear in mind, that, though food may be now superabundant, it is not so at all seasons of each recurring year.

THE TERM, STRUGGLE FOR EXISTENCE, USED IN A LARGE SENSE.

I should premise that I use this term in a large and metaphorical sense including dependence of one being on another, and including (which is more important) not only the life of the individual, but success in leaving progeny. Two canine animals, in a time of dearth, may be truly said to struggle with each other which shall get food and live. But a plant on the edge of a desert is said to struggle for life against the drought, though more properly it should be said to be dependent on the moisture. A plant which annually produces a thousand seeds, of which only one of an average comes to maturity, may be more truly said to struggle with the plants of the same and other kinds which already clothe the ground. The mistletoe is dependent on the apple and a few other trees, but can only in a far-fetched sense be said to struggle with these trees, for, if too many of these parasites grow on the same tree, it languishes and dies. But several seedling mistletoes, growing close together on the same branch, may more truly be said to struggle with each other. As the mistletoe is disseminated by birds, its existence depends on them; and it may metaphorically be said to struggle with other fruit-bearing plants, in tempting the birds to devour and thus disseminate its seeds. In these several senses, which pass into each other, I use for convenience' sake the general term of Struggle for Existence.

GEOMETRICAL RATIO OF INCREASE.

A struggle for existence inevitably follows from the high rate at which all organic beings tend to increase. Every being, which during its natural lifetime produces several eggs or seeds, must suffer destruction during some period of its life, and during some season or occasional year, otherwise, on the principle of geometrical increase, its numbers would quickly become so inordinately great that no country could support the product. Hence, as more individuals are produced than can possibly survive, there must in every case be a struggle for existence, either one individual with another of the same species, or with the individuals of distinct species, or with the physical conditions of life. It is the doctrine of Malthus applied with manifold force to the whole animal and vegetable kingdoms; for in this case there can be no artificial increase of food, and no prudential restraint from marriage. Although some species may be now increasing, more or less rapidly, in numbers, all cannot do so, for the world would not hold them.

There is no exception to the rule that every organic being naturally increases at so high a rate, that, if not destroyed, the earth would soon be covered by the progeny of a single pair. Even slow-breeding man has doubled in twenty-five years, and at this rate, in less than a thousand years, there would literally not be standing-room for his progeny. Linnæus has calculated that if an annual plant produced only two seeds—and there is no plant so unproductive as this—and their seedlings next year produced two, and so on, then in twenty years there should be a million plants. The elephant is reckoned the slowest breeder of all known animals, and I have taken some pains to estimate its probable minimum rate of natural increase; it will be safest to assume that it begins breeding when thirty years old, and goes on breeding till ninety years old, bringing forth six young in the interval, and surviving till one hundred years old; if this be so, after a period of from 740 to 750 years there would be nearly nineteen million elephants alive, descended from the first pair.

But we have better evidence on this subject than mere theoretical calculations, namely, the numerous recorded cases of the astonishingly rapid increase of various animals in a state of nature, when circumstances have been favourable to them during two or three following seasons. Still more striking is the evidence from our domestic animals of many kinds which have run wild in several parts of the world; if the statements of the rate of increase of slow-breeding cattle and horses in South America, and latterly in Australia, had not been well authenticated, they would have been incredible. So it is with plants; cases could be given of introduced plants which have become common throughout whole islands in a period of less than ten years. Several of the plants, such as the cardoon and a tall thistle, which are now the commonest over the whole plains of La Plata, clothing square leagues of surface almost to the exclusion of every other plant, have been introduced from Europe; and there are plants which now range in India, as I hear from Dr. Falconer, from Cape Comorin to the Himalaya, which have been imported from America since its discovery. In such cases, and endless others could be given, no one supposes, that the fertility of the animals or plants has been suddenly and temporarily increased in any sensible degree. The obvious explanation is that the conditions of life have been highly favourable, and that there has consequently been less destruction of the old and young, and that nearly all the young have been enabled to breed. Their geometrical ratio of increase, the result of which never fails to be surprising, simply explains their extraordinarily rapid increase and wide diffusion in their new homes.

In a state of nature almost every full-grown plant annually produces seed, and amongst animals there are very few which do not annually pair. Hence we may confidently assert, that all plants and animals are tending to increase at a geometrical ratio,—that all would rapidly stock every station in which they could anyhow exist,—and that this geometrical tendency to increase must be checked by destruction at some period of life. Our familiarity with the larger domestic animals tends, I think, to mislead us: we see no great destruction falling on them, but we do not keep in mind that thousands are annually slaughtered for food, and that in a state of nature an equal number would have somehow to be disposed of.

The only difference between organisms which annually produce eggs or seeds by the thousand, and those which produce extremely few, is, that the slow-breeders would require a few more years to people, under favourable conditions, a whole district, let it be ever so large. The condor lays a couple of eggs and the ostrich a score, and yet in the same country the condor may be the more numerous of the two; the Fulmar petrel lays but one egg, yet it is believed to be the most numerous bird in the world. One fly deposits hun-

dreds of eggs, and another, like the hippobosca, a single one; but this difference does not determine how many individuals of the two species can be
supported in a district. A large number of eggs is of some importance to those
species which depend on a fluctuating amount of food, for it allows them
rapidly to increase in number. But the real importance of a large number of
eggs or seeds is to make up for much destruction at some period of life; and
this period in the great majority of cases is an early one. If an animal can in
any way protect its own eggs or young, a small number may be produced, and
yet the average stock be fully kept up; but if many eggs or young are destroyed,
many must be produced, or the species will become extinct. It would suffice to
keep up the full number of a tree, which lived on an average for a thousand
years, if a single seed were produced once in a thousand years, supposing that
this seed were never destroyed, and could be ensured to germinate in a fitting
place. So that, in all cases, the average number of any animal or plant depends
only indirectly on the number of its eggs or seeds.

In looking at Nature, it is most necessary to keep the foregoing considerations always in mind—never to forget that every single organic being may be
said to be striving to the utmost to increase in numbers; that each lives by a
struggle at some period of its life; that heavy destruction inevitably falls either
on the young or old, during each generation or at recurrent intervals. Lighten
any check, mitigate the destruction ever so little, and the number of the
species will almost instantaneously increase to any amount.

STRUGGLE FOR LIFE MOST SEVERE BETWEEN INDIVIDUALS AND VARIETIES OF THE SAME SPECIES.

As the species of the same genus usually have, though by no means invariably,
much similarity in habits and constitution, and always in structure, the struggle will generally be more severe between them, if they come into competition
with each other, than between the species of distinct genera. We see this in
the recent extension over parts of the United States of one species of swallow
having caused the decrease of another species. The recent increase of the
missel-thrush in parts of Scotland has caused the decrease of the song-thrush.
How frequently we hear of one species of rat taking the place of another
species under the most different climates! In Russia the small Asiatic cock-
roach has everywhere driven before it its great congener. In Australia the
imported hive-bee is rapidly exterminating the small, stingless native bee.
One species of charlock has been known to supplant another species; and so
in other cases. We can dimly see why the competition should be most severe
between allied forms, which fill nearly the same place in the economy of

nature; but probably in no one case could we precisely say why one species has been victorious over another in the great battle of life.

A corollary of the highest importance may be deduced from the foregoing remarks, namely, that the structure of every organic being is related, in the most essential yet often hidden manner, to that of all the other, organic beings, with which it comes into competition for food or residence, or from which it has to escape, or on which it preys. This is obvious in the structure of the teeth and talons of the tiger; and in that of the legs and claws of the parasite which clings to the hair on the tiger's body. But in the beautifully plumed seed of the dandelion, and in the flattened and fringed legs of the water-beetle, the relation seems at first confined to the elements of air and water. Yet the advantage of plumed seeds no doubt stands in the closest relation to the land being already thickly clothed with other plants; so that the seeds may be widely distributed and fall on unoccupied ground. In the water-beetle, the structure of its legs, so well adapted for diving, allows it to compete with other aquatic insects, to hunt for its own prey, and to escape serving as prey to other animals.

The store of nutriment laid up within the seeds of many plants seems at first sight to have no sort of relation to other plants. But from the strong growth of young plants produced from such seeds, as peas and beans, when sown in the midst of long grass, it may be suspected that the chief use of the nutriment in the seed is to favour the growth of the seedlings, whilst struggling with other plants growing vigorously all around.

Look at a plant in the midst of its range, why does it not double or quadruple its numbers? We know that it can perfectly well withstand a little more heat or cold, dampness or dryness, for elsewhere it ranges into slightly hotter or colder, damper or drier districts. In this case we can clearly see that if we wish in imagination to give the plant the power of increasing in number, we should have to give it some advantage over its competitors, or over the animals which prey on it. On the confines of its geographical range, a change of constitution with respect to climate would clearly be an advantage to our plant; but we have reason to believe that only a few plants or animals range so far, that they are destroyed exclusively by the rigour of the climate. Not until we reach the extreme confines of life, in the Arctic regions or on the borders of an utter desert, will competition cease. The land may be extremely cold or dry, yet there will be competition between some few species, or between the individuals of the same species, for the warmest or dampest spots.

Hence we can see that when a plant or animal is placed in a new country amongst new competitors, the conditions of its life will generally be changed in an essential manner, although the climate may be exactly the same as in its former home. If its average numbers are to increase in its new home, we should have to modify it in a different way to what we should have had to do in its native country; for we should have to give it some advantage over a different set of competitors or enemies.

It is good thus to try in imagination to give to any one species an advantage over another. Probably in no single instance should we know what to do. This ought to convince us of our ignorance on the mutual relations of all organic beings; a conviction as necessary, as it is difficult to acquire. All that we can do, is to keep steadily in mind that each organic being is striving to increase in a geometrical ratio; that each at some period of its life, during some season of the year, during each generation or at intervals, has to struggle for life and to suffer great destruction. When we reflect on this struggle, we may console ourselves with the full belief, that the war of nature is not incessant, that no fear is felt, that death is generally prompt, and that the vigorous, the healthy, and the happy survive and multiply.

SOUCE: Chapter 3 in *The Origin of Species (1859) and The Descent of Man (1871)* (New York: Modern Library, 1936), 75–82, 93–96.

On the Formation of the
Races of Man

CHARLES DARWIN

In some cases the crossing of distinct races has led to the formation of a new race. The singular fact that the Europeans and Hindoos, who belong to the same Aryan stock, and speak a language fundamentally the same, differ widely in appearance, whilst Europeans differ but little from Jews, who belong to the Semitic stock, and speak quite another language, has been accounted for by Broca,[1] through certain Aryan branches having been largely crossed by indigenous tribes during their wide diffusion. When two races in close contact cross, the first result is a heterogeneous mixture: thus Mr. Hunter, in describing the Santali or hill-tribes of India, says that hundreds of imperceptible gradations may be traced "from the black, squat tribes of the mountains to the tall olive-coloured Brahman, with his intellectual brow, calm eyes, and high but narrow head;" so that it is necessary in courts of justice to ask the witnesses whether they are Santalis or Hindoos.[2] Whether a

1. 'On Anthropology,' translation 'Anthropolog. Review,' Jan. 1868, p. 38.
2. 'The Annals of Rural Bengal,' 1868, p. 134.

heterogeneous people, such as the inhabitants of some of the Polynesian islands, formed by the crossing of two distinct races, with few or no pure members left, would ever become homogeneous, is not known from direct evidence. But as with our domesticated animals, a cross-breed can certainly be fixed and made uniform by careful selection[3] in the course of a few generations, we may infer that the free intercrossing of a heterogeneous mixture during a long descent would supply the place of selection, and overcome any tendency to reversion; so that the crossed race would ultimately become homogeneous, though it might not partake in an equal degree of the characters of the two parent-races.

Of all the differences between the races of man, the colour of the skin is the most conspicuous and one of the best marked. It was formerly thought that differences of this kind could be accounted for by long exposure to different climates; but Pallas first shewed that this is not tenable, and he has since been followed by almost all anthropologists.[4] This view has been rejected chiefly because the distribution of the variously coloured races, most of whom must have long inhabited their present homes, does not coincide with corresponding differences of climate. Some little weight may be given to such cases as that of the Dutch families, who, as we hear on excellent authority,[5] have not undergone the least change of colour after residing for three centuries in South Africa. An argument on the same side may likewise be drawn from the uniform appearance in various parts of the world of gipsies and Jews, though the uniformity of the latter has been somewhat exaggerated.[6] A very damp or a very dry atmosphere has been supposed to be more influential in modifying the colour of the skin than mere heat; but as D'Orbigny in South America, and Livingstone in Africa, arrived at diametrically opposite conclusions with respect to dampness and dryness, any conclusion on this head must be considered as very doubtful.[7]

Various facts, which I have given elsewhere, prove that the colour of the skin and hair is sometimes correlated in a surprising manner with a complete immunity from the action of certain vegetable poisons, and from the attacks of certain parasites. Hence it occurred to me, that negroes and other dark

3. 'The Variation of Animals and Plants under Domestication,' vol. ii. p. 95.

4. Pallas, 'Act. Acad. St. Petersburg,' 1780, part ii. p. 69. He was followed by Rudolphi, in his 'Beyträge zur Anthropologie,' 1812. An excellent summary of the evidence is given by Godron, 'De l'Espèce,' 1859, vol. ii. p. 246, &c.

5. Sir Andrew Smith, as quoted by Knox, 'Races of Man,' 1850, p. 473.

6. See De Quatrefages on this head, 'Revue des Cours Scientifiques,' Oct. 17, 1868, p. 731.

7. Livingstone's 'Travels and Researches in S. Africa,' 1857, pp. 338, 339. D'Orbigny, as quoted by Godron, 'De l'Espèce,' vol. ii. p. 266.

races might have acquired their dark tints by the darker individuals escaping from the deadly influence of the miasma of their native countries, during a long series of generations.

I afterwards found that this same idea had long ago occurred to Dr. Wells.[8] It has long been known that negroes, and even mulattoes, are almost completely exempt from the yellow-fever, so destructive in tropical America.[9] They likewise escape to a large extent the fatal intermittent fevers, that prevail along at least 2600 miles of the shores of Africa, and which annually cause one-fifth of the white settlers to die, and another fifth to return home invalided.[10] This immunity in the negro seems to be partly inherent, depending on some unknown peculiarity of constitution, and partly the result of acclimatisation. Pouchet[11] states that the negro regiments recruited near the Soudan, and borrowed from the Viceroy of Egypt for the Mexican war, escaped the yellow-fever almost equally with the negroes originally brought from various parts of Africa and accustomed to the climate of the West Indies. That acclimatisation plays a part, is shewn by the many cases in which negroes have become somewhat liable to tropical fevers, after having resided for some time in a colder climate.[12] The nature of the climate under which the white races have long resided, likewise has some influence on them; for during the fearful epidemic of yellow fever in Demerara during 1837, Dr. Blair found that the death-rate of the immigrants was proportional to the latitude of the country whence they had come. With the negro the immunity, as far as it is the result of acclimatisation, implies exposure during a prodigious length of time; for the aborigines of tropical America who have resided there from time immemorial, are not exempt from yellow fever; and the Rev. H. B. Tristram states, that there are districts in Northern Africa which the native inhabitants are compelled annually to leave, though the negroes can remain with safety.

That the immunity of the negro is in any degree correlated with the colour of his skin is a mere conjecture: it may be correlated with some difference in his blood, nervous system, or other tissues. Nevertheless, from the facts above

8. See a paper read before the Royal Soc. in 1813, and published in his Essays in 1818. I have given an account of Dr. Wells' views in the Historical Sketch (p. xvi.) to my 'Origin of Species.' Various cases of colour correlated with constitutional peculiarities are given in my 'Variation of Animals under Domestication,' vol. ii. pp. 227, 335.

9. See, for instance, Nott and Gliddon, 'Types of Mankind,' p. 68.

10. Major Tulloch, in a paper read before the Statistical Society, April 20th, 1840, and given in the 'Athenæum,' 1840, p. 353.

11. 'The Plurality of the Human Race' (translat.), 1864, p. 60.

12. Quatrefages, 'Unité de l'Espèce Humaine,' 1861, p. 205. Waltz, 'Introduct. to Anthropology,' translat. vol. i. 1863, p. 124. Livingstone gives analogous cases in his 'Travels.'

alluded to, and from some connection apparently existing between complexion and a tendency to consumption, the conjecture seemed to me not improbable. Consequently I endeavoured, with but little success,[13] to ascertain how far it holds good. The late Dr. Daniell, who had long lived on the West Coast of Africa, told me that he did not believe in any such relation. He was himself unusually fair, and had withstood the climate in a wonderful manner. When he first arrived as a boy on the coast, an old and experienced negro chief predicted from his appearance that this would prove the case. Dr. Nicholson, of Antigua, after having attended to this subject, writes to me that dark-coloured Europeans escape the yellow fever more than those that are light-coloured. Mr. J. M. Harris altogether denies that Europeans with dark hair withstand a hot climate better than other men: on the contrary, experience has taught him in making a selection of men for service on the coast of Africa, to choose those with red hair.[14] As far, therefore, as these slight indications go, there seems no foundation for the hypothesis, that blackness has resulted

13. In the spring of 1862 I obtained permission from the Director-General of the Medical department of the Army, to transmit to the surgeons of the various regiments on foreign service a blank table, with the following appended remarks, but I have received no returns. "As several well-marked cases have been recorded with our domestic animals of a relation between the colour of the dermal appendages and the constitution; and it being notorious that there is some limited degree of relation between the colour of the races of man and the climate inhabited by them; the following investigation seems worth consideration. Namely, whether there is any relation in Europeans between the colour of their hair, and their liability to the diseases of tropical countries. If the surgeons of the several regiments, when stationed in unhealthy tropical districts, would be so good as first to count, as a standard of comparison, how many men, in the force whence the sick are drawn, have dark and light-coloured hair, and hair of intermediate or doubtful tints; and if a similar account were kept by the same medical gentleman, of all the men who suffered from malarious and yellow fevers, or from dysentery, it would soon be apparent, after some thousand cases had been tabulated, whether there exists any relation between the colour of the hair and constitutional liability to tropical diseases. Perhaps no such relation would be discovered, but the investigation is well worth making. In case any positive result were obtained, it might be of some practical use in selecting men for any particular service. Theoretically the result would be of high interest, as indicating one means by which a race of men inhabiting from a remote period an unhealthy tropical climate, might have become dark-coloured by the better preservation of dark-haired or dark-complexioned individuals during a long succession of generations."

14. 'Anthropological Review,' Jan. 1866, p. xxi. Dr. Sharpe also says, with respect to India ('Man a Special Creation,' 1873, p. 118), "that it has been noticed by some medical officers that Europeans with light hair and florid complexions suffer less from diseases of tropical countries than persons with dark hair and sallow complexions; and, so far as I know, there appear to be good grounds for this remark." On the other hand, Mr. Heddle, of Sierra Leone, "who has had more clerks killed under him than any other man," by the climate of the West African Coast (W. Reade, 'African Sketch Book,' vol. ii. p. 522), holds a directly opposite view, as does Capt. Burton.

from the darker and darker individuals having survived better during long exposure to fever-generating miasma.

Dr. Sharpe remarks,[15] that a tropical sun, which burns and blisters a white skin; does not injure a black one at all; and, as he adds, this is not due to habit in the individual, for children only six or eight months old are often carried about naked, and are not affected. I have been assured by a medical man, that some years ago during each summer, but not during the winter, his hands became marked with light brown patches, like, although larger than freckles, and that these patches were never affected by sun-burning, whilst the white parts of his skin have on several occasions been much inflamed and blistered. With the lower animals there is, also, a constitutional difference in liability to the action of the sun between those parts of the skin clothed with white hair and other parts.[16] Whether the saving of the skin from being thus burnt is of sufficient importance to account for a dark tint having been gradually acquired by man through natural selection, I am unable to judge. If it be so, we should have to assume that the natives of tropical America have lived there for a much shorter time than the negroes in Africa, or the Papuans in the southern parts of the Malay archipelago, just as the lighter-coloured Hindoos have resided in India for a shorter time than the darker aborigines of the central and southern parts of the peninsula.

Although with our present knowledge we cannot account for the differences of colour in the races of man, through any advantage thus gained, or from the direct action of climate; yet we must not quite ignore the latter agency, for there is good reason to believe that some inherited effect is thus produced.[17]

We have seen in the second chapter that the conditions of life affect the development of the bodily frame in a direct manner, and that the effects are transmitted. Thus, as is generally admitted, the European settlers in the United States undergo a slight but extraordinary rapid change of appearance. Their bodies and limbs become elongated; and I hear from Col. Bernys that during the late war in the United States, good evidence was afforded of this fact by the ridiculous appearance presented by the German regiments, when

15. 'Man a Special Creation,' 1873, p. 119.

16. 'Variation of Animals and Plants under Domestication,' vol. ii. pp. 336, 337.

17. See, for instance, Quatrefages ('Revue des Cours Scientifiques,' Oct. 10, 1868, p. 724) on the effects of residence in Abyssinia and Arabia, and other analogous cases. Dr. Rolle ('Der Mensch, seine Abstammung,' &c., 1865, s. 99) states, on the authority of Khanikof, that the greater number of German families settled in Georgia, have acquired in the course of two generations dark hair and eyes. Mr. D. Forbes informs me that the Quichuas in the Andes vary greatly in colour, according to the position of the valleys inhabited by them.

dressed in ready-made clothes manufactured for the American market, and which were much too long for the men in every way. There is, also, a considerable body of evidence shewing that in the Southern States the house-slaves of the third generation present a markedly different appearance from the field-slaves.[18]

If, however, we look to the races of man as distributed over the world, we must infer that their characteristic differences cannot be accounted for by the direct action of different conditions of life, even after exposure to them for an enormous period of time. The Esquimaux live exclusively on animal food; they are clothed in thick fur, and are exposed to intense cold and to prolonged darkness; yet they do not differ in any extreme degree from the inhabitants of Southern China, who live entirely on vegetable food, and are exposed almost naked to a hot, glaring climate. The unclothed Fuegians live on the marine productions of their inhospitable shores; the Botocudos of Brazil wander about the hot forests of the interior and live chiefly on vegetable productions; yet these tribes resemble each other so closely that the Fuegians on board the "Beagle" were mistaken by some Brazilians for Botocudos. The Botocudos again, as well as the other inhabitants of tropical America, are wholly different from the Negroes who inhabit the opposite shores of the Atlantic, are exposed to a nearly similar climate, and follow nearly the same habits of life.

Nor can the differences between the races of man be accounted for by the inherited effects of the increased or decreased use of parts, except to a quite insignificant degree. Men who habitually live in canoes, may have their legs somewhat stunted; those who inhabit lofty regions may have their chests enlarged; and those who constantly use certain sense-organs may have the cavities in which they are lodged somewhat increased in size, and their features consequently a little modified. With civilised nations, the reduced size of the jaws from lessened use—the habitual play of different muscles serving to express different emotions—and the increased size of the brain from greater intellectual activity, have together produced a considerable effect on their general appearance when compared with savages.[19] Increased bodily stature, without any corresponding increase in the size of the brain, may (judging from the previously adduced case of rabbits), have given to some races an elongated skull of the dolichocephalic type.

Lastly, the little-understood principle of correlated development has sometimes come into action, as in the case of great muscular development and

18. Harlan, 'Medical Researches,' p. 532. Quatrefages ('Unité de l'Espèce Humaine,' 1861, p. 128) has collected much evidence on this head.

19. See Prof. Schauffhausen, translat. in 'Anthropological Review,' Oct. 1868, p. 429.

strongly projecting supra-orbital ridges. The colour of the skin and hair are plainly correlated, as is the texture of the hair with its colour in the Mandans of North America.[20] The colour also of the skin, and the odour emitted by it, are likewise in some manner connected. With the breeds of sheep the number of hairs within a given space and the number of excretory pores are related.[21] If we may judge from the analogy of our domesticated animals, many modifications of structure in man probably come under this principle of correlated development.

We have now seen that the external characteristic differences between the races of man cannot be accounted for in a satisfactory manner by the direct action of the conditions of life, nor by the effects of the continued use of parts, nor through the principle of correlation. We are therefore led to enquire whether slight individual differences, to which man is eminently liable, may not have been preserved and augmented during a long series of generations through natural selection. But here we are at once met by the objection that beneficial variations alone can be thus preserved; and as far as we are enabled to judge, although always liable to err on this head, none of the differences between the races of man are of any direct or special service to him. The intellectual and moral or social faculties must of course be excepted from this remark. The great variability of all the external differences between the races of man, likewise indicates that they cannot be of much importance; for if important, they would long ago have been either fixed and preserved, or eliminated. In this respect man resembles those forms, called by naturalists protean or polymorphic, which have remained extremely variable, owing, as it seems, to such variations being of an indifferent nature, and to their having thus escaped the action of natural selection.

SOURCE: Chapter 7 in *The Origin of Species (1859) and The Descent of Man (1871)* (New York: Modern Library, 1936), 550–56.

20. Mr. Catlin states ('N. American Indians,' 3rd edit. 1842, vol. i. p. 49) that in the whole tribe of the Mandans, about one in ten or twelve of the members, of all ages and both sexes, have bright silvery grey hair, which is hereditary. Now this hair is as coarse and harsh as that of a horse's mane, whilst the hair of other colours is fine and soft.
21. On the odour of the skin, Godron, 'Sur l'Espèce,' tom. ii. p. 217. On the pores of the skin, Dr. Wilckens, 'Die Aufgaben der Landwirth. Zootechnik,' 1869, s. 7.

Excerpt from "Darwin"
DIGAIN WILLIAMS

IV

The story told with careful art,
Is not the whole although sublime,
For other things will come with time
But now we only "know in part."

While seeking for an ancient goal
'Twas given one to find the new
For all these millions, not the few;
Within the new to find the whole

Was given thee. We stood beside
Locked gates of worlds. God gave to thee
A strong and precious golden key,
The universe is open wide.

We see what He, the Lord, hath done
In Being's temple on each wall,
He is "the Lord that maketh all,"
And He "spread forth the heavens alone."

We love as true the great and small,
Without the tiniest little wheel
The master timepiece now would reel,
And into chaos black would fall.

We trace the highest suns that soar,
And belt them as they whirl and dance;
And note the star above the glance
Of humming birds in Ecuador.

We cross those lands long since no more,
And sweep o'er continents unformed,
We sail o'er oceans never stormed
Which never knew nor sand nor shore.

We bask in suns not born to men,
And cool in shades no breath hath stirred,
We hear hosannas never heard
With far off ages shout "Amen."

And down creation's aisles we walk
So far with trembling and with fear,
We feel, O Lord, that thou art here,
Our silence take, we cannot talk.

Ah! finished man, for he creates,
And with a little lump of clay
He up to beauty starts a way.
What courage! God he imitates.

He there for God began to grope,
And there he once began to nod
With but a dreamy smile on God:
The germ of everlasting hope.

We see the dawn of higher race,
The dawn of beauty from the mind,
We see the triumph of the kind,
We see the ape go from thy face.

We hail thee, "Dawn Man," mixed thy rays,
Three-fourths a man, a fraction brute,
For through thine eye a mind doth shoot,
While round thy mouth a simian stays.

There is some keenness in thy look,
There jabbering to a common flint,
To thee more precious than a mint
Of gold, while sitting by that brook.

We hear thee babbling to thy child
Who softens much thine iron heart,
Unknown, he knows the highest art,
The art that turns the fierce to mild.

The morn is moist, and rich and warm,
The lion's roar awakes the tree
That at the sound lets down on thee
The shower resting on her arm.

We see the time a grain of choice
Disturbed the sea of instinct still,
And count the days of mind and will
To where all tongues are but a voice.

Born is the rose of holy fame,
And Nature blushes like a maid
That ages hence in some cool shade
Will blush when love will give the same.

.   .   .

And still far down the ages through
We travel towards that holy light
That's on the altar ever bright,
And transubstantiation true!

For when was gone the heated strife,
And Peace gave earth such rich contents,
God somehow mixed the elements
With drop of self, and there was life.

Man yet will sing his pean best,
And all the ages flood with light,
When many letters come to sight
Now hid in Nature's palimpsest.

SOURCE: In *Darwin* (San Diego: Frye and Smith, 1922), 19–25.

Comparative Physiognomy
JAMES W. REDFIELD

CHAPTER I

Aristotle, or some other equally sage philosopher, has said, "Man is an animal." If man was not well aware of this fact long before the saying was uttered, he has certainly confirmed it in innumerable instances since, not only in words, but in actions. It is a humiliating truth, of which many people seem proud; but, as humility is a rare and inestimable virtue, it is well that we should be reminded of our frailty by a just comparison of ourselves with the brute creation. What does hinder man from speaking like an angel on the topic that most interests him, and upon which he most wishes to interest

others? It is the animal nature that oppresses and clouds his mind, alas! alas! But there is a divine fire within him that struggles against the superincumbent mass, and ever and anon casts it high in air, mingled and confounded with substances of a lighter and more ethereal nature; and there is a sun of truth and love that clears away the dark mists that obscure his vision.

If, now, we were going to write a poem, we would commence with an invocation, like that with which Milton introduces his "Paradise Lost;" but, "gentle reader," we claim for our subject a scientific character, and we intend to treat it accordingly. An invocation, uttered within the chamber of the soul, is none the less appropriate on that account.

We commence, then, with the admission that "man is an animal." A comparison of himself with the inferior animals has led him, in all ages of the world, to apply the names of animals to men, and the names of men to animals, on the ground of a resemblance between them. There is often great significance in the words *calf, goose, dog, monkey,* and so on, when applied contemptuously. They betray fragments of a true science, perverted to the degradation of human beings. There is equal evidence of the rudiments of this science in the popular mind in the use of the words *kitty, lamb, duck, dove,* and the names of other gentle and favorite pets, applied to those who have corresponding traits. In a rude and simple state of society, the designation of an individual by some ruling trait of character, embodied in the form of some animal, shows what foundation this department of Physiognomy has in nature and in the human mind, and how easily and naturally it is learned. It is not probable that the American Indians are indebted to our modern civilization for an observation of those correspondences which have led them to apply the terms *wild-oat, black-hawk, alligator, snapping-turtle,* and the like, to their chiefs and warriors.

But, lest the reader should suppose that his estimation of man is much higher than our own, we will here state that, in our opinion, the essential attributes of a human being elevate him to a point beyond comparison with the animal creation. The term *man,* in its highest sense, is synonymous with *angel.* Men are not born, and peradventure we are not men when we "come to man's estate." It may be that we are but "children of an older growth." Man

is the result of education, of improvement. He is
"self-made," if he be made at all, and the character
which he forms for himself is indicated in his
countenance. But if truly a man, he considers himself the workmanship of a higher power, for in his
own creation he works from a sense of duty, and in
opposition to himself, or to the animal which Na-
ture has made him. We say emphatically—

"Man is a name of honor for a king"—
though, according to the definition, most men who are promoted to royalty
are worthy of the title of "king of beasts."

"Man is an animal," but he is more. He has the privilege of naming all the
fowls of the air, the beasts of the field, and the fishes of the sea. The lion is to
eat straw like the ox, but he is no less a lion on that account; and so it is with
every other savage beast, or passion in the human beast. If the beast be made
human, the comparison is favorable to the man; but if the man be made
animal, the comparison is favorable to the beast. Dear reader, we do not wish
to puzzle you, but do you not see the difference between comparing a beast
with a man, and comparing a man with a beast? Yes, you see there is some
difference between calling an ass a faithful servant and calling a faithful
servant an ass! If, therefore, in the following pages, we fail to observe this
distinction, you will, for humanity's sake, pardon us, knowing that it was not
intentional.

The inferior races are like infants, who, as is well known, go on all-fours.
The Ethiopian who opened this chapter is like a brat just learning to stand.
Observe the posture—the arms, body, legs, and feet—and you will be struck

with the similarity. What a reminiscence of infancy is awakened by that physiognomy! Let it teach thee not to despise one who is as Nature made him, until thou canst deny that thou wast ever a child. Thou wert misshapen, and some time in coming to the condition even of a quadruped, from which thou mightst have grown a satyr—

——"Thy face itself
Half mated with the royal stamp of man,
And half o'ercome with beast!"

Plato's definition of man was, "A bird without feathers." This is carrying the comparison rather too far, but it may be said that in many respects man has a striking resemblance to the bird. The bird aspires to a similar standing, though wisely he never takes advantage of his position. The feathered gentry are, we believe, biped animals without an exception and it is upon his position upon two legs that man prides himself. Birds show something of the same vanity, without therefore laying any claim to superiority. They do, indeed, make use of all-fours in travelling, but it is never with more than two at a time. Birds, however, have a greater likeness to some people than to others.

There are certain persons for ever flying about, making a greater flourish with their arms than with their feet: they preserve their hands in gloves, as carefully as a bird does his in feathers; and when they are not swinging their arms, in imitation of rapid travelling, they carry their hands tucked under their coat-tails, behind their backs. They are bound at all events not to show their hands, lest people should know that they have any, and should insist upon their making use of them. The man who very much resembles a bird invariably attempts to live by his wits, however little his noddle may contain. But he is not, by any means, the only person who adopts this method of gaining a livelihood. Those who resemble foxes and pussy-cats do the same.

But as every person has an individuality of his own, which is not to be confounded with that of any other, it is necessary that we should be more particular. Here is a person (see next figure) with a sharp, bird-like countenance, who is trying to assure himself that he has a genuine bill, or that it is not a jaw with teeth in it, by which he is in danger of being bitten. The result of the examination will probably be, that he has a long bill, and that he feels like a bird. He is evidently of the kind that was forbidden to the Jews, for the reason probably that he is too much like them to be "taken in;" and his partiality for bills is entirely on account of the  havoc they make among the frogs, and young lizards, and other small-fry, that are found in shallow places. His ear is a mighty small one, just fitted to be the lodging-place of a quill; and you might know, without asking his attention for a few moments, that he is a "deaf adder." Think you he makes any great use of the quill upon which he prides himself so amazingly? It is an apology for not grasping with his hands something more substantial than a feather, and it is a token that he plumes himself upon his ability.

Here is a bird on a roost, sharpening his wit with a penknife, a mighty labor of his hands, considering the disposition of his feet to take upon themselves the office of handling. Examine him from top to toe, and you will expect that when anything comes in his way, he will remove it with his foot; and that when he wishes to draw anything nearer to him, his feet will be found more accommodating than his hands. The hand, in his opinion, has a higher office to perform. It is a quill-holder, and there is no knowing what high flights this gray goose may take into the regions of *space,* to bring down fancies and imaginations—

> "Such as take lodgings in a head
> That's to be let unfurnished"—

 into the regions of tangible reality.

What have we here? A bird, saving the feathers, which might be supplied with a few tatters, or else with a coat more smooth and glossy. This also is one of the creations of Darley, who seems ambitious to have his creations classed with those of Nature. Those legs!—there is something in their position that beggars description. What need we to speak of the body, the arms, the head, the features, the expression? they speak for themselves, and it is fortunate for a good example that it teaches its own lesson.

By dwelling too long on the subject of birds, we are in danger of becoming flighty. We will simply say that the specimens of the *rara avis* are, if the popular opinion be true, very frequently met with. The individual above, no more than those preceding him, can be accused of soiling his hands by very hard labor, and will certainly get his living in some easy way, without any greater tax upon his wit than is natural to him.

On the following page is a real "fly-away"—and she is but one of a multitude of the same variety. Whether it be a robin, a tomtit, or a lady-bird, it is not important to decide. But let us, if our subject does not keep us up in spite of ourselves, descend from birds in general to birds in particular. We can not make minute observations upon the wing—and are not so skilled in marksmanship as not to require our bird to be at rest in order to hit him.

When the artist has made a capital hit, and fixed his quarry to the spot on which it stood, which is generally some old limb of a tree, we are prepared to aim at the mark, and may stand some chance of hitting it too.

CHAPTER VI

What executioner is this, come to wield his monstrous lash, more effective than the club of Hercules? He is inclined to try the stability of those mathematical certainties which the rhinoceros puts his trust in—to feel the ground upon which he treads, and to make impressions on defences that bid defiance to attack. Everything about him is formed to be the counterpart of that which is discovered in the rhinoceros. That trunk of his, which is the only thing of the kind in existence, is curiously and wonderfully made. It is a maul unparalleled, and has at its end an instrument for pinching, so that it is suitable to the execution of every sentence. He punishes both great and minor offences, with an exactness of justice that is truly admirable. As he is physically suited to carry it into execution, so his belief is—

> "That when a man is past his sense,
> The method to reduce him thence
> Is twinging by the ears and nose,
> Or laying on of heavy blows."

He has the feeling that he is formed to be an executioner. When the sentence has gone forth, it is never revoked. The punishment must come if ever the opportunity offers; his duty must be discharged. In the East, he is chosen to execute the laws. There is no variety of execution short of infernal that he is

not prepared to inflict. The man who is so wanting in Sensibility as to play a hoax upon the elephant, will have it dinged into him by the elephant's trunk if ever he comes within the reach of that flexible instrument. By "the elephant," be it understood, we mean the man who resembles the elephant, and by "the rhinoceros" the man who resembles the rhinoceros.

The animal we are now speaking of may be styled the "Executive." He is the very embodiment of "physical force." As the rhinoceros represents Endurance, so does the elephant represent Effectiveness. Like an immense water-wheel, he rolls, and tumbles, and pours the water over him; and the *animus* which he applies, or the motive-power, is like water tumbling over a precipice, to which his forehead and descending trunk bear a close resemblance. His countenance is all dripping, and seems to invite a torrent of water to be poured over it. His whole body is like a sea, with its ebb and flow, and moving forward with a slow current to its outlet, where the mighty force of descent invites to the demonstration of the principle that "knowledge is power." He is the wisest of the brute creation, for physical force should be governed by intellectual, to which it corresponds. He represents all things mighty—the water-power, the ponderous wheel, and the whole

machinery through which power overcomes a resistance equal to itself in the production of the most wonderful results.

As there is in the rhinoceros that which involves the principles of mathematics, so there is in the elephant that which involves the principles of mechanics; and as Nature illustrates these principles in the animal economy of both, so Art, in those who resemble the rhinoceros and the elephant, applies them to the demonstration of the laws which govern the material creation, and to the production of machinery. Astronomy is the result of the one, and wheels and their complicated revolutions are the result of the other. The Effectiveness that resides in the human frame is still greater in the instrument that man produces. There is a resemblance to the elephant, not only in those who make an extensive application of machinery, but in those who invent it.

The *inferior* class who bear this resemblance, are suited physically to perform the function of executioners, and to be the instruments of power. The stoutest laborers—in size, form, motions, and expressions of the countenance—resemble the elephant. This is so with herculean negroes particularly, and they have been regarded as the executors and as the labor-saving machinery of the world from time immemorial. This is doubtless in some degree a perversion of

the grand principle which they illustrate, but it shows an instinctive recognition of this resemblance, not only in those who make a slave of the negro, but in the negro himself. There is something peculiarly noble, dutiful, and trustworthy, in the features of the "black fellow" who bears this resemblance—rude when caught, and yet beautiful from his adaptation to his various uses.

The elephant exhibits this beauty of adaptation the very day that he is captured; he takes to service almost immediately, which can be said of no other animal. His susceptibility of improvement is uncommonly great. This is true of the African, and hence he is capable of attaining to the highest condition morally and intellectually, the correspondent of which is the lowest

physical condition when the former and the latter are not united. But his development is exceedingly slow, as is also that of the elephant.

The negro presented in the first of these chapters is a mere babe. Precocity in the human family, although highly flattered, is less to be desired than the tardy development of the negro. Every one may judge what the difference will be in the final result. Mrs. Harriet Beecher Stowe has some fine remarks on this subject, in her popular work entitled "Uncle Tom's Cabin, or Life among the Lowly," which it would be superfluous to quote, since it must be taken for granted that everybody has read them. The features which resemble the elephant are characteristic of childhood, as in this

and the preceding examples. There is also characteristic childhood in a child like this, who is exceedingly fond of a ride on the elephant's back, and whose features are seen to bear a striking resemblance to the profile of that animal. It must be confessed, too, that he has reason to be grateful for affection on the part of his bearer, for they are congenial spirits. In the negro-looking female who stands above, we can hardly fail to see that the features are elephantine, and to ascribe to her all the docility, faithfulness, caution, substitution, and love of children, that are characteristic of the elephant.

The African may be called deformed and monstrous, like the elephant but there is an old proverb which says, "Homely in the cradle, handsome in the saddle." Besides this, the highest beauty is the result of the highest use, and is founded on the lowest. In his adaptation to the lowest, which is that of a dutiful child, the African is still handsome:—

——"his mother's eye,
That looks upon him from his parent sky,
Sees in his flexile limbs untutored grace,
Power in his forehead, beauty in his face."

This beauty is latent in him, and will be developed. It should be observed, however, that certain negro races do not resemble elephants, and these in market value are good for nothing except to play the banjo, and exhibit white collars and pocket handkerchiefs: but we shall speak of these in another chapter.

SOURCE: Chapters 1 and 6 in *Comparative Physiognomy, or Resemblances Between Men and Animals* (New York: W. J. Widdleton, 1866), 13–20, 49–54. Redfield's other pseudoscientific works include *Comparative Anatomy* and *New System of Physiognomy: Illustrated by Numerous Engravings.*

Excerpts from *The Future of Science*

ERNEST RENAN

[Ernest (Joseph) Renan (1823–1892) was a French Catholic who abandoned Catholicism after studying the Greek and Hebrew biblical traditions; he became a professor of Hebrew at the College de France in 1870. Renan is renowned for his linguistic and philological interpretations of cultures. Some of his significant works include *The Life of Jesus* (1863), *On the Origin of Languages* (1864), *History of the People of Israel* (1887), *Caliban: A Philosophical Drama Continuing "The Tempest" of William Shakespeare* (1896), and *Poetry of the Celtic Races* (1896).]

II

To know is the keyword of the creed of natural religion; for to know is the first condition of the commerce of mankind with the things that are, of the penetrating study of the universe, which is the intellectual life of the individual; to know is self-initiation to God. By ignorance man is as it were sequestrated from nature, shut up within himself, and reduced to make himself a fanciful *non-ego* on the model of his personality. Hence arises the strange world in which infancy lives, in which primitive man lived. Man is only capable of communing with things by knowledge and love; without science he only loves so many chimeras. Science only can supply the foundation of reality necessary to life. If like Leibnitz we conceive the individual soul as a mirror in which the universe is reflected, it is by science that it will be able to reflect a smaller or greater portion of what is, and travel towards its final aim; namely, towards its perfect harmony with the universality of things.

To know is of all acts of life the least profane, for it is the most disinterested, the most independent of gratifications, the most *objective*, to employ the language of the schools. It is a waste of time to prove its sanctity, for those only for whom there is nothing sacred would dream of denying it. Those who go no further than the mere facts of human nature without venturing upon a qualification on the value of things, even those will not deny that science at any rate is the first and foremost necessity of mankind. Man face to face with things is necessarily impelled to seek their secret. The problem suggests itself, and that by virtue of man's faculty of penetrating beyond the phenomenon he perceives. It is first of all nature itself which whets this craving to know, and he attacks the latter with the impatience bred of a naïve presumption, which fancies itself able to draw up a system of the universe at the first attempt and in a few pages. Then his curiosity is tempted by the wish to know all about himself, and much later on by the desire to solve the problem of his species, of humanity at large, of its history. Then comes the final problem, the great cause, the supreme law. The problem gets varied, grows larger and larger, according to the horizons appertaining to each age, but it never ceases suggesting itself; face to face with the unknown man always experiences a dual sentiment; a reverence for the mysterious, a noble recklessness that prompts him to rend the veil in order to know what is beyond it.

To remain indifferent face to face with the universe is utterly impossible to man. As soon as he begins to think, he begins to seek, he puts problems to himself and solves them; he must needs have a system on the world, on himself, on the primary cause, on his origin, on his end. He lacks the necessary data to answer the questions he puts to himself, but no matter. He supplies them himself. Hence, primitive religions, improvised solutions of a problem that required long centuries of research, but to which an immediate answer was necessary. The scientific method is capable of resigning itself to no-knowledge, or it does at any rate submit to delay; primitive science wanted there and then to grasp the meaning of things. In fact, to ask man to adjourn certain problems, to postpone to future centuries the knowledge of what he is, what kind of place he occupies in the world, what is the cause of the world and of himself, to ask him to do this is to ask him to achieve the impossible. Even if he did get to know the enigma insoluble, one could not prevent him from worrying and wearing himself out about it.

I am aware that there is something irreverent, something unlawful, something savouring of high treason against the divine in this bold act of man by which he endeavours to penetrate the mystery of things. At any rate that is how all ancient peoples looked at it. According to them science was a robbery committed to the prejudice of God, an act of defiance and disobedience. In the beautiful myth with which the Pentateuch opens, it is the genius of evil that prompts man to emerge from his state of innocent ignorance in order to become like God by the knowledge distinct and antithetic of good and evil. The fable of Prometheus has no other meaning than that; the conquests of civilization presented as an attempt against, an illicit rape upon, a jealous divinity who wished to keep them to himself. Hence, the proud character of daring against the gods borne by the first inventors, hence, the theme developed in so many mythological legends: that the wish for a better state is the source of all evil in the world. It will be easily understood that, antiquity not having the "key-word" of the enigma, progress was, as it were, bound to feel a respectful dread in shattering the barriers erected, according to it by a superior power, that not daring to rely upon the future for a state of happiness, it conceived it as having existed in a primitive golden age, that it should have said, *Audax Iapeti genus,* that it called the conquest of the perfect a *vetitum nefas.* Humanity, in those days, had the sentiment of the obstacle, not that of victory, but though calling itself all the while audacious and daring, it kept marching onward and onward. As for us who have reached the grand moment of our consciousness, it is no longer a question of saying, "*Cœlum ipsum petimus stultitia!*" and to go on committing sacrileges as it were. We must proceed with proudly uplifted head and fearlessly towards that which is ours and when we do violence to things in order to drag their secret from them, feel perfectly convinced that we are acting for ourselves, for them and for God.

Man does not at once become fully conscious of his strength and creative power. Among primitive peoples, all the marvellous exploits of the human intellect are attributed to the Divinity; the wise men believe themselves inspired and thoroughly convinced of their mysterious relations with higher beings and boast of them. Often the supernatural agents themselves are credited with the authorship of works that seemingly exceed the powers of man. In Homer it is Hephæstos who creates all the ingenious mechanisms. The credulous centuries of mediævalism attribute all eminent science or all skill above the common level to secret faculties, to commerce with the Evil One. As a rule the non-reflecting or "little-reflecting" centuries are given to substitute theological for psychological explanations. It seems natural to believe that *grace* comes from on high; it is only later on discovered to emanate from the inmost conscience. The untutored fancies that the dew drops from the sky; he scarcely believes the *savant* who assures him that it emanates from the plants themselves.

When I wish to picture to myself fact as of the progenitor of science in all its primitive simplicity and disinterested impulse, I revert with a feeling of inexpressible charm to the first-rational philosophers of Greece. To the psychologist there is a priceless ingenuousness and truth in this spontaneous ardour of a few men who without traditional precedent or official motive but from mere inward impulse of their nature take to grappling with the eternal problem in its true form. Aristotle is already a deep-thinking *savant* conscious of his process who produces science and philosophy as Virgil produces verse. Those first thinkers, on the contrary, are moved by their spontaneous curiosity in a totally different manner. The object is before them, whetting their appetite; they attack it like the child who, growing impatient when confronted with a complicated piece of machinery, tries it in every way in order to get at its secret, and does not stop until he has found the to him sufficiently satisfactory explanation. This primitive science is nothing more than the constantly repeated "*Why?*" of infancy; with this difference though that with us the child finds an instructed person to supply the answer to his question while there it is the child itself who gives the answer with the same simplicity. It seems to me as difficult to understand the true point of view of science without having studied those primitive *savants* as to have the lofty sense of poetry without having studied primitive poesy.

A busy civilization like ours is by no means favourable to the glorifying of those speculative wants. Nowhere is curiosity more keen, more disinterested, more attracted by the outward than in the child and the savage. How sincerely and simply interested they are in nature, in animals, without a single second thought or a respect for humanity. The busy man, on the contrary, is bored in the company of nature and of animals; those disinterested enjoyments are no part or parcel of his egoism. Unsophisticated man, left to his own thought, often conceives a more complete and far-reaching system of things than he who has only received a conventional and fictitious education. The habits of practical life weaken the instinct of pure curiosity; but there is comfort to the lover of science in the thought that nothing can destroy it, that the monument to which he has added a stone is eternal, that like morality, it has its guarantee in the very instincts of human nature.

As a rule science is only looked at from the standpoint of its practical results and its civilizing effects. There is no great difficulty in finding out that modern society is indebted to it for its principal improvements. This is very true, but nevertheless, putting the thesis in a dangerous way. One might just as well, in order to establish the claims of morality point exclusively to the benefits society derives from it. Science, as well as morality is valuable in itself and independently of all beneficent results.

These results are, moreover, nearly always conceived in a mean and shabby spirit. As a rule people remain blind to anything but practical applications which no doubt have their importance inasmuch as by their rebound they powerfully contribute to mental progress but which in themselves have little or no ideal value. Moral applications, in fact, almost always lead science astray from its true aim. To study history for no other purpose than the lessons of morality or practical wisdom to be deduced from it is simply to revive the ridiculous theory of those poor interpreters of Aristotle who considered the only object of dramatic art to be the cure of the passions it puts into action. The spirit against which I am especially tilting here is that of English science, so lacking in loftiness, in philosophy. I know of no Englishman, Byron perhaps excepted, who has deeply grasped the philosophy of things. To order one's life in accordance with reason, to avoid error, not to embark upon enterprises that cannot be carried out, to provide for one's self a gentle and assured existence, to recognize the simplicity of the laws of the universe, to get hold of a few views of natural theology seems to be to the Englishman who thinks the sovereign aim of science. There is never as much as an idea of lofty and harassing speculation, never a deep glance at that which is. This, no doubt, arises from the fact that with our neighbours, positive religion, kept under a conservative sequestration, is held to be unassailable, is still considered as capable of giving the key to the enigma of great things. But science, in fact, being only of value in as far as it is capable of replacing religion, what becomes of it under such a system? A kind of petty process to knock a little bit of understanding into folk, a kind of help in obtaining a social status, a means of acquiring useful and interesting knowledge. All this is not worth a moment's consideration. As for myself, I only admit of one result of science, namely, the solution of the enigma, the final explanation to mankind of the meaning of things, the explanation of man to himself, the giving to him in the name of the sole legitimate authority which is the whole of human nature itself, of the creed which religion gave him ready made and which he can no longer accept. To live without a system whereby to explain things is not to live the life of man.

CHAPTER IX

What then is the meaning of this superficial and idle contempt? Why is the philologist, manipulating as he does, things human in order to extract from them the science of humanity, less understood than the student of chemistry and the physicist, manipulating nature, in order to get at the theory of nature? No doubt the existence of the curious man of erudition who has spent his life in amusing himself learnedly and in treating serious things frivolously has been a profitless existence indeed. Men and women of the world are not altogether wrong in looking upon such a role as a mere clever trick of memory, suited to those who have only been endowed with second rate qualities. But theirs is a short and narrow view, in that they fail to perceive that the knowledge of many arts and sciences is the condition of the high æsthetic, moral, religious, poetical intelligence. A philosopher who thinks that he can evolve everything from his own bosom, that is, from the study of the soul and from purely abstract consideration must necessarily despise erudition and look upon it as prejudicial to the progress of reason. From this point of view, the fretful temper of Descartes, of Malebranche and of the Cartesians in general with regard to erudition is legitimate and accounted for by reason. Leibnitz was the first to realize in a magnificent harmony that elevated conception of a *critical philosopher* to which Bayle could not attain through insufficient concentration of mind. The nineteenth century is destined to be called upon to realize it and to introduce the positive method in every branch of knowledge. M. Cousin's glory will lie in his having proclaimed criticism as a new method in philosophy, a method which may lead to results as dogmatic as abstract speculation. His eclecticism has only lost its strength when outward necessities, which he could not resist, have compelled it to embrace exclusively particular doctrines which have made it as narrow as they themselves are, and to screen itself behind certain names, which should be honoured otherwise than by fanaticism. Such was not the grand eclecticism of 1828 and 1829, and of the preface to Tennemann. The new philosophical generation will understand the necessity of transporting itself to the living centre of things, of no longer making philosophy a collection of speculations without unity, of restoring to it at last its ancient and broad acceptation, its eternal mission of giving vital truths to man.

Philosophy, in fact, is not a science apart, it is one side of all sciences. In each science we should distinguish the technical and special part, which has no value except in so far as it contributes to discovery and exposition, from the general results which the science in question provides on its own account towards the solution of the problem of things. Philosophy constitutes the common head, the central part of the grand fabric of human knowledge, the focus where all the rays touch one another in an identical light. There is not a line which traced to the very end does not lead to that focus. Psychology which one has become accustomed to consider as the whole of philosophy is after all one of many sciences, nay, it may not even provide the most philosophical results. Logic understood as the analysis of reason is only a part of psychology; considered as a repertory of processes to lead the mind to the discovery of the truth, it is simply useless, seeing that it is impossible to give recipes for the discovery of truth. Refined culture and the multiple training of the intellect are from this point of view the only legitimate logical methods. Morality and the theory of divine justice are not sciences apart, they become heavy and ridiculous, when one pretends to treat them according to a definite and scientific programme, they should only be the divine resonance resulting from all things or at most the æsthetic education of the pure instincts of the soul, the analysis of which belongs to psychology. By what right then can we constitute a whole, having the right to assume the name of philosophy, seeing that this whole, in the only limits one can assign to it, has already a particular name, that is psychology? Antiquity grasped this lofty and broad acceptation of philosophy in a marvellous manner. Philosophy was to it the sage, the investigator, Jupiter on Mount Ida, the spectator taking up his stand in the world. "Among those who rush to the public festivals of Greece, some are attracted by the wish to contest and to dispute the palm; others come thither to transact their commercial business; a few again come neither for glory, nor for profit, but merely to *see;* and these are the noblest, for the spectacle is provided for them, and they are there for no one's sake but their own. So on entering life, some aspire to mingle in the strife, others are ambitious to make a fortune; but there are some noble souls who despise vulgar cares and while the common herd of combatants rend one another to pieces in the arena, look upon themselves as spectators in the vast amphitheatre of the universe. They are the philosophers."—Never has philosophy been more perfectly defined.

If the final aim of philosophy be the truth on the general system of things, how then could it remain indifferent to the science of the universe? Has not cosmology the same claim to holiness as the psychological sciences? Does not it start problems the solution of which is as imperatively demanded by our nature as that of questions related to ourselves and to the primary cause? Is not the world the first object that excites the curiosity of the human intellect, is it not the first to whet the craving to know which is the marked trait of our rational nature, and which makes of us beings capable of philosophizing? Take the mythologies, which give us the true measure of the spiritual needs of man; they all open with a cosmogony; the cosmological myths occupy a space in them at least as great as those relating to morals or theosophy. And even in our days though the particular sciences are far from having reached their final form, how many precious data have they not afforded to the mind that aspires to know philosophically? He who has not learnt from geology the history of our globe and of the beings who have successively populated it; from physiology the laws of life; from zoology and botany, the laws of form of all breathing things, and the general plan of animate nature; from astronomy, the structure of the universe; from ethnography and from history, the science of humanity in its evolution; he who has not learned this can he pretend to know the law of things, nay, to know man whom he only studies in the abstract and in individual manifestations?

I will endeavour to explain by an instance the manner in which one might use the particular sciences in the solution of a philosophical question. I select the problem which from the very first years that I began to philosophize has occupied my mind most; the problem of the *origins of mankind.*

There can be no doubt as to the existence of mankind having had a beginning. It is equally certain that the appearance of mankind on earth was accomplished in accordance with the permanent laws of nature, and that the first facts of his psychological and physiological life, though so strangely different from those that characterize his actual condition were the development pure and simple of the laws that are still in force to-day, operating in a medium profoundly different. Hence we are confronted by an important problem, if ever there was one, and from the solution of which would spring data of capital importance on the whole of the meaning of human life. And in my opinion this problem should be divided into six subordinate questions all of which should be solved by different sciences.

1st. *Ethnographic Question.*—If and up to what point the races actually existent are deducible from one another. Were there several centres of creation? which are they, etc.?—The investigator should therefore have at command the *ensemble* of the whole of modern ethnography, in its certain as well as hypothetical parts, also the anatomical and linguistic knowledge without which the study of ethnography is impossible.

2nd. *Chronological Question.*—At what epoch did mankind or each race make its appearance on earth?—This question should be resolved by the collating of two means; on the one hand, the geological data; on the other, the data supplied by the antique chronologies and above all by the monuments. Hence the author must be learned in geology, and well versed in the antiquities of China, Egypt, of India, of the Hebrews, etc.

3rd. *Geographical Question.*—At which point of the globe did mankind or the diverse races take their starting point?—Here the knowledge of geography in its most philosophic part would be necessary and above all the deepest scientific knowledge of antique literatures and the traditions of the various peoples. Languages in this instance supplying the principal element the author should be an able linguist, or if not, he should at any rate have at his disposal the results acquired by comparative philology.

4th. *Physiological Question.*—Possibility and mode of apparition of organic life and of human life. The laws that have produced that apparition, which is still continued in the hidden corners of nature. To deal with this side of the question, a thorough knowledge of comparative physiology is necessary. The author should be able to form an opinion on the most delicate point of that science.

5th. *Psychological Question.*—The condition of mankind and of the human intellect at the first stages of its existence. Primitive languages. Origin of thought and of language. Must have a deep insight into the secrets of spontaneous psychology, an habitual practice of the higher branches of psychology and philosophical sciences. Must be thoroughly versed in the experimental study of the child and the first exercise of its reason, in the experimental study of the savage, consequently must be extensively acquainted with the literature of the great travellers, and as much as possible have travelled himself among the primitive peoples which are fast disappearing from the face of the earth, at any rate in their original condition of spontaneous impulse; must have a knowledge of all primitive literatures, of the comparative genius of the various peoples, of comparative literature, a refined and scientific taste, tact, and spontaneous initiative; a childlike and at the same time serious nature, susceptible of great enthusiasm with regard to the spontaneous and capable of reproducing it within himself, within the very seat of deeply reflected thought.

6th. *Historical Question.*—The history of mankind before the definite apparition of reflected thought.

I am convinced that there is a science of the origins of mankind, and that it will be constructed one day not by abstract speculation but by scientific research. What human life in the actual condition of science would suffice to explore all the sides of this single problem? And still, how can it be resolved without the scientific study of the positive data? And if it be not resolved how can we say that we know man and mankind? He who would contribute to the solution of this problem, even by a very imperfect essay, would do more for philosophy than by half a century of metaphysical meditations.

SOURCE: Chapters 2 and 9 in *The Future of Science* (Boston: Roberts Brothers, 1893), 11–17, 142–51.

SELF-GOVERNANCE

Nation-Making

WALTER BAGEHOT

[Walter Bagehot (1826–1877) was a journalist, literary critic, and economist; he became editor of the *Economist* in 1860. Bagehot's best-known works include *The English Constitution* (1867) and *Lombard Street: A Description of the Money Market* (1892). His collection of *Biographical Studies* (1895) includes essays on the Reform Act of 1832, Sir Robert Peel, Gladstone and Disraeli, William Cobden, and Lord Palmerston.]

In still ruder ages the religion of savages is a thing too feeble to create a schism or to found a community. We are dealing with people capable of history when we speak of great ideas, not with prehistoric flint-men or the present savages. But though under very different forms, the same essential causes—the imitation of preferred characters and the elimination of detested characters—were at work in the oldest times, and are at work among rude men now. Strong as the propensity to imitation is among civilized men, we must conceive it as an impulse of which their minds have been partially denuded. Like the far-seeing sight, the infallible hearing, the magical scent of the savage, it is a half-lost power. It was strongest in ancient times, and *is* strongest in uncivilized regions.

This extreme propensity to imitation is one great reason of the amazing sameness which every observer notices in savage nations. When you have seen one Fuegian, you have seen all Fuegians—one Tasmanian, all Tasmanians. The higher savages, as the New Zealanders, are less uniform; they have more of the varied and compact structure of civilized nations, because in other respects they are more civilized. They have greater mental capacity—larger stores of inward thought. But much of the same monotonous nature clings to them too. A savage tribe resembles a herd of gregarious beasts; where the leader goes they go too; they copy blindly his habits, and thus soon become that which he already is. For not only the tendency, but also the power to imitate is stronger in savages than civilized men. Savages copy quicker, and they copy better. Children, in the same way, are born mimics; they cannot help imitating what comes before them. There is nothing in their minds to resist the propensity to copy. Every educated man has a large inward supply of ideas to which he can retire, and in which he can escape from or alleviate unpleasant outward objects. But a savage or a child has no resource. The external movements before it are its very life; it lives by what it sees and hears. Uneducated people in civilized nations have vestiges of the same condition. If you send a housemaid and a philosopher to a foreign country of which neither knows the language, the chances are that the housemaid will catch it before the philosopher. He has something else to do; he can live in his own thoughts. But unless she can imitate the utterances, she is lost; she has no life till she can join in the chatter of the kitchen. The propensity to mimicry, and the power of mimicry, are mostly strongest in those who have least abstract minds. The most wonderful examples of imitation in the world are perhaps the imitations of civilized men by savages in the use of martial weapons. They learn the *knack*, as sportsmen call it, with inconceivable rapidity. A North American Indian—an Australian even—can shoot as well as any white man. Here the motive is at its maximum, as well as the innate power. Every savage cares more for the power of killing than for any other power.

The persecuting tendency of all savages, and, indeed, of all ignorant people, is even more striking than their imitative tendency. No barbarian can bear to see one of his nation deviate from the old barbarous customs and usages of their tribe. Very commonly all the tribe would expect a punishment from the gods if any one of them refrained from what was old, or began what was new. In modern times and in cultivated countries we regard each person as responsible only for his own actions, and do not believe, or think of believing, that the misconduct of others can bring guilt on them. Guilt to us is an individual taint consequent on choice and cleaving to the chooser. But in early ages the act of one member of the tribe is conceived to make all the tribe impious, to offend its peculiar god, to expose all the tribe to penalties from heaven. There is no "limited liability" in the political notions of that time. The early tribe or nation is a religious partnership, on which a rash member by a sudden impiety may bring utter ruin. If the state is conceived thus, toleration becomes wicked. A permitted deviation from the transmitted ordinances becomes simple folly. It is a sacrifice of the happiness of the greatest number. It is allowing one individual, for a moment's pleasure or a stupid whim, to bring terrible and irretrievable calamity upon all. No one will ever understand even Athenian history who forgets this idea of the old world, though Athens was, in comparison with others, a rational and sceptical place, ready for new views,

and free from old prejudices. When the street statues of Hermes were mutilated, all the Athenians were frightened and furious; they thought that they
should *all* be ruined because some *one* had mutilated a god's image and so
offended him. Almost every detail of life in the classical times—the times
when real history opens—was invested with a religious sanction; a sacred
ritual regulated human action; whether it was called "law" or not, much of it
was older than the word "law"; it was part of an ancient usage conceived as
emanating from a superhuman authority, and not to be transgressed without
risk of punishment by more than mortal power. There was such a *solidarité*
then between citizens that each might be led to persecute the other for fear of
harm to himself.

It may be said that these two tendencies of the early world—that to persecution and that to imitation—must conflict; that the imitative impulse
would lead men to copy what is new, and that persecution by traditional habit
would prevent their copying it. But in practice the two tendencies co-operate.
There is a strong tendency to copy the most common thing, and that common thing is the old habit. Daily imitation is far oftenest a conservative force,
for the most frequent models are ancient. Of course, however, something new
is necessary for every man and for every nation. We may wish, if we please,
that tomorrow shall be like today, but it will not be like it. New forces will
impinge upon us; new wind, new rain, and the light of another sun; and we
must alter to meet them. But the persecuting habit and the imitative combine
to ensure that the new thing shall be in the old fashion; it must be an alteration, but it shall contain as little of variety as possible. The imitative impulse
tends to this, because men most easily imitate what their minds are best prepared for—what is like the old, yet with the inevitable minimum of alteration;
what throws them least out of the old path, and puzzles least their minds. The
doctrine of development means this—that in unavoidable changes men like
the new doctrine which is most of a "preservative addition" to their old
doctrines. The imitative and the persecuting tendencies make all change in
early nations a kind of selective conservatism, for the most part keeping what
is old, but annexing some new but like practice—an additional turret in the
old style.

It is this process of adding suitable things and rejecting discordant things
which has raised those scenes of strange manners which in every part of the
world puzzle the civilized men who come upon them first. Like the old head-
dress of mountain villages, they make the traveller think not so much whether
they are good or whether they are bad as wonder how anyone could have
come to think of them; to regard them as "monstrosities," which only some
wild abnormal intellect could have hit upon. And wild and abnormal indeed

would be that intellect if it were a single one at all. But in fact such manners are the growth of ages, like Roman law or the British Constitution. No one man—no one generation—could have thought of them—only a series of generations trained in the habits of the last and wanting something akin to such habits could have devised them. Savages *pet* their favourite habits, so to say, and preserve them as they do their favourite animals; ages are required, but at last a national character is formed by the confluence of congenial attractions and accordant detestations.

Another cause helps. In early states of civilization there is a great mortality of infant life, and this is a kind of selection in itself—the child most fit to be a good Spartan is most likely to survive a Spartan childhood. The habits of the tribe are enforced on the child; if he is able to catch and copy them he lives; if he cannot he dies. The imitation which assimilates early nations continues through life, but it begins with suitable forms and acts on picked specimens. I suppose, too, that there is a kind of parental selection operating in the same way and probably tending to keep alive the same individuals. Those children which gratified their fathers and mothers most would be most tenderly treated by them, and have the best chance to live, and as a rough rule their favourites would be the children of most "promise"; that is to say, those who seemed most likely to be a credit to the tribe according to the leading tribal manners and the existing tribal tastes. The most gratifying child would be the best looked after, and the most gratifying would be the best specimen of the standard then and there raised up.

Even so, I think there will be a disinclination to attribute so marked, fixed, almost physical a thing as national character to causes so evanescent as the imitation of appreciated habit and the persecution of detested habit. But, after all, national character is but a name for a collection of habits more or less universal. And this imitation and this persecution in long generations have vast physical effects. The mind of the parent (as we speak) passes somehow to the body of the child. The transmitted "something" is more affected by habits than it is by anything else. In time an ingrained type is sure to be formed, and sure to be passed on if only the causes I have specified be fully in action and without impediment.

As I have said, I am not explaining the origin of races, but of nations, or, if you like, of tribes. I fully admit that no imitation of predominant manner, or prohibitions of detested manners, will of themselves account for the broadest contrasts of human nature. Such means would no more make a Negro out of a Brahmin, or a red man out of an Englishman, than washing would change the spots of a leopard or the colour of an Ethiopian. Some more potent causes must co-operate, or we should not have these enormous diversities. The minor causes I deal with made Greek to differ from Greek, but they did not make the Greek race. We cannot precisely mark the limit, but a limit there clearly is.

If we look at the earliest monuments of the human race, we find these race-characters as decided as the race-characters now. The earliest paintings or sculptures we anywhere have give us the present contrasts of dissimilar types as strongly as present observation. Within historical memory no such differences have been created as those between Negro and Greek, between Papuan and red Indian, between Eskimos and Goth. We start with cardinal diversities; we trace only minor modifications, and we only see minor modifications. And it is very hard to see how any number of such modifications could change man as he is in one race-type to man as he is in some other. Of this there are but two explanations; *one,* that these great types were originally separate creations, as they stand—that the Negro was made so, and the Greek made so. But this easy hypothesis of special creation has been tried so often, and has broken down so very often, that in no case, probably, do any great number of careful inquirers very firmly believe it. They may accept it provisionally, as the best hypothesis at present, but they feel about it as they cannot help feeling as to an army which has always been beaten; however strong it seems, they think it will be beaten again. What the other explanation is exactly I cannot pretend to say. Possibly as yet the data for a confident opinion are not before us. But by far the most plausible suggestion is that of Mr. Wallace, that these race-marks are living records of a time when the intellect of man was not as able as it is now to adapt his life and habits to change of region; that consequently early mortality in the first wanderers was beyond conception great; that only those (so to say) haphazard individuals throve who were born with a protected nature—that is, a nature suited to the climate and the country, fitted to use its advantages, shielded from its natural diseases. According to Mr. Wallace, the Negro is the remnant of the one variety of man who without more adaptiveness than then existed could live in interior Africa. Immigrants died off till they produced him or something like him, and so of the Eskimos or the American.

Any protective habit also struck out in such a time would have a far greater effect than it could afterwards. A gregarious tribe, whose leader was in some imitable respects adapted to the struggle for life, and which copied its leader, would have an enormous advantage in the struggle for life. It would be sure to win and live, for it would be coherent and adapted, whereas, in comparison, competing tribes would be incoherent and unadapted. And I suppose that in early times, when those bodies did not already contain the records and the traces of endless generations, any new habit would more easily fix its mark on the heritable element, and would be transmitted more easily and more certainly. In such an age, man being softer and more pliable, deeper race-marks would be more easily inscribed and would be more likely to continue legible.

But I have no pretence to speak on such matters; this paper, as I have so often explained, deals with nation-making and not with race-making. I assume a world of marked varieties of man, and only want to show how less marked contrasts would probably and naturally arise in each. Given large homogeneous populations, some Negro, some Mongolian, some Aryan, I have tried to prove how small contrasting groups would certainly spring up within each—some to last and some to perish. These are the eddies in each race-stream which vary its surface, and are sure to last till some new force changes the current. These minor varieties, too, would be infinitely compounded, not only with those of the same race, but with those of others. Since the beginning of man, stream has been a thousand times poured into stream— quick into sluggish, dark into pale—and eddies and waters have taken new shapes and new colours, affected by what went before, but not resembling it. And then on the fresh mass the old forces of composition and elimination again begin to act, and create over the new surface another world. "Motley was the wear" of the world when Herodotus first looked on it and described it to us, and thus, as it seems to me, were its varying colours produced.

If it be thought that I have made out that these forces of imitation and elimination be the main ones, or even at all powerful ones, in the formation of national character, it will follow that the effect of ordinary agencies upon that character will be more easy to understand than it often seems and is put down in books. We get a notion that a change of government or a change of climate acts equally on the mass of a nation, and so are we puzzled—at least, I have been puzzled—to conceive how it acts. But such changes do not at first act equally on all people in the nation. On many, for a very long time, they do not act at all. But they bring out new qualities, and advertise the effects of new habits. A change of climate, say from a depressing to an invigorating one, so acts. Everybody feels it a little, but the most active feel it exceedingly. They labour and prosper, and their prosperity invites imitation. Just so with the contrary change, from an animating to a relaxing place—the naturally lazy look so happy as they do nothing that the naturally active are corrupted. The effect of any considerable change on a nation is thus an intensifying and accumulating effect. With its maximum power it acts on some prepared and congenial individuals; in them it is seen to produce attractive results, and then the habits creating those results are copied far and wide. And, as I believe, it is in this simple but not quite obvious way that the process of progress and of degradation may generally be seen to run.

SOURCE: In *Physics and Politics: Or, Thoughts on the Application of the Principles of "Natural Selection" and "Inheritance" to Political Society* (1869; New York: Alfred Knopf, 1948), 104–15.

The Primitive Man—Intellectual

HERBERT SPENCER

[Herbert Spencer (1820–1903), the father of social Darwinism, was one of the earliest evolutionary philosophers to apply Charles Darwin's theories to contemporary cultures and communities. Spencer synthesized the theories of natural selection and "survival of the fittest"—a phrase Spencer coined and Darwin adopted—with biological, social, psychological, and ethical disciplines. His best-known works include *System of Synthetic Philosophy* (9 vols., 1862–1893), *Descriptive Sociology: Or, Groups of Social Facts* (1873–1881), *The Data of Ethics* (1879), and *Education: Intellectual, Moral, and Physical* (1896).]

§ 39. The three measures of mental evolution which, in the last chapter, helped us to delineate the emotional nature of the primitive man, will, in this chapter, help us to delineate his intellectual nature. And further to aid ourselves we must recall, in connexion with these measures, those traits of thought which, in the *Principles of Psychology* (§§ 484-93), were shown to characterize a lower evolution as compared with a higher.

Conceptions of *general facts* being derived from experiences of particular facts and coming later, are deficient in the primitive man. Consciousness of a general truth implies more heterogeneous correspondence than does consciousness of any included particular truth; it implies higher representativeness, since it colligates more numerous and varied ideas; and it is more remote from reflex action—will not, indeed, of itself, excite action at all.

Having no records, man, in his uncivilized state, cannot recognize long sequences. Hence *provision of distant results*, such as is possible in a settled society having measures and written language, is impossible to him: correspondence in times comes within narrow limits. The representations include few successions of phenomena, and these not comprehensive ones. And there is but a moderate departure from the reflex life in which stimulus and act stand in immediate connexion.

Ignorant of localities outside his own, the associations of ideas the primitive man forms are little liable to be changed. As experiences (multiplying in number, gathered from a wider area, and added to by those which other men record) become more heterogeneous, the narrow notions first framed are shaken and made more plastic—there comes greater *modifiability of belief.* In his relative rigidity of belief we see a smaller correspondence with an environment containing adverse facts; less of that representativeness which simultaneously grasps and averages much evidence; and a smaller divergence from those lowest actions in which impressions cause, irresistibly, the appropriate motions.

Conditioned as he is, the savage lacks *abstract ideas.* Drawn from many concrete ideas, an abstract idea becomes detachable from them only as fast as their variety leads to mutual cancellings of differences, and leaves outstanding that which they have in common. This implies growth of the correspondence in range and heterogeneity; wider representation of the concretes whence the idea is abstracted; and greater remoteness from reflex action. Such abstract ideas as those of *property* and *cause,* belong to a still higher stage. For only after many special properties and many special causes have been abstracted, can there arise the re-abstracted ideas of property in general and cause in general.

The conception of *uniformity* in the order of phenomena, develops simultaneously. Only along with the use of *measures* does there grow up the means of ascertaining uniformity; and only after a great accumulation of measured results does the idea of *law* become possible. Here, again, the indices of mental evolution serve. The conception of natural order presupposes an advanced correspondence; it involves re-representativeness in a high degree; and the implied divergence from reflex action is extreme.

Until the notion of uniformity has developed along with the use of measures, thought cannot have much *definiteness.* In primitive life, there is little to yield the idea of agreement; and so long as there are few experiences of exact equality between objects, or perfect conformity between statements and facts, or complete fulfilment of anticipations by results, the notion of *truth* cannot become clear. Once more our general tests answer. The conception of truth, being the conception of correspondence between Thoughts and Things, implies advance of that correspondence; it involves representations which are higher, as being better adjusted to realities; and its growth causes a decrease of the primitive credulity allied to reflex action—allied, since it shows us single suggestions producing sudden beliefs which forthwith issue in conduct. Add that only as this conception of truth advances, and therefore the correlative conception of untruth, can *scepticism* and *criticism* grow common.

Lastly, such imagination as the primitive man has, small in range and heterogeneity, is *reminiscent* only, not *constructive.* An imagination which invents, shows extension of the correspondence from the region of the actual into that of the potential; implies a representativeness not limited to combinations which have been, or are, in the environment, but including non-existing combinations thereafter made to exist; and exhibits the greatest remoteness from reflex action, since the stimulus issuing in movement is unlike any that ever before acted.

And now, having enumerated these leading traits of intellectual evolution in its latter stages, as deduced from psychological principles, we are prepared to observe the significance of the facts as described by travellers.

§ 40. Testimonies to the acute senses and quick perceptions of the uncivilized, are given by nearly everyone who describes them.

Lichtenstein says the vision of the Bushman is telescopic; and Barrow speaks of his "keen eye always in motion." Of Asiatics may be named the Karens, who see as far with naked eyes as we do with opera-glasses; and the inhabitants of the Siberian steppes are celebrated for their "distant and perfect sight." Of the Brazilians, Herndon writes—"The Indians have very keen senses, and see and hear things that are inaudible and invisible to us;" and the like is remarked of the Tupis. The Abipones, "like apes, are always in motion;" and Dobrizhoffer asserts that they discern things which escape "the most quick-sighted European." Respecting hearing, too, there is similar, if less abundant, evidence. All have read of the feats of North American Indians in detecting faint sounds; and the acute hearing of the Veddahs is shown by their habit of finding bees' nests by the hum.

Still more abundant are the testimonies respecting their active and minute observation. "Excellent superficial observers," is the characterization Palgrave gives of the Bedouins. Burton refers to the "high organization of the perceptive faculties" among them; and Petherick proved, by a test, their marvellous powers of tracking. In South Africa the Hottentots show astonishing quickness "in everything relating to cattle;" and Galton says the Damaras "have a wonderful faculty of recollecting any ox that they have once seen." It is the same in America. Burton, speaking of the Prairie Indians, comments on the "development of the perceptions which is produced by the constant and minute observations of a limited number of objects." Instances are given showing what exact topographers the Chippewayans are; and the like is alleged to the Dakotahs. Bates notices the extraordinary "sense of locality" of the Brazilian Indians. Concerning the Arawaks, Hillhouse says—"Where an European can discover no indication whatever, an Indian will point out the footsteps of any number of negroes, and will state the precise day on which they have passed; and if on the same day he will state the hour." A member of a Guiana tribe "will tell how many men, women, and children have passed, where a stranger could only see faint and confused marks on the path." "Here passes one who does not belong to our village," said a native of Guiana searching for tracks; and Schomburgh adds that their power "borders on the magical."

Along with this acuteness of perception there naturally goes great skill in those actions depending on immediate guidance of perception. The Esquimaux show great dexterity in all manual works. Kolben asserts that the Hottentots are very dexterous in the use of their weapons. Of the Fuegians it is said that "their dexterity with the sling is extraordinary." The skill of the Andamanese is shown in their unerring shots with arrows at forty or fifty yards. Tongans "are great adepts in managing their canoes." The accuracy with which an Australian propels a spear with his throwing-stick, is remarkable; while all have heard of his feats with the boomerang. And from the Hilltribes of India, the Santals may be singled out as so "very expert with the bow and arrow" that they kill birds on the wing, and knock over hares at full speed.

Recognizing some exceptions to this expertness, as among the now-extinct Tasmanians and the Veddahs of Ceylon; and observing that survival of the fittest must ever have tended to establish these traits among men whose lives from hour to hour depended on their keen senses, quick observations, and efficient uses of their weapons; we have here to note this trait as significant in its implications. For in virtue of a general antagonism between the activities of simple faculties and the activities of complex faculties, this dominance of the lower intellectual life hinders the higher intellectual life. In proportion as the mental energies go out in restless perception, they cannot go out in deliberate thought. This truth we will contemplate from another point of view.

§ 41. Not having special senses by which to discriminate, the worm swallows bodily the mould containing vegetal matter partially decayed: leaving its alimentary canal to absorb what nutriment it can, and to eject, in the shape of worm-cast, the 95 per cent. or so that is innutritive. Conversely, the higher annulose creature, with special senses, as the bee, selects from plants concentrated nutritive matters wherewith to feed its larvæ, or, as the spider, sucks the ready-prepared juices from the flies it entraps. The progress from the less intelligent to the more intelligent and the most intelligent among the *Vertebrata*, is similarly accompanied by increasing ability in the selection of food. By herbivorous mammals the comparatively innutritive parts of plants have to be devoured in great quantities, that the requisite amounts of nutriment may be obtained; while carnivorous animals, which are mostly more sagacious, live on concentrated foods of which small quantities suffice. Though the monkey and the elephant are not carnivorous, yet both have powers which, certainly by the one and probably by the other, are used in choosing the nutritive parts of plants when these are to be had. Coming to mankind, we observe that the diet is of the most concentrated kind obtainable; but that the uncivilized man is less choice in his diet than the civilized. And then among the highly civilized the most nutritive food is carefully separated from the rest: even to the extent that at table fragments of inferior quality are uneaten.

My purpose in naming these seemingly-irrelevant contrasts, is to point out the analogy between progress in bodily nutrition and progress in mental nutrition. The psychically higher, like the physically higher, have greater powers of selecting materials fit for assimilation. Just as by appearance, texture, and odour, the superior animal is guided in choosing food, and swallows only things which contain much organizable matter; so the superior mind, aided by what we may figuratively call intellectual scent, passes by multitudes of unorganizable facts, but quickly detects facts full of significance, and takes them in as materials out of which cardinal truths may be elaborated. The less-developed intelligences, unable to decompose these more complex facts and assimilate their components, and having therefore no appetites for them, devour with avidity facts which are mostly valueless; and out of the vast mass absorb very little that helps to form general conceptions. Concentrated diet furnished by the experiments of the physicist, the investigations of the political economist, the analyses of the psychologist, is intolerable to them, indigestible by them; but instead, they swallow with greediness the trivial details of table-talk, the personalities of fashionable life, the garbage of the police and divorce courts; while their reading, in addition to trashy novels, includes memoirs of mediocrities, volumes of gossiping correspondence, with an occasional history, from which they carry away a few facts about battles and the doings of conspicuous men. By such minds, this kind of intellectual provender is alone available; and to feed them on a higher kind would be as impracticable as to feed a cow on meat.

Suppose this contrast exaggerated—suppose the descent from the higher to the lower intellects among ourselves, to be continued by a second descent of like kind, and we get to the intellect of the primitive man. A still greater attention to meaningless details, and a still smaller ability to select facts from which conclusions may be drawn, characterize the savage. Multitudes of simple observations are incessantly made by him; but such few as have significance, lost in the mass of insignificant ones, pass through his mind without leaving behind any data for thoughts, worthy to be so called. Already in a foregoing section, the extreme perceptive activity of the lowest races has been illustrated; and here may be added a few illustrations showing the reflective inactivity going along with it. Of the Brazilian Indian Mr. Bates remarks—"I believe he thinks of nothing except the matters that immediately concern his daily material wants." "He observes well, but he can deduce nothing profitable from his perceptions," says Burton, describing the East African; and he adds that the African's mind "will not, and apparently cannot, escape from the circle of sense, nor will it occupy itself with aught but the present." Still more definite testimony is there respecting the Damara, "who never generalizes." Mr. Galton states that one "who knew the road perfectly from A to B and again from B to C would have no idea of a straight cut from A to C: he has no map of the country in his mind, but an infinity of local details." Even the Bedouin, as Mr. Palgrave remarks, "judges of things as he sees them present before him, not in their causes or consequences." Some semi-civilized peoples, as the Tahitians, Sandwich-Islanders, Javans, Sumatrans, Malagasy, do, indeed, manifest "quickness of apprehension, . . . penetration and sagacity." But it is in respect of simple things that their powers are shown; as witness the assertion of Mr. Ellis concerning the Malagasy, that "facts, anecdotes, occurrences, metaphors, or fables, relating to or derived from sensible and visible objects, appear to form the basis of most of their mental exercises." And how general is this trait of unreflectiveness among inferior races, is implied by Dr. Pickering's statement that, in the course of much travel, the Fijians were the only savage people he had met with who could give reasons, and with whom it was possible to hold a connected conversation.

§ 42. "The eccentricity of genius" is a current phrase implying the experience that men of original powers are prone to act in ways unlike ordinary ways. To do what the world does, is to guide behaviour by imitation. Deviating from ordinary usages is declining to imitate. And the noticeable fact is that a smaller tendency to imitate goes along with a greater tendency to evolve new ideas. Under its converse aspect we may trace this relationship back through early stages of civilization. There was but little originality in the middle ages; and there was but little tendency to deviate from the modes of living established for the various ranks. Still more was it so in the extinct societies of the East. Ideas were fixed; and prescription was irresistible.

Among the partially-civilized races, we find imitativeness a marked trait. Everyone has heard of the ways in which Negroes, when they have opportunities, dress and swagger in grotesque mimicry of the whites. A characteristic of the New Zealanders is an aptitude for imitation. The Dyaks, too, show "love of imitation;" and of other Malayo-Polynesians the like is alleged. Mason says that "while the Karens originate nothing they show as great a capability to imitate as the Chinese." We read that the Kamschadales have a "peculiar talent of mimicking men and animals;" that the Nootka-Sound people "are very ingenious in imitating;" that the Mountain Snake Indians imitate animal sounds "to the utmost perfection." South America yields like evidence. Herndon was astonished at the mimetic powers of the Brazilian Indians. Wilkes speaks of the Patagonians as "admirable mimics." And Dobrizhoffer joins with his remark that the Guaranis can imitate exactly, the further remark that they bungle stupidly if you leave anything to their intelligence. But it is among the lowest races that proneness to mimicry is most conspicuous. Several travellers have commented on the "extraordinary tendency to imitate" shown by the Fuegians. They will repeat with perfect correctness each word in any sentence addressed to them—mimicking the manner and attitude of the speaker. So, too, according to Mouat, the Andamanese show high imitative powers; and, like the Fuegians, repeat a question instead of answering it. Sturt gives a kindred account of the South Australians, who, he says, "evinced a strange perversity" "in repeating words" which "they knew were meant as questions."

In this imitativeness, shown least by the highest members of civilized races and most by the lowest savages, we see again the antagonism between perceptive activity and reflective activity. Among inferior gregarious creatures, as rooks that rise in a flock when one rises, or as sheep that follow a leader in leaping, we see an almost automatic repetition of actions witnessed in others; and this peculiarity, common to the lowest human types—this tendency to "ape" others, as we significantly call it—implies a smaller departure from the brute type of mind. It shows us a mental action which is, from moment to moment, chiefly determined by outer incidents; and is therefore but little determined by causes involving excursiveness of thought, imagination, and original idea.

§ 43. Our conception of the primitive man—intellectual, will grow clearer when, with the above inductions, we join illustrations of his feeble grasp of thought.

Common speech fails to distinguish between mental activities of different grades. A boy is called clever who takes in simple ideas rapidly, though he may prove incapable of taking in complex ideas; and a boy is condemned as stupid because he is slow in rote-learning, though he may apprehend abstract truths more quickly than his teacher. Contrasts of this nature must be recognized, if we would interpret the conflicting evidence respecting the capacities of the uncivilized. Even of the Fuegians we read that they "are not usually deficient in intellect;" even the Andamanese are described as "excessively quick and clever;" and the Australians are said to be as intelligent as our own peasants. But the ability thus referred to as possessed by men of the lowest types, is one for which the simpler faculties suffice; and goes along with inability when any demand is made on the complex faculties. A passage which Sir John Lubbock quotes from Mr. Sproat's account of the Ahts may be taken as descriptive of the average state:—

> "The native mind, to an educated man, seems generally to be asleep. . . . On his attention being fully aroused, he often shows much quickness in reply and ingenuity in argument. But a short conversation wearies him, particularly if questions are asked that require efforts of thought or memory on his part. The mind of the savage then appears to rock to and fro out of mere weakness."

Spix and Martius tell us of the Brazilian Indian that "scarcely has one begun to question him about his language, when he grows impatient, complains of headache, and shows that he is unable to bear the exertion;" and according to Mr. Bates, "it is difficult to get at their notions on subjects that require a little abstract thought." When the Abipones "are unable to comprehend anything at first sight, they soon grow weary of examining it, and cry—'What is it after all?'" It is the same with Negroes. Burton says of the East Africans, "ten minutes sufficed to weary out the most intellectual" when questioned about their system of numbers. And even of so comparatively superior a race as the Malagasy, it is remarked that they "do not seem to possess the qualities of mind requisite for close and continued thought."

On observing that to frame the idea of a species, say trout, it is needful to think of the characters common to trout of different sizes, and that to conceive of fish as a class, we must imagine various kinds of fish, and see mentally the likenesses which unite them notwithstanding their unlikenesses; we perceive that, rising from the consciousness of individual objects to the consciousness of species, and again to the consciousness of genera, and orders, and classes, each further step implies more power of mentally grouping numerous things with approximate simultaneity. And perceiving this, we may understand why, lacking the needful representativeness, the mind of the savage is soon exhausted with any thought above the simplest. Excluding those referring to individual objects, our most familiar propositions, such even as "Plants are green," or "Animals grow," are propositions never definitely framed in his consciousness; because he has no idea of a plant or an animal, apart from kind. And of course until he has become familiar with general ideas and abstract ideas of the lowest grades, those a grade higher in generality and abstractness are inconceivable by him. This will be elucidated by an illustration taken from Mr. Galton's account of the Damaras, showing how the concrete, made to serve in place of the abstract as far as possible, soon fails, and leaves the mind incapable of higher thought:—

> They puzzle very much after five [in counting], because no spare hand remains to grasp and secure the fingers that are required for units. Yet they seldom lose oxen; the way in which they discover the loss of one is not by the number of the herd being diminished, but by the absence of a face they know. When bartering is going on, each sheep must be paid for separately. Thus, suppose two sticks of tobacco to be the race of exchange for one sheep, it would sorely puzzle a Damara to take two sheep and give him four sticks."

This mental state is, in another direction, exemplified by the statement of Mr. Hodgson concerning the Hill-tribes of India. "Light," he says, "is a high abstraction which none of my informants can grasp, though they readily give equivalents for sunshine and candle or fire-flame." And Spix and Martius further exemplify it when they say that it would be vain to seek in the language of the Brazilian Indians "words for the abstract ideas of plant, animal, and the still more abstract notions, colour, tone, sex, species, etc.; such a generalization of ideas is found among them only in the frequently used infinitive of the verbs to walk, to eat, to drink, to dance, to sing, to hear, etc."

§ 44. Not until there is formed a general idea, by colligating many special ideas which have a common trait amid their differences—not until there follows the possibility of connecting in thought this common trait with some other trait also possessed in common, can there arise the idea of a causal relation; and not until many different causal relations have been observed, can there result the conception of causal relation in the abstract. By the primitive man, therefore, such distinction as we make between natural and unnatural cannot be made. Just as the child, ignorant of the course of things, gives credence to an impossible fiction as readily as to a familiar fact; so the savage, similarly without classified and systematized knowledge, feels no incongruity between any absurd falsehood propounded to him and some general truth which we class as established: there being, for him, no such established general truth.

Hence his credulity. If the young Indian takes as his totem, and thereafter regards as sacred, the first animal he dreams about during a fast—if the Negro, when bent on an important undertaking, chooses for a god to help him the first object he sees on going out, and sacrifices to it and prays to it—if the Veddah, failing in a shot with his arrow, ascribes the failure not to a bad aim but to insufficient propitiation of his deity; we must regard the implied convictions as normal accompaniments of a mental state in which the organization of experiences has not gone far enough to evolve the idea of natural causation.

§ 45. Absence of the idea of natural causation, implies absence of rational surprise.

Until there has been reached the belief that certain connexions in things are constant, there can be no astonishment on meeting with cases seemingly at variance with this belief. The behaviour of the uncultivated among ourselves teaches us this. Show to a rustic a remarkable experiment, such as the rise of liquid in a capillary tube, or the spontaneous boiling of warm water in an exhausted receiver, and instead of the amazement you expected he shows a vacant indifference. That which struck you with wonder when first you saw it, because apparently irreconcilable with your general ideas of physical processes, does not seem wonderful to him, because he is without those general ideas. And now if we suppose the rustic divested of what general ideas he has, and the causes of surprise thus made still fewer, we get the mental state of the primitive man.

Of the lowest races, disregard of novelties is almost uniformly alleged. According to Cook, the Fuegians showed utter indifference in presence of things that were entirely new to them. The same voyager observed in the Australians a like peculiarity; and Dampier says those he had on board "did not notice anything else in the ship" than what they had to eat. So, too, the Tasmanians were characterized by Cook's surgeon as exhibiting no surprise. Wallis asserts of the Patagonians, that they showed the most "unaccountable indifference" to everything around them on shipboard; even the looking-glass, though it afforded great diversion, excited no astonishment; and Wilkes describes like conduct. I also find it stated of the village Veddahs that two of them "showed no surprise at a looking-glass." And of the Samoiedes we read that "nothing but the looking-glasses caused any surprise in them for an instant; again a moment and this ceased to draw their attention."

§ 46. Along with absence of surprise there goes absence of curiosity; and where there is least faculty of thought, even astonishment may be excited without causing inquiry. Illustrating this trait in the Bushmen, Burchell says—"I showed them a looking-glass; at this they laughed, and stared with vacant surprise and wonder to see their own faces; but expressed not the least curiosity about it." Where curiosity exists we find it among races of not so low a grade. That of the New Caledonians was remarked by Cook; and that of the New Guinea people by Earl and by Jukes. Still more decided is an inquiring nature among the relatively-advanced Malayo-Polynesians. According to Boyle, the Dyaks have an insatiable curiosity. The Samoans, too, "are usually very inquisitive;" and the Tahitians "are remarkably curious and inquisitive."

Evidently this absence of desire for information about new things, which characterizes the lowest mental state, prevents the growth of that generalized knowledge which makes rational surprise, and consequent rational inquisitiveness, possible. If his "want of curiosity is extreme," as Mr. Bates says of the Cucáma Indian, the implication is that he "troubles himself very little concerning the causes of the natural phenomena around him." Lacking ability to think, and the accompanying desire to know, the savage is without tendency to speculate. Even when there is raised such a question as that often put by Park to the Negroes—"What became of the sun during the night, and whether we should see the same sun, or a different one, in the morning," no reply is forthcoming. "I found that they considered the question as very childish: . . . they had never indulged a conjecture, nor formed any hypothesis, about the matter."

The general fact thus exemplified is one quite at variance with current ideas respecting the thoughts of the primitive man. He is commonly pictured as theorizing about surrounding appearances; whereas, in fact, the need for explanations of them does not occur to him.

§ 47. One more general trait must be named—I mean the lack of constructive imagination. This lack naturally goes along with a life of simple perception, of imitativeness, of concrete ideas, and of incapacity for abstract ideas.

The collection of implements and weapons arranged by General Pitt-Rivers, to show their relationships to a common original, suggests that primitive men are not to be credited with such inventiveness as even their simple appliances seem to indicate. These have arisen by small modifications; and the natural selection of such modifications has led unobtrusively to various kinds of appliances, without any distinct devising of them.

Evidence of another kind, but of like meaning, is furnished by Sir Samuel Baker's paper on the "Races of the Nile Basin," in which he points out that the huts of the respective tribes are as constant in their types as are the nests of birds: each tribe of the one, like each species of the other, having a peculiarity. The like permanent differences he says hold among their head-dresses; and he further asserts of head-dresses, as of huts, that they have diverged from one another in proportion as the languages have diverged. All which facts show us that in these races the thoughts, restrained within narrow established courses, have not the freedom required for entering into new combinations, and so initiating new modes of action and new forms of product.

Where we find ingenuity ascribed, it is to races such as the Tahitians, Javans, etc., who have risen some stages in civilization, who have considerable stocks of abstract words and ideas, who show rational surprise and curiosity, and who thus evince higher intellectual development.

§ 48. Here we come to a general truth allied to those with which, in the two foregoing chapters, I have preluded the summaries of results—the truth that the primitive intellect develops rapidly, and early reaches its limit.

In the *Principles of Psychology*, § 165, I have shown that the children of Australians, of Negroes in the United States, of Negroes on the Nile, of Andamanese, of New Zealanders, of Sandwich Islanders, are quicker than European children in acquiring simple ideas, but presently stop short from inability to grasp the complex ideas readily grasped by European children, when they arrive at them. To testimonies before quoted I may add the remark of Mr. Reade, that in Equatorial Africa the children are "absurdly precocious;" the statement of Captain Burton, that "the negro child, like the East Indian, is much 'sharper' than the European . . . at the age of puberty this precocity . . . disappears;" and the description of the Aleuts of Alaska, who "up to a certain point are readily taught." This early cessation of development implies both low intellectual nature and a great impediment to intellectual advance; since it makes the larger part of life unmodifiable by further experiences. On reading of the East African, that he "unites the incapacity of infancy with the unpliancy of age," and of the Australians that "after twenty their mental vigour seems to decline, and at the age of forty seems nearly extinct;" we cannot fail to see how greatly this arrest of mental evolution hinders improvement where improvement is most required.

The intellectual traits of the uncivilized, thus made specially difficult to change, may now be recapitulated while observing that they are traits recurring in the children of the civilized.

Infancy shows us an absorption in sensations and perceptions akin to that which characterizes the savage. In pulling to pieces its toys, in making mudpies, in gazing at each new thing or person, the child exhibits great tendency to observe with little tendency to reflect.

There is, again, an obvious parallelism in the mimetic propensity. Children are ever dramatizing the lives of adults; and savages, along with their other mimicries, similarly dramatize the actions of their civilized visitors.

Want of power to discriminate between useless and useful facts, characterizes the juvenile mind, as it does the mind of the primitive man. This inability to select nutritive facts necessarily accompanies low development; since, until generalization has made some progress, and the habit of generalizing has become established, there cannot be reached the conception that a fact has a remote value apart from any immediate value it may have.

Again, we see in the young of our own race a similar inability to concentrate the attention on anything complex or abstract. The mind of the child, as well as that of the savage, soon wanders from sheer exhaustion when generalities and involved propositions have to be dealt with.

From feebleness of the higher intellectual faculties comes, in both cases, an absence, or a paucity, of ideas grasped by those faculties. The child, like the savage, has few words of even a low grade of abstractedness, and none of a higher grade. For a long time it is familiar with cat, dog, horse, cow, but has no conception of animal apart from kind; and years elapse before words ending in *ion* and *ity* occur in its vocabulary. Thus, in both cases, the very implements of developed thought are wanting.

Unsupplied as its mind is with general truths, and with the conception of natural order, the civilized child when quite young, like the savage throughout life, shows but little rational surprise or rational curiosity. Something startling to the senses makes it stare vacantly, or perhaps cry; but let it see a chemical experiment, or draw its attention to the behaviour of a gyroscope, and its interest is like that shown in a common-place new toy. After a time, indeed, when the higher intellectual powers it inherits are beginning to act, and when its stage of mental development represents that of such semi-civilized races as the Malayo-Polynesians, rational surprise and rational curiosity about causes, begin to show themselves. But even then its extreme credulity, like that of the savage, shows us the result of undeveloped ideas of causation and law. Any story, however monstrous, is believed; and any explanation, however absurd, is accepted.

And here, in final elucidation of these intellectual traits of the primitive man, let me point out that, like the emotional traits, they could not be other than they are in the absence of the conditions brought about by social evolution. In the *Principles of Psychology*, §§ 484—493, it was shown in various ways that only as societies grow, become organized, and gain stability, do there arise those experiences by assimilating which the powers of thought develop. It needs but to ask what would happen to ourselves were the whole mass of existing knowledge obliterated, and were children with nothing beyond their nursery-language left to grow up without guidance or instruction from adults, to perceive that even now the higher intellectual faculties would be almost inoperative, from lack of the materials and aids accumulated by past civilization. And seeing this, we cannot fail to see that development of the higher intellectual faculties has gone on *pari passu* with social advance, alike as cause and consequence; that the primitive man could not evolve these higher intellectual faculties in the absence of a fit environment; and that in this, as in other respects, his progress was retarded by the absence of capacities which only progress could bring.

SOURCE: Chapter 7 in *Principles of Sociology*, vol. 1 (1906; Osnabrück, Germany: Otto Zeller, 1966), 73–91.

The Principles of the Relations of Our
Civilization to the Tropics
BENJAMIN KIDD

In any forecast of the future of our civilization, one of the most important of the questions presenting themselves for consideration is that of the future relationship of the European peoples to what are called the lower races. Probably one of the most remarkable features of the world-wide expansion the European peoples are undergoing will be the change that this relationship is destined to undergo in the near future. In estimates which have been hitherto made of our coming relations to the coloured races, a factor which will in all probability completely dominate the situation in the future has received scarcely any attention.

The relationships of the Western peoples to the inferior races, with which they have come into contact in the course of the expansion they have undergone, is one of the most interesting subjects in history. Confused though these relationships may appear, it may be distinguished that they have passed through certain well-marked stages of development. We must set aside, as being outside our present field of vision, those races which have inhabited countries suitable for European colonization. The fate of all races occupying territories of this kind has been identical. Whether wars of extermination have been waged against them, or whether they have been well treated and admitted to citizenship, they have always tended to disappear before the more vigorous incoming race. It is with the inhabitants of regions unsuitable for European settlement, and mostly outside the temperate zone, that we are concerned.

The alteration observable in our relations to these races since the sixteenth and seventeenth centuries has been very gradual, but its general character is unmistakable. During the sixteenth, seventeenth, and eighteenth centuries, a great part of the richest regions in the tropical countries of the earth passed under the dominion of the four great sea powers of Western Europe—Spain,

Holland, France, and England have successively engaged in the keenest rivalry for the possession of vast regions of this kind, unsuitable for permanent colonization, but possessing rich natural resources. The general idea which lay behind this extension of dominion was in the main that of military conquest. The territories of the weaker peoples were invaded, taken possession of, and exploited for the benefit of the more vigorous invader. The interests of the original occupiers were little, if at all, regarded. The main end in view was the immediate profit and advantage of the conquerors. In the West India Islands the native population was worked in the mines and the plantations until it became in great part extinct, and the Spaniards began to introduce negroes from Africa. Operations were conducted on so great a scale that in the 20 years before the opening of the eighteenth century 300,000 slaves were exported from Africa by the English, and in the 80 years which followed, over 600,000 slaves were landed in the Island of Jamaica alone. Slave labour was employed to an enormous extent in most of the countries of which possession was obtained. The natural resources of the territories occupied were, however, developed to a considerable degree. The enormous wealth which Spain drew from her conquests and undertakings in tropical America was long a very powerful factor in the wars and politics of Europe: Holland, France, and England also enriched themselves both directly and indirectly. In the Spanish, Dutch, and English settlements and plantations in the eastern hemisphere, and in those in the West Indies and South America, under Spanish, Dutch, French, and English rule, great enterprises in trade, agriculture, and mining were successfully undertaken. Order and government were introduced, and large cities sprung up rivalling European cities in size and magnificence. This first period was one of feverish activity, and of universal desire on the part of the invaders to quickly enrich themselves. There was much cruelty to weaker races, and although all the powers were not equally guilty in this respect, none, at least, were innocent. But looking at the period as a whole, and regarding the enterprises undertaken in their true light,—namely, as an attempt to develop, by forced coloured labour under European supervision, the resources of countries not suitable for European settlement,—a certain degree of success must be admitted to have been attained, and the enterprises undoubtedly contributed to increase, for the time being, the material wealth and resources of the powers concerned.

Towards the end of the eighteenth century the tendency of the change that was taking place began to be visible. It had become clear that the European peoples could not hope to settle permanently in the tropical lands they had occupied, and that, if the resources were to be developed, it must be by native labour under their supervision. Already, however, the effects of the altruistic development which had been so long in progress were becoming generally evident, and before the opening of the nineteenth century men had glimpses of the nature of the social revolution it was eventually to accomplish in our civilization. The institution of slavery in tropical lands under European auspices was clearly doomed. So also, to the more far-reaching minds, seemed another institution upon which depended, to all appearance, the continued maintenance of European enterprise and European authority in lands not suitable for the permanent settlement of the Western races.

The right of occupation and government in virtue of conquest or force tended, it was felt, to become an anachronism; it was antagonistic to, and it involved a denial of, the spirit which constituted the mainspring of that onward movement which was taking place in our civilization, and which was slowly bringing the people into the rivalry of life on conditions of equality. Although almost every European people, that had attained to any consciousness of national strength, had in the past endeavoured to imitate the military ideals of the ancient empires, and to extend their rule by conquest over other peoples of equal civilization, they had done so with ever-diminishing success. The growth of influences and conditions tending to render the realization of such aims more and more difficult was unmistakable. Any nation which would embark upon such an enterprise, on a great scale and against a European people, would, it was felt, find in the near future forces arrayed against it of which the ancient world had no experience, and which no military skill, however great, and no national strength and resolution, however concentrated and prolonged, could entirely subdue. To keep in subjection, therefore, by purely military force a people of even greatly lower development must, it was felt, become correspondingly difficult; and this, not so much because of the fear of effective resistance in a military sense, but because of the lack of moral force on the part of the stronger peoples to initiate an effort involving a principle antagonistic to the spirit governing the development which these peoples were themselves undergoing.

Throughout the early and middle decades of the nineteenth century we have, therefore, to watch the development of this spirit and the effects it produced. Before the close of the eighteenth century the agitation against the slave-trade in the colonies had assumed large proportions. In England a motion was carried in the House of Commons in 1792, providing for the gradual abolition of the traffic. In 1794 the French Convention decreed that all slaves throughout the French colonies should be admitted to the rights of French citizens; and, although slavery did not cease in the French dominions for some fifty years after, the Convention in this as in other matters only anticipated the future. The agitation in England against the slave-trade having been largely successful, the feeling against the employment of slaves continued to grow in strength until an Act was at length obtained in 1834, finally abolishing slavery in the British settlements, the slave-owners being awarded £20,000,000 as indemnification. The negroes in the French settlements were emancipated in 1848, those in the Dutch colonies in 1863; while the slaves in the Southern States of the American Union obtained their freedom as the result of the Civil War of 1862–65.

Meanwhile the growth of the other influence tending to undermine the position of the European races in the tropical countries they had occupied had continued. By the end of the eighteenth century the coloured races of Hayti, under the influence of the ideas of the French Revolution, had thrown off the rule of France. Before the first quarter of the nineteenth century had passed away the Spanish territories of Central and South America—often still spoken of as if they were inhabited by Europeans, although in most of which, it must be remembered, the vast bulk of the population consists of native Indians, imported negroes, and mixed races—had, one after another, declared their independence of European rule. It came to be looked upon as only natural and inevitable that it should be so; and it was held to be only a question of time for the Dutch possessions and the remaining Spanish settlements to follow suit. The English settlements in the West Indies, it was supposed, would become independent too. They came to be regarded as being as good as gone. We have Mr. Froude's word for it that he had it on high official authority, about 1860, that all preparations for the transition had been already made. "A decision had been irrevocably taken. The troops were to be withdrawn from the Islands, and Jamaica, Trinidad, and the English Antilles were to be masters of their own destiny." The withdrawal did not take place, but the general feeling in the minds of politicians in England at the time was undoubtedly such as might have prompted such a decision.

If we turn now to the condition of affairs accompanying these events in the countries in question, we have presented to us what is probably one of the most extraordinary spectacles the world has beheld. The enterprise that once attempted to develop the resources of the countries concerned, has been to a large extent interrupted. Regarding the West Indies first, we have to note that their former prosperity has waned. The black races under the new order of things have multiplied exceedingly. Where left to themselves under British rule, whether with or without the political institutions of the advanced European peoples, they have not developed the natural resources of the rich and fertile lands they have inherited. Nor do they show any desire to undertake the task. The descriptions we have had presented to us for many years past by writers and politicians of some of the West India Islands read like accounts of a former civilization. Decaying harbours, once crowded with shipping; ruined wharves, once busy with commerce; roofless warehouses; stately buildings falling to ruins and overgrown with tropical creepers; deserted mines and advancing forests,—these are some of the signs of the change. In Hayti, where the blacks have been independent of European control for the greater part of a century, we have even a more gloomy picture. Revolution has succeeded revolution, often accompanied by revolting crime; under the outward forms of European government every form of corruption and license has prevailed; its commerce has been more than once almost extinguished by its political revolutions; the resources of the country remain undeveloped; intercourse with white races is not encouraged, and the Black Republic, instead of advancing, is said to be drifting slowly backwards.

Turning to the mainland of Central America and the vast territories embraced in tropical South America, once under the rule of the Spaniards and Portuguese, the spectacle is in some respects more noteworthy. In this expanse, which includes over three-fourths of the entire continental area south of the territory of the United States, we have one of the richest regions of the earth. Under the outward forms of European government it appears, however, to be slowly drifting out of our civilization. The habit has largely obtained amongst us of thinking of these countries as inhabited by European races and as included in our Western civilization;—a habit doubtless due to the tendency to regard them as colonies of European powers which have become independent after the manner of the United States. As a matter of fact this view has little to justify it. In the republics comprising the territory in question, considerably over three-fourths of the entire population are descendants of the original Indian inhabitants, or imported negroes, or mixed races. The pure white population appears to be unable to maintain itself for more than a limited number of generations without recruiting itself from the outside. It is a gradually diminishing element, tending to ally itself to an increasing degree with "colour." Both for climatic reasons, and in obedience to the general law of population already noticed, by which the upper strata of society (to which the white population for the most part belongs) are unable to maintain themselves apart for any considerable period, we must, apparently, look forward to the time when these territories will be almost exclusively peopled by the Black and Indian races.

Meanwhile the resources of this large region remain almost undeveloped or run to waste. During the past fifty years, the European powers may be said to have endeavoured to develop them in a manner that apparently promised to be advantageous to both parties, and not inconsistent with the spirit of the new altruistic ideas which have come to govern men's minds. Since the period of their independence, immense sums have been borrowed by the republics of central and northern South America, with the object of developing their resources, and large amounts have also been invested by private persons in public enterprises undertaken by Europeans in these countries. But the general prevalence of those qualities which distinguish peoples of low social efficiency has been like a blight over the whole region. In nearly all the republics in question, the history of government has been the same. Under the outward forms of written laws and constitutions of the most exemplary character, they have displayed a general absence of that sense of public and private duty which has always distinguished peoples who have reached a state of high social development. Corruption in all departments of the government, insolvency, bankruptcy, and political revolutions succeeding each other at short intervals have become almost the normal incidents of public life—the accompanying features being a permanent state of uncertainty, lack of energy and enterprise amongst the people, and general commercial stagnation. Much of the territory occupied by these states is amongst the richest in the world in natural resources. Yet we seem to have reached a stage in which the enterprise of the Western races is almost as effectively excluded therefrom, or circumscribed therein, as in the case of China. Not, however, through any spirit of exclusiveness in the people or desire to develop these resources themselves, but by, on the one hand, the lack in the inhabitants of qualities contributing to social efficiency, and, on the other, by the ascendency in the minds of the Western peoples of that altruistic spirit which, except in a clear case of duty or necessity, deprives any attempt to assume by force the government and administration of the resources of other peoples of the moral force necessary to ensure its success.

Now it would appear probable that we have, in the present peculiar relationship of the Western peoples to the coloured races, the features of a transition of great interest and importance, the nature of which is, as yet, hardly understood. It is evident that, despite the greater consideration now shown for the rights of the lower races, there can be no question as to the absolute ascendency in the world to-day of the Western peoples and of Western civilization. There has been no period in history when this ascendency has been so unquestionable and so complete as in the time in which we are living. No one can doubt that it is within the power of the leading European people of to-day—should they so desire—to parcel out the entire equatorial regions of the earth into a series of satrapies, and to administer their resources, not as in the past by a permanently resident population, but from the temperate regions, and under the direction of a relatively small European official population. And this without any fear of effective resistance from the inhabitants.

Always, however, assuming that there existed a clear call of duty or necessity to provide the moral force necessary for such action.

It is this last stipulation which it is all-important to remember in any attempt which is made to estimate the probable course of events in the future. For it removes at once the centre of interest and observation to the lands occupied by the European peoples. It is, in short, in the development in progress amongst these peoples, and not in the events taking place to-day in lands occupied by the black and coloured races; that we must seek for the controlling factor in the immediate future of the tropical regions of the world.

Now, stress has been laid, in the preceding chapters, on the fact that we have, in the altruistic development that has been slowly taking place amongst the European peoples, the clue to the efficiency of our civilization. It is this development which—by its influence in breaking down an earlier organization of society, and by its tendency to bring, for the first time in the history of the race, all the people into the rivalry of life on a footing of equality of opportunity—has raised our Western civilization to its present position of ascendency in the world. It must be always remembered, however, that a principal cause operating in producing it has been the doctrine peculiar to the ethical system upon which our civilization is founded—the doctrine, steadfastly and uncompromisingly held, of the native equality of all men. So great has been the resistance to be overcome, so exceptional in the history of the race has been the nature of the process of expansion through which we have passed, that only a doctrine held as this has been, and supported by the tremendous sanctions behind it, could have effected so great a social transformation. Of such importance has been the character of this process, and so strong has been the social instinct that has recognized its vital significance to the Western peoples themselves, that everything has gone down before the doctrine which produced it. It is this doctrine which has raised the negro in the Southern States of North America to the rank of citizen of the United States, despite the incongruous position which he now occupies in that country. It is before this doctrine (because of its predominant importance to ourselves), and not before the coloured races, that the European peoples have retreated in those tropical lands which, being unsuitable for colonization, could have been ruled and developed only under a system of military occupation.

We must, therefore, in any attempt to estimate our future relationship to the coloured races outside the temperate regions, keep clearly in mind the hitherto supreme importance to the Western peoples of this altruistic development, and, therefore, of the doctrine of the native equality of men which has accompanied it.

Now, there are two great events which will, in all probability, fill a great part in the history of the twentieth century. The first will be the accomplishment, amongst the Western peoples, of the last stage of that process of social development which tends to bring all the people into the rivalry of life on conditions of social equality. The other will be the final filling up, by these peoples, of all those tracts in the temperate regions of the earth suitable for permanent occupation. As both these processes tend towards completion, it would appear that we must expect our present relationship towards the coloured races occupying territories outside the temperate zones to undergo further development. With the completion of that process of social evolution in which the doctrine of the native equality of men has played so important a part,—and, therefore, with the probable modification of that instinct which has hitherto recognized the vital necessity to ourselves of maintaining this doctrine in its most uncompromising form,—it seems probable that there must arise a tendency to scrutinize more closely the existing differences between ourselves and the coloured races, as regards the qualities contributing to social efficiency; this tendency being accompanied by a disposition to relax our hitherto prevalent opinion that the doctrine of equality requires us to shut our eyes to those differences where political relations are concerned.

As the growth of this feeling will be coincident with the filling up to the full limit of the remaining territories suitable for European occupation, and the growing pressure of population therein, it may be expected that the inexpediency of allowing a great extent of territory in the richest region of the globe—that comprised within the tropics—to remain undeveloped, with its resources running largely to waste under the management of races of low social efficiency, will be brought home, with ever-growing force, to the minds of the Western peoples. The day is probably not far distant when, with the advance science is making, we shall recognize that it is in the tropics, and not in the temperate zones, that we have the greatest food-producing and material-producing regions of the earth; that the natural highways of commerce in the world should be those which run north and south; and that we have the highest possible interest in the proper development and efficient administration of the tropical regions, and in an exchange of products therewith on a far larger scale than has been yet attempted or imagined.

The question that will, therefore, present itself for solution will be: How is the development and efficient administration of these regions to be secured? The ethical development that has taken place in our civilization has rendered the experiment, once made to develop their resources by forced native labour, no longer possible, or permissible, even if possible. We have already abandoned, under pressure of experience, the idea, which at one time prevailed, that the tropical regions might be occupied, and permanently colonized by European races, as vast regions in the temperate climes have been. Within a measurable period in the future, and under pressure of experience, we shall probably also have to abandon the idea which has in like manner prevailed for a time, that the coloured races left to themselves possess the qualities necessary to the development of the rich resources of the lands they have inherited. For, a clearer insight into the laws that have shaped the course of human evolution must bring us to see that the process which has gradually developed the energy, enterprise, and social efficiency of the race northwards, and which has left less richly endowed in this respect the peoples inhabiting the regions where the conditions of life are easiest, is no passing accident or the result of circumstances changeable at will, but part of the cosmic order of things which we have no power to alter.

It would seem that the solution which must develop itself under pressure of circumstances in the future is, that the European races will gradually come to realize that the tropics must be administered from the temperate regions. There is no insurmountable difficulty in the task. Even now all that is required to ensure its success is a clearly defined conception of moral necessity. This, it would seem, must come under the conditions referred to, when the energetic races of the world, having completed the colonization of the temperate regions, are met with the spectacle of the resources of the richest regions of the earth still running largely to waste under inefficient management.

In discussing the present condition of the tropical regions of America no reference was made to the experiment which, in the corresponding regions of the eastern hemisphere, has been taking place under British rule in India. For the past half-century the relationship existing between England and India has been the cause of considerable heart-searching and conflict of opinion amongst politicians of the more advanced school in England. The means whereby a footing was at first obtained in that country had little to distinguish them from those already mentioned which led the European races at one time to occupy vast territories in tropical regions. In the altruistic development of the nineteenth century which has so profoundly affected the relationships of the European peoples to other races, it has come to be felt by many politicians that the position of Great Britain in India involved a denial of the spirit actuating the advanced peoples, and that it tended to become in consequence morally indefensible. This was undoubtedly the feeling in the minds of a considerable section of persons in England at no distant date in the past.

Nevertheless, as time has gone by, other features of the position have pressed themselves with growing force upon the minds of the British people. Exceptionally influenced as the British nation has been by the altruistic spirit underlying our civilization, its administration of the Indian peninsula has never been marked by those features which distinguished Spanish rule in the American Continent. English rule has tended more and more to involve the conscientious discharge of the duties of our position towards the native races. We have respected their rights, their ideas, their religions, and even their independence to the utmost extent compatible with the efficient administration of the government of the country.

The result has been remarkable. There has been for long in progress in India a steady development of the resources of the country which cannot be paralleled in any other tropical region of the world. Public works on the most extensive scale and of the most permanent character have been undertaken and completed; roads and bridges have been built; mining and agriculture have been developed; irrigation works, which have added considerably to the fertility and resources of large tracts of country, have been constructed; even sanitary reform is beginning to make considerable progress. European enterprise too, attracted by security and integrity in the government, has been active. Railways have been gradually extended over the Peninsula. Indian tea, almost unknown a short time ago, has, through the planting and cultivation of suitable districts under European supervision, already come into serious competition with the Chinese article in the markets of the world. The cotton industry of India has already entered on friendly rivalry with that of Lancashire. Other industries, suited to the conditions of the country, are in like manner rising into prominence, without any kind of artificial protection or encouragement; the only contribution of the ruling powers to their welfare being the guarantee of social order and the maintenance of the conditions of efficiency and integrity in the administration of the departments of government.

The commerce of the country has expanded in a still more striking manner. In the largest open market in the world, that which Great Britain provides, India now stands third on the list as contributor of produce, ranking only below the United States and France, and above Germany and all the British Australian colonies together. She takes, too, as much as she gives, for her exports to and imports from the United Kingdom nearly balance each other. In the character of importer she is, indeed, the largest of all the customers of Great Britain, the Australasian colonies and the United States coming after her on the list. This exchange of products has all the appearance of being as profitable as it is creditable to both parties concerned.

Very different, too, is the spirit animating both sides in this development of the resources of India as compared with that which prevailed in past times. There is no question now of the ruling race merely exploiting India to their own selfish advantage. Great Britain desires to share in the prosperity she has assisted in creating, it is true; but, for the most part, she shares indirectly and in participation with the rest of the world. India sends her products to British markets, but she is equally free to send them elsewhere. As her development proceeds she offers a larger market for the products of British industries; but England has reserved to herself no exclusive advantages in Indian markets. Under the principle of free trade all the rest of the world may compete with her on equal terms in those markets. Her gain tends to be a gain, not only to India, but to civilization in general.

The object-lesson that all this has afforded has not been without its effect on English public opinion—an effect which deepens as the true nature of the relationship existing between the two countries is more generally understood. Nor is there lack of similar experiences elsewhere. The work undertaken by France in Algeria and Tunis, although it has differed in many important respects from that performed by Great Britain in India, and although it has been undoubtedly more directly inspired by the thought of immediate benefit to French interests, has been on the whole, it must be frankly confessed, work done in the cause of civilization in general. Within the past decade we have had a more striking lesson still in the case of Egypt. Some seventeen years ago that country, although within sight of, and in actual contact with, European civilization, had reached a condition of disaster through misgovernment, extravagance, and oppression without example, as a recent writer, who speaks with authority, has insisted, "in the financial history of any country from the remotest ages to the present time." Within thirteen years the public debt of a country of only 6,000,000 inhabitants had been increased from 3,000,000 to 89,000,000, or nearly thirty-fold. With a submissive population, a corrupt bureaucracy, and a reckless, ambitious, and voluptuous ruler, surrounded by adventurers of every kind, we had all the elements of national bankruptcy and ruin. Things drifted from bad to worse, but it was felt that nothing could be more at variance, theoretically, with the principles of the Liberal party then in power in England, than active interference by the English people in the affairs of that country. Yet within a few years circumstances had proved stronger than prevailing views, and England found herself most unwillingly compelled to interfere by force in the government of Egypt; and obliged to attempt, in the administration of its affairs, what, in the peculiar conditions prevailing, appeared to be one of the most hopeless, difficult, and thankless tasks ever undertaken by a nation.

Yet the results have been most striking. Within a few years the country had emerged from a condition of chronic and apparently hopeless bankruptcy, and attained to a position of solvency, with a revenue tending to outrun expenditure. Great improvements in the administration of the state departments had been effected. Public works which have greatly contributed to the prosperity of the country had been completed. The Kurbash had been suppressed; the Corvée had been reduced; the Barrage had been repaired; the native administration of justice had been improved. Under an improved system of irrigation the area of land won from the desert for cultivation was enormously increased. The cotton crop, representing one-third of the entire agricultural wealth of the country, had increased 50 per cent in a few years. The foreign trade increased to the highest point it had ever attained; and the credit of the country so far improved that within nine years the price of its Unified stock had risen from 59 to 98.

All these results were attained by simple means; by the exercise of qualities which are not usually counted either brilliant or intellectual, but which nevertheless are, above all others, characteristic of peoples capable of attaining a high degree of social efficiency, and of those peoples only. British influence in Egypt, Mr. Milner maintains, "is not exercised to impose an uncongenial foreign system upon a reluctant people. It is a force making for the triumph of the simplest ideas of honesty, humanity, and justice, to the value of which Egyptians are just as much alive as any one else."

Nor can it be said that Great Britain has exploited Egypt in her own interest, or obtained any exclusive advantage by the development of the resources of the country. It is true that she does benefit, and benefit considerably, by the improvement which has followed. But it is in the same manner as in India. For, says Mr. Milner, "the improvement of Egyptian administration leads directly to the revival of Egyptian trade, and in that increase, England, who has more than half the trade of Egypt in her hands, possesses a direct interest of the most unmistakable kind. Our own country does thus, after all, obtain a recompense, and a recompense at once most substantial and most honourable for any sacrifices she may make for Egypt. She gains, not at the expense of others, but along with others. If she is the greatest gainer, it is simply because she is the largest partner in the business." But "neither directly nor indirectly has Great Britain drawn from her predominant position any profit at the expense of other nations." Her gain is there also the gain of civilization.

It is to be expected that as time goes on, and an approach is made to the conditions before mentioned, such object-lessons as these will not be without their effect on the minds of the European races. It will probably come to be recognized that experiments in developing the resources of regions unsuitable for European colonization, such as that now in progress in India, differ essentially both in character and in spirit from all past attempts. It will probably be made clear, and that at no distant date, that the last thing our civilization is likely to permanently tolerate is the wasting of the resources of the richest regions of the earth through the lack of the elementary qualities of social efficiency in the races possessing them. The right of those races to remain in possession will be recognized; but it will be no part of the future conditions of such recognition that they shall be allowed to prevent the utilization of the immense natural resources which they have in charge. At no remote date, with the means at the disposal of our civilization, the development of these resources must become one of the most pressing and vital questions engaging the attention of the Western races. The advanced societies have, to some extent, already intuitively perceived the nature of the coming change. We have evidence of a general feeling, which recognizes the immense future importance of the tropical regions of the earth to the energetic races, in that partition of Africa amongst the European powers which forms one of the most remarkable signs of the times at the end of the nineteenth century. The same feeling may be perceived even in the United States, where the necessity for the future predominance of the influence of the English-speaking peoples over the American Continents is already recognized by a kind of national instinct that may be expected to find clearer expression as time goes on.

Lastly, it will materially help towards the solution of this and other difficult problems, if we are in a position, as it appears we shall be, to say with greater clearness in the future, than we have been able to do in the past, what it is constitutes superiority and inferiority of race. We shall probably have to set aside many of our old ideas on the subject. Neither in respect alone of colour, nor of descent, nor even of the possession of high intellectual capacity, can science give us any warrant for speaking of one race as superior to another. The evolution which man is undergoing is, over and above everything else, a social evolution. There is, therefore, but one absolute test of superiority. It is only the race possessing in the highest degree the qualities contributing to social efficiency that can be recognized as having any claim to superiority.

But these qualities are not as a rule of the brilliant order, nor such as strike the imagination. Occupying a high place amongst them are such characteristics as strength and energy of character, humanity, probity and integrity, and simple-minded devotion to conceptions of duty in such circumstances as may arise. Those who incline to attribute the very wide influence which the English-speaking peoples have come to exercise in the world to the Machiavellian schemes of their rulers are often very wide of the truth. This influence is, to a large extent, due to qualities not at all of a showy character. It is, for instance, a fact of more than superficial significance, and one worth remembering, that in the South American Republics, where the British peoples move amongst a mixed crowd of many nationalities, the quality which has come to be accepted as distinctive of them is simply "the word of an Englishman." In like manner it is qualities such as humanity, strength, and uprightness of character, and devotion to the immediate calls of duty without thought of brilliant ends and ideal results, which have largely contributed to render English rule in India successful when similar experiments elsewhere have been disastrous. It is to the exercise of qualities of this class that we must also chiefly attribute the success which has so far attended the political experiment of extraordinary difficulty which England has undertaken in Egypt. And it is upon just the same qualities, and not upon any ideal schemes for solving the social problem, that we must depend to carry us safely through the social revolution which will be upon us in the twentieth century, and which will put to the most severe test which it has yet had to endure, the social efficiency of the various sections of the Western peoples.

It must be noticed that the conclusion here emphasized is the same towards which the historian with the methods hitherto at his command has been already slowly feeling his way. Said Mr. Lecky recently, speaking of the prosperity of nations, and the causes thereof as indicated by history: "Its foundation is laid in pure domestic life, in commercial integrity, in a high standard of moral worth and of public spirit, in simple habits, in courage, uprightness, and a certain soundness and moderation of judgment which springs quite as much from character as from intellect. If you would form a wise judgment of the future of a nation, observe carefully whether these qualities are increasing or decaying. Observe especially what qualities count for most in public life. Is character becoming of greater or less importance? Are the men who obtain the highest posts in the nation, men of whom in private life, and irrespective of party, competent judges speak with genuine respect? Are they of sincere convictions, consistent lives, indisputable integrity? . . . It is by observing this moral current that you can best cast the horoscope of a nation."

This is the utterance of that department of knowledge which, sooner or later, when its true foundations are perceived, must become the greatest of all the sciences. It is but the still, small voice which anticipates the verdict which will be pronounced with larger knowledge, and in more emphatic terms, by evolutionary science, when at no distant date it must enable us, as we have never been enabled before, "to look beyond the smoke and turmoil of our petty quarrels, and to detect, in the slow developments of the past, the great permanent forces that are steadily bearing nations onward to improvement or decay."

SOURCE: Appendix to *The Control of the Tropics* (New York: Macmillan Company, 1898), 63–101. Benjamin Kidd was born in 1858 and died in 1916.

———

Excerpts from *Kafir Socialism*
DUDLEY KIDD

PREFACE

Racial questions, democratic ideals, and the problems of Socialism are in the air. The world is filling up fast, and aggregates, whether of nations, races or classes, are now being sifted drastically by the process of natural selection. Aristocracies, majorities, and minorities, whether of races or classes, seem to have entered on the acute stage of their probation. No matter where we turn, whether to South Africa with its Boer and Native problems, to America with its Negro and Japanese difficulties, to Russia with its nightmare, to India and Egypt with their agitations for self-government, to the Balkans with its tangle, to the Congo with its struggles and tragedies amid primæval forests, to Australia with its fear of Kanakas and Japanese, to Mohammedans with their aspirations for Pan-Islamism, to Asia in its awakening, or to Europe with its rising tide of Democracy and Socialism, we are face to face with the struggle for existence that is taking place between groups of men that are fighting for very life. In the case of races and classes, just as in the case of individuals, those that are the most efficient in their adaptation to environment, and not those that simply give expression to the loftiest sentiment, will survive and dominate all rivals; while the weak and inefficient will go to the wall.

We shall be occupied in these pages with but a single race; though the future of the Kafir, and our duty to him, will take us into several fields of thought. The present volume deals with but one aspect of the Native Problem, namely, the conflict of Western conceptions of Individualism with the ingrained Socialism of the Kafir. This aspect of the problem is isolated for several reasons.

In the first place, no treatment of all the aspects of the Native Problem can hope to be altogether satisfactory unless it takes the form of a symposium in which experts in native thought, economics, politics, education, and missions combine to present the various aspects of this many-sided problem. There seems to be no person who possesses all the qualities necessary for such a work.

In the second place, so far as I know—and I think I have read every book that has been written on the subject—the very existence of the above-mentioned aspect of the problem has not even been recognized by any previous writer.

In the third place, the conflict of European Individualism with Kafir Socialism constitutes the very heart of the problem. No one has written more wisely about the Native Problem than Mr. Colquhoun; and yet he not only failed to recognise the existence of this conflict of Socialism and Individualism, but has actually stated that the socialistic ideal is a conception that cannot possibly take hold of the Kafir. I shall quote presently the actual words used by Mr. Colquhoun; and hope to prove that, so far from being alien to native thought, Socialistic ideals affect almost every conception of the Kafirs, giving colour and form even to their ideas about such widely different things as justice and witchcraft.

There is a further and final reason for not attempting a complete discussion of the Native Problem. It is a most unsuitable time to make such an attempt, because the present Liberal Government, by reserving the affairs of the Kafirs in the Transvaal and Orange River Colony for its own special care, and by interfering in the native affairs of Natal, is virtually stifling discussion; for what colonist cares to waste his time in presenting a reasoned statement of his views concerning a thousand details of administration when he has every reason for feeling certain that the Party that meditates interference in the domestic affairs of South Africa will be guided, not by facts and sound sense, but by the uninformed sentiment of "moral experts"?

For the above reasons—and assured that Home interference is the transient whim of a political clique rather than the settled will of the people—I have decided to make this volume simply an introduction to, and not a detailed study of, the Native Problem. The native point of view, which I have sought to explain, is of great importance, though it is not the only point of view. Unless we clearly understand native conceptions and ideals, we shall but reckon without our host.

In South Africa we are all aware that we are building up our commercial, industrial, political and social structure at the foot of a volcano; but like all Pompeians, we have become so accustomed to the manifold dangers of the situation that we do not worry very much about our Vesuvius. Every now and then we feel some very disquieting and ominous rumblings beneath our feet, and occasionally see a flash of fire and a puff of smoke, and feel a few ashes falling on our heads; but the anxiety soon wears off; officials assure us that the natives are quiet again; and every one goes about his work as though there were no danger brewing. The problem is so many-sided and complicated that most of us are content to postpone all serious consideration of the subject. We talk about the natives in vague terms, for most of us know but little about the inscrutable Kafirs. There are comparatively few people who have any first-hand and intimate knowledge of the *kraal-life* of the natives; and so most of us are content to accept the many floating, commonplace statements that abound in our towns and villages. Opinion takes the place of knowledge, and we are apt to adopt a sort of nonchalant optimism based on our national reputation of muddling through most of our difficulties. The law-abiding nature of the Kafir tends to confirm us in the delusion that the natives are reconciled to a rule which we know to be just and fair.

As the result of this attitude towards the subject, the ground is simply littered with half-truths, and with antiquated though inveterate prejudices. The Kafir that the average white man knows is the semi-civilised barbarian who has suffered from the degenerative influences of civilisation in our centres of industry, on our farms, or in domestic service. The visitor to South Africa picks up some specious and delusive myths about such Kafirs, and if he should write a book, he can scarcely resist the temptation to give the most picturesque of these half-truths a fresh lease of life, a wider currency, and an additional distortion due to his imperfect understanding of a strange and alien race. From the nature of the case, it is impossible even for the globe-trotting Member of Parliament to get to the heart of a racial problem in a visit, the brevity of which makes it impossible for the out-of-the-way Kafir kraals to be visited. Yet the writer feels bound to spatchcock into his book a chapter dealing with the subject. It is no cause for wonder that Home criticism should so often be wide of the mark, and that the most ludicrous suggestions should from time to time appear in the Press, or should be proposed in the House of Commons.

In addition to these sources of information, we have some valuable Blue Books—studies in the anatomy of the subject—that only few people seem to read until the contents are boiled down into magazine articles. There are also among the annual crop of South African books some volumes in which the writers manage to find space for a short chapter on the Native Problem. Though writers who are experts in economics or sport, or some kindred subject, naturally view the Native Problem through their own special keyhole, the result is interesting and not without value; for it is of great importance to know the bearing of such a side-issue as the Rand Labour-Supply on the Native Problem, even though the writer may assure us that this side-issue is not only the heart but the whole of the problem. The Kafirs say that no elephant ever felt its own trunk to be a burden, and we may therefore safely take some discount off the opinion of the man with but one idea.

But it is not only the mine-owner who is in danger of ignoring the native in his insistence of the importance of some side-issue of the problem: the philanthropist, the person who asks hysterical questions in the House of Commons, and the members of the Aborigines Protection Society are just as much in danger of forgetting the actual Kafir owing to their concentration on their own hobby. It is fatally easy to set up in the mind some unreal image of an oppressed and voiceless black man, who is too gentle and peaceable, and withal too guileless, to provoke hostilities except under the most provoking oppression of some wicked white men. This mental image affords a splendid occasion for giving expression to those most pleasurable and luxurious of all emotions, indignation and pity. A meeting is held, and there is set up an emotional storm in many a tea-cup; the actual savage is lost sight of, and the "brutality" of the colonist and the humanity of the people at home are apt to become the twin-centres of what the Kafirs call a crab's dance. The question then ceases to be the *native,* and becomes the *white,* problem. Under the influence of prejudice or passion, the native, who is the subject of the contention, is lost sight of; and the real war is waged round such problems as the moral character of the colonist, the nature of the British Constitution, or the abstract idea of Justice, for every one thinks he knows all about these things. The Kafir becomes the ostensible subject of debate in which people exploit their special and peculiar obsessions. The argument becomes practically independent of the actual Kafir of the kraal, and would not be modified much if the aborigines of South Africa were Siamese, Red Indians or even Martians. Every conceivable side-interest, prejudice, and false analogy is discussed by these people, whom Carlyle would call Professors of Things in General, and who entirely ignore the real wishes of the Kafir.

The Native Problem is the problem of the native. This is so obvious when once stated that one would be ashamed to say it unless it were so constantly forgotten. Before we can understand the bearings of the Native Problem we must study native customs and thought. We shall never get any nearer a solution of the problem by concentrating our attention on the relative values of Home and Colonial sentiment and ethical sense, or on political panaceas for imaginary and non-existent needs, for it is the Kafir, and not our emotion, that is the determining factor in the problem.

I have not dealt with the subject of the religious aspect of Missions, though missionaries have done so much to exploit individualism amongst the Kafirs. There is not space available for the treatment of the subject. I fear to say too little or too much, and feel that any inadequate statement would but raise many undesirable misunderstandings. That aspect of the subject must therefore be reserved for a future volume.

I am not without hope that the picture of the "savage" that I present may do something to undermine the distorted mental image that is ordinarily awakened by that word. Many a race has opprobriously called another race, that it did not understand, barbarian or savage; even though that despised race was in some directions the more advanced of the two. The Kafir, contrary to ordinary belief, has the most extraordinarily well-developed spirit of altruism and *camaraderie,* which is very rarely equalled amongst Western nations. Ethnologists are slowly forcing us to admit that the savage is not so savage as has been supposed.

CAN THE ETHIOPIAN CHANGE HIS SKIN?

(1) *Can the Ethiopian become a European?*—When we seek to put all race-prejudice aside and examine the capacity of the Kafir to absorb and assimilate Western civilisation in such a way that he shall practically cease to exhibit the peculiarities of the negro, and shall become Western in thought and feeling, I think we must admit, from cases before our very faces to-day, that he can apparently sometimes do this to a much greater extent than is thought by most people to be possible. But yet there seems to remain something—is it in the texture of the man's mind?—that prevents him, even in the best cases, from becoming altogether Western. It is doubtful whether he can quite adopt the European standpoint in anything, for he seems to lack that indefinable something which, after all, makes so much difference even in the best instances. There is lacking a subtle quality, illusive and difficult to define, that somehow or other makes us say,

> The little more, and how much it is:
> The little loss, and what worlds away.

And it is difficult to believe that this illusive *x* could be gained—I doubt whether it could ever be gained—without a greatly preponderating loss of some essentially good Kafir qualities. I am talking of to-day's practical politics, and do not pause at present to ask whether this difficulty might not be overcome in, say, ten more centuries of help from the white man. At present the individual Kafir may occasionally rise very high, and yet he does not cease to be a Kafir. Progress is a social product, and it may be that in the absence of the "evolution of his environment" no educated Kafir has yet enjoyed the stimulating atmosphere, formed by a sufficient number of his equally educated and congenial fellows, which might enable him to rise to greater heights. And I do not think that it would be a good thing to place a few Kafirs in a hothouse so that they might outstrip the rest of their race in their mental growth.

The average colonist feels that "Exeter Hall" ambitions and methods lead but to a coating of Western veneer over the savage nature. He asks what can be the good of such an accretion of an unabsorbable civilisation which leaves the savage still a savage at heart. Even in the preliminary stages, this philan-thropic elevating of the Kafir tends to make the most immature native think he is equal to the white man. While a few exceptional Kafirs have advanced surprisingly high, the *average* educated Kafir has, of course, not in the slight-est degree changed his nature: he has only added to it some highly unsuitable and discordant elements of a very superficial character. He has put on some-thing over his skin—usually dirty clothes—rather than made a change be-neath it. But though we recognise that this has been the result of our philan-thropy in the great majority of cases, we need not jump to the conclusion that the few exceptional natives who have been wisely handled, and who have enjoyed most favourable environment, have not advanced as far beyond the average Kafir as they are yet behind the average white man. And, once more, it does not follow because we believe the Kafir to be capable of advancing very far toward Western ideals that therefore it is wise for us to help a few natives to do so at once. It may be better to help on a larger number to a lesser degree. What may be good for the individual, viewed in the abstract, and in isolation from his race-duties, may be bad for him when this immensely important aspect of the matter is considered. But because one does not wish to see a few Kafirs educated far beyond the bulk of their fellows, one need not deny that they are capable of such development. And it is important to recognise what I believe may safely be called a fact, namely, that the Kafir cannot as yet advance much if left to himself without European guidance. When free from that guidance he will ape the white man in mere externals; and this can be stated definitely, not by appealing to analogy, and by showing that it is what has actually occurred in Hayti where Black rules White, but, because the Kafir in South Africa has actually done so when left to himself. The Ethiopian move-ment shows how utterly superficial, pernicious, and bizarre is the civilisation of the natives who break loose from European guidance.

I, for one, am not inclined to blame the colonist for being sceptical as to the Kafir's capacity to develop. Very much has been done by friends of the Kafirs to break down colonial belief in the capacity of the Kafir. The renowned Dr. Philip was a very pugnacious man, and he fought the colonists most rigor-ously—not to say cruelly—about the Kafir. In Mr. Theal's words, he "laid down a theory that the coloured races were in all respects, except education, mentally equal to the European colonists, and that they were wrongfully and cruelly oppressed by the white people and the Government. With this as a professed motive for exertion, he stood forth as their champion."[1] Later on in life he found out how disastrous had been his advocacy—even from the

---

1. "History of South Africa," vol. 1795–1834, pp. 345, 340.

standpoint of Kafir interests. "After he had enjoyed almost unlimited political influence, and had seen the schemes which he devised result in bloodshed and confusion, he became a comparatively gentle old man, and abandoned politics."[2] He was but an example of the man who willed the good, and yet who thereby wrought the bad. Apart from the immediate suffering his mistaken philanthropy brought to the Kafirs, he did very much, by his intemperate advocacy of the natives, to wreck colonial belief in the capacity of the Kafirs to advance at all. That the average colonist should, in the face of the extreme advocacy of Kafir equality to the whites, run to the opposite extreme, and say that the Kafir is scarcely capable of any improvement at all, is very natural and very human, even if it is not fully accurate.

In answer to our first question, I should be tempted to reply that there is good evidence for saying that while the individual Kafir can, nay, does now and then in exceptional cases under suitable white guidance, reach a surprisingly close approximation to the European, yet at present he always falls short, and moreover falls short in some strange way that makes it quite impossible for the most kindly critic to regard him as the equal of the white man. In this sense the Ethiopian, probably, can never change his skin.

(2) *Can the individual Kafir rise immensely higher than the average of his race?*—It is certainly a pity that our race-prejudice should sometimes hide from us the fact that it is immensely to our interest that the Ethiopian should change his skin. Unless he can do so, it will be a very bad look-out for the white man in South Africa: if the native is to remain, for example, as ruthless as he was during the Border Wars, if he is to foster for ever the hatred of the white man that he now undoubtedly cherishes, if he is to continue to become top-heavy and unbalanced when educated, then the fate of South Africa is sealed, for it is only a matter of time before the whites will either be massacred or squeezed out of the country. But if the Ethiopian can change his skin there is hope.

It is most interesting to read what an American negro has to say on the latent capacity of the black races to rise in the scale of civilisation. Du Bois, at least so I have been told by an old friend of his, is more white than black, and yet glories far more in his negro than in his European inheritance. Perhaps it is not fair to take him as a specimen of the height to which the average Kafir may hope to attain. Yet it is instructive to read what he has written as to the capacity of the negro to rise.

"The silently growing assumption of this age is that the probation of races is past, and that the backward races of to-day are of proven inefficiency, and are

2. *Op. cit.* p. 345.

not worth saving. Such an assumption is the arrogance of peoples irreverent towards Time, and ignorant of the deeds of men. A thousand years ago such an assumption, easily possible, would have made it difficult for the Teuton to prove his right to life. Two thousand years ago such a dogmatism, readily welcome, would have scouted the idea of blonde races ever leading civilisation. So woefully unorganised is sociological knowledge that the meaning of progress and the meaning of 'swift' and 'slow' in human doing and the limits of human perfectibility are veiled, unanswerable sphinxes on the shore of science."[3] Yet we are sometimes told by colonists in South Africa that the individual Kafir comes of a bad stock, and "inherits" no civilised traits or "characters," and therefore cannot make up for his hopeless handicap. It will be interesting to seek to trace where the truth lies in this matter.

Those who have studied recent developments of biology do not need to be told that an organism has great, and often unsuspected, capacity for responding to suitable stimuli. Nature is fuller of resources than our imagination, or the lack of it, would sometimes lead us to believe; and we are coming to perceive that the individual can respond to stimuli far more than we had thought. There are three factors to be considered in all questions of possible progress in the animal kingdom: these are heredity, capacity for variation, and the power of the environment to modify the organism: but for the present let us confine ourselves to the subject of heredity, for we shall approach the two other subjects at a later stage of our argument.

Popular thought on the subject of heredity has been so misled by the exuberant, though inexact, fancy of novelists that people are slow to listen to and grasp the facts that have been observed by trained biologists. It is popularly thought that we "inherit" our culture and civilisation through parents who pass on to their children the "modifications" they have acquired during life. The word "inherit" is used in the vaguest way by popular writers, and would cover the inheritance of a quick temper as well as that of money or lands: but in biological circles the word has a very definite connotation which must be explained. The "characters" of an organism are divided into two distinct categories. On the one hand we find *inborn* characters which are passed on from generation to generation by the germ-plasm, and on the other hand the modifications or *acquired* characters that are the result of individual use or of the environment. These acquired characters are the result of the play of the environment, or of personal habits, on the stock of previously inborn characters. All inborn characters take their origin from the germ, while all— or nearly all—acquired characters seem to be acquired by the individual by his

3. W. E. B. Du Bois, "The Souls of Black Folk," p. 262.

own direct action, and are but modifications of inborn characters. It is becoming more and more clear that—at least in animals—acquired characters—or "use-acquirements" or "modifications" as they are often called—cannot at the present stage of evolution be passed on by heredity. The term "heredity" is therefore used to connote the passing on of characters by the germ-cells. Civilisation and culture are use-acquirements and not inborn characters: therefore, on our hypothesis, they cannot be passed on by germinal means, and so are not hereditary. "Man," says Dr. Reid, "has not evolved into a civilised being; he has merely developed into one. The change in him consists solely or principally in a change of mental acquirements, not in a germinal change. He transmits his civilised habits by tradition and not by inheritance." This would seem to be the reason why a high state of civilisation was difficult, if not impossible, to attain until man had invented some method of writing that would render tradition more permanent. Had culture been passed on by heredity, the progress of mankind should have been enormously rapid. The fact that, previous to the invention of writing, human progress was so slow would seem to be corroborative evidence of the hypothesis that acquired habits are not hereditary.

At first sight all this may seem to offer but a depressing and pessimistic view of life, for an appalling amount of individual effort thus seems to be ephemeral. Is this, we ask, the fact of all the "struggling sighs of sacrifice"? But a little further reflection will show us that there is a very bright side to this hypothesis. *First*, no man is hopelessly doomed to cultural poverty because his ancestors have been slack. No Kafir can be pronounced incapable of rising simply because his father did not rise. We cannot say the stock is bad until successive generations have had a fair chance, for mental capacity can lie dormant for ages and yet ultimately awake to life. *Secondly*, the hypothesis indicates to us how to set to work. Philanthropists in the past have thought they could quickly improve *the stock* by educating the individual: they were therefore apt to work at a high tension for a short period, and then to leave their *protégés* to stand or fall by themselves. The moment they saw a slight improvement in the individual, they mistakenly thought they had permanently improved the stock. But germinal changes are very slowly brought about; and we now see that if we would directly improve the stock, we must pay attention to artificial selection rather than to education. To this subject we shall return presently. *Thirdly*, we now know that, when we look away from the stock to the individual, we can, by maintaining through successive generations a sort of *external* heritage of culture—a very laborious process that must never be relaxed—uplift each successive generation; for men everywhere possess much more capacity for making acquirements, when placed under suitable conditions, than they can ever hope to make use of in their lifetime. But we see that this culture does not affect the germ-plasm, and so it is essential that we should not relax our stimulus. We cannot make human nature perfect, and then leave it to take care of itself, for each successive generation must see to its own culture. Civilisations have waxed and waned because cultural atmospheres are easily destroyed. And past civilisations have left no impress on the germ-cells, for it is not in the power of culture to effect such changes. Yet the individual, if rightly handled, is capable of almost endless advance because he possesses enormous, and somewhat unlooked-for, capacity for responding to suitable stimuli. Science joins hands with poetry at this point, and Browning's "Rabbi Ben Ezra" will occur to all:

> All instincts immature,
> All purposes unsure
> That weighed not as his work, yet swelled the man's account.
>
> .   .   .
>
> All I could never be,
> All men ignored in me,
> This was I worth to God, whose wheel the pitcher shaped.

Instead of saying that the individual Kafir cannot rise above the level of his race, we must admit that if he can respond to stimuli—and if suitable stimuli can be applied—there is every hope that the individual thus stimulated may rise surprisingly high above the present low level of his fellows. And all the Kafirs may be raised enormously, though to different degrees, if all are suitably stimulated. The capacity for responding to stimuli varies with the personal equation; and one Kafir, like one white man, can rise higher than another. Each man has to work up his own cultural fortune, and we can never say that the individual Kafir cannot rise until we have exhausted every kind of stimulus that might help him to do so. In this matter we must be empiricists, and indeed pragmatists, seeking to make real and actual what we now suspect to be but a latent possibility. The individual Kafir is not doomed to remain a savage *because* his ancestors were savages. The only thing that could condemn him to remain a savage would be his own individual incapacity to respond to a stimulus. It is idle, therefore, to say that the individual Ethiopian cannot change his skin until we have tried all possible methods for enabling him to do so and have failed in our attempts. And I submit that we *have* tried the experiment in the past, though in the most bungling and unintelligent fashion; and yet amidst the many failures we have, as a matter of fact, produced educated Kafirs who seem centuries ahead of the bulk of the people.

It is also necessary for us to remember that progress is a social product, and that we cannot expect amongst the Kafirs Beethovens, Newtons, or Shakespeares, who did but give expression to the simmering ideas and emotions of their age, until we lift up the low average of the Kafirs *as a whole,* so that it may be somewhat comparable to the state of European society when it threw up such men. These men were but the mountain peaks arising out of national mountain ranges or table-lands. They did not rise in isolation out of the ocean. Until we lift up the general level of the Kafirs, we cannot expect to find some of them towering above the ordinary European, for all they can do is to tower above their submerged fellow Kafirs. And a mountain peak arising out of a submerged bed of ocean may seem a mountain peak to creatures living on that bed, though it is not conspicuous to people living far above that level. We think of Caliban upon Setebos, or of the young witch in "Pauline," and remember how her blue eyes drew down a god, who said even in his perishing, "I am still a god—to thee": and we begin to see that, though the Kafir genius may be no genius to us, he may be one to his fellows.

I conclude, therefore, that in this second sense of the words the Ethiopian can change his skin. He may not be able to become a European, but he can become a Super-Kafir.

SOURCE: "Preface" and "Can the Ethiopian Change His Skin?" in *Kafir Socialism and the Dawn of Individualism: An Introduction to the Study of the Native Problem* (London: Adam and Charles Black, 1908), v–xi, 213–26. Dudley Kidd was also the author of *South Africa* (1908), *The Essential Kafir* (n.d.), and *Savage Childhood* (n.d.).

─────────

How the Leopard Got His Spots
RUDYARD KIPLING

[While best known for his depictions of Anglo-India, Rudyard Kipling (1865–1936) spent several important years in South Africa, years that coincided with the Anglo-Boer War (1899–1902). His African experience informs the tales collected in the *Just So Stories,* as biographer Angus Wilson points out with regard to their "pleasing little Darwinian send-up": "The whale's throat, the camel's hump, the rhinoceros's skin, the leopard's spots, the elephant's trunk, the kangaroo's physique, the armadillo altogether, are all jokes about evolutionary adaptation. And, as such, they are closely related to the natural scene, the surroundings—Kipling's forte—and they are most fully realised in the two stories with South African settings" (*The Strange Ride of Rudyard Kipling* [London: Pimlico, 1977], 229).]

In the days when everybody started fair, Best Beloved, the Leopard lived in a place called the High Veldt. 'Member it wasn't the Low Veldt, or the Bush Veldt, or the Sour Veldt, but the 'sclusively bare, hot shiny High Veldt, where there was sand and sandy-colored rock and 'sclusively tufts of sandy-yellowish grass.

The Giraffe and the Zebra and the Eland and the Koodoo and the Harte-beest lived there, and they were 'sclusively sandy-yellow-brownish all over; but the Leopard, he was the 'sclusivest, sandiest-yellowest-brownest of them all—a grayish-yellowish catty-shaped kind of beast, and he matched the 'sclusively yellowish-grayish-brownish color of the High Veldt to one hair.

This was very bad for the Giraffe and the Zebra and the rest of them, for he would lie down by a 'sclusively yellowish-grayish-brownish stone or clump of grass, and when the Giraffe or the Zebra or the Eland or the Koodoo or the Bush-Buck or the Bonte-Buck came by he would surprise them out of their jumpsome lives. He would indeed!

And, also, there was an Ethiopian with bows and arrows (a 'sclusively grayish-brownish-yellowish man he was then), who lived on the High Veldt with the Leopard, and the two used to hunt together—the Ethiopian with his bows and arrows, and the Leopard 'sclusively with his teeth and claws—till the Giraffe and the Eland and the Koodoo and the Quagga and all the rest of them didn't know which way to jump, Best Beloved. They didn't indeed!

After a long time—things lived for ever so long in those days—they learned to avoid anything that looked like a Leopard or an Ethiopian, and bit by bit—the Giraffe began it, because his legs were the longest—they went away from the High Veldt. They scuttled for days and days till they came to a great forest, 'sclusively full of trees and bushes and stripy, speckly, patchy-blatchy shadows, and there they hid: and after another long time, what with standing half in the shade and half out of it, and what with the slippery-slidy shadows of the trees falling on them, the Giraffe grew blotchy, and the Zebra grew stripy, and the Eland and the Koodoo grew darker, with little wavy gray lines on their backs like bark on a tree-trunk, and so, though you could hear them and smell them, you could very seldom see them, and then only when you knew precisely where to look.

They had a beautiful time in the 'sclusively speckly-spickly shadows of the forest, while the Leopard and the Ethiopian ran about over the 'sclusively grayish-yellowish-reddish High Veldt outside, wondering where all their breakfasts and their dinners and their teas had gone.

At last they were so hungry that they ate rats and beetles and rock-rabbits, the Leopard and the Ethiopian, and then they had the Big Tummy-ache, both together: and then they met Baviaan—the dog-headed, barking baboon, who is Quite the Wisest Animal in All South Africa.

Said the Leopard to Baviaan (and it was a very hot day), 'Where has all the game gone?'

And Baviaan winked. He knew.

Said Ethiopian to Baviaan, 'Can you tell me the present habitat of the aboriginal Fauna?' (That meant just the same thing, but the Ethiopian always used long words. He was a grown-up.)

And Baviaan winked. He knew.

Then said Baviaan, 'The game has gone into other spots: and my advice to you, Leopard, is to go into other spots as soon as you can.'

And the Ethiopian said, 'That is all very fine, but I wish to know whither the aboriginal Fauna has migrated.'

Then said Baviaan, 'The aboriginal Fauna has joined the aboriginal Flora because it was high time for a change; and my advice to you, Ethiopian, is to change as soon as you can.'

That puzzled the Leopard and the Ethiopian, but they set off to look for the aboriginal Flora, and presently, after ever so many days, they saw a great, high, tall forest full of tree-trunks all 'sclusively speckled and sprottled and spottled, dotted and splashed and slashed and hatched and cross-hatched with shadows. (Say that quickly aloud, and you will see how very shadowy the forest must have been.)

'What is this,' said the Leopard, 'that is so 'sclusively dark, and yet so full of little pieces of light?'

'I don't know,' said the Ethiopian, 'but it ought to be the aboriginal Flora. I can smell Giraffe, and I can hear Giraffe, but I can't see Giraffe.'

'That's curious,' said the Leopard. 'I suppose it is because we have just come in out of the sunshine. I can smell Zebra, and I can hear Zebra, but I can't see Zebra.'

'Wait a bit,' said the Ethiopian. 'It's a long time since we've hunted 'em. Perhaps we've forgotten what they were like.'

'Fiddle!' said the Leopard. 'I remember them perfectly on the High Veldt, especially their marrow-bones. Giraffe is about seventeen feet high, of a 'sclusively fulvous golden-yellow from head to heel: and Zebra is about four and a half feet high, of a 'sclusively gray-fawn color from head to heel.'

'Umm,' said the Ethiopian, looking into the speckly-spickly shadows of the aboriginal Flora-forest. 'Then they ought to show up in this dark place like ripe bananas in a smokehouse.'

But they didn't. The Leopard and the Ethiopian hunted all day; and though they could smell them and hear them, they never saw one of them.

'For goodness' sake,' said the Leopard at tea-time, 'let us wait till it gets dark. This daylight hunting is a perfect scandal.'

So they waited till dark, and then the Leopard heard something breathing sniffily in the starlight that fell all stripy through the branches, and he jumped at the noise, and it smelt like Zebra, and it felt like Zebra, and when he knocked it down it kicked like Zebra, but he couldn't see it. So he said, 'Be quiet, O you person without any form. I am going to sit on your head till morning, because there is something about you that I don't understand.'

Presently he heard a grunt and a crash and a scramble, and the Ethiopian called out, 'I've caught a thing that I can't see. It smells like Giraffe, and it kicks like Giraffe, but it hasn't any form.'

'Don't you trust it, said the Leopard. 'Sit on its head till the morning—same as me. They haven't any form—any of 'em.'

So they sat down on them hard till bright morning-time, and then Leopard said, 'What have you at your end of the table, Brother?'

The Ethiopian scratched his head and said, 'It ought to be 'sclusively a rich fulvous orange-tawny from head to heel, and it ought to be Giraffe; but it is covered all over with chestnut blotches. What have you at your end of the table, Brother?'

And the Leopard scratched his head and said, 'It ought to be 'sclusively a delicate grayish-fawn, and it ought to be Zebra; but it is covered all over with black and purple stripes. What in the world have you been doing to yourself, Zebra? Don't you know that if you were on the High Veldt I could see you ten miles off? You haven't any form.'

'Yes,' said the Zebra, 'but this isn't the High Veldt. Can't you see?'

'I can now,' said the Leopard, 'But I couldn't all yesterday. How is it done?'

'Let us up,' said the Zebra, 'and we will show you.'

They let the Zebra and the Giraffe get up; and Zebra moved away to some little thorn-bushes where the sunlight fell all stripy, and the Giraffe moved off to some tallish trees where the shadows fell all blotchy.

'Now watch,' said the Zebra and the Giraffe. 'This is the way it's done. One, two, three! And where's your breakfast?'

Leopard stared, and Ethiopian stared, but all they could see were stripy shadows and blotched shadows in the forest, but never a sign of Zebra and Giraffe. They had just walked off and hidden themselves in the shadowy forest.

'Hi! Hi!' said the Ethiopian. 'That's a trick worth learning. Take a lesson by it, Leopard. You show up in this dark place like a bar of soap in a coal-scuttle.'

'Ho! Ho!' said the Leopard. 'Would it surprise you very much to know that you show up in this dark place like a mustard-plaster on a sack of coals?'

'Well, calling names won't catch dinner,' said the Ethiopian. 'The long and the little of it is that we don't match our backgrounds. I'm going to take Baviaan's advice. He told me I ought to change: and as I've nothing to change except my skin I'm going to change that.'

'What to?' said the Leopard, tremendously excited.

'To a nice working blackish-brownish color, with a little purple in it, and touches of slaty-blue. It will be the very thing for hiding in hollows and behind trees.'

So he changed his skin then and there, and the Leopard was more excited than ever: he had never seen a man change his skin before.

'But what about me?' he said, when the Ethiopian had worked his last little finger into his fine new black skin.

'You take Baviaan's advice too. He told you to go into spots.'

'So I did,' said the Leopard. 'I went into other spots as fast as I could. I went into this spot with you, and a lot of good it has done me.'

'Oh,' said the Ethiopian. 'Baviaan didn't mean spots in South Africa. he meant spots on your skin.'

'What's the use of that?' said the Leopard.

'Think of Giraffe,' said the Ethiopian. 'Or if you prefer stripes, think of Zebra. They find their spots and stripes give them perfect satisfaction.'

'Umm,' said the Leopard. 'I wouldn't look like Zebra—not for ever so.'

'Well, make up your mind,' said the Ethiopian, 'because I'd hate to go hunting without you, but I must if you insist on looking like a sunflower against a tarred fence.'

'I'll take spots, then,' said the Leopard; 'but don't make 'em too vulgar-big. I wouldn't look like Giraffe—not for ever so.'

'I'll make 'em with the tips of my fingers,' said the Ethiopian. 'There's plenty of black left on my skin still. Stand over!'

Then the Ethiopian put his five fingers close together (there was plenty of black left on his new skin still) and pressed them all over the Leopard, and wherever the five fingers touched they left five little black marks, all close together. You can see them on any Leopard's skin you like, Best Beloved. Sometimes the fingers slipped and the marks got a little blurred; but if you look closely at any Leopard now you will see that there are always five spots— off five black finger-tips.

'Now you are a beauty!' said the Ethiopian. 'You can lie out on the bare ground and look like a heap of pebbles. You can lie out on the naked rocks and look like a piece of pudding-stone. You can lie out on a leafy branch and look like sunshine sifting through the leaves; and you can lie right across the center of a path and look like nothing in particular. Think of that and purr!'

'But if I'm all this,' said the Leopard, 'why didn't you go spotty too?'

'Oh, plain black's best,' said the Ethiopian. 'Now come along and we'll see if we can't get even with Mr One-Two-Three-Where's-Your-Breakfast!'

So they went away and lived happily ever afterwards, Best Beloved. That is all.

Oh, now and then you will hear grown-ups say, 'Can the Ethiopian change his skin or the Leopard his spots?' I don't think even grown-ups would keep on saying such a silly thing if the Leopard and the Ethiopian hadn't done it once—do you? But they will never do it again, Best Beloved. They are quite contented as they are.

SOURCE: In *Just So Stories* (1902; New York: Doubleday, 1952): 19–25.

III

THE POLITICAL CORPS

THE MISSION

INTRODUCTION
The Mission: Christianity, Civilization, and Commerce
MIA CARTER AND BARBARA HARLOW

The Powers of Europe are happy in rivalry to promote the means of civilising Africa. . . . The black man will get the best of the bargain; the railway will be the precursor of commerce, education, civilisation, Christianity, conveying those native and white missionaries who will carry the glad tidings of salvation to the millions who now sit in darkness and the shadow of death.—Rev. W. Hughes, *Dark Africa and the Way Out*, 1892

ALTHOUGH MISSIONARY ACTIVITY in Africa began under the direction of Portugal's Prince Henry in the fifteenth century, the missionary enterprise vastly expanded in the eighteenth and nineteenth centuries. The brutal realities of slavery inspired British evangelists to campaign for the cessation of the British slave trade (abolished in 1807); the end of England's sinful trade in bodies led to the expansion of what was referred to as legitimate commerce. Missionary-explorers like David Livingstone wanted to uplift Africa by means of commercialization and Christian conversion. The missionaries' work on behalf of African "development" was depicted as a generous endeavor, one that would save the Africans from spiritual darkness and moral debasement. Western emissaries would encourage the Africans to evolve and join the ranks of the civilized races and nations.

The missionaries' early rhetoric combined idealistic discourses of enlightenment and salvation with aggressive militaristic jingoism; the Christian mission was to enact a war on barbarism and heathenism. The Salvation Army handbook and Henry Stanley's *How I Found Livingstone* reflect the "humanizing" campaign's incorporation of the metaphors of warfare; one song includes the refrain, "We'll march with song and band and flag, / And godless crowds to the cross we'll drag." Stanley depicts Livingstone the missionary as the ultimate white warrior. "His is the Spartan heroism, the inflexibility of the Roman, the enduring resolution of the Anglo-Saxon." But Livingstone's own commentaries on the "civilizing mission" suggest the difference between his generation's sense of their mission and that of Stanley and his coevals. As Andrew Ross has pointed out, the senior missionary-pioneer had asserted "human unity in what was becoming a losing battle in the English-speaking world against the rising tide of the complex of ideas that came to be called, depending on the perspective, scientific racism or Anglo-Saxonism" (in de Gruchy, *London Missionary Society*, 37). A representative of the London Missionary Society (LMS), and Livingstone's father-in-law, Robert Moffat, translated the Bible into Setswana, for example, and it was well-received when published in London in 1837–1838; only decades later, however, Bishop Colenso's Zulu renderings of the Pentateuch would be excoriated as nothing short of blasphemous by Matthew Arnold. Race served more and more emphatically as a cultural marker dividing the superior and inferior specimens of humanity and delimiting their differential access to political participation. Meanwhile, however, the missionary statesmen celebrated the missionaries' efforts on behalf of the eradication of cannibalism, human sacrifice, suttee, polygamy, and infanticide, revealing the competitive and mercenary nature of the industry of doing good.

In many of the missionaries' narratives, Africa is represented as a charnel house, a site in which the atmosphere of disease and death is omnipresent. Africa is also recognized as a potential breadbasket, a source of abundant agricultural material resources that could help feed the empire's growing metropolitan centers and employ its displaced factory workers and impoverished working classes. Indeed, Jean and John Comaroff have argued in their study of the southern African Tswana that agriculture was central to colonial evangelism: "At the turn of the seventeenth century, Edmund Spenser had blamed the barbarity and belligerence of the 'wild Irish' on their seminomadic, pastoral pursuits. In order to allay the threat they posed to England, and to bring them within the compass of its civilisation, they had to be made to live settled agrarian lives. The Bible might have spoken of a chosen people who herded at least as much as they tilled—a point not lost on the Tswana—but, to the modernist imagination, evolution depended on cultivation. Like their contemporaries in England, the evangelists absorbed the axiom that agriculture made men peaceful, law-abiding and amenable to education" (in de Gruchy, *London Missionary Society,* 57). The consequence was, according to the Comaroffs, "enclosure after the 'English fashion,'" a system of land distribution that laid the grounds for the eventual dispossession and disenfranchisement of the Africans following the passage of various "land laws." But the extension of African colonies and missions was thought at the time to provide a solution to the increasing economic difficulties for European expansionist and imperialist nations; Africans became empire's new workforce, and the "surplus" British subjects displaced by industrialization became their exported overseers, colonialism's burgeoning managerial staff.

By the time that Stanley described how it was that he "found Livingstone," it was "becoming commonplace to see destiny as willing the removal of inferior groups if they stood in the way of progress" (Ross, in de Gruchy, *London Missionary Society,* 38). For Count Arthur Gobineau, as for Robert

Knox, for example, race was crucial to all dimensions of human history and distinguished among political and social cultures. Gobineau thus considered missionary work to be a useless enterprise; Africans could never be fully uplifted because their intellectual disparities could not be eradicated. In Gobineau's eyes, the missionaries' aims of successful development could not be implemented because the Africans were a separate species and because Christianity was not a total culture. He concluded that Christianity was a civilizing instrument but not a civilization; therefore, its influence on the lowly Africans could be minimal and superficial, at best. In Gobineau's terms, the missionary project was characterized by misplaced faith and useless expenditure.

Benefactors or betrayers? Were the missionaries agents of conquest, carriers of cultural imperialism, or advocates on behalf of their converts against the depredations of colonizing zeal and the "civilizing mission"?

BIBLIOGRAPHY

Ajayi, J. F. Ade. *Christian Missions in Nigeria 1841–1891: The Making of a New Elite.* Evanston, Ill.: Northwestern University Press, 1961.

Attwell, David. "Reprising Modernity: Black South African 'Mission' Writing." *Journal of Southern African Studies* 25, no. 2 (June 1999): 267–85.

Beidelman, T. O. *Colonial Evangelism: A Socio-Historical Study of an East African Mission at the Grassroots.* Bloomington, Ind.: Indiana University Press, 1982.

Berman, Edward H. *African Reactions to Missionary Education.* New York: Columbia Teachers College Press, 1975.

Comaroff, Jean, and John Comaroff. *Of Revelation and Revolution: The Dialectics of Modernity on a South African Frontier.* 2 vols. Chicago: University of Chicago Press, 1991.

De Gruchy, John, ed. *The London Missionary Society in Southern Africa: Historical Essays in Celebration of the Bicentenary of the LMS in Southern Africa 1799–1999.* Claremont, South Africa: David Philip, 1999.

Elder, Gregory P. *Chronic Vigour: Darwin, Anglicans, Catholics, and the Development of a Doctrine of Providential Evolution.* Lanham, Md.: University Press of America, 1996.

Groves, C.P. *The Planting of Christianity in Africa.* 4 vols. London: Lutterworth Press, 1948–1958.

Hastings, Adrian. *The Church in Africa 1450–1950.* Oxford: Clarendon Press, 1994.

Hattersley, Roy. *Blood and Fire: William and Catherine Booth and Their Salvation Army.* London: Little, Brown and Company, 1999.

Hughes, Rev. W. *Dark Africa and the Way Out: A Scheme for Civilizing and Evangelizing the Dark Continent.* London, 1892; New York: Negro University Press, 1969.

Lagergren, David. *Mission and State in the Congo.* Uppsala, Sweden: Gleerup, 1970.

Leibowitz, Daniel. *The Physician and the Slave Trade: John Kirk, the Livingstone Expeditions, and the Crusade against Slavery in East Africa.* New York: W. H. Freeman and Company, 1999.

Knox, Robert. *The Races of Men.* London, 1860; Miami, FL: Mnemosyne Pub, 1969.

MacKenzie, D. F. "The Sociology of a Text: Oral Culture, Literacy, and Print in Early New

Zealand." In *Bibliography and the Sociology of Texts*. Cambridge: Cambridge University Press, 1999.

Majeke, Nosipho (Doris Taylor). *The Role of the Missionaries in Conquest*. Johannesburg: Society of Young Africa, 1952.

Miller, Jon. *The Social Construction of Religious Zeal: A Study of Organizational Contradictions*. New Brunswick, N.J.: Rutgers University Press, 1994.

Mobley, Harris W. *The Ghanaian's Image of the Missionary: An Analysis of the Published Critiques of Christian Missionaries by Ghanaians, 1897–1965*. Leiden: Brill, 1970.

Murray, Jocelyn. *Proclaim the Good News: A Short History of the Church Missionary Society*. London: n.p., 1985.

National Portrait Gallery. *David Livingstone and the Victorian Encounter with Africa*. London: National Portrait Gallery, 1996. Catalog.

Schweitzer, Albert. "The Relations of the White and Coloured Races." *Contemporary Review* 133 (1928): 65–70.

Wolf, Eric, ed. *Religious Regimes and State-Formation: Perspectives from European Ethnology*. Albany, N.Y.: State University of New York Press, 1991.

Excerpts from *Salvation Army Songs*

WILLIAM BOOTH

[Methodist minister "General" William Booth (1829–1912) began his missionary career with the establishment of the Christian Mission in London's East End; that organization later became the Salvation Army, with battalions of followers, which ringed the world from Scandinavia to South America, from South Africa to Indonesia. Booth was assisted in his enterprise by his wife, Catherine, who enlisted female officers and advocated the importance of a "woman's ministry." Playing on references to Africa as the dark continent, Booth wrote *In Darkest England: The Way Out* (1890), a devastating critique of the deplorable conditions in Victorian slums. That same year, Henry M. Stanley would produce his own—rather less reformist—*In Darkest Africa* (1890). William Booth also published a series of missionary instructional books, including *Salvation Soldiery: A Series of Addresses on the Requirements of Jesus Christ's Service* (1883) and *How to Make the Children into Saints and Soldiers of Jesus Christ* (1888). He was succeeded as head of the Salvation Army by his eldest son, Bramwell Booth; his other children also committed their lives to missionary work.]

WAR

SOLDIERS PRAYING

507   God bless our Army brave.
      Soon shall our colours wave
      O'er land and sea.
  Clothe us with righteousness,
  Our faithful soldiers bless,
  And crown with great success
    Our Army brave.
  The "blood and fire" bestow,

Go with us when we go
    To fight for Thee.
Still with our Army stay,
Drive sin and fear away,
Give victory day by day
    On Israel's side.
God bless our General,
Our Officers as well—
    God bless them all.
Oh, give us power to fight,
To put all hell to flight,
Let victory still delight
    Our Army brave.

535   Onward! upward! blood-washed soldier;
    Turn not back, nor sheathe thy sword,
Let its blade be sharp for conquest,
    In the battle for the Lord.
      To arms, to arms, ye brave;
      See, see the standard wave!
      March on, march on, the trumpet sounds.
        To victory or death.
From the great white throne eternal
    God Himself is looking down;
He it is who now commands thee—
    Take the cross and win the crown!
Onward! upward! doing, daring
    All for Him who died for thee;
Face the foe, and meet with boldness
    Danger, whatsoe'er it be.
From the battlements of glory
    Holy ones are looking down;
Thou canst almost hear them shouting,
    "On! let no one take thy crown!"
Onward! till thy course is finished,
    Like the ransomed ones before;
Keep the faith through persecution,
    Never give the battle o'er.
Onward! upward! till, victorious,
    Thou shalt lay thine armour down,

And thy loving Saviour bids thee
　　At His hand receive thy crown.

SOLDIERS PRAYING

508　O Thou God of every nation,
　　　We now for Thy blessing call;
　　　　Fit us for full consecration,
　　　　　Let the fire from heaven fall;
　　Bless our Army! With Thy power baptise us all.
　　　Fill us with Thy Holy Spirit,
　　　　Make our soldiers white as snow;
　　　Save the world through Jesus' merit,
　　　　Satan's kingdom overthrow!
　　Bless our Army! Send us where we ought to go!
　　　Give us all more holy living,
　　　　Fill us with abundant power;
　　　Give The Army more thanksgiving;
　　　　Greater victories every hour.
　　Bless our Army! Be our Rock, our Shield, our Tower.
　　　Bless our General, bless our Leaders,
　　　　Bless our Officers as well!
　　　Bless Headquarters—bless our Soldiers;
　　　　Bless the foes of sin and hell!
　　Bless our Army! We will all Thy goodness tell.

WAR

510　Jesus, give Thy blood-washed Army
　　　Universal liberty;
　　　　Keep us fighting, waiting calmly
　　　　　For a world-wide jubilee.
　　Hallelujah! We shall have the victory.
　　　Thou hast bound brave hearts together,
　　　　Clothed us with the Spirit's might,
　　　Made us warriors for ever,
　　　　Sent us in the field to fight;
　　In the Army We will serve Thee day and night.
　　　'Neath Thy sceptre foes are bending,
　　　　And Thy name makes devils fly;

Christless kingdoms Thou art rending,
    And Thy blood doth sin destroy;
For Thy glory We will fight until we die.
    Lift up valleys, cast down mountains,
        Make all evil natures good;
    Wash the world in Calvary's fountain,
        Send a great salvation flood;
All the nations We shall win with fire and blood.

561   Salvation soldiers, full of fire,
        From battle never stay;
Keep up the fire, keep aiming higher,
    Make ready, fire away!
        With The Army we will go,
        To the world our colours show,
        Never, never fear the foe,
            But fire away!
            Fire away! fire away!
            Fire away! fire away!
        With the gospel gun we will fire away;
            Mighty victories have been won
            With the great salvation gun!
        Stand your ground and fire away!
Salvation soldiers, every hour
    King Jesus we'll obey;
He loads our guns with saving power;
    In faith we'll fire away!
Salvation soldiers bound for heaven,
    Keep fighting night and day;
Use every gun that God has given—
    Make ready! fire away!

SONGS OF VICTORY

564   Hark, hark, my soul, what warlike
        songs are swelling   [to door;
    Through all the land and on from door
How grand the truths those burning strains are
        telling
    Of that great war till sin shall be no more.

Salvation Army, Army of God,
　　Onward to conquer the world with fire and blood
　　Onward we go, the world shall hear our singing,
　Come, guilty souls, for Jesus bids you come;
And through the dark its echoes, loudly ringing,
　Shall lead the wretched, lost, and wandering
　　home.
Far, far away, like thunder grandly pealing,
　We'll send the call for mercy full and free
And burdened souls by thousands humbly
　　kneeling,　　　　　　　　　[Thee
　Shall bend, dear Lord, their rebel necks to
Conquerors at last, though the fight be long
　　and dreary,　　　　　　　[be past
　Bright day shall dawn and sin's dark night
Our battles end in saving sinners weary,
　And Satan's kingdom down shall fall at last.

WAR

529　A world in rebellion our Jesus defied,
　　　His soldiers they faltered, for others
　　　　He cried;
　　　Just then our dear Saviour the blood and
　　　　fire waved,
　　　And said He'd ne'er furl it, till all men
　　　　were saved.
　Saving the world through the blood of the Lamb.
We care not though foes may be crowding our
　　track.　　　　　　　　　　[back;
All earth, hell, and devils shall ne'er keep us
King Jesus is leading, we trust in His might,
So down with the wrong, and up with the right.
Heaven-born is our purpose, the wide world our
　　field,
We hold a commission by Jesus' blood sealed;
How sacred our duty, how honoured our post,
We follow our Captain, to bring home the lost.
If ready for battle with me take your stand,
If ready to suffer in this cause so grand,

If ready for conquest, dark millions to win,
Then fix every bayonet and help me to sing.

574   We are sweeping through the land,
         With the sword of God in hand;
     We are watching, and we're praying while
             we fight,
         On the wings of love we'll fly,
         To the souls about to die,
     And we'll force them to behold the
             precious light.
             With the conquering Son of God,
             Who has washed us in His blood,
             Dangers braving, sinners saving,
             We are sweeping through the land.
         Oh, the blessed Lord of Light,
         We will serve Him with our might,
     And His arm shall bring salvation to the poor;
         They shall lean upon His breast,
         Know the sweetness of His rest,
     Of His pardon He the vilest will assure.
         We are sweeping on to win
         Perfect victory over sin,
     And we'll shout the Saviour's praises evermore;
         When the strife on earth is done,
         And some million souls we've won,
     We'll rejoin our conquering comrades gone before.
             Burst are all our prison bars,
             And we'll shine in heaven like stars,
     For we'll conquer 'neath our blessed Lord's
             command.
             See, salvation's morning breaks,
             And our country now awakes,
     The Salvation Army's sweeping through the land.

SOURCE: William Booth, *Salvation Army Songs* (London: Salvation Publishing and Supplies, n.d.).

Dr. Livingstone's Cambridge Lectures
DAVID LIVINGSTONE

["Between 1890 and 1960," observes Andrew Ross, "hardly a child who attended a Protestant Sunday school in the English-speaking world could have escaped receiving, as a prize, a book on Livingstone" (quoted in De Gruchy, John, ed., *The London Missionary Society in Southern Africa: Historical Essays in Celebration of the Bicentenary of the LMS in Southern Africa 1799–1999* [Claremont, South Africa: David Philip, 1999], 41). David Livingstone (1813–1873), who began as a child factory worker, was ordained by the London Missionary Society in 1840 and went on to become nothing less than a national hero. He arrived in South Africa in 1841 and traveled 600 miles into the interior to join Robert Moffat's LMS mission at Kuruman, south of the Kalahari Desert. Three years later he married Moffat's daughter, Mary, who would accompany him on several of his African expeditions, but who would, in 1852, return to England with their children. Livingstone was the "first European to have made an authenticated crossing of the continent from coast to coast" (National Portrait Gallery, *David Livingstone and the Victorian Encounter with Africa* [London: National Portrait Gallery, 1996], 13). His explorations in Africa became internationally renowned due in part to the uncertainty of his fate in the continental interior. Henry Morton Stanley's recovery of Livingstone provided the nineteenth-century audience with one of its most sensational "rescue" stories. Livingstone's travel and adventure narratives include his *African Journal, 1853–56, Missionary Travels* (1857), *Explorations in Africa* (1872), and *The Last Journals of David Livingstone* (1875). On his demise, Livingstone was buried in Westminster Abbey.]

LECTURE I

Delivered before the University of Cambridge, in the Senate-House, on Friday, 4th December, 1857. Dr. Philpott, Master of St Catharine's College, Vice-Chancellor, in the chair. The building was crowded to excess with all ranks of the University and their friends. The reception was so enthusiastic that lite-rally there were volley after volley of cheers. The Vice-Chancellor introduced Dr Livingstone to the meeting, who spoke nearly as follows:—

When I went to Africa about seventeen years ago I resolved to acquire an accurate knowledge of the native tongues; and as I continued, while there, to speak generally in the African languages, the result is that I am not now very fluent in my own; but if you will excuse my imperfections under that head, I will endeavour to give you as clear an idea of Africa as I can. If you look at the map of Africa you will discover the shortness of the coast-line, which is in consequence of the absence of deep indentations of the sea. This is one reason why the interior or Africa has remained so long unknown to the rest of the world. Another reason is the unhealthiness of the coast, which seems to have reacted upon the disposition of the people, for they are very unkindly, and opposed to Europeans passing through their country. In the southern part of Africa lies the great Kalahari desert, not so called as being a mere sandy plain, devoid of vegetation: such a desert I never saw until I got between Suez and Cairo. Kalahari is called a desert because it contains no streams, and water is obtained only from deep wells. The reason why so little rain falls on this extensive plain, is, because the winds prevailing over the greater part of the interior country are easterly, with a little southing. The moisture taken up by the atmosphere from the Indian Ocean is deposited on the eastern hilly slope; and when the moving mass of air reaches its greatest elevation, it is then on the verge of the great valley, or, as in the case of the Kalahari, the great heated inland plains there meeting with the rarefied air of that hot, dry surface, the ascending heat gives it greater capacity for retaining all its remaining humidity, and few showers can be given to the middle and western lands in consequence of the increased hygrometric power. The people living there, not knowing the physical reasons why they have so little rain, are in the habit of sending to the mountains on the east for rain-makers, in whose power of making rain they have a firm belief.[1] They say the people in those mountains have plenty of rain, and therefore must possess a medicine for making it. This faith in rain-making is a remarkable feature in the people in the country, and

---

1. Rain-makers are a numerous race in Southern Africa; and rain-making is an inveterate prejudice in the minds of large numbers of people. At pages 20–25 of the book of *Travels* is given an amusing, yet pathetic, account of this quackery among the Bakwains. These people try to help themselves to rain by a variety of preparations, such as charcoal made of burnt bats, jackals' livers, baboons' and lions' hearts, serpents' skins and *vertebrae*, in addition to the means mentioned above. They take a philosophical view of the question, and say that they do not pretend to make the rain themselves, but that God Himself makes it in answer to their prayers, and as a consequence of their preparations. They pray by means of their medicines, which act makes the rain theirs. A practice somewhat similar exists among the medicine men of the North-American Indians. It is somewhat striking that the Bakwains were so long afflicted with drought during Dr Livingstone's residence among them. They attributed this partly to his wizard powers, and partly to the presence of the Bible; regarding him with a suspicion corresponding with this belief. The dialogue between the medical doctor and the rain-doctor is highly entertaining, and shews great acuteness on the part of the untutored savage.

they have a good deal to say in favour of it. If you say you do not believe that these medicines have any power upon the clouds, they reply that that is just the way people talk about what they do not understand. They take a bulb, pound it, and administer an infusion of it to a sheep: in a short time the sheep dies in convulsions, and then they ask, Has not the medicine power? I do not think our friends of the homœopathic "persuasion" have much more to say than that. The common argument known to all those tribes is this—"God loves you white men better than us: He made you first, and did not make us pretty like you: He made us afterwards, and does not love us as He loves you. He gave you clothing, and horses and waggons, and guns and powder, and that Book, which you are always talking about. He gave us only two things—cattle and a knowledge of certain medicines by which we can make rain. We do not despise the things that you have; we only wish that we had them too; we do not despise that Book of yours, although we do not understand it: so you ought not to despise our knowledge of rain-making, although you do not understand it." You cannot convince them that they have no power to make rain. As it is with the homœopathist, so it is with the rain-maker—you might argue your tongue out of joint, and would convince neither.

I went into that country for the purpose of teaching the doctrines of our holy religion, and settled with the tribes on the border of the Kalahari desert. These tribes were those of the Bakwains, Bushmen and Bakalahari. Sechele[2] is the chief of the former. On the occasion of the first religious service held, he asked me if he could put some questions on the subject of Christianity, since such was the custom of their country when any new subject was introduced to their notice. I said, "By all means." He then inquired "If my forefathers knew of a future judgment?" I said, "Yes;" and began to describe the scene of the great white throne, and Him who should sit on it, from whose face the

2. This interesting man is the son of the Bakwain Chief, Mochoasele. He was uniformly kind to the Livingstones, sending them food constantly during their stay with him at Shokuane, his place of residence, and becoming our traveller's guide in 1850, when going to visit Sebituane. As a child his life was spared by Sebituane when attacking the Bakwains, who gave him his father's chieftainship. He married the daughters of three of his under-chiefs, and afterwards became Dr Livingstone's Sergius Paulus, or first influential Christian convert. He had family prayers in his house, and became a missionary to his own people, sending his children to Mr Moffat, at Kuruman, to be instructed "in all the knowledge of the white man." He learnt to read with great diligence, and succeeded well, getting quite fat through becoming a student instead of a hunter. The Bible was his constant study, he being particularly fond of Isaiah's book of prophecy. Once he said, in reference to St Paul, "He was a fine fellow, that Paul."

The Boers hate him for his resolute independence, and love of the English. He values everything European, and desires to trade with white men. Some further details are found in the Lectures about him.

heavens shall flee away, and be no more seen; interrupting he said, "You startle me, these words make all my bones to shake, I have no more strength in me. You have been talking about a future judgment, and many terrible things, of which we know nothing," repeating, "Did your forefathers know of these things?" I again replied in the affirmative. The chief said, "All my forefathers have passed away into darkness, without knowing anything of what was to befall them; how is it that your forefathers, knowing all these things, did not send word to my forefathers sooner?" This was rather a poser; but I explained the geographical difficulties, and said it was only after we had begun to send the knowledge of Christ to Cape Colony and other parts of the country, to which we had access, that we came to them; that it was their duty to receive what Europeans had now obtained the power to offer them; and that the time would come when the whole world would receive the knowledge of Christ, because Christ had promised that all the earth should be covered with a knowledge of Himself. The chief pointed to the Kalahari desert, and said, "Will you ever get beyond that with your Gospel? We, who are more accustomed to thirst than you are, cannot cross that desert; how can you?" I stated my belief in the promise of Christ; and in a few years afterwards that chief was the man who enabled me to cross that desert; and not only so, but he himself preached the Gospel to tribes beyond it. In some years, more rain than usual falls in the desert, and then there is a large crop of water-melons. When this occurred, the desert might be crossed: in 1852, a gentleman crossed it, and his oxen existed on the fluid contained in the melons for twenty-two days. In crossing the desert, different sorts of country are met with; up to 20th south latitude, there is a comparatively dry and arid country, and you might travel for four days, as I have done, without a single drop of water for the oxen. Water for the travellers themselves was always carried in the waggons, the usual mode of travelling south of the 20th degree of latitude being by ox-waggon. For four days, upon several occasions, we had not a drop of water for the oxen; but beyond 20th south latitude, going to the north, we travelled to Loanda, 1,500 miles, without carrying water for a single day. The country in the southern part of Africa is a kind of oblong basin, stretching north and south, bounded on all sides by old schist rocks. The waters of this central basin find an exit through a fissure into the river Zambesi, flowing to the east, the basin itself being covered with a layer of calcareous tufa.

My object in going into the country south of the desert was to instruct the natives in a knowledge of Christianity, but many circumstances prevented my living amongst them more than seven years, amongst which were considerations arising out of the slave system carried on by the Dutch Boers. I resolved to go into the country beyond, and soon found that, for the purposes of commerce, it was necessary to have a path to the sea. I might have gone on instructing the natives in religion, but as civilization and Christianity must go on together, I was obliged to find a path to the sea, in order that I should not sink to the level of the natives.[3] The chief[4] was overjoyed at the suggestion, and furnished me with twenty-seven men, and canoes, and provisions, and presents for the tribes through whose country we had to pass. We might have taken a shorter path to the sea than that to the north, and then to the west, by which we went; but along the country by the shorter route, there is an insect called the tsetse, whose bite is fatal to horses, oxen, and dogs, but not to men or donkeys.—You seem to think there is a connexion between the two.—The habitat of that insect is along the shorter route to the sea. The bite of it is fatal to domestic animals, not immediately, but certainly in the course of two or

3. After leaving Lake Ngami, Dr Livingstone took his family back to the Cape, and then set out on his first great journey. He visited Sebituane, at whose death he recommenced his exploring labours. During the course of these, he floundered through the marshy country south of Lin-yanti, and came so unexpectedly upon Secheletu, that the people said "he dropped from the clouds, riding on a hippopotamus."

4. This is Secheletu, chief of the Makololo, being the son of Sebituane. When Dr Livingstone first knew him he was eighteen years old, being of a coffee and milk colour. He became chief through the resignation and at the desire of his sister, Mamochisáne, whom Sebituane, at his death, had appointed to govern. Secheletu had a rival, 'Mpepe, who, while alive, rendered his position somewhat insecure. This 'Mpepe attempted to assassinate him as he was escorting our traveller to explore the river Chobe, and visiting his possessions. Dr Livingstone unintentionally prevented this design by stepping between them just as the murderer was about to strike the chief down.

Secheletu behaved so generously towards Dr Livingstone, at all times and in so many ways, that the civilized world and Africa are deeply indebted to him for contributing so largely towards the opening of the interior of that vast continent. He found the escort of twenty-seven men, as here mentioned, for the first, and that of one hundred and fourteen men for the second, great journey; also, ten tusks of ivory to help to defray the costs of the former, and thirty for the latter.

He is a man of enlightened mind, and a peace-maker. When our traveller set out from Linyanti on his journey towards the Barotse country, he accompanied him with one hundred and sixty at-tendants. During this journey they ate together, dwelt in the same tent, and returned to Linyanti after a nine weeks' tour. When Dr Livingstone and his party set out for Loanda, he lent his own canoes, and sent orders for their maintenance wherever they came in his dominions, and gave them a most touching and spirit-stirring reception on their return to Linyanti. On this occasion the presents received, story told, and greetings given, were of a most satisfactory character.

To shew the eagerness of Secheletu to trade with the white man, he immediately dispatched another party to Loanda, who arrived safely there after our traveller's arrival in England. To the latter he gave all the ivory in his country, and asked him to bring from England, as well as a sugar-mill, "any beautiful thing you may see in your own country." He eagerly and confidently awaits our traveller's promised return.

three months; the animal grows leaner and leaner, and gradually dies of emaciation: a horse belonging to Gordon Cumming died of a bite five or six months after it was bitten.

On account of this insect, I resolved to go to the north, and then westwards to the Portuguese settlement of Loanda. Along the course of the river which we passed, game was so abundant that there was no difficulty in supplying the wants of my whole party: antelopes were so tame that they might be shot from the canoe. But beyond 14 degrees of south latitude the natives had guns, and had themselves destroyed the game, so that I and my party had to live on charity. The people, however, in that central region were friendly and hospitable: but they had nothing but vegetable productions: the most abundant was the cassava, which, however nice when made into tapioca pudding, resembles in its more primitive condition nothing so much as a mess of laundress' starch. There was a desire in the various villages through which we passed to have intercourse with us, and kindness and hospitality were shewn us; but when we got near the Portuguese settlement of Angola the case was changed, and payment was demanded for every thing.[5] But I had nothing to pay with. Now the people had been in the habit of trading with the slavers, and so they said I might give one of my men in payment for what I wanted. When I shewed them that I could not do this, they looked upon me as an interloper, and I was sometimes in danger of being murdered.

As we neared the coast, the name of England was recognized, and we got on with ease. Upon one occasion, when I was passing through the parts visited by slave-traders, a chief[6] who wished to shew me some kindness offered me a slave-girl: upon explaining that I had a little girl of my own, whom I should not like my own chief to give to a black man, the chief thought I was displeased with the size of the girl, and sent me one a head taller. By this and other means I convinced my men of my opposition to the principle of slavery; and when we arrived at Loanda I took them on board a British vessel, where I took a pride in shewing them that those countrymen of

5. This was often a sort of black-mail levied for a right of way, and was generally demanded in the shape of "a man, a tusk, an ox, or a gun."

6. This was Shinte, or Kabombo, a Balonda chief. He gave our traveller a grand reception, and treated him kindly. The kidnapping of children and others by night, to sell for slaves, was an unhappy practice of his.

Dr Livingstone mentions five other Balonda chiefs, with four of whom he had intercourse. Matiamvo, the paramount chief of all the Balonda tribes, he did not visit, as he resides too far away to the North. Those whom he saw were Manenko and Nyamoana, two female chiefs; also Masiko and Kawawa, two other chieftains. Interesting notices of these are scattered through the book, especially of Shinte and Manenko, who are related as uncle and niece.

mine and those guns were there for the purpose of putting down the slave-trade. They were convinced from what they saw of the honesty of English-men's intentions; and the hearty reception they met with from the sailors made them say to me, "We see they are your countrymen, for they have hearts like you." On the journey, the men had always looked forward to reaching the coast: they had seen Manchester prints and other articles imported there-from, and they could not believe they were made by mortal hands. On reach-ing the sea, they thought that they had come to the end of the world. They said, "We marched along with our father, thinking the world was a large plain without limit; but all at once the land said 'I am finished, there is no more of me;'" and they called themselves the true old men—the true ancients—having gone to the end of the world. On reaching Loanda, they commenced trading in firewood, and also engaged themselves at sixpence a day in unloading coals, brought by a steamer for the supply of the cruiser lying there to watch the slave-vessels. On their return, they told their people "we worked for a whole moon, carrying away the stones that burn." By the time they were ready to go back to their own country, each had secured a large bundle of goods. On the way back, however, fever detained them, and their goods were all gone, leaving them on their return home, as poor as when they started.[7]

7. These men behaved well to our traveller, and shewed much simplicity and shrewdness both in their conduct and remarks. On one or two trying occasions they behaved with real courage. They carried home with them seeds, plants, pigeons, &c., not there to be found. We cannot but be struck with the unity of the human race, as asserted in Scripture, by seeing it from independent quarters in oneness of thought, feeling, desire, and affection, all the world over, despite other differences. These men were genuine Africans, chiefly Makalolo, with a mixture of several other tribes. The ships on board which our traveller took them were her Majesty's cruisers, *Pluto* and *Philomel*. Here they were delighted with their reception, and all they saw. The cannons for "putting down the slave trade with" especially delighted them. The officers won their affections by their cordiality, and the sailors by like kindness and by sharing their bread and beef with them. Respecting the ships they said, "This is not a canoe at all; it is a town." They looked on the decks and rigging as being "a town upon town." The party left Loanda on the return journey on the 20th September, 1854. The account they gave of themselves, when arrived in their own country, was singularly amusing. "We are the true ancients, who can tell wonderful things." Pitsane, the head-man, related all they had seen, heard, and felt; and this account did not lose in the telling. At Linyanti, all had a grand reception; Secheletu himself wearing the officers' uniform sent him by the Portuguese authorities at Loanda, while the men appeared in dashing white dresses and red caps, calling themselves our traveller's "braves," and trying to walk like Portuguese soldiers. They spoke of the wonderful things they had met with, adding as a climax, "that they had finished the whole world, and had turned only when there was no more land." One glib old gentleman asked, "Then you reached Ma-Robert (Mrs Livingstone)?" They were obliged to confess "that she lived a little beyond the world." (*Travels*, p. 501.)

I had gone towards the coast for the purpose of finding a direct path to the sea, but on going through the country we found forests so dense that the sun had not much influence on the ground, which was covered with yellow mosses, and all the trees with white lichens. Amongst these forests were little streams, each having its source in a bog; in fact nearly all the rivers in that country commence in bogs. Finding it impossible to travel here in a wheel conveyance, I left my waggon behind, and I believe it is standing in perfect safety, where I last saw it, at the present moment. The only other means of conveyance we had was ox-back, by no means a comfortable mode of travelling. I therefore came back to discover another route to the coast by means of the river Zambesi.

The same system of inundation that distinguishes the Nile, is also effected by this river, and the valley of the Barotse is exceedingly like the valley of the Nile between Cairo and Alexandria. The inundations of the Zambesi, however, cause no muddy sediment like those of the Nile, and, only that there are no snow-mountains, would convey the impression that the inundations were the result of the melting of snow from adjoining hills. The face of the country presents no such features, but elevated plains, so level that rain-water stands for months together upon them. The water does not flow off, but gradually soaks into the soil, and then oozes out in bogs, in which all the rivers take their rise. They have two rainy seasons in the year, and consequently two periods of inundation. The reason why the water remains so clear is this; the country is covered by such a mass of vegetation that the water flows over the grass, &c., without disturbing the soil beneath.

There is a large central district containing a large lake formed by the course of the Zambesi, to explore which would be well worthy of the attention of any individual wishing to distinguish himself.

Having got down amongst the people in the middle of the country, and having made known to my friend the chief my desire to have a path for civilization and commerce on the east, he again furnished me with means to pursue my researches eastward; and, to shew how disposed the natives were to aid me in my expedition, I had 114 men to accompany me to the east, whilst those who had travelled to the west with me only amounted to 27.[8] I carried

8. There is something really affecting in the manner how this wonderful man attached these savages to himself. It must be remembered, too, that the Makololo are justly regarded with dread by their neighbours as incurable marauders. At any rate this spectacle shows what kindness, tact and firmness will do. His service is now so popular, that he gets one hundred and fourteen volunteers to accompany him in his second journey. These, like the others, belong to different tribes. On several occasions, "when before the enemy," they behaved with temper and courage. Their general conduct was good, though there were some black sheep among them. One

with me thirty tusks of ivory; and, on leaving my waggon to set forth on my journey, two warriors of the country offered a heifer a-piece to the man who should slay any one who molested it. Having proceeded about a hundred miles, I found myself short of ammunition, and despatched an emissary back to the chief to procure more percussion caps from a box I had in my waggon. Not understanding the lock, the chief took a hatchet and split the lid open, to get what was wanted; and notwithstanding the insecure state in which it remained, I found, on returning two years after, that its contents were precisely as I left them. Such honesty is rare even in civilised Christian England, as I know from experience; for I sent a box of fossils to Dr Buckland, which, after arriving safely in England, was stolen from some railway, being probably mistaken for plate.

I could not make my friend the chief understand that I was poor: I had a quantity of sugar, and while it lasted the chief would favour me with his company to coffee; when it was gone, I told the chief how it was produced from the cane, which grew in central Africa, but as they had no means of extracting the saccharine matter, he requested me to procure a sugar-mill. When I told him I was poor, the chief then informed me that all the ivory in the country was at my disposal, and he accordingly loaded me with tusks, ten of which on arriving at the coast I spent in purchasing clothing for my followers; the rest were left at Quillimane, that the impression should not be produced in the country that they had been stolen in case of my non-return.

Englishmen are very apt to form their opinion of Africans from the elegant figures in tobacconists' shops: I scarcely think such are fair specimens of the African. I think at the same time, that the African women would be much handsomer than they are if they would only let themselves alone: though unfortunately that is a failing by no means peculiar to African ladies; but they

---

hundred and thirteen of these are now awaiting our traveller's return at Teté. The Portuguese commandant there, Major Sicard, gave them land to till, food, clothing, and permission to hunt elephants. He writes to England to say that they killed four in two months.

The Doctor tried to bring to England one remarkable man, Sekwebu, his interpreter and chief guide, who had been of great service during the journey from Linyanti to Teté. Of him we must sorrowfully say, "One is not." His loss must be severe and painful to our traveller. He knew the Zambesi well, as also the dialects spoken on its banks. On arriving at Quillimane, and on attempting to board the *Frolic*, the sea ran mountains high. Poor Sekwebu in terror asked, "Is this the way you go? Is this the way you go?" He became a favourite on board, but was bewildered with the novelty of every thing. He said, "People are very agreeable," but "what a strange country is this, all water together!" Now comes the climax. When off Mauritius, a steamer approaches. This must be fairy land—see that monster. These white men surely are gods or demons. His senses reel—insanity seizes his brain. He tries to spear a sailor—jumps overboard—pulls himself down by the chains, and Sekwebu in this life is seen no more!

are, by nature, not particularly goodlooking, and seem to take all the pains they can to make themselves worse. The people of one tribe knock out all their upper front teeth, and when they laugh are perfectly hideous. Another tribe of the Londa country file all their front teeth to a point, like cats' teeth, and when they grin put one in mind of alligators: many of the women are comely, but spoil their beauty by such unnatural means. Another tribe has a custom of piercing the cartilage of the nose, and inserting a bit of reed, which spreads it out, and makes them very disagreeable looking: others tie their hair, or rather wool, into basket-work, resembling the tonsorial decorations of the ancient Egyptians; others, again, dress their hair with a hoop around it, so as to resemble the gloria round the head of the Virgin; rather a different application of the hoop to that of English ladies![9]

The people of central Africa have religious ideas stronger than those of the Caffres and other southern nations, who talk much of God but pray seldom. They pray to departed relatives, by whom they imagine illnesses are sent to punish them for any neglect on their part. Evidences of the Portuguese Jesuit missionary operations are still extant, and are carefully preserved by the natives: one tribe can all read and write, which is ascribable to the teaching of the Jesuits: their only books are, however, histories of saints, and miracles effected by the parings of saintly toe-nails, and such-like nonsense: but, surely, if such an impression has once been produced, it might be hoped that the efforts of Protestant missionaries, who would leave the Bible with these poor people, would not be less abiding.

In a commercial point of view communication with this country is desirable. Angola is wonderfully fertile, producing every kind of tropical plant in rank luxuriance. Passing on to the valley of Quango, the stalk of the grass was as thick as a quill, and towered above my head, although I was mounted on

9. The Batoka tribes, on the Zambesi, knock out their upper front teeth, in order that they may, as they say, "look like oxen." They pronounce those who keep their teeth to "look like zebras." Surely this is some vestige of the animal worship of Egypt. The members of the Babimpo tribe pull out both their upper and lower front teeth, as a distinction. Sheakonda's people, and those on the Tambra, file their teeth to a point; as also do the Chiboque, a hostile tribe on the borders of Angola. This, too, is the practice of the Bashinge; these people flatten their noses by inserting bits of reed, or stick, into the septum. The Balonda gentlemen so load their legs with copper rings, that they are obliged to walk in a straggling way, the weight being a serious hindrance to walking. A man seeing our traveller smile at another with no rings, imitating his betters as though he wore them, said, "That is the way in which they shew off their lordship in these parts." It is the ladies on the Loajima who wear the hoop round the head. The women on the Zambesi and among the Maravi pierce the upper lip, and gradually enlarge the orifice until they can insert a shell. The lip is thus drawn out beyond the perpendicular of the nose. Sekwebu said of them, "These women want to make their mouths like those of ducks."

my ox; cotton is produced in great abundance, though merely woven into common cloth; bananas and pine-apples grow in great luxuriance; but the people having no maritime communication, these advantages are almost lost. The country on the other side is not quite so fertile, but in addition to indigo, cotton, and sugar-cane, produces a fibrous substance, which I am assured is stronger than flax.

The Zambesi has not been thought much of as a river by Europeans, not appearing very large at its mouth; but on going up it for about seventy miles, it is enormous. The first three hundred miles might be navigated without obstacle: then there is a rapid, and near it a coal-field of large extent. The elevated sides of the basin, which form the most important feature of the country, are far different in climate to the country nearer the sea, or even the centre. Here the grass is short, and the Angola goat, which could not live in the centre, had been seen on the east highland by Mr Moffat.

My desire is to open a path to this district, that civilization, commerce, and Christianity might find their way there. I consider that we made a great mistake, when we carried commerce into India, in being ashamed of our Christianity; as a matter of common sense and good policy, it is always best to appear in one's true character. In travelling through Africa, I might have imitated certain Portuguese, and have passed for a chief; but I never attempted anything of the sort, although endeavouring always to keep to the lessons of cleanliness rigidly instilled by my mother long ago; the consequence was that the natives respected me for that quality, though remaining dirty themselves.

I had a pass from the Portuguese consul, and on arriving at their settlement, I was asked what I was. I said, "A missionary, and a doctor too." They asked, "Are you a doctor of medicine?"—"Yes."—"Are you not a doctor of mathematics too?"—"No."—"And yet you can take longitudes and latitudes."— Then they asked me about my moustache; and I simply said I wore it, because men had moustaches to wear, and ladies had not. They could not understand either, why a sacerdote should have a wife and four children; and many a joke took place upon that subject. I used to say, "Is it not better to have children with than without a wife?" Englishmen of education always command respect, without any adventitious aid. A Portuguese governor left for Angola, giving out that he was going to keep a large establishment, and taking with him quantities of crockery, and about five hundred waistcoats; but when he arrived in Africa, he made a 'deal' of them. Educated Englishmen seldom descend to that sort of thing.

A prospect is now before us of opening Africa for commerce and the Gospel. Providence has been preparing the way, for even before I proceeded to the Central basin it had been conquered and rendered safe by a chief named Sebituane,[10] and the language of the Bechuanas made the fashionable tongue, and that was one of the languages into which Mr Moffat had translated the Scriptures. Sebituane also discovered Lake Ngami some time previous to my explorations in that part. In going back to that country my object is to open up traffic along the banks of the Zambesi, and also to preach the Gospel. The natives of Central Africa are very desirous of trading, but their only traffic is at present in slaves, of which the poorer people have an unmitigated horror: it is therefore most desirable to encourage the former principle, and thus open a way for the consumption of free productions, and the introduction of Christianity and commerce. By encouraging the native propensity for trade, the advantages that might be derived in a commercial point of view are incalculable; nor should we lose sight of the inestimable blessings it is in our power to bestow upon the unenlightened African, by giving him the light

10. This man, according to Dr Livingstone, is the most remarkable African who has lived for many an age. He has been truly called the Napoleon of these parts. His interesting biography can be found at pages 84–90, *Travels*. Here we can only refer to him. Unlike other African warrior chiefs, such as Africaner, Dingaan, and Mosilikatse, his own determined opponent, he led his men to battle in person. Terrible and successful he was in battle. Lake Ngami was known to him before it was discovered by our traveller and his companions. Sebituane was forty-five years old when first known to Dr Livingstone, who describes him as being somewhat bald, of middle height, frank, cordial, wonderfully fleet of foot, very popular, and of a coffee and milk colour. He was from the South, and probably of Caffre extraction. His fortunes were various, and his narrative is somewhat like the *Commentaries of Cæsar,* or the history of the British in India. He, like his son Secheletu, was touchingly kind to Dr Livingstone, coming one hundred miles to meet and escort him to his capital, Seshaké. His desire for intercourse with white men was most passionate. The period and circumstances of his death were solemn and striking. As we have before seen, he died soon after that meeting had occurred which both so much desired. War was the object of his life and the cause of his death, which occurred through an old wound in the lungs turning to inflammation. On his death-bed he said to our traveller, "Come near and see if I am any longer a man; I am done." The native doctors said to Dr Livingstone, who spoke to him of another life, "Why do you speak of death? Sebituane will never die."

Our traveller proceeds: "After sitting with him some time, and commending him to the mercy of God, I rose to depart, when the dying chieftain, raising himself up a little from his prone position, called a servant, and said, 'Take Robert to Maunku (one of his wives), and tell her to give him some milk.' These were the last words of Sebituane.

"He was decidedly the best specimen of a native chief I ever met. I never felt so much grieved by the loss of a black man before; and it was impossible not to follow him in thought into the world of which he had just heard before he was called away, and to realise somewhat of the feelings of those who pray for the dead. The deep dark question of what is to become of such as he, must, however, be left where we find it, believing that, assuredly, the 'Judge of all the earth will do right.'"

of Christianity. Those two pioneers of civilization—Christianity and commerce—should ever be inseparable; and Englishmen should be warned by the fruits of neglecting that principle as exemplified in the result of the management of Indian affairs. By trading with Africa, also, we should at length be independent of slave-labour, and thus discountenance practices so obnoxious to every Englishman.

Though the natives are not absolutely anxious to receive the Gospel, they are open to Christian influences. Among the Bechuanas the Gospel was well received. These people think it a crime to shed a tear, but I have seen some of them weep at the recollection of their sins when God had opened their hearts to Christianity and repentance. It is true that missionaries have difficulties to encounter; but what great enterprise was ever accomplished without difficulty? It is deplorable to think that one of the noblest of our missionary societies, the Church Missionary Society, is compelled to send to Germany for missionaries, whilst other societies are amply supplied. Let this stain be wiped off.—The sort of men who are wanted for missionaries are much as I see before me;—men of education, standing, enterprise, zeal, and piety. It is a mistake to suppose that *any one*, as long as he is pious, will do for this office. Pioneers in every thing should be the ablest and best qualified men, not those of small ability and education. This remark especially applies to the first teachers of Christian truth in regions which may never have before been blest with the name and Gospel of Jesus Christ. In the early ages the monasteries were the schools of Europe, and the monks were not ashamed to hold the plough. The missionaries now take the place of those noble men, and we should not hesitate to give up the small luxuries of life in order to carry knowledge and truth to them that are in darkness. I hope that many of those whom I now address will embrace that honourable career. Education has been given us from above for the purpose of bringing to the benighted the knowledge of a Saviour. If you knew the satisfaction of performing such a duty, as well as the gratitude to God which the missionary must always feel, in being chosen for so noble, so sacred a calling, you would have no hesitation in embracing it.

For my own part, I have never ceased to rejoice that God has appointed me to such an office. People talk of the sacrifice I have made in spending so much of my life in Africa. Can that be called a sacrifice which is simply paid back as a small part of a great debt owing to our God, which we can never repay?—Is that a sacrifice which brings its own blest reward in healthful activity, the consciousness of doing good, peace of mind, and a bright hope of a glorious destiny hereafter?—Away with the word in such a view, and with such a thought! It is emphatically no sacrifice. Say rather it is a privilege. Anxiety, sickness, suffering, or danger, now and then, with a foregoing of the common conveniences and charities of this life, may make us pause, and cause the spirit to waver, and the soul to sink, but let this only be for a moment. All these are nothing when compared with the glory which shall hereafter be revealed in, and for, us. I never made a sacrifice. Of this we ought not to talk, when we remember the great sacrifice which He made who left His Father's throne on high to give Himself for us;—"Who being the brightness of that Father's glory, and the express image of His person, and upholding all things by the word of His power, when He had by Himself purged our sins, sat down on the right hand of the majesty on high."

English people are treated with respect; and the missionary can earn his living by his gun,—a course not open to a country curate. I would rather be a poor missionary than a poor curate.

Then there is the pleasant prospect of returning home and seeing the agreeable faces of his countrywomen again. I suppose I present a pretty contrast to you. At Cairo we met a party of young English people, whose faces were quite a contrast to the skinny, withered ones of those who had spent the latter years of their life in a tropical clime: they were the first rosy cheeks I had seen for sixteen years; you can hardly tell how pleasant it is to see the blooming cheeks of young ladies before me, after an absence of sixteen years from such delightful objects of contemplation. There is also the pleasure of the welcome home, and I heartily thank you for the welcome you have given me on the present occasion; but there is also the hope of the welcome words of our Lord, "Well done, good and faithful servant."

I beg to direct your attention to Africa;—I know that in a few years I shall be cut off in that country, which is now open; do not let it be shut again! I go back to Africa to try to make an open path for commerce and Christianity; do you carry out the work which I have begun. I leave it with you!

LECTURE II

The following Lecture was delivered in the Town-Hall, on the day after the delivery of the other. Although the notice was so short, crowds of persons came to hear, who could not gain admittance. Swann Hurrell, Esq., the Mayor, took the chair, and some members of the Town Council were present. The anxiety of all classes to see and hear Dr Livingstone is pleasing, since it shews the state of public opinion on several vital topics, especially the civilization and evangelization of Africa. After being introduced to the assembly, the Doctor, without any prefatory remarks, took his wand, and began to point towards some maps of Africa just above his head, in his usual manner speaking as follows:—

In turning to the map of South Africa, I want to draw your attention to three imaginary zones, on the southern part, all different in population and climate. You will see that this part of Africa forms a kind of cone. This cone can be divided into three longitudinal bands or zones, just spoken of: the eastern band comprises what is generally known as Kafirland, which has been rather a difficult nut to crack for the English nation. However, the Kafir war has at length ended, both parties owning themselves tired; only we had to pay two millions of money, and lost a great many valuable lives as well. That part of the country is mountainous and well watered. The central zone, or Bechuana country, is comparatively dry, being seldom visited by rain; and its inhabitants, the Bechuanas, Bushmen, and Bakalahari, &c., are not nearly so warlike as the Caffres. Passing towards the West, we come to a level plain called the Kalahari desert, not consisting of barren sands, like the generally received notions of deserts, but covered with grass, bushes and trees, and containing a population of Bushmen and other people called the Bakalahari. I lived sixteen years on the borders of the Kalahari desert; and having gone to the country in 1841, I was naturally anxious to ascertain the effect the teaching of the missionaries had produced.

I must own that I was disappointed in what I saw, having formed rather sanguine expectations. I forwarded the result of my inquiries to the London Missionary Society, by whom I was sent out, and after a little time went to the country beyond, where I found the people in just the same state as the missionaries found those I had left; and when I compared those I had just come amongst with the people with whom I had recently lived, the benefit of the missionary teaching then appeared great indeed. True, the African when Christianised is not so elevated as we who have had the advantages of civilization and Christianity for ages; but still, when rescued from the degradation and superstitions of heathenism, he evinced improvement in an eminent degree. We should compare new converts who are still surrounded with all their old associations of heathenism, rather with the churches first planted by the Apostles, than with ourselves. Public opinion, law, custom, and general manners, with us who have enjoyed the inestimable blessings of the Gospel so long, are so essentially different from those which governed the converts of the first Christian age, and which still influence those new disciples of the better way among whom our modern Missionaries labour. If these latter soldiers of the cross have sometimes to mourn over the inconsistencies of their converts, it must be remembered that such was also the case with the Apostles, as their writings prove; especially those of St Paul, the great Apostle of the Gentiles.

I was not at all anxious to enter on the labours of other men; for I consider that the young missionary should devote himself as much as possible to his own field of duty, and not interfere with any other man's labour, but go to the real heathen, who may not as yet have heard Christ's name, or received his Gospel. Through the instrumentality of Mr Moffat, the Bechuanas have the Bible in their own language. To shew the value put on the sacred volume, in the first editions there were two sorts, one rather cheaper than the other and the binding less costly. The natives, who are rather inclined to be niggardly, purchased the cheap edition, thinking the binding stronger; but finding it was not so, they soon bought all the more costly Bibles with avidity.

Mr Moffat's labours, for the first ten years of his ministration, were not attended with any apparent success; and a large body of the tribe left the district in which he preached; and went a hundred miles away, in order to get out of the reach of his preaching, thinking to live in their own way without any stings of conscience; but in the latter respect they were mistaken, for the seed of the Gospel had taken root in their hearts, and they were obliged to send to the missionaries for assistance, and their chiefs used to go backwards and forwards for teaching: there was a constant relay going to the missionaries and coming back to teach those whom they left at home. When first visited by the missionary, one hundred were considered proper subjects for baptism, and the Church there now numbers upwards of three hundred in that one village. Many native missionary stations are dispersed around. It is an indisputable fact that when a man feels the value of the Gospel himself, in his own heart, he is ever anxious to impart its blessing to others. Travelling still in the south, I determined to visit a tribe called the Bakwains, resolving to go to the country beyond Kuruman, and when I commenced preaching the Gospel to them, I seemed as one who came with a lie or with some political object in view; hence they received me with suspicion, saying, "It is too good to be true," adding, "this man has some other design, which we shall soon see;" for they thought it strange that a man should leave his own tribe to preach to others: this caution was rather a good trait in their character, for it prevented them making sudden professions like the South Sea Islanders.

Their chief[11] is a remarkable man, not an average specimen of his people. He resolved at once to learn to read; and on the very first day of my visit

11. The chief here mentioned is Sechele. For an account of him, see note 2.

acquired the alphabet. Sechele one day said to me, after I had been preaching to the tribe, "Do you imagine you will get these people to believe by just talking to them? I can do nothing without thrashing them. If you want them to believe, I, and my under-chiefs, will get our whips of Rhinoceros' hide, and soon make them all believe." That was before he understood the Gospel; he soon after began to feel its influence, but, as he expressed himself, could not disentangle himself from his country's custom of having more wives than one. This was a source of disquietude to him. Feeling the Gospel at heart, he talked no longer of thrashing his people, but suggested frequent prayer-meetings. Accordingly, when he consulted me on the subject pressing so much on his mind, and especially about baptism, for which he applied about two years after he professed Christianity, I simply asked him if he thought he was doing right? What he thought he ought to do? I never *preached* against polygamy, but left the matter to take its course.[12] Sechele went away, and sent home four of his wives, giving each a new dress, &c., saying he had no fault to find with them, but the sole reason for parting with them was conviction in the truth of the Gospel, and therefore the separation was a relief to his mind; hence I was saved from many anxious thoughts on this matter. These women and their friends henceforth became the determined enemies both of myself and Sechele. Now, among the Africans, if a chief is fond of hunting, dancing, or drinking, his people are ever anxious to follow in the same pursuits; but with Christianity this was not the case. Sechele was both astonished and disappointed at finding the people stand aloof from his meetings, and his under-chiefs oppose both him and me. I and my cause were now unpopular. Unfortunately at this time there was a four years' drought; and the people believed implicitly that their chief had the power of making rain, and since none had come for so long a time, they suspected me of having thrown a charm over him, and would not allow him to make the rain. He was the rain-maker of the tribe; and this fact was easily connected with my instruments and movements, to them so unfathomable. If Sechele was thus the accredited rain-maker of the tribe, I was now the self-appointed necromancer, and he had become my unconscious victim.

Many of these people waited on me, begging me to allow them to make only a few showers, really thinking that I was purposely preventing the rain from descending. One old man used to come to me, and say, "The corn is yellow for want of rain; the cattle want grass; the children require milk; the

12. The reason stated for so doing, in answer to a question put at the conversazione at my house, is very striking, "I never preached against polygamy, since I was sure that when the Gospel took effect, it would operate on the mind just as it did with Sechele."

people lack water, therefore only let our chief make the showers to come, and then he may sing and pray as long as he likes." Looking at my peculiar circumstances, this drought was remarkable. I watched the clouds as anxiously as they; and many a cloudy morning, promising refreshing showers, turned into a cloudless day as parching as ever. They declared that the people would starve, or all leave the district, and I should have no one to preach to. It was quite heart-rending to hear them, seeing their distress; and especially keeping in mind their mental, moral, and spiritual degradation.

I endeavoured to persuade them that no mortal could control the rain, and their argument was, "We know very well that God makes the rain; we pray to him by means of medicines. You use medicines to give to a sick man, and sometimes he dies: you don't give up your medicine, because one man dies; and when any one is cured by it, you take the credit. So, the only thing we can do is to offer our medicines, which, by continued application, may be successful." The only way to eradicate such absurdities from the minds of these poor people is to give them the Gospel. They entertain a horror of Christianity, because they imagine that every one who becomes a Christian does not want rain, regarding me as the leader of the anti-rain faction. Those who became converted, therefore, cannot be regarded as hypocrites; for hypocrites do not generally take the line that ensures an empty stomach. I have no doubt the Gospel is entering into their hearts; for when I have been passing their houses, I have frequently heard them engaged in prayer, in a loud tone of voice. It is considered very disgraceful for men to cry in Africa; a stoical indifference to all sorrow or suffering is their educated practice. Yet have I seen stern men in public assemblies, crying out, like the jailor at Philippi, and weeping in the most piteous manner about the concerns of their souls. I doubt not, though I may not live to see it, but that God will bring my ministry in that region to a good result.

The difficulty of the chief Sechele, as I said before, was with regard to his five wives. The father of this man had been murdered, and four of the principal men had assisted in restoring the son to the chieftainship of the tribe: to shew his gratitude for which service, he had married a daughter of each of his benefactors; now, he could not very well put them away without appearing ungrateful. I found great difficulty in this matter: the wives were my aptest scholars, and I wished to save them as well as the Chief. In consequence of being sent away, these women and their friends became bitter enemies of Christianity. Furthermore, the African has a passion for an alliance with great men; on being introduced, he is sure to tell you that he is the remote cousin, relation or descendant, of some noted man; or some friend or hanger-on will tell you for him. Such alliances too have a political importance for the chief himself; since they attach powerful men to his interests and service. Hence my difficulties were increased by these facts. But the most difficult opponents I had to contend against were the Dutch Boers.[13]

Two hundred years ago, a number of Dutch and French people, the descendants of pious families, fled from the persecutions in Holland and France, and settled at and around the Cape. But their descendants fled from the British dominion in Cape Colony, on account of the emancipation by the government of their Hottentot slaves. They said, they did not like a government that made no difference between a black man and a white one: they therefore made forays and slavery incursions, and established themselves where they could pursue their slave-holding propensities with impunity. No fugitive slave-law being in operation, hundreds of Africans fled from the Boers to Sechele, and the Dutch consequently desired to get rid of that chief. They attacked the Bakwains while I was staying among them; and had fre-

---

13. Dr Livingstone often discusses these people, and has little reason to remember them favourably. He is too liberal-minded and straight-forward for them, and hence they threatened his life. They now reside chiefly near the Kalahari desert, being also numerous about the Kuruman station, where they are characterized for industry and successful irrigation. The more distant or transversal Boers reside behind the Cashan mountains. These were particularly furious against the Doctor. These people increase rapidly, and are sheep-farmers; being somewhat deservedly held in low estimation by the Cape community. In manners they are kind one towards another, but cruel to the natives. The word "Boer" simply means "farmer." Frequent fights occur between them and the Hottentots, Griquas, and Bechuanas, with varied results. Our traveller considers the British policy of allowing them and the Kafirs to have arms and ammunition, while the Bechuanas and Griquas are debarred therefrom, to be suicidal.

The most disaffected are those who have fled from English law. They have set up a republic, in order to carry out what they call "the proper treatment of the blacks," which is making them render compulsory unpaid labour, in return for what they call protection! These tender-hearted *Christians* have introduced a new species of slavery. The Bechuanas will not sell their people: hence the Boers seize children for domestic slaves. The reason why they do this is a shrewd one. As we have seen, there can be no fugitive slave-law in Africa; hence if a slave runs away, it is not very probable that he will be recovered. If a child is taken away, he does not know his tribe, forgets his mother-tongue, and possibly his very parents; hence he has less inducement to run away. On the occasion of the attack on Sechele (see *Introduction*, pp. v–viii), they carried away the two hundred children above-named, with the motives and for the purposes stated. In truth they are inveterate slave-hunters and dealers, the more distant revelling in slothful idleness on the industry of the natives. Themselves they call "Christians;" the natives, "black property," or "creatures;" saying, that God has given them, "the heathen for an inheritance."

This accursed system has made them fraudulent and mean-spirited; English missionaries, traders and travellers are their abomination, fearing that they will enlighten the natives, and especially give them firearms. Hear our traveller's decision about the matter, as far as he is concerned: "The Boers resolved to shut up the interior, and I determined to open the country; and we shall see who have been most successful in resolution, they or I."—*Travels*, p. 39.

quent battles with the people, killing many of them in these unequal conflicts. As an illustration as to how far exaggeration can be carried, on one occasion, I lent the chief a cooking-pot, which the Boers afterwards magnified into a cannon! and 5 guns into 500; writing to the English authorities, to inform them that I was protecting the Bakwains with cannon; and even some Boers were killed with guns. The reputation of this cannon kept the Boers away for seven years; but when their independence was declared by the Colonial government, they again made war upon the Bakwains, and being mounted and possessing guns, had the advantage, but it so happened that the Bakwains killed some of the Boers in one foray, and the latter gave me all the credit for it: asserting as a reason, "These people knew nothing of shooting till this Englishman came among them, and he has taught it them." The Boers, however, ultimately were victorious, and carried off 200 children of the Bakwains into slavery, killing 60 adults.

Sechele, knowing that such a proceeding was contrary to their engagements, and all law, set off to go to the Queen of England, to tell her of their conduct. I met him on his way to the Cape, and endeavoured to persuade him from going any further; on explaining the difficulties of the way, and endeavouring to dissuade him from the attempt, he put the pointed question:— "Will the Queen not listen to me, supposing I should reach her?" I replied, "I believe she would listen, but the difficulty is to get to her." He had many conversations with me on the subject, but he was determined, however, in his course, and proceeded to Cape Town.

Now, it so happened, that the Governor of Cape Colony had just sent home a flaming account of the peace and happiness that would prevail under his plan, and had he taken any notice of Sechele it would have been a virtual confession, that he had made a mull: consequently the chief and myself met with little encouragement. He had an interview with the Governor, to whom he delivered a letter from me, offering to point out the whole of the children, but all to no purpose: it is convenient sometimes for governors to be deaf, and shrug their shoulders, and to put political expediency before individual right. The British officers at the Cape, however—for English officers, wherever they are, are always fond of fair play—advised Sechele to go on, and subscribed £113 for him; but not knowing the value of money, he soon spent it all, giving a sovereign where sixpence would do, and so on; so that he found himself, at length, a thousand miles from home, and as poor as when he started. Instead of feeling angry at the ill-success of his mission, he began to preach to the natives around, and many anti-slavery tribes enlisted under him: consequently he has now many more people than he had before, and finds it hard work to be both priest and king. He opened a prayer-meeting, and, in fact, became his own missionary among his own people. He built himself a house and a school, and was the means of converting his wife. The people clustered around him, and there is every reason to believe that he is a sincere Christian.

What we greatly need is more missionaries to sow the seed of spiritual truth. The fields are white to the harvest. Glorious is the prospect of the outpouring of the Holy Spirit on all the ends of the earth. Labourers are wanted in the heathen vineyard of the Lord. As yet the missionary has only put in the thin end of the wedge towards the advancement of the kingdom of heaven in those dark places of the earth, which are still full of the habitations of cruelty—Africa, especially. Where, as yet, are the mission stations of North or South central Africa? Yet there are numbers of tribes,

> In those romantic regions men grow wild,
> There dwells the negro, Nature's outcast child.

As an encouragement to those who think of being missionaries, I need not say more than call to remembrance those Reformers who founded our Colleges here. The missionary's work is one of the most honourable a man can desire. Think of those Reformers; who would not like to be one of them? The missionaries now are just in their position. Those who now go forth as missionaries, and endeavour to advance the knowledge of Christ and His Gospel, are pre-eminently their representatives. Like the morning star before the dawn, they entered into the thick darkness, and began the glorious work of making known the promises of Christ, for which posterity will bless their name. Indeed to be a missionary is a great privilege and honour. The work is so great and glorious, that it has this promise of Him who "is the same yesterday, to-day, and for ever:"—"I will never leave thee, nor forsake thee,"—encouraging both itself and its promoters.

Finding that I could not successfully carry on the work of a missionary among the Bakwains, I conceived the idea of becoming a traveller. The question came across my mind, Whither will you go, to the North or to the South? I resolved to go to the North, to endeavour to open the country to the coast. Having got into the country beyond the Kalahari desert, bounded to the south by Lake Ngami, I came into quite a different country, where there are a great many rivers which flow from the sides into the centre. They form a very large river. The Zambesi is very much broader than the Thames at London Bridge. This large river flows out at the east end until it gets into the central basin by means of a fissure, which is 600 feet above the level of the sea. It was highly necessary for that fissure to be made. If it had not, a lake would have had to be formed for the purpose of getting away the very large amount of water which flows into the central basin. The rivers there are not like those in our country, since their sides are perpendicular. The region beyond the Kalahari desert is in the form of a basin, covered with a layer of calcareous tufa, intersected by the course of the Zambesi, which flows Southward until it reaches near Linyanti, and then branches off to the East. In the Kalahari desert there is not a single flowing stream, and the only water there is found in deep wells; but at certain periods of the year water-melons are found in abundance, upon the fluid of which oxen and men have subsisted for days, obviating thereby the necessity for carrying water. Animals are also plentiful; and though they took care to keep out of bow-shot, I found that with my gun I could kill as many as were wanted. In my journey beyond the desert, I met with many antelopes of a kind before unknown to naturalists, besides elephants, buffaloes, zebras, &c.

The chief of the central basin I have described, is named Sekeletu. I proposed to teach him to read, but he said he was afraid it would change his heart, and make him content with only one wife, like Sechele. I told him if he were content with one, what did it matter? But he said, "No, no; I always want to have five. I intend to keep them." Seeing I was anxious that he should learn to read, he subjected his father-in-law to learn first, as some men like to see the effect of medicines on other people, before they imbibe them themselves; and finding that it did him no harm, Sekeletu was taught long enough to gain the ability to read.

I entered this central basin, in order to find out a path to the sea: I might have gone to the west from Linyanti, but the country in that direction is infested with an insect called Tsetse, whose bite is fatal to most tame animals. To escape the insect plague, I resolved to go northwards and westwards to Loanda, the capital of Angola, a large city containing 12,000 inhabitants, a cathedral, and a Jesuit college. Having got down to the West coast, I found I had not accomplished my object of finding a path to the sea, the way being beset with difficulties and almost impassable. In fact, the only conveyance was ox-back, and dense forests had to be passed through by tortuous paths. I resolved, therefore, to go back, and try if the Zambesi did not furnish a good pathway to the eastern coast.

I did not find the people in that direction quite so well disposed towards me as the western tribes: the former were accustomed to the slave-trade, and asked payment for every thing: they prayed to the departed spirits of dead men, and believed that the deceased had power to influence the living. When I was at Cassange, the farthest inland station of the Portuguese, the governor, with whom I was stopping, had a sick child, and the nurse sent for a diviner to tell the cause of its illness. This man worked himself into frenzy, foamed at the mouth, and, pretending to be speaking under the influence of the fit, said the child was being killed by the soul of a trader, whose goods its father had stolen, and he said he should make an offering to appease the vengeance of the departed spirit. Now, it so happened that a native of Cassange had recently died, leaving an assignment, under which the governor had taken his goods; and the natives, not understanding the circumstances, said he had robbed him. This was the diviner's cue. The governor quietly sent to a friend of his, and they each took a stick, and applied them with such force to the back of the diviner, that he fled in the most undignified manner. I have never read of clairvoyance or spirit-rapping being tested similarly, but probably the trial would be equally successful.

My journey to Loanda was productive of delight among the natives whom I had left, and on returning to Linyanti the chief sent several tusks to Loanda for sale; the men also got goods, but by the time they got back to Linyanti, had been so afflicted with fever, that they were all expended. Only 27 accompanied me to Loanda, but when the people found I was going to find a path to the east, 114 volunteered to join me.

The people of that central part were anxious to have intercourse with white men, and their productions of cotton, indigo, &c. cannot fail to render commerce with them advantageous. Without the central basin, also, besides cotton, there are extensive coal-fields, with nine seams upon the surface, as well as an abundance of iron ore of the best quality. There is also produced a fibrous plant worth £50 or £60 a ton; and I have the authority of an English merchant to state, that a fabric finer and stronger than flax might be woven from it. The wild vine grows here in great luxuriance, and might be brought, by cultivation, to bear the most delicious grapes.

On each side of the southern portion of Africa is an elevated ridge, in the centre of which flows the Zambesi, forming an oblong inclosure. The climate on the sides of each elevation is different to that of the centre; Mr Moffat having found a species of the Angola goat, which flourishes in the Northern part of Asia, on the high-land; wheat also grows there well. This climate is, therefore, not open to the usual objection that Europeans could not live there. Some of the elevations in this part are about 5000 feet above the level of the sea. The country hereabout is one of gradual elevation; still there are different climates, ridges, and elevations, and the heat at times very great; the highlands generally are cool and salubrious, and fit for European residence. The Zambesi was full when I passed it, but even at low water it was as deep as the Thames in London, and therefore, might be traversed by a tolerably sized steamer. At the junction of other rivers with the Zambesi there is a rapid, and the coal-field to which I have alluded is near it; but the river is otherwise free from obstruction, and I trust will be the means of conveying the productions of that country to this, and thus opening the way for commerce and civilization to the benighted Africans upon its banks.

The people of the interior are very desirous to hold intercourse with white men. Having been cradled in wars' alarms, they ask, "When will you bring us sleep?" "We want sleep!" meaning peace. One reason of my being well received in the country was, because it had got noised abroad that I had come for that purpose. One report told to the Portuguese governor at Teté was, "That the Son of God was coming, with the moon under his arm," alluding to me and my sextant. Several deputations from towns and villages in the interior, in waiting on me, asked for "sleep." Such was also the topic of the songs, and talk of the women.

All this evidences a certain preparedness for receiving the Gospel, and it is for Christian England to answer the inquiry with the pure Gospel of the Prince of Peace. Already Providence is clearing the way for that Gospel; the hand of God has been at work in a striking manner. When I first went to that country, I found Providence paving the way before me: a chieftain had invaded the central basin, before I went there; had conquered the country, discovered Lake Ngami; and the language of the Bechuanas, into which Mr Moffat had translated the Scriptures, had become diffused in the district.

The natives formerly used to cut off the heads of strangers, and stick them on poles; but the chief[14] who conquered them had made the country safe, otherwise my cranium might have adorned one of their villages. I am convinced that the Portuguese have never gone into this district, because their maps gave a different course to the Zambesi; and I am strengthened in that opinion from the quantity of ivory tusks I saw adorning the graves of chieftains, and put to other uses, thereby proving that there was no market for them. Another reason is, that they sent all the way to Mozambique for lime, when there were large marble quarries within a comparatively short distance. I therefore believe that I am the first European who has entered that region. But now they have the Bible in their own language, it is the fashionable language, and the missionary has no difficulty in communicating with them; thus shewing that the hand of Providence has been at work.

When I was at Loanda, I was laid up with the fevers of the country, and being very weak, Captain Bedingfield, with whom I was upon intimate terms, strongly persuaded me to go home, offering a free passage; however, I having brought the twenty-seven men from Sekeletu, had no desire to leave them;

14. The chief here referred to is Sebituane; for an account of him, see note 10. The natives here referred to are the Batoka, with several of whom our traveller had some difficulties.

and committing certain papers and maps to the care of that officer, bade him farewell. Soon after, I received intelligence that the ship had gone down off Madeira, and my papers with it. Several lives were lost, but my friend was saved; but probably had I gone with the ship, I should have been drowned; and had I, on the other hand, first travelled eastward, I should have gone in the midst of the skirmishes that were then going on between the Portuguese and the Kafirs, and might have been cut off among them. Even when I travelled in that direction, I was in some danger; but when I said I was an Englishman, I was allowed to pass. I was told that if I went to the East, the people who were for the support of the Portuguese government would per-haps kill me; I said that I loved a black man as well as a white man. I often found that I rose in the estimation of the people among whom I passed, when it was told I was an Englishman, one of that country which is engaged in putting down slavery: they called me "the right sort of white man."

In the middle of the country they passed me off in a way that I scarcely liked. The people imagine that all white people, and the manufactures they import, come out of the sea, and suppose that the whites live under the water; also, that if they leave slaves, fruits, &c. on the sea-shore, that then the white men come up and take them away. My men were asked, Whether I came out of the sea? "Yes," said they, "don't you see how straight the water has made his hair?" Not relishing the idea of being passed off as a merman, I endeavoured to dissipate the idea, but the story was too good to be easily got rid of. The Africans, whose hair is all wool, could not understand my head, and some of them declared that I wore a wig made of a lion's mane.[15]

---

15. This idea of the white man actually living in the sea is largely prevalent in Africa. One cause of the terror of the natives at the European is, a report maliciously spread about that the white man takes the slaves into the sea, and actually eats them. Major Laing's experience was somewhat like Dr Livingstone's. He penetrated into Africa, in 1822, from Sierra Leone, as far as Soolimana, and relates the following piece of African droll simplicity concerning himself. Among the Kooranko people he was hailed with delighted astonishment, as being the first white man they had ever seen. All classes vied in doing him honour. The men and women sung in alternate choruses as follows: the men sung, "Of the white man who came out of the water to live among the Kooranko people; the white man ate nothing but fish when he lived in the water, and that is the cause of his being so thin. If he came among black men he would get fat, for they would give him cows, goats, and sheep to eat, and his thirst should be quenched with draughts of milk."

The women were less complimentary, and shewed a spirit not quite so kindly as those did to Mungo Park. The burden of the ladies' song, after the dance, was, "Of the white man who had come to their town; of the houseful of money which he had, such cloth, such beads, such fine things as had never been seen in Kooranko before. If their husbands were men, and wished to see their wives well dressed, they ought to take some of the money from the white man!" This counsel had a bad effect, and was mainly set aside by the major's native attendant, Tamba,

My object in labouring as I have in Africa, is to open up the country to commerce and Christianity. This is my object in returning thither. I contend that we ought not to be ashamed of our religion, and had we not kept this so much out of sight in India, we should not be now in such straits in that country. Let us appear just what we are. For my own part, I intend to go out as a missionary, and hope boldly, but with civility, to state the truth of Christianity and my belief that those who do not possess it are in error. My object in Africa is not only the elevation of man, but that the country might be so opened, that man might see the need of his soul's salvation.

I propose in my next expedition to visit the Zambesi, and to propitiate the different chiefs along its banks, endeavouring to induce them to cultivate cotton, and to abolish the slave-trade: already they trade in ivory and gold-dust, and are anxious to extend their commercial operations. There is thus a probability of their interests being linked with ours, and thus the elevation of the African would be the result.

I believe England is alive to her duty of civilizing and Christianizing the heathen. We cannot all go out as missionaries, it is true; but we may all do something towards providing a substitute: moreover, all may especially do that which every missionary highly prizes, viz. commend the work in their prayers. I hope that those whom I now address, will both pray for, and help those who are their substitutes.

SOURCE: "Lecture I" and "Lecture II" in *Dr. Livingstone's Cambridge Lectures* (London: Deighton, Beli, 1858), 1–23, 24–47.

———

Excerpts from *How I Found Livingstone*
HENRY M. STANLEY

[Henry Morton Stanley (1841–1904) was born John Rowlands, the illegitimate son of John Rowlands and Elizabeth Parry. He was abandoned in a British workhouse as a young child. Stanley obtained a job as a cabin boy on a ship bound for New Orleans, Louisiana, in 1859. New Orleans merchant Henry Hope Stanley adopted him and gave the orphan boy his own name. In 1867 Stanley joined the staff of the *New York Herald* as a special

———

shrewdly slipping in and singing, "Of Sierra Leone, of houses a mile in length filled with money; that the white man who was here had nothing compared with those at Sierra Leone; if therefore they wished to see some of these rich men come into Kooranko, they must not trouble this one; whoever wanted to see a snake's tail must not strike it on the head."—*Lond. Encyclop.* Vol. 1. p. 259.

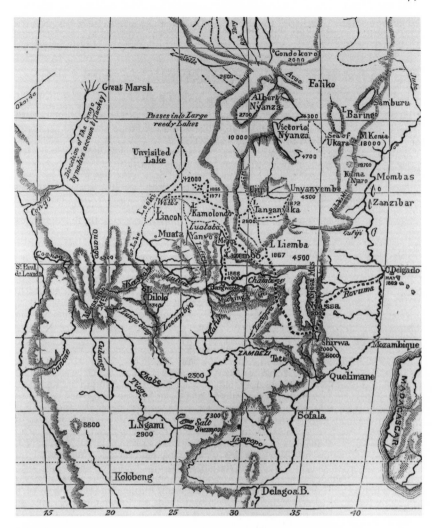

Sketch map of Livingstone's journeys 1841–1856.
Good Words (London: Daldy, Ibister, 1874).

correspondent. His editor James Gordon Bennett's desire to have Stanley, the traveling correspondent, locate Livingstone would forever change Stanley's life. Stanley's success led some of the British members of the press to charge him with fictionalizing his mission. The Royal Geographical Society also resented his achievement and doubted his geographical findings; however, the society would eventually award Stanley a gold medal for his scientific discoveries. When David Livingstone died in 1873, Stanley took up his unsuccessful search for the source of the Nile. Stanley's roving reporter activities gave him both physical and political-national mobility; when the reports of his discoveries failed to raise British interest in the Congo, for example, he put himself in the service of King Leopold II of Belgium. Stanley's citizenship status was similarly fluid: he became a U.S. citizen in 1885 and re-naturalized as a British citizen in 1892, when the English recognized and applauded his achievements. Stanley served as a member of Parliament for North Lambeth from 1895 to 1900. He was knighted in 1900. Some of Stanley's significant works include *Coomassie and Magdala: The Story of Two British Campaigns in Africa* (1874), *In Darkest Africa* (1890), *The Congo and the Founding of Its Free State: A Story of Work and Exploration* (1885), and *The Flaming Torch in Darkest Africa* (1898).]

INTRODUCTORY

On the sixteenth day of October, in the year of our Lord one thousand eight hundred and sixty-nine, I am in Madrid, fresh from the carnage at Valencia. At 10 A.M. Jacopo, at No.—Calle de la Cruz, hands me a telegram: on opening it I find it reads, "Come to Paris on important business." The telegram is from Jas. Gordon Bennett, jun., the young manager of the "New York Herald."

Down come my pictures from the walls of my apartments on the second floor, into my trunks go my books and souvenirs, my clothes are hastily collected, some half washed, some from the clothes-line half dry, and after a couple of hours of hasty hard work my portmanteaus are strapped up, and labelled for "Paris."

The express-train leaves Madrid for Hendaye at 3 P.M. I have yet time to say farewell to my friends. I have one at No. 6 Calle Goya, fourth floor, who happens to be a contributor to several London dailies. He has several children, in whom I have taken a warm interest. Little Charlie and Willie are fast friends of mine; they love to hear of my adventures, and it has been a pleasure to me to talk to them. But now I must say farewell.

Then I have friends at the United States Legation whose conversation I admire—there has come a sudden ending of it all. "I hope you will write to us, we shall always be glad to hear of your welfare." How often have I not during my feverish life as a flying journalist heard the very same words, and how often have I not suffered the same pang at parting from friends just as warm as these.

But a journalist in my position must needs suffer. Like a gladiator in the arena, he must be prepared for the combat. Any flinching, any cowardice, and he is lost. The gladiator meets the sword that is sharpened for his bosom—the flying journalist or roving correspondent meets the command that may send him to his doom. To the battle or the banquet it is ever the same—"Get ready and go."

At 3 P.M. I was on my way, and being obliged to stop at Bayonne a few hours, did not arrive at Paris until the following night. I went straight to the "Grand Hotel," and knocked at the door of Mr. Bennett's room.

"Come in," I heard a voice say.

Entering, I found Mr. Bennett in bed.

"Who are you?" he asked.

"My name is Stanley!" I answered.

"Ah, yes! sit down; I have important business on hand for you."

After throwing over his shoulders his robe-de-chambre, Mr. Bennett asked, "Where do you think Livingstone is?"

"I really do not know, sir!"

"Do you think he is alive?"

"He may be, and he may not be!" I answered.

"Well, I think he is alive, and that he can be found, and I am going to send you to find him."

"What!" said I, "do you really think I can find Dr. Livingstone? Do you mean me to go to Central Africa?"

"Yes; I mean that you shall go, and find him wherever you may hear that he is, and to get what news you can of him, and perhaps"—delivering himself thoughtfully and deliberately—"the old man may be in want:—take enough with you to help him should he require it. Of course you will act according to your own plans, and do what you think best—BUT FIND LIVINGSTONE!

Said I, wondering at the cool order of sending one to Central Africa to search for a man whom I, in common with almost all other men, believed to be dead, "have you considered seriously the great expense you are likely to incur on account of this little journey?"

"What will it cost?" he asked, abruptly.

"Burton and Speke's journey to Central Africa cost between £3,000 and £5,000, and I fear it cannot be done under £2,500."

"Well, I will tell you what you will do. Draw a thousand pounds now; and when you have gone through that, draw another thousand, and when that is spent, draw another thousand, and when you have finished that, draw another thousand, and so on; but, FIND LIVINGSTONE.

Surprised but not confused at the order, for I knew that Mr. Bennett when once he had made up his mind was not easily drawn aside from his purpose, I yet thought, seeing it was such a gigantic scheme, that he had not quite considered in his own mind the pros and cons of the case; I said, "I have heard that should your father die you would sell the 'Herald' and retire from business."

"Whoever told you that is wrong, for there is not money enough in New York city to buy the 'New York Herald.' My father has made it a great paper, but I mean to make it greater. I mean that it shall be a news paper in the true sense of the word. I mean that it shall publish whatever news will be interesting to the world at no matter what cost."

"After that," said I, "I have nothing more to say. Do you mean me to go straight on to Africa to search for Dr. Livingstone?"

"No! I wish you to go to the inauguration of the Suez Canal first and then proceed up the Nile. I hear Baker is about starting for Upper Egypt. Find out what you can about his expedition, and as you go up describe as well as possible whatever is interesting for tourists; and then write up a guide—a practical one—for Lower Egypt, tell us about whatever is worth seeing and how to see it.

"Then you might as well go to Jerusalem; I hear Captain Warren is making some interesting discoveries there. Then visit Constantinople, and find out about that trouble between the Khedive and the Sultan.

"Then—let me see—you might as well visit the Crimea and those old battle-grounds. Then go across the Caucasus to the Caspian Sea, I hear there is a Russian expedition bound for Khiva. From thence you may get through Persia to India; you could write an interesting letter from Persepolis.

"Bagdad will be close on your way to India; suppose you go there, and write up something about the Euphrates Valley Railway. Then, when you have come to India, you can go after Livingstone. Probably you will hear by that time that Livingstone is on his way to Zanzibar; but if not, go into the interior and find him, if alive. Get what news of his discoveries you can; and, if you find he is dead, bring all possible proofs of his being dead. That is all. Good-night, and God be with you."

"Good-night, sir," I said; "what it is in the power of human nature to do I will do; and on such an errand as I go upon, God will be with me."

I lodged with young Edward King, who is making such a name in New England. He was just the man who would have delighted to tell the Journal he was engaged upon what young Mr. Bennett was doing, and what errand I was bound upon.

I should have liked to exchange opinions with him upon the probable results of my journey, but I dared not do so. Though oppressed with the great task before me, I had to appear as if only going to be present at the Suez Canal. Young King followed me to the express-train bound for Marseilles, and at the station we parted—he to go, and read the newspapers at Bowles' Reading-room—I to Central Africa and—who knows?

There is no need to recapitulate what I did before going to Central Africa.

I went up the Nile, and saw Mr. Higginbotham, chief-engineer in Baker's Expedition, at Philæ, and was the means of preventing a duel between him and a mad young Frenchman, who wanted to fight Mr. Higginbotham with pistols, because that gentleman resented the idea of being taken for an Egyptian, through wearing a fez cap. I had a talk with Capt. Warren at Jerusalem, and descended one of the pits with a sergeant of engineers to see the marks of the Tyrian workmen on the foundation stones of the Temple of Solomon. I visited the mosques of Stamboul with the Minister Resident of the United States, and the American Consul General. I travelled over the Crimean battle-grounds with Kinglake's glorious books for reference in my hand. I dined with the widow of General Liprandi at Odessa. I saw the Arabian traveller Palgrave at Trebizond, and Baron Nicolay, the Civil Governor of the Caucasus, at Tiflis. I lived with the Russian Ambassador while at Teheran, and wherever I went through Persia I received the most hospitable welcome from the gentlemen of the Indo-European Telegraph Company; and following the examples of many illustrious men, I wrote my name upon one of the Persepolitan monuments. In the month of August, 1870, I arrived in India.

On the 12th of October I sailed on the barque "Polly" from Bombay to Mauritius. As the "Polly" was a slow sailer, the passage lasted thirty-seven days. On board this barque was a William Lawrence Farquhar—hailing from Leith, Scotland—in the capacity of first-mate. He was an excellent navigator, and thinking he might be useful to me, I employed him; his pay to begin from the date we should leave Zanzibar for Bagamoyo. As there was no opportunity of getting to Zanzibar direct, I took ship to Seychelles. Three or four days after arriving at Mahé, one of the Seychelles group, I was fortunate enough to get a passage for myself, William Lawrence Farquhar, and Selim— a Christian Arab boy of Jerusalem, who was to act as interpreter—on board an American whaling vessel, bound for Zanzibar, at which port we arrived on the 6th of January, 1871.

I have skimmed over my travels thus far, because these do not concern the reader. They led over many lands, but this book is only a narrative of my search after Livingstone, the great African traveller. It is an Icarian flight of journalism, I confess; some even have called it Quixotic; but this is a word I can now refute, as will be seen before the reader arrives at the "Finis."

I have used the word "soldiers" in this book. The armed escort a traveller engaged to accompany him into East Africa is composed of free black men, natives of Zanzibar, or freed slaves from the interior, who call themselves "askari," an Indian name which, translated, means "soldiers." They are armed and equipped like soldiers, though they engage themselves also as servants; but it would be more pretentious in me to call them servants, than to use the word "soldiers;" and as I have been more in the habit of calling them soldiers, than my watuma—servants—this habit has proved too much to be overcome. I have therefore allowed the word "soldiers" to appear, accompanied, however, with this apology.

I have also used the personal pronoun first person singular, "I," oftener, perhaps, than real modesty would admit.

But it must be remembered that I am writing a narrative of my own adventures and travels, and that until I meet Livingstone, I presume the greatest interest is attached to myself, my marches, my troubles, my thoughts, and my impressions. Yet though I may sometimes write, "my expedition," or "my caravan," it by no means follows that I arrogate to myself this right. For it must be distinctly understood that it is the "'New York Herald' Expedition," and that I am only charged with its command by Mr. James Gordon Bennett, the proprietor of the 'New York Herald,' as a salaried employé of that gentleman.

One thing more; I have adopted the narrative form of relating the story of the search, on account of the greater interest it appears to possess over the diary form, and I think that in this manner I avoid the great fault of repetition for which some travellers have been severely criticised.

Having explained so much, I do not think it necessary to say any more in the Introduction, and shall therefore commence my narrative.

Henry M. Stanley
8, *Duchess Street, Portland Place, London.*
October, 1872.

November 3rd

What contention have we not been a witness to these last three days! What anxiety have we not suffered ever since our arrival in Uvinza! The Wavinza are worse than the Wagogo, and their greed is more insatiable. We got the donkey across with the aid of a mganga, or medicine man, who spat some chewed leaves of a tree which grows close to the stream over him. He informed me he could cross the river at any time, day or night, after rubbing his body with these chewed leaves, which he believed to be a most potent medicine.

About 10 A.M. appeared from the direction of Ujiji a caravan of eight Weguhha, a tribe which occupies a tract of country on the south-western side of the Lake Tanganika. We asked the news, and were told a white man had just arrived at Ujiji from Manyuema. This news startled us all.

"A white man?" we asked.

"Yes, a white man," they replied.

"How is he dressed?"

"Like the master," they answered, referring to me.

"Is he young, or old?"

"He is old. He has white hair on his face, and is sick."

"Where has he come from?"

"From a very far country away beyond Uguhha, called Manyuema."

"Indeed! and is he stopping at Ujiji now?"

"Yes, we saw him about eight days ago."

"Do you think he will stop there until we see him?"

"*Sigue*" (don't know).

"Was he ever at Ujiji before?"

"Yes, he went away a long time ago."

Hurrah! This is Livingstone! He must be Livingstone! He *can* be no other; but still;—he may be some one else—some one from the West Coast—or perhaps he is Baker! No; Baker has no white hair on his face. But we must now march quick, lest he hears we are coming, and runs away.

I addressed my men, and asked them if they were willing to march to Ujiji without a single halt, and then promised them, if they acceded to my wishes, two doti each man. All answered in the affirmative, almost as much rejoiced as I was myself. But I was madly rejoiced; intensely eager to resolve the burning question, "Is it Dr. David Livingstone?" God grant me patience, but I do wish there was a railroad, or, at least, horses in this country. With a horse I could reach Ujiji in about twelve hours.

We set out at once from the banks of the Malagarazi, accompanied by two guides furnished us by Usenge, the old man of the ferry, who, now that we had crossed, showed himself more amiably disposed to us. We arrived at the village of Isinga, Sultan Katalambula, after a little over an hour's march across a saline plain, but which as we advanced into the interior became fertile and productive. We were warned after camping that to-morrow's march would have to be made with caution, as a band of Wavinza, under Makumbi, a great chief of Nzogera's, were returning from war, and it was the custom of Makumbi to leave nothing behind him after a victory. Intoxicated with success, he attacked even the villages of his own tribe, capturing the live stock—slaves and cattle. The result of a month's campaign against Lokanda-Mira was the destruction of two villages, the killing of one of the children of that chief, and the slaughter of several men; Makumbi also lost five men from thirst during the crossing of a saline desert south of the Malagarazi.

November 4th

Started early with great caution, maintaining deep silence. The guides were sent forward, one two hundred yards ahead of the other, that we might be warned in time. The first part of the march was through a thin jungle of dwarf trees, which got thinner and thinner until finally it vanished altogether, and we had entered Uhha—a plain country. Villages were visible by the score among the tall bleached stalks of dourra and maize. Sometimes three, sometimes five, ten, or twenty beehive-shaped huts formed a village. The Wahha were evidently living in perfect security, for not one village amongst them all was surrounded with the customary defence of an African village. A narrow dry ditch formed the only boundary between Uhha and Uvinza. On entering Uhha, all danger from Makumbi vanished.

We halted at Kawanga, the chief of which lost no time in making us understand that he was the great Mutware of Kimenyi under the king, and that he was the tribute gatherer for his Kiha majesty. He declared that he was the only one in Kimenyi—an eastern division of Uhha—who could demand tribute; and that it would be very satisfactory to him, and a saving of trouble to ourselves, if we settled his claim of twelve doti of good cloths at once. We did not think it the best way or proceeding, knowing as we did the character of the native African; so we at once proceeded to diminish this demand; but, after six hours' hot argument, the Mutware only reduced it by two. This claim was then settled, upon the understanding that we should be allowed to travel through Uhha as fas as the Rusugi River without being further mulcted.

November 5th

Leaving Kawanga early in the morning, and continuing our march over the boundless plains, which were bleached white by the hot equatorial sun, we were marching westward full of pleasant anticipations that we were nearing the end of our troubles, joyfully congratulating ourselves that within five days we should see that which I had come so far from civilisation, and through so many difficulties, to see, and were about passing a cluster of villages, with all the confidence which men possess against whom no one had further claim or a word to say, when I noticed two men darting from a group of natives who were watching us, and running towards the head of the Expedition, with the object, evidently, of preventing further progress.

The caravan stopped, and I walked forward to ascertain the cause from the two natives. I was greeted politely by the two Wahha with the usual "Yambos," and was then asked,

"Why does the white man pass by the village of the King of Uhha without salutation and a gift? Does not the white man know there lives a king in Uhha, to whom the Wangwana and Arabs pay something for right of passage?"

"Why, we paid last night to the chief of Kawanga, who informed us that he was the man deputed by the King of Uhha to collect the toll."

"How much did you pay?"

"Ten doti of good cloth."

"Are you sure?"

"Quite sure. If you ask him, he will tell you so."

"Well," said one of the Wahha, a fine, handsome, intelligent-looking youth, "it is our duty to the King to halt you here until we find out the truth of this. Will you walk to our village, and rest yourselves under the shade of our trees until we can send messengers to Kawanga?"

"No; the sun is but an hour high, and we have far to travel, but, in order to show you we do not seek to pass through your country without doing that which is right, we will rest where we now stand, and we will send with your messengers two of our soldiers, who will show you the man to whom we paid the cloth."

The messengers departed; but, in the meantime, the handsome youth, who turned out to be the nephew of the King, whispered some order to a lad, who immediately hastened away, with the speed of an antelope, to the cluster of villages which we had just passed. The result of this errand, as we saw in a short time, was the approach of a body of warriors, about fifty in number, headed by a tall, fine-looking man, who was dressed in a crimson robe called Joho, two ends of which were tied in a knot over the left shoulder; a new piece of American sheeting was folded like a turban around his head, and a large curved piece of polished ivory was suspended to his neck. He and his people were all armed with spears, and bows and arrows, and their advance was marked with a deliberation that showed they felt perfect confidence in any issue that might transpire.

We were halted on the eastern side of the Pombwe stream, near the village of Lukomo, in Kimenyi, Uhha.

The gorgeously-dressed chief was a remarkable man in appearance. His face was oval in form, high cheekbones, eyes deeply sunk, a prominent and bold forehead, a fine nose, and a well-cut mouth; he was tall in figure, and perfectly symmetrical.

When near to us, he hailed me with the words,

"Yambo, bana?—How do you do, master?" in quite a cordial tone.

I replied cordially also, "Yambo, mutware?—How do you do, chief?"

We, myself and men, interchanged "Yambos" with his warriors; and there was nothing in our first introduction to indicate that the meeting was of a hostile character.

The chief seated himself, his haunches resting on his heels, laying down his bow and arrows by his side; his men did likewise.

I seated myself on a bale, and each of my men sat down on their loads, forming quite a semicircle. The Wahha slightly outnumbered my party; but, while they were only armed with bows and arrows, spears, and knob-sticks, we were armed with rifles, muskets, revolvers, pistols, and hatchets.

All were seated, and deep silence was maintained by the assembly. The great plains around us were as still in this bright noon as if they were deserted of all living creatures. Then the chief spoke:

"I am Mionvu, the great Mutware of Kimenyi, and am next to the King, who lives yonder," pointing to a large village near some naked hills about ten miles to the north. "I have come to talk with the white man. It has always been the custom of the Arabs and the Wangwana to make a present to the King when they pass through his country. Does not the white man mean to pay the King's dues? Why does the white man halt in the road? Why will he not enter the village of Lukomo, where there is food and shade—where we can discuss this thing quietly? Does the white man mean to fight? I know well he is stronger than we are. His men have guns, and the Wahha have but bows and arrows, and spears; but Uhha is large, and our villages are many. Let him look about him everywhere—all is Uhha, and our country extends much further than he can see or walk in a day. The King of Uhha is strong; yet he wishes friendship only with the white man. Will the white man have war or peace?"

A deep murmur of assent followed this speech of Mionvu from his people, and disapprobation, blended with a certain uneasiness, from my men. When about replying, the words of General Sherman, which I heard him utter to the chiefs of the Arapahoes and Cheyennes at North Platte, in 1867, came to my mind; and something of their spirit I embodied in my reply to Mionvu, Mutware of Kimenyi.

"Mionvu, the great Mutware, asks me if I have come for war. When did

Mionvu ever hear of white men warring against black men? Mionvu must understand that the white men are different from the black. White men do not leave their country to fight the black people, neither do they come here to buy ivory or slaves. They come to make friends with black people; they come to search for rivers, and lakes, and mountains; they come to discover what countries, what peoples, what rivers, what lakes, what forests, what plains, what mountains and hills are in your country; to know the different animals that are in the land of the black people, that, when they go back, they may tell the white kings, and men, and children, what they have seen and heard in the land so far from them. The white people are different from the Arabs and Wangwana; the white people know everything, and are very strong. When they fight, the Arabs and the Wangwana run away. We have great guns which thunder, and when they shoot the earth trembles; we have guns which carry bullets further than you can see: even with these little things" (pointing to my revolvers) "I could kill ten men quicker than you could count. We are stronger than the Wahha. Mionvu has not spoken the truth, yet we do not wish to fight. I could kill Mionvu now, yet I talk to him as to a friend. I wish to be a friend to Mionvu, and to all black people. Will Mionvu say what I can do for him?"

As these words were translated to him—imperfectly, I suppose, but still, intelligibly—the faces of the Wahha showed how well they appreciated them. Once or twice I thought I detected something like fear, but my assertions that I desired peace and friendship with them soon obliterated all such feelings.

Mionvu replied:

"The white man tells me he is friendly. Why does he not come to our village? Why does he stop on the road? The sun is hot. Mionvu will not speak here any more. If the white man is a friend he will come to the village."

"We must stop now. It is noon. You have broken our march. We will go and camp in your village," I said, at the same time rising and pointing to the men to take up their loads.

We were compelled to camp; there was no help for it; the messengers had not returned from Kawanga. Having arrived in his village, Mionvu had cast himself at full length under the scanty shade afforded by a few trees within the boma. About 2 P.M. the messengers returned, saying it was true the chief of Kawanga had taken ten cloths; not, however for the King of Uhha, but for himself!

We made a short halt at noon, for rest and refreshment. I was shown the hills from which the Tanganika could be seen, which bounded the valley of the Liuche on the east. I could not contain myself at the sight of them. Even with this short halt I was restless and unsatisfied. We resumed the march again. I spurred my men forward with the promise that to-morrow should see their reward. Fish and beer should be given them, as much as they could eat and drink.

We were in sight of the villages of the Wakaranga; the people caught sight of us, and manifested considerable excitement. I sent men ahead to reassure them, and they came forward to greet us. This was so new and welcome to us, so different from the turbulent Wavinza and the black-mailers of Uhha, that we were melted. But we had no time to loiter by the way to indulge our joy. I was impelled onward by my almost uncontrollable feelings. I wished to re-solve my doubts and fears. Was He still there? Had He heard of my coming? Would He fly?

How beautiful Ukaranaga appears! The green hills are crowned by clusters of straw-thatched cones. The hills rise and fall; here denuded and cultivated, there in pasturage, here timbered, yonder swarming with huts. The country has somewhat the aspect of Maryland.

We cross the Mkuti, a glorious little river! We ascend the opposite bank, and stride through the forest like men who have done a deed of which they may be proud. We have already travelled nine hours, and the sun is sinking rapidly towards the west; yet, apparently, we are not fatigued.

We reach the outskirts of Niamtaga, and we hear drums beat. The people are flying into the woods; they desert their villages, for they take us to be Ruga-Ruga—the forest thieves of Mirambo, who, after conquering the Arabs of Unyanyembe, are coming to fight the Arabs of Ujiji. Even the King flies from his village, and every man, woman, and child, terror-stricken, follows him. We enter into it and quietly take possession, and my tent is set. Finally, the word is bruited about that we are Wangwana, from Unyanyembe.

"Well, then, is Mirambo dead?" they ask.

"No," we answer.

"Well, how did you come to Ukaranga?"

"Oh—hi-le!" Then they laugh heartily at their fright, and begin to make excuses. The King is introduced to me, and he says he had only gone to the woods in order to attack us again—he meant to have come back and killed us all, if we had been Ruga-Ruga. But then we know the poor King was terribly frightened, and would never have dared to return, had we been Ruga-Ruga—not he. We are not, however, in a mood to quarrel with him about an idio-matic phrase peculiar to him, but rather take him by the hand and shake it well, and say we are so very glad to see him. And he shares in our pleasure, and immediately three of the fattest sheep, pots of beer, flour, and honey are brought to us as a gift, and I make him happier still with two of the finest cloth I have in my bales; and thus a friendly pact is entered into between us. While I write my diary of this day's proceedings, I tell Selim to lay out my new flannel suit, to oil my boots, to chalk my helmet, and fold a new puggaree around it, that I may make as presentable an appearance as possible before the white man with the grey beard, and before the Arabs of Ujiji; for the clothes I have worn through jungle and forest are in tatters. Good-night; only let one day come again, and we shall see what we shall see.

November 10th. Friday.

The 236th day from Bagamoyo, and the 51st day from Unyanyembe. General direction to Ujiji, west-by-south. Time of march, six hours.

It is a happy, glorious morning. The air is fresh and cool. The sky lovingly smiles on the earth and her children. The deep woods are crowned in bright green leafage; the water of the Mkuti, rushing under the emerald shade afforded by the bearded banks, seems to challenge us for the race to Ujiji, with its continuous brawl.

We are all outside the village cane fence, every man of us looking as spruce, as neat, and happy as when we embarked on the dhows at Zanzibar, which seems to us to have been ages ago—we have witnessed and experienced so much.

"Forward!"

"Ay Wallah, ay Wallah, bana yango!" and the light-hearted braves stride away at a rate which must soon bring us within view of Ujiji. We ascend a hill overgrown with bamboo, descend into a ravine through which dashes an impetuous little torrent, ascend another short hill, then, along a smooth footpath running across the slope of a long ridge, we push on as only eager, light-hearted men can do.

In two hours I am warned to prepare for a view of the Tanganika, for, from the top of a steep mountain the kirangozi says I can see it. I almost vent the feelings of my heart in cries. But wait, we must behold it first. And we press forward and up the hill breathlessly, lest the grand scene hasten away. We are at last on the summit. Ah! not yet can it be seen. A little further on—just yonder, oh! there it is—a silvery gleam. I merely catch sight of it between the trees, and—but here it is at last! True—the Tanganika! and there are the blue-black mountains of Ugoma and Ukaramba. An immense broad sheet, a burnished bed of silver—lucid canopy of blue above—lofty mountains are its valances, palm forests form its fringes! The Tanganika!—Hurrah! and the men respond to the exultant cry of the Anglo-Saxon with the lungs of Stentors, and the great forests and the hills seem to share in our triumph.

"Was this the place where Burton and Speke stood, Bombay, when they saw the lake first?"

"I don't remember, master; it was somewhere about here, I think."

"Poor fellows! The one was half-paralyzed, the other half-blind," said Sir Roderick Murchison, when he described Burton and Speke's arrival in view of the Tanganika.

And I? Well, I am so happy that, were I quite paralyzed and blinded, I think that at this supreme moment I could take up my bed and walk, and all blindness would cease at once. Fortunately, however, I am quite well; I have not suffered a day's sickness since the day I left Unyanyembe. How much would Shaw be willing to give to be in my place now? Who is happiest—he, revelling in the luxuries of Unyanyembe, or I, standing on the summit of this mountain, looking down with glad eyes and proud heart on the Tanganika?

We are descending the western slope of the mountain, with the valley of the Liuche before us. Something like an hour before noon we have gained the thick matete brake, which grows on both banks of the river; we wade through the clear stream, arrive on the other side, emerge out of the brake, and the gardens of the Wajiji are around us—a perfect marvel of vegetable wealth. Details escape my hasty and partial observation. I am almost overpowered with my own emotions. I notice the graceful palms, neat plots, green with vegetable plants, and small villages surrounded with frail fences of the matete-cane.

We push on rapidly, lest the news of our coming might reach the people of Bunder Ujiji before we come in sight, and are ready for them. We halt at a little brook, then ascend the long slope of a naked ridge, the very last of the myriads we have crossed. This alone prevents us from seeing the lake in all its vastness. We arrive at the summit, travel across and arrive at its western rim, and—pause, reader—the port of Ujiji is below us, embowered in the palms, only five hundred yards from us! At this grand moment we do not think of the hundreds of miles we have marched, of the hundreds of hills that we have ascended and descended, of the many forests we have traversed, of the jungles and thickets that annoyed us, of the fervid salt plains that blistered our feet, of the hot suns that scorched us, nor the dangers and difficulties, now happily surmounted. At last the sublime hour has arrived!—our dreams, our hopes, and anticipations are now about to be realized! Our hearts and our feelings are with our eyes, as we peer into the palms and try to make out in which hut or house lives the white man with the grey beard we heard about on the Malagarazi.

"Unfurl the flags, and load your guns!"

"Ay Wallah, ay Wallah, bana!" respond the men, eagerly.

"One, two, three—fire!"

A volley from nearly fifty guns roars like a salute from a battery of artillery: we shall note its effect presently on the peaceful-looking village below.

"Now, kirangozi, hold the white man's flag up high, and let the Zanzibar flag bring up the rear. And you men keep close together, and keep firing until we halt in the market-place, or before the white man's house. You have said to me often that you could smell the fish of the Tanganika—I can smell the fish of the Tanganika now. There are fish, and beer, and a long rest waiting for you. March!"

Before we had gone a hundred years our repeated volleys had the effect desired. We had awakened Ujiji to the knowledge that a caravan was coming, and the people were witnessed rushing up in hundreds to meet us. The mere sight of the flags informed every one immediately that we were a caravan, but the American flag borne aloft by gigantic Asmani, whose face was one vast smile on this day, rather staggered them at first. However, many of the people who now approached us remembered the flag. They had seen it float above the American Consulate, and from the masthead of many a ship in the harbor of Zanzibar, and they were soon heard welcoming the beautiful flag with cries of "Bindera Kisungu!"—a white man's flag! "Bindera Merikani!"—the American flag!

Then we were surrounded by them: by Wajiji, Wanyamwezi, Wangwana, Warundi, Waguhha, Wamanyuema and Arabs, and were almost deafened with the shouts of "Yambo, yambo bana! Yambo, bana! Yambo, bana!" To all and each of my men the welcome was given.

We were now about three hundred yards from the village of Ujiji, and the crowds are dense about me. Suddenly I hear a voice on my right say,

"Good morning, sir!"

Startled at hearing this greeting in the midst of such, a crowd of black people, I turn sharply around in search of the man, and see him at my side, with the blackest of faces, but animated and joyous—a man dressed in a long white shirt, with a turban of American sheeting around his woolly head, and I ask:

"Who the mischief are you?"

"I am Susi, the servant of Dr. Livingstone," said he, smiling, and showing a gleaming row of teeth.

"What! Is Dr. Livingstone here?"

"Yes, sir."

"In this village?"

"Yes, sir."

"Are you sure?"

"Sure, sure, sir. Why, I leave him just now."

"Good morning, sir," said another voice.

"Hallo," said I, "is this another one?"

"Yes, sir."

"Well, what is your name?"

"My name is Chumah, sir."

"What! are you Chumah, the friend of Wekotani?"

"Yes, sir."

"And is the Doctor well?"

"Not very well, sir."

"Where has he been so long?"

"In Manyuema."

"Now, you Susi, run, and tell the Doctor I am coming."

"Yes, sir," and off he darted like a madman.

But by this time we were within two hundred yards of the village, and the multitude was getting denser, and almost preventing our march. Flags and streamers were out; Arabs and Wangwana were pushing their way through the natives in order to greet us, for, according to their account, we belonged to them. But the great wonder of all was, "How did you come from Unyanyembe?"

Soon Susi came running back, and asked me my name; he had told the Doctor that I was coming, but the Doctor was too surprised to believe him, and, when the Doctor asked him my name, Susi was rather staggered.

But, during Susi's absence, the news had been conveyed to the Doctor that it was surely a white man that was coming, whose guns were firing and whose flag could be seen; and the great Arab magnates of Ujiji—Mohammed bin Sali, Sayd bin Majid, Abid bin Suliman, Mohammed bin Gharib, and others—had gathered together before the Doctor's house, and the Doctor had come out from his veranda to discuss the matter and await my arrival.

In the meantime, the head of the Expedition had halted, and the kirangozi was out of the ranks, holding his flag aloft, and Selim said to me, "I see the Doctor, sir. Oh, what an old man! He has got a white beard." And I—what would I not have given for a bit of friendly wilderness, where, unseen, I might vent my joy in some mad freak, such as idiotically biting my hand, turning a somersault, or slashing at trees, in order to allay those exciting feelings that were well-nigh uncontrollable. My heart beats fast, but I must not let my face betray my emotions; lest it shall detract from the dignity of a white man appearing under such extraordinary circumstances.

So I did that which I thought was most dignified. I pushed back the crowds, and, passing from the rear, walked down a living avenue of people, until I came in front of the semicircle of Arabs, in the front of which stood the white man with the grey beard. As I advanced slowly towards him I noticed he was pale, looked wearied, had a grey beard, wore a bluish cap with a faded gold band round it, had on a red-sleeved waistcoat, and a pair of grey tweed trousers. I would have run to him, only I was a coward in the presence of such a mob—would have embraced him, only he being an Englishman, I did not know how he would receive me;[1] so I did what cowardice and false pride suggested was the best thing—walked deliberately to him, took off my hat, and said:

"Dr. Livingstone, I presume?"

"Yes," said he, with a kind smile, lifting his cap slightly.

I replace my hat on my head, and he puts on his cap, and we both grasp hands, and I then say aloud:

"I thank God, Doctor, I have been permitted to see you."

He answered, "I feel thankful that I am here to welcome you."

I turn to the Arabs, take off my hat to them in response to the saluting chorus of "Yambos" I receive, and the Doctor introduces them to me by name. Then, oblivious of the crowds, oblivious of the men who shared with me my dangers, we—Livingstone and I—turn our faces towards his tembe. He points to the veranda, or, rather, mud platform, under the broad over-hanging eaves; he points to his own particular seat, which I see his age and experience in Africa has suggested, namely, a straw mat, with a goatskin over it, and another skin nailed against the wall to protect his back from contact with the cold mud. I protest against taking this seat, which so much more befits him than me, but the Doctor will not yield: I must take it.

We are seated—the Doctor and I—with our backs to the wall. The Arabs

1. "This Englishman, as I afterwards found, was a military man returning to his country from India, and crossing the Desert at this part in order to go through Palestine. As for me, I had come pretty straight from England, and so here we met in the wilderness at about half-way from our respective starting-points. As we approached each other, it became with me a question whether we should speak; I thought it likely that the stranger would accost me, and in the event of his doing so, I was quite ready to be as sociable and chatty as I could be, according to my nature; but still I could not think of anything particular that I had to say to him; of course among civilized people, the not having anything to say is no excuse at all for not speaking, but I was shy, and indolent, and I felt no great wish to stop, and talk like a morning visitor, in the midst of those broad solitudes. The traveller perhaps felt as I did, for except that we lifted our hands to our caps, and waved our arms in courtesy, we passed each other as if we had passed in Bond Street."
—Kinglake's *Eōthen*.

take seats on our left. More than a thousand natives are in our front, filling the whole square densely, indulging their curiosity, and discussing the fact of two white men meeting at Ujiji—one just come from Manyuema, in the west, the other from Unyanyembe, in the east.

Conversation began. What about? I declare I have forgotten. Oh! we mutually asked questions of one another, such as:

"How did you come here?" and "Where have you been all this long time?—the world has believed you to be dead." Yes, that was the way it began; but whatever the Doctor informed me, and that which I communicated to him, I cannot correctly report, for I found myself gazing at him, conning the wonderful man at whose side I now sat in Central Africa. Every hair of his head and beard, every wrinkle of his face, the wanness of his features, and the slightly wearied look he wore, were all imparting intelligence to me—the knowledge I craved for so much ever since I heard the words, "Take what you want, but find Livingstone." What I saw was deeply interesting intelligence to me, and unvarnished truth. I was listening and reading at the same time. What did these dumb witnesses relate to me?

Oh, reader, had you been at my side on this day in Ujiji, how eloquently could be told the nature of this man's work! Had you been there but to see and hear! His lips gave me the details; lips that never lie. I cannot repeat what he said; I was too much engrossed to take my note-book out, and begin to stenograph his story. He had so much to say that he began at the end, seemingly oblivious of the fact that five or six years had to be accounted for. But his account was oozing out; it was growing fast into grand proportions—into a most marvellous history of deeds.

The Arabs rose up, with a delicacy I approved, as if they intuitively knew that we ought to be left to ourselves. I sent Bombay with them, to give them the news they also wanted so much to know about the affairs at Unyanyembe. Sayd bin Majid was the father of the gallant young man whom I saw at Masange, and who fought with me at Zimbizo, and who soon afterwards was killed by Mirambo's Ruga-Ruga in the forest of Wilyankuru; and, knowing that I had been there, he earnestly desired to hear the tale of the fight; but they had all friends at Unyanyembe, and it was but natural that they should be anxious to hear of what concerned them.

After giving orders to Bombay and Asmani for the provisioning of the men of the Expedition, I called "Kaif-Halek," or "How-do-ye-do," and introduced him to Dr. Livingstone as one of the soldiers in charge of certain goods left at Unyanyembe, whom I had compelled to accompany me to Ujiji, that he might deliver in person to his master the letter-bag he had been entrusted with by Dr. Kirk. This was that famous letter-bag marked "Nov. 1st, 1870," which was now delivered into the Doctor's hands 365 days after it left Zanzibar! How long, I wonder, had it remained at Unyanyembe had I not been despatched into Central Africa in search of the great traveller?

The Doctor kept the letter-bag on his knee, then, presently, opened it, looked at the letters contained there, and read one or two of his children's letters, his face in the meanwhile lighting up.

He asked me to tell him the news. "No, Doctor," said I, "read your letters first, which I am sure you must be impatient to read."

"Ah," said he, "I have waited years for letters, and I have been taught patience. I can surely afford to wait a few hours longer. No, tell me the general news: how is the world getting along?"

"You probably know much already. Do you know that the Suez Canal is a fact—is opened, and a regular trade carried on between Europe and India through it?"

"I did not hear about the opening of it. Well, that is grand news! What else?"

Shortly I found myself enacting the part of an annual periodical to him. There was no need of exaggeration—of any penny-a-line news, or of any sensationalism. The world had witnessed and experienced much the last few years. The Pacific Railroad had been completed; Grant had been elected President of the United States; Egypt had been flooded with savans; the Cretan rebellion had terminated; a Spanish revolution had driven Isabella from the throne of Spain, and a Regent had been appointed; General Prim was assassinated; a Castelar had electrified Europe with his advanced ideas upon the liberty of worship; Prussia had humbled Denmark, and annexed Schleswig-Holstein, and her armies were now around Paris; the "Man of Destiny" was a prisoner at Wilhemlshöhe; the Queen of Fashion and the Empress of the French was a fugitive; and the child born in the purple had lost for ever the Imperial crown intended for his head; the Napoleon dynasty was extinguished by the Prussians, Bismarck and Von Moltke; and France, the proud empire, was humbled to the dust.

What could a man have exaggerated of these facts? What a budget of news it was to one who had emerged from the depths of the primeval forests of Manyuema! The reflection of the dazzling light of civilization was cast on him while Livingstone was thus listening in wonder to one of the most exciting pages of history ever repeated. How the puny deeds of barbarism paled before these! Who could tell under what new phases of uneasy life Europe was laboring even then, while we, two of her lonely children, rehearsed the tale of her late woes and glories? More worthily, perhaps, had the tongue of a lyric Demodocus recounted them; but, in the absence of the poet, the newspaper correspondent performed his part as well and truthfully as he could.

Not long after the Arabs had departed, a dishful of hot hashed-meat cakes was sent to us by Sayd bin Majid, and a curried chicken was received from Mohammed bin Sali, and Moeni Kheri sent a dishful of stewed goat-meat and rice; and thus presents of food came in succession, and as fast as they were brought we set to. I had a healthy, stubborn digestion—the exercise I had taken had put it in prime order; but Livingstone—he had been complaining that he had no appetite, that his stomach refused everything but a cup of tea now and then—he ate also—ate like a vigorous, hungry man; and, as he vied with me in demolishing the pancakes, he kept repeating, "You have brought me new life. You have brought me new life."

"Oh, by George!" I said, "I have forgotten something. Hasten, Selim, and bring that bottle; you know which; and bring me the silver goblets. I brought this bottle on purpose for this event, which I hoped would come to pass, though often it seemed useless to expect it."

Selim knew where the bottle was, and he soon returned with it—a bottle of Sillery champagne; and, handing the Doctor a silver goblet brimful of the exhilarating wine, and pouring a small quantity into my own, I said,

"Dr. Livingstone, to your very good health, sir."

"And to yours," he responded.

And the champagne I had treasured for this happy meeting was drunk with hearty good wishes to each other.

But we kept on talking and talking, and prepared food was being brought to us all that afternoon; and we kept on eating every time it was brought, until I had eaten even to repletion, and the Doctor was obliged to confess that he had eaten enough. Still, Halimah, the female cook of the Doctor's establishment, was in a state of the greatest excitement. She had been protruding her head out of the cookhouse to make sure that there were really two white men sitting down in the veranda, when there used to be only one, who would not, because he could not, eat anything; and she had been considerably exercised in her mind about this fact. She was afraid the Doctor did not properly appreciate her culinary abilities; but now she was amazed at the extraordinary quantity of food eaten, and she was in a state of delightful excitement. We could hear her tongue rolling off a tremendous volume of clatter to the wondering crowds who halted before the kitchen to hear the current of news with which she edified them. Poor, faithful soul! While we listened to the noise of her furious gossip, the Doctor related her faithful services, and the terrible anxiety she evinced when the guns first announced the arrival of another white man in Ujiji; how she had been flying about in a state of the utmost excitement, from the kitchen into his presence, and out again into the square, asking all sorts of questions; how she was in despair at the scantiness of the general larder and treasury of the strange household; how she was anxious to make up for their poverty by a grand appearance—to make up a sort of Barmecide feast to welcome the white man. "Why," said she, "is he not one of us? Does he not bring plenty of cloth and beads? Talk about the Arabs! Who are they that they should be compared to white men? Arabs, indeed!"

The Doctor and I conversed upon many things, especially upon his own immediate troubles, and his disappointment, upon his arrival in Ujiji, when told that all his goods had been sold, and he was reduced to poverty. He had but twenty cloths or so left of the stock he had deposited with the man called Sherif, the half-caste drunken tailor, who was sent by the British Consul in charge of the goods. Besides which he had been suffering from an attack of dysentery, and his condition was most deplorable. He was but little improved on this day, though he had eaten well, and already began to feel stronger and better.

This day, like all others, though big with happiness to me, at last was fading away. We, sitting with our faces looking to the east, as Livingstone had been sitting for days preceding my arrival, noted the dark shadows which crept up above the grove of palms beyond the village, and above the rampart of mountains which we had crossed that day, now looming through the fast approaching darkness; and we listened, with our hearts full of gratitude to the great Giver of Good and Dispenser of all Happiness, to the sonorous thunder of the surf of the Tanganika, and to the chorus which the night insects sang. Hours passed, and we were still sitting there with our minds busy upon the day's remarkable events, when I remembered that the traveller had not yet read his letters.

"Doctor," I said, "you had better read your letters. I will not keep you up any longer."

"Yes," he answered, "it is getting late; and I will go and read my friends' letters. Good-night, and God bless you."

"Good-night, my dear Doctor; and let me hope that your news will be such as you desire."

And now, dear reader, having related succinctly "How I found Livingstone," I bid you also "Good-night."

SOURCE: Henry M. Stanley, *How I Found Livingstone: Travels and Discoveries in Central Africa* (New York: Scribner, Armstrong, 1872), xv–xxiii, 384–391, 403–419.

<hr/>

Preparing the Empire: Livingstone and Stanley in Central Africa
M. B. SYNGE

"I have opened the door; I leave it to you to see
that no one closes it after me."—Dr. Livingstone.

While Captain McClintock was bringing home the last news of Sir John Franklin to England (1859) another of England's bravest sons was preparing the way for civilisation in Central Africa, enduring untold hardships and "facing fearful odds" for the sake of his high mission.

And in this connection it is interesting to note how many great tracts of our Empire have been first opened up by missionaries and what brave pioneers and explorers they have proved themselves to be.

A few years after the Queen's accession, Livingstone, a young Scotsman, started on a five months' voyage to the Cape of Good Hope to take up missionary work among the natives of South Africa. Landing at Algoa Bay, after a long ox-wagon journey of 700 miles, he arrived at the Mission-station in the very heart of the country now known as British Bechuanaland. There he gained a knowledge of native languages, native customs, and laws which enabled him to do such good work later on. But the Boers, who had recently trekked to the Transvaal, looked toward Bechuanaland for the extension of their boundaries, and they raided the little Mission-station, carrying off the little black children as their slaves.

So Livingstone started northwards; he crossed the Kalahari Desert—a great wilderness of rocks and sand and lifeless scrub—and discovered the Lake Nyami, for which the Royal Geographical Society voted him twenty-five guineas.

He was as enthusiastic about his Mission work as his exploration.

"Cannot the love of Christ carry the missionary where the slave-trade carries the dealer?" he said. "I shall open up a path to the interior or perish."

The discovery of the Zambesi—the largest river in South Africa—added to his fame as a missionary. Into regions now owning Britain's sway he carried the name of Christian England. While performing the unparalleled feat of crossing Africa from ocean to ocean, east and west, he discovered the great Victoria Falls in that country, now known as Rhodesia. Then, after years of hardship, he took ship for England. The grief of his black attendants was pitiful. "Take us; we will die at your feet," they cried. Finally he agreed to take the chief, but the sea was wild and stormy, and the terrified man threw himself overboard and was drowned.

It is hard in these days, when books of travel are so common, to realise the immense interest created in England by the publication of Livingstone's Journals in 1857.

Englishmen had been interesting themselves more of late in the great African continent, that was to play so large a part in her history. Natal had been added to the Empire, the independence of the Transvaal had been recognised by this country. Lake Tanganyika and Victoria Nyanza had been discovered by Englishmen. The mysteries of the "Dark Continent" have exercised a great fascination over the minds of men and the "great spaces washed by sun" have attracted Englishmen before the famous days of Cecil Rhodes.

Livingstone's next achievement was the discovery of Lake Nyassa, now forming the boundary between Rhodesia and Portuguese Africa. He opened up the new country of Nyassaland, "for commerce and Christianity" which to-day is the heart of the Central African Protectorate, administered by an English Commissioner under our Colonial Office. It would take too long to follow the missionary explorer on his travels through Central Africa. Strong in purpose, high in courage, his toil was incessant, his industry unflagging.

In 1867 news reached England of his discovery of Lake Bangweolo, now included in Rhodesia and the waters of the Upper Congo, though he did not realise it was the Congo at all. Time passed on and a rumour reached England that he was dead. The last letter from him bore the date 1867. There was a repetition of that silence that surrounded the fate of Franklin. The silence was broken by H. M. Stanley, a journalist sent by the *New York Herald* to discover whether Livingstone was alive or dead. How the two men met in the very heart of Africa forms one of the romances of history.

Livingstone was one day sitting in his hut on the shores of Lake Tanganyika, when news arrived that a white man had made his way from the coast and was searching for a friend. Soon the two English-speaking men were face to face.

"Dr. Livingstone, I presume?" said Stanley, as he looked at the old man before him with long, white beard and tired face, his form reduced to a mere skeleton for want of proper food. He wore an official cap with faded gold band, a red-sleeved waist-coat, and much-patched tweed trousers.

"Yes," answered the old explorer.

A warm grasp of hands followed.

"You have brought me new life—new life," murmured Livingstone, as the two men compared experiences. But in vain Stanley begged him to return to England; the old man resolutely turned away from home, with its well-earned comforts and honours; he could not rest till he had cleared up the mystery of Lake Tanganyika watershed. Stanley accompanied him some little way on his last heroic journey and then turned sadly back.

Two years after this Livingstone died. He died kneeling by his rough camp bed in that attitude of prayer which had dominated his life.

His faithful black servants buried his heart in the still forest near the shores of Lake Bangweolo and carried his body to the coast through swamp and desert, whence it was taken to England. Ever proud of her brave sons, Englishmen laid his body, "brought by faithful hands over land and sea," in Westminster Abbey with a simple record of his great work.

> "Open the Abbey doors and bear him in
> To sleep with kings and statesmen, chief and sage,
> The missionary come of weaver kin
> But great by work that brooks no lower wage."

The death of his friend Livingstone before the completion of his life-work made a deep impression on Stanley, and he resolved to follow in his steps and carry on the work.

In the year 1874, fresh back from the English expedition to Koomassie, he started for Zanzibar, bound for the great African lakes. As yet little was known of Victoria Nyanza and most of Central Africa was blank upon our maps. The expedition, numbering some 356, started inland on November 17th, carrying a cedar canoe, the *Lady Alice,* in sections to explore the lakes further. It was the end of February when, after 740 miles of marching, the first sight of Victoria Nyanza came into view and the men burst into cheers of delight. The little canoe was soon afloat and the lake was circumnavigated.

Having proved that the Nile left the northern end of the lake and for 300 miles raced between high rocky walls over rapids and cataracts till it flowed through Albert Nyanza to Khartum, Stanley made his way to the famous region of Uganda—the "Pearl of Africa"—where he was warmly received by the black king Mtesa. Stanley was greatly struck by the intelligence of the king, and grasped the possibilities of Uganda as a centre of civilisation. "With the aid of Mtesa the civilisation of equatorial Africa becomes possible;" he wrote home begging that missionaries might be sent at once to carry on the work, that he himself had begun.

Stanley now turned his attention to the watershed between the Nile and the Congo, making his way south to Lake Tanganyika, which he completely explored. Yet greater discoveries were before him as he now started on an eventful journey that was to "flash a torch of light across the western half of the Dark Continent." His wanderings had already lasted two years, and his men were reduced to less than half the original number, when he turned westward through dense jungle to the still unknown basin of the Congo, at this time known as the River Livingstone and supposed to be the Nile. Great were the obstacles; fierce tribes attacked the little party and sickness broke out in their midst.

On Christmas Day, 1876, a crisis arose. Stanley's resolution alone saved the situation.

"My children, make up your minds as I have made up mine: we shall continue our journey and toil on and on by this river till we reach the great salt sea."

So the twenty-three canoes started off on the unknown river, heading for the Equator. A weary twenty days followed, cannibals appeared on the banks, the stream grew wild and turbulent, cataracts abounded, and at last the river suddenly narrowed and flung its waters over a wide precipice—the Stanley Falls. Then the river widened and Stanley knew he must be sailing down the great Congo river. All through the months of February and March he struggled with the raging waters—day after day it seems as if the little canoe must be dashed to pieces—until in August, 1877, the coast was reached.

Stanley had explored the whole course of the Congo—a river three thousand miles in length—the second largest river in the world. Though the Congo State is administered by Belgium, England has many interests there, and Stanley's book "Through the Dark Continent" made no small stir in England when it appeared.

Such men as Franklin, Livingstone, and Stanley were not only makers of history and pioneers of civilisation; they were very giants of perseverance and endurance—scorners of that luxury which tends to sap away the strength of our manhood and weaken our national character.

SOURCE: In *The Great Victorian Age for Children* (London: Hodder and Stoughton, 1908), 132–38.

————

In Memory of Dr. Livingstone
ELIZABETH RUNDLE CHARLES (?)

[This unsigned poem appears to have been written by Elizabeth Rundle Charles (1828–1896), who is listed as the author of *The Schönberg-Cotta Family*. The initials "B. C." at the poem's end may stand for Beth Charles.]

By the Author of *The Schönberg-Cotta Family*

Most mournful his dying seems;
　Yet glorious and good his death;
For meanings and hopes beyond our dreams
　Breathe from his dying breath.

With consciously failing force,
　Yet steadfastly forward face,
Still pressing on to the hidden source,
　To rescue and raise a race.

On to the mystical hill
　Whence[1] flow the four rivers of old,
Failing through years, yet following still
　As the Father of History told.

Not only the riddle to read
　Which had baffled the world from its youth—
Of science the foremost van to lead,
　And widen the bounds of truth;

But the fetters of ages to break,
　To wipe out the world's disgrace,
Through the mighty river he hoped to make
　The channel of life to a race.

He found not the source he sought—
　Finished not what he hoped to do;
The shadows fell deeper o'er heart and thought:
　No sign from his friends broke through.

1. In his later years he was stimulated by a constantly recurring report of a mountain which contained the sources of four great rivers.

Still on o'er the pestilent plain,
   True, though all seemed untrue.
The shadows fell deeper o'er heart and brain,
   Till scarcely a gleam broke through.

Forsaken of country and friend,
   Forgotten, unanswered, unheard;
Whilst England was roused from end to end
   To her noblest work at his word.

Dying, the world he moved;
   As he crept alone through the land,
By tens of thousands the race he loved
   Were saved from the spoiler's hand.

Dying, the race he served
   Which, loving, he loved to the end.
Dead, he their hearts to service nerved
   True as friend renders friend.

Who would not die in the dark
   And the loneliness, as he died,
To help the world on to its noblest mark,
   And stem, as he stemmed, the tide?

For once we can pierce the cloud
   O'er this fragment of life below,
And see the shrine through the veils which shroud,
   As he sees it ever now.

Beyond the clouds that brood
   Ever this dim earth o'er;
Misunderstanding, misunderstood,
   Forgotten, alone, no more.

Led by the Hand he knew
   To the fountains of life and bliss,
Where those who have served the Faithful and True
   Their goal shall never miss.

B. C.

SOURCE: In *Good Words* (London: Daldy, Isbister, 1874), 360.

Dr. Livingstone

BY THE RIGHT HON. SIR BARTLE FRERE

[Sir Bartle Frere (1816–1884) wrote a number of books and essays on imperialism, reform, and Indian culture; his significant works include *Correspondence Showing the Measures Taken by the Syuds of Tatta in Sind to Reduce the Expenses of Their Birth, Marriage* (1859), *Old Deccan Days: Or, Old Fairy Legends in India* (1868), and *Memoirs of a Hindoo* (1877). His imperial activities subsequently took him, as they took many other officers and diplomats of the British Empire, from the Indian subcontinent to the African continent, where he participated in wars with the Zulus, disputes with Boers, and in the contest over the Congo.]

For some weeks and months past the fate of a single man has divided the attention of many minds with the destinies of kingdoms and the disasters of empires. As, day by day, the news of distant regions arrived in England, the progress of our campaign against the Ashantees, or the gathering gloom of the Bengal famine were among the topics of most general interest, but few would lay down the daily journal without seeing whether it contained any tidings of Dr. Livingstone; and, wherever men met, for business or for pleasure, every one who was supposed to have any means of information regarding Africa, was sure to be asked, "Do you really think that Dr. Livingstone is dead?"

It is not often that the fate of a single man in distant lands thus affects multitudes, even of his own countrymen; but the great Scotch traveller had made himself the benefactor of the world at large, and all mankind, who cared to know the doings of civilised nations, were interested in his fate. At first, we were glad to think the wildly improbable story told untrue; but day by day brought some new fact to prove it and to confirm our worst fears; and when, at last, it seemed certain that his body was being conveyed to the coast, we read everywhere tales of his eventful life, and of mourning over his loss couched in language generally reserved for the greatest of mankind.

Nor was the tone in which so much of regret was expressed, in any way unbefitting the event which called it forth. The periods of Milton or of Dryden were not too stately to chronicle what Livingstone had done for mankind, and no poet's fancy could imagine deeds more fitted to be sung in heroic verse; but, while we await the remains which we believe are now being brought to his native land, let us give a few moments to think soberly over what he has accomplished, and to glance at the place which his work is likely to fill in future history.

The leading facts of Dr. Livingstone's life are sufficiently well known. We have been told of his birth, fifty-eight years ago, of one of those old Scotch families which, however ill-supplied with worldly gear, always seem to remind their members that they are bound to carry the loftiest qualities of ancient nobility into whatever work they may undertake. All know how, when his mind was first awakened to obey the parting command of his Saviour to preach the gospel in distant lands, while he worked steadily at his mechanical calling that he might not eat the bread of idleness, he devoted every moment of spare time to storing his mind with such knowledge as might fit him to be a preacher of the gospel—how he was called to the ministry, and went forth in the service of the London Missionary Society—how he joined Mr. Moffat's mission, beyond what was then the utmost boundary of European civilisation, north of the Cape Colony—how he married, and worked for years as a minister among the frontier tribes, and perfected himself in that knowledge of the country and people which was afterwards so valuable to him in all his wanderings—all this is well known. We, in India, first heard of him some thirty or forty years ago. The Cape was then a place of great resort for men whose health had broken down under an Indian climate. The young Indian soldier, or civilian, would in those days wander, when his health returned, far beyond the limits of the Cape Colony, and exercise his renewed strength in pursuing the large game which then abounded on the Cape frontier. There he would fall in with Mr. Moffat and his fellow-labourers, and rarely failed to be struck with their simple kindly earnestness and self-devotion. There are many grey-haired old Indians who can remember how they, or their friends, used to hear of the Scotch missionaries among the Basutos; and often, at an Indian messtable, while discussing, as young men will, the little prospect of any good ever coming of attempts to teach the Kaffirs Christianity, they would make an exception, and say, "But if all missionaries were like Moffat or Livingstone, something might be done."

Livingstone's earliest attempts to travel beyond the missionary stations were made in an expedition to Lake Ngami in 1849, and in 1852 he commenced that wonderful journey which first made his name known throughout Christendom, crossing and recrossing the continent of Africa from the mouths of the Zambesi to St. Paul de Loando through regions which it was not supposed that a white man had ever crossed before. He returned home in 1856, and found himself at once famous; and he might have been the greatest lion of the day, but he declined all the hospitalities and indulgences offered to him with the simple remark "that he had three pieces of work to do, and he found that he could do none of them without devoting his whole attention to them." He had to write his book of travels, which his kind friend Mr. Murray had promised to publish for him; he had to assist Arrowsmith to reduce to proper form and map down the rough notes of those careful observations, which he had taken during his long and adventurous journeys; above all, he had to work in various ways for his mission, and to obtain the means for further labour in the great work he had undertaken. He made one exception, in accepting the hospitality of his early friend, Mr. Webb, of Newstead Abbey, who had learned to understand and love him while exploring with him the shores of Lake Ngami, and much of his first volume of travels was written in the quiet shades already rendered famous by the memory of Byron.

His work produced an immense effect on thinking men of every class, but especially among those who had at heart the civilisation and conversion to Christianity of the tribes of Africa. His obviously truthful pictures of scenery and manners would have at any time interested the lover of books of travel; but his descriptions of fertile regions which had always been supposed to be barren, of kindly and improvable races which had ever been accounted hopelessly savage, his narrative of Portuguese oppression and misgovernment, but, above all, the prevailing tone of cheerful confidence in the ultimate victory of good over evil, stirred the hearts of his countrymen. They had often been touched before by what Bruce or Mungo Park, Denham or Clapperton, had related, but they had never perhaps been so moved as by the modest record of what Livingstone had, single-handed, accomplished.

Among other results, the great universities of England and Ireland agreed to join in sending out a joint mission to preach Christianity in the countries he had visited, and a high-minded and self-devoted man having been found in Bishop Mackenzie to head that mission, Livingstone undertook to join him in his arduous task, and to lead him and his zealous followers to the lands of promise, to whose redemption from slavery and idolatry they had resolved to devote themselves. Others joined the mission as men of science, and in the hope of aiding to develop the commercial and agricultural resources of the country. Few expeditions have ever been so well manned and equipped, or started with so fair a prospect of achieving great results.

Livingstone's second book of travels contains the record of this expedition, begun with such high hopes, marked by such zealous self-devotion, but ending in what, for a time, appeared, even to the most sanguine of its projectors, akin to a disastrous failure. The book, which contains the record of this enterprise from 1858 to 1864, was written under great difficulties, for, while recording the disappointment of many lofty aspirations; he wished to avoid anything like blame or disparagement of those who had been his companions in misfortune. Yet the results were in truth by no means disproportioned to the sacrifices made; a vast extent of new country was explored, much useful information and experience was gained, and though the death of Bishop Mackenzie and of Mrs. Livingstone who had subsequently joined them, and of other fellow-travellers, threw a gloom over the expedition from which it did not recover, great real progress was made towards opening the interior of the country to European explorers. The expedition added to the character Livingstone had already established as the most sagacious and intrepid of modern travellers; and when, commissioned by the Government of the day to inquire into and report on the Slave Trade, and accredited as British Consul to the chiefs of Central Africa he again set forth, alone, on the work of African exploration, his countrymen felt that they might rely upon his accomplishing what no other living man could have ventured to attempt.

When his expedition in Africa in 1864 came to an end he found himself at Zanzibar burdened with the lake steamer *Lady Nyassa,* in providing which he had embarked a large portion of such worldly fortune as his writings and the kindness of his friends had enabled him to command. Finding that he could not dispose of her advantageously at Zanzibar, he formed, and immediately executed, his resolution to take her to Bombay; his crew consisted of sixteen negro lads, who had been released by him from slavery, and who, a few weeks before, had never seen the sea; no one but himself knew how to navigate, or to direct the working of the engines; but he started, as he had so often done before, putting his trust in God, with a stout heart and firm will, and arrived at Bombay, where the little craft had been a whole day in the great harbour, before she was discovered by the Custom-House officers, he having meantime gone ashore to report his proceedings to the Governor, and to seek counsel among his Christian friends.

This visit to Bombay was, in many ways, important to him, for he saw at once the intimate connection between Western India and Eastern Africa, a connection not confined to features of physical geography or climate, but extending to characteristics in the zoology and ethnology of the countries, which led him to think that each might help the other in the race of civilisation and human progress. Among the missionaries in India he met several who not only sympathized with his great objects, but could help him in various ways, and among them, Dr. John Wilson, of the Presbyterian Free Kirk, who had long devoted much of his time and attention to training Abyssinian youths at the excellent educational institution which the Free Kirk maintains at Bombay; and he found, under the charge of the Rev. William Price, of the Church Missionary Society, at Nassick, great numbers of released negro slaves of both sexes, who were receiving a good Christian and industrial education from the

Nassick missionaries. Leaving some of the youths whom he had chosen from among his late companions, under the charge of Dr. Wilson, he returned to England, and when he again resolved on visiting Africa in 1865, he took Bombay in his way, where he found some of the youths he had left, much improved by their attendance at the schools of the Free Kirk mission, and selected a number of the Nassick negro youths, who volunteered to accompany him back to their native land. He also took with him some natives of India, Sepoys in the Marine Battalion, who he thought likely to make good fellow-travellers, and a number of buffaloes, of the kind commonly used in India in carrying heavy burdens, thinking they might be of similar service in Africa, and be able to resist the attacks of the Tzetze fly, there so fatal to horses and ordinary cattle. At Zanzibar he added to his party a number of Johannah men, islanders, who had the best reputation of any on that coast, as intelligent, trustworthy voyagers; and, thus equipped, he started on his last journey.

Landing near the mouth of the Rovuma, and travelling in a north-westerly direction towards the lake region, every kind of discouragement awaited him: his buffaloes died, his Johannah men deserted him and returned with false stories of his death, and the Indian sepoys behaved so badly that he had to send back those who did not run away. But nothing could daunt or stop him; and attended only by Chuma and his two or three companions of the Nyassa men, a few of the Nassick boys, and such porters as he picked up in the country, he continued his ceaseless journeyings on foot in the pathless wilds of the Central African lake region, and was, for many years, never heard of by his countrymen.

At length, two years ago, the world was astounded by the intelligence that Mr. Stanley, a special correspondent of the *New York Herald,* had found Dr. Livingstone just after his return to Ujiji, the farthest post of the coast Arabs, where his wants had been relieved; and that he had again started to prosecute his journeyings, with a fresh supply of goods and six more Christian negro volunteers from Nassick, who had joined him at the call of the Church Missionary Society as soon as it was known that he was within reach. What little we know of the sad history of the later months of his life is too fresh in our recollection to need repeating. He probably died about October in last year; and we are told that his faithful fellow-Christian servants have now brought his remains to the coast, having met on their way the expedition sent in 1872, under Lieutenant Cameron, to search for and relieve him.[1]

---

1. For details of his last journeyings I would refer to the "Reports and Proceedings" of the Royal Geographical Society for 1872–73; to the "Ocean Highways" for the same years; and to an excellent letter from Mr. Finlay in the *Athenaum* for February 28th, 1874.

We frequently hear the question asked what were the objects of Livingstone's last expedition. People complain that he embarked upon it without telling the world what he was going to do, and that they are consequently often unable to judge how far he accomplished what he had purposed. When he last stayed with me in India, on his way out to Africa in 1865, I asked him as to his plan of operations, and he then told me that he had purposely abstained from publishing his projects before he left England, and he wished little to be said about them while he was travelling in Africa, because, as he very truly observed, it was certain that he must disappear from European view for many months together, that it was possible after he had disappeared into the heart of Africa that attempts would be made to relieve him, and he was anxious not to encourage such attempts by any mention of his intentions, while he was naturally averse to announce plans which he might be prevented by unavoidable and unforeseen circumstances from carrying out. But his main object was, he told me, to fulfil the wishes of Sir Roderick Murchison that the limits of the Nile basin should be defined, and he proposed, after ascertaining the water-parting between the Nile basin and other eastern or southern tributaries to the ocean, to follow the watershed round the whole margin of the basin, and thus, if possible, to mark the limits within which future travellers might search for whatever particular streams, of the many thousand affluents, might have the best claim to the honour of being the source of the Nile.

But in this, as in every other of his undertakings, geographical discovery was entirely subordinate to higher objects; he desired to solve the most difficult problem of African geography simply as a necessary preliminary to letting light into the heart of Africa. He knew that the Traveller must precede both the Merchant and the Missionary, but he looked to all he could accomplish as a discoverer, mainly as being useful to the spread of Christianity and civilisation. His uniform object was to elevate the negro race of Africa. The abolition of the Slave Trade and slavery, the progress of civilisation and commerce were subsidiary in his mind to the preaching of the gospel, which he looked upon as the one only effectual panacea for all the ills which have been for so many ages the heirloom of Africa.

This may help us in part to answer another question which is very frequently asked, "why did he not, many years ago, come back to his own country and his family?" The simple answer is, that his work was not done; and, while it remained undone, no yearning for country, no anxiety about himself or his family, which he loved much more than himself, could make him swerve from the prosecution of the work he had undertaken. It is very probable that when we have all the notes of his journeyings before us we may find that he had done much more than he believed himself to have accomplished; that we may discover the missing links to many a chain of communication across the continent; and that when his work is joined to that of the able and accomplished travellers who have followed his example since he first published his narrative of his early wanderings in Africa, the blanks in the maps of those regions may prove to have been filled up to an extent far beyond what we can at present anticipate. But Livingstone could not have known even what we now know, of the vast amount of work that has recently been accomplished; how, to use a common phrase, the neck of the African difficulty may be pronounced fairly broken, so that a multitude of future travellers may, in a few years, fill up what is wanting in the great outlines which have been furnished by Livingstone and other great explorers of our generation.

But if the letters and journals of his last journeyings contain no more than minor details of what we already know, what a vast amount of work has this one man achieved! In geography it is no exaggeration to say that to him, and to the example he set, may be fairly attributed the filling up of the blank which the maps of the interior of Africa presented to our grandfathers. It derogates nothing from Livingstone's claim to this honour that we are now aware how much was known to Portuguese travellers of a former generation. Their memories must often pay the penalty imposed on them by the reticence of their government and countrymen regarding all that the Portuguese have discovered during the last century in Africa. They wished to exclude all other nations from that continent, and to keep their knowledge of the interior to themselves, and they succeeded but too well. It would be idle to estimate to what extent the misery which Africa has suffered since is due to this policy of concealment; but we may fairly credit those who have done their best to pour light into the darkness, with all the good results which are likely to follow our better acquaintance with the great central home of the negro races.

Geographers may, I think, accept, without reserve, Livingstone's estimate of geographical discoverers as being simply the pioneers of commerce and civilisation. Regarding commerce, exaggeration is simply impossible in speaking of the probable results of Livingstone's labours in opening up the interior of Africa. It may be briefly but truly said, that there are few things which that country can produce which we do not need, and shall not be willing to pay for—few manufactures which Europe, Asia, and America produce which will not find a ready market in Africa. It is clear that the Negroes are far removed from those races in Asia and America, who are found to be incapable of industrial arts, and insensible to the value of foreign manufacturers, which they are too ignorant or apathetic to make for themselves. The Negroes, as a rule, are obviously fond of fine clothes, of metal work, and of that infinite variety of manufactured goods which Europe, Asia, and America can supply. They are also well disposed to labour as far as may be necessary to pay for them, in such things as their country produces in the grain, the cotton and other fibres, the oils, the metals, the timber, the skins, the dyes, and the multitude of other articles which they can send to us. Protection to the trader, and the abolition of traffic in human flesh are the only two requisites to a growth of commerce, which will probably exceed anything witnessed in our dealings with other nations in modern days. It is clearly from no cause, but the want of means to possess themselves of clothing materials, that the Africans generally are content with so little clothing. If they could be once assured that they would be allowed to enjoy the fruits of their own agricultural labour, and that the trader would be protected in dealing with them, all the looms of Europe would not suffice to supply the material which Africa could consume; and so of metal work, and hardware, of earthenware and other manufactured goods, which are even now eagerly bought for raw produce, wherever trade and traders can exist.

We already see that the apparently inscrutable problem presented by the persistent barbarism of the negro races, was mainly due to their practical isolation from all contact with more civilised peoples; and since the country has been opened up by travellers, we may reasonably hope that the same improvement in civilisation will follow which is observable where similar facilities have, in other continents, been afforded to barbarous races for communicating with the civilised nations which touch their frontiers.

Everywhere following close upon the traveller and the trader we find the Christian missionary, and from every point of the compass efforts are now directed by the missionaries of Europe and America, and even of Asia, to carry the light of the gospel into the lands which Livingstone and his followers have discovered.

Men will differ in their estimates of the results of missionary labour among the Negroes, not only according to their varying views of the capacity of the negro races, but according to the different degrees in which they may be themselves impressed by the power of the gospel. Those, however, who are the most sceptical as to our ever being able to make anything of Negroes, or who estimate at the lowest point the power of the gospel to elevate and improve the races of mankind, must feel that it is physically, morally, and intellectually impossible for the great civilised nations of Europe and America to send men eminent in their own land for energy of character and moral elevation of spirit, to labour in Africa for the improvement of Africans, without their effecting a great change, even in the most hopeless material which presents itself to us in that continent.

Two things are abundantly clear regarding the great mass of the negro race.

First, it is a physical impossibility to remove them, as might be thought desirable by some, off the face of the earth. They are so prolific, so full of life, that even a Tamerlane or Gengis Khan would find their destruction impossible in any sense analogous to that which has swept or is sweeping from the face of the earth the Red Indian, the Polynesian, and many other of the races of Europe and Asia. The Negro seems positively to defy physical extinction, and the few years of rest which are imposed on the exterminator by the desolation of the country and by the exhaustion of the conqueror, suffice to repeople the fertile plains of Africa with a race as light-hearted, as careless of all but animal enjoyment, and as prolific as those which seem to have inhabited the same plains from the remotest ages.

On the other hand it is equally clear that even a very imperfect amount of civilisation supplies much that is wanting in the negro character, and converts the weakest and most timid of the negro tribe into races distinctly superior in physical as well as moral characteristics. Witness the changes everywhere effected by the propagandists of Islam. There can be no doubt that wherever Islam has extended itself into negro-land, there the Mussulman Negro is a vastly superior being to the Fetish worshipper. Philosophers may dispute as to whether monotheism, or the law of the Kuran, or the brotherhood of Islam, has the greater share in the change; to the practical observer the results are everywhere the same. The Moslem Negro is everywhere a finer, stronger, more energetic, and a more trustworthy being than the idolater. And however much we may dispute as to the relative civilising power of Christianity as compared with Islam, the practical observer will also come unhesitatingly to the conclusion that, without reference to the superior truth or morality of either system, there can be no doubt that the civilising power of Christianity is vastly greater than that of Islam.

If any one has doubts upon this subject, let him consider the different teachings of the two religions on only three points, one intellectual, the other two moral or social.

As the civilisation propagated by Islam advances, the intellectual inquirer finds that whatever may be its abstract teachings regarding the value of truth, the pursuit of truth by man's unfettered intellect is prohibited. In some directions of historical research the true believer may inquire at will, and according to the best canons of modern historical investigation; but woe be to him if he applies the same mode of investigation to any part of the history of the Prophet, or of his followers, or their teachings;—he immediately becomes a helpless heretic and infidel. There are not, as in other religions, any two opinions tolerable on the subject. A perfectly free investigation of all historical problems is utterly inconsistent with the orthodox teachings of Islam, so with geography—so with astronomy—so with every branch of physical science. The tyranny of the Syllabus is a cobweb compared with the bonds of Moslem orthodoxy, and the disciple of Islam must either abandon his faith in the Kuran and its teachings, or all hope of free intellectual inquiry.

It is needless to point to the contrast afforded by Christianity. Whatever terrors the freest intellectual inquiry may have at times for some very sincere and excellent Christians, there can be no doubt that in the long-run the spread of Christianity has everywhere been marked by a corresponding impulse to intellectual investigation of every kind. The fear of the freest intellectual inquiry prevails only where there has been a deadness or partial paralysis of religious fervour; and every fresh manifestation of religious enthusiasm among Christians has invariably been marked in the history of the last two thousand years by a fresh manifestation of intellectual energy and inventive effort, in every department of human knowledge and progress. We may dispute for ever as to which is cause and which is effect; but that the two results are always as far as possible contemporaneous admits of no doubt, whether we study history in Egypt or Italy, in Spain or Gaul, in England, in Germany, or in the United States.

Nor is the result of the comparative effects of Islam and Christianity at all different when we come to mixed problems of morality and civil policy or social order. There can be no doubt that while the spirit of Christianity condemns slavery and polygamy, the spirit of Islam tolerates both. Either slavery or polygamy by itself would be quite sufficient to infuse decay into any system of civilisation. This is not so observable when the civilisation of Islam is contrasted with that of some African superstition, for Islam greatly mitigates both the slavery and the polygamy of the unconverted African; but it becomes immediately conspicuous when brought in contrast with the teachings of Christianity. There may be many who still talk of, and some who still believe in the inevitable destiny of the black races to be slaves to all eternity, but there can be but very few who do not recognise that the presence of slavery is incompatible with advancing Christianity, and that either Christianity must stand still and decay, or slavery must be extinguished. So with polygamy. The system may be tolerated in a simple pastoral or agricultural people, where few are rich and where none but the very rich can afford more than one wife; but it is a certain social canker whenever society settles down into civilised forms, and wealth increases. The stagnation and decrease of population, the ruin of aristocracies, and the destruction of dynasties are among the smallest evils of polygamy; but they are inevitable results. And here again the general law of Christendom which allows but one wife, is found in its practical results to be a certain safeguard for social progress.

If, then, as we see proved on every side, the imperfect teachings of Islam immediately and immensely elevate the Negro, may we not hope with Livingstone that the teaching of Christianity will indeed be life to the dead?

Of Livingstone's character it is difficult for those who knew him intimately to speak without appearance of exaggeration. Of his intellectual force and energy he has given such proof as few men can afford. Any five years of his life might, in any other occupation, have established a character, and raised for him a fortune, such as none but the most energetic of our race can realise. His powers of observation and practical sagacity I have never seen exceeded. Both, possibly, were rendered more acute by the life he led; but he had the quickness of eye and the power of judging of forces and results which belong only to the great organizer, politician, or general. Equally remarkable was his knowledge of character and penetration. No flattery could blind him, no allurements could lead him aside; his estimate of men was unfailing.

But his great characteristic was his perfect simplicity and single-mindedness. People might think his object eccentric and unaccountable; but no one could possibly suspect him for a moment of duplicity, or of seeking anything but the object he announced, and seeking it by the most direct and open path. He was not wanting in the cautious reserve and practical sagacity of his countrymen; but no man could be more open in all that he had a right to tell, or in all that his inquirer had a right to ask, and this was one great element of his strength in dealing with uncivilised as well as civilised men. Powerful as was his energy and perseverance, it was the straightness, and directness, and openness of his aim, that constituted his greatest strength.

Next to this I would rank as his prominent characteristic his patience. Some men who had to deal with him, said he had an incapacity and dislike for combined action with other people; the truth undoubtedly was, he felt so strong himself, and so little needed the advice and help which others could give, that he generally found he did best alone, and this sometimes gave an appearance of impracticability to his propositions, and joined to his quick intuition, for which he could not always give full reasons, occasionally brought on him the charge of obstinacy in combined action. But he was rarely, if ever, mistaken; when he had entirely his own way no man could be more safely trusted to lead aright, and however he might differ in opinion from those with whom he came in contact, nothing could be less arrogant than his expression of dissent, however firm and decided. Like all men of iron frame and unbending will, he often seemed intolerant of weakness. When he saw his object clearly within reach, he could not stop to count the cost of attaining it, and the determination which in the general or surgeon would have been at once accepted as the inspiration of genius, was sometimes set down by his fellow-travellers as want of sympathy with their sufferings. To himself Livingstone had long since died, and he expected from all the same self-devotion to his work which had become a part of his very nature.

In his intercourse with the poor or the weak, with children or with women, no pastor could be more gentle or tolerant or more full of the highest characteristics of a Christian gentleman. It was, in fact, his Christian faith which was the mainspring of his character in all its relations. In his courage, in his energy, in his patience, and in his large toleration and unfailing charity for all mankind, the most superficial observer could not but recognise the devoted follower of his Divine Master and Exemplar. He had no love for theological controversy, little toleration for theological bitterness, but his whole soul was possessed with the spirit of the gospel, and his every thought, word, and deed could be recognised as inspired by the Spirit of Christ.

Men sometimes said he did not give them much the idea of a great missionary. He was full of observation and of quiet humour, and no man enjoyed cheerful society more than he did; but this was mainly due to the fact that he had found the peace which passeth all understanding. If he sometimes seemed to lay less claim to the office of a minister of the gospel than he might have done, it was because he regarded his own office as that simply of a pioneer, to prepare the way for those who should come after him, to teach and preach the gospel in more distinct terms to the millions he might render accessible to it. Had he lived in earlier ages, he might have seen less of hope or joy in what he undertook, and have been more of an ascetic; but though he was full of joy as well as of peace in believing, no man in these days realised more completely the great work of the forerunner who is everywhere needed to go before, to prepare the way for Him who is coming—no man of our time has done more the work of the Baptist in making straight the paths by which shall be brought Him who gives sight to the blind, hearing to the deaf, freedom to the captive.

It is not in our day that we can realise the greatness of the work he has accomplished. His life may be written in terms which shall make it the chosen volume of the young and old, like the pages which tell of the daring of Nelson, or the adventures of the shipwrecked hero of Defoe; but it will yet be generations ere our children shall know how vast a work was done by the strong-willed and firm-hearted Scotchman who, in his solitary tramp, traversed for years the forest and marsh that he might open the path for the missionary and the merchant to reach the dusky millions of Central Africa.

No greater proof of his power could be given than that which his followers are said to have now afforded, in bearing his lifeless body back to his fellow-countrymen. Be it remembered these men were not chosen or well-educated specimens of African aristocracy. They were one and all liberated slaves, with nothing to direct them but the precepts, nothing to sustain them but the example and their memories of one devoted Christian. For a thousand miles and more they have borne coastward those remains which no old African traveller believed any bribe would have induced them, or could have enabled them, to carry a score of leagues. If they succeed in restoring Livingstone's relics to his native land, let no man henceforth ever say that the people of Africa are incapable of acts of the highest and most sustained heroism and self-devotion.

Every one naturally asks, Where shall the remains rest, if we are allowed to receive them? Had Livingstone been consulted, he would perhaps have preferred to be buried where he fell, in the same land which contains the remains of his beloved wife. From the little that I used to hear from him on such subjects it always seemed to me that his hopes were fixed on resting near where she had rested; but he may at the time of his death have felt that this would have exposed his faithful followers to much unmerited suspicion and obloquy, and that it would lead his countrymen to attempt to unravel the mystery which would have still surrounded his disappearance, and thus might risk many valuable lives; and so he may have charged his followers to carry to the coast the only indubitable evidence of his death. None but they who know practically the difficulties of African travel can rightly appreciate the marvellous devotion with which this undertaking has been accomplished.

Many of his countrymen, again, might wish his remains to rest by the side of the parents whom he so loved and reverenced, or in the old cathedral of the town where he learnt and laboured in his youth; but his remains belong not to Scotland alone, or to any county or kingdom, but to the English empire.

There is one place where for ages past the men of these lands have been in the habit of laying those who have contributed in any conspicuous degree to build up this empire—whether kings or princes, warriors or statesmen, great lawyers, great nobles, or the poets, the orators, and the authors who have helped to perfect our language and literature. That is the only fitting place for him to rest who has opened to the English nation and to all mankind, a quarter of the globe which had for thousands of years remained practically a closed country more jealously shut up from the eye of foreign intruder, by nature and the evil passions of man, than China or Japan. When Dean Stanley wrote from St. Petersburg, as soon as he heard of Dr. Livingstone's death, to offer his remains a resting-place in Westminster Abbey, he rightly divined what would be the feeling of the whole people of the British Empire, and it will be long ere we see received within those walls one of our time and race worthier to rest among the greatest men of these Islands.

H. B. E. F.

March 18th, 1874.

SOURCE: In *Good Words* (London: Daldy, Isbister, 1874), 280–87.

———

Influence of Christianity upon Moral and Intellectual Diversity of Races

COUNT JOSEPH ARTHUR GOBINEAU

[Count Arthur Gobineau (1816–1882) was an aristocrat, novelist, and orientalist. For a brief time, he was employed as the secretary to Alexis de Tocqueville during his term as foreign minister of France (1849). Gobineau's theory of racial determinism was developed, in part, in response to the fervent republicanism and socialism that were influencing French, British, and European politics and culture; his investment in the idea of a strict social, class, and caste hierarchy informed his orientalist interpretations and pseudoscientific racial and anthropological theories. Ironically, this passionate defender of aristocratic order and Aryan privilege was born on Bastille Day. Gobineau's works include the novels *Pléiades* (The Pleiads) (1874) and *Souvenirs de Voyage* (The Crimson Handkerchief) (1872); he is also known for his *Histoire des Perses* (History of the Persians) (1869) and the influential, four-volume *Essai sur l'Inégalité des Races Humaines* (Essay on the inequality of the human races) (1853–1855)—the work that would impress Richard Wagner, Friedrich Nietzsche, Houston Stewart Chamberlain, and Adolf Hitler.]

The term Christian civilization examined—Reasons for rejecting it—Intellectual diversity no hindrance to the universal diffusion of Christianity—Civilizing influence of Christian religion by elevating and purifying the morals, etc.; but does not remove intellectual disparities—Various instances—Cherokees—Difference between imitation and comprehension of civilized life.

By the foregoing observations, two facts seem to me clearly established: first, that there are branches of the human family incapable of spontaneous civilization, so long as they remain unmixed; and, secondly, that this innate incapacity cannot be overcome by external agencies, however powerful in their nature. It now remains to speak of the civilizing influence of Christianity, a subject which, on account of its extensive bearing, I have reserved for the last, in my consideration of the instruments of civilization.

The first question that suggests itself to the thinking mind, is a startling one. If some races are so vastly inferior in all respects, can they comprehend the truths of the gospel, or are they forever to be debarred from the blessing of salvation?

In answer, I unhesitatingly declare my firm conviction, that the pale of salvation is open to them all, and that all are endowed with equal capacity to enter it. Writers are not wanting who have asserted a contrary opinion. They dare to contradict the sacred promise of the Gospel, and deny the peculiar characteristic of our faith, which consists in its accessibility to all men. According to them, religions are confined within geographical limits which they cannot transgress. But the Christian religion knows no degrees of latitude or longitude. There is scarcely a nation, or a tribe, among whom it has not made converts. Statistics—imperfect, no doubt, but, as far as they go, reliable— show them in great numbers in the remotest parts of the globe: nomad Mongols, in the steppes of Asia, savage hunters in the table-lands of the Andes; dark-hued natives of an African clime; persecuted in China;[1] tortured in Madagascar; perishing under the lash in Japan.

But this universal capacity of receiving the light of the gospel must not be confounded, as is so often done, with a faculty of entirely different character, that of social improvement. This latter consists in being able to conceive new wants, which, being supplied, give rise to others, and gradually produce that perfection of the social and political system which we call civilization. While the former belongs equally to all races, whatever may be their disparity in other respects, the latter is of a purely intellectual character, and the prerogative of certain privileged groups, to the partial or even total exclusion of others.

With regard to Christianity, intellectual deficiencies cannot be a hindrance to a race. Our religion addresses itself to the lowly and simple, even in preference to the great and wise of this earth. Intellect and learning are not

---

1. Although the success of the Chinese missions has not been proportionate to the self-devoting zeal of its laborers, there yet are, in China, a vast number of believers in the true faith. M. Hue tells us, in the relation of his journey, that, in almost every place where he and his fellow-traveller stopped, they could perceive, among the crowds that came to stare at the two "Western devils" (as the celestials courteously call us Europeans), men making furtively, and sometimes quite openly, the sign of the cross. Among the nomadic hordes of the tables-lands of Central Asia, the number of Christians is much greater than among the Chinese, and much greater than is generally supposed. (See *Annals of the Propagation of the Faith*, No. 135, et seq.)—H.

necessary to salvation. The most brilliant lights of our church were not always found among the body of the learned. The glorious martyrs, whom we venerate even above the skilful and erudite defender of the dogma, or the eloquent panegyrist of the faith, were men who sprang from the masses of the people; men, distinguished neither for worldly learning, nor brilliant talents, but for the simple virtues of their lives, their unwavering faith, their self-devotion. It is exactly in this that consists one great superiority of our religion over the most elaborate and ingenious systems devised by philosophers, that it is intelligible to the humblest capacity as well as to the highest. The poor Esquimaux of Labrador may be as good and as pure a Christian as the most learned prelate in Europe.

But we now come to an error which, in its various phases, has led to serious consequences. The utilitarian tendency of our age renders us prone to seek, even in things sacred, a character of material usefulness. We ascribe to the influence of Christianity a certain order of things, which we call *Christian civilization*.

To what political or social condition this term can be fitly applied, I confess myself unable to conceive. There certainly is a Pagan, a Brahmin, and Buddhistic, a Judaic civilization. There have been, and still are, societies so intimately connected with a more or less exclusive theological formula, that the civilizations peculiar to them, can only be designated by the name of their creed. In such societies, religion is the sole source of all political forms, all civil and social legislation; the groundwork of the whole civilization. This union of religious and temporal institutions, we find in the history of every nation of antiquity. Each country had its own peculiar divinity, which exercised a more or less direct influence in the government,[2] and from which laws and civiliza-

---

2. The tutelary divinity was generally a typification of the national character. A commercial or maritime nation, would worship Mercury or Neptune; an aggressive and warlike one, Hercules or Mars; a pastoral one, Pan; an agricultural one, Ceres or Triptolemus; one sunk in luxury, as Corinth, would render almost exclusive homage to Venus.

As the author observes, all ancient governments were more or less theocratical. The regulations of castes among the Hindoos and Egyptians were ascribed to the gods, and even the most absolute monarch dared not, and could not, transgress the limits which the immortals had set to his power. This so-called divine legislation often answered the same purpose as the charters of modern constitutional monarchies. The authority of the Persian kings was confined by religious regulations, and this has always been the case with the sultans of Turkey. Even in Rome, whose population had a greater tendency for the positive and practical, than for the things of another world, we find the traces of theocratical government. The sibylline books, the augurs, etc., were something more than a vulgar superstition; and the latter, who could stop or postpone the most important proceedings, by declaring the omens unpropitious, must have possessed very considerable political influence, especially in the earlier periods. The rude, liberty-loving tribes of

tion were said to be immediately derived. It was only when paganism began to wane, that the politicians of Rome imagined a separation of temporal and religious power, by attempting a fusion of the different forms of worship, and proclaiming the dogma of legal toleration. When paganism was in its youth and vigor, each city had its Jupiter, Mercury, or Venus, and the local deity recognized neither in this world nor the next any but compatriots.

But, with Christianity, it is otherwise. It chooses no particular people, prescribes no form of government, no social system. It interferes not in temporal matters, has naught to do with the material world, "its kingdom is of another." Provided it succeeds in changing the interior man, external circumstances are of no import. If the convert fervently embraces the faith, and in all his actions tries to observe its prescriptions, it inquires not about the built of his dwelling, the cut of his garments, or the materials of which they are composed, his daily occupations, the regulations of his government, the degree of despotism, or of freedom, which pervades his political institutions. It leaves the Chinese in his robes, the Esquimaux in his seal-skins; the former to his rice, the latter to his fish-oil; and who would dare to assert that the prayers of both may not breathe as pure a faith as those of the *civilized* European? No mode of existence can attract its preference, none, however humble, its disdain. It attacks no form of government, no social institution; prescribes none, because it has adopted none. It teaches not the art of promoting worldly comforts, it teaches to despise them. What, then, can we call a Christian civilization? Had Christ, or his disciples, prescribed, or even recommended any particular political or social forms,[3] the term would then be applicable.

Scandinavia, Germany, Gaul, and Britain, were likewise subjected to their druids, or other priests, without whose permission they never undertook any important enterprise, whether public or private. Truly does our author observe, that Christianity came to deliver mankind from such trammels, though the mistaken or interested zeal of some of its servants, has so often attempted, and successfully, to fasten them again. How ill adapted Christianity would be, even in a political point of view, for a theocratical formula, is well shown by Mr. Guizot, in his *Hist. of Civilization*, vol. i. p. 213.—H.

3. I have already pointed out, in my introduction (p. 41–49), some of the fatal consequences that spring from that doctrine. It may not, however, be out of place here to mention another. The communists, socialists, Fourierites, or whatever names such enemies to our social system assume, have often seduced the unwary and weak-minded, by the plausible assertion that they wished to restore the social system of the first Christians, who held all goods in common, etc. Many religious sectaries have created serious disturbances under the same pretence. It seems, indeed, reasonable to suppose, that if Christianity had given its exclusive sanction to any particular social and political system, it must have been that which the first Christian communities adopted.—H.

But his law may be observed under all—of whatever nature—and is therefore superior to them all. It is justly and truly called the *Catholic*, or Universal.

And has Christianity, then, no civilizing influence? I shall be asked. Undoubtedly; and a very great one. Its precepts elevate and purify the soul, and, by their purely spiritual nature, disengage the mind from worldly things, and expand its powers. In a merely human point of view, the material benefits it confers on its followers are inestimable. It softens the manners, and facilitates the intercourse between man and his fellow-man; it mitigates violence, and weans him from corrosive vices. It is, therefore, a powerful promoter of his worldly interests. But it only expands the mind in proportion to the susceptibility of the mind for being expanded. It does not give intellect, or confer talents, though it may exalt both, and render them more useful. It does not create new capacities, though it fosters and develops those it finds. Where the capacities of an individual, or a race, are such as to admit an improvement in the mode of existence, it tends to produce it; where such capacities are not already, it does not give them. As it belongs to no particular civilization, it does not compel a nation to change its own. In fine, as it does not level all individuals to the same intellectual standard, so it does not raise all races to the same rank in the political assemblage of the nations of the earth. It is wrong, therefore, to consider the equal aptitude of all races for the true religion, as a proof of their intellectual equality. Though having embraced it, they will still display the same characteristic differences, and divergent or even opposite tendencies. A few examples will suffice to set my idea in a clearer light.

The major portion of the Indian tribes of South America have, for centuries, been received within the pale of the church, yet the European civilization, with which they are in constant contact, has never become their own. The Cherokees, in the northern part of the same continent, have nearly all been converted by the Methodist missionaries. At this I am not surprised, but I should be greatly so, if these tribes, without mixing with the whites, were ever to form one of the States, and exercise any influence in Congress. The Moravians and Danish Lutheran missionaries in Labrador and Greenland, have opened the eyes of the Esquimaux to the light of religion; but their neophytes have remained in the same social condition in which they vegetated before. A still more forcible illustration is afforded by the Laplanders of Sweden, who have not emerged from the state of barbarism of their ancestors, though the doctrine of salvation was preached to them, and believed by them, centuries ago.

I sincerely believe that all these peoples may produce, and, perhaps, already have produced, persons remarkable for piety and pure morals; but I do not expect ever to see among them learned theologians, great statesmen, able military leaders, profound mathematicians, or distinguished artists;—any of those superior minds, whose number and perpetual succession are the cause of power in a preponderating race; much less those rare geniuses whose meteor-like appearance is productive of permanent good only when their countrymen are so constituted as to be able to understand them, and to advance under their direction. We cannot, therefore, call Christianity a promoter of civilization in the narrow and purely material sense of some writers.

Many of my readers, while admitting my observations in the main to be correct, will object that the modifying influence of religion upon the manners must produce a corresponding modification of the institutions, and finally in the whole social system. The propagators of the gospel, they will say, are almost always—though not necessarily—from a nation superior in civilization to the one they visit. In their personal intercourse, therefore, with their neophytes, the latter cannot but acquire new notions of material well-being. Even the political system may be greatly influenced by the relations between instructor and pupil. The missionary, while he provides for the spiritual welfare of his flock, will not either neglect their material wants. By his teaching and example, the savage will learn how to provide against famine, by tilling the soil. This improvement in his condition once effected, he will soon be led to build himself a better dwelling, and to practise some of the simpler useful arts. Gradually, and by careful training, he may acquire sufficient taste for things purely intellectual, to learn the alphabet, or even, as in the case of the Cherokees, to invent one himself. In course of time, if the missionaries' labors are crowned with success, they may, perhaps, so firmly implant their manners and mode of living among this formerly savage tribe, that the traveller will find among them well-cultivated fields, numerous flocks, and, like these same Cherokees, and the Creeks on the southern banks of the Arkansas, black slaves to work on their plantations.

Let us see how far facts correspond with this plausible argument. I shall select the two nations which are cited as being the furthest advanced in European civilization, and their example will, it seems to me, demonstrate beyond a doubt, how impossible it is for any race to pursue a career in which their own nature has not placed them.

The Cherokees and Creeks are said to be the remnants or descendants of the Alleghanian Race, the supposed builders of those great monuments of which we still find traces in the Mississippi Valley. If this be the case, these two nations may lay claim to a natural superiority over the other tribes of North America.

Deprived of their hereditary dominions by the American government, they were forced—under a treaty of transplantation—to emigrate to regions selected for them by the latter. There they were placed under the superintendence of the Minister of War, and of Protestant missionaries, who finally succeeded in persuading them to embrace the mode of life they now lead. Mr. Prichard,[4] my authority for these facts, and who derives them himself from the great work of Mr. Gallatin,[5] asserts that, while all the other Indian tribes are continually diminishing, these are steadily increasing in numbers. As a proof of this, he alleges that when Adair visited the Cherokee tribes, in 1762, the number of their warriors was estimated at 2,300; at present, their total population amounts to 15,000 souls, including about 1,200 negroes in their possession. When we consider that their schools, as well as churches, are directed by white missionaries; that the greater number of these missionaries—being Protestants—are probably married and have children and servants also white, besides, very likely, a sort of retinue of clerks and other European employees;—the increase of the aboriginal population becomes extremely doubtful,[6] while it is easy to conceive the pressure of the white race upon its pupils. Surrounded on all sides by the power of the United States, incommensurable to their imagination; converted to the religion of their masters, which they have, I think, sincerely embraced; treated kindly and judiciously by their spiritual guides; and exposed to the alternation of working or of starving in their contracted territory;—I can understand that it was possible to make them tillers of the earth.

It would be underrating the intelligence of the humblest, meanest specimen of our kind, to express surprise at such a result, when we see that, by dexterously and patiently acting upon the passions and wants of animals, we succeed in teaching them what their own instincts would never have taught them. Every village fair is filled with animals which are trained to perform the

4. *Natural History of Man*, p. 390. London, 1843.

5. *Synopsis of the Indian Tribes of North America.*

6. Had I desired to contest the accuracy of the assertions upon which Mr. Prichard bases his arguments in this case, I should have had in my favor the weighty authority of Mr. De Tocqueville, who, in speaking of the Cherokees, says: "What has greatly promoted the introduction of European habits among these Indians, is the presence of so great a number of half-breeds. The man of mixed race—participating as he does, to a certain extent, in the enlightenment of the father, without, however, entirely abandoning the savage manner of the mother—forms the natural link between civilization and barbarism. As the half-breeds increase among them, we find savages modify their social condition, and change their manners." (*Dem. in Am.*, vol. i. p. 412.) Mr. De Tocqueville ends by predicting that the Cherokees and Creeks, albeit they are half-breeds, and not, as Mr. Prichard affirms, pure aborigines, will, nevertheless, disappear before the encroachments of the whites.

oddest tricks, and is it to be wondered at that men submitted to a rigorous system of training, and deprived of the means of escaping from it, should, in the end, be made to perform certain mechanical functions of civilized life; functions which, even in the savage state, they are capable of understanding, though they have not the will to practise them? This were placing human beings lower in the scale of creation than the learned pig, or Mr. Leonard's domino-playing dogs.[7] Such exultation on the part of the believers in the equality of races is little flattering to those who excite it.

I am aware that this exaggeration of the intellectual capacity of certain races is in a great measure provoked by the notions of some very learned and distinguished men, who pretend that between the lowest races of men, and the highest of apes there was but a shade of distinction. So gross an insult to the dignity of man, I indignantly reject. Certainly, in my estimation, the different races are very unequally endowed, both physically and mentally; but I should be loath to think that in any, even in the most degraded, the un-mistakable line of demarcation between man and brute were effaced. I recog-nize no link of gradation which would connect man mentally with the brute creation.

But does it follow, that because the lowest of the human species is still unmistakably human, that all of that species are capable of the same develop-ment? Take a Bushman, the most hideous and stupid of human families, and by careful training you may teach him, or if he is already adult, his son, to learn and practise a handicraft, even one that requires a certain degree of intelligence. But are we warranted thence to conclude that the nation to which this individual belongs, is susceptible of adopting our civilization? There is a vast difference between mechanically practising handicrafts and arts, the products of an advanced civilization, and that civilization itself. Let us suppose that the Cherokee tribes were suddenly cut off from all connection with the American government, the traveller, a few years hence, would find among them very unexpected and singular institutions, resulting from their mixture with the whites, but partaking only feebly of the character of Euro-pean civilization.

We often hear of negroes proficient in music, negroes who are clerks in counting-rooms, who can read, write, talk like the whites. We admire, and conclude that the negroes are capable of everything that whites are. Notwith-

7. "When four pieces of cards were laid before them, each having a number pronounced *once* in connection with it, they will, after a re-arrangement of the pieces, select any one named by its number. They also play at domino, and with so much skill as to triumph over biped opponents, whining if the adversary plays a wrong piece, or if they themselves are deficient in the right one."—*Vest. of Cr.*, p. 236.—H.

standing this admiration and these hasty conclusions, we express surprise at the contrast of Selavonian civilization with ours. We aver that the Russian, Polish, Servish nations, are civilized only at the surface, that none but the higher classes are in possession of our ideas, and this, thanks to their intermixture with the English, French, and German stock; that the masses, on the contrary, evince a hopeless inaptitude for participating in the forward movement of Western Europe, although these masses have been Christians for centuries, many of them while our ancesetors were heathens. Are the negroes, then, more closely allied to our race than the Selavonic nations? On the one hand, we assert the intellectual equality of the white and black races; on the other, a disparity among subdivisions of our own race.

There is a vast difference between imitation and comprehension. The imitation of a civilization does not necessarily imply an eradication of the hereditary instincts. A nation can be said to have adopted a civilization, only when it has the power to progress in it unprompted, and without guidance. Instead of extolling the intelligence of savages in handling a plough, after being shown; in spelling and reading, after they have been taught; let a single example be alleged of a tribe in any of the numerous countries in contact with Europeans, which, with our religion, has also made the ideas, institutions, and manners of a European nation so completely its own, that the whole social and political machinery moves forward as easily and naturally as in our States. Let an example be alleged of an extra-European nation, among whom the art of printing produces effects analogous to those it produces among us; where new applications of our discoveries are attempted; where our systems of philosophy give birth to new systems; where our arts and sciences flourish.

But, no; I will be more moderate in my demands. I shall not ask of that nation to adopt, together with our faith, all in which consists our individuality. I shall suppose that it rejects it totally, and chooses one entirely different, adapted to its peculiar genius and circumstances. When the eyes of that nation open to the truths of the Gospel, it perceives that its earthly course is as encumbered and wretched as its spiritual life had hitherto been. It now begins the work of improvement, collects its ideas, which had hitherto remained fruitless, examines the notions of others, transforms them, and adapts them to its peculiar circumstances; in fact, erects, by its own power, a social and political system, a civilization, however humble. Where is there such a nation? The entire records of all history may be searched in vain for a single instance of a nation which, together with Christianity, adopted European civilization, or which—by the same grand change in its religious ideas—was led to form a civilization of its own, if it did not possess one already before.

On the contrary, I will show, in every part of the world, ethnical characteristics not in the least effaced by the adoption of Christianity. The Christian Mongol and Tartar tribes lead the same erratic life as their unconverted brethren, and are as distinct from the Russian of the same religion, who tills the soil, or plies his trade in their midst, as they were centuries ago. Nay, the very hostilities of race survive the adoption of a common religion, as we have already pointed out in a preceding chapter. The Christian religion, then, does not equalize the intellectual disparities of races.

SOURCE: Chapter 7 in *The Moral and Intellectual Diversity of Races, with Particular Reference to Their Respective Influence in the Civil and Political History of Mankind* (Philadelphia: J. B. Lippincott, 1856), 215–33.

The Bishop and the Philosopher
MATTHEW ARNOLD

[John William Colenso, the first Anglican bishop in Natal (South Africa), gained both prestige and notoriety for his translations of the first five books of the Bible into Zulu. Colenso was assisted in this project by William Ngidi, but their accomplishment was not necessarily appreciated by all his audience in England. Among his critics was Matthew Arnold. As Jeff Guy points out, Arnold's "scathing attack on Colenso's work did much to ruin the bishop's reputation as a serious thinker on religious matters" ("Class, Imperialism, and Literary Criticism: William Ngidi, John Colenso, and Matthew Arnold," *Journal of Southern African Studies* 23, no. 2 [1997]: 219–441.)]

"Der Engländer ist eigentlich ohne Intelligenz," said Goethe; by which he meant, not that the Englishman was stupid, but that he occupied himself little with the *rationale* of things. He meant that an Englishman held and uttered any given opinion as something isolated, without perceiving its relation to other ideas, or its due place in the general world of thought; without, therefore, having any notion of its absolute value. He meant, in short, that he was uncritical.

Heedless of what may be said about him, the Englishman is generally content to pursue his own way, producing, indeed, little in the sphere of criticism, but producing from time to time in the sphere of pure creation masterpieces which attest his intellectual power and extort admiration from his detractors. Occasionally, however, he quits this safe course. Occasionally, the uncritical spirit of our race determines to perform a great public act of self-humiliation. Such an act it has recently accomplished. It has just sent forth as its scapegoat into the wilderness, amidst a titter from educated Europe, the Bishop of Natal.

The Bishop's book on the Pentateuch has been judged from a theological point of view by members of his own profession; and critics too, who were not members of that profession, have judged it from the same point of view. From the theological point of view I do not presume to judge it. But a work of this kind has to justify itself before another tribunal besides an ecclesiastical one; it is liable to be called up for judgment, not only before a Court of Arches, but before the Republic of Letters. It is as a humble citizen of that republic that I wish to say a few words about the Bishop of Natal's book. But what, it may be asked, has literary criticism to do with books on religious matters? That is what I will in the first instance try to show.

Literary criticism's most important function is to try books as to the influence which they are calculated to have upon the general culture of single nations or of the world at large. Of this culture literary criticism is the appointed guardian, and on this culture all literary works may be conceived as in some way or other operating. All these works have a special professional criticism to undergo: theological works that of theologians, historical works that of historians, philosophical works that of philosophers, and in this case each kind of work is tried by a separate standard. But they have also a general literary criticism to undergo, and this tries them all, as I have said, by one standard—their effect upon general culture. Every one is not a theologian, a historian, or a philosopher, but every one is interested in the advance of the general culture of his nation or of mankind. A criticism therefore which, abandoning a thousand special questions which may be raised about any book, tries it solely in respect of its influence upon this culture, brings it thereby within the sphere of every one's interest. This is why literary criticism has exercised so much power. The chief sources of intellectual influence in Europe, during the last century and a half, have been its three chief critics—Voltaire, Lessing, Goethe. The chief sources of intellectual influence in England during the same period, have been its chief organs of criticism—Addison, Johnson, the first Edinburgh Reviewers.

Religious books come within the jurisdiction of literary criticism so far as they affect general culture. Undoubtedly they do affect this in the highest degree: they affect it whether they appeal to the reason, or to the heart and feelings only; whether they enlighten directly, or, by softening and purifying, prepare the way for enlightenment. So far as by any book on religious matters the raw are humanised or the cultivated are advanced to a yet higher culture, so far that book is a subject for literary criticism. But, undoubtedly, the direct promotion of culture by intellectual power is the main interest of literary criticism, not the indirect promotion of this culture by edification. As soon, therefore, as a religious work has satisfied it that it pursues no other end than edification, *and that it really does pursue this,* literary criticism dismisses it without further question. Religious books, such as are sold daily are round us by thousands and tens of thousands, of no literary merit whatever, which do not pretend to enlighten intellectually, which only profess to edify, and do in some way fulfil their profession, literary criticism thus dismisses with respect, without a syllable of disparaging remark. Even a work like that of M. Hengstenberg on the Pentateuch, which makes higher claims without fulfilling them, literary criticism may dismiss without censure, because it is honestly written for purposes of edification. Over works, therefore, which treat of religious matters, literary criticism will only in certain cases linger long. One case is, when, through such works, though their object be solely or mainly general edification, there shines an ethereal light, the presence of a gifted nature; for this entitles the "Imitation," the "Spiritual Works" of Fénelon, the "Pilgrim's Progress," the "Christian Year," to rank with the works which inform, not with those which edify simply; and it is with works which inform that the main business of literary criticism lies. And even over works which cannot take this high rank, but which are yet freshened, as they pursue their aim of edification, with airs from the true poetical sky—such as the "Mother's Last Words" of Mrs. Sewell—literary criticism will be tempted to linger; it will, at least, salute them in passing, and say: "There, too, is a breath of Arcadia!"

This is one case: another is, when a work on religious matters entirely foregoes the task of edifying the uninstructed, and pursues solely that of informing the instructed, of raising the intellectual life of these to a yet higher stage. Such an attempt to advance the highest culture of Europe, of course powerfully interests a criticism whose especial concern is with that culture. There is a third and last case. It is, when a work on religious matters is neither edifying nor informing; when it is neither good for the many nor yet for the few. A Hebrew moralist, in the "Ethics of the Fathers," says: "Every dispute that is instituted for God's sake will in the end be established; but that which is not for God's sake will not be established." What may be considered as a dispute for God's sake? Literary criticism regards a religious book, which tends to edify the multitude, as a dispute for God's sake; it regards a religious book which tends to inform the instructed, as a dispute for God's sake; but a religious book which tends neither to edify the multitude nor to inform the instructed, it refuses to regard as a dispute for God's sake; it classes it, in the language of the moralist just cited, not with the speaking of Hillel and

Shamai, but with the gainsaying of Korah. It is bound, if the book has notoriety enough to give it importance, to pass censure on it.

According to these principles, literary criticism has to try the book of the Bishop of Natal, which all England is now reading. It has to try it in respect of the influence which it is naturally calculated to exercise on the culture of England or Europe; and it asks: "Does this book tend to advance that culture, either by edifying the little-instructed, or by further informing the much-instructed?"

Does it tend to edify the little-instructed—the great majority? Perhaps it will be said that this book professes not to edify the little-instructed, but to enlighten them; and that a religious book which attempts to enlighten the little-instructed by sweeping away their prejudices, attempts a good work and is justifiable before criticism, exactly as much as a book which attempts to enlighten on these matters the much-instructed. No doubt, to say this is to say what seems quite in accordance with modern notions; the *Times* tells us day after day how the general public is the organ of all truth, and individual genius the organ of all error; nay, we have got so far, it says, that the superior men of former days, if they could live again now, would abandon the futile business of running counter to the opinions of the many, of persisting in opinions of their own: they would sit at the feet of the general public, and learn from its lips what they ought to say. And, no doubt, this doctrine holds out, both for the superior man and the general public, a prospect in a high degree tempting; the former is to get more pudding than formerly, and the latter more praise. But it is a doctrine which no criticism that has not a direct interest in promulgating it can ever seriously entertain. The highly-instructed few, and not the scantily-instructed many, will ever be the organ to the human race of knowledge and truth. Knowledge and truth, in the full sense of the words, are not attainable by the great mass of the human race at all. The great mass of the human race have to be softened and humanised through their heart and imagination, before any soil can be found in them where knowledge may strike living roots. Until the softening and humanising process is very far advanced, intellectual demonstrations are uninforming for them; and, if they impede the working of influences which advance this softening and humanising process, they are even noxious; they retard their development, they impair the culture of the world. All the great teachers, divine and human, who have ever appeared, have united in proclaiming this. "Remember the covenant of the Highest, and wink at ignorance," says the Son of Sirach. "Unto you," said Christ to a few disciples, "it is given to know the mysteries of the kingdom of heaven, but to them (the multitude) it is not given." "My words," said Pindar, "have a sound only for the wise." Plato interdicted the entry of his school of philosophy to all who had not first undergone the discipline of a severe science. "The vast majority," said Spinoza, "have neither capacity nor leisure to follow speculations." "The few (those who can have a saving knowledge) can never mean the many," says, in one of his noblest sermons, Dr. Newman. Old moral ideas leaven and humanise the multitude: new intellectual ideas filter slowly down to them from the thinking few; and only when they reach them in this manner do they adjust themselves to their practice without convulsing it. It was not by the intellectual truth of its propositions concerning purgatory, or prayer for the dead, or the human nature of the Virgin Mary, that the Reformation touched and advanced the multitude: it was by the moral truth of its protest against the sale of indulgences, and the scandalous lives of many of the clergy.

Human culture is not, therefore, advanced by a religious book conveying intellectual demonstrations to the many, unless they be conveyed in such a way as to edify them. Now, that the intellectual demonstrations of the Bishop of Natal's book are not in themselves of a nature to edify the general reader, that is, to serve his religious feeling, the Bishop himself seems well aware. He expresses alarm and misgivings at what he is about, for this very reason, that he is conscious how, by shaking the belief of the many in the Inspiration of Scripture, he may be shaking their religious life—working, that is, not to their edification. He talks of "the sharp pang of that decisive stroke which is to sever their connexion with the ordinary view of the Mosaic story for ever." Again: "I tremble," he says, "at the results of my own inquiry—the momentous results" (he elsewhere calls them) "to which it leads." And again: "I cannot but feel, that having thus been impelled to take an active part in showing the groundlessness of that notion of Scripture Inspiration which so many have long regarded as the very foundation of their faith and hope, a demand may be made upon me for something to supply the loss, for something *to fill up the aching void* which will undoubtedly be felt at first." Even if he had not been himself conscious of the probable operation of his book, there were plenty of voices to tell him beforehand what it would be. He himself quotes these words of Mr. Cook: "One thing with the Englishman is fixed and certain;—a narrative purporting to be one of positive facts, which is wholly, or in any considerable portion, untrue, can have no connexion with the Divine, and cannot have any beneficial influence on mankind" (*der Engländer est eigentlich ohne Intelligenz*). He quotes Mr. Burgon as expressing the common belief of English Christians when he says: "Every verse of the Bible, every word of it, every syllable of it, every letter of it, is the direct utterance of the Most High." And so, too, since the publication of the Bishop of Natal's book, a preacher in the Oxford University pulpit has declared, that if the historical credit of a single verse of the Bible be shaken, all belief in the Bible is gone.

But indeed, without looking at all to these momentous results of his demonstrations, the Bishop would probably have no difficulty in admitting that these demonstrations can have in themselves nothing edifying. He is an excellent arithmetician, and has published an admirable Manual of Arithmetic; and his book is really nothing but a series of problems in this his favourite science, the solution to each of which is to be the *reductio ad absurdum* of that Book of the Pentateuch which supplied its terms. The Bishop talks of the "multitude of operatives" whose spiritual condition we must care for: he allows that to the pious operative his proceedings must give a terrible shock; but will the impious operative be softened or converted by them? He cannot seriously think so; for softening and converting are positive processes, and his arithmetical process is a purely negative one. It is even ruthlessly negative; for it delights in nothing so much as in triumphing over attempts which may be made to explain or attenuate the difficulties of the Bible narrative. Such an attempt Dr. Stanley has made with respect to the history of the sojourn of the Israelites in the wilderness; the quotations on this matter from Dr. Stanley's "Sinai and Palestine" are the refreshing spots of the Bishop of Natal's volume, but he cites them only to refute them. In a similar spirit he deals with M. Hengstenberg. M. Hengstenberg is, in general, only too well contented to remain with his head under water, raking about in the sand and mud of the letter for the pearl which will never be found there; but occasionally a mortal commentator must come up to breathe. M. Hengstenberg has hardly time to gasp out a rational explanation of any passage, before the remorseless Bishop pushes him under water again.

So we must look for the edifying part of the Bishop of Natal's work elsewhere than in his arithmetical demonstrations. And I am bound to say, that such a part the Bishop does attempt to supply. He feels, as I have said, that the work he has been accomplishing is not in itself edifying to the common English reader, that it will leave such a reader with an "aching void" in his bosom; and this void he undoubtedly attempts to fill. And how does he fill it? "I would venture to refer him," he says, "to my lately published Commentary on the Epistle to the Romans . . . which I would humbly hope by God's mercy may minister in some measure to the comfort and support of troubled minds under present circumstances." He candidly adds, however, that this Commentary was written "when I had no idea whatever of holding my present views." So as a further support he offers "the third and sixth chapters of Exodus " (that Exodus on which he has just been inflicting such severe blows), "the noble words of Cicero preserved by Lactantius" in the eighth section of the sixth book of his "Divine Institutions," "the great truths revealed to the Sikh Gooroos" as these truths are set forth in Cunningham's "History of the Sikhs," pp. 355, 356, and lastly a Hindoo prayer, to be found in the *Journal of the Asiatic Society of Bengal,* vol. vi. pp. 487, 750, 756, beginning "Whatever Rám willeth." And this is positively all. He finds the simple everyday Englishman going into church, he buries him and the sacred fabric under an avalanche of rule-of-three sums; and when the poor man crawls from under the ruins, bruised, bleeding, and bewildered, and begs for a little spiritual consolation, the Bishop "refers him" to his own Commentary on the Romans, two chapters of Exodus, a fragment of Cicero, a revelation to the Sikh Gooroos, and an invocation of Rám. This good Samaritan sets his battered brother on his own beast (the Commentary), and for oil and wine pours into his wounds the Hindoo prayer, the passage of Cicero, and the rest of it.

Literary criticism cannot accept this edification as sufficient. The Bishop of Natal must be considered to have failed to edify the little-instructed, to advance the lower culture of his nation. It is demanded of him, therefore, that he shall have informed the much-instructed, that he shall have advanced the higher culture of his nation or of Europe.

Literary criticism does not require him to edify this; it is enough if he informs it. We may dismiss the Commentary on the Romans and the truths revealed to the Sikh Gooroos from our consideration, for the Bishop himself has told us that it is the weak vessel, the little-instructed, whom he refers to these. There remain his arithmetical demonstrations. And, indeed, he himself seems to rely for his justification upon the informing influence which these are calculated to exercise upon the higher culture of his nation; for he speaks of the "more highly educated classes of society," and of the "intelligent operative" (that favourite character of modern disquisition)—those, that is, who have either read much or thought much—as the special objects of his solicitude. Now, on the higher culture of his nation, what informing influence can the Bishop of Natal's arithmetical demonstrations exercise? I have already said what these are: they are a series of problems, the solution of each of which is meant to be the *reductio ad absurdum* of that Book of the Pentateuch which supplied its terms. This being so, it must be said that the Bishop of Natal gives us a great deal too many of them. For his purpose a smaller number of problems and a more stringent method of stating them would have sufficed. It would then have been possible within the compass of a single page to put all the information which the Bishop's book aspires to convey to the mind of Europe. For example: if we take the Book of Genesis, and the account of the family of Judah there related—"*Allowing* 20 *as the marriageable age, how many years are required for the production of* 3 *generations?*" The answer to that sum disposes (on the Bishop's plan) of the Book of Genesis. Again, as to the account in the Book of Exodus of the Israelites dwelling in tents—"*Allowing* 10 *persons for each tent* (*and a Zulu hut in Natal contains on an average only* 3 ½), *how many tents would* 2,000,000 *persons require?*" The parenthesis in that problem is hardly worthy of such a master of arithmetical statement as Dr. Colenso; but, with or without the parenthesis, the problem, when answered, disposes of the Book of Exodus. Again, as to the account in Leviticus of the provision made for the priests: "*If three priests have to eat* 264 *pigeons a day, how many must each priest eat?*" That disposes of Leviticus. Take Numbers, and the total of firstborns there given, as compared with the number of male adults: "*If, of* 900,000 *males,* 22,273 *are firstborns, how many boys must there be in each family?*" That disposes of Numbers. For Deuteronomy, take the number of lambs slain at the Sanctuary, as compared with the space for slaying them: "*In an area of* 1,692 *square yards, how many lambs per minute can* 150,000 *persons kill in two hours?*" Certainly not 1,250, the number required; and the Book of Deuteronomy, therefore, shares the fate of its predecessors. *Omnes eodem cogimur.*

Even a giant need not waste his strength. The Bishop of Natal has, indeed, other resources in his conflict with the Pentateuch, if these are insufficient; he has the overcrowding of the Tabernacle doorway, and the little difficulty about the Danites; but he need not have troubled himself to produce them. All he designed to do for the higher culture of his nation has been done without them. It is useless to slay the slain.

Such are the Bishop of Natal's exploits in the field of biblical criticism. The theological critic will regard them from his own point of view; the literary critic asks only in what way can they be informing to the higher culture of England or Europe? This higher culture knew very well already that contradictions were pointed out in the Pentateuch narrative; it had heard already all that the Bishop of Natal tells us as to the "impossibility of regarding the Mosaic story as a true narrative of actual historical matters of fact;" of this impossibility, of which the Bishop of Natal "had not the most distant idea" two years ago, it had long since read expositions, if not so elaborate as his, at least as convincing. That which the higher culture of Europe wanted to know is,—*What then?* What follows from all this? What change is it, if true, to produce in the relations of mankind to the Christian religion? If the old theory of Scripture Inspiration is to be abandoned, what place is the Bible henceforth to hold among books? What is the new Christianity to be like? How are Governments to deal with national Churches founded to maintain a very different conception of Christianity? It is these questions which the higher culture of Europe now addresses to those who profess to enlighten it in the field of free religious speculation, and it is intellectually informed only so far as these questions are answered. It is these questions which freethinkers who really speak to the higher culture of their nation or of Europe—men such as Hegel was in Germany, such as M. Rénan now is in France—attempt to answer; and therefore, unorthodox though such writers may be, literary criticism listens to them with respectful interest. And it is these questions which the Bishop of Natal never touches with one of his fingers.

I will make what I mean yet clearer by a contrast. At this very moment is announced the first English translation of a foreign work which treats of the same matter as the Bishop of Natal's work—the interpretation of Scripture—and, like the Bishop of Natal's work, treats of it in an unorthodox way. I mean a work signed by a great name—to most English readers the name of a great heretic, and nothing more—the *Tractatus Theologico-Politicus* of Spinoza. It is not so easy to give a summary of this book as of the book of the Bishop of Natal. Still, with the aim of showing how free religious speculation may be conducted so as to be informing to the much-instructed, even though it be not edifying to the little-instructed, I will attempt the task.

The little-instructed Spinoza's work could not unsettle, for it was inaccessible to them. It was written in Latin, the language of the instructed few—the language in which Coleridge desired that all novel speculations about religion should be written. Spinoza even expressly declares that he writes for the instructed few only, and that his book is not designed for the many—*reliquis hunc tractatum commendare non stuleo.* Not only the multitude, but all of a higher culture than the multitude who yet share the passions of the multitude, he intreats not to read his book: they will only, he says, do harm to others, and no good to themselves. So sincere was this author's desire to be simply useful, his indifference to mere notoriety, that when it was proposed to publish a Dutch translation of his work, and thus bring it within the reach of a wider public, he requested that the project might be abandoned. Such a publication could effect no benefit, he said, and it might injure the cause which he had at heart.

He was moved to write, not by admiration at the magnitude of his own sudden discoveries, not by desire for notoriety, not by a transport of excitement, not because he "had launched his bark on the flood and was carried along by the waters;" but because, grave as was the task to be attempted, and slight as was the hope of succeeding, the end seemed to him worth all the labour and all the risk. "I fear that I have taken this work in hand too late in the day; for matters are nearly come to that pass that men are incapable, on these subjects, of having their errors cleared away, so saturated with prejudices are their minds. Still, I will persevere, and continue to make what effort I can; for the case, after all, is not quite hopeless." For the instructed few he was convinced that his work might prove truly informing—*his hoc opus perquem utile fore confido.*

Addressing these, he tells them how, struck with the contrast between the precepts of Christianity and the common practice of Christians, he had sought the cause of this contrast and found it in their erroneous conception of their own religion. The comments of men had been foisted into the Christian religion; the pure teaching of God had been lost sight of. He had determined to go again to the Bible, to read it over and over with a perfectly unprejudiced mind, and to accept nothing as its teaching which it did not clearly teach. He began by constructing a method, or set of conditions indispensable for the adequate interpretation of Scripture. These conditions are such, he points out, that a perfectly adequate interpretation of Scripture is now impossible: for example, to understand any Prophet thoroughly, we ought to know the life, character, and pursuits of that Prophet, under what circumstances his book was composed, and in what state and through what hands it has come down to us; and, in general, most of this we cannot now know. Still, the main sense of the Books of Scripture may be clearly seized by us. Himself a Jew with all the learning of his nation, and a man of the highest natural powers, he had in the difficult task of seizing this sense every aid which special knowledge or preeminent faculties could supply.

In what then, he asks, does Scripture, interpreted by its own aid, and not by the aid of Rabbinical traditions or Greek philosophy, allege its own divinity to consist? In a revelation given by God to the Prophets. Now all knowledge is a Divine revelation; but prophecy, as represented in Scripture, is one of which the laws of human nature, considered in themselves alone, cannot be the cause. Therefore nothing must be asserted about it, except what is clearly declared by the Prophets themselves; for they are our only source of knowledge on a matter which does not fall within the scope of our ordinary knowing faculties. But ignorant people, not knowing the Hebrew genius and phraseology, and not attending to the circumstances of the speaker, often imagine the Prophets to assert things which they do not.

The Prophets clearly declare themselves to have received the revelation of God through the means of words and images—not, as Christ, through immediate communication of the mind with the mind of God. Therefore the Prophets excelled other men by the power and vividness of their representing and imagining faculty, not by the perfection of their mind. This is why they perceived almost everything through figures, and express themselves so variously, and so improperly, concerning the nature of God. Moses imagined that God could be seen, and attributed to Him the passions of anger and jealousy; Micaiah imagined Him sitting on a throne, with the host of heaven on his right and left hand; Daniel as an old man, with a white garment and white hair; Ezekiel as a fire; the disciples of Christ thought they saw the Spirit of God in the form of a dove; the Apostles, in the form of fiery tongues.

Whence, then, could the Prophets be certain of the truth of a revelation which they received through the imagination, and not by a mental process?— for only an idea can carry the sense of its own certainty along with it, not an imagination. To make them certain of the truth of what was revealed to them, a reasoning process came in; they had to rely on the testimony of a sign, and (above all) on the testimony of their own conscience, that they were good men, and spoke for God's sake. Either testimony was incomplete without the other. Even the good prophet needed for his message the confirmation of a sign; but the bad prophet, the utterer of an immoral doctrine, had no certainty for his doctrine, no truth in it, even though he confirmed it by a sign. This, the testimony of a good conscience, was, therefore, the prophet's grand source of certitude. Even this, however, was only a moral certitude, not a mathematical; for no man can be perfectly sure of his own goodness.

The power of imagining, the power of feeling what goodness is, and the habit of practising goodness, were therefore the sole essential qualifications of a true prophet. But for the purpose of the message, the revelation, which God designed him to convey, these qualifications were enough. The sum and substance of this revelation was simply: *Believe in God, and lead a good life.* To be the organ of this revelation, did not make a man more learned; it left his scientific knowledge as it found it. This explains the contradictory and speculatively false opinions about God, and the laws of Nature, which the Patriarchs, the Prophets, the Apostles entertained. Abraham and the Patriarchs knew God only as *El Sadai,* the Power which gives to every man that which suffices him; Moses knew Him as *Jehovah,* a self-existent being, but imagined Him with the passions of a man. Samuel imagined that God could not repent of His sentences; Jeremiah, that He could. Joshua, on a day of great victory, the ground being white with hail, seeing the daylight last longer than usual, and imaginatively seizing this as a special sign of the help divinely promised to him, declared that the sun was standing still. To be obeyers of God themselves, and inspired leaders of others to obedience and good life, did not make Abraham and Moses metaphysicians, or Joshua a natural philosopher. His revelation no more changed the speculative opinions of each prophet, than it changed his temperament or style. The wrathful Elisha required the natural sedative of music, before he could be the messenger of good fortune to

Jehoram. The high-bred Isaiah and Nahum have the style proper to their condition, and the rustic Ezekiel and Amos the style proper to theirs. We are not therefore bound to pay heed to the speculative opinions of this or that prophet, for in uttering these he spoke as a mere man: only in exhorting his hearers to obey God and lead a good life was he the organ of a Divine revelation.

To know and love God is the highest blessedness of man, and of all men alike; to this all mankind are called, and not any one nation in particular. The Divine Law, properly so named, is the method of life for attaining this height of human blessedness: this law is universal, written in the heart, and one for all mankind. Human law is the method of life for attaining and preserving temporal security and prosperity; this law is dictated by a lawgiver, and every nation has its own. In the case of the Jews, this law was dictated, by revelation, through the Prophets; its fundamental precept was to obey God and to keep His commandments, and it is therefore, in a secondary sense, called Divine; but it was, nevertheless, framed in respect of temporal things only. Even the truly moral and divine precept of this law, to practise for God's sake justice and mercy towards one's neighbour, meant for the Hebrew of the Old Testament his Hebrew neighbour only, and had respect to the concord and stability of the Hebrew Commonwealth. The Jews were to obey God and to keep His Commandments, that they might continue long in the land given to them, and that it might be well with them there. Their election was a temporal one, and lasted only so long as their State. It is now over; and the only election the Jews now have is that of the *pious*, the *remnant*, which takes place, and has always taken place, in every other nation also. Scripture itself teaches that there is a universal divine law, that this is common to all nations alike, and is the law which truly confers eternal blessedness. Solomon, the wisest of the Jews, knew this law, as the few wisest men in all nations have ever known it; but for the mass of the Jews, as for the mass of mankind everywhere, this law was hidden, and they had no notion of its moral action—its *vera vita* which conducts to eternal blessedness—except so far as this action was enjoined upon them by the prescriptions of their temporal law. When the ruin of their State brought with it the ruin of their temporal law, they would have lost altogether their only clue to eternal blessedness. Christ came when that fabric of the Jewish State, for the sake of which the Jewish Law existed, was about to fall; and He proclaimed the universal Divine Law. A certain moral action is prescribed by this law, as a certain moral action was prescribed by the Jewish Law; but he who truly conceives the universal Divine Law conceives God's decrees adequately as eternal truths, and for him moral action has liberty and self-knowledge; while the Prophets of the Jewish Law inadequately conceived God's decrees as mere rules and commands, and for them moral action had no liberty and no self-knowledge. Christ, who beheld the decrees of God as God himself beholds them—as eternal truths—proclaimed the love of God and the love of our neighbour as *commands* only because of the ignorance of the multitude: to those to whom it was "given to know the mysteries of the kingdom of God," He announced them, as He himself perceived them, as eternal truths. And the Apostles, like Christ, spoke to many of their hearers "as unto carnal not spiritual:" presented to them, that is, the love of God and their neighbour as a Divine command authenticated by the life and death of Christ, not as an eternal idea of reason carrying its own warrant along with it. The presentation of it as this latter their hearers "were not able to bear." The Apostles, moreover, though they preached and confirmed their doctrine by signs as prophets, wrote their Epistles, not as prophets, but as doctors and reasoners. The essentials of their doctrine, indeed, they took not from reason, but, like the Prophets, from fact and revelation; they preached belief in God and goodness of life as a catholic religion, existing by virtue of the Passion of Christ, as the Prophets had preached belief in God and goodness of life as a national religion existing by virtue of the Mosaic Covenant; but while the Prophets announced their message in a form purely dogmatical, the Apostles developed theirs with the forms of reasoning and argumentation according to each apostle's ability and way of thinking, and as they might best commend their message to their hearers; and for their reasonings they themselves claim no Divine authority, submitting them to the judgment of their hearers. Thus each apostle built essential religion on a non-essential foundation of his own, and, as St. Paul says, avoided building on the foundations of another apostle, which might be quite different from his own. Hence the discrepancies between the doctrine of one apostle and another—between that of St. Paul, for example, and that of St. James; but these discrepancies are in the non-essentials not given to them by revelation, and not in essentials. Human Churches, seizing these discrepant non-essentials as essentials, one maintaining one of them, another another, have filled the world with unprofitable disputes, have "turned the Church into an academy, and religion into a science, or rather a wrangling," and have fallen into endless schism.

What, then, are the essentials of Religion according both to the Old and to the New Testament? Very few and very simple. The precept to love God and our neighbour. The precepts of the first chapter of Isaiah: "Wash you, make you clean; put away the evil of your doings from before mine eyes; cease to do evil; learn to do well; seek judgment; relieve the oppressed; judge the fatherless; plead for the widow." The precepts of the Sermon on the Mount, which add to the foregoing the injunction that we should cease to do evil and learn to do well, not to our brethren and fellow-citizens only, but to all mankind. It is by following these precepts that belief in God is to be shown; if we believe in Him we shall keep His commandment; and this is His commandment, that we love one another. It is because it contains these precepts that the Bible is properly called the Word of God, in spite of its containing much that is mere history, and, like all history, is sometimes true, sometimes false; in spite of its containing much that is mere reasoning, and, like all reasoning, is sometimes sound, sometimes hollow. These precepts are also the precepts of the universal Divine Law written in our hearts; and it is only by this that the Divinity of Scripture is established;—by its containing, namely, precepts identical with those of this inly-written and self-proving law. This law was in the world, as St. John says, before the doctrine of Moses or the doctrine of Christ. And what need was there, then, for these doctrines? Because the world at large "knew not" this original Divine Law, in which precepts are ideas, and the belief in God the knowledge and contemplation of Him. Reason gives us this law, Reason tells us that it leads to eternal blessedness, and that those who follow it have no need of any other. But Reason could not have told us that the moral action of the universal Divine Law—followed not from a sense of its intrinsic goodness, truth, and necessity, but simply in proof of obedience (for both the Old and New Testament are but one long discipline of obedience), simply because it is so commanded by Moses in virtue of the Covenant, simply because it is so commanded by Christ in virtue of His life and passion—can lead to eternal blessedness, which means, for Reason, eternal knowledge. Reason could not have told us this, and this is what the Bible tells us. This is that "thing which had been kept secret since the foundation of the world." It is thus that by means of the foolishness of the world God confounds the wise, and with things that are not brings to nought things that are. Of the truth of the promise thus made to obedience without knowledge, we can have no mathematical certainty; for we can have a mathematical certainty only of things deduced by Reason from elements which she in herself possesses. But we can have a moral certainty of it; a certainty such as the Prophets had themselves, arising out of the goodness and pureness of those to whom this revelation has been made, and rendered possible for us by its contradicting no principles of Reason. It is a great comfort to believe it; because "as it is only the very small minority who can pursue a virtuous life by the sole guidance of reason, we should, unless we had this testimony of Scripture, be in doubt respecting the salvation of nearly the whole human race."

It follows from this that Philosophy has her own independent sphere, and Theology hers, and that neither has the right to invade and try to subdue the other. Theology demands perfect obedience, Philosophy perfect knowledge: the obedience demanded by Theology and the knowledge demanded by Philosophy are alike saving. As speculative opinions about God, Theology requires only such as are indispensable to the reality of this obedience; the belief that God is, that He is a rewarder of them that seek Him, and that the proof of seeking Him is a good life. These are the fundamentals of Faith, and they are so clear and simple that none of the inaccuracies provable in the Bible narrative the least affect them, and they have indubitably come to us uncorrupted. He who holds them may make, as the Patriarchs and Prophets did, other speculations about God most erroneous, and yet their faith is complete and saving. Nay, beyond these fundamentals, speculative opinions are pious or impious, not as they are true or false, but as they confirm or shake the believer in the practice of obedience. The truest speculative opinion about the nature of God is impious if it makes its holder rebellious; the falsest speculative opinion is pious if it makes him obedient. Governments should never render themselves the tools of ecclesiastical ambition by promulgating as fundamentals of the national Church's faith more than these, and should concede the fullest liberty of speculation.

But the multitude, which respects only what astonishes, terrifies, and overwhelms it, by no means takes this simple view of its own religion. To the multitude Religion seems venerable only when it is subversive of Reason, confirmed by miracles, conveyed in documents materially sacred and infallible, and dooming to damnation all without its pale. But this religion of the multitude is not the religion which a true interpretation of Scripture finds in Scripture. Reason tells us that a miracle—understanding by a miracle a breach of the laws of Nature—is impossible, and that to think it possible is to dishonour God: for the laws of Nature are the laws of God, and to say that God violates the laws of Nature is to say that He violates His own nature. Reason sees, too, that miracles can never attain their professed object,—that of bringing us to a higher knowledge of God; since our knowledge of God is raised only by perfecting and clearing our conceptions, and the alleged design of miracles is to baffle them. But neither does Scripture anywhere assert, as a general truth, that miracles are possible. Indeed, it asserts the contrary; for Jeremiah declares that Nature follows an invariable order. Scripture, however, like Nature herself, does not lay down speculative propositions (*Scriptura definitiones non tradit, ut nec etiam Natura*). It relates matters in such an order and with such phraseology as a speaker (often not perfectly instructed himself) who wanted to impress his hearers with a lively sense of God's greatness and goodness would naturally employ; as Moses, for instance, relates to the Israelites the passage of the Red Sea without any mention of the East Wind which attended it, and which is brought accidentally to our knowledge in another place. So that to know exactly what Scripture means in the relation of each seeming miracle, we ought to know (besides the tropes and phrases of the Hebrew language) the circumstances, and also—since every one is swayed in his manner of presenting facts by his own preconceived opinions, and we have seen what those of the prophets were—the preconceived opinions of each speaker. But this mode of interpreting Scripture is fatal to the vulgar notion of its verbal inspiration, of a sanctity and absolute truth in all the words and sentences of which it is composed. This vulgar notion is, indeed, a palpable error. It is demonstrable from the internal testimony of the Scriptures themselves, that the Books from the first of the Pentateuch to the last of Kings were put together, after the first Destruction of Jerusalem, by a compiler (probably Ezra) who designed to relate the history of the Jewish people from its origin to that destruction: it is demonstrable, morever, that the compiler did not put his last hand to the work, but left it, with its extracts from various and conflicting sources sometimes unreconciled—left it with errors of text and unsettled readings. The prophetic books are mere fragments of the Prophets, collected by the Rabbins where they could find them, and inserted in the Canon according to their discretion. They, at first, proposed to admit neither the Book of Proverbs nor the Book of Ecclesiastes into the Canon, and only admitted them because there were found in them passages which commended the Law of Moses. Ezekiel also they had determined to exclude; but one of their number remodelled him, so as to procure his admission. The Books of Ezra, Nehemiah, Esther, and Daniel are the work of a single author, and were not written till after Judas Maccabeus had restored the worship of the Temple. The Book of Psalms was collected and arranged at the same time. Before this time, there was no Canon of the Sacred Writings, and the great synagogue, by which the Canon was fixed, was first convened after the Macedonian conquest of Asia. Of that synagogue none of the prophets were members; the learned men who composed it were guided by their own fallible judgment. In like manner the uninspired judgment of human councils determined the Canon of the New Testament.

Such, reduced to the briefest and plainest terms possible, stripped of the developments and proofs with which he delivers it, and divested of the metaphysical language in which much of it is clothed by him, is the doctrine of Spinoza's treatise on the interpretation of Scripture. Certainly it is not the doctrine of any of the old Churches of Christendom; of the Church of Rome, or the Church of Constantinople, or the Church of England. But Spinoza was not a member, still less a minister, of any one of these Churches. When he made a profession of faith widely different from that of any of them, he had not vowed to minister the doctrine of one of them "as that Church had received the same." When he claimed for Churchmen the widest latitude of speculation in religious matters, he was inviting Governments to construct a new Church; he was not holding office in an old Church under articles expressly promulgated to check "disputations, altercations, or questions." The Bishop of Natal cries out, that orders in the Church of England without full liberty of speculation are an intolerable yoke. But he is thus crying out for a new Church of England, which is not that in which he has voluntarily taken office. He forgets that the clergy of a Church with formularies like those of the Church of England, exist in virtue of their relinquishing in religious matters full liberty of speculation. Liberal potentates of the English Church, who so loudly sound the praises of freedom of inquiry, forget it also. It may be time for the State to institute, as its national clergy, a corporation enjoying the most absolute freedom of inquiry; but that corporation will not be the present clergy of the Church of England. Coleridge maintained that the whole body of men of letters or science formed the true clergy of a modern nation, and ought to participate in the endowments of the National Church. That is a beautiful theory; but it has not hitherto been cordially welcomed by the clergy of the Church of England. It has not hitherto been been put in practice by the State. Is it to be put in practice for the future? To any eminent layman of letters, who presents himself on the other side the river with the exterminating Five Problems, the passage of Cicero, and the prayer to Rám as his credentials, will the gates of Lambeth fly open?

Literary criticism, however, must not blame the Bishop of Natal because his personal position is false, nor praise Spinoza because his personal position is sound. But, as it must deny to the Bishop's book the right of existing, when it can justify its existence neither by edifying the many nor informing the few, it must concede that right to Spinoza's for the sake of its unquestionably philosophic scope. Many and many are the propositions in Spinoza's work, which, brought by him to us out of the sphere of his unaccepted philosophy, and presented with all the calm inflexibility of his manner, are startling, repellent, questionable. Criticism may take many and many objections to the facts and arguments of his Treatise. But, by the whole scope and drift of its argument, by the spirit in which the subject is throughout treated, his work undeniably becomes interesting and stimulating to the general culture of Europe. There are alleged contradictions in Scripture; and the question which the general culture of Europe, informed of this, asks with real interest is, as I have said,—*What then?* To this question Spinoza returns an answer, and the Bishop of Natal returns none. The Bishop of Natal keeps going round for ever within the barren sphere of these contradictions themselves; he treats them as if they were supremely interesting in themselves, as if we had never heard of them before, and could never hear enough of them now. Spinoza touches these verbal matters with all possible brevity, and presses on to the more important. It is enough for him to give us what is indispensably necessary of them. He points out that Moses could never have written, "And the Canaanite was then in the land," because the Canaanite was in the land still at the death of Moses. He points out that Moses could never have written, "There arose not a prophet since in Israel like unto Moses." He points out how such a passage as "These are the kings that reigned in Edom *before there reigned any king over the children of Israel,"* clearly indicates an author writing not before the times of the Kings. He points out how the account of Og's iron bedstead—"Only Og the king of Bashan remained of the remnant of giants; behold, his bedstead was a bedstead of iron; is it not in Rabbath of the children of Ammon?"—probably indicates an author writing after David had taken Rabbath, and found there "abundance of spoil," amongst it this iron bedstead, the gigantic relic of another age. He points out how the language of this passage, and of such a passage as that in the Book of Samuel—"Beforetime in Israel, when a man went to inquire of God, thus he spake: Come and let us go to the seer; for he that is now called Prophet was aforetime called seer"—is certainly the language of a writer describing the events of a long-past age, and not the language of a contemporary. But he devotes to all this no more space than is absolutely necessary. He, too, like the Bishop of Natal, touches on the family of Judah; but he devotes one page to this topic, and the Bishop of Natal devotes thirteen. To the sums in Ezra—with which the Bishop of Natal, "should God, in His providence, call him to continue the work," will assuredly fill folios—Spinoza devotes barely a page. He is anxious to escape from the region of these verbal matters, which to the Bishop of Natal are a sort of intellectual land of Beulah, into a higher region; he apologises for lingering over them so long: *non est cur circa hæc diu detinear: nolo tædiosâ lectione lectorem detinere.* For him the interesting question is, not whether the fanatical devotee of the letter is to continue, for a longer or for a shorter time, to believe that Moses sate in the land of Moab writing the description of his own death, but what he is to believe when he does not believe this. Is he to take for the guidance of his life a great gloss put upon the Bible by theologians, who "not content with going mad themselves with Plato and Aristotle, want to make Christ and the Prophets go mad with them too,"—or the Bible itself? Is he to be presented by his National Church with metaphysical formularies for his creed, or with the real fundamentals of Christianity? If with the former, religion will never produce its due fruits. A few elect will still be saved; but the vast majority of mankind will remain without grace and without good works, hateful and hating one another. Therefore he calls urgently upon Governments to make the National Church what it should be. This is the conclusion of the whole matter for him; a fervent appeal to the State, to save us from the untoward generation of metaphysical Article-makers. And therefore, anticipating Mr. Gladstone, he called his book "The Church in its Relations with the State."

Thus Spinoza attempts to answer the crucial question, *"What then?"* and by the attempt, successful or unsuccessful, he interests the higher culture of Europe. The Bishop of Natal does not interest this, neither yet does he edify the unlearned. His book, therefore, satisfies neither of the two conditions, one of which literary criticism has a right to impose on all religious books: *Edify the uninstructed,* it has a right to say to them, *or inform the instructed.* Fulfilling neither of these conditions, the Bishop of Natal's book cannot justify itself for existing. When, in 1861, he heard for the first time that the old theory of the verbal inspiration of Scripture was untenable, he should, instead of proclaiming this news (if this was all he could proclaim) in an octavo volume, have remembered that excellent saying of the Wise Man: "If thou hast heard a word, let it die with thee; and behold, it will not burst thee."

These two conditions, which the Bishop of Natal's book entirely fails to fulfil, another well-known religious book also—that book which made so much noise two years ago, the volume of *Essays and Reviews*—fails, it seems to me, to fulfil satisfactorily. Treating religious subjects and written by clergymen, the compositions in that volume have in general, to the eye of literary criticism, this great fault—that they tend neither to edify the many, nor to inform the few. There is but one of them—that by Mr. Pattison on the *Tendencies of Religious Thought in England*—which offers to the higher culture of Europe matter new and instructive. There are some of them which make one, as one reads, instinctively recur to a saying which was a great favourite—so that Hebrew moralist whom I have already quoted tells us—with Judah Ben-Tamar: "The impudent are for Gehiman, and the modest for Paradise." But even Dr. Temple's Essay on the *Education of the World,* perfectly free from all faults of tone or taste, has this fault—that while it offers nothing edifying to the uninstructed, it offers to the instructed nothing which they could not have found in a far more perfect shape in the works of Lessing. Mr. Jowett's Essay, again, contains nothing which is not given, with greater convincingness of statement and far greater fulness of consequence in Spinoza's seventh chapter, which treats of the Interpretation of Scripture. The doctrines of his Essay, as mere doctrine, are neither milk for babes nor strong meat for men; the weak among his readers will be troubled by them; the strong would be more informed by seeing them handled as acquired elements for further speculation by freer exponents of the speculative thought of Europe, than by seeing them hesitatingly exhibited as novelties. In spite of this, however, Mr. Jowett's Essay has one quality which, at the tribunal of literary criticism, is sufficient to justify it—a quality which communicates to all works where it is present an indefinable charm, and which is always, for the higher sort of minds, edifying;—it has *unction*. From a clergyman's essay on a religious subject theological criticism may have a right to demand more than this; literary criticism has not. For a court of literature it is enough that the somewhat pale stream of Mr. Jowett's speculation is gilded by the heavenly alchemy of this glow.

Unction Spinoza's work has not; that name does not precisely fit any quality which it exhibits. But he is instructive and suggestive even to the most instructed thinker; and to give him full right of citizenship in the Republic of Letters this is enough. And yet, so all-important in the sphere of religious thought is the power of edification, that in this sphere a great fame like Spinoza's can never be founded without it. A court of literature can never be very severe to Voltaire: with that inimitable wit and clear sense of his, he can never write a page in which the fullest head may not find something suggestive: still because, with all his wit and clear sense, he handles religious ideas wholly without the power of edification, his fame as a great man is equivocal. Strauss treated the question of Scripture Miracles with an acuteness and fulness which even to the most informed minds is instructive; but because he treated it wholly without the power of edification, his fame as a serious thinker is equivocal. But in Spinoza there is not a trace either of Voltaire's passion for mere mockery or of Strauss's passion for mere demolition. His whole soul was filled with desire of the love and knowledge of God, and of that only. Philosophy always proclaims herself on the way to the *summum bonum;* but too often on the road she seems to forget her destination, and suffers her hearers to forget it also. Spinoza never forgets his destination: "The love of God is man's highest happiness and blessedness, and the final end and aim of all human actions;—The supreme reward for keeping God's Word is that Word itself—namely, to know Him and with free will and pure and constant heart love Him:" these sentences are the keynote to all he produced, and were the inspiration of all his labours. This is why he turns so sternly upon the worshippers of the letter,—the editors of the *Masora*, the editor of the *Record*—because their doctrine imperils our love and knowledge of God. "What!" he cries, "our knowledge of God to depend upon these perishable things, which Moses can dash to the ground and break to pieces like the first tables of stone, or of which the originals can be lost like the original book of the Covenant, like the original book of the Law of God, like the book of the Wars of God! . . . which can come to us confused, imperfect, miswritten by copyists, tampered with by doctors! And you accuse others of impiety! It is you who are impious, to believe that God would commit the treasure of the true record of Himself to any substance less enduring than the heart!" And his life was not unworthy of this elevated strain. A philosopher who professed that knowledge was its own reward—a devotee who professed that the love of God was its own reward, this philosopher and this devotee believed in what he said! Spinoza led a life the most spotless, perhaps, to be found among the lives of philosophers; he lived simple, studious, even-tempered, kind; declining honours, declining riches, declining notoriety. He was poor, and his admirer, Simon de Vries, sent him two thousand florins—he refused them: the same friend left him his fortune—he returned it to the heir. He was asked to dedicate one of his works to the magnificent patron of letters in his century, Louis the Fourteenth; he declined. His great work, his *Ethics,* published after his death, he gave injunctions to his friends to publish anonymously, for fear he should give his name to a school. Truth, he thought, should bear no man's name. And, finally,—"Unless," he said, "I had known that my writings would in the end advance the cause of true religion, I would have suppressed them—*taeuissem.*" It was in this spirit that he lived; and this spirit gives to all he writes not exactly unction—I have already said so,—but a kind of sacred solemnity. Not of the same order as the Saints, he yet follows the same service: *Doubtless Thou are our Father, though Abraham be ignorant of us, and Israel acknowledge us not.*

Therefore he has been, in a certain sphere, edifying, and has inspired in many powerful minds an interest and an admiration such as no other philosopher has inspired since Plato. The lonely precursor of German philosophy, he still shines when the light of his successors is fading away: they had celebrity, Spinoza has fame. Not because his peculiar system of philosophy has had more adherents than theirs; on the contrary, it has had fewer. But schools of philosophy arise and fall; their bands of adherents inevitably dwindle; no master can long persuade a large body of disciples that they give to themselves just the same account of the world as he does; it is only the very young and the very enthusiastic who can think themselves sure that they possess the whole mind of Plato, or Spinoza, or Hegel at all. The very mature and the very sober can even hardly believe that these philosophers possessed it themselves enough to put it all into their works, and to let us know entirely how the world seemed to them. What a remarkable philosopher really does for human thought, is to throw into circulation a certain number of new and striking ideas and expressions, and to stimulate with them the thought and imagination of his century or of after-times. So Spinoza has made his distinction between adequate and inadequate ideas a current notion for educated Europe. So Hegel seized a single pregnant sentence of Heracleitus, and cast it, with a thousand striking applications, into the world of modern thought. But to do this is only enough to make a philosopher noteworthy; it is not enough to make him great. To be great, he must have something in him which can influence character, which is edifying; he must, in short, have a noble and lofty character himself, a character—to recur to that much-criticised expression of mine—*in the grand style.* This is what Spinoza had; and because he had it, he stands out from the multitude of philosophers, and has been able to inspire in powerful minds a feeling which the most remarkable philosophers, without this grandiose character, could not inspire. "There is no possible view of life but Spinoza's" said Lessing. Goethe has told us how he was calmed and edified by him in his youth, and how he again went to him for support in his maturity. Heine, the man (in spite of his faults) of truest genius that Germany has produced since Goethe—a man with faults, as I have said, immense faults, the greatest of them being that he could reverence so little—reverenced Spinoza. Hegel's influence ran off him like water: "I have seen Hegel," he cries, "seated with his doleful air of a hatching hen upon his unhappy eggs, and I have heard his dismal clucking.—How easily one can cheat oneself into thinking that one understands everything, when one has learnt only how to construct dialectical formulas!" But of Spinoza, Heine said: "His life was a copy of the life of his Divine kinsman, Jesus Christ."

Still, the *Tractatus Theologico-Politicus* was deemed by Spinoza himself a work not suitable to the general public, and here is Mr. Trübner offering it to the general public in a translation! But a little reflection will show that Mr. Trübner is not therefore to be too hastily blamed. Times are changed since Spinoza wrote; the reserve which he recommended and practised is being repudiated by all the world. Speculation is to be made popular, all reticence is to be abandoned, every difficulty is to be canvassed publicly, every doubt is to be proclaimed; information which, to have any value at all, must have it as part of a series not yet complete, is to be flung broadcast, in the crudest shape, amidst the undisciplined, ignorant, passionate, captious multitude.

> "Andax omnia perpeti
> Gens humana ruit per vetitum nefas:"

and in that adventurous march the English branch of the race of Japhet is, it seems, to be headed by its clergy in full canonicals. If so it is to be, so be it. But, if this is to be so, the Editor of the *Record* himself, instead of deprecating the diffusion of Spinoza's writings, ought rather to welcome it. He would prefer, of course, that we should all be even as he himself is; that we should all think the same thing as that which he himself thinks. This desire, although all might not consent to join in it, is legitimate and natural. But its realisation is impossible; heresy is here, it is pouring in on all sides of him. If we must have heresy, he himself will admit that we may as well have the informing along with the barren. The author of the *Tractatus Theologico-Politicus* is not more unorthodox than the author of the *Pentateuch Critically Examined,* and he is far more edifying. If the English clergy must err, let them learn from this outcast of Israel to err nobly! Along with the weak trifling of the Bishop of Natal, let it be lawful to cast into the huge caldron, out of which the new world is to be born, the strong thought of Spinoza!

Matthew Arnold

SOURCE: In *Macmillans* 39, no. 7 (January 1863): 241–56.

Excerpts from *The Surplus*
INTRODUCTORY NOTE BY GENERAL BOOTH

[The long subtitle for the Emigration Office's pamphlet is "Being a Restatement of the Emigration Policy and Methods of the Salvation Army, Together with a Report upon Last Year's Work, an Introductory Note by General Booth, and Prefatory Remarks by Representative Men on the Subject of Emigration and Colonization." The "Representative Men" selected include literary figures, statesmen, politicians, eccentric women, and administrators of imperial institutes—all of whom were called on to assist with the "problem" of Great Britain's primarily working-class "surplus" population.]

The problem of insufficient employment in the British Isles and elsewhere is upon all our hearts, and no apology is needed in presenting a restatement of the principles of our Emigration operations and offering an account of work which has done at least something towards the relief of the congestion of the labour market.

Surely, there is no more pathetic sight than that of a crowd of honest, sober men, willing and able to work, but who cannot find it. Altered laws might ameliorate their condition, but in the immediate present, and as far as I can see for a long time to come, a system of organized emigration is calculated to most effectually meet the difficulty; for in addition to the large standing army of unemployed which already confronts us, the displacement of labour by machinery and inventions of various kinds goes on adding to the number.

I have long contended that a scheme of colonization, on a scale adapted to meet the need, under proper management and control, would be the best method for dealing with a large proportion of the overflowing populations of these Isles and the older countries of the world. But at present, as was the case when I first undertook emigration work, this road does not lie open.

It seemed to me then, that failing colonization on the lines I would lay down, organized emigration was the immediate remedy which offered to meet the evil of lack of employment, and after five years practical testing of the theory, I am, if possible, more firmly of this belief than ever.

Emigration as undertaken by The Salvation Army combines a system of careful selection and direction at the outset, with a system of sympathetic reception and oversight in the early days of settlement in the new circumstances in which the settler finds himself placed. The facilities of The Army for undertaking such a work are, by all who have any acquaintance with them, confessedly unique. Of the work that has already been accomplished I need say nothing here. The difficulties of the task have not consisted in the detail of organization and investigation. Nor has there been at any time a lack of suitable people ready to go to whatever part of the world it seemed to us best to direct them. Our drawbacks have chiefly arisen from professional and official jealousies, want of funds, and of an 'open door', into countries where the new arrivals would be assured of a warm welcome.

It is first and foremost in my mind that 'the British Empire for the British' should still be a foundation principle to any statesmanlike policy of emigration from this country. It seems natural and desirable that a Home Government, distracted by the burden of tens of thousands of honest and sober out-of-works, should sit in council with the Governments of her lands across the seas, whose millions of acres of virgin soil call for workers, as to the best and wisest method of transportation of 'the landless man to the manless land". That some whole-hearted scheme of mutual benefit would be the outcome seems a reasonable result to be expected, and the summoning of such a conference should not be long delayed.

The recent dispatch of parties of emigrants to lands outside the Empire was a development of this work to which I somewhat reluctantly consented. But there was no alternative, for the calls of humanity know no bounds of Empire.

Meanwhile this Department must go on with its beneficent work, and the £5,000 required to enable it to continue and extend its operations during the coming season should be, I think, quickly forthcoming. Of all the remedies propounded for the solution of the recurring problem of unemployment I am satisfied that for the immediate and permanent relief of thousands of the selected Surplus, *Emigration still holds the field.*

William Booth
International Headquarters,
London, E.C. Christmas, 1908.

LETTER FROM MR. RUDYARD KIPLING

Bateman's, Burwash, Sussex,
September 5, 1908.
Dear Colonel Lamb,

Many thanks to your letter about emigration matters. I have always taken an interest in that side of The Army's work since I met General Booth when he was beginning it.

It looks to me as though the average English emigrant is not used to raw land, and does not as a rule care to go far from his neighbours. He is more easily planted by the hundred than by the head, and that is where I think The Army's system is so sound, if, as is usually the case, there are good, understanding Officers to meet and explain things to the new arrivals.

The Army began in towns, and I believe can manage an urban or semi-urban community better than most other agencies. Perhaps the best play now might be to press forward settlement by townships or villages; sending out families to an already half-developed section, and if any of them chose to get away farther off on their own initiative, to let them go and not to worry them too much to pay their advances. You might lose a little money this way at first, but you would gain in other ways, as I understand most men who are helped by The Army pay up sooner or later, and can be depended upon to help others.

I am all for Army settlements and villages, which, in addition to keeping those who care to live in them, can be used as training dépôts and hostels for people passing through. Everything of course depends on the officer on the spot; but then you, of all people, know that everything in the world is a one man job.

I don't dispute your statement that an able-bodied emigrant even without capital is an asset for a new country. Canada, Australia, New Zealand, and in large part South Africa (read Pringle's account of the settlement of the

Eastern Provinces), were built up by that very class, but, human nature being what it is, you will not find that fact admitted in present-day labour legislation. There is a material Calvinism which would limit worldly prosperity to a few of the electors—just as there is a spiritual Calvinism which confines Salvation to a few elect. That, I imagine, you have discovered in more than one quarter of the Empire, and I should very much like to know how you get round it.

The trouble is that when the able-bodied man has been planted in a new country, the very strangeness of it—climatic differences, variations in tools, equipment and methods—often throws him into a sort of bewildered daze which lasts a long time—an additional reason why he ought to be handled at some Army settlement or settlement under Army influences before going up country. It is not much more trouble after all, than one would take for an imported horse or dog, which one wished to see do well.

I think too it often happens that families imported *en bloc*, will by their clinging together in their loneliness, confirm each other in their unwillingness to accept new conditions, and the lonelier they are, the more will they face inwards—just like a mob of strange horses on a run. They also need to be worked over in an Army settlement by people who will not laugh at them, or tell tales of their pride (which is only their shyness), behind their backs.

So for single men and families The Army settlement on its own lands, seems to me most useful at present. There is a type of man, as there is of family, which only needs to be taken out of England to adapt itself to a new land as trout take to a new brook; but there are not very many of them, and in England they sometimes live on the outskirts of good reputation—a quick, acquisitive, not too truthful breed, enormously satisfied with themselves. But they are a splendid cross on slower blood in the second generation, and it has struck me that they are the people you could reach by means of travelling vans and lectures with limelight views, in the village halls. Of course the cry would go up at once: 'You are draining England of its best blood'; but isn't there something to be said for the idea of drafting out the First Eleven and so giving the Second Eleven a chance.

There never was an Empire that offered such opportunities to all men as ours, and I sometimes think that there never was an Empire whose people took less advantage of those opportunities.

But I have already inflicted much too long a letter upon you, so I will content myself by wishing you all success in your work.

Yours very sincerely,

Rudyard Kipling

THE PROSPECT FOR THE SELECTED SURPLUS

Concerning the British Empire

The British Empire, as is well known, is represented by about one-fourth of the people of the world, and comprises about one-fifth of the world's land, 11,000,000 square miles of territory being under British rule. Many of its possessions are not adapted to the permanent settlement of a white population, but serve as an outlet for the exploitation of British capital and as a field for the exercise of Christianizing and civilizing influences: the greater part of these have tropical climatic conditions and dense native populations. In this category may be placed parts of British East Africa, British possessions in West Africa, India, Ceylon; many islands in the Indian Ocean, British Guiana, British Honduras, Jamaica, and many West Indian islands. On the other hand, there are vast territories in the British Empire which have become hers because they are eminently suited to the permanent settlement of a white population, and so have offered an outlet for that legitimate spirit of enterprise which has helped to build up the Empire; and which, in the result of no other output of energy, finds such complete satisfaction as it finds in the harvest which accrues from the conquering and subduing of the land. The territories referred to may be found in Canada, New Zealand, Australia, and Africa south of the Zambezi, all of which have been through, or are going through, a struggle to find their feet and walk alone subsequent upon the grant of self-government. These younger territories are larger, certainly, but on the whole they often remember that the Old Country has her size in another way. And yet do they sometimes chafe at the bond which binds them to her across the seas? Theoretically they are proud of it, but will they help her practically by letting her use it, when advisable, as a channel through which some of her surplus population may pass to relieve her internal strain? Or is there any truth in the idea, gaining prevalence now, that such of the Great Dominions as could come to her aid are closing their doors against her need? If so, it may be truly said that there has been 'a screw loose' in the Imperial idea. With some justice the Mother Country, straining beneath the burden of her over-population, might take herself to task on the score of foolishness for having severed her connexion for all practical purposes with her hands across the seas. In this she might well ask herself what she gained when, in giving self-government to her Dominions, she parted with their mineral, timber, and fishing rights, not even reserving to herself in return a claim with regard to the peopling of their surplus lands.

The Alternatives

There is no doubt that, at least for some time to come, emigration on a scale somewhat adequate to the need, will be one practical method of meeting the heart-rending problem of unemployment in this country. Then, in dealing with our would-be emigrant to the Colonies, will the time come when we shall be obliged to point to the doors of the various Dominions in the Empire, explaining that through some which are open it would not be desirable to enter, and that another, to which common sense would otherwise direct him, is closed? In reply to his question as to whether there would be a chance for him in the Colonies, we should then be bound, in his interest, to give a negative reply. His attention, doubtless, would turn next in the direction of the United States of America, with their immense resources and wide possibilities. Here he knows he would find a people speaking his own language. Here also political institutions would not be widely different from those at home. It would be for us, however, to explain to him that, though doubtless there will be a vast field here at some future time, immigration prospects in the United States are poor just now. Then to guide him wisely would be to point out to him the 'open door' of South America. To do so would be to direct him to the country, of all others, to which the emigrant from a colony-less land would do best to turn his face. It would be to direct him to a land, the policy of whose thoughtful statesmen would assure him of a welcome—a land capable of absorbing thousands, and of offering, in return, the inducement of good material prospects. Here the English mechanic could secure work and good wages without any difficulty, because of his superior skill and industry. There would be a demand for him in the arsenals, and he would be assured of work, while he was acquiring a knowledge of the language and of the country. An artisan, plumber, shoemaker, or tradesman might make his way up country, and settle in one of the smaller towns where, perhaps, he would be the only Englishman. If he merited success he would be assured of it, perhaps of prosperity. But what price would he be paying in return? He would no longer be beneath the protection of a country flying the British flag. He would be giving up more than the German Jew gives up when he settles in England, for, as far as nationality is concerned, he would inevitably be absorbed. The process of his adoption into this country would be very different from that of his settlement in one of the Colonies. He would lose his language and his sense of sonship to the Empire, whilst any children born to him after his immigration would probably be subject to conscription. Then, to secure for himself the right to live, will he be forced to such a step as this by the closed colonial door? There would still be the alternative of remaining at home. Few, however, will deny that the prospect in the British Isles for the surplus portion of the population is blacker than ever it was. Given a little less than an average chance, a persevering and intelligent man will succeed; but, given no chance at all, this man must sink beneath the wave of overwhelming circumstance.

NOTABLE UTTERANCES

There need be no hesitation in affirming that Colonization in the present state of the world, is the very best affair of business in which the capital of an old and wealthy country can possibly engage.—John Stuart Mill

It is necessary and very interesting to observe that Colonization has a tendency to increase employment for capital and labour at home. When a Hampshire peasant emigrates to Australia, he very likely enables an operative to live in Lancashire and Yorkshire. Besides making food in the Colony for himself, he makes some more to send home for the manufacturer, who, in his turn, makes clothes or implements for the Colonist.—Edward Gibbon Wakefield (*The Founder of the Colonies of South Australia and New Zealand.*)

It is the strange and unaccountable neglect of our opportunities for Colonizing which I firmly believe is one of the most pregnant sources of the various social evils by which at home we are surrounded.—Sir Frederick Young, K.C.M.G. (*Vice-President of the Royal Colonial Institute, etc.*)

No man in England has done more than I have to try and impress upon the nation the absolute necessity of trying to populate their own land. But there has been no result; now I say if you won't populate your own country, rather than let the people rot in the towns like herrings in a barrel, it is better to send them to the Colonies where, at any rate, they will help to build up the Empire.—H. Rider Haggard. (*Author of 'Rural England', etc.*)

The cities have their own problems, as we have, and they do not welcome nor offer any encouragement, even to skilled tradesmen. This must be borne in mind by the intending Emigrant—that it is to the land he must go, that only upon the land there is room. . . . And further, I saw and talked with many who had striven long and encountered only bitter failure in the Old Country, who here have established homesteads and made a position for themselves, such as they could never have achieved in the British Islands. Innumerable cases came under my own immediate and personal observation of men who had no

knowledge of agriculture until they went out, who had to buy their experience day by day. There was no pretension that it had been or was an easy life. Pioneering needs strength and courage and almost unremitting toil. But it has its compensations; for the family man, such compensations as can never be told.—Annie S. Swan in 'The Outsiders'.

His Excellency (Earl Grey) Governor-General of Canada, cabled from Ottawa to our first party last year—Bon Voyage to the first of this year's shipment of Canadian settlers you are sending off to-morrow in SS. *Southwark*. If they are as good as the 20,000 you sent out in 1905 and 1906 they will be a blessing to Canada. They will find here kindly welcome—new opportunities—new hopes.

Sir Wilfrid Laurier, the Premier of the Dominion of Canada, says—We are well-pleased with the settlers you have sent out. Send us more, and send some English and Scotch lasses for the North-West.

The Hon. J. P. Whitney, the Premier of Ontario, speaking at a public meeting in the City of Bath, said—The Salvation Army Officers who had previously found for the Immigrants places saw them straight into their situations, and I am here to say that The Army has had a smaller percentage of failures than any other organization engaged in this work. This being the truth, it is right that the truth should be told. The methods of The Army have been criticized. I have nothing to do with them. It was the results that commended themselves to me, and by the results I am satisfied.

SOURCE: International Emigration Office, *The Surplus* (London: International Emigration Office, 1909), 3–9, 72–75, 90–91.

Excerpts from *The Salvation Army British Empire Exhibition Handbook*

[At the time during which the 1924 Exhibition Book was published, Bramwell Booth (1856–1929), the eldest son of General William Booth, was leading the missionary organization. During Bramwell Booth's tenure as general of the Salvation Army, the colonial missionary project was coupled with the nation's domestic missionary and uplift campaigns. Bramwell Booth's significant works include *Work in Darkest England in 1894* (1894), *Servants of All: A*

Brief Review of the Call, Character, and Labours of Officers of the Salvation Army (1900?), and *Echoes and Memories* (1926).]

THE SALVATION ARMY:
ITS MESSAGE AND WHAT IT IS

The Salvation Army has a message of hope, of forgiveness, of Salvation for the whole human race resting on the Crucifixion of Jesus Christ, His resurrection, and the coming of the Holy Spirit.

It calls men to repentance and the service of their fellows.

It believes that God, the Father, speaks direct to the hearts of men everywhere.

The Salvation Army emerged from the void through the travailing of one man's spirit over the sufferings and wretchedness and hopelessness of great masses of the people who had not the wherewithal sufficiently to clothe and feed themselves or religion to sustain or console them.

General William Booth, the Founder of The Salvation Army, did not start a new sect, but he was the pioneer of new methods of bringing religion to the lives of the people. He gave a wider and broader interpretation of the duties and responsibilities of those who professed the Christian religion than had hitherto been accepted under the ordinary conventions.

He lit his spiritual torch in the fires of what many termed 'fanaticism,' but as its beam enlarged to become a world inspiration the light it shed grew more mellow and humanizing.

To him were attracted men and women of a militant religious fervour, all rugged revivalists, who were never happier than when attacking the cohorts of sin in whatever form they presented themselves in the world around them. Vice was a hydra-headed monster. It was their business to give the Devil no quarter.

These stout-hearted warriors of a bygone day gave momentum to a movement which, as the years roll on, is gaining more and more power in the execution of its mission. The Army seeks to remove some of the evils that darken the lives of men and women, to direct them to the fountain of all light, and free them from the burdens that oppress them.

The Army was not designed. It grew. In his early days William Booth was a Methodist minister. But, finding his sphere of labour too narrow and circumscribed for one fired with his zeal, he, with his wife, Catherine Booth, decided to come out and stand alone to be free to proclaim the message of Salvation to the churchless crowds who moved in the streets of East London.

It was in 1865 that these two courageous souls started the Christian Mission, which in 1878 took the name of 'The Salvation Army.' Since then The Army has gone on from strength to strength. It is now established in seventy-nine countries and colonies and its message is published in fifty-three languages.

Within the British Empire it exercises a most potent influence. It is a powerful spiritual force in Australia, New Zealand, Canada, Newfoundland, India, Ceylon, South Africa, and the West Indies.

But The Army Flag is unfurled in almost every habitable part of the globe. In the United States of America it is a mighty instrument for good. On the Continent of Europe it operates in almost every country, and in South America, China, Japan, Korea, and the Dutch East Indies its activities are steadily extending.

All over the world the Organization has come to be known, as some one aptly termed it, 'The Army of the Helping Hand.' In the eyes of The Army the supreme title of a person's claim to help is his necessity.

It is not a charitable Organization merely—a giver of alms and a sermon. It has large ideals, but its ideals are intensely practical, and it is the impetus of this practical idealism that carries it on its helpful progress.

An erring woman is not merely rescued from the streets, an opportunity is afforded her of living a clean life. The Army sets the broken man who is down and out on his feet and inspires him with new heart of grace and a desire to make a fresh start.

The Army is the stay of the widow and the fatherless.

Its motto is 'Service,' and that, it can be claimed, is well expressed in the comprehensiveness of its social work in most countries of the world, and its great missionary enterprises in India, China, Japan, and in other lands where the light of Christianity is but dimly burning.

Almost wherever there is a hopeless man or woman, wherever there is an outrageous open offender, a persistent drunkard or drug fiend, a harlot, a poor girl in trouble, an unwanted babe doomed to neglect, misery, or death, a starving stomach, a thief, a planner of iniquities, a would-be suicide, an ignorant untaught or tortured child, a victim of superstition or mental terrors, a reviler of all that is holy, doer of all that is ill, a wanderer in the darkness, a dweller in the pit of despair there, in peace or war, almost from pole to pole, is The Salvation Army to comfort, to uplift, to feed the body and the spirit; to prove that until everything is lost everything can be regained, and to declare by countless examples the truth of the old saying that out of the foulest sinners may still be fashioned the most perfect saints.

It carries out its purposes irrespective of creed or nationality. It is not a rich society. While its ramifications and interests are vast and widespread yet for its maintenance it is wholly dependent upon the voluntary contributions of its friends and supporters. Its local branches publish balance sheets every year, and the accounts of its Central Funds in each country are audited by well-known firms of Chartered Accountants.

THE CHRISTENING OF THE SALVATION ARMY

General Bramwell Booth recalls the incident which definitely gave The Salvation Army its name. He and the late Commissioner Railton, one of the pioneers of the Organization, and one who by his ability as a writer and the influence of his life did much to advance its progress, were summoned early one morning to his father's bedroom to compare notes and to receive instructions for the day's work of the Christian Mission, as The Army was then known. Commissioner Railton sat at a table writing; Mr. Bramwell Booth occupied a chair at his side; William Booth, the Founder, in a long yellow dressing gown and felt slippers, was walking up and down, dictating his instructions. At that time the Volunteer movement was established, and was receiving derisive treatment at the hands of the public. The phrase occurred in the article which Commissioner Railton was writing, 'We are a volunteer Army'; and when he came to read this out, young Bramwell Booth leaned back in his chair, glanced over his shoulder at the perambulating General Superintendent, and exclaimed: 'Volunteer! Here, I'm not a volunteer. I'm a regular or nothing!' William Booth, who had stopped walking at this interruption, studied his son for a moment, and then coming to the table, leaned over Commissioner Railton's shoulder, took the pen from his hand, scratched out the word 'Volunteer' and wrote in its place the word 'Salvation.'

'The effect,' says General Bramwell Booth, 'of that one word upon Railton and me was really quite extraordinary. We both sprang from our chairs. I remember that I exclaimed, "Thank God for that!" And Railton was equally enthusiastic.'

WITH THE LEGION OF THE LOST
BY SIR RIDER HAGGARD

'No Man Need Beg, Steal, or Commit Suicide'[1]

The following extracts are from an article by the well-known novelist, Sir Rider Haggard, a great friend of The Salvation Army, describing a scene at a Salvation Army Free Breakfast to the broken men of the streets of London

I entered the great hall, in which were gathered this Sunday morning nearly 600 men seated upon benches, every one of which was filled. The faces and general aspect of these men were eloquent of want and sorrow. Some of them appeared to be intent upon the religious service that was going on, attendance at this service being the condition on which the free breakfast is given to all who need food and have passed the previous night in the street. Others were gazing about them vacantly, and others, sufferers from the effects of drink, debauchery, or fatigue, seemed to be half comatose or asleep.

This congregation, the strangest that I have ever seen, comprised men of all classes. Some might once have belonged to the learned professions, while others had fallen so low that they looked scarcely human. Every grade of rag-clad misery was represented here, and every stage of life from the lad of sixteen up to the aged man whose allotted span was almost at an end. Rank upon rank of them, there they sat in their infinite variety, linked only by the common bond of utter wretchedness, the most melancholy sight that ever my eyes beheld.

It was a wonderful thing to see the spiritually faced man on the platform pleading with his sordid audience, and to watch them stirring beneath his words. To see, also, a uniformed woman flitting to and fro among that audience, whispering, exhorting, invoking—a temptress to Salvation; then to note the response and its manner that were stranger still. Some poor wretch would seem to awaken, only to relapse into a state of sullen, almost defiant, torpor. A little while and the leaven begins to work in him. He flushes, mutters something, half rises from his seat, sits down again, rises once more, and with a peculiar, unwilling gait staggers to the penitent-form, in an abandonment of grief and repentance.

---

1. Such was the notice published by Commissioner Elijah Cadman in the Army's Shelters 30 years ago. It is true to-day. The Army offers food and shelter, and work to the destitute and despairing, and also operates an Anti-Suicide Bureau.

The Army's Official Organs—Published in Twenty-Five Languages

Now the ice is broken. Another comes, and another, and another, till there is no room at the penitent-form. They swarm on to the platform which is cleared for them, and there kneel down, and I observed the naked feet of some of them showing through the worn-out boots.

It is done, and the watcher feels that he has witnessed the very uttermost of tragedies, human and spiritual.

The age of miracles has passed, we are told; but I confess that while watching this strange sight I wondered more than once that if this were so, what that age of miracles had been like. Of one thing I am sure, that it must have been to such as these that He who is acknowledged even by sceptics to have been the very Master of mankind would have chosen to preach, had this been the age of His appearance, He who came to call sinners to repentance.

SOURCE: *The Salvation Army British Empire Exhibition Handbook* (London: Salvation Army, 1924), 3–4, 19.

THE ADMINISTRATION:
LUGARD AND THE
ROYAL NIGER COMPANY

It may be said that as Faith, Hope, and Charity are the Christian creed, so are Decentralisation, Co-operation, and Continuity to African Administration—and the greatest of these is Continuity.—Lord Frederick Lugard, *The Dual Mandate in British Tropical Africa*, 1922

The Commissioner went away, taking three or four of the soldiers with him. In the many years in which he had toiled to bring civilisation to different parts of Africa he had learnt a number of things. One of them was that a District Commissioner must never attend to such undignified details as cutting down a hanged man from the tree. Such attention would give the natives a poor opinion of him. In the book which he planned to write he would stress that point. As he walked back to the court he thought about that book. Every day brought him some new material. The story of this man who had killed a messenger and hanged himself would make interesting reading. One could almost write a whole chapter on him. Perhaps not a whole chapter but a reasonable paragraph at any rate. There was so much else to include, and one must be firm in cutting out the details. He had already chosen the title of the book, after much thought: *The Pacification of the Primitive Tribes of the Lower Niger.*—Chinua Achebe, *Things Fall Apart*, 1958

INTRODUCTION
Inheritors of Empire, Agents of Change:
Lord Lugard and Mary Kingsley
MIA CARTER AND BARBARA HARLOW

ALMOST . . . A WHOLE CHAPTER . . . a reasonable paragraph at any rate"—howsoever, it was necessary to "be firm," whether in "cutting out details" from the narration, or in the imposition of "indirect rule." Lord Frederick Lugard's philosophy and practice of managing "British tropical Africa," as elaborately presented in his various writings as it was implemented in his governance, might well have been a source for the Nigerian novelist's recall of pre-independence history. Chinua Achebe's first novel describes the difficult transition—and its coming pitfalls—from British imperial rule in West Africa to Nigerian independence. The district commissioner was a linchpin in that process—and Frederick Lugard was key to the story. Mary Kingsley provided an important and telling counterpoint in its eventual reconstructions.

Both Frederick Lugard and Mary Kingsley were born into families whose forebears had illustrious military careers. Lugard's father and grandfather, Frederick Junior and Senior, were famous soldiers and national heroes, and Kingsley's paternal side of the family had been distinguished military men for more than six hundred years. The children of these families were beneficiaries of imperial power, of its moral and political lessons and legacies; and Lugard and Kingsley were also beneficiaries of modern scientific theories and philosophies. Both were unabashed and enthusiastic supporters of empire; however, each was what one might call an "enlightened imperialist." Lugard and Kingsley believed in the scientific administration of empire rather than in the preceding era's aggressive militarism, violent policies of seizure, and oppressive control.

Kingsley believed that "true knowledge" of Africa could be obtained with the assistance of cultural anthropology and the biological study of tropical diseases. In her terms, the modern science of anthropology and its careful

habits of observation—as opposed to ethnology's racial myths and stereo-
types—would be central in providing colonial administrators useful and accurate information. Sympathy for African cultures and acknowledgment of
Africans' cultural, moral, philosophical, and religious differences would enable the British to rule Africa efficiently, economically, benignly, and hu-
manely. The study of tropical diseases would additionally enable British administrators and colonial servants to maintain their physical health and the
economic health of the empire. Kingsley understood that colonization of a
culture involved the disruption and destruction of indigenous values and
traditions. For example, she recognized the Hut Tax, which the British administration had imposed on Africans to raise funds for policing and expanding inland territories, as being "fundamentally abhorrent to the principles of
African law" because taxation violated Africans' rights of property and destroyed feelings of African national pride and autonomy. She likened the Hut
Tax War in Sierra Leone to a "little Indian Mutiny." Kingsley recognized the
integrity of African cultures and appreciated their uniqueness; these feelings
caused her to disparage missionary conversion and domineering administrative practices. She made it her mission to represent Africans to the British
public as she knew and understood them and encouraged British statesmen
and citizens to think of the tropical possessions as small towns that were as
distinctive and valuable as English towns like Sheffield, Birmingham, Manchester, or Leeds. Kingsley hoped the British public could feel as connected
to and concerned about the African territories as they did to those local
industrial centers.

Kingsley's familiarity with Africans was extremely atypical. After her parents' deaths, she used her inheritance to travel to the African continent. She
traveled to the Canary Islands where her contacts with the "Coasters"—the
European agents of West African trading firms—gave her the information
and inspiration to plan her own exploration of the African interior. Kingsley
visited West Africa in 1893 and collected fish specimens along the way; her
biological specimens were donated to the British Museum, which presented
her with a collector's outfit for future African expeditions. When Kingsley's
finances dwindled, she raised funds by adopting the lessons that she learned
from the traders and merchants, lived on local foods, resided in native villages, and traded rubber, ivory, and other local goods with the villagers in
order to continue her travels. The success and ease of her own trade led Mary
Kingsley to place her political and administrative faith in policies of free
trade; for Kingsley, the alleged mutual benefits of capitalism and commerce
were the ideal deterrents to violent conquest and native unrest.

Kingsley looked like the typical Victorian spinster, traveling in bonnet, crisp, white blouse, and full, woolen skirts; however, she was mobile and politically influential as only a few Victorian women had managed to be. But she shared both the onus and the privilege of precedent-setting. She unofficially served as adviser to Colonial Secretary Joseph Chamberlain and customarily argued on behalf of African traders and against the Colonial Office's direct rule of Africa. Kingsley believed that traders like George Goldie, the creator of the Royal Niger Company, whom she greatly admired, would more effectively implement the innovative, cooperative, and indirect systems of rule that she championed. Goldie became Frederick Lugard's administrative superior in 1894. Kingsley's books, *Travels in West Africa* and *West African Studies*, were both best-sellers; her lively wit, expertise, and unusual opinions on Africa made her a popular speaker and, for some, a highly entertaining one. Mary Kingsley died in South Africa at the age of thirty-four; the crusader for the study of tropical diseases succumbed to typhoid fever, which she contracted while nursing South African prisoners of war.

Frederick Lugard was another colonial administrator who frequently consulted Mary Kingsley. Like the lady traveler, Lugard was a visionary student of empire and colonial administration. Cecil Rhodes had considered Lugard for an administrative appointment but decided he was an uncontrollable maverick and a too-independent firebrand. Lugard, who was born at Fort Saint George in Madras, India, in January 1858, the year of the Sepoy Mutiny, considered himself a gentlemanly imperialist and modern pioneer. He knew well what he described as the terror and thrill of warfare, having served during the Afghan Wars (1879), the Suakin (Sudan) Campaign (1885), the Burma Wars (1886), and the Nyasa Campaign against Arab slave-traders (1888–1889); however, Lugard claimed to be uncomfortable with the hypermasculine imperial ideal. In his diary confessions Lugard attributed his self-defensive soldierly beliefs to his womanly character.

After his active military service, Lugard accepted a series of jobs for African charter companies, including the Imperial British East Africa Company (1889), the Royal Niger Company (1894–1895), and the diamond-prospecting British West Charterland Company (1896–1897). He distinguished himself by successfully negotiating treaties that would rout the French and German competitors and expand Britain's African territories. Lugard described the plot of the "Old African Life" as "battle, murder, sudden death." He was a reluctant but efficient warrior who believed in "civilization by applied science," which for him involved the development and efficient management of human and material resources, the eradication of disease, the implementation of fair trade, and annexation by legitimate treaty. The fairness of the treaties negotiated by Lugard was certainly questionable, and the gentleness of his administration can also be challenged; however, Lugard did implement many of the more efficient and economical theories of indirect rule that Mary Kingsley advocated. He developed administrative policies that would rely on cooperation with native rulers and recognition of African traditions and cultural and political hierarchies. Lugard also maintained a lifelong interest in African languages.

In 1902 Lugard's administrative career was substantially bolstered by his marriage to another famous lady traveler, the *London Times'* African correspondent Flora Shaw (Lady Lugard). Shaw was a lionhearted ultra-imperialist who traveled in highly influential political circles; she was a suspected go-between for Cecil Rhodes and Joseph Chamberlain during the Jameson Raid scandal, and was a friend and admirer of George Goldie. Flora Shaw reportedly coined the name Nigeria for the expanded territories gained by her husband. She also relentlessly campaigned on Lugard's behalf and on behalf of expansionist policies. Imperial expansion was increasingly under attack by the "Little Englanders" at home, some of whom were opposed to expansionism for moral and ideological reasons; others were fiscal conservatives who were concerned about the increasing expenditures involved with the maintenance and protection of colonial territories. Lugard's and Kingsley's writings contain stereotypical and traditional racial and imperialist attitudes; their writings also reflect the reformist energies and experimental philosophies of the modern agents of empire.

BIBLIOGRAPHY

Asiegbu, Johnson U. J. *Nigeria and Its British Invaders, 1851–1920: A Thematic Documentary History.* New York: NOK Publishers International, 1984.

Birkett, Dea. *Spinsters Abroad: Victorian Lady Explorers.* Oxford: Blackwell, 1989.

Blunt, Alison. *Travel, Gender, and Imperialism: Mary Kingsley and West Africa.* New York: Guilford Press, 1994.

Callaway, Helen. *Gender, Culture, and Empire: European Women in Colonial Nigeria.* Basingstroke, England: Macmillan, 1987.

Chaudhuri, Napur, and Margaret Strobel, eds. *Western Women and Imperialism: Complicity and Resistance.* Bloomington, IN: Indiana University Press, 1992.

Dusgate, Richard H. *The Conquest of Northern Nigeria.* London: Frank Cass, 1985.

Falola, Toyin. *Nationalism and African Intellectuals.* Rochester, N.Y.: University of Rochester Press, 2001.

Hertslet, Edward. *The Map of Africa by Treaty.* 3 vols. London: Harrison and Sons, 1909.

Lugard, Frederick. *The Rise of Our East African Empire: Early Efforts in Nyasaland and Uganda.* London: W. Blackwood and Sons, 1893.

—. *Memorandum on the Taxation of Natives in Northern Nigeria.* London: Darling and Son, 1907.

Manson, Janet. "Margery Perham, the Fabians, and Colonial Policy." In *Women in the Milieu of Leonard and Virginia Woolf: Peace, Politics and Education,* edited by Wayne Chapman and Janet M. Manson, 170–90. New York: Pace University Press, 1998.

Perham, Margery. *Africans and British Rule.* London: Oxford University Press, 1941.

—. *African Discovery: An Anthology of Exploration.* London: Faber and Faber, 1942.

Woolf, Leonard. *Empire and Commerce in Africa: A Study in Economic Imperialism.* Westminster: Labour Research Department; London: Allen and Unwin, 1919.

Royal Charter Granted to the National African Company, Later Called the Royal Niger Company

[Colonial administrator Sir George Taubman Goldie (1846–1925) was educated at the Royal Military Academy; he briefly served as a Royal Engineer in 1856–1857. Goldie formed a series of African charter companies, including the Central African Trading Company (1876) and the Royal Niger Company (1886). In 1879 Goldie attempted to gain control of the Niger region by uniting several private British trading companies; the charter for this organization, the amalgamated United African Company, however, was denied due to French and German competition in the region and due to Great Britain's lack of influence in the area. After the European nations defined their respective areas of conquest at the Berlin Conference (1884–1885), the charter for the Royal Niger Company was granted, and Goldie became governor of the company in 1895. Increasing difficulties dealing with international politics caused the company to be transferred to the imperial British government (31 December 1899). Goldie eventually lost interest in the company and the African territories; he later destroyed all of his African papers and memoranda. For another book-length study of George Goldie's life and colonial career, see Dorothy Wellesley's *Sir George Goldie, Founder of Nigeria* (1934; New York: Arno Press, 1977).]

Victoria, by the Grace of God, of the United Kingdom of Great Britain and Ireland, Queen, Defender of the Faith. To all to whom these Presents shall come Greeting:

Whereas an humble Petition has been presented to Us, in Our Council, by the National African Company, Limited, of 34 to 40, Ludgate Hill, in the City of London (hereinafter referred to as 'the Company').

And whereas the said Petition states (among other things) that the Petitioner Company was incorporated in the year 1882, under the Companies Acts, 1862 to 1880, as a Company limited by Shares. And that the Capital of the Company is 1,000,000*l.*, divided into 100,000 Shares of 10*l.* each, with power to increase. And 91,675 of such Shares have been subscribed for and issued; and a further 6,000 of such Shares have been subscribed for and are about to be issued, making in all, 97,675 of such Shares. And that the objects of the Company as declared by the Memorandum of Association of the Company, are (amongst others) the following, that is to say:

> To carry on business and to act as merchants, bankers, traders, commission agents, shipowners, carriers, or in any other capacity, in the United Kingdom, Africa, or elsewhere, and to import, export, buy, sell, barter, exchange, pledge, make advances upon, or otherwise deal in goods, produce, articles, and merchandise according to the custom of merchants, or otherwise.
>
> To form or acquire and carry on trading stations, factories, stores and depôts in Africa or elsewhere, and to purchase, lease, or otherwise acquire, carry on, develop, or improve any business or any real or personal property in the United Kingdom, Africa, or elsewhere, or any undivided or other interest whatsoever therein respectively.
>
> To apply for, acquire, and hold any Charters, Acts of Parliament, privileges, monopolies, licenses, concessions, patents, or other rights or powers from the British Government, or any other Government or State, or any potentate or local or other authority in Africa or elsewhere; to exercise, carry on, and work any powers, rights, or privileges, so obtained; and to constitute or incorporate the Company as an anonymous or other Society in any foreign Country or State.
>
> To purchase, or otherwise acquire, open and work mines, forests, quarries, fisheries, and manufactories; and to stock, cultivate and improve any of the lands of the Company, erect buildings thereon, and sell the produce thereof.
>
> To do all other things whatsoever, whether of the like or other nature, which the Company may consider in any way incidental or conducive to the foregoing objects or any of them.

And whereas the Petition further states that the Kings, Chiefs, and peoples of various territories in the basin of the River Niger, in Africa, fully recognising after many years' experience, the benefits accorded to their countries by their intercourse with the Company and their predecessors, have ceded the whole of their respective territories to the Company by various Acts of Cession specified in the Schedule hereto.

And whereas, in consideration of such Cessions, the Company agreed, amongst other things, not to interfere in any of the native laws and not to encroach on or to interfere with any private property unless the value should be agreed upon by the Owner and the said Company, and payment made to such value.

And whereas the Petitioners further state that the Company, since their incorporation, have been actively engaged in carrying into effect the objects stated in the aforesaid Memorandum of Association, and have purchased the business of all European traders in the regions aforesaid, and are now the sole European traders there, and are now engaged in developing the resources of such regions and in extending trade further into the interior.

And whereas the Petition further states that the Company and their predecessors, whose businesses they purchased, have, during many years past, expended large sums of money and made great exertions in and about acquiring the confidence of the said native Kings, Chiefs, and peoples, which have resulted in the said Cessions of territory, and large expenditure will be incurred in carrying the same into effect and discharging the obligations arising thereunder.

And whereas the Petition further states that the condition of the natives inhabiting the aforesaid territories would be materially improved, and the development of such territories and those contiguous thereto, and the civilization of their peoples would be greatly advanced if We should think fit to confer on the Company, and the Petitioner Company therefore most humbly pray that We will be graciously pleased to grant by Our Royal Charter authority to accept the full benefit of the several Cessions aforesaid, and all such other powers and authorities in relation to the premises as to Us may seem meet, subject nevertheless to such conditions as We may think fit to impose.

And whereas the Petitioner further states that if such authority were conferred on the Petitioner Company they would thereby be enabled to render to Our Dominions services of much value, and to promote the commercial prosperity of many of Our Subjects.

Now, therefore, We, having taken the said Petition into Our Royal consideration, in Our Council, and being satisfied that the intentions of the Petitioner Company are praiseworthy and deserve encouragement, do hereby will, ordain, grant, and declare as follows, that is to say:

AUTHORISATION TO COMPANY

1. The said National African Company, Limited (in this Our Charter referred to as 'the Company'), is hereby authorised and empowered to hold and retain the full benefit of the several Cessions aforesaid, or any of them, and all rights, interests, authorities, and powers for the purposes of government, preservation of public order, protection of the said territories, or otherwise, of what nature or kind soever, under or by virtue thereof, or resulting therefrom, and ceded to or vested in the Company, in, over, or affecting the territories, lands, and property, in the neighbourhood of the same, and to hold, use, enjoy, and exercise the same territories, lands, property, rights, interests, authorities, and powers respectively for the purposes of the Company and on the terms of this Our Charter.

FULFILMENT BY THE COMPANY OF PROMISES GIVEN

2. The Company shall be bound by and shall fulfil all and singular the stipulations on their part contained in the Acts of Cession aforesaid, subject to any subsequent agreement affecting those stipulations approved by one of Our Principal Secretaries of State (in this Our Charter referred to as 'Our Secretary of State').

BRITISH CHARACTER OF THE COMPANY

3. The Company shall always be and remain British in character and domicile, and shall have its principal Office in England; and its principal representative in the Territories aforesaid, and all the Directors shall always be natural born British subjects, or persons who have been naturalised as British subjects, by or under an Act of Parliament of Our United Kingdom.

RESTRICTION OF TRANSFER BY COMPANY

4. The Company shall not have power to transfer, wholly or in part, the benefit of the Cession aforesaid, or any of them, except with the consent of Our Secretary of State.

FOREIGN POWERS

5. If at any time Our Secretary of State thinks fit to dissent from or object to any of the dealings of the Company with any foreign Power, and to make the Company any suggestion founded on that dissent or objection, the Company shall act in accordance therewith.

SLAVERY

6. The Company shall, to the best use of its power, discourage and, as far as may be practicable, abolish by degrees any system of domestic servitude existing among the native inhabitants; and no foreigner, whether European or not, shall be allowed to own Slaves of any kind in the Company's territories.

RELIGIONS OF INHABITANTS

7. The Company as such, or its Officers as such, shall not in any way interfere with the religion of any class or tribe of the people of its territories, or of any of the inhabitants thereof, except so far as may be necessary in the interests of humanity; and all forms of religious worship and religious ordinances may be exercised within the said territories, and no hindrance shall be offered thereto except as aforesaid.

ADMINISTRATION OF JUSTICE TO INHABITANTS

8. In the administration of Justice by the Company to the peoples of its territories, or to any of the inhabitants thereof, careful regard shall always be had to the customs and laws of the class, or tribe, or nation to which the parties respectively belong, especially with respect to the holding, possession, transfer, and disposition of lands and goods, and testate or intestate succession thereto, and marriage, divorce, and legitimacy, and other rights of property and personal rights.

TREATMENT OF INHABITANTS GENERALLY

9. If at any time Our Secretary of State thinks fit to dissent from or object to any part of the proceedings or system of the Company relative to the people of its territories, or to any of the inhabitants thereof, in respect of slavery or religion, or the administration of Justice, or other matter, and to make the

Company any suggestion founded on that dissent or objection, the Company shall act in accordance therewith.

FACILITIES FOR BRITISH NATIONAL SHIPS

10. The Company shall freely afford all facilities requisite for Our Ships in the harbours of the Company.

FLAG

11. The Company may hoist and use on its buildings, and elsewhere in its territories, and on its vessels, such distinctive flag indicating the British character of the Company as Our Secretary of State and the Lords Commissioners of the Admiralty shall from time to time approve.

GENERAL POWERS OF THE COMPANY

12. The Company is hereby further authorised and empowered, subject to the approval of Our Secretary of State, to acquire and take by purchase, cession, or other lawful means, other rights, interests, authorities, or powers of any kind or nature whatever, in, over, or affecting other territories, lands, or property in the region aforesaid, and to hold, use, enjoy, and exercise the same for the purposes of the Company, and on the terms of this Our Charter.

QUESTIONS OF TITLE

13. If at any time Our Secretary of State thinks fit to object to the exercise by the Company of any authority or power within any part of the territories comprised in the several Cessions aforesaid, or otherwise acquired by the Company, on the ground of there being an adverse claim to that part, the Company shall defer to that objection.

PROHIBITION OF MONOPOLY

14. Nothing in this Our Charter shall be deemed to authorise the Company to set up or grant any monopoly of trade; and subject only to customs duties and charges as hereby authorised, and to restrictions on importation similar in character to those applicable in Our United Kingdom, trade with the Company's territories under our protection shall be free and there shall be no differential treatment of the subjects of any Power as to settlement or access to

markets, but foreigners alike with British subjects will be subject to administrative dispositions in the interests of commerce and of order.

The customs duties and charges hereby authorised shall be levied and applied solely for the purpose of defraying the necessary expenses of government, including the administration of justice, the maintenance of order, and the performance of Treaty obligations, as herein mentioned, and including provision to such extent and in such a manner as Our Secretary of State may from time to time allow for repayment of expenses already incurred for the like purposes or otherwise, in relation to the acquisition, maintenance, and execution of Treaty rights.

The Company from time to time, either periodically or otherwise, as may be directed by Our Secretary of State, shall furnish accounts and particulars in such form, and verified, in such manner as he requires, of the rates, incidence, collection, proceeds, and applications of such duties, and shall give effect to any direction by him as to any modification of the description, rate, incidence, collection, or application of such duties.

CONFORMITY TO TREATIES

15. The Company shall be subject to and shall perform, observe and undertake all the obligations and stipulations relating to the River Niger, its affluents, branches, and outlets, or the territories neighbouring thereto, or situate in Africa, contained in and undertaken by Ourselves under the General Act of the Conference of the Great Powers at Berlin, dated the twenty-sixth February, One thousand eight hundred and eighty-five, or in any other Treaty, Agreement, or Arrangement between Ourselves and any other State or Power, whether already made or hereafter to be made.

FOREIGN JURISDICTION

16. In all matters relating to the observance of the last preceding Article or to the exercise within the Company's territories for the time being of any jurisdiction exercisable by Us under the Foreign Jurisdiction Acts, or the said General Act of the twenty-sixth February, One thousand eight hundred and eighty-five, the Company shall conform to and observe and carry out all such directions as may from time to time be given in that behalf by Our Secretary of State, and the Company shall, at their own expense, appoint all such Officers to perform such duties and provide such Courts and other requisites for the administration of Justice as he directs.

GENERAL PROVISIONS

And We do further will, ordain, and declare that this Our Charter shall be acknowledged by Our Governors, and Our Naval and Military Officers, and Our Consuls, and Our other Officers in Our Colonies and possessions, and on the high seas and elsewhere, and they shall severally give full force and effect to this Our Charter, and shall recognize and be in all things aiding to the Company and its Officers.

And We do further will and ordain, and declare that this our Charter shall be taken, construed, and adjudged in the most favourable and beneficial sense for and to the best advantage of the Company, as well in Our Courts in Our United Kingdom, and in Our Courts in Our Colonies or possessions, and in Our Courts in Foreign Countries, or elsewhere, notwithstanding that there may appear to be in this Our Charter any non-recital, mis-recital, uncertainty or imperfection.

And We do further will, ordain, and declare that this Our Charter shall subsist and continue valid, notwithstanding any lawful change in the name of the Company, or in the Articles of Association thereof, such change being made with the previous approval of Our Secretary of State signified under his hand.

And We do, lastly, will, ordain, and declare that in case at any time it is made to appear to Us in Our Council expedient that this Our Charter should be revoked, it shall be lawful for Us, Our heirs and successors, and We do hereby expressly reserve and take to Ourselves, Our heirs and successors, the right and power, by writing, under the Great Seal of Our United Kingdom, to revoke this Our Charter, without prejudice to any power to repeal the same by law belonging to Us or them, or to any of Our Courts, Ministers, or Officers, independently of this present declaration and reservation.

SCHEDULE OF TREATIES

[Here follow the numbers of treaties made by the Company on certain dates in 1884.]

In witness whereof We have caused these Our Letters to be made Patent.

Witness Ourself at Westminster, the tenth day of July, in the fiftieth year of Our Reign.

By Warrant under the Queen's Sign Manual,
Muir Mackenzie.

SOURCE: Can be found in John E. Flint, *Sir George Goldie and the Making of Nigeria* (1884; London: Oxford University Press, 1960), appendix 2, 330–36.

———

Selected Correspondence:
The Royal Niger Company

GEORGE TAUBMAN GOLDIE AND FREDERICK LUGARD

[*Inserted from Lugard Papers*]

The Royal Niger Company, Chartered & Limited,
London, W.C. 2 July 1894.

Dear Capt Lugard,

Before we come to a final arrangement, it is necessary that I should put formally before you matters relating to your position and duties, which I have already referred to in conversation.

The Company, ever since its foundation, has been engaged in a work—that of opening up tropical Africa—which a great number of persons still believe to be impracticable. The Company believes it practicable on one condition; namely that, in view of the difficulties resulting from the climate, the difficulty of access to inner Africa, the barbarism of the populations and other abnormal causes, abnormal energy, persistence, patience and, above all, *discipline* should be displayed by all the officials of The Company from the Governor and Council down to the junior Customs clerk. Engaged in a campaign against natural and other forces which would overwhelm us if we made mistakes, it is essential that every person working for The Company should observe the same *discipline* that is expected from an officer on active service.

The two greatest dangers at home are the apathy of public opinion, as a general rule, about western Africa, and the excitability of public opinion, for short periods, when led astray on some popular hobby, by one sided or exaggerated reports.

This latter danger can only be averted by the *discipline* to which I have above referred. Every official of The Company, whether a member of the Council or a judge or an Executive officer or a soldier is very properly bound not to publish, nor to communicate to anyone likely to publish, anything connected with The Company as a Government or as a commercial society, or the Company's Territories or regions visited when in The Company's service, without the previous assent of the Governing Body of The Company.

You will understand that in the difficult and complicated game which The Company is playing, every move of which has to be calculated with the greatest care, it would be intolerable that any individual should be allowed to be the judge of what he might (directly or indirectly) publish or communicate to other persons than the Council of The Company.

But whether you agree or not with the necessity of the above policy, I must on behalf of the Governor and Council, make it quite clear to you, in this formal and official letter, that The Company cannot make an exception in anyone's favour, and I shall be obliged by your returning me this letter with its appended assent on your part. I will then send you a duplicate to keep.

There will be no difficulty about your publishing books or delivering addresses after your return, *provided that all proofs are subject to the revision of the Council.*

I am, &c, &c,
(Sgd) George Taubman Goldie,
Deputy Governor.

[*Printed letter enclosed*]

London   18
Dear Sir,

In accordance with an arrangement adopted with other officers of The Company, I shall feel obliged by your signing the letter annexed to this and returning the whole to me. You will probably understand why this is desirable, but I think it only proper to state in writing why these conditions are necessary. With the Governments of European States it is an understood thing that their officials are bound to keep inviolate, as a matter of honour, all matters that come officially to their knowledge. The principle should of course apply equally to the Government of the Niger Territories, authorized by Royal Charter, but it is quite conceivable that some person in The Company's service might, in the event of a dispute, commit indiscretions and salve his conscience with the plea that it was not a Government he was serving, but only a Trading Company. Moreover, some of the clauses of your agreement relate to matters about which a Government does not, as a rule, trouble itself. In Europe, as a rule, a judge is nothing but a judge; an administrator has only administrative work to perform; a soldier, only soldier's work; a doctor, medical work; and a trader is only a trader. But in Central Africa, where every European is, more or less, thrown in contact with all manner of people, it might happen that the judge or the officer might have some important discovery communicated to him; or might be, out of policy, compelled to receive valuable presents from some native prince; or, if exploring either the Territories or the extra-territorial regions, he might be able, and if able, might find it desirable to conclude important agreements with native chiefs or individuals.

The Company is most willing to reward liberally all such discoveries or all such advantages gained for it *so soon as they produce actual pecuniary results*, but it holds jealously to its sole and entire proprietary right in such matters.

With reference to the engagement not to divulge matters to any outside person, official or private, it must not be imagined that The Company has any desire to hide its actions under a bushel, but it claims and insists on its right to state its own case. What, indeed, would otherwise be the effect of a number of Judges, Constabulary Officers, Executive Officers, Trading Agents, &c., all contradicting each other, or splitting up into factions in newspaper squabbles, or in communications to other Governments? With reference to pamphlets, books, &c., I have no reason to doubt that whatever you might write would pass the necessary revision in this office with but little alteration; but it is only fair to say that there are a great number of matters on which it would be decidedly inadvisable that anything should as yet be published.

Like other officials of The Company, you are bound to comply with these restrictions under 'liquidated damages' to the extent of £1,000, without prejudice to the right of The Company to restrain a continuance of the breach of the agreement. While retaining their legal right to pursue you for damages, or to obtain an injunction against you, the Council rely more on your honourable pledge to fulfil to the best of your powers the conditions referred to, in spirit as well as in letter, even in the extremely unlikely event of a dispute or lawsuit occurring between you and The Company.

Yours faithfully,

London, 2nd July 1894.
Dear Sir G. Goldie,

I have carefully read the above letter and pledge myself to observe the conditions required of me, not only during my term of service with The Company, but for five years after its conclusion.

Yours faithfully,
(Sgd) F. D. Lugard. Capt.

MEMORANDUM of AGREEMENT between Capt. Lugard and the Royal Niger Company, dated the Twenty fourth day of July 1894.

Capt. Lugard will leave Liverpool for the Niger Territories on the 28th July to carry out the instructions contained in Sir George Goldie's letter of even date. The Company will pay Capt. Lugard's passage to and from the Territories and will give him pay at the rate of One Thousand Pounds per annum from the day of his leaving Liverpool to the day of his return to England. The total period of his services with The Company including his passages to and fro will not be less than eight months nor more than Sixteen months unless by mutual agreement. The Company finds all the necessary material for Capt. Lugard's Expedition and allows him a sum not exceeding Fifty Pounds for his personal outfit. The Company has already advanced Capt. Lugard One Hundred Pounds in respect of such pay and outfit and will give him the balance on his return home subject to such further reasonable advances as The Company may make to Capt. Lugard or his assigns at his written request; and in the event of Capt. Lugard's prior decease his pay would be calculated up to the day of his decease. Capt. Lugard undertakes to keep careful accounts of the expenditure of his Expedition for the information of the Council. He understands that the barter goods supplied to him for payments to native Kings and Chiefs and for the other expenses of the Expedition are considered by The Company to be largely in excess of what he will require and have been furnished by The Company on the principle that it would be better that Capt. Lugard should bring back a large balance of unused goods than that the slightest risk should be run of the Expedition being unable to do valuable work from any deficiency whatsoever. Capt. Lugard undertakes to hand over any unused balance of such goods as well as of such remaining material of the Expedition as belongs to The Company to some responsible official of The Company and to see that a proper inventory is taken by such official, that it is signed and forwarded to the Council in London.

SIGNED on behalf of the Royal Niger Company, Chartered & Limited by
           (Sgd.) George Taubman Goldie Deputy Governor.
           (Sgd.) F. D. Lugard Captain, 9th Foot.
WITNESS to the signature of Sir George Taubman Goldie
           J. Carden, 185 Barry Road, E. Dulwich, S.E. Clerk
WITNESS to the signature of the said Capt. Lugard
        Joshua Berkeley, Junior Army & Navy Club, St. James's Street.

Royal Niger Company.
24 July 1894.
Dear Capt Lugard,
    The following will serve you as concise general instructions—more for your own satisfaction than for any need of written instructions after our numerous and lengthy conversations.

ITINERARY TO JEBBA

Berths have been secured for yourself and Mr. Mottram in the steamer leaving Liverpool for Akassa on the 28th inst. I have received a promise of a separate cabin for yourself and probably—but this is not certain—for Mr. Mottram. Doubtless Mr. Flint, our Agent General and Chief of the Executive Power in the Territories, will meet you at Akassa, as he has full instructions about your expedition, which he will assist to the utmost of his power. But should it prove that, owing to his being up country when our letters arrived, he has not been able to reach Akassa in time to meet you, you are furnished, herewith, with a letter for the local authority at Akassa to pass your expedition up to Lokoja as rapidly as possible. Mr. Watts, our Senior Executive Officer in the Nupe Districts (which include Jebba and Bajibo) cannot sail with you as I had hoped, owing to urgent private affairs; but he will follow the next week in a steamer which will land him in the Forcados River, whence he will make his way up to reach you at Lokoja or higher up and assist in collecting and starting your expedition. You cannot do better than trust to the experience of Mr. Flint and Mr. Watts to get together all the men, horses, donkeys etc that you require. Mr. Flint has instructions to detach from our staff an able young man, Mr. Reynolds, to accompany you. You will find him docile and active, while his constitution is thoroughly acclimatized—an immense advantage in Western Africa. I believe him to be thoroughly sober, but there are few men in West Africa whom I should trust too far with the care of liquors: the depressing climate predisposing the best men to take stimulants unduly. I say nothing of your journey from Akassa to Jebba or Bajibo, leaving this for you to arrange with the local authorities: but if you decide to make your start from Bajibo instead of Jebba, please to insist that no launch is used in that dangerous stretch of river for the transport of either your men or stores. The officials might feel bound to press this civility on you, instead of transporting by land; but the Council could not recover the insurance on a vessel lost in these dangerous rapids.

ITINERARY WESTWARD

In the event of your not receiving a cablegram 'Lugard Kuka', you will, at the very earliest possible date, complete your caravan and leave Jebba (or opposite) Bajibo for Kiama. Your westward journey will follow, generally, the pencil lines traced in the maps handed to you; but it is very desirable (a) to visit *Nikki* either on the homeward or outward journey and obtain a treaty unless you discover that *Nikki* is no longer the capital of an extensive region, or on the other hand you obtain the assurance that our Boussa treaty is really given by the Nikki King; (b) to touch that point on the 9th parallel of north latitude which is the eastern and northern limit of the present French Dahomey sphere and to advance from that point about W.N.W. so as to pass between Tschautscho land and Sugu. (c) to skirt but on no account to make treaties in the 'neutral zone' marked in the maps handed to you; (d) to reach, if convenient, the 4th meridian West of Greenwich, but not to go west of it unless you find you are likely to have time to spare, in which case the further west you penetrate the more successful your journey will be from a diplomatic point of view; (e) to visit Mossi, if you find from the Hausa (and other) caravans that you meet, that this country is, as I expect, a congeries of independent tribes, with whom you can therefore make treaties without regard to any treaty that Monteil may have made with Wogodogho; (f) to return by any route that you like, bearing in mind Nikki and also what will have been done by the expedition just returning under Mr. Wallace, of whose work you will obtain full information when you arrive in the Territories—that is, it would be of no use your making for Say and working your way down river, if Mr. Wallace has been able to carry out his instructions to do this; but if he has failed to do so, then such work would be most valuable, as we want treaties *south* and *west* of Say, even with people who are really tributary to Gandu. In your itinerary westwards it may be necessary for you to zig-zag a good deal, so as to run networks of treaties across and between the few treaties obtained by Monteil, Crozat and (in a portion of your region) Binger, for France.

OBJECTS OF YOUR JOURNEY WEST

The last sentence conveys the objects of your journey. France has obtained a few treaties with powerful chiefs on the strength of which she claims immense regions in the great bend of the Niger, known in France as 'le boucle du Niger'. Yet although her own rights in these vast regions are so slight and unfounded, she sends her adventurers into a recognized British Sphere to make treaties with persons who are undoubtedly subjects or tributaries of kings having treaties with England, and she defends this policy in the only possible manner by asserting the independence of these subject or tributary princes. I do not think that in your journey westward you will need to follow her example; as it is probable that great numbers of tribes and States are really quite independent of the chiefs with whom the French explorers have made treaties. I do not for a moment anticipate that you will be able to found a continuous British Protectorate from the Niger to Long. 4° W. It will be sufficient to secure great numbers of small regions, which can be reached by strips (however narrow and however circuitous) either from Gandu or Borgu or Illorin or the Gold Coast Colony—including the Neutral Zone, over which free transit exists. Your objects will therefore be as follows:—

(a) In places where the French pretend that they have made treaties, to obtain a written declaration from the rulers that such statements are false, and then to make treaties for us.

(b) In places where no such pretence has been made, to secure treaties accompanied by a short declaration that no previous treaties have been made with any European. Wherever you cannot obtain a written declaration in Hausa, or some other language which your interpreter can read, you had better have the verbal declaration written in English and after carefully explaining each point to the Chief, ask him to set his X to it and have that mark duly attested by your companions.

(c) To collect the fullest information as to the extent (mileage in every direction) of the jurisdiction of *all* the above places, so as to enable the fullest claims to be made for British rights and proper limits to be set to the pretensions of France.

(d) To collect general information of every kind about the regions you visit, which you will remember is one of the most important objects of your expedition, but especially to make inquiries as to the existence of gold, either alluvial or in reefs, and to bring home for investigation any specimens of rock or sand which the natives assure you contain gold. The gradual lightening of your loads as you proceed will enable you to do this on a considerable scale.

(e) To check Mr. Mottram's astronomical observations by your own calculations of your marches, and to insist on his taking as many independent observations as possible in each place so that mistakes can be rejected.

(f) To urge on all chiefs and men of influence the importance to them of Europeans bringing goods to their country, which can only be done if they sign the treaties.

(g) To obtain from natives and especially from caravan men (Hausas and others) the greatest possible number of lists of itineraries, with the number of days march, from every town of importance to every other. These lists cannot be obtained from too many independent persons, so as to enable us to reject those which differ too widely from the average.

(h) To note specially prevalence of Gum trees, Shea Butter trees and rubber vines.

(i) To remember, above all, that diplomacy and not conquest is *the* object of your expedition westwards. The French Press for the last six years have incessantly boasted that French officers and travellers, with (or even without) a single French companion and with very few native carriers and armed men, are able to cross new regions peacefully, and acquire valuable treaty rights where Englishmen can only make their way by force, leaving behind them a hatred and fear of Europeans. I do not for a moment admit the truth of this; but it is possible that, in regions where Europe has absolutely no military power, the gaiety, cajolery and sympathetic manner of the French have more effect in obtaining treaties than the sterner and colder manners of our countrymen. I suggest this only to emphasize the fact that in your expedition west, the exercise of force cannot further your objects, but must on the contrary prevent them being attained. On the other hand, it is vital that by constant vigilance, entrenching yourself and other precautions, you should secure yourself against treachery and violence. The above remarks are made not because you, with your experience, need them, but only to discharge our Council of a heavy responsibility.

POSSIBLE ALTERNATIVE ITINERARY EASTWARD

As you have been informed verbally, it is just possible that you may, before leaving Jebba or Bajibo, receive a cablegram 'Lugard Kuka', meaning that instead of proceeding *westward*, you will retrace your steps to Lokoja and make your way to Bornu and Lake Chad. There are several routes by which you can do this. You might ascend the Benue to Loko, thence to Zaria, Kano and Kuka. Or you might go to Ibi and thence to Yakoba (in Bautshi) and Kuka. This would be the most interesting route. Or you might ascend the Benue to Yola and thence to Kuka. To meet this last possibility, I enclose the itinerary of Mr. Charles McIntosh's journey to and from Kuka. But one point must be noted. He started from Ribago, which was then a station of The Company but has since been ceded to Germany. You have a map showing the Anglo-German frontier, which starts from a point Five Kilometres (3 ⅛ miles) below the confluence of the Faro with the Benue and runs to a point on the southern shore of Lake Chad. It is very desirable that you should slightly modify the route of the previous expedition so as not to cross into the German sphere.

OBJECTS OF KUKA JOURNEY

The conquest of Bornu by Rabeh and the subsequent defeat and death of the latter has no doubt created great changes, of which we are still unaware, in the political conditions of the country hitherto known as Bornu. Your work would be to ascertain in whose hands power now rests; to conciliate and if possible obtain treaties with the person or persons holding such power; to obtain every information which may enable you to report fully to our Council

on the present state of affairs and the probable course of events in the immediate future; to perform the same work of mapping and obtaining astronomical observations which you would have carried out on the itinerary westward;
and, generally, to exercise your discretion in doing your best in the interests of
The Company and Great Britain.

If a special crisis were to occur, which should render your remaining in
Bornu desirable, you would be at liberty to do so, and utilize any native allies
you could gain for the purpose of extending the effective jurisdiction of The
Company over those regions; but it must be distinctly and positively understood that The Company is not prepared, without full knowledge and consideration of the facts, to incur large expenditure for this purpose. The Council
cannot delegate to anyone, no matter how competent and experienced, the
authority to involve The Company, on his own responsibility, in undertakings
or liabilities which would seriously involve the prosperity of The Company.

YOUR PERSONAL POSITION

As our Council's representative deputed to arrange matters with you, it is my
duty to put formally on record, what is already fully understood between us,
that you go out altogether as a Special Agent of The Company and in no way
of Her Majesty's Government, to whom our Council and our Council alone
are responsible, as the Governing Body of the Royal Niger Company.

> Believe me,
> Yours sincerely,
> (Sgd.) George Taubman Goldie
> Deputy Governor.

SOURCE: In *The Diaries of Lord Lugard: Nigeria, 1894–5 and 1898*, vol. 4, ed. Margery Perham and
Mary Bull (Evanston, Ill.: Northwestern University Press, 1959–1963), 52–61. George Taubman
Goldie was born in 1846 and died in 1925; Frederick Lugard was born in 1858 and died in 1945.

Exerpts from
The Diaries of Lord Lugard: Nigeria
FREDERICK LUGARD

[In Frederick Lugard's early journal entries, the soldier and colonial civil
servant assessed what he considered his disappointing career; his period of
African service, however, provided a dramatic professional turning point.

Lugard (1858–1945) raised and commanded the West African Frontier Force (1897) and was appointed commissioner of northern Nigeria in 1900. Lugard and his wife, Flora Shaw, were obliged to leave Africa, due to her adverse reaction to the African climate. Lugard was appointed governor of Hong Kong (1907–1912), where he founded the University of Hong Kong. When the opportunity to return to Africa came about, Lugard accepted it; he served as governor-general of Nigeria from 1912 to 1919. On his return to England, Lord Lugard was appointed a member of the Permanent Mandates Commission of the League of Nations (1923), the International Slavery Committee (1924), and the International Labour Organisation Committee on Forced Labour (1927). He was made a Peer of the Realm in 1928. Frederick Lugard also served as the chairman of the International Institute of Languages and Cultures from 1926 to 1945.]

6th [November 1894]

At last the Caravan book is complete. The Long Roll contains every man's name—soldiers, Hausa-porters, Yorubas, and Nupes, Headmen, Interpreters, Horse and donkey attendants, servants &c; all advances are entered, each man and also date of engagement. Every man is shewn who left Jebba with us. This agrees with the 'Present State' which is completed and done to October 31st, shewing all changes. The Itinerary of each day is written up to date. All orders signed by me on Jebba Store are shewn in their place. Private accounts of Europeans also. The barter goods are balanced to October 31st. The treaty presents are tabulated and issues noted—this will be balanced *quarterly*. Once well started it will not be difficult to keep it written up accurately, and it will save a lot of useless book-keeping work. It forms my own personal record and check on every detail of the expedition. Entries are made by myself and the book kept by myself, and no expenditure of a single cowrie is authorised unless passed through it. At the final paying off of the expedition I can account for every single thing.

I sent Joseph and Omoro to the King early this morning with my salaams and to make an appointment for me to come and see him formally at mid-day today. They returned to say that whenever traders and people had come here they had always sent a present to the King and unless my messengers brought a present in their hands they could not be received. The Liman sent a private message to say he was going to see the King, and would do his best to explain &c. I replied that we had not come to trade, but to make friends. We had come at the wish of the King himself and guided by his own Envoy, we were guests. If we had brought goods for trade it would be a different matter, we should then desire to remain here a long time, and make profits. We merely wished to make friends and pass on, and as I had already told him, if he did not want us we would have gone elsewhere. As guests it is always the custom—which has happened to us everywhere—that the King sends us some food for the night—nothing had come. Of course the King would receive a present, before we went, if everything went well. Omoro again saw the Liman first as he was going off to see the King, and told him what I said, and asked him from me, to come and have a talk with me. He said he would come secretly by night.

17th

Nothing to do but wait until His Gracious Majesty shall be pleased to summon us to an audience. We sent salaams to him early by Joseph. Worked very hard all day at various camp jobs, made the magazine for sporting amtn., collecting box, canvas hold-all for tools, &c.

In the afternoon a summons came from the King about 4 P.M. Went up with Watts, who is still very shaky with fever, and we were kept waiting in the sun for nearly half an hour. I got terribly out of patience. It is a radical mistake, this abasement of the European before *very* petty African chieflets. I would not be treated so at any Government Department in England. I brought the scarlet coat emblazoned with gold lace and stars and foolery, but I wrapped it up in a towel and only put it on at the door. I detest this mummery, it is more irksome to me to dress myself up like a Punch and Judy show than to visit a dentist. The King of all the Bussas turned out to be a specially dirty and mean-looking savage, seated on a filthy and greasy carpet and Musnud, surrounded by a group of ordinary savages. The door-ways were blocked with gazing crowds of naked girls and semi-nude women—sheep, goats and fowls wandered about. And *this* man is subsidised by the Royal Niger Company to the tune of £50 a year. And on his whim the representative of the Company has to stand in the sun and wait, with fever on him! &c. At Rome we must do as the Romans do, but my heart sinks at the thought that I must submit to such customs and indignities for another year! On entering no-one made way for us, and I asked somewhat brusquely if he could not provide a chair. Thereupon he sent for one, and I sat opposite him. He made no courteous overture—and on a former occasion had refused Watts' hand when he offered it! I said I had been sent from England to make friends with Kings here, and had come to him first, on my return I should report of his friendliness &c. This was only an official and formal visit, would he name a time when I could see him privately and say what I had to say. He said he would let me know—I thanked him for his hospitality, (he has not sent us a single yam I believe!) and with many polite phrases I withdrew.

I had intended going shooting and was promised a guide, but he turned up to say it was too late, the place was far &c. and I must wait till early tomorrow. With an ill grace I had to do so.

19*th*

We were to have left today, but there is now no chance of it. I would greatly have liked to go out shooting this morning but refrained lest the King's message might come in my absence. Instead of this a message was returned by Joseph (whom I had sent to ask if the letter &c. was ready) to say that before writing it he wished to see us again, that today he had some ceremonies to perform in the vicinity of my camp near the river, about 2 P.M., and later in the evening would see us. Bye and bye another message came to ask me to take my tent away as his horses must be tethered on the spot. So I had to pack up, strike my tent, and move to Watts' house!—*Quousque tandem!* Later again a message came to ask for spirits as he was making holiday, tho' he well knows they are prohibited. I replied we had not a drop public or private.

I asked Watts if all this is the customary procedure. He says it is, and that when he goes to Bida he prepares to wait 10 days! I asked if Macdonald was treated like this, for he came as a *Government* Official and put on full uniform, with Ferryman as a Lieutenant, and hundreds of porters carrying every conceivable luxury, and with large presents. Watts replied that Bida refused to see him in a hurry thereupon M. said he would go, and would not give him his present. Bida replied he could keep the present for he did not want it! Macdonald sent the present and left! The King of Yola was even worse, and refused to see Macdonald at all!

I don't see my way clearly in this business I have undertaken. I am altogether the wrong man. The 'intrepid French explorers' who have succeeded in penetrating these countries with a handful of men and no goods or rifles, and have brought back packets of treaties, are roundly accused here of never having translated the real contents of these treaties. Facts seem to point to this conclusion. To secure a treaty with Sokoto, Thomson spent £500. Macdonald's futile trip to Bida when he never was received by the king at all cost £80. Bida gets presents of £500 at a time, and a subsidy of about £3000. Even a petty chief like Bussa gets a small subsidy—how then could Frenchmen secure important treaties for nothing at all? Again they say here, that once a Frenchman has got his *soi disant* treaty he clears out, and if the French want to come into the country with which they have made a treaty they invariably have to fight, which shews that the treaty was Nil. Mizon's methods of which we have some accurate knowledge are a case in point. Now I am *not* that class of man, so success on *those* lines is denied me. The alternative is apparently a man who will eat any amount of dirt. Bida threatened to cut off Wallace's head and he is deputy to Flint and Agent General when he [Flint] is at home. Nothing was done; MacTaggart was tied to a tree and shot at—and another agent was flogged! A man used to *trading,* arguing, haggling, and *not* to ruling or asserting himself might succeed but I could hardly have been chosen on those grounds!

Meanwhile yesterday and today the people I have sent to purchase food cannot get a single yam. The men in camp pick up some, but there are few if any women hawking goods, as at Yashikera, Kaiama &c. where the air resounded from morning till night, with the monotonous cry of the women, crying their goods for sale. There is a report in camp that the King has given orders that no provisions are to be sold to us. I trust it may not prove true—for 415 rations are daily wanted. Borgu is a trying country to travel in!

The Liman was all the afternoon with the King, and came as he had promised to me after night-fall. He is an old man, somewhat garrulous but shrewd. I found out from him that the real obstacle is that the King—or rather the people—are possessed by this prophecy that if the King sees a European he will die within 3 months. He said that nothing would induce them to allow me to see the King. Moreover, as he justly remarked, supposing that the King, who is old and blind, *did* happen in the course of nature to die within 3 months, what would happen to the prince of Yashikera who had so strongly urged our coming, and to himself? Mentally I went a step further and thought what a hole we should be in if the silly old pagan died *now!* The whole population of Borgu would rise to rend us—*ergo* let us reduce the chance as far as may be by getting away as soon as possible. I thanked the old man, and said I was glad to know the real reason, and not to have evasive answers and false reasons. I had before once been placed in this identical position (at Ankole), but the King agreed to send his son who made blood brotherhood with me, and 4 old Councillors to whose words he pledged himself. The Liman said that *he* would be the King's proxy, and would bring a confidential slave from the King who would witness everything he said or did. I pressed the matter of 4 leading chiefs, but it seems that *they* are as afraid to see a White man as the King is. I don't believe this, for the King's son came to see me yesterday, and later the old Liman said incidentally that so soon as the matter was settled I should be flooded with visitors. He wishes, of course, to keep the whole game in his hands, and aggrandise himself, and secure a regal present in consequence. It will be a difficult matter to handle for if I offend him my chance is gone.

I then said that as he professed to be a man of such influence—he said that it was he who put the King of Kaiama on his throne, and the King was wholly guided by him—how was it that he came to see me secretly by night? This hit the root of the matter, for I well knew that the absence of any present of a single yam or of water meant that things were not yet right. The King had insisted on my messengers bringing a present. I had refused, and said that as his guest it was right he should first send me food and water *at once* on my arrival. We had *not* come to trade, nor was I a trader, but an officer, and his guest by invitation. It was on this subject mainly that the Liman had gone to the King. He now said he had wholly succeeded, that the King had had the drums beaten round the town, for everyone to bring yams, and tomorrow or next day they would be here, with the water. It is the custom to send (as at Kaiama) a great number of women carrying gourds of water—not only I take it is this a civility to save our drawing it, but it means, I suppose, that we are welcome to the water (viz. to the country) an entirely African idea. Thus in East Africa it is for permission to draw water that Hongo is demanded. Till the King had sent these presents the Liman said he could not come openly— all the people were most eager to see us, and to see our camp, but dare not come till this had taken place, not knowing the King's attitude towards us. If true I have scored a point, and made the King climb down. It appears, however, that the reason chiefs have not visited me is *not* because they fear the prophecy which refers to the King only, but because the King has not yet sent yams and water.

After this interview I gave the old man a piece of brocade, and a quire or so of the crested Mohammedan paper. He was greatly pleased—it seems now as though everything depends on him at the moment. I told him with great force the urgent necessity of haste. Traders come and settle down for a month to sell their goods, we have no such object but are bound for a distant country, and each day's halt costs us a bale of cloth to feed our men. Nothing can be done till the King's present comes, and he assures me it will be here tomorrow. I then told Joseph to take him off and have a quiet talk, and broach the subject of the treaty, and tell him its main provisions from memory. This he says he did, and that the Liman said there would be no difficulty now that the matter was in his hands. I hope it may prove so.

Miscellaneous work today—completed the Caravan book, wrote up diary, wrote a few letters &c.

7th

A fowl and salutations from the Liman. Then another 'King's son' to visit me. Then a man to complain that my men had stolen food and yams from his fields. I made the Crier cry round camp that any man caught stealing from the natives or forcing women—for there was also a complaint that the men pretended to buy, and then got the food from the natives and refused to pay, and also tried to get the women into the bush—should get 70 lashes (my old punishment in East Africa). That in this matter there was one law for every man in the caravan from top to bottom—Headmen, soldiers and porters alike. I begged the natives to catch a man in the act and bring him to me, or to run and tell me when it occurred so that I might catch the man. I gave the plaintiff a piece of cloth, warning them at the same time that it was useless in future to come to me for compensation unless they caught the thief. I was wondering only last evening that I have had no case of this sort, for food is expensive and hard to get, and these long halts always result naturally in the men tampering with women. In East Africa my halts were always employed in building stockades and the men were *very* hard worked.

At the same time I sent out a corporal and 2 men in the direction of the nearest fields—they caught a man stealing in the act. He got a handsome flogging straight away, before the whole caravan. The Crier then went round again saying that was what every man would get who was caught stealing from the natives. I also gave orders that the Sergeants on duty should send out a patrol continually every day to catch such thieves. I said I was very pleased that they had caught this man, and if they caught more I should recognise that they were doing the work for which they were here—viz. helping me to enforce the law of the Expedition. If *not* then I should order them daily parades, and fatigue duties while in camp.

There has been a great improvement the last few days in the C.S.T.—I only hope it may continue. It came about thus. On arrival at Wenn I called Bela-ribe, and told him that I had not done with the matter of his reply regarding their rations the day we left Yashikera. That after bothering me to buy their rations because they thought I should not be able to buy the amount with the cloth issued, he had had the insolence to come and say that now it was bought (and was the full ration) they could not carry it. If I gave them their ration a day in advance they said they could not carry it, if I waited till arrival in camp, and till I could then buy, they complained of delay. If I gave them cloth, they complained they could not get the rations; if I gave them yams, they said I favoured the porters, who could with their cloth buy varieties of food. Of all this I was heartily sick. He himself told me that the men troubled him greatly, and would listen to no orders. Though pleased with him as an individual, he was worthless as a Sergeant. I pointed out how that very day my orders had not been enforced. Porters allowed to pass in front of the advance guard, the loads laid out late &c. I would promote Abdr Rahman as senior sergeant, and see if things went better. Belaribe was in a great state of agitation. Said he had been 9 years in the C.S.T. and never a fault before &c. He also said—and it appears to be the case—that Abdr Rahman told him to go with that message to me. As Abdr Rahman did not deny this, I said I could not promote him over Belaribe for a fault in which he was equally a participator so things should remain as they were, but unless orders were better obeyed the matter would only be deferred. Since then I have not seen Belaribe's face. He has utterly collapsed, and Abdr Rahman has represented him, on the plea I believe that Belaribe has toothache, and things have been *much* better.

I wrote letters most of today, as I shall send back mails by the Kaiama guides and envoys. Mottram hard at observations trying to find the cause of the collapse of his longitudes. The latitudes are apparently right. So soon as he has got some clearly worked out, I am going through them with him.

In the evening the late King's son came to see me, with a very unprepossessing crew. Also a small present from the Magija (chief woman adviser) a personage who seems to be a great swell in all Borgu towns. Each of these 'princes' &c. brings a fowl and from 6 to 15 yams, and I *have* to give a piece of cheap cloth, and even *that* is so little that I am on tenter-hooks lest the recipient should enact the rôle of the Beteh man. The present, however, is not worth half a piece at purchasing price, and this runs away with our cloth, about which I am getting very anxious indeed.

The Nupes ration is due today, and there was a rumpus. Food is hard to buy here, and after careful inquiry I found that the utmost I could make a piece go for, was for 5 days (instead of 6 as at Yashikera) between 8 men. This the Nupes refused, and so did the Yorubas—so I had the cloth done up again. Tomorrow the Hausas' are due. I sent for Derrie and asked him if the Hausas intended to try the same game. He said that the Hausas knew that I had to calculate how far my cloth would go, and provide against starvation in the future. *Whatever* I gave would be accepted without a word and *made* to last. I told him to go and tell the men that a piece would be given for 5 days.

8th

Issued to the Hausas who were quite contented, and chaff and laughter prevailed, not a trace of sulkiness. Then the Yorubas were called, and told that the cloth was for 5 days—they had lost yesterday's ration by refusing. They replied that they wanted a regular fixed ration to last for so many days—a head of cowries per week per man for instance. What was the buying price was not my business. I told them that it was my business to provide against starvation, to give the men the food necessary and no more. They could take the cloth or leave it as they preferred. They got up and went away in a body. I told the Headman to let it be known that any single individual could have his cloth if he came for it—there is apparently no response.

What these 167 men intend to do I have not an idea. I wish that sufficient goods had been sent that I might not have to cut corners so fine. My last issue was a piece of Baft at 3/3 (14 yards of the cheapest possible cloth) for a man for 48 days (Viz. 8 men for 6 days). This issue is at the rate of a piece for 40 days—and it really is *barely* sufficient. Yet even thus we consume a bale a day and *more*. As it is 167 men out of 281 are in a state of mutiny.

I sent Joseph at daybreak today to the Liman, to ask about the 'King's water' viz. his present of welcome, which was to have come yesterday and didn't. Here are 3 or 4 days gone and nothing done, and I am very worried about it. He returned to say that the King had been very vexed that his order of yesterday had not been carried out, and that assuredly the present would come today. If the people did not bring it quickly he would send to their fields and seize it. He had heard of the man complaining to me about theft from his fields, and how I had given him a bit of cloth, and how the Crier had cried round my camp, and how I had caught a man and flogged him, and he was astonished and said that it was indeed true that Europeans were quite different in their methods from other people, and it was wrong of him to [keep] such people waiting. Joseph also added that these princes and people who have been to see us with presents are the very people who opposed our coming! This is all very satisfactory *talk*—Inshallah the *event* will prove equally so.

Later. The 'King's water' has at last arrived—viz. a wretched-looking sheep and 35 very medium yams—a very different present from Kaiama's! *He* sent me a very large cow, 4 goats, corn, yams (daily) &c. and lastly a horse. However, I replied that I was very pleased indeed, and now the King had sent the 'water' I knew I was welcome to the country. It was the custom of every country that, after the guest had received his welcome, he went to pay a formal visit, and to render his thanks &c. But I had heard that the King feared to see me personally therefore his messengers must return my thanks for me, and ask him to appoint someone to whom I might speak of the matters which had brought me here—either the Liman alone, or better still the Liman and some other chiefs.

At the same time I sent to tell the Liman, and to say that as his interview with me was secret I had not divulged its purport, but had given this reply—and now he had better get the King to appoint him as his representative. I also asked him to come and see me openly as the King's present had now come. It appears there was much discussion around the King; some wanted the Liman alone to deal with me, others desired several chiefs should come. As the argument was protracted the Liman could not come to see me.

The Nupes and Yorubas have caved in and taken their rations, but I am vexed to hear that the Hausas too—those from Lokoja—are clamouring for advances from their pay, or a higher ration. I am more bothered about them than about these cackling Nupes. If I say the cloth is only to last 4 days instead of 5 it means a whole bale expenditure. Then these return presents to 'Princes' and 'Princesses', leading councillors, Magajis &c. &c. run away with so much. In this country it is the custom (a custom the Niger Company have created and fostered on the Niger I am told) that if a man brings a present he expects double its value—if he be a 'Prince' he probably expects 6 times the value. I have cut this down to the narrowest possible limits, but when a big chief (as here) sends a fowl and a dozen yams one *can't* give him less than a *'piece'* of the commonest cloth—viz. the value of 40 men's rations!

So again in the matter of the C.S.T. They are entitled to 6 oz. of meat a day = 17 ½ lbs. of meat—a goat or sheep of the country is barely the ration of clear meat, and that would cost 5 or 6 heads. That is to say that I should have to give each man of the C.S.T. the value of 3 rations a day!—I have declined this *in toto*. I give them the sheep and goats and oxen which we receive as presents, keeping only the *very* small ones (sucking kids &c.) and the fowls for ourselves. Thus the whole expedition is on the very minimum of ration which is adequate and just, the presents are cut down to the very least I can possibly give. We practically spend nothing on the cookhouse, except to buy occasionally a little country grain for our bread or a bunch of bananas; I am positive in my mind that no such economy has been practised before. I use every possible expedient to reduce the number of loads, and have employed women and temporary carriers from village to village &c. at the cost of a very great deal of extra work and anxiety, and have sent back *all* the spare men—yet our expenditure to date is 34 loads of cloth and this in spite of the enormous reduction in the ration scale which I made since leaving Kaiama—a reduction which I have already had to alter back partly, and which will vanish and more than vanish as we go south and come upon Lagos goods, or West towards Salaga. Besides cloth *must* be issued in small quantities for clothing. It is a bale a day roughly (for the expedition was rationed for 7 days at starting) and we had 145 bales to start with, including the expensive cloths which will not realise their value in food purchase. All this I have written about and asked for a caravan of cloth to be sent to meet me at Kwampanissa. If it does not come the expedition cannot last more than 5 months or so, I fear. If it *does* come we can go on for the 10 months arranged. This matter worries me considerably.

The crux of the whole difficulty about food &c. seems to me to arise from the following circumstances. The men composing this expedition are mostly men engaged at Lokoja. These are not regular porters—(either Hausas, Yoru-bas or Nupes) they are all discontented and mutinous because (1) I will not make them a fixed allowance for food regardless of how cheap or expensive it may be where we are. If I acceded it would of course mean that so long as food was cheap the men would get double or treble rations, and if there was a dearth of food they would come crying to me for more. Such a system is impossible, and the regular travelling porters engaged at Jebba know that, and say not a word and give no trouble. (2) Because I will not give them a portion of their pay here on the march in cloth. If I did that of course the expedition would collapse for want of goods to buy food. The reason that these men were engaged appears to be that there was a general strike among the regular men, consequent on some extreme bitterness at Mr. Wallace's settlement after the Sokoto expedition. I found this to be the case when I sent Omoro and Derrie to Langwa to enlist some. They said, I am told, that they would never serve the Company again. I thought of sending back every spare man I could from here, under charge of the returning envoys from Kaiama. I might have got rid of some 24 porters, and 6 donkey and horse-men, say 30 in all—but I do not think I shall attempt it now. It would probably lead to trouble, and as the men are at the moment discontented, many would be clamouring to go back, or if they are contented those selected to go and their friends would be a trouble as they considered they are engaged for the whole expedition. I should have to give these men at least 10 or 12 days ration to reach Jebba, and probably by that time we should be in Kwampanissa. However I shall see how things go.

9th

The Liman came today, and went off to see the King and finally arrange about who was to represent him, regarding the business I wanted to speak of. He promised to be back again by 1 or 2 P.M. He duly turned up with two more chiefs who with himself were deputed to represent the King. We went though the treaty very carefully, as before I explained and paraphrased every sentence, and those who understood Hausa re-translated it into Borgu for those who did not. The Liman of course speaks Hausa. He led the way the moment Joseph had translated each sentence in saying 'Keoh' (good, excellent) with the air of a man calling for '3 cheers'. The other principal chief only spoke Borgu, and a man of his own, I think, translated it for him, when he too was quite pleased with everything. So we finished by sunset.

I have written a great number of English letters today. I showed them the King of Ilorin's letter, also Kaiama's—one of the men read them. They took Ilorin's letter as a sample to write me another like it to carry me on my way.

[Treaty inserted from Foreign Office Records]

(A copy of the Nikki treaty was sent to the Foreign Office by the Niger Company and is in F.O. 2/167, p. 194. The printed treaty form is used, with insertions copied by hand; here these insertions are given in italics.)

(Form No. 12.) (For Moslems.) Treaty made on the *10th* day of *November* 1894, between *The King of Nikki (which is the capital of Borgu)*, on the one hand, and THE ROYAL NIGER COMPANY, Chartered and Limited, for themselves and their assigns, for ever, hereinafter called 'The Company', on the other hand.

1. I, *Lafia (also called Absalamu, son of Wurukura)*, *King of Nikki and of all Borgu country*, with the view of bettering the condition of my country and people, hereby give to The Company and their assigns, for ever, full criminal and civil jurisdiction of every kind over all Foreigners to my country, including the rights of protection and taxation, and I pledge myself and my successors not to exercise any jurisdiction whatsoever over such Foreigners without the sanction of The Company.

2. I bind myself not to have any intercourse, as representing my tribe or State, on tribal or State affairs with any Foreigner or Foreign Government other than The Company; but this provision shall not be interpreted as authorizing any monopoly of trade, direct or indirect, by The Company or others, nor any restriction of private or commercial intercourse with any person or persons; subject, however, to such administrative measures as may be taken by The Company, as a Government, in the interests of order and of commerce.

3. I recognize that the Company, as a Government, represents Her Majesty the Queen of Great Britain and Ireland, and I accept the protection of the British Flag, but I understand that such protection against the attacks of neighbouring tribes can only be afforded as far as practicable.

4. I give to The Company and their assigns, for ever, the sole right to mine or dispose of mining rights in any portion of my territory.

5. In consideration of the foregoing, The Company bind themselves not to interfere with any of the native laws or customs of the country, consistently with the maintenance of order and good government and the progress of civilization.

6. As a pledge of their good faith, The Company have this day paid the said *Lafia, King of Nikki and Borgu,* a donation, receipt of which is hereby acknowledged.

This Treaty having been interpreted to *us* (*the representation deputed to act for him by* the above-mentioned *Lafia, King of Nikki and of Borgu*), we hereby approve and accept it for *the King* and for *his* successors for ever.

(Signature of Native Ruler.)

Arabic signatures of The Leman, The Sirkin Powa, The Naimin

(Attestation.) *Witness to all signatures:*

(*Signed*) *T. A. Reynolds, Guy N. Mottram.*

I, *Captain F. D. Lugard,* for and on behalf of The Company, do hereby approve and accept the above Treaty, and hereby affix my hand.

(*Signed*) *F. D. Lugard, Captain Commanding Borgu Expedition.*

I certify and solemnly declare that I was sent to the King Lafia by Captain Lugard to carry to him a present from The Company, and that at that interview, in accordance with my instructions, I asked the King myself, in the presence of various Chiefs and people, whether he had himself deputed the Leman and Sirkin Powa and Naimin to act for him in the matter of this Treaty, and that he thrice declared to me that he had done so.

(*Signed*) *T. F. Joseph*

Witnesses: (*Signed*) *T. A. Reynolds. Guy N. Mottram.*

Declaration by Interpreter

I, *T. F. Joseph,* native of *Sierra Leone,* do hereby solemnly declare that I am well acquainted with the *Hausa* language, and that on the *10th* day of *November, 1894,* I truly and faithfully explained the above Treaty to the *representatives deputed by the said Lafia,* and that *they* understand its meanings.

Signature or mark of Interpreter *(Signed) T. F. Joseph*

Witnesses to the above Interpreter's mark or signature:

(Signed) T. A. Reynolds, Guy N. Mottram.

Done in triplicate at *Nikki, Borgu,* this 10*th* day of *November,* 1894.

The King being blind, and also having a superstitious dread of personally meeting any European, has deputed the Leman and the Sirkin Powa to be his representatives and proxy, and to sign the treaty on his behalf. In the presence of these and other important men the treaty has been translated word by word, and fully explained in Hausa—many understanding that language—and retranslated again, sentence by sentence, into Borgu dialect.

(*Signed*) *F. D. Lugard, Captain, Commanding Borgu Expedition.*

10*th*

Signed the treaty early this morning. Made out the present or donation which the Company gives. I gave about £6 to the King, £5 to the Liman and 15/- each to the two chiefs. Reynolds all day opening bales and getting it out. It goes early tomorrow.

Tomorrow the letter is to be ready and also the guide. The 3 guides from Kaiama return, and will take my letters to Jebba for me. They are *excellent* fellows, and very great friends of ours. It is largely due to them that we have got on here—they are interpreters and go-betweens and work all day. I made out presents for them, also for the guide the King of Nikki sent to bring us here. I found out some information about routes, trade, &c. today, and wrote more home letters. The question of sending back men from here is no longer on the *tapis* for the Kaiama guides decline to take them.

Twice lately we have had a *dense* fog at sunrise, which has lifted about 7 A.M. and been succeeded by a blazing hot day.

11*th*

Joseph took the present to the King, and I instructed him to ask the King if he had in reality deputed the 3 men to act for him in the matter of the treaty. He did so three times over, and each time the King said 'Yes'. The King, who is old and blind, was behind a screen. He was very cordial, and said that never before had Europeans entered Borgu. Now he thanked God that it was in his life-time they had first come, and even if he died tomorrow that fact and honor would remain. Now we had made a treaty of friendship, and from North to South and East to West, whichever direction we wished to go in at any time, the country was open to us and we were welcome. Guides and envoys would be provided, both to precede us and to go with us, and make us welcome everywhere. I sincerely and most earnestly hope after the treaties that I have made, which are *thorough* and not a farce, that the Company will never 'swap' or abandon Borgu to France, but get it included in the British Empire eventually.

SOURCE: In *The Diaries of Lord Lugard: Nigeria, 1894–5 and 1898*, vol. 4, ed. Margery Perham and Mary Bull (Evanston, Ill.: Northwestern University Press, 1959–1963), 176–88.

Duties of Political Officers and
Miscellaneous Subjects

FREDERICK LUGARD

[Lugard was a proponent of the policy of indirect rule, for which he remained a major spokesperson. According to his biographer and admirer, Margery Perham, this system eventually "helped bridge the gap between tribal systems and the new movements toward democracy and unity" (http://www .britannica.com/eb/article?ev=50479). Later critics, however, have been less appreciative. Mahmood Mamdani, the Ugandan historian, has argued recently that "the colonial powers dismantled the single legal universe of direct rule, employing instead a system of indirect rule. In so doing they created a series of parallel universes: non-natives continued to have rights in the realm of civic law, as under direct rule, but natives were to be governed differently. Each ethnic group was now said to have its own set of customary laws, to be enforced by its own 'native authority'—its chief—in its own 'home area.' In this way, the aggregate category 'native' was legally abolished and different kinds of natives were created. The political aim was to fracture the native population into ethnic groups. With each group governed through its own 'customary law,' a plural legal order produced plural political identities; these identities were said to stem from tribes, cultures, and traditions that predated the colonial encounter. This shift to indirect rule signified a retreat from colonization's original project of civilization: the natives were to remain natives, forever proscribed from the realm of civil law" ("A Brief History of Genocide," *Transition* 10, no. 3 [2001]: 26–47).]

1. The duties of Administrative and Political Officers form, for the most part, the subject of the following series of Memoranda, and, consequently the more important of the subjects touched upon in this Memo. will be found much more fully dealt with elsewhere. A synopsis of them, may, however, be found useful, so that newly-appointed Officers may have some idea of what their work will be, and where to find the more detailed instructions on each subject. This Memo. deals also with various matters which hardly require a Memo. to themselves.

2. "Napoleon said, '*á la guerre les hommes ne sont rien, c'est un homme qui est tout.*' It is a part of the false idea of greatness that the men employed in giving effect to it are nothing, and that the whole is to be the outcome of one man's conception, imposed on others. Not so. Great and enduring things grow

gradually from the first efforts of every individual engaged in producing them. One man has perhaps a conception. That makes him a leader, but every man who works with him, adds his bit, not only to the accomplishment of the ideal, but to the ideal itself. The whole scheme grows like a tree that puts out new branches, and personal touch between the leader and the workers helps greatly to develop this vital spirit."

This quotation admirably expresses the co-operation in a common task which has, and will always, I trust, continue to be a feature of the work of Administration in Nigeria.

3. The British rôle here is to bring to the country all the gains of civilisation by applied science (whether in the development of material resources, or the eradication of disease, &c.), with as little interference as possible with Native customs and modes of thought. Where new ideas are to be presented to the native mind, patient explanation of the objects in view will be well rewarded, and new methods may often be clothed in a familiar garb. Thus the object of Vaccination and its practical results may be sufficiently obvious, while the prejudice which exists among some Moslems may perhaps be removed by pointing out that it is a preventive of disease by contagion, no less than the circumcision enforced by their own law.

. . . .

6. The degree to which a Political Officer may be called upon to act in an administrative capacity, will thus depend upon the influence and ability of the Native Chiefs in each part of the Province, though in every case he will endeavour to rule through the Native Chiefs.

In those parts of Provinces which are under the immediate authority of a Chief of the first or of the second grade, the primary duty and object of a Political Officer will be to educate them in the duties of Rulers according to a civilised standard; to convince them that oppression of the people is not sound policy, or to the eventual benefit of the rulers; to bring home to their intelligence, as far as may be, the evils attendant on a system which holds the lower classes in a state of slavery or serfdom, and so destroys individual responsibility, ambition, and development amongst them; to impress upon them the advantage of delegating the control of districts to subordinate Chiefs, and of trusting and encouraging these subordinates, while keeping a strict supervision over them; to see that there is no favouritism in such appointments; and to inculcate the unspeakable benefit of justice, free from bribery and open to all.

Where taxation exists the consequent duty of assessing all the towns and villages himself, will throw upon the Political Officer a considerable amount of purely Administrative work, even in such districts. In this work he should invite the cooperation of the Chief, and endeavour to enlist his cordial assistance by making it clear to him that his own interests are deeply involved.

In districts where there is no Chief of the first or second grade, a Political Officer's functions become more largely Administrative, and among uncivilised Pagan tribes he must assume the full onus of Administration, to the extent to which time and opportunity permit. In such communities he will constantly endeavour to support the authority of the Chief, and encourage him to show initiative. If there is no Chief who exercises authority beyond his own village, he will encourage any village Chief of influence and character to control a group of villages, with a view to making him Chief of a district later if he shows ability for the charge. Native Court clerks or scribes, constables or couriers will never be allowed to usurp the authority of the Native Chief or Village Head. The position and status of Native Chiefs is dealt with in Memo. 9.

9. A Resident acting, but not in permanent charge of a Province, will not delimit Provincial boundaries, select Native Chiefs for appointment, make pledges in the name of Government, alter assessment of taxes, or undertake any such matter of great importance, nor will he change the office system, nor cut down trees and alter the lay out of the station, unless with the express sanction of the Lieutenant-Governor, but will endeavour to carry out the policy of the Resident in charge, and inaugurate nothing without the concurrence of the Lieutenant-Governor.

13. All Officers of the Political Staff are required to pass an examination in the Ordinances and Regulations of Nigeria, in the General Orders, and in one of the chief Native languages of Nigeria. Proficiency in a Native language is an important qualification for promotion. Promotion will ordinarily be provisional only unless an officer has passed, and he will be liable to revert if he does not do so within the period prescribed. Assistant District Officers must pass the Lower Standard to qualify for promotion, and a Resident should have passed the Higher Standard, especially if the language he has adopted is Hausa.

14. I regard continuity of Administration as a matter of paramount and indeed of vital importance in African Administration. It is only after many years of personal contact that the African—naturally reserved and suspicious towards strangers—will give his confidence unreservedly. More can often be accomplished in half-an-hour by an officer well known and trusted by the

people, than by another, though his superior in ability, after months of patient effort.

It has, therefore, been my general rule, that the more senior an officer becomes the less liable he is for transfer from his Province. An Assistant District Officer may be posted to two or three Provinces in succession, in order that he may gain experience, and the Lieutenant-Governor may decide whether his abilities are best adapted for work in an advanced, or a backward Province. As a Second Class District Officer he has become more of a fixture, and finally when he becomes Resident in substantive charge of a Province he is never taken away from it.

These rules are of course liable to violation owing to sudden vacancies, &c., more especially of late under war conditions, but though a Senior Officer may be removed for a time he will be restored to the Province he knows and to the people who know and trust him as soon as circumstances permit. Now that there is a single Administrative roster for all Nigeria, a Southern Provinces Officer may find himself posted on promotion to the Northern Provinces and *vice versa.* But here again the change will not as a rule be permanent, especially amongst the Senior Officers, and I should endeavour to restore an Officer to the people whose language he has learnt, and among whom he can do more efficient work, as soon as an exchange could be effected. Residents in like manner will avoid changing their Staff from one division to another if it can be helped.

. . .

17. A Resident will establish a Native Court in every city or district where it appears advisable to do so, and will constantly supervise its work, especially in the lower grades of Courts. He must of course carefully study the Native Courts Ordinance and Memo. 8. In Courts of Grades A and B he will watch the integrity of the Native Judges, and note their comparative ability for promotion to more important centres, and see that their sentences are in accord with British conceptions of humanity. In the lower grades he will take care that the initiative of the Chiefs who compose the Court is not interfered with by the clerk or scribe, that they do not exceed their powers, and that their sentences and findings are free from bias.

. . .

19. A Political Officer has to represent various Departments and to exercise divers functions in the Province to which he belongs. He acts as *Postal Officer,* in the absence of an European Officer of the Department, and is responsible for the despatch of mails in transit, and for the various duties laid down in the Regulations under the Postal Ordinance. The Postal and Telegraph Clerks,

under his general supervision, will undertake the duties of issuing stamps, and preparing receipts for parcels and registered letters, &c.

The *Police* in his Province are under the general orders of the Resident, whose relation to them and to the Commissioner or Assistant Commissioner of Police is laid down in Police Regulations and in General Orders and elsewhere. Isolated Police Constables should never be stationed in villages since it deprives the Village Headman of responsibility and initiative; and men placed in such a position of power are apt to misuse their authority. Detachments without a European are always to be deprecated. When in charge of the Government prison, the District Officer will inspect it frequently and check the prisoners with the warrants at least once a month.

Political Officers will also assist the *Customs* on those inland frontiers where it is not possible for the Department to have an European representative, and also in the collection of Customs due on Postal parcels; and in such capacity they exercise the powers of Customs Officers, and any preventive staff is under their orders.

.   .   .

23. As soon as possible after the close of each year, the Resident will submit to the Lieutenant-Governor, through the Secretary, a report of the work done in his Province, and on all matters of interest connected therewith for the past year. The report will be written by the Resident in substantive charge of the Province. If he is absent on leave at the end of the year he will write it on his return if he is due back before the end of February. Otherwise he will leave a draft completed as far as possible to the date of his leaving, and the fact that this draft was left and forms the basis of the report will be stated by the Officer who completes and signs it.

The report will be typewritten on foolscap paper, on one side of the page only, and a third margin will be left. The pages will be numbered, and fastened together at the extreme left-hand corner only. Paragraphs will be numbered *consecutively from beginning to end.* It will be on fairly strong paper and sent unfolded. One copy only will be sent to Headquarters (the duplicate being retained in the Provincial Office), but in order to avoid unnecessary re-typing, a copy of paragraphs relating to trade should be sent for transmission to the Officer charged with the duty of compiling trade statistics. Reports will be written in the first person, and the use of slang terms or of vernacular words such as 'Doki,' 'Mammie,' &c., where they have English equivalents should be avoided, as also the term "Whiteman" instead of "the Government" or "boys" where men are meant.

It is desirable that the Annual Report should be a complete and self-contained record for reference, and with this object in view it will contain a brief summary of any important correspondence which has taken place during the year, included under its appropriate heading, setting out the conclusions and decisions arrived at without too much detail. It will aim at being a full statement of facts and events—even though some repetition is involved—including any matters already reported in the interim half-yearly report. Recommendations, requisitions, questions, and discussions of policy, and departmental criticism, should be reserved for separate correspondence, the report being as I have said limited to a statement of events, facts and conclusions.

The report should be in terse phraseology in order that the maximum information may be included within reasonable length. The progress of each division should be separately related as part of the single unit of the Province, when dealing with various subject-heads as a whole. Any passage of interest from the Divisional Officers' report may be quoted, but their reports should not be attached in their entirety, or the Resident's report becomes a mere bundle of attachments.

Reports on subjects which are dealt with by a Departmental Officer will not repeat the statistics and details which would find a place in the latter Officer's report, but will give a general summary, with especial regard to the bearing of the work of the Department on the Provincial Administration. The Annual Reports will be transmitted to the Governor with the Lieutenant-Governor's comments upon them.

The Governor's notes on these reports must necessarily be so terse, that they may sometimes possibly read as though they conveyed dispraise, when no such intention existed. Residents will bear in mind that the pressure of work necessitates brevity in these replies, and that the report is only one of many (including all Departmental ones) with which the Governor has to deal. When answering the Governor's or Lieutenant-Governor's comments and questions, the context should be briefly stated in order to save reference.

The Annual Report cannot of course be finished until all the accounts and returns of the year are completed, but it should reach Headquarters not later than February, accompanied by the returns laid down in Memo. 2 and by a map of the Province. The printed or sun-printed map on scale of 1 to 500,000 will have enfaced upon it all changes, and additional information acquired during the year. Areas, the assessment of which has been "approved," will be coloured, those completed during the year being shown in a different colour. Special care must be taken in compiling this report, since it is the most important of the Provincial archives, which in future years may become of great interest and value.

24. The following should always form headings of the report, and may of course be added to as required:—

I. General Administrative:—This section should deal first with the Province as a whole, and with matters which refer to all Divisions alike, and then with each Division separately, quoting from the Divisional Officers' reports as to the general progress, the conduct of the Native Administration, and any matters especially affecting the Division. The class of subjects which are referred to in this section include (*inter alia*) the following: Progress and efficiency of the Native Administration, its finances and officials (especially the efficiency of the Head Chief and District Heads)—village grouping and self-contained districts. The police and prisons and the employment and health of prisoners—the latter are dealt with in detail under Head II. Where no Native Administration exists, the attitude of the Pagan Chiefs towards Government, and progress made in training them as Rulers. The area and population of the Province and its divisions; the principal events of the year; progress made in organisation and assessment; the material acquired for inclusion in the historical, ethnological and general statistics of the Province; any surveys executed, settlements of boundaries, and whether involving any additions to or subtractions from the area of the Province or divisions; any coercive expeditions in which troops or armed police have been employed, and the causes of any unrest or disturbances; mileage and condition of roads; any facts relating to *Jujus*, secret societies or similar organisations; efficiency of the Native Staff; any exceptional calls for recruits or labour; emigration and immigration; the travelling done by the Resident and Staff; housing, water supply, exiles and deportees; and game preservation, &c.

II. Judicial:—The returns laid down in Memo. 2 contain full statistics of cases tried in the Provincial Courts and nature of sentences passed. Allusion should be made to any case of particular interest, whether tried by the Supreme or Provincial Court, especially if it involves any question of principle or policy affecting the Administration. Extra-judicial comments on any case, or advice and assistance asked for, should form the subject of separate letters, accompanying the minutes of the case, and do not find a proper place in the Annual Report. The number of cases tried by Judges of the Supreme Court and their results; the working of the Commissioner's Courts in the "local limits" of the Supreme Court; the efficiency of the Commissioners of the Provincial Court, and the powers held by each should be noted; cases in which collective punishments have been inflicted under the Ordinance and their recovery; the extent to which Provincial Courts have made use of Assessors; and the number of informal cases dealt with, are all matters falling under this head. An explanation should be given of any notable increase or decrease of trials, or of exceptional severity of sentences.

The number of each grade of Native Tribunal in the Province, and their efficiency, integrity, and progress will be described. The number added during the year (if any), and whether they are popular and command the confidence of the people in primitive areas, are matters of interest. Repetition of the statistics embodied in the returns is unnecessary, but any cases of particular interest should be described. The number of prisons connected with these Courts, their location, adequacy, and cost; the average number of prisoners and how they are employed may with advantage be noted.

III. Revenue and Taxation:—Explanatory observations on the figures contained in the Returns, and the reasons of increase or of decrease are of value. The items which accrue to Government, such as licences, land rents, &c., should first be commented on, followed by a full report on the progress of Assessment, and in carrying out the policy outlined in Memo. 5. All matters of interest such as the approximation to the authorised rate of 10 per cent. (especially as regards wealthy traders); Remissions; "Taki"; efficiency of Native Treasury control in those districts in which taxation is fully established should be noted, while in areas in the Southern Provinces in which it has not yet (or only recently) been introduced, the feeling of the Chiefs and people towards the scheme of taxation, and any difficulties anticipated, should be fully described.

IV. Expenditure:—The items of Government expenditure will first be dealt with. The usual sub-votes from which the Lieutenant-Governor allots a sum to each Province are the following:—

(*a*) *Petty Expenses.*—Includes guides, river tolls, lodging for interpreters and others on the march if in the rains, small office expenses, lighting, &c.

(*b*) *Extra Services.*—The payment of such temporary Staff, at time of pressure, as has been previously sanctioned.

(*c*) *Special Runners.*—Conveyance of mails between the postal stations notified in the Postal Regulations will be paid for by the Postmaster-General from his regular vote. Mails despatched to places not so included, or to a Resident on tour, will be charged to this vote, and also the cost of conveying an urgent despatch too important to await the ordinary mail. Opportunities of sending such mails by any Police or other Government servant who may be going in the required direction, or who can be spared for the duty, will never be neglected.

(*d*) *Secret Service.*—Means the pay of Secret Agents, and gratuities for obtaining political information, only when Government Agents are impracticable, *see* § 34. Each payment will be entered in the Cash Book and on the Pay Voucher, simply as expended on Secret Service, giving no details as to mode or recipient of the payment in the case of small sums, but for larger disbursements when the accounts are rendered to the Treasurer, a confidential letter will be sent to the Lieutenant-Governor, quoting the number of the Pay Voucher and giving any necessary details. The name of a Secret Agent will never be mentioned in the letter.

(*e*) *Judicial.*—Includes the maintenance of witnesses (who should always receive subsistence), and any Court expenses. It does not include transport and maintenance of prisoners before or after trial, or rewards to Police, or "Sheriff's expenses" in carrying out sentences, which are debitable to the Police or Prisons votes.

(*f*) *Stipends to Chiefs.*—Will include only any authorised subsidies or gratuities. Where Native Treasuries exist, such charges will usually be met by them. Payments for road-making will be charged to Public Works Department votes, and must of course have been previously sanctioned.

(*g*) *Sanitation.*—A small sum will in some cases be allotted to a Province for necessary sanitation in Government stations where no prison labour is available. In townships where a local authority administers Municipal funds these will be available to supplement prison labour. If additional funds are required they will be drawn from Sanitary Department votes. The cost of sanitation and improvement of Native cities will be borne by Native Treasuries, if they exist; if not, some assistance may be given by providing tools and material from this vote. Expenditure against Departmental votes, such as Police, Prisons, Sanitation, Public Works Department, Education, &c., will be incurred with the concurrence of the Head of Department, who will provide the money required.

(*h*) *Transport.*—To this vote is debited the cost of carriers, canoes, &c., according to the authorised scale when travelling on any duty. Political Officers should, whenever possible, employ pack-animals and especially carts, with the three-fold object of affording an object lesson to the Natives, of avoiding the withdrawal of labour from productive occupation, and of saving cost to Government.

Full instructions on matters of accounting will be found in General Orders and elsewhere. I will here merely emphasise the fact that financial requisitions are *anticipatory*. If an Officer expends public money before the sanction is received, he does so at his own risk. It is the duty of an Officer in a high and responsible position to accept such risks where the matter is one of real urgency, and in such a case he will of course submit a full explanation of the reasons which prompted him. Even though the Lieutenant-Governor should disagree with his view and even express disapproval of his action, he would never be called upon to refund the money expended, if the Governor was satisfied that he had acted to the best of his discretion in the interests of the Public Service. If a number of instances occurred where expenditure had been made by a Resident (or other Officer) in circumstances in which urgency was alleged, and previous sanction could not be obtained, but in the necessity or urgency of which the Lieutenant-Governor did not concur, he would be driven to the conclusion that the Officer lacked discrimination, and was not suitable for his post. If, however, several cases of unauthorised expenditure occurred, which might and ought to have been anticipated and sanction obtained, the Lieutenant-Governor might in certain cases order the amount to be charged against an officer personally, in accordance with the financial instructions. He would, of course, have a right to appeal through the Lieutenant-Governor to the Governor, or even to the Secretary of State.

Following the notes on Government expenditure, the report will deal with the expenditure during the year of the Native Administration, explaining more particularly any items which were not borne on the approved estimates for the year; investments and balances.

V. Trade and Economic:—This head will embrace matters dealt with in § 26 and will detail any steps taken to develop new products; a description of products not previously reported on, and of any samples sent in for examination. It will describe in general terms the conditions and prospects of trade, with notes on the progress of agriculture and industries, and the cultivation of waste lands. Increases and decreases of produce for export, and of horses and livestock may be added. Information regarding exports should be given in some detail, with names of exporting firms. Notes on any special industry— model farms, ranches, horse breeding, &c.—and on the principal class of trade in the Province are of use. The circulation of coinage, and the extent to which European traders continue to deal by barter or accept and offer cash; the prices obtainable by the Native producers for staple products, and whether higher or lower than in the previous year, the quantities brought to market, and the part played by Native middle-men are all matters upon which information is desirable. Full information should be given regarding cotton, the quantity exported during the year as compared with the last year, and the quantity anticipated in the coming year. Statistics of the value of imports and exports are only required in so far as they are not rendered by the Customs Department. Notes on transport (carts and motors), on roads, waterways, and ferries as affecting trade, and on rainfall should be added.

VI. Departmental:—A Resident is not required to give information and statistics under this head which are already included in departmental reports. A few notes, based on his own original information or inquiry, as to the working of each Department, as it affects the Political service and the Natives, with suggestions as to how it can be made more efficient, and comments as to its conduct by the local representative are all that is required.

(a) *Police.*—The numbers, efficiency, mode of employment of the Force, and class of recruits.

(b) *Prisons.*—The average number of prisoners in the Government prison, the nature of the work on which convicts have been employed, and the number of "prison days," with any remarks as to the prison, food, health of prisoners, prison farm, &c.

(c) *Military.*—Any observations which a Resident may desire to make regarding the military detachment and reservists, movements of troops, supply of food and forage, and the behaviour of soldiers and their followers towards the civil population.

(d) *Medical.*—General health of Europeans and Natives, improvements in Government stations (sanitation, housing, &c.), progress in vaccination and dispensary work, leper camps and similar institutions, and in regard to the sanitation of native capitals; epidemics, and treatment of lunatics.

(e) *Postal.*—Efficiency of the service, and progress (if any) in Telegraph Construction.

(f) *Education.*—Progress in the Government Schools—leaving details to the Education Department. The attitude of the Native Chiefs and communities towards them, and any points of interest. New Mission Schools, and the method on which they are being conducted.

(g) *Public Works.*—Buildings and road construction with special reference to the treatment of Natives, and supply of labour and food. Progress made in motor and animal transport and use of carts.

(h) *Customs.*—Whether smuggling of dutiable goods occurs over inland frontiers.

(i) *Agriculture, Forestry and Veterinary.*—The relations of these Departments to the Native Administration, and progress made.

(j) *Railway.*—With special regard to labour employed, treatment of Native passengers, thefts, &c.

These notes should be brief and made from the administrative point of view only, not attempting to anticipate the detailed report of the Head of Department. A duplicate copy should be sent in case the Lieutenant-Governor desires to transmit it to any Head of Department.

Finally, a brief statement should be made of the European and Native Political Staff. The average number of the former in the Province during the year, and reliefs effected. The efficiency, number and aggregate pay of the Clerical Staff, and local provincial employees (Political Agents, Interpreters, &c.), and whether the latter have proved honest and capable. The tendency to go into great detail regarding each Officer and his reliefs, &c., should be avoided. The separate confidential reports will give details as to character.

VII. Slavery:—The prescribed return gives all the statistical information required. Any notes on special cases, particularly as regards the relation of concubinage and slavery, and other matters dealt with in Memo. 6, would be of great interest. Any recrudescence of the traffic in small children, and any new devices of the slave-traders should be noted, together with the progress made in the establishment of a free labour market.

These headings appear voluminous but they are intended merely as suggestions. Many may be omitted where there is nothing definite to report, and many others do not apply to all Provinces. The necessity for terse diction, and for recording only what is of definite interest should never be lost sight of. Tabular statements will as far as possible be included in the body on the report, following the paragraphs to which they refer. Only the more elaborate ones on printed forms will be added as Appendices. The statement of provincial Staff, and the period during which each officer has been present in the Province, should be shown in the form of graphic chart.

The Annual Report on each second class Township (none is required from third class) will be transmitted by the "Local Authority" under flying seal through the Resident.

25. An interim report will be submitted as soon as possible after June 30th in each year. The annual returns will not be attached to this report, but a return of touring should be made. Only such extracts from this report will be submitted to the Governor as the Lieutenant-Governor may consider useful to keep him in touch with progress, or as are suggestive or informative. Any paragraph in the interim report which deals fully with some particular matter can be transcribed verbatim in the Annual Report.

.   .   .

29. Transactions of importance with Natives, whether for Government Departments or for private enterprise, should be undertaken by the Political Officer, as, for instance, the purchase in bulk of supplies for troops (food and forage), engagement of gangs of labourers for road-making or other public works, or the supply of wood-fuel for steamers or engines. Negotiations for ranches, for mining or prospecting areas, for trading sites or for agricultural leases by unofficials should also usually be conducted by the Political Staff, in so far as they refer to acquisition from the Natives, and choice of locality. Full and prompt payment should be secured to the Natives for value or services rendered.

As far as may be done, without interfering with the law of supply and demand, a scale of prices to be paid for food at various halting-places on roads frequented by Europeans will be laid down, alike in the interest of the natives—so that their supplies may not be arbitrarily taken for a price current elsewhere, but less than the market value at that place—and in the interest of the travellers, so that they shall not be compelled, in their need, to pay exorbitant prices. These rates will be fixed from time to time in consultation with the local Chief, who will be warned that he will be held responsible if higher rates are demanded. Rates thus fixed will be posted in every Rest House, and a copy of them will be given to the local Chief for presentation to any European passing through. If a traveller takes supplies by force at a lower rate, the offence can be dealt with under the Criminal Code. When the market prices of supplies at a station have become inflated without good cause, the Resident should represent the matter to the Emir or Head Chief, and direct him, according to custom, to send round a crier to warn the traders to reduce their charges. If no notice is taken, and the Resident is satisfied that exorbitant prices are being charged to Government employees, he may direct that the market dues be temporarily increased, reporting the matter at once to the Lieutenant-Governor.

.   .   .

35. The question of the sanitation of Native towns is of sufficient importance to merit a word here. Beyond doubt the insanitary condition of Native towns and villages increases the prevalence of disease, and is a primary cause of the very high rate of infant mortality. In districts in which the Native Administration is effective, Residents will encourage Native Rulers to devote attention to this matter. Simple rules (which require the approval of the Governor-General) may be made under Section 2 of Ordinance 4 of 1918 (amending the Native Authority Ordinance), enforcing elementary sanitary regulations, and imposing penalties for non-observance in Native cities and towns.

In Districts where a more "direct rule" has at present to be exercised, it may still be feasible to require the Native Authority to pass some very simple rules; and in the last resort a few of the obligations imposed under the Public Health Ordinance may, under the conditions therein prescribed, be applied and enforced by the Provincial Court, but it is greatly preferable that such matters should be dealt with by the Native Authority and the Native Courts. The Native Executive Authority should not only see that such Regulations as may have been enacted are carried out, but, apart from definite Regulations enforceable by the authority of the Courts, should enforce general cleanliness, and should be encouraged to provide *salgas* and incinerators, to construct camping places and markets outside the villages, and to see to their sanitation. Village Headmen may be warned that the tenure of their position will depend on their ability to enforce reasonable reform in these matters.

.   .   .

37. Wherever Europeans reside care will be taken to give effect to the Government policy of Segregation (*see* Memo. II, § 24), more especially in those places which may possibly in the future expand into Townships. It is not invariably obligatory for Missionaries and traders in remote places to live at a distance from Native villages, if there is no possibility of such expansion, and if they have strong reasons for selecting the particular site, but whenever it is feasible to maintain the principle it should be adhered to, both in the interest of their own health, and in the interest of the vital statistics of the country. Residents should not recommend the grant of a lease or right of occupancy outside a Township if there is one in the vicinity, except in special circumstances (mining camps, etc.), and in no case will a right of occupancy for a European be commended inside a Native city. Residents in conjunction with the Local Authority of a Township will take steps to exclude from residence in the Native reservation all Natives who are ordinarily under the jurisdiction of the local Native Courts. Such persons should live in a Native town adjacent to the Township and under Native Authority.

· · ·

41. Permits for arms of precision, and a specified quantity of ammunition, may be issued to non-natives, as prescribed by the Arms Ordinance, by a Resident, and with the consent of the Lieutenant-Governor to individual Natives, especially to those in Government employ, the nature of whose duties demands a means of self-defence in case of emergency. Permits will not be issued to a group of Natives in a community without the authority of the Governor-General. All firearms not held under permit will be seized, except flint-locks with unrifled barrels. Though I do not consider a "Dane gun" to be so formidable a weapon as a bow and arrow in the hands of tribes who are expert bowmen, the case is different among communities in the Southern Provinces, where the bow and arrow has fallen out of use. There is no doubt that the possession of arms gives great confidence and prompts lawless characters to crimes which they would not otherwise attempt, and occasionally leads to defiance of Government. This is especially the case since an improved type of gun and better powder has been imported. The matter is being dealt with. The number of guns in the Egba, Yoruba, and Ijebu countries is enormous, and recent events have shown that it is desirable that their possession should be controlled and limited. For this purpose any district may be proclaimed under the Arms Ordinance. Dane guns are also being converted into cap guns by local blacksmiths. Since these are illegal they will be seized at sight, and every effort will be made to detect any person importing caps.

42. Prisoners may be employed in sanitary work about a Township and in assisting the Local Authority or Public Works Department in any works

which are in progress. In the Southern Provinces where food is very expensive, a prison farm will be attached to each convict and provincial prison. In the Northern Provinces, wherever possible, prisoners should be employed in permanent works, such as brick and tile making. Light labour men may be usefully employed in making rope, twine and gunny-bags.

.   .   .

44. The duties of Political Officers in regard to mineral development are for the most part limited to seeing that the Natives are fairly treated. It devolves upon the Resident to assess compensation due for disturbance and for loss of crops, &c., on land, over which surface rights have been acquired; to see that the prospector pays full compensation for any damage he may do; to assess on behalf of Government the small surface rent charged to holders of mining leases and rights according to its value as arable, grazing, or barren land; and, finally, to see that there is no encroachment on the rights of the villagers, that no land is occupied except under lease or certificate of occupancy, and that no trees are cut down except as permitted by Law. Since the tin and gold industries are both so far entirely alluvial, surface rights are of course necessary. A Resident is required to state whether there is any political objection to the grant of each application in whole or part. Should he consider that there is an objection, he will give his reasons fully, in order that the Governor may decide whether the minerals (which are the sole property of Government) should be worked or not. He may recommend the exclusion of the site occupied by a village, and temporarily at any rate of such land as they require for their crops, but if the ground is highly mineralised it will usually be advisable to award an ample compensation for removal. The most probable objection would arise if the lives of the lessee and his agents would be endangered. This objection should seldom occur, since all such districts should have been already "closed to prospecting," and the application would not therefore be possible. Any person prospecting in such an area or entering one declared to be "unsettled," would of course be prosecuted. Political Officers will also keep a careful eye on the welfare of Natives in the labour camps, and take up any complaints of irregular punishment or underpayment. They will see that the camps are properly laid out in accordance with the rules prescribed.

The Minerals Ordinance and Regulations are now so clear (and I believe satisfactory) that they call for no comment. The bulk of the work falls on the Secretariat and Mines Departments. Political Officers will, of course, assist the mining industry in every way in their power, more especially in procuring labour on fair terms, but no compulsion whatever will be exercised. All escorts for specie or other special protection will be charged for at full cost. In exercising the right to exclude prospectors from certain districts, Government does not profess to act primarily in the interest of the prospector, whose risks are his own affair, but in its own interests, with the object of avoiding a serious political situation, or the necessity for reprisals in case of insult or injury to a prospector.

If a Political Officer discovers minerals it is his duty to disclose the fact to Government. Prospectors should never be allowed to accompany a District Officer on tour. The Niger Company is entitled to half of all royalties and taxes imposed on the mining industry as such, in the area lying between the Niger, and a line drawn from Yola to Zinder. The fact must not be lost sight of, that except in this area they can claim no share.

45. It may not be out of place to add a short paragraph here for the benefit of new arrivals, on the avoidance of common diseases.

Malaria.—Take 5 grains of quinine daily, preferably in liquid form. Tabloids sometimes become so hard that they pass through the system without dissolving. If unavoidably exposed to mosquitos, take an extra dose on alternate days for 10 days. See that your mosquito net is well tucked in, and that your feet or hands do not lie against it while asleep.

Sun.—Wear a small hat when under an insufficient roof, or in a verandah. On no account go into the sun without a hat even for a moment.

Dysentry and Enteric.—Boil all drinking water, and milk and butter bought from Natives. Eat sparingly of salads and uncooked vegetables. Personally see to the cleanliness of all cooking utensils by frequent inspection.

SOURCE: *Political Memoranda 1913–18* (London: Frank Cass, 1970), 9–16, 18–20, 22–29, 31, 33–39.

Excerpts from *The Dual Mandate*
in British Tropical Africa
FREDERICK LUGARD

INTRODUCTION

Contrast between Africa and the rest of the world—Its isolation—Causes which led to the penetration of Africa—Moral progress—The respective tasks of the eighteenth, nineteenth, and twentieth centuries—Object of this book.

Africa has been justly termed "the Dark Continent," for the secrets of its peoples, its lakes, and mountains and rivers, have remained undisclosed not merely to modern civilisation, but through all the ages of which history has any record. There are many regions in Asia—in Persia, Assyria, Arabia, and Western China—in which modern explorers have claimed to have made discoveries. But all these countries were the seats of ancient civilisations, some of them highly developed, and exploration was concerned rather with piecing together chapters of past history than in discovery. The penetration into the interior of Africa, on the other hand, may as truly be described as discovery as that of America by Columbus.

The Muscat Arabs from Zanzibar were pioneers in the exploration of the region of the great lakes and the Congo basin, while in Western Africa the zeal of the Moslem Arabs and Berbers led them across the Sahara. Here indeed a great empire, famed for its culture, boasted a fragmentary history dating back to the eighth or ninth centuries; but in this or any other part of tropical Africa, from the frontiers of Egypt to the Zambesi, there are no traces of antecedent civilisations—no monuments or buried cities—like those of the prehistoric civilisations of Asia and South America.

That portion of the north of Africa which is included in the temperate zone, and contiguous to Europe, had been the home of the most ancient civilisations, first of Egypt, dating back to perhaps 4000 B.C., and later of the Phœnicians. But Egypt had penetrated no further south than Ethiopia, while the Carthagenians (though they had trade routes with the interior)[1] for the most part confined their efforts to the establishment of colonies on the coast. We read of one or two expeditions to the interior both by Pharaoh Necho and by Carthage, but they were barren of results. So were the expeditions of the Greeks, who founded their first colony at Cyrene 1000 years before Christ, and of the Romans, who later incorporated all North Africa as a Roman province.

Accurate knowledge even of the coast-line, and the establishment of European settlements upon it, dates only from the fifteenth century—synchronising with the discovery of America. The outlet for commerce and the new fields which this great discovery—together with the development of India—afforded to adventurous pioneers, diverted for some three centuries or more the tide of exploration which might otherwise have set towards Africa. The voyages of Da Gama and others in the fifteenth century had, however, already produced one very notable result. Hitherto the gateway which led to the great unknown interior had been situated in the north. Access to Timbuktu was by caravan across the desert from Tripoli or Algeria. The sea route discovered by Da Gama disclosed a back door, which was henceforth to become the princi-

---

1. Heeren's Historical Researches—vol. African Nations, p. 17 *et seq.*

pal entrance. As modern railways have rendered the desert route obsolete, they may in the not distant future restore it.

Thus the interior of Africa remained unknown. It appeared on the map as a great blank space, with a fringe of names all round its coasts, till Livingstone, Barth, and others began its systematic exploration about seventy years ago. For thirty or forty years tropical Africa remained a field for adventurous and sensational exploration, and it was not till 1885—when the Berlin Act was passed—that the modern development of Africa began to assume definite and recognised form.

What, then, were the causes which led to the opening up of Africa, a continent which all the preceding ages of the world's history had left untouched, though it lay close to the homes of the early civilisations in Europe and Asia—a continent containing a fifth of the earth's land surface and a ninth of its population?

The dominant cause of Africa's isolation was, no doubt, that the world had not hitherto had urgent need of its products, and that its warlike tribes were able to repel unwelcome visitors armed but little better than themselves. Even when the economic pressure caused by the rapidly increasing population of Europe began to exert its inevitable influence, in driving men to seek for new markets and fresh supplies of food and raw material, the discovery of America, and the new fields for commerce in India, more than met the demand for several centuries. It was not until the great industrial revival which followed the Civil War in America that America began herself to compete in the world's markets, and to utilise her own resources primarily for the needs of her own industry.[2]

One of the more immediate causes which led to the opening up of Africa

2. It is interesting to note that it was the conquest of the ocean which directly led to the expansion of the peoples of Europe, and relieved them from the age-long pressure of Asia on their frontiers. In 1492 Columbus discovered America, and in 1494 Vasco da Gama rounded the Cape and opened up the way to India. At that time (A.D. 1500) the population of Europe was about 70 millions. At the end of the next three centuries (A.D. 1800) it is said to have been 150 millions, an additional 10 millions having migrated overseas. But at the close of the succeeding century—which witnessed the industrial revolution, and the advent of steam navigation—it is estimated (A.D. 1900) at nearly 450 millions, with 100 million additional emigrants. Thus while the population of Europe only doubled itself in the three centuries prior to 1800, it more than trebled itself in the following century. The figures for Great Britain are: population in 1600 (England only), 4,800,000; in 1800 about 16,000,000; and in 1900 about 42,000,000.—(Stoddard, 'The Rising Tide of Colour,' p. 155, Whittaker, &c.)

An additional reason for the demand for increased supplies of food and raw materials at the close of the nineteenth century was to be found in the immensely improved standard of living of the people.

was the Franco-Prussian War of 1870. Crippled by her defeat, France proclaimed by the mouth of her principal statesmen and writers[3]—just as she is doing to-day—that it was to Greater France beyond the seas, and especially in West and North-West Africa, that she must look for rehabilitation. At that time, moreover, colonisation in tropical Africa was believed to be both possible and desirable. Germany, on the other hand, found herself with a great and increasing industrial population in urgent need of raw materials and additional food supplies. Not content with the wholly unrestricted market offered by British colonies, where Germans were welcomed, and exercised every privilege equally with their British rivals, she not unnaturally desired to have colonies of her own. We have since learnt that she had other motives—the creation of naval bases and world-wide wireless stations, and the raising of negro armies for world conquest.

Humanitarian motives—the desire to suppress the slave-trade, &c.—also played their part, but it was the rivalry of these two great Continental Powers which was the immediate cause of the modern "partition of Africa." By the Berlin Act of 1885, and the Brussels Act of 1892, Europe and America endeavoured in some feeble way to safeguard the interests of the natives—but these Acts were practically ineffective for their purpose. The one thing they did succeed in effecting was the restriction of the import of arms of precision to the natives, theoretically as a check to the slave-trade, but with the practical result of rendering the African more powerless than ever to resist conquest by Europeans.

England was unwillingly forced into the competition. On the one hand her colonies on the West Coast demanded some effort, to save them from being cut off from all access to the interior by hostile foreign tariffs, and becoming mere coast enclaves. Her vital interests in India, on the other hand, compelled her to protect her route thither—Egypt, the Suez Canal, and the eastern shores of Africa. The essential interests of Egypt, for which she had become responsible, demanded the protection of the Nile sources.

For a decade and more the "scramble" went on till it was brought to a close by the conventions with France of 1898 and 1899, and the Fashoda incident of the latter year. Germany had secured large colonies in East, West, and South Africa, at the expense of prior British claims, but we recognised her right to a place in the tropical sun. France added largely to her territory in West and Central Africa, and annexed the great island of Madagascar.

It was towards the close of this period of rivalry that Mr Joseph Chamberlain became Colonial Secretary, and for the first time in our history a

3. See M. Leroy Beaulieu, 'Histoire de la Colonisation chez les peuples modernes.'

policy of progress and development found favour at Whitehall. The colonies were encouraged to raise loans, supported if necessary by Imperial credit, for the development of their resources, and had it not been for the South African War this policy would, I know, have been carried much further. During the twelve years which elapsed between the South African and the recent world war, great progress was made in the construction of roads and railways, and the opening up of waterways—for the material development of Africa may be summed up in the one word "transport."

Though we may perhaps at times entertain a lingering regret for the passing of the picturesque methods of the past, we must admit that the locomotive is a substantial improvement on head-borne transport, and the motor-van is more efficient than the camel. The advent of Europeans has brought the mind and methods of Europe to bear on the native of Africa for good or for ill, and the seclusion of ages must perforce give place to modern ideas. Material development is accompanied by education and progress.

The condition of Africa when Europe entered the continent, which Isaiah so graphically describes as "the land shadowing with wings, which is beyond the rivers of Ethiopia . . . a people scattered and peeled," was deplorable. On the East Coast, Arabs and half-castes were engaged in a lucrative trade in slaves for export to Arabia and to Turkish possessions. In the west, powerful armies of Moslem States depopulated large districts in their raids for slaves. Europe had failed to realise that throughout the length and breadth of Africa inter-tribal war was an ever-present condition of native life, and that extermination and slavery were practised by African tribes upon each other.

It was the task of civilisation to put an end to slavery, to establish Courts of Law, to inculcate in the natives a sense of individual responsibility, of liberty, and of justice, and to teach their rulers how to apply these principles; above all, to see to it that the system of education should be such as to produce happiness and progress. I am confident that the verdict of history will award high praise to the efforts and the achievements of Great Britain in the discharge of these great responsibilities. For, in my belief, under no other rule—be it of his own uncontrolled potentates, or of aliens—does the African enjoy such a measure of freedom and of impartial justice, or a more sympathetic treatment, and for that reason I am a profound believer in the British Empire and its mission in Africa.

In brief, we may say that the eighteenth century was chiefly remarkable for the acquisition of large and almost uninhabited portions of the earth, situated in the temperate zone. The nineteenth century saw the development of these great colonies into nations enjoying self-government. Its closing decade witnessed the dawning recognition of the vital importance of the tropics to civilisation, and the "discovery" and acquisition of large non-colonisable areas in tropical Africa—no longer regarded as picturesque appanages of Empire, but as essential to the very existence of the races of the temperate climes.

To the twentieth century belongs the heritage of the tropics and the task of their development. Two decades have already passed and wonderful progress has been made, not only in the improvement of the quality and quantity of the material output, by scientific research, by organised method, and by the expenditure of capital, but also in methods of administration for the welfare of the subject races, education, free labour, taxation, and other similar problems.

A comparative study of the methods by which these various problems—administrative and economic—have been approached in the several tropical dependencies of the Empire and by other nations would form a fascinating study and a useful guide,[4] but the racial differences between Asiatics and Africans are so great (as my own experience in India and China have taught me) that methods applicable to the one may be quite misplaced with the other. The tropical dependencies in Africa, on the other hand, offer almost identical problems.

"No serious attempt," says Mr Kidd, "has so far been made to set forth the principles which should underlie our future relations with the tropical regions of the world. . . . Nowhere is there to be found any whole-hearted or consistent attempt either to justify the political relations which already exist, or to define the principles of any relations which ought to exist in the future."[5] The following pages have been written in the hope that an experience, with short intervals, of forty years in the tropics, and of over thirty in responsible positions in Africa, may enable me to make some useful contribution to the study of these subjects. During the first half of these thirty years it was my privilege to assist in some degree in bringing under British control portions of Nyasaland, East Africa, Uganda, and Nigeria, where the difficulties of the pioneer had to be encountered. During the second fifteen it has been my good fortune to be entrusted with the development of Nigeria, and with the aid of capable colleagues to lay the foundations of a system of administration upon which others may build. I shall endeavour to describe the difficulties encountered, the methods used, and the results obtained in administration—which forms the most important part of our task in Africa.

4. The great value of a bureau to collate and publish the results of administrative experience in various tropical countries was urged by Sir T. Morison in a letter to the 'Times' of 21st July 1920.
5. Compare the 'Times' (1st Oct. 1901). "No attempt has been made to ascertain what are the special conditions of the administrative problem in Equatorial Africa, no attempt has been made to formulate the general lines of a well-considered policy in dealing with that problem, and no machinery has been devised for maintaining continuity of administration."

It is, moreover, also of great moment that the British democracy, faced with problems which portend great changes in our social organisation, should understand the relation which our overseas dependencies bear to the economic well-being of this country—how vital to our industrial life are the products of the tropics, and its markets for our manufactures. It is indeed essential that democracy should take an intelligent and well-informed interest in questions which affect the Empire of which it is the inheritor and trustee.

SOME GENERAL PRINCIPLES OF ADMINISTRATION

Nature and functions of the administration—Constitution of a Crown colony—Two principles of administration: (a) Decentralisation—Decentralisation and amalgamation—Reasons for amalgamation—The case of Nigeria—Decentralisation in departments—Method of amalgamation in Nigeria—The principles involved—(b) Continuity: of personnel—Of records—Of Governor's instructions and policy—Continuity in office of Governor—Scheme of continuous responsibility—Anticipated advantages—The former system—Objections by permanent officials—Object and limitations—The "Man on the Spot"—The scheme abandoned—Suggestions for promoting continuity and co-operation—Tenure of office of Governor.

The British Empire, as General Smuts has well said, has only one mission— for liberty and self-development on no standardised lines, so that all may feel that their interests and religion are safe under the British flag. Such liberty and self-development can be best secured to the native population by leaving them free to manage their own affairs through their own rulers, proportionately to their degree of advancement, under the guidance of the British staff, and subject to the laws and policy of the administration.

But apart from the administration of native affairs the local Government has to preserve law and order, to develop the trade and communications of the country, and to protect the interests of the merchants and others who are engaged in the development of its commercial and mineral resources. What, then, are the functions of the British staff, and how can the machinery of Government be most efficiently constituted for the discharge of its duties in those countries in Africa which fall under British control?

The staff must necessarily be limited in numbers, for if the best class of men are to be attracted to a service which often involves separation from family and a strain on health, they must be offered adequate salaries and inducements in the way of leave, housing, medical aid—or their equivalents in money—for their maintenance in health and comfort while serving abroad, and this forms a heavy charge on the revenues. Policy and economy alike demand restriction in numbers, but the best that England can supply.

Obviously a consideration of the machinery of British administration in the tropics involves a review of its relations to the home Government on the one hand, and of its local constitution and functions on the other. I will take the latter first.

The Government is constituted on the analogy of the British Government in England. The Governor represents the King, but combines the functions of the Prime Minister as head of the Executive. The Councils bear a certain resemblance to the Home Cabinet and Parliament, while the detailed work of the administration is carried out by a staff which may be roughly divided into the administrative, the judicial, and the departmental branches.

The administrative branch is concerned with the supervision of the native administration and the general direction of policy; with education, and the collection and control of direct taxes, which involve assessment and close relations with the native population; with legislation and the administration of justice in courts other than the Supreme Court; and with the direct government and welfare of the non-native section of the population.

The departmental staff is charged with duties in connection with transport, communications, and buildings (railways, marine, and public works); with the development of natural resources (mines, collieries, forestry, agriculture, and geology); with the auxiliary services of government (medical, secretarial, accounting, posts and telegraphs, surveys, &c.); and the collection of customs duties.

The task of the administrative branch is to foster that sympathy, mutual understanding, and co-operation between the Government and the people, without which, as Sir O. Ilbert has observed, no Government is really stable and efficient. Its aim is to promote progress in civilisation and justice, and to create conditions under which individual enterprise may most advantageously develop the natural resources of the country. The task of the departments, on the other hand, is to maintain the Government machine in a state of efficiency, and to afford direct assistance in material development. Their motto is efficiency and economy. The two branches work together, and their duties overlap and are interdependent in every sphere. The efficient discharge of those duties in combination constitutes the white man's title to control.

There are in my estimation two vital principles which characterise the growth of a wise administration—they are Decentralisation and Continuity. Though, as Lord Morley said of India, "perfectly efficient administration has an inevitable tendency to over-centralisation," it is a tendency to be combated. It has indeed been said that the whole art of administration consists in judicious and progressive delegation, and there is much truth in the dictum, provided that delegation of duties be accompanied by public responsibility. This is not applicable to the head of the Government alone or in particular, but to every single officer, from the Governor to the foreman of a gang of daily labourers. The man who is charged with the accomplishment of any task, and has the ability and discrimination to select the most capable of those who are subordinate to him, and to trust them with ever-increasing responsibility, up to the limits of their capacity, will be rewarded not only with confidence and loyalty, but he will get more work done, and better done, than the man who tries to keep too much in his own hands, and is slow to recognise merit, originality, and efficiency in others. His sphere of work becomes a training school, and he is able to recommend his best men for promotion to greater responsibility than he himself can confer. The Governor who delegates to his Lieut.-Governors, Residents, and heads of departments the widest powers compatible with his own direct responsibility to the Crown, will witness the most rapid progress.

But delegation to an individual who is not equal to the responsibility obviously means disaster, and it is therefore often advisable to entrust extended powers to the individual rather than to incorporate them as a part of the duties of his office. His successor, who must obviously have less experience, and may or may not be his equal in ability, will not then automatically enjoy the same latitude, until he has proved his capacity in the higher office.

Increased latitude to the individual is not, however, inconsistent with increased delegation of duties to the office, more especially in the administrative branch of the service, where posts must of necessity grow in importance as the country as a whole develops. It is a frequent ground of criticism that the Colonial Office has been somewhat backward in appreciating the value of this principle in these young and rapidly-growing dependencies.

The Governor, by delegating work to others, would seem to lighten his own task, but in point of fact the more he delegates the more he will find to do in co-ordinating the progress of the whole. Moreover, in order to have a right appreciation of the abilities, and of the personal character of each principal administrative officer and head of department, he must be in close personal touch with them, and make absolutely clear to them the essential features of his policy. He must be the directing brain, and leave the execution to others. The task he undertakes is no light one, and if he should be called on to create an administration *ab ovo*, or to lay down new lines of policy in an old one, the work may become more than the time at his command suffices for, and the personal touch with his officers may temporarily suffer from the insistent demands of his office, until he is able gradually to delegate to those in whom he has confidence.

In applying the principle of decentralisation it is very essential to maintain a strong central co-ordinating authority, in order to avoid centrifugal tendencies, and the multiplication of units without a sufficiently cohesive bond. I shall revert to this point when discussing the grouping of colonies.

There are in British tropical Africa several blocks of territory under separate administrations which are contiguous to each other, and the question arises whether it would be more advantageous that they should be placed under a single directing authority, with a single fiscal system, a common railway policy, and identical laws—more especially if one controls the coast area, and the other has no access to the seaboard. Such a process would, of course, be in no way opposed to decentralisation of the machinery of Government. Amalgamation (that is, unification) and federation are both natural processes of evolution, as we have seen in the United States, in Canada, Australia, and South Africa, and more recently in Nigeria. The French have gone even further, and placed colonies widely separated from each other under a central authority. I will deal here only with the question of amalgamation. The federation or grouping of colonies raises a separate issue, which I shall discuss later.

Where one administration comprises the coast area, and collects the customs dues (which have hitherto formed the bulk of the revenue in most African dependencies), while another forms its hinterland, the latter must either establish an inland fiscal frontier, or share the duties collected by its neighbour. The former expedient adds to the cost of all imports—already enhanced by the inherent expense of long and costly transport services (involving a slower turnover of commercial capital),—and is obviously opposed to the progress of trade and development, apart from the heavy cost of the administration of an effective customs and preventive service. The latter course is rendered most difficult by the impossibility of arriving at a division of the customs revenue which will not be resented by both. Imported goods which have paid duty on the coast pass into the hands of native middlemen, and their ultimate destination, by a thousand byways of trade, may be in the hinterland; or the exportable produce for which they are bartered may originate in the interior territory. It is clearly impossible to discriminate with any accuracy in such circumstances between the value and volume of the trade properly belonging to each administration. The Liverpool Chamber of Commerce in July 1893 made strong representations in this sense to Lord Rosebery regarding Nigeria. The French Governor-General, M. Roume, referring to the fiscal reorganisation of the French West African colonies, observed that "it was not right to continue to allow the coast colonies alone to benefit by trade, a large proportion of which was destined for the interior," and Senegal had to make a subsidy to its hinterland.

A hinterland Government has not only to bear heavy transport charges from and to the coast on its imports and exports, but upon it falls the burden of frontier defence. In order to balance its budget it will probably have to depend on a grant from Parliament, paid by the British taxpayer, while the coast Government may have a surplus revenue. A grant-in-aid involves control by the Imperial Treasury—a department which knows nothing of local needs, and is solely concerned in reducing the charges—and the dual control of two departments of State is inimical to all progress.

With an increase of material prosperity, new and disturbing factors arise. An interior administration depends largely for its development on railways and improved waterways, for which capital is required—but loans are not permissible while as yet a country depends on an Imperial grant. Even if sufficient revenue for its needs were raised by taxation, payment of taxes must be largely made in kind, which can only be realised by conveying it to the coast. Some small part may be sold to merchants for cash, but they will not establish themselves, unless means of transport are available.

The organisation and control of railways, waterways, and telegraph lines traversing both territories must of necessity be in the hands of a central administration. It would obviously be inadvisable for one administration to treat the other as foreign territory, and to conclude railway and postal conventions with it in order to exercise separate control over its own section. Increased cost of administration, obstacles to trade, unnecessary accounting, and the certainty of friction must result. A comprehensive and far-sighted railway policy, to which the efforts of both would be consistently devoted, becomes impossible.[6]

When legislation pursues two different channels, differences in policy in regard to native administration, the courts of law, and other vital matters are bound to arise, and it is obviously inadvisable that contiguous communities should be under different systems of taxation, and different penal codes. The evil is accentuated by the fact that the frontiers between the two—often fixed

6. The railway in East Africa does not actually traverse Uganda, and the difficulty is therefore not so acute, but it depends largely for its earnings on the carriage of merchandise to and from Uganda. Hitherto Kenya has appropriated its revenue. A railway Board has now been formed on which both countries are represented. The control of the Board (unless amalgamation of the two Governments is carried out) must presumably be exercised from Downing Street,—a retrograde step opposed to decentralisation, and tending towards that absentee control from London, which the Indian Railway Committee has so unanimously condemned.—See Cmd. 1512/1921.

at a time when their geography and ethnology were almost unknown, by lines of latitude and longitude instead of by distinctive natural features—must inevitably intersect tribal boundaries. It goes without saying that a single co-ordinated effort will achieve more for the permanent good of a country than the separate efforts of two administrators, not focussed on a common objective.

Such conditions were applicable to Nigeria, and are still probably applicable to Kenya and Uganda. They were fully described by me in a Memo. dated May 1905; but the amalgamation of Nigeria, though supported by the Governors of the coastal administrations, was not decided upon till 1912, when Mr Harcourt charged me with the task. To administer such enormous territories as East Africa or Nigeria as a single unit, decentralisation is more than ever necessary, but how it can best be effected is not an easy problem.

In the administrative branch the chain of responsibility from the most junior grade to the head of the Government—the District Officer, the Resident of a Province, the Lieut.-Governor—is easily forged, but the departments offer a more difficult problem. If on the one hand each department is under a single head, responsible to the Governor, the tendency is towards a highly-centralised Government, in which the Lieut.-Governors are deprived of initiative and financial control, and there is a danger lest their instructions to the local representative of the department may conflict with those of the departmental head. The Lieut.-Governor for all practical purposes ceases to frame his own budget. On the other hand, the duplication of departmental heads in each area under a Lieut.-Governor involves extra cost, and some loss of technical efficiency and co-ordination. There are, moreover, a number of departments whose functions are indivisible, and they must remain under the direct control of the central authority—such as the judicial, railway, military, &c.

The scheme of amalgamation adopted in Nigeria was designed to involve as little dislocation of existing conditions as possible, while providing for the introduction later of such further changes as were either foreseen, but not immediately necessary, or might be suggested by future experience. They would then be rather in the nature of natural evolution than of reversal. There are twenty-one provinces in Nigeria—exclusive of the Mandate territory in the Cameruns and of the colony proper—each with an average area of 16,000 square miles, and a population of 800,000. To invest each Resident of a province with large powers of autonomy, or at the least to create half a dozen Lieut.-Governorships, would not be a measure of decentralisation but the reverse, for the work arising from each of the separate units—as well as from all the departments—would be centralised in the hands of the Governor. The truest principle of decentralisation was to make the area placed under a Lieut.-Governor so large and important that the officer appointed to its charge could relieve the Governor of all the routine functions of administration, leaving him to direct the general policy, initiate legislation, and control those departments which must necessarily be centralised.

The old northern and southern divisions of Nigeria were retained intact (the colony being a separate entity), and placed under Lieut.-Governors, pending the unification of the laws, the judicial system, and the general policy. It was thought that when the fundamental divergencies in these should have been removed, it would be possible (should the experience gained point in that direction) to create a third Lieut.-Governorship, or to make other changes. The task of amalgamating and re-enacting the statute-books of the two administrations was one which would necessarily take some time.

The difficulty regarding the decentralisation of the departments to which I have alluded was dealt with in the following way. A central secretariat (which would naturally later become the principal secretariat of Nigeria) was set up, while Lieut.-Governors retained their own secretariats. The departments which I have described as necessarily indivisible remained under the Governor and the Central Secretary. The other large departments, such as the Medical and Public Works, were retained in each unit as fully organised entities, and their receipts and expenditure were included in the Lieut.-Governor's budget, but they were placed under the general supervision of an officer senior to both the departmental heads, who, without interfering with the Lieut.-Governor's control, preserved uniformity and technical efficiency, and acted as adviser to Government.[7] Minor departments, such as Police, Education, &c., whose spheres of action do not overlap, remained separate in each unit. Departmental promotion was in all cases to be determined by a common roster.

In fiscal matters the whole of Nigeria became a single entity. All revenue was paid into the common Treasury (a "central" department), and each Lieut.-Governor and the heads of the central departments framed and submitted his own estimates to the Governor, who personally examined them with him, and assigned such funds for new works or for departmental expansion as the requirements of the country as a whole permitted. I shall describe more fully the functions and powers of the Lieut.-Governor and other officers in the next chapter. It suffices to note here that the methods by which it was sought to secure effective decentralisation were (a) by the delegation of execu-

---

7. In proportion as the head of a department ceases to exercise executive functions, and acts as adviser to Government, he approaches to the position of a "Minister" in a self-governing colony, and the germ of a future development is introduced.

tive, financial, and administrative powers to Lieut.-Governors who would exercise responsibility and initiative, and not be merely Deputy-Governors with no executive powers of their own;[8] (b) the administration of native affairs, being regarded not merely as a department, but as the most important duty of the administration, the Resident of a Province was as far as possible relieved of all other administrative duties, in order that he might devote his undivided time and thought to this work; (c) the authority of its head over a department was unfettered, and subject only to the control of the Governor or Lieut.-Governor, as the case might be. This scheme of amalgamation was adopted in the particular circumstances then existing in Nigeria; and its general principles would of course require adaptation if applied elsewhere, and will require modification to the changing conditions of the development of Nigeria itself.[9]

To what extent the principles of decentralisation may be applied as between the Colonial Office and the local Government is a question I shall discuss in chapters viii. and ix.

The second of the two principles which I have described as vital in African administration is Continuity, and this, like Decentralisation, is applicable to every department and to every officer, however junior, but above all to those officers who represent the Government in its relations with the native population. The annually recurrent absence on leave, which withdraws each officer in West Africa from his post for about a third of his time, the occasional invalidings and deaths, and the constant changes rendered unavoidable of late years by a depleted and inadequate staff, have made it extremely difficult to preserve in that part of Africa any continuity whatever. The African is slow to give his confidence. He is suspicious and reticent with a newcomer, eager to resuscitate old land disputes—perhaps of half a century's standing—in the hope that the new officer in his ignorance may reverse the decision of his predecessor. The time of an officer is wasted in picking up the tangled threads and informing himself of the conditions of his new post. By the time he has acquired the necessary knowledge, and has learnt the character of the people he has to deal with, and won their confidence, his leave becomes due, and if on his return he is posted elsewhere, not only is progress arrested but retrogression may result.

It is also essential that each officer should be at pains to keep full and accurate records of all important matters, especially of any conversation with

8. Decentralisation is the key-note of the Sudan administration, where Governors of provinces have the widest powers.

9. A full report was submitted to the Secretary of State, and published as Cd. 468 of 1920.

native chiefs, in which any pledge or promise, implied or explicit, has been made. It is not enough that official correspondence should be filed—a summary of each subject should be made and decisions recorded and brought up to date, so that a newcomer may be able rapidly to put himself *au courant.* The higher the post occupied by an officer, the more important does the principle become.

It is especially important that the decisions of the Governor should be fully recorded in writing, and not merely by an initial of acquiescence or a verbal order. This involves heavy office work, but it is work which cannot be neglected if misunderstandings are to be avoided and continuity preserved. The very detailed instructions regarding the duties of each newly-created department which were issued when the administration of Northern Nigeria was first inaugurated, served a very useful purpose in maintaining continuity of policy, till superseded on amalgamation by briefer general orders.

In the sphere of administration there are obviously many subjects—education, taxation, slavery and labour, native courts, land tenure, &c.—in which uniformity and continuity of policy is impossible in so large a country, unless explicit instructions are issued for guidance. By a perusal of the periodical reports of Residents, the Governor could inform himself of the difficulties which presented themselves in the varying circumstances of each province, and think out the best way in which they could be met, and could note where misunderstandings or mistakes had been made. By these means a series of Memoranda were compiled, and constantly revised as new problems came to light, and as progress rendered the earlier instructions obsolete. They formed the reference book and authority of the Resident and his staff.

In a country so vast, which included communities in all stages of development, and differing from each other profoundly in their customs and traditions, it was the declared policy of Government that each should develop on its own lines; but this in no way lessens the need for uniformity in the broad principles of policy, or in their application where the conditions are similar. It was the aim of these Memoranda to preserve this continuity and uniformity of principle and policy. Newcomers, by studying them, could make themselves fully acquainted with the nature of the task before them, the problems to be dealt with, and the attitude of Government towards each of those problems. Senior officers were spared the labour and loss of time involved in frequent iteration, when noting any misunderstanding or ignorance in the reports of their subordinates, by simply inviting attention to the pertinent paragraph of the Memorandum. Subversive policies cannot gradually creep in, and any change must be deliberately inaugurated by the formal cancellation of the particular instructions in the Memoranda. Though the preparation of the Memoranda involves considerable labour, they result in an eventual saving in the time both of the Governor and of senior officers. They are the embodiment of the experience of the most capable officers, co-ordinated by the head of the Government, who has access to the reports and is familiar with circumstances of all. When any point of particular difficulty presents itself where opinions are in conflict, and the information insufficient to form a clear judgment on the principles involved, the governor may perhaps cause a précis to be circulated before a final decision is reached. The little volume of 'Political Memoranda' has been of much use in Nigeria. It deals solely with the actual problems of practical administration.

The Statute Book, the Regulations and Orders made under the laws, the General Orders, and the Governor's Memoranda on administrative subjects, contain between them in a readily accessible and compact form the whole structural policy of the Administration and constitute the "Laws and Usages" of the country. Had such a quartette existed, revised decennially since the earliest origin of our Indian Empire and of our Crown colonies, they would have formed valuable material for the history of the Empire. In Africa we are laying foundations. The superstructure may vary in its details, some of which may perhaps be ill-designed, but the stability of the edifice is unaffected. You may pull down and re-erect cupolas, but you cannot alter the design of the foundations without first destroying all that has been erected upon them.

Important as it is that the British Staff, so long as they are efficient, should remain in the same posts without more interruption than is necessary for the preservation of health, and the prevention of ennui or "staleness," it is of still greater importance that continuity should be maintained in the case of an efficient Governor, who directs the policy of the whole country.[10] For in a rapidly-progressing country policy and legislation are developed from day to day, Regulations and Orders in Council for the carrying out of laws are matters of daily consideration; and in spite of every effort to decentralise and to delegate powers, the Governor has to deal daily with large numbers of Minute papers, each calling for a considered judgment on some problem of sufficient importance for reference to him.

It is above all important that he should be present towards the close of the year, when the estimates are framed in which the programme of material

---

10. The 'Times,' discussing the "Administrative problem in Equatorial Africa," in a well-informed article some years ago (1st Oct. 1901), pointed out that the entire absence of continuity in the administration of Uganda had produced results which were alike "deplorable and discreditable." The bewildering rapidity of the changes in Commissioners, each of whom experimented with the unfortunate country by introducing new and subversive policies, made it impossible to fix any responsibility.

progress—railways, roads, buildings—and increases of staff, &c., are settled. These months, and the first quarter of the new year, are far more important from an administrative and business point of view than the remaining months, which form the rainy season in the tropics north of the Equator. The accounts are completed; annual reports from all departments begin to come in, and must be reviewed; and the yearly report to the Secretary of State, for which they form material, must be compiled. Communications are no longer impeded by washouts, or roads too soft from rain to carry vehicles, and the season permits of travel and inspection. In order always to be present at this season, a Governor in West Africa must take his leave either after eight or after about seventeen months in the country, and so make his absence coincide with the rainy season. By which arrangement will continuity be best preserved?

The seventeen months' tour of service involves a heavy strain. The Governor's absence on completing it would extend over a period of about 6½ months, including voyages, thus seriously encroaching on the working season. During so long a period many matters of first-class importance must be decided without awaiting his return, new legislation must be put through, and even questions of policy may be affected. By so long an absence continuity is seriously sacrificed. Another hand must guide the helm, or there must be a period of stagnation and delay. Important questions await his return, and leave him but little time to read up all that has transpired during his long absence, so that he finds himself wasting precious time in the hopeless endeavour to overtake arrears at a moment of exceptional pressure, or dealing with questions with which he is perforce imperfectly acquainted.

The eight months' period of residential service offers less disadvantage in these respects, and is already applicable to the judges in Nigeria. But even an absence of four months in each year (including voyages) is a distressing break in continuity, if the Governor during this period is wholly detached from his work. It was, however, found necessary by Lord Cromer—though the climate of Cairo or Alexandria is better than that of West Africa,—and I believe he attributed much of his success to his annual holiday. The Governor-General of the Sudan also takes an annual leave, bringing home with him during the rainy season many of his senior officers, and transacting much business for his Government during his time in England. During the absence of Lord Cromer, or Sir R. Wingate, the *locum tenens* could not initiate any new policy or legislation. This was the Foreign Office solution of the problem. The Niger Chartered Company had found it no less necessary for their highest officers (the Agent-General and Chief Justice) to come home yearly, though in their case the administration was directed from London.

After six years' experience in West Africa, during which an exceptionally robust constitution enabled me to adopt the sixteen to eighteen months' period of foreign service, and so to avoid absence at the essential period of the year, I realised very fully its disadvantages, and submitted to Mr Lyttelton, then Secretary of State for the Colonies, a proposal by which I hoped that this lack of continuity might be overcome, and at the same time a closer touch assured between the Governor and the Secretary of State and commercial interests in England. The proposal was seen by Mr Chamberlain, who had recently left the Colonial Office, and he was inclined to approve it. The principle was also approved by Lord Cromer and other statesmen.[11] Mr Lyttelton declared his intention of giving it a trial in Nigeria.

In brief, I suggested that "the Governor-General (of an amalgamated Nigeria) should spend six months of each year in Africa, and six in England, being on duty and not on leave while at home . . . whether in England or in Africa he would remain the sole working head of the administration." The scheme was not cordially accepted by the permanent officials, and did not at that time take effect; but when in 1912 I was invited by Mr (now Lord) Harcourt to undertake the amalgamation of the two Nigerias, he agreed to adopt it on the basis of seven months' residence abroad and five months' absence, including voyages—which I think is better than six and six. With rapid sea passages it might even be eight and four months.

The scheme was in operation for some years, and I doubt whether the task of amalgamation, with the added difficulties of the war, could have been satisfactorily carried through without it. Arrangements had been made so that the rôle of the permanent officials at the Colonial Office should in no way be interfered with by the presence of the Governor, while his residence in England for four months during the rains each year involved an absence from Nigeria no longer, though more frequent, than the normal period of leave. He was in point of fact more closely in touch with his deputy than if he had been travelling in a distant part of Nigeria. His deputy in Africa was vested with full powers to deal with any emergency which might arise, and to carry on routine work.

It was hoped that the arrangement would have beneficial results in relieving the Governor for a period in each year, when he could best be spared, of the burden of routine work, and enable him to devote time to the study of

11. Sir A. Hemming, who had served for thirty years in the Colonial Office, latterly as head of the West African Department, and subsequently as Governor of two Crown colonies, warmly supported it in a letter to the 'Times' (26th December 1905).

larger problems,[12] and to maintain a close touch with commercial interests in England. For the latter reason it was welcomed by the merchants.[13] It was anticipated also that the Governor's presence in England—not on leave but on duty—might, if duly utilised, prove of value to the home authorities, and minimise despatch-writing.

Under the normal Colonial Office system, the Governor when on leave was rarely consulted, except on a matter of very exceptional importance, and was at liberty to leave England if he desired. No doubt it was the kindly intention that he should have complete rest. The Acting-Governor was vested with full powers, and for the time being entirely superseded the Governor, and was alone recognised by the Colonial Office. Since the Governor did not see the despatches sent to or received from his Government, he lost all touch, and on his return he had a heavy task to overtake arrears and possess himself of what had transpired in his absence. The Foreign Office, as Lord Lansdowne told the House of Lords, like the French Government, has a different tradition.

Experience did not lessen the hostility of the permanent officials to the scheme.[14] It was, they considered, contrary to all precedent, and even to constitutional usage. This could not indeed be gainsaid, but the experiment could be, and was, legalised like other experiments in Empire Administration, by Letters Patent and Royal instructions. The apprehensions of the permanent officials were not unnatural, for the presence of the Governor at the Colonial Office seemed to threaten the anonymity of the Secretary of State, from which they derived the powers so absolutely essential to the working of the Colonial Office system. Regarding this system I shall have some remarks to make in chapter viii.; but in so far as this scheme is concerned, no interference with the functions of the permanent officials was ever

12. Compare Burke, addressing a member of the French National Assembly in 1791: "They who always labour can have no true judgment. You never give yourselves time to cool. You can never survey from its proper point of sight the work you have finished before you decree its final execution. You can never plan the future by the past. . . . These are among the effects of unremitted labour, when men exhaust their attention, burn out their candles, and are left in the dark."

13. One of them had in fact advocated a very similar scheme—viz., that a Governor "should return home for six months after nine in Africa, and be responsible for his *locum tenens* and all his acts during the interval."

14. An obviously well-informed article appeared in the 'Glasgow Herald' of 13th July 1912, before the scheme was brought into effect, stating that Mr Harcourt's decision "was strongly resented by the permanent officials . . . no other Crown Colony [they said] is carried on in this way, which means the practical supersession of the permanent Under-Secretaries."

contemplated, or alleged while it was in operation. The Governor, though working in close relation with the department, was not part of it, and had no claim to see the Office Minutes.

The primary object of the scheme, as I have explained, was to promote a true continuity of responsibility and control, in lieu of a continuity which was not real. That there is a tendency on the part of an Acting-Governor, vested with the fullest powers, to inaugurate policies of his own, had been the experience of more than one West African colony. It may not go so far as the reversal of legislation—which could be vetoed by the Secretary of State—and it may even be due to misunderstanding rather than to deliberate intention, but the result is equally deplorable.

The practicability of the principle of continuous responsibility of the Governor when absent from his post, and of his annual return to England, must, of course, depend largely on the distance of the colony and the time taken in sea voyages. It is adapted only to a group of colonies under a Governor-General—and the two Nigerias, in size, population, and wealth, might be said to represent such a group—and to colonies within a comparatively short sea voyage of England. A scheme which has been found feasible for West Africa, Egypt, and the Sudan would not be suitable for the Straits Settlements, Ceylon, or Mauritius, unless aviation introduces new possibilities in the future. The French system in West Africa—which I shall presently describe—is not dissimilar.

British public opinion is in favour of trusting the "Man on the Spot," who represents the King, and is held responsible by the nation. If trouble occurs through the action of his deputy, it is the Governor's policy which is blamed. He should therefore have the same control over his deputy when he is in London as he would have were he absent in some distant part of the protectorate, where for all practical administrative purposes he would be less in touch than when in London. But the scheme, as Mr Churchill wittily said, involves an enlarged definition of the "Spot," due to the rapid means of transport and communications which steam and telegraphy have introduced, in order to give effect to the essential principle—control by the man who is held responsible.

No project can, however, be successfully carried out to which one party is consistently opposed, and the scheme has been abandoned,—nor should I have devoted so much space to it were it not that its revival—possibly in some modified form—would certainly in my view be desirable, if the proposal to "group" colonies—which I shall deal with in chapter ix.—were adopted.

How, then, in the meantime can continuity of responsibility and co-operation best be preserved? It has been said that continuity is maintained by the permanency of the officials at the Colonial Office, whose rôle it is to oppose subversive policy by a new Governor based on insufficient experience, or the assumption of too wide powers by an Acting-Governor. This is, of course, an essential function of the Colonial Office under the present system—a function which, as we have seen, the Foreign Office had been accused of failing to perform in Uganda. The duty of acting as a drag on the wheels may indeed preserve continuity, but it is not necessarily a continuity of progress, and may even produce an attitude of mind tolerant of delays, and hostile to new lines of thought.

If it were made manifest to a Governor on leave that his presence and assistance is welcomed at the Colonial Office; if he saw all correspondence with the Acting-Governor, and were informed of all proposed changes; if the atmosphere of secrecy were exchanged for one of absolute frankness, not only by the seniors but by the juniors of the Office, and he were consulted in matters regarding his sphere of work, and invited to Conferences and Committees; if his period of leave were invariably to coincide with the rainy season—either annually with an absence of three to four months only, or (since conditions in West Africa now admit of longer residence) every alternate year, with a total absence not exceeding six months (say, from mid-March to mid-September); and finally, if the powers of the Acting-Governor were strictly curtailed, and the continuous responsibility of the Governor were officially recognised—much might be done not only to promote continuity, but also to forward the best interests of the country.

In the latter direction clear rules should be laid down and published. The initiation of legislation, the approval of important leases, and the appropriation of any considerable sums unprovided in the estimates, should be reserved to the Governor. His deputy should have no power to cancel or alter existing Regulations, General Orders, or Governor's instructions, or to issue any instructions contrary to these in letter or spirit, or incompatible with the general policy in regard to the native administration. He should not alter the boundaries of provinces, depose or appoint chiefs of the highest rank, alter the permanent distribution of the military forces, or give pledges to merchants or missionaries which involve important principles, without prior reference to the Governor.

The prosperity of a colony, and the welfare of its population, must obviously depend very largely on the character and energy of its Governor. It is therefore of the first importance that the best men should be selected for these posts, and that during their tenure of office the Secretary of State should have frequent opportunities of judging of their ability and sustained energy and enthusiasm.

The work and character of a Governor cannot be gauged by his popularity, or by the hearsay evidence of juniors, or of those whose pecuniary interests may have been affected by measures needed for the good of the country, for they are necessarily inadequately informed. Unpopularity arising from questions of public policy may indeed be a proof of strength of character and of a disinterested sense of duty.

It is manifest that when the right man is in the right place, it is to the benefit of the country that his tenure of office should be prolonged; but in order to avoid the retention of a man who has not come up to the expectations formed of him, or who, though thoroughly capable, is unsuited to the particular post, the period of Governorship should be limited as now to six years (though earlier transfers could, of course, be made), and the extension of this term should carry with it an increase of emoluments, so that the Governor may not suffer in pocket or status, and the extension may be regarded as a recognition of merit. There is a widespread feeling in the senior ranks of the service—the bitterness of which is probably not appreciated in Downing Street—that present methods provide no safeguard against inefficiency, and no guarantee for the selection of the best men.

A Governor is often a married man with a family. In the conditions hitherto prevailing in Africa, except in the eastern Highlands, he must be separated from the latter, even if his wife (probably no longer young) is able to accompany him. The best men, therefore, are apt to look for promotion to a colony which does not necessitate such separations. It is only within the last dozen years that Governors have remained for their full period of office in West Africa. Formerly they rarely remained for more than three years. Continuity again suffers, for Governors appointed from the eastern colonies (as so many have been in West Africa) have much to learn and unlearn before they become familiar with African conditions and African character—so essentially different from those of the East.

In the self-governing colonies limitation of tenure of office has special advantages. Continuity is maintained, not by the Governor-General, but by his ministers. Past controversies are buried with the advent of a new Governor, and the progress of democratic institutions in the Mother Country, and her relations towards the colony, are more accurately represented. The new Governor is, in fact, more up-to-date as the representative of the feelings and changes in Great Britain. In the tropical dependencies the case is otherwise. Personality counts for so much with native races that the departure of a man who has gained their confidence may set the clock back and delay progress— and the same may be said of material development. Given the right man, the longer he stays the better, provided he retains his energy and enthusiasm—as results have proved in Egypt and elsewhere. On the other hand, as decentralisation proceeds, the force of these arguments decreases. Continuity of method and policy is better assured, and the "new blood" which the Colonial Office constantly endeavours to infuse into the colonies has its advantages in bringing new ideas and new experience, and in preventing an administration from becoming limited in its channels of progress under the continued control of the same man.

Continuity may therefore suffer in three ways: first, by the short tenure of his post by a Governor; secondly, by his long absence on leave; and thirdly, by the indefinite powers given to his temporary deputy.

It may be said that as Faith, Hope, and Charity are to the Christian creed, so are Decentralisation, Co-operation, and Continuity to African Administration—and the greatest of these is Continuity.

SOURCE: Introduction and chapter 5 in *The Dual Mandate in British Tropical Africa* (1922; London: Frank Cass, 1965), 1–7, 94–113.

The Clash of Cultures
MARY KINGSLEY

[Mary Kingsley's (1862–1900) inspiration for her African journeys was her father, George Henry Kingsley; the lady traveler hoped to complete his unfinished book of African studies. Kingsley was reportedly the first European to enter parts of Gabon. Her travel through the Fang "cannibals" territory and journeys through the Congo, the French Congo, and Gabon contributed to her celebrity status and popularity on the lecture circuit.]

Wherein this student, realising as usual, when too late, that the environment of such opinions as are expressed above is boiling hot water, calls to memory the excellent saying, "As well be hung for a sheep as a lamb," and goes on.

I have no intention, however, of starting a sort of open-air steam laundry for West African washing. I have only gone into the unsatisfactory-to-all-parties-concerned state of affairs there not with the hope, but with the desire, that things may be improved and further disgrace avoided. It would be no good my merely stating that, if England wishes to make her possessions there morally and commercially pay her for the loss of life that holding them entails, she must abolish her present policy of amateur experiments backed by good intentions, for you would naturally not pay the least attention to a bald statement made by merely me. So I have had to place before you the opinions of others who are more worthy of your attention. I must however for myself disclaim any right to be regarded as the mouthpiece of any party concerned, though Major Lugard has done me the honour to place me amongst the Liverpool merchants. I can claim no right to speak as one of them. I should be only too glad if I had this honour, but I have not. There was early this year a distressing split between Liverpool and myself—whom I am aware they call behind my back "Our Aunt"—and I know they regard me as a vexing, if even a valued, form of relative.

This split, I may say (remembering Mr. Mark Twain's axiom, that people always like to know what a row is about), arose from my frank admiration of both the Royal Niger Company and France, neither of which Liverpool at that time regarded as worthy of even the admiration of the most insignificant; so its *Journal of Commerce* went for me. The natural sweetness of my disposition is most clearly visible to the naked eye when I am quietly having my own way, so naturally I went for its *Journal of Commerce.* Providentially no one outside saw this deplorable family row, and Mr. John Holt put a stop to it by saying to me, "Say what you like, you cannot please all of us;" had it not been for this I should not have written another line on the maladministration of West Africa beyond saying, "Call that Crown Colony system you are working there a Government! England, at your age, you ought to be ashamed of yourself!" But you see, as things are, I am not speaking for any one, only off on a little lone fight of my own against a state of affairs which I regard as a disgrace to my country.

Well but, you may say, after all what you have said points to nothing disgraceful. You have expressly said that there is no corruption in the government there, and the rest of the things—the change of policy arising from the necessity for white men to come home at the least every twelve months, the waste of money necessary to local exigencies, and the fact that officers and gentlemen cannot be expected to understand and look after what one might call domestic expenses—may be things unavoidable and peculiar to the climate. To this I can only say, Given the climate, why do you persist in ignoring the solid mass of expert knowledge of the region which is in the hands of the mercantile party, and go on working your Governors from a non-expert base? You have in England an unused but great mass of knowledge among men of all classes who have personally dealt with West Africa—yet you do not work from that, organise it, and place it at the service of the brand new Governors who go out; far from it, I know hardly any more pathetic sight than the new official suddenly appointed to West Africa buzzing round trying to find out "what the place is really like, you know." I know personally one of the greatest of our Governors who have been down there, a man with iron determination and courage, who was not content with the information derivable from a list of requisites for a tropical climate, the shorter Hausa grammar and a nice cherry-covered little work on diseases—the usual fillets with which England binds the brows of her Sacrifices to the Coast—but went and read about West Africa, all by himself, alone in the British Museum. He was a success, but still he always declares that the only book he found about this particular part was a work by a Belgian, with a frontispiece depicting the author, on an awful river, in the act as per inscription, of shouting, "Row on, brave men of Kru!" which, as subsequent knowledge showed him that bravery was not one of the main qualities of the Kru men, shook him up about all his British Museum education. So in the end he, like the rest, had to learn for himself, out there. Of course, if the Governors were carefully pegged down to a West African place and lived long enough, and were not by nature faddists, doubtless they would learn, and in the course of a few years things would go well; but they are not pegged down. No sooner does one of them begin to know about the country he is in charge of than off he is whisked and deposited again, in a brand new region for which West Africa has not been a fitting introduction.

Then, as for the domestic finance, why expect officers and lawyers, doctors and gentlemen from clubland to manage fiscal matters? Of course they naturally don't know about trade affairs, or whether the Public Works Department is spending money, or merely wasting it. You require professional men in West Africa, but not to do half the work they are now engaged on in connection with red tape and things they do not understand. Of course, errors of this kind may be merely Folly, you may have plenty more men as good as these to replace them with, so it may matter more to their relations than to England if they are wasted alike in life and death, and you are so rich that the gradual extinction of your tropical trade will not matter to your generation. But as a necessary consequent to this amateurism, or young gentlemen's academy system, the Crown Colony system, there is disgrace in the injustice to and disintegration of the native races it deals with.

Now when I say England is behaving badly to the African, I beg you not to think that the philanthropic party has increased. I come of a generation of Danes who when the sun went down on the Wulpensand were the men to make light enough to fight by with their Morning Stars; and who, later on, were soldiers in the Low Countries and slave owners in the West Indies, and I am proud of my ancestors; for whatever else they were, they were not humbugs; and the generation that is round me now seems to me in its utterances at any rate tainted with humbug. I own that I hate the humbug in England's policy towards weaker races for the sake of all the misery on white and black it brings; and I think as I see you wasting lives and money, sowing debt and difficulties all over West Africa by a hut tax war in Sierra Leone, fighting for the sake of getting a few shillings you have no right to whatsoever out of the African—who are you that you should point your finger in scorn at my tribe? I, as one of that tribe, blush for you, from the basis that you are a humbug and not scientific, which I presume you will agree is not the same thing as my being a philanthropist.

I had the honour of meeting in West Africa an English officer who had previously been doing some fighting in South Africa. He said he "didn't like being a butterman's nigger butcher." "Oh! you're all right here then," I said; "you're out now for Exeter Hall, the plane of civilisation, the plough, and the piano." I will not report his remarks further; likely enough it was the mosquitoes that made him say things, and of course I knew with him, as I know with you, butchery of any sort is not to your liking, though war when it's wanted is; the distinction I draw between them is a hard and fast one. There is just the same difference to my mind between an unnecessary war on an unarmed race and a necessary war on the same race, as there is between killing game that you want to support yourself with or game that is destructive to your interests, and on the other hand the killing of game just to say that you have done it. This will seem a deplorably low view to take, but it is one supported by our history. We have killed down native races in Australasia and America, and it is no use slurring over the fact that we have profited by so doing. This argument, however, cannot be used in favour of killing down the African in tropical Africa, more particularly in Western Tropical Africa. If you were to-morrow to kill every native there, what use would the country be to you? No one else but the native can work its resources; you cannot live in it and colonise it. It would therefore be only an extremely interesting place for the zoologist, geologist, mineralogist, &c., but a place of no good to any one else in England.

This view, however, of the profit derivable from and justifying war you will refuse to discuss; stating that such profit in your wars you do not seek; that they have been made for the benefit of the African himself, to free him from his native oppressors in the way of tyrannical chiefs and bloody superstitions, and to elevate him in the plane of civilisation. That this has been the intention of our West African wars up to the Sierra Leone war, which was forced on you for fiscal reasons, I have no doubt: but that any of them advanced you in your mission to elevate the African, I should hesitate to say. I beg to refer you to Dr. Freeman's opinions on the Ashantee wars on this point,[1] but for myself I

1. *Ashantee and Jaman*, Freeman (Constable and Co., 1898).

should say that the blame of the failure of these wars to effect their desired end has been due to the want of power to re-organise native society after a war; for example, had the 1873 Ashantee war been followed by the taking over of Ashantee and the strong handling of it, there would not have been an 1895 Ashantee war; or, to take it the other way, if you had followed up the battle of Katamansu in 1827, you need not have had an 1874 war even. Dr. Freeman holds, that if you had let the Ashantis have a seaport and generally behaved fairly reasonably, you need hardly have had Ashantee wars at all. But, however this may be, I think that a good many of the West African wars of the past ten years have been the result of the humbug of the previous sixty, during which we have proclaimed that we are only in Africa for peaceful reasons of commerce, and religion, and education, not with any desire for the African's land or property: that, of course, it is not possible for us to extend our friendship or our toleration to people who go in for cannibalism, slave-raiding, or human sacrifices, but apart from these matters we have no desire to meddle with African domestic affairs, or take away their land. This, I own, I believe to have honestly been our intention, and to be our intention still, but with our stiff Crown Colony system of representing ourselves to the African, this intention has been and will be impossible to carry out, because between the true spirit of England and the spirit of Africa it interposes a distorting medium. It is, remember, not composed of Englishmen alone, it includes educated natives, and yet it knows the true native only through interpreters.

But why call this humbug? you say. Well, the present policy in Africa makes it look so. Frankly, I do not see how you could work your original policy out unless it were in the hands of extremely expert men, patient and powerful at that. Too many times in old days have you allowed white men to be bullied, to give the African the idea that you, as a nation, meant to have your way. Too many times have you allowed them to violate parts of their treaties under your nose, until they got out of the way of thinking you would hold them to their treaties at all, and then suddenly down you came on them, not only holding them to their side of the treaties, but not holding to your own, imposing on them restrictions and domestic interference which those treaties made no mention of at all. I have before me now copies of treaties with chiefs in the hinterland of our Crown Colonies, wherein there is not even the anti-slavery clause—treaties merely of friendship and trade, with the undertaking on the native chief's part to hand over no part or right in his territories to a foreign power without English Government consent. Yet, in the districts we hold from the natives under such treaties, we are contemplating direct taxation, which to the African means the confiscation of the property taxed. We have, in fact, by our previous policy placed ourselves to the

African with whom we have made treaties, in the position of a friend. "Big friend," it is true, but not conqueror or owner. Our departure now from the "big friend" attitude into the position of owner, hurts his feelings very much; and coupled with the feeling that he cannot get at England, who used to talk so nicely to him, and whom he did his best to please, as far as local circumstances and his limited power would allow, by giving up customs she had an incomprehensible aversion to, it causes the African chief to say "God is up," by which I expect he means the Devil, and give way to war, or sickness, or distraction, or a wild, hopeless, helpless, combination of all three; and then, poor fellow, when he is only naturally suffering from the dazzles your West African policy would give to an iron post, you go about sagely referring to "a general antipathy to civilisation among the natives of West Africa," "anti-white-man's leagues," "horrible secret societies," and such like figments of your imagination; and likely enough throw in as a dash for top the statement that the chief is "a drunken slave-raider," which as the captain of the late s.s. *Sparrow* would say, "It may be so, and, again, it mayn't." Anyhow it seems to occur to you as an argument only after the war is begun, though you have known the man some years; and it has not been the ostensible reason for any West African war save those in the Niger Company's territories, which run far enough inland to touch the slave-raiding zone, and which are entirely excluded from my arguments because they have been in the hands of experts on West Africa in war-making and in war-healing.

Our past wars in West Africa, I mean all our wars prior to the hut-tax war, have been wars in order to suppress human sacrifice, to protect one tribe from the aggression of another, and to prevent the stopping of trade by middlemen tribes. These things are things worth fighting for. The necessity we have been under to fight them has largely arisen from our ancestors shirking a little firm-handedness in their generation.

There is very little doubt that, owing to a want of reconstruction after destruction, these wars have not been worth to the Empire the loss of life and money they have cost; but this is nothing against us as fighters nor any real disgrace to our honour, but merely a slur on our intellectual powers in the direction of statecraft. They are wars of a totally different character to those of the hut-tax kind, which arise from aggressions on native property; the only thing in common between them is the strain of poor statecraft. This imperfection, however, exists to a far greater extent in hut-tax war, for to it we owe that general feeling of dislike to the advance of civilisation you now hear referred to. That, to a certain extent, this dislike already exists as the necessary outcome of our policy of late years, and that it will increase yearly, I fear there is very little doubt. It is the toxin produced by the microbe. It is the consequence of our attempt to introduce direct taxation, which seems to me to be an affair identical with your greased cartridges for India. Doubtless, such people ought not to object to greased cartridges; but, doubtless, such people as we are ought not to give them, and commit, over again, a worthless blunder, with no bad intention be it granted, but with no common sense.

It has been said that the Sierra Leone hut-tax war is "a little Indian mutiny"; those who have said it do not seem to have known how true the statement is, for these attacks on property in the form of direct taxation are, to the African, treachery on the part of England, who, from the first, has kept on assuring the African that she does not mean to take his country from him, and then, as soon as she is strong enough, in his eyes, starts deliberately doing it. When you once get between two races the feeling of treachery, the face of their relationship is altered for ever, altered in a way that no wholesome war, no brutality of individuals, can alter. Black and white men for ever after a national breach of faith tax each other with treachery and never really trust each other again.

The African, however, must not be confounded with the Indian. Externally, in his habits he is in a lower culture state; he has no fanatical religion that really resents the incursions of other religions on his mind; Fetish can live in and among all sorts and kinds of religions without quarrelling with them in the least, grievously as they quarrel with Fetish; he has no written literature to keep before his eyes a glorious and mythical past, which, getting mixed up with his religious ideas, is liable in the Indian to make him take at times lobster-like backward springs in the direction of that past, though it was never there, and he would not have relished it if it had been. Nevertheless, the true negro is, I believe, by far the better man than the Asiatic; he is physically superior, and he is more like an Englishman than the Asiatic; he is a logical, practical man, with feelings that are a credit to him, and are particularly strong in the direction of property; he has a way of thinking he has rights, whether he likes to use them or no, and will fight for them when he is driven to it. Fight you for a religious idea the African will not. He is not the stuff you make martyrs out of, nor does he desire to shake off the shackles of the flesh and swoon into Nirvana; and although he will sit under a tree to any extent, provided he gets enough to eat and a little tobacco, he won't sit under trees on iron spikes, or hold a leg up all the time, or fakirise in any fashion for the benefit of his soul or yours. His make of mind is exceedingly like the make of mind of thousands of Englishmen of the stand-no-nonsense, Englishman's-house-is-his-castle type. Yet, withal, a law-abiding man, loving a live lord, holding loudly that women should be kept in their place, yet often grievously henpecked by his wives, and little better than a slave to his mother, whom he

loves with a love he gives to none other. This love of his mother is so dominant a factor in his life that it must be taken into consideration in attempting
to understand the true negro. Concerning it I can do no better than give you
the Reverend Leighton Wilson's words; for this great missionary knew, as
probably none since have known, the true negro, having laboured for many
years amongst the most unaltered negro tribes—the Grain Coast tribes—and
his words are as true to-day of the unaltered negro as on the day he wrote
them thirty-eight years ago, and Leighton Wilson, mind you, was no blind
admirer of the African.

"Whatever other estimate we may form of the African, we may not doubt
his love for his mother. Her name, whether dead or alive, is always on his lips
and in his heart. She is the first being he thinks of when awakening from his
slumbers and the last he remembers when closing his eyes in sleep; to her he
confides secrets which he would reveal to no other human being on the face of
the earth. He cares for no one else in time of sickness, she alone must prepare
his food, administer his medicine, perform his ablutions, and spread his mat
for him. He flies to her in the hour of his distress, for he well knows if all the
rest of the world turn against him she will be steadfast in her love, whether he
be right or wrong.

"If there by any cause which justifies a man using violence towards one of
his fellow men it would be to resent an insult offered to his mother. More
fights are occasioned among boys by hearing something said in disparagement of their mothers than all other causes put together. It is a common
saying among them, if a man's mother and his wife are both on the point of
being drowned, and he can save only one of them, he must save his mother,
for the avowed reason if the wife is lost he may marry another, but he will
never find a second mother."[2]

Among the tribes of whom Wilson is speaking above, it is the man's true
mother. Among the Niger Delta tribes it is often the adopted mother, the
woman who has taken him when, as a child, he has been left motherless, or, if
he is a boughten child, the woman who has taken care of him. Among both,
and throughout all the bushmen tribes in West Africa, however, this deep
affection is the same; next to the mother comes the sister to the African, and
this matter has a bearing politically.

There is little doubt that there exists a distrustful feeling towards white
culture. Up to our attempt to enforce direct taxation it was only a distrustful
feeling which a few years' careful, honest handling would have disposed of.
Since our attempt there is no doubt there is something approaching a panicky

2. *Western Africa*, Wilson, 1856, p. 116.

terror of white civilisation in all the native aristocracies and property owners. It is not, I repeat, to be attributed to Fetish priests. Certainly, on the whole, it is not attributable to a dislike of European customs or costumes; it is the reasonable dislike to being dispossessed alike of power and property in what they regard as their own country. A considerable factor in this matter is undoubtedly the influence of the women—the mothers of Africa. Just as your African man is the normal man, so is your African woman the normal woman. I openly own that if I have a soft spot in my feelings it is towards African women; and the close contact I have lived in with them has given rise to this, and, I venture to think, made me understand them. I know they have their faults. For one thing they are not so religiously minded as the men. I have met many African men who were philosophers, thinking in the terms of Fetish, but never a woman so doing. Be it granted that on the whole they know more about the details of Fetish procedure than the men do. Yet though frightened of them all, a blind faith in any mortal Ju Ju they do not possess. Your African lady is artful with them, not philosophic, possibly because she has other things to do—what with attending to the children, the farm, and the market— than go mooning about as those men can. For another thing they go in for husband poisoning in a way I am unable to approve of.

Well, it may be interesting to inquire into the reasons that make the West African woman a factor against white civilisation. These reasons are—firstly, that she does not know practically anything about it; and, secondly, she has the normal feminine dislike to innovations. Missionary and other forms of white education have not been given to the African women to anything like the same extent that they have been given to the men. I do not say that there are not any African women who are not thoroughly educated in white education, for there are, and they can compare very favourably from the standpoint of their education with our normal women; but these have, I think I may safely say, been the daughters of educated African men, or have been the women who have been immediately attached to some mission station. I have no hesitation in saying that, considering the very little attention that has been given to the white education of the African women, they give evidence of an ability in due keeping with that of the African men. But all I mean to say is, that our white culture has not had a grasp over the womankind of Africa that can compare with that it has had over the men; for one woman who has been brought home to England and educated in our schools, and who has been surrounded by English culture, &c., there are 500 men. But into the possibilities of the African woman in the white education department I do not mean to go; I am getting into a snaggy channel by speaking on woman at all. It is to the mass of African women, untouched by white culture, but with an enormous influence over their sons and brothers that I am now referring as a factor in the dislike to the advance of white civilisation; and I have said they do not like it because, for one thing, they do not know it; that is to say, they do not know it from the inside and at its best, but only from the outside. Viewed from the outside in West Africa white civilisation, to a shrewd mind like hers, is an evil thing for her boys and girls. She sees it taking away from them the restraints of their native culture, and in all too many cases leading them into a life of dissipation, disgrace, and decay; or, if it does not do this, yet separating the men from their people.

The whole of this affair requires a whole mass of elaborate explanations to place it fairly before you, but I will merely sketch the leading points now. (1) The law of mütterrecht makes the tie between the mother and the children far closer than that between the father and them: white culture reverses this, she does not like that. (2) Between husband and wife there is no community in goods under native law; each keeps his and her separate estate. White culture says the husband shall endow his wife with all his worldly goods; this she knows usually means, that if he has any he does not endow her with them, but whether he has or has not he endows himself with hers as far as any law permits. Similarly he does not like it either. These two white culture things, saddling him with the support of the children and endowing his wife with all his property, presents a repulsive situation to the logical African. Moreover, white culture expects him to think more of his wife and children than he does of his mother and sisters, which to the uncultured African is absurd.

Then again both he and his mother see the fearful effects of white culture on the young women, who cannot be prevented in districts under white control from going down to the coast towns and to the Devil: neither he nor the respectable old ladies of his tribe approve of this. Then again they know that the young men of their people who have thoroughly allied themselves to white culture look down on their relations in the African culture state. They call the ancestors of their tribe "polygamists," as if it were a swear-word, though they are a thousand times worse than polygamists themselves: and they are ashamed of their mothers. It is a whole seething mass of stuff all through, and I would not mention it were it not that it is a factor in the formation of anti-white-culture opinion among the mass of the West Africans, and that it causes your West African bush chief to listen to the old woman whom you may see crouching behind him, or you may not see at all, but who is with him all the same, when she says, "Do not listen to the white man, it is bad for you." He knows that the interpreter talking to him for the white man may be a boughten man, paid to advertise the advantages of white ways; and he knows that the old woman, his mother, cannot be bought where his interest is concerned: so he listens to her, and she distrusts white ways.

I am aware that there is now in West Africa a handful of Africans who have mastered white culture, who know it too well to misunderstand the inner spirit of it, who are men too true to have let it cut them off in either love or sympathy from Africa—men that, had England another system that would allow her to see them as they are, would be of greater use to her and Africa than they now are; but I will not name them: I fight a lone fight, and wish to mix no man, white or black, up in it, or my heretical opinions. That handful of African men are now fighting a hard enough fight to prevent the distracted, uninformed Africans from rising against what looks so like white treachery, though it is only white want of knowledge; and also against those "water flies" who are neither Africans nor Europeans, but who are the curse of the Coast— the men who mislead the white man and betray the black.

Next to this there is another factor almost equally powerful, with which I presume you cannot sympathise, and which I should make a mess of if I trusted myself to explain. Therefore I call in the aid of a better writer, speaking on another race, but talking of the identical same thing. "In these days the boot of the ubiquitous white man leaves its mark on all the fair places of the earth, and scores thereon an even more gigantic track than that which affrighted Robinson Crusoe in his solitude. It crushes down the forest, beats out roads, strides across the rivers, kicks down native institutions, and generally tramples on the growths of natives and the works of primitive man, reducing all things to that dead level of conventionality which we call civilisation.

"Incidentally it stamps out much of what is best in the customs and characteristics of the native races against which it brushes; and though it relieves him of many things which hurt or oppressed him ere it came, it injures him morally almost as much as it benefits him materially. We who are white men admire our work not a little—which is natural, and many are found willing to wear out their souls in efforts to convert the thirteenth century into the nineteenth in a score of years. The natives, who for the most part are frank Vandals, also admire efforts of which they are aware that they are themselves incapable, and even the *laudator temporis acti* has his mouth stopped by the cheap and often tawdry luxury which the coming of the white man has placed within his reach. So effectually has the heel of the white man been ground into the face of Pérak and Selangor, that these native states are now only nominally what their name implies. The white population outnumbers the people of the land in most of the principal districts, and it is possible for a European to spend weeks in either of these states without coming into contact with any Asiatics save those who wait at table, clean his shirts, or drive his cab. It is possible, I am told, for a European to spend years in Pérak or Selangor without acquiring any profound knowledge of the natives, of the country or of the language which is their special medium. This being so, most of the white men who live in the protected native states are somewhat apt to disregard the effect their actions have upon the natives, and labour under the common European inability to view natives from a native standpoint. Moreover, we have become accustomed to existing conditions; and thus it is that few perhaps realise the precise nature of the work which the British in the Peninsula have set themselves to accomplish. What we are really attempting, however, is nothing less than to crush into twenty years the revolution in facts and in ideas, which, even in energetic Europe, six long centuries have been needed to accomplish. No one will, of course, be found to dispute that the strides made in our knowledge of the art of government since the thirteenth century are prodigious and vast, nor that the general condition of the people of Europe has been immensely improved since that day; but nevertheless one cannot but sympathise with the Malays who are suddenly and violently translated from the point to which they have attained in the natural development of their race, and are required to live up to the standard of a people who are six centuries in advance of them in national progress. If a plant is made to blossom or bear fruit three months before its time it is regarded as a triumph of the gardener's art; but what then are we to say of this huge moral forcing system we call 'protection'? Forced plants we know suffer in the process; and the Malay, whose proper place is amidst the conditions of the thirteenth century, is apt to become morally weak and seedy and lose something of his robust self respect when he is forced to bear nineteenth century fruit."[3]

Now, the above represents the state of affairs caused by the clash of different culture levels in the true Negro States, as well as it does in the Malay. These two sets of men, widely different in breed, have, from the many points of agreement in their State-form, evidently both arrived in our thirteenth century. The African peoples in the Central East, and East, and South, except where they are true Negroes, have not arrived in the thirteenth century, or, to put it in other words, the True Negro stem in Africa has arrived at a political state akin to that of our own thirteenth century, whereas the Bantu stem has not; this point, however, I need not enter into here.

There are, of course, local differences between the Malay Peninsula and West Africa, but the main characteristics as regards the State-form among the natives are singularly alike. They are both what Mr. Clifford aptly likens

3. *East Coast Etchings*. H. Clifford, Singapore, 1896.

to our own European State-form in the thirteenth century; and the effect of the white culture on the morals of the natives is also alike. The main difference between them results from the Malay Peninsula being but a narrow strip of land and thinly peopled, compared to the densely populated section of a continent we call West Africa. Therefore, although the Malay in his native state is a superior individual warrior to the West African, yet there are not so many of him; and as he is less guarded from whites by a pestilential climate, his resistance to the white culture of the nineteenth century is inferior to the resistance which the West African can give.

The destruction of what is good in the thirteenth century culture level, and the fact that when the nineteenth century has had its way the main result is seedy demoralised natives, is the thing that must make all thinking men wonder if, after all, such work is from a high moral point of view worth the nineteenth century doing. I so often think when I hear the progress of civilisation, our duty towards the lower races, &c., talked of, as if those words were in themselves Ju Ju, of that improving fable of the kind-hearted she-elephant, who, while out walking one day, inadvertently trod upon a partridge and killed it, and observing close at hand the bird's nest full of callow fledglings, dropped a tear, and saying "I have the feelings of a mother myself," sat down upon the brood. This is precisely what England representing the nineteenth century is doing in thirteenth century West Africa. She destroys the guardian institution, drops a tear and sits upon the brood with motherly intentions; and pesky warm sitting she finds it, what with the nature of the brood and the surrounding climate, let alone the expense of it. And what profit she is going to get out of such proceedings there, I own I don't know. "Ah!" you say, "yes, it is sad, but it is inevitable." I do not think it is inevitable, unless you have no intellectual constructive Statecraft, and are merely in that line an automaton. If you will try Science, all the evils of the clash between the two culture periods could be avoided, and you could assist these West Africans in their thirteenth century state to rise into their nineteenth century state without their having the hard fight for it that you yourself had. This would be a grand humanitarian bit of work; by doing it you would raise a monument before God to the honour of England such as no nation has ever yet raised to Him on earth.

There is absolutely no perceivable sound reason why you should not do it if you will try Science and master the knowledge of the nature of the native and his country. The knowledge of native laws, religion, institutions, and state-form would give you the knowledge of what is good in these things, so that you might develop and encourage them; and the West African, having reached a thirteenth century state, has institutions and laws which with a strengthening from the European hand would, by their operation now, stamp out the evil that exists under the native state. What you are doing now, however, is the direct contrary to this: you are destroying the good portion and thereby allowing what is evil, or imperfect, in it as in all things human, to flourish under your protection far more rankly than under the purely native thirteenth century state-form, with Fetish as a state religion, it could possibly do.

I know, however, there is one great objection to your taking up a different line towards native races to that which you are at present following. It is one of those strange things that are in men's minds almost without their knowing they are there, yet which, nevertheless, rule them. This is the idea that those Africans are, as one party would say, steeped in sin, or, as another party would say, a lower or degraded race. While you think these things, you must act as you are acting. They really are the same idea in different clothes. They both presuppose all mankind to have sprung from a single pair of human beings, and the condition of a race to-day therefore to be to its own credit or blame. I remember one day in Cameroons coming across a young African lady, of the age of twelve, who I knew was enjoying the advantages of white tuition at a school. So, in order to open up conversation, I asked her what she had been learning. "Ebberyting," she observed with a genial smile. I asked her then what she knew, so as to approach the subject from a different standpoint for purposes of comparison. "Ebberyting," she said. This hurt my vanity, for though I am a good deal more than twelve years of age, I am far below this state of knowledge; so I said, "Well, my dear, and if you do, you're the person I have long wished to meet, for you can tell me why you are black." "Oh yes," she said, with a perfect beam of satisfaction, "one of my pa's pa's saw dem Patriark Noah wivout his clothes." I handed over to her a crimson silk necktie that I was wearing, and slunk away, humbled by superior knowledge. This, of course, was the result of white training direct on the African mind; the story which you will often be told to account for the blackness and whiteness of men by Africans who have not been in direct touch with European, but who have been in touch with Mohammedan, tradition—which in the main has the same Semitic source—is that when Cain killed Abel, he was horrified at himself, and terrified of God; and so he carried the body away from beside the altar where it lay, and carried it about for years trying to hide it, but not knowing how, growing white the while with the horror and the fear; until one day he saw a crow scratching a hole in the desert sand, and it struck him that if he made a hole in the sand and put the body in, he could hide it from God, so he did; but all his children were white, and from Cain came the white races, while Abel's children are black, as all men were before the first murder. The present way of contemplating different races, though expressed in finer language, is practically identical with these; not only the religious view, but the view of the suburban agnostic. The religious European cannot avoid regarding the races in a different and inferior culture state to his own as more deeply steeped in sin than himself, and the suburban agnostic regards them as "degraded" or "retarded" either by environment, or microbes, or both.

I openly and honestly own I sincerely detest touching on this race question. For one thing, Science has not finished with it; for another, it belongs to a group of subjects of enormous magnitude, upon which I have no opinion, but merely feelings, and those of a nature which I am informed by superior people would barely be a credit to a cave man of the palæolithic period. My feelings classify the world's inhabitants into Englishmen, by which I mean Teutons at large, Foreigners, and Blacks, whom I subdivide into two classes, English Blacks and Foreign Blacks. English Blacks are Africans. Foreign Blacks are Indians, Chinese and the rest. Of course, everything that is not Teutonic is, to put it mildly, not up to what is; and equally, of course, I feel more at home with, and hold in greater esteem the English Black: a great strong Kruman, for example, with his front teeth filed, nothing much on but oil, half a dozen wives, and half a hundred Ju Jus, is a sort of person whom I hold higher than any other form of native, let the other form dress in silk, satin, or cashmere, and make what pretty things he pleases. This is, of course, a general view; but I am often cornered for the detail view, whether I can reconcile my admiration for Africans with my statement that they are a different kind of human being to white men. Naturally I can, to my own satisfaction, just as I can admire an oak tree or a palm; but it is an uncommonly difficult thing to explain. All I can say is, that when I come back from a spell in Africa, the thing that makes me proud of being one of the English is not the manners or customs up here, certainly not the houses or the climate; but it is the thing embodied in a great railway engine. I once came home on a ship with an Englishman who had been in South West Africa for seven unbroken years; he was sane, and in his right mind. But no sooner did we get ashore at Liverpool, than he rushed at and threw his arms round a postman, to that official's embarrassment and surprise. Well, that is just how I feel about the first magnificent bit of machinery I come across: it is the manifestation of the superiority of my race.

In philosophic moments I call superiority difference, from a feeling that it is not mine to judge the grade in these things. Careful scientific study has enforced on me, as it has on other students, the recognition that the African mind naturally approaches all things from a spiritual point of view. Low down in culture or high up, his mind works along the line that things happen because of the action of spirit upon spirit; it is an effort for him to think in terms of matter. We think along the line that things happen from the action of matter upon matter. If it were not for the Asiatic religion we have accepted, it is, I think, doubtful whether we should not be far more materialistic in thought-form than we are. This steady sticking to the material side of things, I think, has given our race its dominion over matter; the want of it has caused the African to be notably behind us in this, and far behind those Asiatic races who regard matter and spirit as separate in essence, a thing that is not in the mind either of the Englishman or the African. The Englishman is constrained by circumstances to perceive the existence of an extra material world. The African regards spirit and matter as undivided in kind, matter being only the extreme low form of spirit. There must be in the facts of the case behind things, something to account for the high perception of justice you will find in the African, combined with an inability to think out a pulley or a lever except under white tuition. Similarly, taking the true Negro States, which are in their equivalent to our thirteenth century, it accounts for the higher level of morals in them than you would find in our thirteenth century; and I fancy this want of interest and inferiority in materialism in the true Negro constitutes a reason why they will not come into our nineteenth century, but, under proper guidance could attain to a nineteenth century state of their own, which would show a proportionate advance. The analogy of the influence of the culture of Rome, or rather let us say the culture of Greece spread by the force of Rome, upon Barbarian culture is one often used to justify the hope that English culture will have a similar effect on the African. This I do not think is so. It is true the culture of Rome lifted the Barbarians from what one might call culture 9 to culture 17, but the Romans and the Barbarians were both white races. But you see now a similar lift in culture in Africa by the influence of Mohammedan culture, for example in the Hausa States and again in the Western Soudan, where there is no fundamental race difference.

In both English and Mohammedan Berber influence on the African there is another factor, apart from race difference; namely, that the two higher cultures are in a healthier state than that of Rome was at the time it mastered the Barbarian mind; in both cases the higher culture has the superior war force.

This seems to me simply to lay upon us English for the sake of our honour that we keep clean hands and a cool head, and be careful of Justice; to do this we must know what there is we wish to wipe out of the African, and what there is we wish to put in, and so we must not content ourselves by relying materially on our superior wealth and power, and morally on catch phrases. All we need look to is justice. Love of our fellow-man, pity, charity, mercy, we need not bother our heads about, so long as we are just. These things are of value only when they are used as means whereby we can attain justice. It is no use saying that it matters to a Teuton whether the other race he deals with is black, white, yellow—I can quite conceive that we should look down on a pea-green form of humanity if we had the chance. Naturally, I think this shows a very proper spirit. I should be the last to alter any of our Teutonic institutions to please any race; but when it comes to altering the institutions of another race, not for the reason even of pleasing ourselves but merely on the plea that we don't understand them, we are on different ground. If those ideas and institutions stand in the way of our universal right to go anywhere we choose and live as honest gentlemen, we have the power-right to alter them; but if they do not we must judge them from as near a standard of pure Justice as we can attain to.

There are many who hold murder the most awful crime a man can commit, saying that thereby he destroys the image of his Maker; I hold that one of the most awful crimes one nation can commit on another is destroying the image of Justice, which in an institution is represented more truly to the people by whom the institution has been developed, than in any alien institution of Justice; it is a thing adapted to its environment. This form of murder by a nation I see being done in the destruction of what is good in the laws and institutions of native races. In some parts of the world, this murder, judged from certain reasonable standpoints, gives you an advantage; in West Africa, judged from any standpoint you choose to take, it gives you no advantage. By destroying native institutions there, you merely lower the moral of the African race, stop trade, and with it the culture advantages it brings both to England and West Africa. I again refer you to the object lesson before you now, the hut tax war in Sierra Leone. Awful accusations have been made against the officers and men who had the collecting of this tax. In the matter of the native soldiery, there is no doubt these accusations are only too well founded, but the root thing was the murder of institutions. The worst of the whole of this miserable affair is that a precisely similar miserable affair may occur at any time in any of our West African Crown Colonies—to-morrow, any day—until you choose to remove the Crown Colony system of government.

It has naturally been exceedingly hard for men who know the colony and the natives, with the experience of years in an unsentimental commercial way, to keep civil tongues in their heads while their interests were being wrecked by the action of the Government; but whether or no the white officers were or were not brutal in their methods we must presume will be shown by Sir David Chalmers's report. I am unable to believe they were. But there is no manner of doubt that outrages have been committed, disgraceful to England, by the set of riff-raff rascal Blacks, who had been turned out by, or who had run away from, the hinterland tribes down into Sierra Leone Colony, and there been turned, by an ill-informed government, into police, and sent back with power into the very districts from which they had, shortly before, fled for their crimes. I entirely sympathise, therefore, with the rage of Liverpool and Manchester, and of every clear-minded common-sense Englishman who knows what a thing the hut tax war has been. And I want common-sense Englishmen to recognise that a system capable of such folly, and under which such a thing could happen in an English possession, is a system that must go. For a system that gets short of money, from its own want of business-like ability, and then against all expert advice goes and does the most unscientific thing conceivable under the circumstances, to get more, is a thing that is a disgrace to England. Yet the Sierra Leone Colony was capable of this folly, and the people in London were capable of saying to Liverpool and Manchester, that no difficulty was expected from the collection of the tax. If this is so in our oldest colony, what reason have we to believe that in the others we are safer? Any of them, in combination with London, may to-morrow go and do the most unscientific thing conceivable, and disgrace England, in order to procure more local revenue, and fail at that.

The desire to develop our West African possessions is a worthy one in its way, but better leave it totally alone than attempt it with your present machinery; which the moment it is called upon to deal with the administration of the mass of the native inhabitants gives such a trouble. And remember it is not the only trouble your Crown Colony system can give; it has a few glorious opportunities left of further supporting everything I have said about it, and more. But I will say no more. You have got a grand rich region there, populated by an uncommon fine sort of human being. You have been trying your present set of ideas on it for over 400 years; they have failed in a heartbreaking drizzling sort of way to perform any single solitary one of the things you say you want done there. West Africa to-day is just a quarry of paving-stones for Hell, and those stones were cemented in places with men's blood mixed with wasted gold.

Prove it! you say. Prove it to yourself by going there—I don't mean to Blazes—but to West Africa.

source: Chapter 16 in *West African Studies* (London: Macmillan, 1901), 311–34.

―――――

A Letter to the Editor of
"The New Africa"

MARY KINGSLEY

The Union Liner "Moor,"
In the Bay of Biscay.
Dear Sir,

I have been anxious to write and thank you for the review of my book, *West African Studies,* which you published in the November number of the *New Africa.*

I have been prevented from so doing up to now by wretched health, caused by repeated attacks of influenza, and by pressure of work. I now take the opportunity of the leisure I have on board ship to attempt to thank you for having so sympathetically understood what my views on the subject of African culture were. I own it is no easy matter to do this, because I do not belong to any well-known party in this matter and my method of expression is, I know, bad; and I am therefore all the more grateful to those few who will take the trouble to understand what I mean.

This subject of the relationship between European and African culture is one in which I am quite deeply interested. I am quite sure that the majority of the Anglo-Saxons are good men, and I am equally sure the majority of the true Negroes are good men—possibly the percentage of perfect angels and calm scientific minds in both races is less than might be desired, but that we cannot help. Now it seems to me a deplorable thing that the present state of feeling between the two races should be so strained; and that unsatisfactory state, I cannot avoid thinking, arises largely from mutual misunderstanding. It does not seem to me to be unavoidable—a natural race hatred—but a thing removable by making the two people understand each other, and by avoiding rousing a hatred in either for the other by forcing them into interference with each other's institutions.

The great difficulty is of course how to get the people to understand each other. The white race seems to me to blame in saying that all the reason for its interference in Africa is the improvement of the native African, and then proceeding to alter African institutions without in the least understanding them; while the African is to blame for not placing clearly before the Anglo-Saxon what African institutions really are, and so combating the false and exaggerated view given of them by stray travellers, missionaries and officials, who for their own aggrandisement exaggerate the difficulties and dangers with which they have to deal. It is mere human nature for them to do this thing, but the effect produced on the minds of our statesmen has terrible consequences. The stay-at-home statesmen think that Africans are awful savages or silly children—people who can only be dealt with on a reformatory penitentiary line. This view you know is not mine, nor that of the very small party—the scientific ethnologists—who deal with Africa; but it is the view of the statesmen and the general public and the mission public, in African affairs. And it will remain so until you who know European culture, who are educated in our culture, and who also know African culture, will take your place as true ambassadors and peacemakers between the two races and place before the English statesmen the true African, and destroy the fancy African made by exaggeration, that he has now in his mind. Forgive me for speaking plainly upon a very delicate point, but it seems to me that the leading men among the European-educated Africans have depended too much on the religious side of the question. I know that there is a general opinion among the leading men of both races that Christianity will give the one possible solution to the whole problem. I fail to be able to believe this. I fail to believe Christianity will bring peace between the two races, for the simple reason that though it may be possible to convert Africans *en masse* into practical Christians, it is quite impossible so to convert Europeans *en masse.* You have only got to look at the history of any European nation—the Dutch, the Spanish, the Italian and German—every one calling themselves Christians, but none the more for that, tolerant and peaceable. Each one of them is ready to take out a patent for a road to Heaven and make that road out of men's blood and bones and the ashes of burnt homesteads. Of course by doing this they are not following the true teaching of Jesus Christ, but that has not and will not become a factor in politics. So I venture to say that you who build on Christianity in this matter are not building on safe ground. You cannot by talking about Christianity to the Europeans save your people. I believe there is a thing you could appeal to more safely in this case of the Anglo-Saxon, particularly the English—that thing is *honour,* the honour of a gentleman. There are thousands of Englishmen who would not mind being told they were no Christians to do so and so, who would mind being told they were no gentlemen to do so and so, and who would not do wrong if they knew the facts of the case; who would not destroy native independence and institutions if they but knew what those things really were; who would respect native law if they knew what it was, and who would give over sneering at the African and respect him if they knew him as he is really and truly, as I have known him; and who, though they might say, as I do, the African is different from the European, yet would say, he is a very fine fellow and we can be friends. Then there is another factor in this matter I wish you to consider carefully and let me some day know your opinion on, namely, the factor of nationalism. I believe that no race can, as a race, advance except on its own line of development, and that it is the duty of England, if she intends really and truly to advance the African on the plane of culture and make him a citizen of the world, to preserve the African nationalism and not destroy it; but destroy it she will unless you who know it come forward and demonstrate that African nationalism is a good thing, and that it is not a welter of barbarism, cannibalism and cruelty. I have had to stand up alone these two years and fight for African freedom and institutions, while Africans equally well and better educated in English culture have been talking about religious matters, etc., to a pack of people who do *not care* about Christianity at all. The Christian general public up here will bring little influence to bear on preserving Africa's institutions. The public, be it granted, is a powerful one, but it has been taught that all African native institutions are bad, and unless you preserve your institutions, above all *your land law,* you cannot, no race can, preserve your liberty.

I should like to direct your attention to a book called *Black Jamaica,* by a Mr. Livingston, recently published. That book is much thought of just now. In it you will see it put down that those Africans who went as slaves to Jamaica were people of no culture of their own; they were, as it were, slates or blank sheets of paper on which any man could write what he chose to. Well, that is not true. Those Africans had a culture of their own—not a perfect one, but one that could be worked up towards perfection, just as European culture could be worked up. I do not say that if Europe does break down the nationality of Africa she will utterly destroy Africans or African culture, but I do say that if she does it, she will make the Africans a people like the Jews—a landless people and an unhappy people. I beg you, Sir, to do your best to prevent this fate falling on your noble race. I believe you can best do it by stating that there is an African law and an African culture; that the African has institutions and a state form of his own. I believe if you do this thing fairly and well, that England at any rate will not destroy the African nationality, nor will she give them an African grievance, as she from *ignorance* not *intention* has given the Irish. If you will look up the old Irish Brehon laws, you will find there the same form of land law you have in Africa. The English have only during the past 50 years or so known that law. Had they known it in Elizabeth's day, we should have had no Irish land question. You have the chance. God is always giving chances of teaching men in time how to prevent a repetition of the Irish tragedy. I think if you will do the work it will be good work. Mr. Sarbah is at present the only man who has worked on the question, in his book on *Fanti Customary Law*. That book has done a great deal, and Mr. Sarbah deserves well of his countrymen, who wish to be free citizens and not slaves, *however cultured in European culture.*

Forgive this ill-written letter. I am writing in the Bay of Biscay, an unrestful place for writing in. I am on my way over to nurse fever cases in South Africa. I may never see West Africa again, but if I do, I hope it will be Liberia. I assure you I shall always feel grateful for the invitation to come there. I know I have been a nuisance. I know I have spoken words in wrath about the educated missionary-made African, and I am glad to hear you will tolerate me, I who desire to get on with the utter Bushman and never sneer or laugh at his native form of religion, a pantheism which I confess is a form of my own religion. I yield to no one in the admiration for Jesus Christ, and I believe in the Divine origin, but the religion His ministers preached I have never been able to believe in.

I hear my friend, Dr. Blyden, is in Liberia; if he is, please ask him if he got the books I sent him to Sierra Leone, Le Bon's *Psychology of People* and another, all right. Please give him my kindest regards, and ask him to write me a line saying how he is to Miss Kingsley, in care of the Standard Bank, Cape Town, South Africa, and believe me, Sir,

Yours gratefully,
M. H. Kingsley

SOURCE: Appendix in Stephen Gwynn's *The Life of Mary Kingsley* (London: Macmillan, 1932), 264–67.

———

Excerpts from *A Tropical Dependency*
FLORA L. SHAW (LADY LUGARD)

CHAPTER I. INTRODUCTORY

It has become the habit of the British mind to think of the British Empire as a white empire. But, as a matter of fact, we all know that ours is not a white empire. Out of an estimated population of 413,000,000, only 52,000,000, or one in eight, are white. Out of a territory of 16,000,000 square miles, which extends over a quarter of the globe, about 4,000,000 square miles, or a quarter of the whole, lies within the tropics.

The administration of this quarter of the Empire cannot be conducted on the principle of self-government as that phrase is understood by white men. It must be more or less in the nature of an autocracy which leaves with the rulers full responsibility for the prosperity of the ruled. The administration of India, where this aspect of the question has been long appreciated, is among the successes of which the British people is most justly proud. The work done by England in Egypt is another proof of our capacity for autocratic rule. We are justified therefore in thinking of ourselves as a people who may face with reasonable hopes of success still vaster questions of tropical administration.

We stand now at an interesting moment in our history. The most pressing questions which are connected with the self-governing colonies would seem to have been settled; attention and interest are set free to turn themselves towards other channels; and simultaneously with this liberation of public sympathy the direction of a new development is indicated by circumstances of almost irresistible significance.

Within the last five-and-twenty years we have acquired in tropical Africa alone territories of which the area exceeds by one-half the whole extent of British India. These, and other colonies and dependencies which lie within the tropics, now call for some of the same care and attention which have helped to make India what it is.

In nearly all the tropical colonies there is much fertile land which already produces some of the most necessary and valuable raw materials of trade. Cotton, silk, rice, rubber, sugar, coffee, tea, oils, drugs, dyes and spices, gold and gems, and other important elements of civilised industry, are home products of our tropics. But in very few of the colonies have these products been developed to anything approaching the natural capacity of their sources of origin. In many parts of the colonies the resources of nature have not been cultivated at all. Valuable commodities produce themselves and grow wild—unsown, unreaped. The increase which might result to British trade by a mere opening of the markets that lie as yet unapproached within the Empire, is past calculation. Such opening would necessarily be reciprocal in its action, and every market of supply over which our administration extended would automatically become a market of consumption for manufactured goods. At home the very prosperity of our trade creates a demand for expansion. And these potential markets are our own. We may do as we will within them.

The cultivation of our tropical lands involves, we are sometimes told, questions of transport and labour which are too difficult to touch. Of these the question of transport within the limits of our own colonies and protectorates is very largely a question of money, and its difficulties may easily be made to disappear whenever a real demand for transport shall arise. The question of labour is more serious. Tropical labour is coloured labour, and we have not yet faced the question of organising free coloured labour. But that this question has not yet been faced is not a reason why the difficulties attending it should be regarded as insurmountable. They must be reckoned among the most interesting problems of tropical administration.

The industrial development of ancient civilisations was largely based on slavery, and, from the earliest periods of which history has any record, countries lying within the tropics—always prolific of population—were raided to supply the slave-markets of the world. It was thought worth while in the great days of Egypt, Persia, Greece, Rome, and mediæval Spain, to be at the expense of sending caravans into the Soudan for slaves, who had to be hunted and caught in the tropical regions further south. Notwithstanding the cost of the overland journey, the expense and waste of slave-hunting, and the large percentage of deaths which occurred in transit, the labour of Africa was considered valuable enough to be worth transporting to any market in which it was required. The trade was continued through the Middle Ages, and under modern conditions of steam shipping and travelling it was still found worth while less than fifty years ago to carry African labour to America.

We have abolished slavery, and, as a consequence, it has been assumed that the labour which once supplied the great industries of the world has ceased to have any value.

This is a curious anomaly, for which, however, many explanatory reasons might be produced. Coloured labour, without the control which the master exercises over the slave, has its peculiar difficulties. In the face of them the civilised communities of the Western world have abandoned the use of coloured labour, and the introduction of industrial and agricultural machinery, which began almost coincidently with the abolition of slavery, has minimised the consequences of the loss. The fact is not altered that African labour had through many ages of the world's history a very high marketable value. That this labour still exists, that it is native to an immense area of the tropical colonies, and that it will rapidly increase in volume under the conditions of peace and security introduced by British administration, are factors of great importance in considering the possible development of the resources of these colonies. To construct a bridge between the old system of civilisation and the new, by finding means to organise as free labour the labour which preceding generations could only use enslaved, would be to lead the way in a very sensible advance beyond the first and necessary step of the abolition of slavery.

In speaking of ancient civilisations, I have not mentioned the ancient civilisations of the Far East, where industry is believed to have been first carried to the highest pitch. The industries of the Far East were supplied with other than African labour. From the earliest times the Chinese have been famed for manual dexterity, and Eastern industries have been based upon yellow labour. Yellow labour was carried to a far higher degree of perfection than black labour ever seems to have attained, and yellow labour has never been thrown out of employment. The products of its industries were always largely imported by the nations which owned black slaves. It retains to-day the dexterity for which it was famous in the period of the Pharaohs. But the kingdoms of the East having risen earlier to a condition of cohesion in which they were able to protect their subjects, and having also from a very early period maintained the policy of exclusion practised by Egypt in its greatest days, yellow labour has never been used to supply the slave-markets of the West. Western communities have felt the same repugnance to the employment of free Chinese labour that they felt to the employment of free African labour, and we have had to wait for the present conjunction of events in order to see yellow labour, under the direction of intelligence as acute as any intelligence of the West, prepare to enter into competition with white labour in the industrial markets of the world.

That Japan, which has now established its military and naval ascendancy on the shores of the Pacific, will proceed to the fuller development of its industrial resources, is scarcely doubtful. The labour of China is under its hand. We have therefore an additional reason to take stock of our imperial and of our industrial position. We have within our Empire a body of coloured labour greater than any which Japan can at present command. There is nothing to prevent us from attracting by immigration as much more as we please. But in order to use our own, or to attract more with profit to the Empire, we must face the whole question of tropical administration. We must study with an open mind the thorny questions of native labour. We must prepare and make known those parts of hitherto undeveloped colonies to which it may be considered desirable to attract labour. We must introduce systems of transport by means of which not only the fruits of labour but labour itself may be able to circulate within the Empire. We must, no doubt, in many instances recast our local labour laws. We must frankly recognise the fact that labour is the foundation upon which development rests.

We may at the same time have the satisfaction, even in our earliest beginnings, of knowing that the development of the tropical colonies, if we undertake it seriously, will not end with industrial development. There are many sides to the history of nations, and in the attempt to introduce order and industry into the at present uncivilised areas of many of our tropical possessions, we shall no doubt meet with innate powers unsuspected now, that in more favourable conditions may blossom into life.

Our fathers, by a self-denying ordinance, did what they could to set the subject populations free. It was nobly conceived, and civilisation has profited by the step in human progress that was made. But the actual enjoyment of freedom is still far from the African native. If we could realise the dream of abolition by carrying freedom to every village, and so direct our administration that under it the use of liberty would be learned, we should be filling a place that any nation might be proud to hold in the annals of civilisation. It is not a mere unworthy dream of gain which turns our eyes towards the tropics. It is a great opportunity which seems to be presenting itself in national life, one which affords scope for the best qualities and highest talents that we can command.

It is not, therefore, surprising that interest in tropical questions should of late have become more general, and it is only when we begin to think about them that we realise how very little we know of some of our newer possessions in the tropics. A recognition of this ignorance on my own part in relation to the interior of West Africa has led me to study such authorities as I could find, and, with a very profound sense of my own incompetence in dealing with a subject which demands the care and attention of an accomplished Oriental scholar, I have put together a little account of the general movement of civilisation in the Western Soudan which may perhaps serve rather as a basis for future criticism than for any of the permanent purposes of history. Fresh information comes almost daily to light in the territories occupied by civilised powers, which will doubtless elucidate many points now left obscure, and rectify mistaken conclusions. In the meantime, what I have been able to gather, in part from original manuscripts, but chiefly from translations of Arab historians, may interest some of those who, like myself, desire to have a connected idea of the civilisations which have preceded our own in our lately acquired territories in the interior of West Africa. I am, of course, chiefly concerned with the territories of the protectorate lying on the watershed of the Niger and the Benué, of which the administration was only assumed by the British Government on the 1st of January 1900. By this occupation an entirely new chapter has been opened in the relations of Great Britain with West Africa.

CHAPTER XLV. THE ESTABLISHMENT OF BRITISH ADMINISTRATION

It will be understood that in attempting, as I am now about to do, to give some account of the establishment of British administration in the midst of the conditions which have been described, I enter upon a difficult portion of my task. The British High Commissioner is my husband. Many members of his staff have become my personal friends. It is impossible for me altogether to clear my mind of favourable prejudice, and I am forced to realise that the detachment which gives the proportion of history is no longer at my command. I can only therefore ask beforehand for indulgence if in this last section of my book personal sentiment tends to warp my judgment of the relative importance of events.

The rulers of the Nigerian territories had placed themselves nominally, for reasons which rendered a choice of European protectors essential to them, under the protection of Great Britain. By their treaties with the Royal Niger Company some of them had nominally surrendered their territory with all sovereign rights. Others, and these the most important, including the emirates of Sokoto and Gando, had agreed to enter into treaty with no other white nation but the British; to give to Great Britain jurisdiction over all foreigners and non-natives in their dominions, with right to tax them; to transfer to Great Britain sovereign rights in the riverine territories of the Niger and the Benué for a distance of ten hours' journey inland from the banks of the two rivers; to confer also rights of mining and trading; and generally, while reserving their own powers of internal rule, to subordinate themselves in external matters to the protecting power. They had, in fact, by treaty, accepted the recognised position of protected native states. The equivalent which was to be given by Great Britain was protection against external powers and respect for internal law and custom. On one side, as on the other, the maintenance of communication and friendly relations was provided for.

Bornu had made no treaty with the Company, but by virtue of international agreement it fell within the territory allotted to the influence of Great Britain.

The relations of protecting powers to protected states are always a question of discussion until they have been placed by the logic of accomplished facts outside the limits of theory. The exact measure of responsibility accepted by Great Britain in Northern Nigeria, at the moment of the establishment of British administration there, would have been difficult to define. The vague title of suzerain covered the position, and, beyond a general desire that slave-raiding should be suppressed and trade routes thrown open, there was probably no wish in any quarter in England to see a rapid advance towards the assumption of more defined duties, or of responsibilities which would involve expense. The public generally knew nothing of the country. Political necessities had imposed the creation of a military force for the defence, not only of the Nigerian, but of all West African frontiers. A small grant in aid to meet other administrative expenses was reluctantly added by the Treasury to the sum required for the maintenance of the West African Frontier Force. These concessions were made rather by respect for the judgment and the wishes of

Mr. Chamberlain, then occupying the position of Secretary of State for the Colonies, than by any strong conviction on the part of the British Government that Northern Nigeria was likely to prove a very valuable acquisition to the Crown; and in the absence of a clearly expressed interest on the part of the House of Commons, in the adoption of a new West African policy, it seemed improbable that funds would be willingly voted for any full development of the Nigerian Protectorate. In these circumstances the wishes of the Government and of the country, if they had to be condensed into one phrase of instruction to the High Commissioner, would perhaps best have been rendered by the words, "Go slow!"

But events upon the spot refused to wait. From the moment in which the British flag ran up at Lokoja on the 1st of January 1900, the High Commissioner and his staff found themselves taxed to the utmost limits of their capacity in the effort to keep pace with the developments which hurried them along.

The first desire of the High Commissioner upon taking up the duties of his position would naturally have been to give effect to British treaty obligations by establishing residents at the native courts, and proceeding to open friendly relations throughout the Protectorate. He found himself face to face with a chaos of civil and inter-tribal war, in which his immediate duty was to endeavour to ascertain the disposition towards the Government which he represented of the dominant powers. He had also everything to learn about the actual condition of the northern country.

The civil staff allotted for the purpose of founding an administration was very small, and its numbers were liable to be reduced by illness and leave. The Ashantee War, which had broken out in another portion of West Africa, shortly claimed all the troops of the West African Frontier Force that could be spared, and the South African War drawing to itself all the best military activity of the nation, rendered it difficult to obtain efficient officers for the remainder of the regiment. Almost single-handed in every administrative department, the little group who formed the government at Lokoja felt that they had every reason during the first year of the administration to wish for their own sakes to "go slow."

There was the machinery of administration to establish, of which the seat was temporarily fixed at Jebba, where the military headquarters had been formed. There was the transfer from the Royal Niger Company, the taking over of their assets, and the work of assigning to them their trading stations, to be attended to. There was the neighbouring country to survey, in the hopes of finding, within friendly territory, a more suitable and central position in which the permanent seat of government could be established, under healthier conditions than those offered by either Lokoja or Jebba, in the malarial valley of the Niger, and there were relations to establish with such chiefs as might prove friendly in the neighbourhood. While the High Commissioner and the civil staff undertook the formation of Administrative Departments, the duty of surveying the country was committed to military expeditions, which, moving in strength sufficient to protect themselves against disaster, were strictly enjoined to avoid all occasion of conflict with the natives, to endeavour as far as possible to win the confidence of the people, and to submit reports on the economic and geographical conditions of the country. Three such parties were sent out to examine the country lying to the north of the confluence of the Niger and the Benué between the river Kaduna and the eastern highlands of Bautchi.

Though Fulani emirs were at the time slave-raiding in these districts, it was believed from information received that the native tribes were friendly and would be willing to welcome Europeans, and here it was thought likely that a permanent administrative centre might be formed in the southern part of the province of Zaria, bordering upon the Kaduna river. In the absence of railroads, necessities of transport rendered it impossible for any position to be taken far from a navigable river. Some little opposition was met by two of the survey parties, who were obliged to reduce some intractable pagan tribes, but no serious fighting occurred; and from the geographical and topographical reports of the surveys, it was, after some discussion, decided that the site for the new seat of government would be most favourably placed in the neighbourhood of the native town of Wushishi, on the river Kaduna. This river, often mentioned in the ancient geography of the country, is one of the important rivers of the Protectorate, and drains the south-western watershed to the Niger. It is navigable for a large portion of the year by steamers, and during the dry season by steel canoes. A small garrison was accordingly left at Wushishi, and relations were in the meantime cultivated with the southern states. The disturbed condition of the country was such that, pending the establishment of the new headquarters, no attempt was made to open relations with the Fulani emirates of the north, otherwise than by the despatch of conciliatory letters informing the Sultans of Gando and Sokoto of the assumption of administration by the British Government, and of the desire of Great Britain to maintain friendly relations.

The southern provinces of Northern Nigeria, as they spread on the south bank of the rivers from west to east, are Ilorin, Kabba, Bassa, part of Muri, and part of Yola. Immediately to the north of these, and with the exception of Borgu, all on the northern side of the rivers, are—taking them again from west to east—Borgu, Kontagora, Southern Zaria, Nupe, Nassarawa, Bautchi, and the northern half of Muri and Yola; in all, eleven provinces out of the seventeen of which Northern Nigeria is composed. Of these provinces three only, Borgu, Ilorin, and Kabba, were, in the first instance, effectively occupied by the British. Jebba, situated on an island in the Niger between the mainland of Ilorin and Kontagora, commanded the southern province.

On the nothern banks the pagan populations welcomed the advent of the British, but the Fulani emirs of Kontagora and Nupe soon removed all doubt as to their hostile attitude. The British occupation was scarcely effected before they were openly slave-raiding to the banks of the river. Their combined armies laid waste their own country from the Niger banks on the west and south to the eastern highlands, and to the north as far as the frontiers of Sokoto and Zaria. The Emir of Zaria, in whose territory the site chosen for the future seat of British government, near Wushishi, was situated, was nominally friendly to Great Britain, but in the beginning of July 1900 information reached the High Commissioner at Jebba that Kontagora and Nupe had planned a combined attack upon the little British garrison at Wushishi, and he hurried there in person with reinforcements under Major O'Neill. The situation became so acute that the population began to desert Wushishi, and in order to obtain supplies for the British troops and to protect the villages which had been friendly, it became necessary to erect some small forts in the neighbourhood, and to order Major O'Neill to patrol the country. This task being admirably performed, and the cavalry of Nupe and Kontagora defeated in a series of brilliant skirmishes, the country was occupied by British troops for some twenty miles south and east of Wushishi. Great loss was inflicted on the slave-raiders in the encounters by which the occupation was effected, and the people, siding as always with the party of success, crowded in thousands to the protected villages for safety. A situation was created in which the British Government already represented in the eyes of the natives a power strong enough to protect them against the scourge of the slave-raider.

But, as a matter of fact, with the body of the troops still absent in Ashantee, the local administration did not feel itself to be in a position to sustain suspended hostilities. A British Resident had been placed at the friendly court of Ilorin, where, while he worked hard at the introduction of domestic reforms, he was made aware that emissaries from Nupe and Kontagora were endeavouring to induce the Emir of Ilorin to join with them in an attempt to overpower the British and drive the white anti-slaver out of the country. The position was dangerous as well as delicate, and while the small force of soldiers at Wushishi held their own, and even on one occasion, somewhat rashly, drove the enemy before them to the walls of the Nupe capital at Bida, the desire of the High Commissioner was to avoid all but strictly necessary fighting. The Resident at Ilorin, Mr. Carnegie, by whose subsequent death the administration lost a most valuable officer, exerted all the tact and the pluck at his command to keep things quiet in Ilorin.

During these months the High Commissioner at headquarters was pressing forward the organisation of the administrative departments, creating a system for dealing with the freed slaves, especially the slave children who were liberated in the encounters with the slave-raiders, endeavouring to get into touch with other provinces who gave friendly indications along the river banks, and evolving the first framework of local legislation.

The creation of a judicial system was among the early necessities of the administration, and in these first few turbulent months the seeds of future order were sown. By legislative proclamation, British Supreme and Provincial Courts were established, and the jurisdiction of each defined. Two Cantonment or Magistrates' Courts were also established in Lokoja and Jebba, and by a Native Courts' proclamation the establishment of Native Courts by British warrant was provided for in all provinces under British jurisdiction. This measure, necessary for the province of Ilorin, was as yet hardly applicable to pagan provinces, where native institutions had not attained to the level of a judicial organisation. A slavery proclamation forbade the enslaving of any person within the Protectorate, and without directly touching the institution of domestic slavery, reaffirmed, under the new administration, the abolition of the legal status of slavery, which had been proclaimed by the Niger Company after their Bida campaign. All children born within the Protectorate after April 1, 1901, were declared free. Laws were also issued against the importation of liquor and firearms.

The busy days as they passed pressed their own conclusions upon the minds of the High Commissioner and his staff, and the theory of a future policy was formed under the light of daily practice. The High Commissioner had the advantage of including in his staff one or two of the servants of the Niger Company, whose knowledge of local conditions was invaluable. The Accounting Department, which he had used in connection with the organisation of the West African Frontier Force, became, with a little reorganisation, the Treasury of the new administration. The vessels which formed the material of a Marine Department were taken over from the Niger Company. The staff included the necessary doctors and legal officers for the formation of Medical and Legal Departments. The Public Works Department, after an unfortunate preliminary delay, during which the European staff was left almost without houses, was formed, under the direction of Mr. Eaglesome, an engineer of Indian experience, into a body of which the efficiency and economy soon became a subject of considerable local pride. The rest of the staff,

loyally supported by a few white noncommissioned officers and civil subordinates, was chiefly composed of that fine type of young Englishmen who,
whether as soldiers or civilians, have it in their minds to serve their country, to
the best of their ability, in some adventurous capacity which will take them
out of the common round of comfortable life. Their experience of Africa was
mostly nil, but they had the training of the public school, the army, and the
university, which fits men equally for the assumption of responsibility and for
loyal subordination to authority. They were ready to go anywhere and to do
anything, and with the few inevitable exceptions, who were rapidly weeded
out, represented, in the eyes of the High Commissioner, the very best stuff of
which the English nation is made.

He had in them the instruments that he wanted, and he worked them
without mercy, as hard as he worked himself. The staff was short-handed.
There was three men's work for every man to do, and during the initial stage
of the establishment of British authority in the country, it is not too much to
say that the whole of the staff, civil as well as military, gave themselves with
entire devotion to their task. There was little of alleviation or of pleasure in
the early conditions. Miserable houses, bad food, a malarial climate, and
ceaseless responsibility, formed the accompaniment of their daily existence.
With the inveterate determination of Englishmen to have some form of
sport, a polo ground was among the earliest of the public institutions established by the soldiers at headquarters. But it was the work itself which furnished the real attraction of the life, and had the small body of Europeans
who formed the first British staff been polled for their opinions, there would
not probably have been found one who wished to turn back from the task
which grew day by day under their hands.

In view of the pessimism which appears in some quarters to be gaining
ground with regard to the capacities of the English race, I may perhaps
without indiscretion quote a passage from one of the latest of my husband's
despatches, which shows at least how in his opinion the staff working under
him have sustained the promise of the first year's performance. "There are no
words of praise," he writes under date of August 1905, "that I can find too
strong to describe the indefatigable efforts and the enthusiasm for their task
which has been shown by the Political Staff. By their ceaseless devotion to
duty they have not only increased the revenue in the way that I have shown,
but have brought order, peace, and security out of chaos, have established an
effective judicial system, and have substituted progress and development for
misrule and stagnation." This is satisfactory reading for those who doubt
whether the Englishmen of to-day are capable of the same achievements as
their fathers, and it must be counted as not the least among the advantages of

the colonial development of the Empire that by its very roughness it gives opportunity for the exercise in individuals of qualities which under less stimulating circumstances might perhaps lie dormant through the whole course of a too easy life. The names, alas, of more than one of the first small Nigerian group are engraved now upon tombstones on that border of the Empire which they helped to make. They live in the memory of good service done, and their work accomplished is, as they would have wished it to be, their monument.

SOURCE: Chapters 1 and 45 in *A Tropical Dependency: An Outline of the Ancient History of the Western Soudan with an Account of the Modern Settlement of Northern Nigeria* (London: James Nisbet, 1905), 1–7, 417–24.

THE ADMINISTRATION:
CECIL J. RHODES AND THE
BRITISH SOUTH AFRICA
COMPANY

INTRODUCTION
Cecil J. Rhodes: Colossus or Caricature?
BARBARA HARLOW

ASTRIDE THE CONTINENT of Africa, from Cape Town to Cairo, Cecil John Rhodes was recognized, even beyond the reach of *Punch* magazine's now nearly prototypical 1892 representation of the nineteenth-century mining and banking magnate, as a determining influence in British imperial policies in southern Africa. Rhodes's ambitions in and for Africa were at once territorial, financial, and political, and his example loomed large both during his lifetime and posthumously. He was the stuff of Trooper Peter Halket's visions of advancement in Olive Schreiner's novel; his decease was commemorated by the poet of empire, Rudyard Kipling; and *Punch*'s pages were regularly graced and glamorized by his various figurations. But as the 1896 cartoon "My Career Is Only Beginning" shows, it was a legend not without its peripeties and precariousness. Surefooted as "the colossus" might have seemed to some at times, his agenda was for others both a challenge and a crisis-ridden set of claims as he sought to straddle the competitions of inter- and intracontinental rivalries and colonial prospects. Rhodes himself, however, was throughout his lifetime an ardently outspoken, if also self-serving, proponent for the development of Africa—by British imperialism. His public speeches as well as his private pleadings addressed topics that ranged from the expansion and the settlement of British interests across the African continent to the reliability and resistances of native labor, colonial governance, and, of course, the agenda of the "chartered company."

Rhodes was born on 5 July 1854 in a small Hertfordshire village north of London, the sixth surviving child of his parents, churchman Francis William Rhodes and his wife, Louisa. For all the splendor of his subsequent, albeit short-lived (he lived not even half a century, dying of a longtime heart ailment at the age of forty-eight) career, his childhood was apparently altogether ordinary. In 1870, however, at the age of seventeen, he went to South Africa, to join his brother who was farming cotton in Natal. But, following up on the discovery of diamonds in Kimberley in 1867, he proceeded north to seek there another kind of fortune, and even while completing a much-desired degree at Oriel College, Oxford, he managed to build up a more-than-successful diamond business in South Africa. The De Beers Mining Company (named for the farmer on whose land the first diamond had been discovered), which Rhodes formed in 1880, won out in the amalgamation struggle against both competitors and the strenuous opposition from supporters of another, freer, kind of trade. Rhodes went on to launch Goldfields of South Africa in 1887 and to charter the British South Africa Company in 1889, thus repeatedly capitalizing on the discovery of diamonds and, later, gold in the Witwatersrand, as well as continuing the chartered company tradition. He secured the charter for his British South Africa Company in part with a "gift" of £10,000 to Charles Stewart Parnell's Irish Home Rule Party in exchange—however paradoxically—for their eighty-five votes in Parliament endorsing his expansionist imperial designs. Rhodes served in the Cape Parliament and then as prime minister of the Cape Colony from 1890 until 1896, when he was forced to resign following the ill-fated raid against Afrikaners in the Transvaal, which was led by his longtime friend Dr. Leander Starr Jameson—some say with the complicit approval of Joseph Chamberlain—in December 1895. As far as Rhodes was concerned, the Transvaal Boers were all too intransigent when it came to English and "uitlander" predilections and predispositions toward control over the province's wealth in mineral resources, and four years later the British and the Boers did go to war over its eventual dispensation. Meanwhile, Rhodes fought to extend British control northward, over all of Africa, in a plan that was to connect British interests by rail and telegraph, thus fulfilling a "Cape to Cairo" dream and painting the continent's map in British red. But as Roger Casement would later write of Rhodes and his southern African example of colonial concupiscence,

> Probe not of England's valour in the field
> Her heart is sick with lust.
> The gold she wins is red with blood, nor can it shield
> Her name from tainted league with men of broken trust.

Others were equally critical of Rhodes's ends and means alike, including radical political economist and anti-imperialist J. A. Hobson and novelist and feminist Olive Schreiner. A public figure, financier, adventurer, entrepreneur, and politician with territorial designs, Rhodes nonetheless lived on into the late twentieth century in the name of Rhodesia (now Zimbabwe), which he claimed to have made his own following his nefarious campaigns against the "natives" in the Matabele and Mashona lands. It was there, too, that he asked to be buried, atop the Matopos, still overseeing his ill-won gains. He died in 1902, a year after Victoria's death and just months before the conclusion of the Anglo-Boer War.

Rhodes's "last will and testament"—edited and executed by his publicist, erstwhile friend, and adamant antiwar activist, W. T. Stead of the *Review of Reviews*—summarizes well the legacy he hoped to leave: his property in Rhodesia, where he would be interred; the preservation of Groote Schuur, his residence by Table Mountain in the Cape Colony; and the Rhodes scholarships at Oxford for the continued "education of young colonists."

BIBLIOGRAPHY

Ally, Russell. *Gold and Empire: The Bank of England and South Africa's Gold Producers 1886–1926.* Johannesburg: Witwatersrand University Press, 1994.

Bennett, Compton, and Andrew Marton, dirs. *King Solomon's Mines.* United States, 1950. Film.

Buchan, John. *A Lodge in the Wilderness.* London: Thomas Nelson and Sons, 1906–1907.

Burns, James. "Biopics and Politics: The Making and Unmaking of the Rhodes Movies." *Biography* 23, no. 1 (2000): 108–26.

Coan, Stephen, ed. *Diary of an African Journey: The Return of H. Rider Haggard.* Pietermaritzburg: University of Natal Press, 2000.

Drury, David, dir. *Rhodes.* London: British Broadcasting Company, 1996. Film.

Galbraith, John S. *Crown and Charter: The Early Years of the British South Africa Company.* Berkeley: University of California Press, 1974.

Haggard, H. Rider. *King Solomon's Mines.* 1885. Oxford: Oxford University Press, 1989.

Kendle, John E. *The Round Table Movement and Imperial Union.* London: Longmans, 1967.

Millin, Sarah Gertrude. *Rhodes.* London: Chatto and Windus, 1933.

Plaatje, Sol T. *Native Life in South Africa.* 1916. Johannesburg: Ravan Press, 1982.

Plomer, William. *Cecil Rhodes.* London: P. Davies, 1933.

Rakoff, Alvin, dir. *King Solomon's Mines.* 1977. Film.

Raphael, Lois A. C. *The Cape-to-Cairo Dream: A Study in British Imperialism.* New York: Columbia University Press, 1936.

Stevenson, Robert, dir. *King Solomon's Mines,* starring Paul Robeson. United Kingdom, 1937. Film.

Thomas, Antony. *Rhodes: The Race for Africa.* London: BBC Books, 1996.

Thompson, J. Lee, dir. *King Solomon's Mines.* United States, 1985. Film.

Viertel, Berthold, dir. *Rhodes of Africa,* produced by Michael Balcon. United Kingdom, 1936. Film.

Excerpt from *Trooper Peter Halket*
of Mashonaland

OLIVE SCHREINER

[Olive Schreiner's (1855–1920) novel tells the story of young Peter Halket, a British soldier in the service of Rhodes's chartered company in Mashonaland. The narrative relays an anti-imperialist perspective as the fledgling recruit is obliged to come to terms with the differences between his entrepreneurial ambitions and the means—such as shooting prisoners—toward those ends.]

All men made money when they came to South Africa,—Barney Barnato, Rhodes—they all made money out of the country, eight millions, twelve millions, twenty-six millions, forty millions; why should not he!

Peter Halket started suddenly and listened. But it was only the wind coming up the kopje like a great wheezy beast creeping upwards; and he looked back into the fire.

He considered his business prospects. When he had served his time as volunteer he would have a large piece of land given him, and the Mashonas and Matabeles would have all their land taken away from them in time, and the Chartered Company would pass a law that they had to work for the white men; and he, Peter Halket, would make them work for him. He would make money.

Then he reflected on what he should do with the land if it were no good and he could not make anything out of it. Then, he should have to start a syndicate; called the Peter Halket Gold, or the Peter Halket Iron-mining, or some such name, Syndicate. Peter Halket was not very clear as to how it ought to be started; but he felt certain that he and some other men would have to take shares. They would not have to pay for them. And then they would get some big man in London to take shares. He need not pay for them; they would give them to him; and then the company would be floated. No one would have to pay anything; it was just the name—'The Peter Halket Gold Mining Company, Limited'. It would float in London; and people there who didn't know the country would buy the shares; *they* would have to give ready money for them, of course; perhaps fifteen pounds a share when they were up!—Peter Halket's eyes blinked as he looked into the fire.—And then, when the market was up, he, Peter Halket, would sell out all his shares. If he gave himself only six thousand and sold them each for ten pounds, then he, Peter Halket, would have sixty thousand pounds! And then he would start another company, and another.

Peter Halket struck his knee softly with his hand.

That was the great thing—'Always sell out at the right time.' That point Peter Halket was very clear on. He had heard it so often discussed. Give some shares to men with big names, and sell out: they can sell out too at the right time.

Peter Halket stroked his knee thoughtfully.

And then the other people, that bought the shares for cash! Well, they could sell out too; they could *all* sell out!

Then Peter Halket's mind got a little hazy. The matter was getting too difficult for him, like a rule of three sum at school when he could not see the relation between the two first terms and the third. Well, if they didn't like to sell out at the right time, it was their own faults. Why didn't they? He, Peter Halket, did not feel responsible for them. Everyone knew that you had to sell out at the right time. If they didn't choose to sell out at the right time, well, they didn't. '*It's the shares that you sell, not the shares you keep, that make the money.*'

But if they *couldn't* sell them?

Here Peter Halket hesitated.—Well, the British Government would have to buy them, if they were so bad no one else would; and then no one would lose. 'The British Government can't let British shareholders suffer.' He'd heard that often enough. The British taxpayer would have to pay for the Chartered Company, for the soldiers, and all the other things, if *it* couldn't, and take over the shares if it went smash, because there were lords and dukes and princes connected with it. And why shouldn't they pay for *his* company? He would have a lord in it too!

Peter Halket looked into the fire completely absorbed in his calculations.— Peter Halket, Esq., Director of the Peter Halket Gold Mining Company, Limited. Then, when he had got thousands, Peter Halket, Esq., M.P. Then, when he had millions, Sir Peter Halket, Privy Councillor!

He reflected deeply, looking into the blaze. If you had five or six millions you could go where you liked and do what you liked. You could go to

The Rhodes Colossus: Striding from Cape Town to Cairo.
SOURCE: *Punch* (10 December 1892): 266.

My Career Is Only Beginning! (*See* Report of Mr. Rhodes's brief speech
before leaving South Africa, Jan. 1896.). Performer (loq.): "Think I will
postpone appearance in public and go back again." "Mr. Rhodes will
immediately return to South Africa. . . . Curiosity will probably be whetted rather
than allayed by this intimation."—*Times,* Feb. 8.
SOURCE: *Punch* (15 February 1896): 74.

Sandringham. You could marry anyone. No one would ask what your mother had been; it wouldn't matter.

A curious dull sinking sensation came over Peter Halket; and he drew in his broad leathern belt two holes tighter.

Even if you had only two millions you could have a cook and a valet, to go with you when you went into the veld or to the wars; and you could have as much champagne and other things as you liked. At that moment that seemed to Peter more important than going to Sandringham.

He took out his flask of Cape Smoke, and drew a tiny draught from it.

Other men had come to South Africa with nothing, and had made everything! Why should not he?

He stuck small branches under the two great logs, and a glorious flame burst out. Then he listened again intently. The wind was falling and the night was becoming very still. It was a quarter to twelve now. His back ached, and he would have liked to lie down; but he dared not, for fear he should drop asleep. He leaned forward with his hands between his crossed knees, and watched the blaze he had made.

Then, after a while, Peter Halket's thoughts became less clear: they became at last, rather, a chain of disconnected pictures, painting themselves in irrelevant order on his brain, than a line of connected ideas. Now, as he looked into the crackling blaze, it seemed to be one of the fires they had made to burn the natives' grain by, and they were throwing in all they could not carry away: then, he seemed to see his mother's fat ducks waddling down the little path with the green grass on each side. Then, he seemed to see his huts where he lived with the prospectors, and the native women who used to live with him; and he wondered where the women were. Then—he saw the skull of an old Mashona blown off at the top, the hands still moving. He heard the loud cry of the native women and children as they turned the maxims on to the kraal; and then he heard the dynamite explode that blew up a cave. Then again he was working a maxim gun, but it seemed to him it was more like the reaping machine he used to work in England, and that what was going down before it was not yellow corn, but black men's heads; and he thought when he looked back they lay behind him in rows, like the corn in sheaves.

SOURCE: From chapter 1 in *Trooper Peter Halket of Mashonaland* (1897; Parklands, South Africa: Ad. Donker, 1992), 32–36.

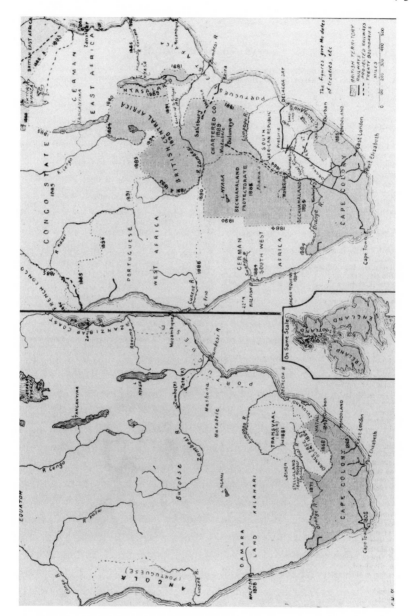

South Africa before and after Cecil Rhodes. SOURCE: *Review of Reviews* 13 (1896): 129.

────────

We Abandon Hope

H. RIDER HAGGARD

[H. Rider Haggard (1856–1925) began his career as a representative of British imperialism in South Africa and, on his return to Britain, translated that early African experience into the adventures of his novels' primary protagonist. Haggard went to South Africa in 1871, at the age of nineteen, as secretary to the governor of Natal, Sir Henry Bulwer, and in 1877, while on the staff of Sir Theophilus Shepstone, hoisted the British flag over the newly annexed territory of Transvaal. The hero of several of Haggard's adventure novels, Alan Quatermain, makes his first appearance in the still popular *King Solomon's Mines* (1885). In the company of Sir Henry Curtis and Captain John Good, whom he has met on board a ship lingering in Durban Harbor, Quatermain, who until then had "made his living as a trader in the old Colony," sets out to follow an ancient map in order to recover Curtis's brother, George, to quest for gold and diamonds, and in the process to liberate a tribe of African natives from their despotic ruler and restore their chief, Umbopa/Ignosi, to his rightful place at the head of his people.]

I can give no adequate description of the horrors of the night which followed. Mercifully they were to some extent mitigated by sleep, for even in such a position as ours, wearied nature will sometimes assert itself. But I, at any rate, found it impossible to sleep much. Putting aside the terrifying thought of our impending doom—for the bravest man on earth might well quail from such a fate as awaited us, and I never had any great pretensions to be brave—the *silence* itself was too great to allow of it. Reader, you may have lain awake at night and thought the silence oppressive, but I say with confidence that you can have no idea what a vivid tangible thing perfect silence really is. On the surface of the earth there is always some sound or motion, and though it may in itself be imperceptible, yet does it deaden the sharp edge of absolute silence. But here there was none. We were buried in the bowels of a huge snow-clad peak. Thousands of feet above us the fresh air rushed over the white snow, but no sound of it reached us. We were separated by a long tunnel and five feet of rock even from the awful chamber of the dead; and the dead make no noise. The crashing of all the artillery of earth and heaven could not have come to our ears in our living tomb. We were cut off from all echoes of the world—we were as already dead.

And then the irony of the situation forced itself upon me. There around us lay treasures enough to pay off a moderate national debt, or to build a fleet of ironclads, and yet we would gladly have bartered them all for the faintest chance of escape. Soon, doubtless, we should be glad to exchange them for a bit of food or a cup of water, and, after that, even for the privilege of a speedy close to our sufferings. Truly wealth, which men spend all their lives in acquiring, is a valueless thing at the last.

And so the night wore on.

'Good,' said Sir Henry's voice at last, and it sounded awful in the intense stillness, 'how many matches have you in the box?'

'Eight, Curtis.'

'Strike one, and let us see the time.'

He did so, and in contrast to the dense darkness the flame nearly blinded us. It was five o'clock by my watch. The beautiful dawn was now blushing on the snow-wreaths far over our heads, and the breeze would be stirring the night mists in the hollows.

'We had better eat something and keep up our strength,' said I.

'What is the good of eating?' answered Good; 'the sooner we die and get it over the better.'

'While there is life there is hope,' said Sir Henry.

Accordingly we ate and sipped some water, and another period of time passed, when somebody suggested that it might be as well to get as near to the door as possible, and halloa, on the faint chance of somebody catching a sound outside. Accordingly Good, who, from long practice at sea, has a fine piercing note, groped his way down the passage and began, and I must say he made a most diabolical noise. I never heard such yells; but it might have been a mosquito buzzing for all the effect it produced.

After a while he gave it up, and came back very thirsty, and had to have some water. After that we gave up yelling, as it encroached on the supply of water.

So we all sat down once more against our chests of useless diamonds in that dreadful inaction, which was one of the hardest circumstances of our fate; and I am bound to say that, for my part, I gave way in despair. Laying my head against Sir Henry's broad shoulder I burst into tears; and I think I heard Good gulping away on the other side, and swearing hoarsely at himself for doing so.

Ah, how good and brave that great man was! Had we been two frightened children, and he our nurse, he could not have treated us more tenderly. Forgetting his own share of miseries, he did all he could to soothe our broken nerves, telling stories of men who had been in somewhat similar circumstances, and miraculously escaped; and when these failed to cheer us, pointing out how, after all, it was only anticipating an end that must come to us all, that it would soon be over, and that death from exhaustion was a merciful one (which is not true). Then, in a diffident sort of a way, as I had once before heard him do, he suggested that we should throw ourselves on the mercy of a higher Power, which for my part I did with great vigour.

His is a beautiful character, very quiet, but very strong.

And so somehow the day went as the night had gone (if, indeed, one can use the terms where all was densest night), and when I lit a match to see the time it was seven o'clock.

Once more we ate and drank, and as we did so an idea occurred to me.

'How is it,' said I, 'that the air in this place keeps fresh? It is thick and heavy, but it is perfectly fresh.'

'Great heavens!' said Good, starting up, 'I never thought of that. It can't come through the stone door, for it is air-tight, if ever a door was. It must come from somewhere. If there were no current of air in the place we should have been stifled when we first came in. Let us have a look.'

It was wonderful what a change this mere spark of hope wrought in us. In a moment we were all three groping about the place on our hands and knees, feeling for the slightest indication of a draught. Presently my ardour received a check. I put my hand on something cold. It was poor Foulata's dead face.

For an hour or more we went on feeling about, till at last Sir Henry and I gave it up in despair, having got considerably hurt by constantly knocking our heads against tusks, chests, and the sides of the chamber. But Good still persevered, saying, with an approach to cheerfulness, that it was better than doing nothing.

'I say, you fellows,' he said, presently, in a constrained sort of voice, 'come here.'

Needless to say we scrambled over towards him quick enough.

'Quatermain, put your hand here where mine is. Now, do you feel anything?'

'I *think* I feel air coming up.'

'Now, listen.' He rose and stamped upon the place, and a flame of hope shot up in our hearts. *It rang hollow.*

With trembling hands I lit a match. I had only three left, and we saw that we were in the angle of the far corner of the chamber, a fact that accounted for our not having noticed the hollow ring of the place during our former exhaustive examination. As the match burnt we scrutinized the spot. There was a join in the solid rock floor, and, great heavens! there, let in level with the rock, was a stone ring. We said no word, we were too excited, and our hearts beat too wildly with hope to allow us to speak. Good had a knife, at the back of which was one of those hooks that are made to extract stones from horses' hoofs. He opened it, and scratched away at the ring with it. Finally he got it under, and levered away gently for fear of breaking the hook. The ring began to move. Being of stone, it had not got set fast in all the centuries it had lain there, as would have been the case had it been of iron. Presently it was upright. Then he got his hands into it and tugged with all his force, but nothing budged.

'Let me try,' I said, impatiently, for the situation of the stone, right in the angle of the corner, was such that it was impossible for two to pull at once. I got hold and strained away, but with no results.

Then Sir Henry tried and failed.

Taking the hook again, Good scratched all round the crack where we felt the air coming up.

'Now, Curtis,' he said, 'tackle on, and put your back into it; you are as strong as two. Stop,' and he took off a stout black silk handkerchief, which, true to his habits of neatness, he still wore, and ran it through the ring. 'Quatermain, get Curtis round the middle and pull for dear life when I give the word. *Now.*'

Sir Henry put out all his enormous strength, and Good and I did the same, with such power as nature had given us.

'Heave! heave! it's giving,' gasped Sir Henry; and I heard the muscles of his great back cracking. Suddenly there came a parting sound, then a rush of air, and we were all on our backs on the floor with a great flag-stone on the top of us. Sir Henry's strength had done it, and never did muscular power stand a man in better stead.

'Light a match, Quatermain,' he said, as soon as we had picked ourselves up and got our breath; 'carefully, now.'

I did so, and there before us was, God be praised! the *first step of a stone stair.*

'Now what is to be done?' asked Good.

'Follow the stair, of course, and trust to Providence.'

'Stop!' said Sir Henry. 'Quatermain, get the bit of biltong and the water that is left; we may want them.'

I went creeping back to our place by the chests for that purpose, and as I was coming away an idea struck me. We had not thought much of the diamonds for the last twenty-four hours or so; indeed, the idea of diamonds was nauseous, seeing what they had entailed upon us; but, thought I, I may as well pocket a few in case we ever should get out of this ghastly hole. So I just stuck my fist into the first chest and filled all the available pockets of my old shooting coat, topping up—this was a happy thought—with a couple of hand-fuls of big ones out of the third chest.

'I say, you fellows,' I sang out, 'won't you take some diamonds with you? I've filled my pockets.'

'Oh! hang the diamonds!' said Sir Henry. 'I hope that I may never see another.'

As for Good, he made no answer. He was, I think, taking a last farewell of all that was left of the poor girl who loved him so well. And, curious as it may seem to you, my reader, sitting at home at ease and reflecting on the vast, indeed the immeasurable, wealth which we were thus abandoning, I can assure you that if you had passed some twenty-eight hours with next to nothing to eat and drink in that place, you would not have cared to cumber yourself with diamonds whilst plunging down into the unknown bowels of the earth, in the wild hope of escape from an agonizing death. If it had not, from the habits of a lifetime, become a sort of second nature with me never to leave anything worth having behind, if there was the slightest chance of my being able to carry it away, I am sure I should not have bothered to fill my pockets.

'Come on, Quatermain,' said Sir Henry, who was already standing on the first step of the stone stair. 'Steady, I will go first.'

'Mind where you put your feet; there may be some awful hole underneath,' said I.

'Much more likely to be another room,' said Sir Henry, as he slowly descended, counting the steps as he went.

When he got to 'fifteen' he stopped. 'Here's the bottom,' he said. 'Thank goodness! I think it's a passage. Come on down.'

Good descended next, and I followed last, and on reaching the bottom lit one of the two remaining matches. By its light we could just see that we were standing in a narrow tunnel, which ran right and left at right angles to the staircase we had descended. Before we could make out any more, the match burnt my fingers and went out. Then arose the delicate question of which way to turn. Of course, it was impossible to know what the tunnel was or where it ran to, and yet to turn one way might lead us to safety, and the other to destruction. We were utterly perplexed, till suddenly it struck Good that when I had lit the match the draught of the passage blew the flame to the left.

'Let us go against the draught,' he said; 'air draws inwards, not outwards.'

We took this suggestion, and feeling along the wall with the hand, whilst trying the ground before us at every step, we departed from that accursed treasure chamber on our terrible quest. If ever it should be entered again by living man, which I do not think it will be, he will find a token of our presence in the open chests of jewels, the empty lamp, and the white bones of poor Foulata.

When we had groped our way for about a quarter of an hour along the passage, it suddenly took a sharp turn, or else was bisected by another, which we followed, only in course of time to be led into a third. And so it went on for some hours. We seemed to be in a stone labyrinth which led nowhere. What all these passages are, of course I cannot say, but we thought that they must be the ancient workings of a mine, of which the various shafts travelled hither and thither as the ore led them. This is the only way in which we could account for such a multitude of passages.

At length we halted, thoroughly worn out with fatigue, and with that hope deferred which maketh the heart sick, and ate up our poor remaining piece of biltong, and drank our last sup of water, for our throats were like lime-kilns. It seemed to us that we had escaped Death in the darkness of the chamber only to meet him in the darkness of the tunnels.

As we stood, once more utterly depressed, I thought I caught a sound, to which I called the attention of the others. It was very faint and very far off, but it *was* a sound, a faint, murmuring sound, for the others heard it too, and no words can describe the blessedness of it after all those hours of utter, awful stillness.

'By heaven! it's running water,' said Good. 'Come on.'

Off we started again in the direction from which the faint murmur seemed to come, groping our way as before along the rocky walls. As we went it got more and more audible, till at last it seemed quite loud in the quiet. On, yet on; now we could distinctly make out the unmistakable swirl of rushing water. And yet how could there be running water in the bowels of the earth? Now we were quite near to it, and Good, who was leading, swore that he could smell it.

'Go gently, Good,' said Sir Henry, 'we must be close.' *Splash!* and a cry from Good.

He had fallen in.

'Good! Good! where are you?' we shouted, in terrified distress. To our intense relief, an answer came back in a choky voice.

'All right; I've got hold of a rock. Strike a light to show me where you are.'

Hastily I lit the last remaining match. Its faint gleam discovered to us a dark mass of water running at our feet. How wide it was we could not see, but there, some way out, was the dark form of our companion hanging on to a projecting rock.

'Stand clear to catch me,' sung out Good. 'I must swim for it.'

Then we heard a splash, and a great struggle. Another minute and he had grabbed at and caught Sir Henry's outstretched hand, and we had pulled him up high and dry into the tunnel.

'My word!' he said, between his gasps, 'that was touch and go. If I hadn't caught that rock, and known how to swim, I should have been done. It runs like a mill-race, and I could feel no bottom.'

It was clear that this would not do; so after Good had rested a little, and we had drunk our fill from the water of the subterranean river, which was sweet and fresh, and washed our faces, which sadly needed it, as well as we could, we started from the banks of this African Styx, and began to retrace our steps along the tunnel, Good dripping unpleasantly in front of us. At length we came to another tunnel leading to our right.

'We may as well take it,' said Sir Henry, wearily; 'all roads are alike here; we can only go on till we drop.'

Slowly, for a long, long while, we stumbled, utterly weary, along this new tunnel, Sir Henry leading now.

Suddenly he stopped, and we bumped up against him.

'Look!' he whispered, 'is my brain going, or is that light?'

We stared with all our eyes, and there, yes, there, far ahead of us, was a faint, glimmering spot, no larger than a cottage window pane. It was so faint that I doubt if any eyes, except those which, like ours, had for days seen nothing but blackness, could have perceived it at all.

With a sort of gasp of hope we pushed on. In five minutes there was no longer any doubt: it *was* a patch of faint light. A minute more and a breath of real live air was fanning us. On we struggled. All at once the tunnel narrowed. Sir Henry went on his knees. Smaller yet it grew, till it was only the size of a large fox's earth—it was *earth* now, mind you; the rock had ceased.

A squeeze, a struggle, and Sir Henry was out, and so was Good, and so was I, and there above us were the blessed stars, and in our nostrils was the sweet air; then suddenly something gave, and we were all rolling over and over and over through grass and bushes, and soft, wet soil.

I caught at something and stopped. Sitting up I halloed lustily. An answering shout came from just below, there Sir Henry's wild career had been stopped by some level ground. I scrambled to him, and found him unhurt, though breathless. Then we looked for Good. A little way off we found him too, jammed in a forked root. He was a good deal knocked about, but soon came to.

We sat down together there on the grass, and the revulsion of feeling was so great, that I really think we cried for joy. We had escaped from that awful dungeon, that was so near to becoming our grave. Surely some merciful Power must have guided our footsteps to the jackal hole at the termination of the tunnel (for that is what it must have been). And see, there on the mountains, the dawn we had never thought to look upon again was blushing rosy red.

Presently the grey light stole down the slopes, and we saw that we were at the bottom, or rather, nearly at the bottom, of the vast pit in front of the entrance to the cave. Now we could make out the dim forms of the three colossi who sat upon its verge. Doubtless those awful passages, along which we had wandered the livelong night, had originally been, in some way, connected with the great diamond mine. As for the subterranean river in the bowels of the mountain, Heaven only knows what it was, or whence it flows, or whither it goes. I for one have no anxiety to trace its course.

Lighter it grew, and lighter yet. We could see each other now, and such a spectacle as we presented I have never set eyes on before or since. Gaunt-cheeked, hollow-eyed wretches, smeared all over with dust and mud, bruised, bleeding, the long fear of imminent death yet written on our countenances, we were, indeed, a sight to frighten the daylight. And yet it is a solemn fact that Good's eye-glass was still fixed in Good's eye. I doubt whether he had ever taken it out at all. Neither the darkness, nor the plunge in the subterranean river, nor the roll down the slope, had been able to separate Good and his eye-glass.

Presently we rose, fearing that our limbs would stiffen if we stopped there longer, and commenced with slow and painful steps to struggle up the sloping sides of the great pit. For an hour or more we toiled steadfastly up the blue clay, dragging ourselves on by the help of the roots and grasses with which it was clothed.

At last it was done, and we stood on the great road, on the side of the pit opposite to the colossi.

By the side of the road, a hundred yards off, a fire was burning in front of some huts, and round the fire were figures. We made towards them, supporting one another, and halting every few paces. Presently, one of the figures rose, saw us, and fell on to the ground, crying out for fear.

'Infadoos, Infadoos! it is us, thy friends.'

We rose; he ran to us, staring wildly, and still shaking with fear.

'Oh, my lords, my lords, it is indeed you come back from the dead!—come back from the dead!'

And the old warrior flung himself down before us, and clasped Sir Henry's knees, and wept aloud for joy.

SOURCE: Chapter 18 in *King Solomon's Mines* (1885; Oxford: Oxford University Press, 1989); 230–40.

———

My Uncle's Gift Is Many Times Multiplied
JOHN BUCHAN

[John Buchan (1875–1940) similarly began his career as a representative of British imperialism in South Africa and, on returning to Britain, likewise translated his early experiences into the adventures of his novel's protagonist. Like Haggard, Buchan had gone to South Africa in secretarial service, as one of the young men who made up Lord Alfred Milner's "kindergarten" in 1901. A mineral no less legendary than the diamonds motivating Haggard's Quatermain animates the exploits of the young Scotsman David Crawfurd in Buchan's *Prester John* (1910). Rather than restore an African chief to his position of leadership, however, Crawfurd, just as much a mercenary as Quatermain, assists instead in the subduing of a native uprising, led by the redoubtable Laputa. Crawfurd succeeds too in recovering the sacred ruby necklace of Solomonic legend and discovering the diamonds alleged to have been pilfered by the African workers from the mines and collected in a secret, ceremonial cave well beyond the mountain passes.]

We got at the treasure by blowing open the turnstile. It was easy enough to trace the spot in the rock where it stood, but the most patient search did not reveal its secret. Accordingly we had recourse to dynamite, and soon laid bare the stone steps, and ascended to the gallery. The chasm was bridged with planks, and Arcoll and I crossed alone. The cave was as I had left it. The bloodstains on the floor had grown dark with time, but the ashes of the sacramental fire were still there to remind me of the drama I had borne a part in. When I looked at the way I had escaped my brain grew dizzy at the thought of it. I do not think that all the gold on earth would have driven me a second time to that awful escalade. As for Arcoll, he could not see its possibility at all.

'Only a madman could have done it,' he said, blinking his eyes at the green linn. 'Indeed, Davie, I think for about four days you were as mad as they make. It was a fortunate thing, for your madness saved the country.'

With some labour we got the treasure down to the path, and took it under a strong guard to Pietersdorp. The Government were busy with the settling up after the war, and it took many weeks to have our business disposed of. At first things looked badly for me. The Attorney-General set up a claim to the whole as spoils of war, since, he argued, it was the war-chest of the enemy we had conquered. I do not know how the matter would have gone on legal grounds, though I was advised by my lawyers that the claim was a bad one. But the part I had played in the whole business, more especially in the visit to Inanda's Kraal, had made me a kind of popular hero, and the Government thought better of their first attitude. Besides, Arcoll had great influence, and the whole story of my doings, which was told privately by him to some of the members of the Government, disposed them to be generous. Accordingly they agreed to treat the contents of the cave as ordinary treasure trove, of which, by the law, one half went to the discoverer and one half to the Crown.

This was well enough so far as the gold was concerned, but another difficulty arose about the diamonds; for a large part of these had obviously been stolen by labourers from the mines, and the mining people laid claim to them as stolen goods. I was advised not to dispute this claim, and consequently we had a great sorting-out of the stones in the presence of the experts of the different mines. In the end it turned out that identification was not an easy matter, for the experts quarrelled furiously among themselves. A compromise was at last come to, and a division made; and then the diamond companies behaved very handsomely, voting me a substantial sum in recognition of my services in recovering their property. What with this and with my half share of the gold and my share of the unclaimed stones, I found that I had a very considerable fortune. The whole of my stones I sold to De Beers, for if I had placed them on the open market I should have upset the delicate equipoise of diamond values. When I came finally to cast up my accounts, I found that I had secured a fortune of a trifle over a quarter of a million pounds.

The wealth did not dazzle so much as it solemnized me. I had no impulse to spend any part of it in a riot of folly. It had come to me like fairy gold out of the void; it had been bought with men's blood, almost with my own. I wanted to get away to a quiet place and think, for of late my life had been too crowded with drama, and there comes a satiety of action as well as of idleness. Above all things I wanted to get home. They gave me a great send-off, and sang songs, and good fellows shook my hand till it ached. The papers were full of me, and there was a banquet and speeches. But I could not relish this glory as I ought, for I was like a boy thrown violently out of his bearings.

Not till I was in the train nearing Cape Town did I recover my equanimity. The burden of the past seemed to slip from me suddenly as on the morning when I had climbed the linn. I saw my life all lying before me; and already I had won success. I thought of my return to my own country, my first sight of the grey shores of Fife, my visit to Kirkcaple, my meeting with my mother. I was a rich man now who could choose his career, and my mother need never again want for comfort. My money seemed pleasant to me, for if men won theirs by brains or industry, I had won mine by sterner methods, for I had staked against it my life. I sat alone in the railway carriage and cried with pure thankfulness. These were comforting tears, for they brought me back to my old commonplace self.

My last memory of Africa is my meeting with Tam Dyke. I caught sight of him in the streets of Cape Town, and running after him, clapped him on the shoulder. He stared at me as if he had seen a ghost.

'Is it yourself, Davie?' he cried. 'I never looked to see you again in this world. I do nothing but read about you in the papers. What for did ye not send for me? Here have I been knocking about inside a ship and you have been getting famous. They tell me you're a millionaire, too.'

I had Tam to dinner at my hotel, and later, sitting smoking on the terrace and watching the flying-ants among the aloes, I told him the better part of the story I have here written down.

'Man, Davie,' he said at the end, 'you've had a tremendous time. Here are you not eighteen months away from home, and you're going back with a fortune. What will you do with it?'

I told him that I proposed, to begin with, to finish my education at Edinburgh College. At this he roared with laughter.

'That's a dull ending, anyway. It's me that should have the money, for I'm full of imagination. You were aye a prosaic body, Davie.'

'Maybe I am,' I said; 'but I am very sure of one thing. If I hadn't been a prosaic body, I wouldn't be sitting here tonight.'

Two years later Aitken found the diamond pipe, which he had always believed lay in the mountains. Some of the stones in the cave, being unlike any ordinary African diamonds, confirmed his suspicions and set him on the track. A Kaffir tribe to the north-east of the Rooirand had known of it, but they had never worked it, but only collected the overspill. The closing down of one of the chief existing mines had created a shortage of diamonds in the world's markets, and once again the position was the same as when Kimberley began. Accordingly he made a great fortune, and to-day the Aitken Proprietary Mine is one of the most famous in the country. But Aitken did more than mine diamonds, for he had not forgotten the lesson we had learned together in the work of resettlement. He laid down a big fund for the education and amelioration of the native races, and the first fruit of it was the establishment at Blaauwildebeestefontein itself of a great native training college. It was no factory for making missionaries and black teachers, but an institution for giving the Kaffirs the kind of training which fits them to be good citizens of the state. There you will find every kind of technical workshop, and the finest experimental farms, where the blacks are taught modern agriculture. They have proved themselves apt pupils, and to-day you will see in the glens of the Berg and in the plains Kaffir tillage which is as scientific as any in Africa. They have created a huge export trade in tobacco and fruit; the cotton promises well; and there is talk of a new fibre which will do wonders. Also along the river bottoms the india-rubber business is prospering.

There are playing-fields and baths and reading-rooms and libraries just as in a school at home. In front of the great hall of the college a statue stands, the figure of a black man shading his eyes with his hands and looking far over the plains to the Rooirand. On the pedestal it is lettered 'Prester John,' but the face is the face of Laputa. So the last of the kings of Africa does not lack his monument.

Of this institution Mr Wardlaw is the head. He writes to me weekly, for I am one of the governors, as well as an old friend, and from a recent letter I take this passage:—

'I often cast my mind back to the afternoon when you and I sat on the stoep of the schoolhouse, and talked of the Kaffirs and our future. I had about a dozen pupils then, and now I have nearly three thousand; and in place of a tin-roofed shanty and a yard, I have a whole countryside. You laughed at me for my keenness, Davie, but I've seen it justified. I was never a man of war like you, and so I had to bide at home while you and your like were straightening out the troubles. But when it was all over my job began, for I could do what you couldn't do—I was the physician to heal wounds. You mind how nervous I was when I heard the drums beat. I hear them every evening now, for we have made a rule that all the Kaffir farms on the Berg sound a kind of curfew. It reminds me of old times, and tells me that though it is peace nowadays we mean to keep all the manhood in them that they used to exercise in war. It would do your eyes good to see the garden we have made out of the Klein Labongo glen. The place is one big orchard with every kind of tropical fruit in it, and the irrigation dam is as full of fish as it will hold. Out at Umvelos' there is a tobacco-factory, and all round Sikitola's we have square miles of mealie and cotton fields. The loch on the Rooirand is stocked with Lochleven trout, and we have made a bridle-path up to it in a gully east of the one you climbed. You ask about Machudi's. The last time I was there the place was white with sheep, for we have got the edge of the plateau grazed down, and sheep can get the short bite there. We have cleaned up all the kraals, and the chiefs are members of our county council, and are as fond of hearing their own voices as an Aberdeen bailie. It's a queer transformation we have wrought, and when I sit and smoke my pipe in the evening, and look over the plains and then at the big black statue you and Aitken set up, I thank the Providence that has guided me so far. I hope and trust that, in the Bible words, "the wilderness and the solitary place are glad for us." At any rate it will not be my fault if they don't "blossom as the rose." Come out and visit us soon, man, and see the work you had a hand in starting. . . .'

I am thinking seriously of taking Wardlaw's advice.

SOURCE: Chapter 23 in *Prester John* (1910; Oxford: Oxford University Press, 1994), 199–203.

Excerpts from *The Speeches of Cecil Rhodes 1881–1900*
CECIL JOHN RHODES

THE NATIVE QUESTION

The ultimate reconciliation and amalgamation into one South African people of the two white races, the English and the Dutch, always under the British flag or the British hegemony, with British civilisation and British institutions, had been, as we have seen, Mr. Rhodes's aim throughout his political life. He had laboured to remove racial feeling by promoting closer intercourse between the two races, and was himself on excellent terms with the Dutch, even with the Cape Dutch leaders, though he did not conceal that his ideal of a United South Africa differed from theirs, because his United South Africa was to remain a part of the British Empire, while theirs required for its realisation an ultimate separation. In his own words, in a speech at Kimberley, 1888: 'We must endeavour to make those who live with us feel that there is no race distinction between us; whether Dutch or English, we are combined in one object, and that is the union of the states of South Africa without abandoning the Imperial tie.'

There was, however, another question which he well knew would be one day of altogether supreme importance, and which had been in the past, and was to some extent still in the present, a cause of separation between the English and Dutch races in South Africa. I mean the native question. The native question was to be in the future the question of questions in South Africa, and in the past it had been the chief operating cause of the separation of the Dutch, when the Great Trek of the discontented Cape Dutchmen led to the formation of the Republics, whose existence and influence have been the means of fostering and maintaining racial feeling at the Cape. It was the British Government's insistence on the rights of the black man which, far more than anything else, produced the exodus of the Dutch from the Cape

Colony. Missionaries from England had constituted themselves from the first the protectors of the natives; and while they seem to have acted often very unwisely and with distinct prejudice, no doubt the natural abuses by individual colonists of the system of slavery which existed till 1834, supplied them with a good deal of actual reason for their interference. This interference with the cherished rights of the slaveowners over beings whom they regarded as their property, produced a state of irritation which was sharply accentuated by the giving of equal civil rights to the free natives in 1828; and the long pent-up indignation burst forth when the emancipation of 1834 was carried out by Downing Street with such stupid maladministration as to deprive the slaveowners of the bulk of the compensation for their property.

The South African Dutchmen at that time regarded the natives as animals, differing essentially from white men, and absolutely without claim to the civil rights which the British Government asserted and conferred. He did so then; and in the Transvaal, where he has full freedom to make his own laws, he does so now. The Transvaal Grondwet, the basis of law in the Republic, is explicit on this subject: 'The people will suffer no equality of whites and blacks either in state or in church.' Among other civil disabilities, landowning is forbidden to natives, and the right of serving on a jury is denied, while the treatment of the natives in the Transvaal has always been characterised by a harshness and habitual refusal of justice to the black man as against the white man which is notorious. The full report given by Mr. Fitzpatrick of the case of the chieftainess Toeremetsjani, head wife of Sekukuni, and since his death head of the tribe, gives a fair notion of the state of things that obtains, especially the cross-examination of a person so high placed in the state as Commandant Cronjé, lately the Boer leader at Magersfontein, then the Superintendent-General of Natives.

Now, this same feeling on the native question has always obtained, though in a modified form, among the Cape Dutchmen. In the Cape Colony black man and white are equal before the law, have practically equal civil rights, though there are certain special police regulations adapted to the present condition of the black man. The question of political rights had, of course, followed upon the establishment of responsible government, and the black man has had a vote ever since, so far as he has been qualified, under the franchise law. In 1892, with Mr. Rhodes, who had formed very definite views on the question, as Prime Minister, a fairly high property qualification, ownership of a house value £75, or receipt of a yearly wage of £50, was fixed by a new act, with the very moderate educational qualification that the voter should be able to sign his name and to write his address and his occupation. This law admits to the franchise those natives who have acquired property and some measure of education, and is a fair attempt to gradually confer political rights as an encouragement to industry and education among the black people. The law applies equally to the white man and the black. The law, of course, denies the vote to natives living in a state of barbarism and communal tenure.

This gradual enfranchisement of the natives had been preceded and accompanied by their education, at first by the missionaries on the basis of a mere book education, which was found a failure; latterly more and more on the basis of good industrial education, of which Lovedale, the great industrial school of the Free Church of Scotland, was long the only and is still the most admirable example.

Obviously, the crux of the native question is their enormous and increasing preponderance of numbers. South of the Zambesi there are, roughly speaking, seven or eight million natives to three-quarters of a million of whites, and even in Cape Colony there are about a million to some four hundred thousand whites. The majority of these are Bantu, and the Bantu race tends to increase under the conditions of civilised rule, the old check of war and massacre being removed. Naturally enough, though unfortunately, the whole feeling at the Cape is largely tinged with the old exclusive view, still held strongly by the Dutch portion of the community, though the English ideal has had a leavening influence, and has, besides, steadily operated through the laws to improve and elevate the natives.

The English view, however, is carried to extremes by a certain section of the English population, who, without any regard to actual conditions, would give the natives at once electoral privileges for which they are quite unprepared. The Dutch view at the Cape is seen (I believe) in the exclusion of natives from the Lord's Supper in the Dutch Reformed Church; the English view, in the fact that they are admitted in all the English churches of all denominations.

In his views on the native question, Mr. Rhodes steers a middle course between the extremes. And just as the broadness of his Imperialism led, in his Bechuanaland settlement, to a cross-fire of attacks and misrepresentations from extreme men, from Jingoes and Dutch Bondsmen alike, so his views on the native question have been assailed by the extreme sections of both sides. He sees the native question, as he sees other questions, as it actually is, and he shapes his policy accordingly. He is not, as he has repeatedly stated in the House, in favour of depriving the black man of the vote, when his growth in civilisation, evidenced by the acquisition of some education and some property, justifies it; but he utterly opposes the giving of the vote to the masses of ignorant and irresponsible natives living under communal tenure and in a state of barbarism.

His position, the thoroughly English one of gradual elevation to full citizenship as the black man gains in civilisation, is well put in a passage of the speech on the Glen Grey Bill, which I give in full at the end of this chapter. 'It will be wise not to deal with the whole native question at once. The natives are children, and we ought to do something for the minds and brains the Almighty has given them. I do not believe they are different from ourselves.' He holds that, as a body, they are ourselves in the state of savagery which we were in in Britain before the coming of the Romans, and while they are in this state of barbarism they are, he says, unfit for full privileges of citizenship. As far back as 1887 he stated in a speech in the Cape House his position as against the extreme negrophilists. 'On account of an extreme philanthropic sympathy there are those who wish to endow the native with the privileges which it has taken the European 1800 years to acquire.' Again: 'I will lay down my policy on this native question: either you have to receive them on an equal footing as citizens, or you have to call them a subject race. Well, I have made up my mind that there must be class legislation, that there must be Pass Laws and Peace Preservation Acts, and that we have got to treat natives, where they are in a state of barbarism, in a different way from ourselves.' He went on to say: 'The missionaries are wrong on the question. When they turn out men who are capable of administering the telegraph and postal system, and of doing carpentry and managing machinery, these are the men who will get the franchise without difficulty.' He had already expressed his admiration for the system of industrial education at Lovedale. What he objected to was the mere book education and Christian doctrine generally taught; and since 1887 the missionaries have generally come round to his view. The old mode of native education is admitted to be a failure; the industrial education, then carried out only at Lovedale, is taking its place everywhere.

On the other hand, on another and most important point, Mr. Rhodes was in 1887 and long before, and has continued to be ever since, against the Dutch view. He knew liquor to be the curse and ruin of the natives by his own observation and experience in Kimberley and elsewhere; he knew the enormous advantage of keeping liquor from the natives, and he has never ceased to insist in the Cape House on the wisdom and justice of doing so. This, of course, was not the Dutch view, not only because liquor kept the natives down, and was the surest means of preventing them acquiring the property qualification for the franchise, but also because the wine industry and the brandy industry at the Cape were almost exclusively Dutch. Mr. Rhodes, when he has a firm conviction, is not afraid of running counter even to those he desires to conciliate, and on the question of keeping liquor from the natives he has fought the strong opposition to his view, in season and out of season, throughout his political life.

The essence of Mr. Rhodes's views on the native question is this: 'We have got to treat the natives, where they are in a state of barbarism, in a different way from ourselves.' 'Where they are in a state of barbarism' is the condition that requires this treatment; but Mr. Rhodes has always been strongly in favour of gradually elevating them out of that state, not only by giving an industrial education, but also by giving them an interest and a part in local government among themselves, as he did in his Glen Grey Act (1894), while encouraging them in education and in habits of industry, which alone could lead to the possession of property, by making the conditions for the franchise an educational and property qualification required of black men and white alike.

Mr. Rhodes has an exceptionally good practical knowledge of the native question, because he knows the natives, from long and close intercourse, extraordinarily well. He has none of that dislike and contempt for the black man, as black, which is so prevalent in South Africa, and has even infected the English, though, of course, to a far less degree than the Dutch. He likes to have black men round him; he treats them as his fellow-men, simply in a lower state of development. His servants are all natives from different parts of Africa; Lobengula's sons, whom he has sent to school, make his house and gardens their own during their holidays, and he treats them just as if they were his own.

In his compound at Kimberley he was in the habit for years of talking with natives from all parts of Africa, knowing enough of their language to make himself understood; while he had seen the prosperity and happiness which his paternal government there had brought to the thousands of black men under him. The shopkeepers and liquor-sellers of Kimberley might grumble and agitate, but Mr. Rhodes looked after 'these poor children,' as he calls them, won their confidence by his friendliness and kindness, and won their affection through that almost animal instinct by which they can tell whether a man has genuine goodwill to them, or is merely professing it; kept the liquor from them, gave them plenty of healthy and harmless recreation, with good education for all who desired it, and thus made the great De Beers Company an instrument in the civilisation of the natives, the influence of which, seeing that the labourers come to the compound from all parts of Africa, and learn the advantages of total abstinence as well as the liking for and the dignity of labour in this practical way, cannot be overestimated.

Of course Mr. Rhodes had studied the native character and native way of thinking, which is very different from the European, in other places than Kimberley. He had begun as a boy in Natal with the Zulus on his brother Herbert's plantation; he had studied it in Basutoland at the beginning of his political life, when he was Commissioner there; he had studied it in Pondo- land and the Transkei; he had studied it in Rhodesia; and thus, in 1894, he was better equipped to undertake a bill to deal with the native question than any other politician living.

With this object in view he took, during his Premiership, the position of Secretary for Native Affairs. The speech in which he moved the second reading of the Glen Grey Bill (July 1894) is a practical attempt to deal with the native question in legislating for the more uncivilised and ignorant natives crowded together in a part of the Cape Colony. It was to be applied first to the Glen Grey district and to Fingoland, and then gradually extended, as it has been since, to new areas. The genuine philanthropy which is often too well concealed beneath the rather rough and downright language of one who loves always to call a spade a spade, and rather enjoys the indignation his plain speaking may produce, betrays itself, to any one who has the seeing eye, in several parts of this speech. That he should have undertaken it at a time when he was loaded with the many anxieties and multifarious business of develop- ing Rhodesia, his time also filled with the ordinary business of his position as Premier, and his mind troubled by the increasing hostility of the Transvaal, says much for his interest in the natives; and the plan he proposed was to elevate the natives to a higher level of humanity by teaching them to govern and to help themselves. Our relation towards the natives in South and Cen- tral Africa is the relation of teachers towards pupils. Mr. Rhodes's comparison of the natives to British tribesmen of the time of the Druids conveys a deep truth in reminding us that the British Empire has to do for the native African exactly what the Roman Empire did for the native Briton, and that the duty of passing on the civilisation we have received and developed will pay us well, makes the performance of the duty a business arrangement. Our profit is the price of their schooling.

The essentials of the measure were its provisions for local self-government and industrial education out of the natives' own resources, while its labour clauses enforced his own maxim, 'The secret of a happy life is work.' The check on the liquor traffic was a kind of local option which was to have an educative influence on the natives by teaching them to make some sacrifices to remove from themselves the pest of drink. The practical wisdom and philanthropy of this measure is a very strong additional claim to the approval of all who value these qualities as characteristics of true statesmanship. The operation of the Act has, as a matter of fact, made for the happiness of the natives, more than any increased facilities for the parliamentary franchise could possibly have done. Six months after the Act came in force the chief inspector of police found the prison at Glen Grey, which was generally crowded, absolutely empty. An inquiry elicited the information that there were no prisoners now, because crime had ceased with the cessation of drink and idleness.

This new development of the policy of stopping the liquor-drinking among the natives could not commend itself to the Dutch wine-growers and brandy-farmers of the West, and would have met with much more serious opposition but for the labour clauses, which redeemed it for them, as for all employers of labour, who were ill supplied owing to the dislike to regular work, which seems almost a primitive instinct among the industrial as well as among the military Bantu. This dislike, of course, may be ascribed to ancestral habit, the old division of duty being war for the men of the tribe, work for the women, which arrangement the polygamous Kaffir finds too satisfactory to change, though his share of this division of duty has ceased to exist. The unskilled labour of the Cape Colony is all, one need scarcely add, native.

This policy of keeping liquor from the natives has, moreover, from the beginning, been placed in the forefront of native administration in Rhodesia, where Mr. Rhodes, as managing director and head of the enterprise, has had about a million of natives under his sway. The laws against selling liquor to natives are very severe, and were from the first stringently enforced, so that a stop was promptly put to the first beginnings of the evil both in Mashonaland and Matabeleland. To treat the natives like children, to let them have what is good for them, and forbid to them what is bad for them, is Mr. Rhodes's policy, to which is joined legislation, such as parts of the Glen Grey Act, the influence of which is carefully designed to be educative as well as protective.

On moving the second reading of the Glen Grey Act in the Cape House, on July 30th, 1894, Mr. Rhodes said:—

'There is, I think, a general feeling that the natives are a distinct source of trouble and loss to the country. Now, I take a different view. When I see the labour troubles that are occurring in the United States, and when I see the troubles that are going to occur with the English people in their own country on the social question and the labour question, I feel rather glad that the labour question here is connected with the native question, for I see that at any rate we do not have here what has lately occurred in Chicago, where, on account of some question as to the management of the Pullman Car Company, the whole of these labour quarrels have broken out, and the city has been practically wrecked. This is what is going on in the older countries on account of the masses as against the classes getting what they term their rights, or, to put it into plain English, those who have not, trying to take from those who have. If they cannot get it by what might be termed Irish legislation, they mean to get it by physical force. That is another aspect of government by the people. The proposition that I would wish to put to the House is this, that I do not feel that the fact of our having to live with the natives in this country is a reason for serious anxiety. In fact, I think the natives should be a source of great assistance to most of us. At any rate, if the whites maintain their position as the supreme race, the day may come when we shall all be thankful that we have the natives with us in their proper position. We shall be thankful that we have escaped those difficulties which are going on amongst all the old nations of the world.

'Now, it happens that in the rearrangement of the Cabinet I was given the charge of the natives, and, naturally, what faced me was the enormous extent of the native problem. In addition to the natives in the colony, I am responsible, on this side of the Zambesi, for half a million of natives, and on the other side of the Zambesi I am responsible for another half-million. By the instrumentality of responsible government, and also by that of another position which I occupy, I feel that I am responsible for about two millions of human beings. The question which has submitted itself to my mind with regard to the natives is this—What is their present state? I find that they are increasing enormously. I find that there are certain locations for them where, without any right or title to the land, they are herded together. They are multiplying to an enormous extent, and these locations are becoming too small. The Transkei could support, perhaps, its present population of 600,000 people, but it is not able to support double that population. The natives there are increasing at an enormous rate. The old diminutions by war and pestilence do not occur. Our good government prevents them from fighting, and the result is an enormous increase in numbers. The natives devote their minds to a remarkable extent to the multiplication of children. The result is an increase in the population. The problem before us is this—What is to become of these people? I am sure that the Transkei cannot support 1,200,000 people, whilst I know that there will be certainly that number of them in about twenty years. What then do we intend to do? As I have stated once before in this House, the natives have had in the past an interesting employment for their minds in going to war and in consulting in their councils as to war. But by our wise government we have taken away all that employment from them. We have given them no share in the government—and I think rightly, too—and no interest in the local development of their country. What one feels is that there are questions like bridges, roads, education, plantations of trees, and various local questions, to which the natives might devote themselves with good results. At present we give them nothing to do, because we have taken away their power of making war—an excellent pursuit in its way—which once employed their minds. Then there arises the question of their land, which cannot continue to provide enough for all of them. There is not room for them all. In the third place, in many parts of their country we have placed canteens. The man who has nothing to do turns to the canteen. We do not teach them the dignity of labour, and they simply loaf about in sloth and laziness. They never go out and work. This is what we have failed to consider with reference to our native population.

'These are my premises. I wish to look at them, not from a philosophical point of view, but from a practical point of view. The natives know nothing about the politics of the country. They have told me time after time that they do not understand these politics. "Leave us alone, but let us try and deal with some of our little local questions." That is the common statement they have made to me. I do not know whether the member for Fort Beaufort would agree with me, though I am not trenching upon the question of no vote at present. I feel, too, that if the people desire it the canteens should be removed from their midst. Further, it is our duty as a Government to remove these poor children from this life of sloth and laziness, and to give them some gentle stimulus to come forth and find out the dignity of labour.

'And then, if I may speak on a general question in the interest of the country, I would say that I have had to face the question of the extraordinary position of the labour problem of the colony. One day I am told that I ought to introduce an irrigation scheme; then the Malmesbury farmers say I must go into the question of the growth of corn; and I am told that my country contains in its natural soil the greatest possible capabilities. And yet I find that nothing is done. This, I am told, is owing to the sluggish conservatism of the people. I might say something about this question. So long as I talk about farming, so long as I talk about what we should do, it is all right. But as soon as anyone of my own race commences to farm, I can almost prophesy that in three years he will collapse. Slow progress—extremely slow progress— is made, it is true; but when I begin to inquire into the reasons for it, I find that the country which grows the greatest quantity of corn is Egypt, at 2d. per diem as the basis of cost of labour. In Nyasaland, where good coffee is pro- duced, wages are 4s. a month, including food 1½d. per diem. It has been stated that it is the laziness of the Western farmer which prevents his produc- ing corn and competing, when he has his labour on this basis—of at least 2s. 6d. to 3s. per diem as against 2d. per diem in these other parts of the world. I am speaking of those countries which are great grain-producing countries. I have seen what these people live on, and their food is not worse than that of the Kaffir. But the wage of the English agricultural labourer averages only about 12s. per week, and he lives certainly at a higher standard of civilisation than our raw Kaffir; and yet the Kaffir is paid almost 50 per cent. more than the Englishman.

'So much for this aspect of the question. Now, as to the Bill itself, I wish to point out that the first clause deals with the question of area. The clause only states Glen Grey, but if the House approves of the Bill, I would propose to apply it to other native areas. If the House approves of the Bill, I will certainly apply that clause to Fingoland. Under the clause, individual title will not be given unless the Divisional Council recommends it. The other provisions I would apply to Fingoland, because I would consider that with the approval of the second reading I had received the approval of the House. Part 1. is simply as to the creation of areas. Glen Grey is not suitable in many respects, and it is mixed up with white farmers, and so we have had to reserve in Glen Grey those parts of the country which are in the occupation of white farmers. Certain other reasons have had to be considered: the Indwe railway, for instance. What I would like in regard to a native area is that there should be no white men in its midst. I hold that the natives should be apart from white men, and not mixed up with them. There are about three hundred morgen of Glen Grey farms which have been already surveyed, which would give about seventy allotments. The Bill proposes that to each of these allotments there should be a village management board of three men, which should be nominated by the Government. And the Government would select first the people whom they thought best to nominate. Perhaps the House is not aware that Glen Grey has been actually settled before. There are five of these farms, which are called mission farms; but they are not mission farms at all, but Crown lands on which there happen to be missionaries. Successive Governments have already settled this question of Glen Grey. They have been giving the titles while the House has been discussing the matter, and I find that they have created these titles and managed them by a village council or board of natives. The Government would give these boards all the powers of the Village Management Act. Under these powers, the boards would limit the amount of stock on each agricultural lot, and therefore overcrowding would be prevented. It rests with the natives to apply for an extra title for building lots which would be pointed out on the commonage.

'As to the cost of surveying, I find on investigation in the district that they have given a title to the Mount Arthur people on what was termed a mission station. It has been said that we should charge them £2, 10s. for each agricultural lot of three to four morgen. But I find that the cost for each has been £5.

After discussing the matter with the magistrate, I think it would not be just to let the difference between the two amounts come out of the revenue, for we should have to issue eight thousand titles to Glen Grey, which would be a loss to the country of nearly £20,000. And this I do not think would be right. I find that they are all anxious to get these titles, and, so as not to lose the other £20,000, the Government has spread the additional cost over four years, to be paid in four instalments. I think that seems fair, as I do not think that the Government should be called upon to pay half the cost. It should be understood that the Government are not asking the natives suddenly to pay the £5, and I do not think that they would feel the other portion of the payment when spread over four years. The natives could always get the four morgen by paying 15s. per annum, and they pay 10s. at present in hut tax. For an extra morgen they would have to pay 3s. With regard to alienation and transfer, it has been thought advisable not to submit these people to the very heavy charges which we have in connection with our farms. The Government looks upon them as living in a native reserve, and desires to make the transfer and alienation of land as simple as possible. These clauses have been drawn after very careful consultation with those gentlemen who are in charge of this matter. In reference to administration and distribution of their estates, the Government have simply taken the Native Succession Law of 1864 and adopted it, the object being to save expense. The next great question is that of primogeniture. These people are given a piece of land, and they are very domestic in their nature. Four morgen of land would not split up into much for each of the family, in case of the death of the native who was the head of the family. The only way to meet this is by the native law of primogeniture. The only way to deal with it is by the law of entail—leave it to the eldest son. We fail utterly when we put natives on an equality with ourselves. If we deal with them differently and say, "Yes, these people have their own ideas," and so on, then we are all right; but when once we depart from that position and put them on an equality with ourselves, we may give the matter up. What we may expect after a hundred years of civilisation I do not know. If I may venture a comparison, I would compare the natives generally, with regard to European civilisation, to fellow-tribesmen of the Druids, and just suppose that they were come to life after the two thousand years which have elapsed since their existence. That is the position. The honourable member for Fort Beaufort simply wants to get rid of the two thousand years that lie between us and the natives.

'To return to the clause under consideration, I consider that the procedure to be adopted with regard to the second wife of the native is a matter for the House to decide. I was in the Transkei the other day, when a native told me that the Government taxed him for each wife. I believe he said he had six, but I am not sure. Now (went on the native), you say you can only recognise the first wife. The missionary tells me that it is very wicked to have more than one wife. But I find in the Old Testament people had from one to one hundred wives. And I do not find any instructions in the Old or New Testaments as to whether I may have a hundred wives or only one. This was just a simple native. I told him, "I had not considered the question." To proceed: of course, the House will have to deal with the matter of entail. As to the question of voting, we say that the natives are in a sense citizens, but not altogether citizens—they are still children. And though we place them in individual positions with regard to certain pieces of agricultural land, we protect them by all sorts of laws. In so far as that land is concerned, the native has no right to claim a vote for it. And so it will be said you are going to take away the vote from the poor native. But if those gentlemen who say that they wish really to consider the welfare of these poor people, would think less about their votes, and more about their future, they would effect more. I know that these gentlemen talk much at missionary meetings about the poor natives, but I say to them, Try to do the natives some real good. Some honourable members may say that I have broken my pledges in interfering with the country by revising the voters' lists in the territories I have referred to. But this is not the case. It may, perhaps, be said that the list of voters clause will rob these poor people of their votes. Nothing of the kind. I have found that nine-tenths of them were not entitled to vote at all at present. I do not propose to interfere with the Franchise Law as it was passed last year, but I say that it has been carried out improperly, and therefore, in dealing with these native areas, if the House approves of it, I propose to extend the law as it at present exists, so that it shall be properly carried out. I think there would be an alteration effected in Aliwal if this were to be carried out. I think that a very large number of voters registered in the district would, on a careful examination, not continue on the roll under the present Franchise Law.

'With reference to the labour tax, some newspapers in the colony take it that all of the natives will have to pay the labour tax whether they work or not. Now, that is not the case. What I have found is this, that we must give some gentle stimulus to these people to make them go on working. There are a large number of young men in these locations who are like younger sons at home, or if you will have it so, like young men about town. These young natives live in the native areas and locations with their fathers and mothers, and never do one stroke of work. But if a labour tax of 10s. were imposed, they would have to work. Their present life is very similar to that of the young man about town who lounges about the club during the day and dresses himself for a tea-party in the afternoon, and in the evening drinks too much, and probably finishes up with immorality. These native young men are not in a position to marry and settle down, because they have not got cows. They are a nuisance to every district in the Transkei, to every magistrate in the Transkei, and to every location. We want to get hold of these young men and make them go out to work, and the only way to do this is to compel them to pay a certain labour tax. But we must prepare these people for the change. Every black man cannot have three acres and a cow, or four morgen and a commonage right. We have to face the question, and it must be brought home to them that in the future nine-tenths of them will have to spend their lives in daily labour, in physical work, in manual labour. This must be brought home to them sooner or later. There is nothing new in this.

'Now is the moment to deal with the question of taxation. I would do away with locations on private farms, the defect of which is that we do not know where the natives are. I propose to use the labour tax for industrial schools and training. I propose that the neglect of labour should provide a fund for instruction in labour. I have called them industrial schools, but I mean that they should be carried on under regulations to be framed by the Government. Why? I have travelled through the Transkei, and have found some excellent establishments where the natives are taught Latin and Greek. They are turning out Kaffir parsons, most excellent individuals, but the thing is overdone. I find that these people cannot find congregations for them. There are Kaffir parsons everywhere—these institutions are turning them out by the dozen. They are turning out a dangerous class. They are excellent so long as the supply is limited, but the country is overstocked with them. These people will not go back and work, and that is why I say that the regulations of these industrial schools should be framed by the Government; otherwise these Kaffir parsons would develop into agitators against the Government. Let me go on and point out the way in which the minds of the natives should be occupied. I find that many of the friends of the natives would hear of their minds being employed in no other pursuit than that of electing members for Parliament. That was the question of the vote. "You must get them to vote for me," was the general position of the friend of the native.

'Now, I say the natives are children. They are just emerging from barbarism. They have human minds, and I would like them to devote themselves wholly to the local matters that surround them and appeal to them. I would let them tax themselves, and give them the funds to spend on these matters— the building of roads and bridges, the making of plantations, and other such works. I propose that the House shall allow these people to tax themselves, and that the proceeds of their taxation shall be spent by them on the development of themselves and of their districts. The honourable member for Cape Town (Mr. Wiener) smiled the other day when I spoke of the natives building bridges, and asked how they could build them with the proceeds of their taxation? If in Fingoland an extra tax of 10s. per agricultural lot, or per head, were put on, and a distict council were formed, that would give them £9000 per annum to spend. The Local Loans Act could be applied, the repayments to extend over eight years. By that means I propose that the country shall gradually be relieved of local expenditure in the Transkei. These people have the best portion of South Africa. I think that any one in charge of the Transkei is doing his duty to these people and to the country when he works with this object, that the Transkei should not be a charge upon our funds for local purposes. So far as roads, bridges, etc., and even so far as education and the appointment of scab inspectors, and indeed all those which I may call local questions, are concerned, I want to ask that these people shall have, through district councils, this kind of representation. Mr. Veldtman, whose name is a household word, has begged me to do something of the kind.

Now as to the liquor question, I have read carefully the proposals of the Labour Commission, and the proposition is that the majority in divisional councils shall have power to make any law for the disposal of liquor licenses. I can say that I have been instrumental in removing the liquor from tens of thousands of these poor children. I refer to the compounds and locations in which they are shut up, and in which the liquor is kept from them. The liquor question is a difficult one, and I know the difficulties of it. When it is said that we should take the licences away from all the hotel and canteen-keepers, I think there is some unfairness in it. We have gone on year after year encouraging these people to improve their dwellings, and have then suddenly turned round and proposed that all these people should shut up shop and have their business taken away from them. This is manifestly unfair. If the majority of the voters decide that a canteen should be closed, we should give compensation. The advantages of the system are plain. No one can then say that the closing of a canteen or hotel is the fad of a teetotal party. The people must put their hands in their own pockets and be willing to pay compensation. If in Fingoland we could raise a fund of £9000 per annum, as I have before pointed out, we shall be able in Glen Grey to have a fund for this compensation. These are the reasons why, in dealing with this liquor question, I have adopted the recommendation of the Labour Commission, but I have also laid down the principle that if the people wish the canteens to be closed they should also pay compensation. Half the people could forward a request through their council and say that they were willing to pay for the closing, and who could say anything against that? If no compensation were paid, we should be open to the charge that it was a temperance move, and that without compensation we were taking the trade away from the people. Then there might be another charge, that the council nominee members would stop this. One half of the council are elected, and the other half nominated. These natives are mixed up with white farmers. I have asked the farmers whether they would object to sitting on the council with people of another colour. They said No. I have made the number of nominees six, for the following reasons: that if it were left to election, there would not be a white on the council. This would not apply to purely native districts, but Glen Grey, unfortunately, is entirely mixed up, and that is the only way out of the difficulty. But for any one to say that the whole of the six white men would vote for no compensation is perfectly ridiculous. I think better of my own countrymen.

'Before I finish dealing with the Bill, I will refer to the question of title. There is the payment of quitrents, and there is that of alienation with consent of the Government. Some newspapers have said that the whole object of the Bill is to get land into the hands of the white men, and I simply refer to the title to refute this. Again, we hear the argument that after five years these people will sell out to the white men. My idea is that the natives should be kept in these native reserves and not be mixed with the white men at all. Are you going to sanction the idea, with all the difficulties of the poor whites before us, that these people should be mixed up with white men, and white children grow up in the middle of native locations? In the interest of the white people themselves we must never let this happen. White labour cannot compete with black labour in this country—physical labour, I mean. As to the argument that some men by assiduous detail could buy out seventy native holders with their three thousand morgen in one bargain, I have dealt with the Diamond Fields and with Charterland, but I would rather do either or both over again than undertake such a job as that. The title means that the holdings cannot be sold without the consent of the Government. There are clauses which lay down that in case of theft the land shall be forfeited; there is a clause that in case of non-cultivation the land shall be taken away and realloted; there is a clause providing that it shall not be sublet; and another clause that there shall not be subdivision.

'I would now deal with a few of the literary criticisms of the Bill. The Bill has puzzled many because it has appealed to the different classes of this country. In one paper I read that the Bill is too sudden. Well, I am sorry. I have not been a year in the Native Affairs Office, but I see terrible crowding of locations going on, and that is my reason for hurrying on the Bill. Another paper remarks that no voting powers would be given. I have explained that before. I have not interfered with the native voting powers at all. If the honourable member for Fort Beaufort raises an objection on that score, then we must come to the conclusion that some persons have voted for him who had no right to do so. I have already dealt with the criticisms in reference to title. There is another criticism, that I am not taking any notice of the recommendations of the Labour Commission. But I would point out that there are no less than ten of these recommendations embodied in the Bill. There are the recommendations in reference to liquor, a labour bureau (for the natives would come and ask to be provided with masters, because otherwise they had to pay a tax of 10s.), forfeiture in case of conviction for theft, subletting, cheap transfer, additional taxation for educational purposes, the agricultural and industrial clause, and vagrancy—in all, ten of the Labour Commission's recommendations embodied in the Bill.

'I submit to this House that there are four propositions that come before us in regard to this question. We have to find land for these people; we have to find them some employment; we have to remove the liquor from them; and we have to stimulate them to work. I submit to this House these propositions, and I hope the House will accept them. Do you admit that the native question is most dangerous? Do you admit that you have done nothing for these people? Do you admit that in many parts of the colony these people have been ruining themselves? Do you admit that century after century these large numbers could not be provided with land? Do you admit that these people are increasing at a great rate? This Bill puts forward various proposals to meet this state of things. I submit to the House that the idea that we could drive them out must be dismissed as regards those parts of the colony which these people have occupied. They are our future labourers, and we cannot permit them in these areas to be ever increasing, and the places to be overstocked. I propose to apply these principles to Fingoland at once. It would be wise not to deal with the whole native question at once. The natives are children, and we ought to do something for the minds and the brains that the Almighty has given them. I do not believe that they are different from ourselves.

'The Bill says to them that we will put them on the land; we will put them under their local magistrate; and we will let them conduct their own local affairs. As to liquor, you will, no doubt, hear that the wine-farmers of the West will object. Still, when the wine-farmers hear that these people are willing to pay compensation for the removal of this pest, I do not think they will continue to object. The last proposition is that we must give the people some stimulus to work. It is impossible to provide them all with land; at the present time their homes are crowded. The question has been met by many countries before, and it is admitted that there has always been a period when the country could not be supported by agriculture alone. Hence the provisions of the Bill to meet this difficulty. I will say one thing in this House—that there was never a greater mistake made than by people who think that the native editor of *Invo*, the native paper, has the confidence of the native people. And so the criticism and abuse which have been poured upon this Bill by this barbarian, who has just partly emerged from barbarism, are not to be taken any notice of. What does this Bill mean? It is an earnest effort to deal with the position of these people. We cannot stand by and do nothing: it is easy to do that. It is an effort to deal with these four propositions I have submitted. Mr. Speaker, this is a Bill with a wide scope. I may say the whole of the north will some time or another come under this Bill if passed by this House. If the Bill gets through, he will be a brave man who will attempt to alter it. I would not be surprised to see Natal—I should say the Transkei—come under this Bill. I will not prophesy that it will be applied to Natal, because the Natal people have too much independence to accept Cape legislation. Indeed, you may say this is a native Bill for Africa. You are sitting in judgment on Africa at the present moment. I have merely submitted to the House my ideas on the question. It is a proposition submitted to provide them with district councils; it is a proposition submitted to employ their minds on simple questions in connection with local affairs; it is a proposition to remove the liquor pest; and last, but not least, by the gentle stimulant of the labour tax to remove them from a life of sloth and laziness; you will thus teach them the dignity of labour, and make them contribute to the prosperity of the state, and give some return for our wise and good government.'

The last speech in this chapter is one made in the Cape House, May 20, 1894, on the annexation of Pondoland. Mr. Rhodes objected to disarmament, as he had done in respect to Basutoland twelve years before, when he said, 'It is hard lines to take from them their guns which they bought with their own money'; for justice to the natives, and consideration for their feelings (the guns being regarded by them as a sign of manhood), were always a part of his native policy.

'I do not ask for congratulations,[1] for what has been done by the Government during the session has simply been a necessity. The House has recognised that once they crossed the Kei, it was merely a matter of time when the boundaries

1. Mr. Rhodes moved:—'That in the opinion of this House it is expedient that the country known as Pondoland, comprising the territories of East and West Pondoland which have been ceded by the Chiefs Sigcau and Nquiliso, should be annexed to this colony, and that the Government take such steps as may be necessary to effect such annexation.'

of the Cape would be conterminous with those of Natal. The maintenance of a barbarian power between two civilised powers has been proved by experience to be almost an impossibility; and the only point for the Cape to consider in connection with Pondoland has for some time been, When would be the right moment for annexation? In the Bluebook upon the matter there will not be found some correspondence which had taken place between the late Government and the Governor of the colony. This has been excluded at the request of the Imperial authorities, but I am allowed to allude to it, and it appears that during the existence of the late Government, when they were asked what course they proposed to pursue, they said that when the right moment came they were prepared to relieve the Imperial Government of all responsibility on condition that the colony had complete control. The whole crux of the question, therefore, was and is this, When is the right moment to annex?

'During the last recess Sigcau and Umhlangaso broke out into hostilities, and the colony of Natal asked the Cape to co-operate with them in dealing with Pondoland. About the same time, too, a native power in the north had been dealt with, and Ministers came to the conclusion that the opportune moment had come to deal with the Pondo question. The next question arose, How was this to be done? The Governor at first rather feared the weakness of the colony, but Ministers felt that in the Cape Mounted Rifles they had a force perfectly capable of successfully carrying through hostilities, should they break out. Major Elliott, the chief magistrate, then came down to the colony, and after consultation with him it was decided that the chiefs should be informed of the proposed annexation, and that it would be sufficient for the purposes of the Cape to move the Cape Mounted Rifles to the boundary and leave to Major Elliott the diplomatic details.'

Mr. Rhodes proceeded to narrate in detail the circumstances of the mission of Major Elliott to Sigcau and Umhlangaso, and said he was supported by physical force, because he (Mr. Rhodes) believed that in dealing with natives a display of physical force went a long way.

'It might be asked, Why did we not consult the neighbouring colony of Natal? But I would point out that there was no time to lose. Hostilities were constantly occurring between the chiefs, and prompt action was necessary, otherwise we should have had serious complications with neighbouring colonies and states, which was not desirable. The position taken up by Natal was an impossible one; it was actually suggested that we should divide the territory with Natal, which meant the handing over of Griqualand East to Natal.

What I would suggest to Natal is the consideration of the question whether the river Umzimkulu, from its source to its mouth, is not the natural boundary between the two colonies. After obtaining cession of the country, I visited Pondoland, and met the two chiefs, when a new difficulty arose, because it appeared that they desired the country to have been annexed on the basis of Basutoland, which meant that their magistrates should advise and not govern. Now, each chief had been found utterly unfit to rule, and though the chiefs tried hard to make me change my mind, I had to tell them that the only basis of annexation the Government could sanction was that the magistrates, and not the chiefs, should govern. This created some unpleasantness at the time, but the chiefs subsequently gave in; and at the present time the magistrates are enforcing the law. Now if the Pondos had intended showing fight, I think they would have done so during the first week, when there were one or two outrages, and magisterial interference was necessary. But the secret of the peace is that the common people are delighted at the change of government, for they know that now there will be law and order.

'The next difficulty that arises is the question of concessions in Pondoland. The Government have decided that no concession shall be recognised. They have been blamed for that decision, but they thought it much better to speak out, otherwise they would have had people, who had *bonâ fide* put their money into concessions, asking them in the future to recognise these concessions, and saying that the Government had not spoken. The Government may be right or wrong, but the position they have taken up is this, that no concession shall be recognised as legal unless sanctioned by the High Commissioner. When you go into a native country you should endeavour to obtain all the attributes of government; and I would remind the House that you would have a hard time of it, if you found the land, minerals, and forests in the hands of different concessionaries. Government then would have the husk and other people the kernel. The Government considers that a sum of £500 a year is enough for the proper maintenance of a native chief. That is the story of the cession. After the cession was made, Government thought it desirable to leave fifty Cape Mounted Rifles with each magistrate, and the result has been that the House will be asked to vote £15,000 to replace the 134 Cape Mounted Rifles taken out of police service in the colony. The actual cost of the occupation of the country is £7500, but we have stores valued at £1812, and although there are incidental expenses, I am confident that we shall come out under £7000. In addition we shall have to pay £8000 a year for magistrates, for we could not get the hut tax in until after next year. That will make in all a sum of £15,000, which, with the cost of the new police, will make £30,000 in all. We hope next year to obtain hut tax sufficient to pay for the maintenance of the police, but I submit that there must be a charge debited to the Transkei, though one hopes that the time will arrive when this portion of the colony will pay for itself. I think we might, indeed, put the cost of the Cape Mounted Rifles against the Customs duties. The House may congratulate itself, if it admits that the annexation of Pondoland was essential, that a happy conjunction of circumstances has permitted it to be effected without great cost or danger. There was of course a considerable difficulty that had to be dealt with in the person of Umhlangaso, whom Sigcau had stipulated that we shall remove from the country. Accordingly Umhlangaso has been brought into the colony, and is now located with a few followers eight miles from Kokstad, and has given a solemn pledge that he will not return to Pondoland. Another difficult question was whether the Government should disarm the natives. But I would ask on what basis we could disarm them. They had submitted without a shot being fired, and I do not think the Government could justly claim to take their guns from them. Even if we had taken the wretched guns they had, the guns would have had to be paid for, and they might then use the money to buy better weapons. There is really no just or logical ground upon which the Government could disarm them, and it is for the House to say whether the decision of the Government was a wise one. With 700,000 natives to rule you may feel almost overweighted with responsibility; but, having taken the step of extending the borders of the colony, we are bound to carry it out. It has been often said that the Cape is unfair to the natives, but it would be as well if the critics knew and studied the conduct of the colony toward native tribes which have frequently rebelled, have been subdued, and are now governed with money drawn from the treasury of the colony. I have pointed out the unselfish position of the colony. To us annexation was an obligation, whereas to the natives it will be a positive relief, for they will be freed from a seething caldron of barbarian atrocities; and I hope that if the House be pleased to adopt this motion, the people will experience the blessing of coming under the kind and beneficent sway of the Cape Colonial Government.'

THE CHARTERED COMPANY AND ITS WORK

Mr. Rhodes's next move was a journey in the spring of 1889 to London. There he had to amalgamate the Exploring Company's interest (the fruit of Mr. Maund's expedition), and there he had to form his own Company and obtain, if possible, a charter. Mr. Rhodes, who had at his back a most powerful financial group, the De Beers Company, the Gold-fields of South Africa, and Mr. Beit, among others, held from the first the reins, and practically directed the whole enterprise. It must have been amusing to those who were then behind the scenes to read the criticisms that have since, with the wisdom that comes after the event, been showered on the allotment of the shares; for at that time the venture was regarded by all, except its moving spirit, Mr. Rhodes, and the few who knew his record and had an almost blind faith in the success of anything he undertook, as extremely hazardous. Mr. Rhodes's optimism, however, is infectious, and he had no difficulty in securing the necessary financial support, and indeed De Beers (which found £200,000), the Gold-fields of South Africa, the great Rhodes-Rudd Gold-mining Corporation, with Mr. Beit and Mr. Rhodes himself, could have easily subscribed the capital of a million among themselves. But no one at the time had any idea that the British public would at once perceive the big possibilities that lay behind the nebulous present and very distant and doubtful future value of the shares, and ignore, as they did, the enormous difficulties of occupation, and the necessarily slow progress and great uncertainty of development.

The business of obtaining a charter from the British Government was not so easy or so expeditious as that of providing the capital. The preliminary negotiations took time, and it was not till July 1889 that the formal application was made, and it was October before it was formally granted.

One of the difficulties which Mr. Rhodes had to overcome was the wish of the Government to limit the charter to the territories south of the Zambesi. Mr. Rhodes was resolved not to be satisfied with such an arrangement, which would have been a terrible blow to his vast scheme of expansion; and by the same untiring perseverance which carried through the De Beers amalgamation, he got what he wanted—freedom to take the unclaimed territory north of the river. Mr. Rhodes's real ambition and aim at this time was nothing less than to secure through the Chartered Company the whole territory north of the Zambesi for the British Empire, and he had no intention of stopping even at Lake Tanganyika, if he could possibly succeed in painting the map red till he reached the Hinterland of Egypt upon the upper Nile. With this object in view, Mr. Rhodes succeeded in getting the northern boundaries of the Chartered Company's realms left undefined, and it was accordingly described in the charter as the region 'lying immediately to the north of British Bechuanaland and to the north and west of the South African Republic, and to the west of the Portuguese dominions,' while the power of further extension was added subject only to the approval of the Government. He had already an eye upon Barotseland, north of the river (which he acquired shortly before the occupation of Mashonaland was completed), on the unexplored territory up to Lakes Bangweolo and Tanganyika, and also on the dominion of Msidi, Katanga, widely celebrated among the natives for its copper, and also supposed to be rich in gold. This last was afterwards successfully claimed by the Congo Free State, though certainly there had never been the most shadowy existence of effective Belgian occupation. He also aimed at making some friendly arrangement with Portugal, and sent a representative to negotiate at Lisbon with a view to acquiring an interest in her East African territories; but this he did not push through, depending here, as in Katanga, a little too much on the policy of action and of accomplished facts.

Further details of his vast schemes might be added, but enough has been told to make plain the immense range of Mr. Rhodes's ambition for the extension of the Empire, and the unhesitating sacrifice of any immediate financial advantage which he was eager to make in order to paint the map red over all unclaimed or unoccupied portions of the last continent that remained open for British expansion. Of course, Mr. Rhodes's associates, who were men of business first and Imperialists after, were somewhat alarmed at the huge schemes of their empire-making chief. Lobengula's dominions would have amply satisfied their acquisitiveness, for they saw very clearly that the occupation of such enormous additional territories would cost money, while a development sufficient to get some return for their money must for a great number of years be practically impossible.

But Mr. Rhodes was not to be denied; he did not rest till he had successfully imposed his policy on his colleagues, and the Chartered Company thus became the great instrument in our time in Imperial expansion. In the spring and early summer of 1889, long before the future of the charter was certain, he was doing practical work to obtain a controlling interest far north of the Zambesi in Nyasaland. This he effected by an agreement with the African Lakes Company, by which the promoters of the yet inchoate Chartered Company, at that time not yet ready even to apply for the charter, subscribed a large sum to the exhausted treasury of the African Lakes Company, undertook to give Chartered shares for the Company's shares, and undertook to find a large sum yearly for the expenses of administration. Mr. Rhodes, on the other hand, obtained the right of taking over the African Lakes Company, a right that was, as regards land and administration, in due time exercised.

When all that could be done in London was accomplished, the restless energy of the empire-builder would not let him await the formal grant of the charter in October; and long before that time he was back in South Africa making preparations to push on at the earliest possible date that effective occupation of territory, which he considered the chief reason for the Company's existence, and, to judge from his tireless devotion to the work of expansion, a main reason for his own. In London Mr. Rhodes had had ample opportunity for consulting a pioneer of the northern territories, Mr. Selous. Mr. Selous, the world-famed hunter, is one of those adventurous English sportsmen, whose hunting expeditions have served so often as the forerunners of the advance of British civilisation into savage lands. His thorough knowledge of Mashonaland and Matabeleland, acquired in the wanderings of many years in the pursuit of big game, his trained habits of observation, his personal, though not very pleasant, experience of Lobengula and the Matabele, made him the best of all possible advisers on the question of occupation. The weight of Mr. Selous's opinion was given in favour of Mashonaland, partly because it was far distant from the home of the Matabele, partly because its high veldt offered a healthy and attractive region for English colonisation, and partly, though in a minor degree, I think, because Mr. Selous, whose humane feelings had been repeatedly outraged by what he had seen of the cruel Matabele massacres of the helpless Mashonas, was anxious to interpose a barrier of Europeans to Lobengula's exterminating *impis.*

The charter was granted at the end of October 1889, and a little after the middle of March 1890 the expedition set out, not without a certain appearance of destiny, from the very place where the dream of empire to the north had first had birth in the young English digger's brain, from Kimberley.

The expedition was as strange and intensely modern in its mode of organisation as it was swift and thorough in its equipment and action. The question of the numbers of men and of the amount of money required for the occupation of Mashonaland was decided by the acceptance of the offer of Mr. Frank Johnson, a man of ample experience and great resource, to contract to raise a small body of Cape colonists and Englishmen, and occupy Mashonaland for the sum of £90,000. Less than two hundred men composed the famous Mashonaland Pioneers, and these, with two troops of mounted police, made up the expedition.

A great difficulty had been to deal with Lobengula, and obtain his countenance and approval to the proposed use of the concession. Mr. Rhodes chose for this extremely delicate work of diplomacy a man whose worth he knew from years of intimate friendship, Dr. Jameson, the successful Kimberley medical man. Dr. Jameson went up to Lobengula in 1889, and stayed three months, cured the beef-eating, beer-drinking monarch's gout, and gained such power over him and his chief Indunas that he succeeded in obtaining his full approval to the objects in view, and particularly to the occupation of Mashonaland. After this was accomplished, Dr. Jameson returned to Kimberley, only to be despatched again to Bulawayo to contend with fresh complications there, and at Bulawayo he remained, keeping Lobengula in a friendly humour to the venture, until the pioneers were on their way to Mashonaland.

Dr. Jameson got away from Bulawayo, however, in time to join the expedition on its way up, and supplied in the work of occupation the place which Mr. Rhodes would have filled himself, had he not been forced by urgent political considerations to remain at the Cape and use the influence he had gained there. It is pretty certain that had not Dr. Jameson gone up the second time to Lobengula and kept that savage despot in good-humour, he would have definitely revoked his permission, and it is probable that the Matabele would, after his departure, have attacked the column, but that it had got through the dangerous bush beyond the Macloutsie River long before the natives expected. Dr. Jameson joined and accompanied the advance guard, and Mr. Selous, at the head of the pioneers, cut the road for the wagons through the thick bush. Once the high veldt, the plateau of Mashonaland, was entered, by a pass discovered by Mr. Selous, the danger was over; for a few hundred mounted men, good riders and good shots, like the pioneers and the police, could have made head in the open against a very large force of natives. The Imperial Government had given some useful aid to the advance, by sending up a force of Bechuanaland police to the south-west borders of Matabeleland, thus drawing off the attention of Lobengula from the expedition.

When one contrasts the unbroken success and the small expense of this occupation with the expense of somewhat similar operations of the Imperial forces, one realises the accurate judgment of Mr. Rhodes in determining to undertake the work of expansion through the Cape Colony and its people, with his own energy and practical abilities to direct the operations, and his own chosen men to see his plans carried through. On the 12th of September 1890 the expedition had reached its destination at Mount Hampden, and there the flourishing town of Salisbury rapidly sprang into existence. The rainy season of 1890–1 brought a great deal of hardship and suffering on the pioneers and on the crowd of gold-seekers who flocked in without any adequate supply of provisions or other necessaries; but the work of expansion, the main object of Mr. Rhodes, went on unchecked. Dr. Jameson, accompanied by Mr. Frank Johnson, explored and mapped out a short route to the east coast by which the Beira railroad now runs. Manica was next explored, and treaties with the chiefs were followed by occupation. After great hardships and privations, Dr. Jameson made his way to Gazaland, to the kraal of the great chief Gungunhana, and, in the face of Portuguese opposition, apparently succeeded in securing the country for the Chartered Company. These advances eastward had, however, brought Mr. Rhodes into conflict with the

Portuguese, who had been making desperate efforts to establish some semblance of an effective occupation of Manicaland and the neighbouring territory they claimed. Umtasa, a Manica chief, had accepted British protection, and when afterwards Portuguese emissaries were found at his kraal, they were arrested by the Chartered Company's officials and sent to Fort Salisbury. This caused a violent agitation in Portugal. The king, believing his crown to be in danger owing to the handle this discontent gave to the Republican party, appealed to the British Crown, and Mr. Rhodes's young men were authoritatively checked, though the difficulty was not finally removed till the *modus vivendi* of November 11, 1890, followed by the Convention of June 1891, by which the greater part of Gazaland (in spite of Gungunhana's efforts to come under the British flag, with which object he sent envoys to England in 1891) remained outside the British Empire, but a preferential right of purchase over Portuguese territory south of the Zambesi was secured.

The same difficulty of shadowy Portuguese claims and active Portuguese aggression was found in what is now North Rhodesia, where Consul-General Sir H. H. Johnston managed to anticipate Serpa Pinto and his army, and made treaties with the chiefs right up to Lake Tanganyika. It was in 1891 that Mr. Johnston became Consul-General for Nyasaland and Administrator of Northern Rhodesia, where, aided by liberal support from Mr. Rhodes and the Chartered Company, he put down the slave-trade by some brilliant operations against the Arab slave-traders and their native allies. This work, of course, belongs to a later period. A far more serious difficulty was the attempt of the Transvaal Boers, backed by General Joubert, but of course ostensibly without the authorisation of President Kruger, to trek into the Company's territories and establish an occupation by force of arms. Some account of this will be given in the next chapter. Mr. Rhodes, not contented with the work of expansion Dr. Jameson and his men were carrying out so expeditiously south of the Zambesi, was not long in sending up an expedition north of the Zambesi under the well-known explorer, Joseph Thomson, and another under Mr. Sharpe, to make treaties, and if possible get possession of Katanga, which, however, it was ultimately decided, belonged to the Congo Free State.

Meanwhile, the empire-builder, who was thus stretching out his arm over Central Africa, had been engaged at the Cape in work which would have been sufficient to occupy all the energies and time of any man of affairs of ordinary ability and ambition. The Chartered Company was bound under the terms of its agreement with the Imperial Government to bear part of the expense of carrying the telegraph line through the Bechuanaland Protectorate, and to build the northern railway from Kimberley to Mafeking. The telegraph and the railway were and are Mr. Rhodes's favourite instruments for rapid development, and he was resolved that they should quickly follow in the wake of his pioneers. The telegraph, being much swifter of construction, as well as cheaper than the railway, was his first care (though he lost no time about the railway), and its beginnings were soon to develop into the great Trans-continental line, which now joins Cape Town to Lake Tanganyika, and is on its way to Egypt, almost entirely at the expense of the private purse of the public-spirited maker of Rhodesia.

While these events were passing in Mashonaland and the neighbouring territory, Mr. Rhodes had accepted the position of Prime Minister at the Cape. Sir Gordon Sprigg's Government had not been a success, and an extravagant railway scheme hastened its downfall. There was really no one but Mr. Rhodes who could command the confidence and support alike of the English colonists and of the Dutch, and a reconciliation and coalition of the two races for the development of South Africa had been all along the great aim of his political life. It was specially important to obtain at this time the support of Mr. Hofmeyr and the Afrikander Bond, as through them some influence might be exerted on President Kruger to stop the inroad of thousands of Transvaal raiders into Mashonaland, which must have resulted in a conflict, the event of which, considering the small number of the pioneers, would have been at least very doubtful. Mr. Rhodes accordingly decided to combine the duties of managing director and virtual head of the Chartered Company with the duties entailed by forming a Ministry at Cape Town. This was early in the latter half of 1890.

Before taking responsibility and forming a Ministry he asked the Bond party to meet him, and obtained an assurance of their support. Here I may point out that Mr. Rhodes, though he was anxious for the support of the Bond, and anxious to work with them, needing their help, and also deeply convinced that the true solvent for racial feeling is co-operation in a common work, and the mutual knowledge such intercourse affords, has never joined the Bond, has never been one of the Bondmen. A short time before this, while Sir Gordon Sprigg was still Premier, Mr. Hofmeyr offered to put him in Sir Gordon Sprigg's place as a nominee of the Bond. Mr. Rhodes refused the offer. He was willing to work with the Bond; he refused to be their instrument. He kept his own independence of action, though willing to do all he could for conciliation. No doubt, Mr. Hofmeyr may have hoped to use Mr. Rhodes for his own scheme of Dutch Supremacy at the time when he and the Bond agreed to support the future Premier; but if he did, he has since learned his mistake. Mr. Rhodes highly esteems the Dutch individually, but naturally, being a Progressive and an Imperialist, is opposed to the idea of the Dutch as a governing body.

The ultimate object of Mr. Rhodes's policy was the union of South Africa, towards which he hoped to work through a Customs Union, a Railway Union, and if possible, in the future, a united native policy. He knew the complete union of South Africa would involve a change in the Transvaal and its policy of isolation and racial distinction, but that he proposed to leave to the workings of inevitable law, by which a large, an enterprising, and increasing industrial population, chiefly of English race, must in one way or other gradually free themselves from the domination of an oligarchy of uneducated Dutch farmers, managed for their personal profit by a clique of Hollander officials and foreign concessionnaires, and strong only in their passionate antipathy to English rule, their skill with the rifle, and their possession of a very powerful and shrewd leader in the dictator who ruled at Pretoria.

The speeches of this period are not numerous, as Mr. Rhodes's energy was finding more congenial expression in action. The first in order is a speech made some time before Mr. Rhodes became Premier, at a banquet given (May 11, 1890) at Bloemfontein to Sir H. Loch (now Lord Loch), then Governor and High Commissioner at the Cape.

In replying for 'The Cape Parliament,' Mr. Rhodes said:—'Mr. Chairman, your Excellency, and Gentlemen,—I could only wish that this night one of the members of the Cape Parliament, who is also a Minister of the Crown, could reply to the kindly words addressed by the gentleman who has proposed the toast of the Cape Parliament. I must say, Mr. Chairman, that I have been for the last ten years a member of the Cape Parliament, and if there is one thing I have seen to be a success in the government of the country, it is the fact that Her Majesty was good enough to grant us the benefits of responsible government. At the time it was granted there were many who thought we were not fitted for it, and could not undertake our own government. I think you will admit in this neighboring State, that though in many respects we have failed, yet it was a credit to the people of the colony that they had the boldness to take into their hands the government of the country. The feeling of the colony was that the time was come, and that they were fitted to undertake the management of government for themselves, and if I may put it to you to-night, when we look back upon the period during which we have had that government, I think we need not be ashamed of ourselves. We have taken upon ourselves the construction of two thousand miles of railway; we have educated ourselves, and have had to rule the races in our charge, and I think you will say that credit is due to us. We had to leave our agricultural pursuits and our mines; we had to educate ourselves to parliamentary life and government; and so we have deserved the confidence of the country. It has fallen to our lot to be put in possession of ports on the sea-coast, and thus we were brought into connection with the neighbouring Republics, and I think that the policy of the Cape Colony has been to cultivate the friendship of these States, and in that policy I think we have not failed generally. I may here refer to very recent transactions which have been entered into with the neighbouring Free State, and I may say that I have to compliment the gentlemen of the Volksraad, seeing that they carried out a political transaction of quite supreme advantage to themselves. When we come to consider a neighbouring State, which is said to be governed by a body of simple farmers, we find that they have made arrangements by which they have obliged the members of another Government to contribute a share of customs, and to spend its money on railways in their State: and when there is any profit on those railways they share it on a half-and-half basis, with the perpetually retained right of adopting full control whenever they see fit to do so. I may say that the neighbouring State does not consist wholly of simple farmers but also of very capable diplomatists. But beyond that there is a doctrine, dated at least thirty years back, regarding customs as the just right of contribution of the coast ports; and I think a speaker to-night placed that as a cardinal fact in the settlement of the question. I think our politicians in the Cape Colony desired not to evade the discussion of these questions. I think that kind of reciprocity will continue. In the railway arrangements you hold, I may say, as a citizen of Kimberley, that I hope your State will claim the rights of further expenditure on the basis of a line between Kimberley and Bloemfontein. Any one who has travelled into the Conquered Territory cannot but perceive what will be the future of the granary of South Africa if only railway extension is afforded to it. The people there must have a market for their industry.'

Mr. Rhodes then alluded to the necessity for running the railways through the coal-mining districts of the Free States, in order that their coal might be used in the Kimberley mines, so that the directors might save the expense of sending 7000 miles for their fuel when it was lying so near their doors. In conclusion, he expressed admiration for a sentiment regarding the possession of a national flag, but said there was still a possibility of a South African Federal Union if they could pursue a course which would give them an arrangement in an equal Customs Union in all the countries from Durban to Walfisch Bay. This and other such equitable understandings would, while not sacrificing sentiment, bring about a practical union in Africa.

The next speech of 1890 is one made, as Premier, at the cradle of his political ambition, Kimberley, on September 6. This speech is in unimportant passages a summary.

'Mr. Mayor and Gentlemen,—I thank you for the very cordial and hearty manner in which you have received the toast just proposed. I cannot say that "A prophet is not without honour save in his own country," for I am not a prophet, and I think the honour done me to-night as one of your citizens, on my being raised to the position of Premier of this colony, is very great indeed; and I appreciate it extremely. Only about two months ago, being much occupied with the North, I had made up my mind not to attend Parliament, but I found there was a huge Railway Bill proposed, and I thought it was my duty to oppose it, as it would place too great a burden upon the revenue of this country. I felt that this community had a very large stake in the prosperity of the country, and a Railway Bill which would cost twelve millions for railways which it was admitted almost on all sides would not pay, would be a heavy burden. I hurried down, and we fought the question, and the result you all know. But events hurried on faster than I expected, and before I knew where I was I saw it would be forced upon me to take the responsibility of the government of this country. I thought of the positions I occupied in De Beers and the Chartered Company, and I concluded that one position could be worked with the other, and each to the benefit of all. At any rate I had the courage to undertake it, and I may say that up to the present I have not regretted it. If there is anything that would give me encouragement, it is the kindly and cordial greeting my fellow-citizens have extended to me to-night.

'I may tell you that before coming to a decision in regard to occupying the position of Premier, I met the various sections of the House. I hope you will not be alarmed when I say that I asked the members of the Bond party to meet me. I trust you will agree with me that when I was undertaking the responsibility of government, the best thing to be done was to ask them to meet me and ask them plainly to give me their support. I put my views before them, and received from them a promise that they would give me a fair chance in carrying on the administration. I think that if more pains were taken to explain matters to the members of the Bond party, many of the cobwebs would be swept away and a much better understanding would exist between the different parties.

'The Government's policy will be a South African policy. What we mean is that we will do all in our power, whilst looking after the interests of the Cape Colony, to draw closer and closer the ties between us and the neighbouring States. In pursuance of this we have arranged to meet in December next in Bloemfontein, and hope to extend the railway from Bloemfontein to the Vaal

River. We feel it is a matter of time to arrive at a settlement of the various questions which divide the States of South Africa. It may not come in our time, but I believe that ultimately the different States will be united. The Government hope that the result of the Swaziland Convention will prove satisfactory to the Transvaal. We feel that if fair privileges were granted to every citizen of the Transvaal, the Transvaal would not be dissatisfied at the terms England will deal out to it. I feel sure that if the Transvaal joins with us and the other States in a Customs Union, the sister colony of Natal will also join, and that would be one great step towards a union of South Africa. The projected extension of the railway will likewise prove that we are getting nearer to a United South Africa.

'It is customary to speak of a United South Africa as possible within the near future. If we mean a complete Union with the same flag, I see very serious difficulties. I know myself that I am not prepared at any time to forfeit my flag. I repeat, I am not prepared at any time to forfeit my flag. I remember a good story about the editor of a leading journal in this country. He was asked to allow a supervision of his articles in reference to native policy, and he was offered a free hand with everything else. "Well," he asked, "if you take away the direction of my native policy, what have I left?" And so it is with me. If I have to forfeit my flag, what have I left? If you take away my flag, you take away everything. Holding these views, I can feel some respect for the neighbouring States, where men have been born under Republican institutions and with Republican feelings. When I speak of South African Union, I mean that we may attain to perfect free trade as to our own commodities, perfect and complete internal railway communication, and a general Customs Union, stretching from Delagoa Bay to Walfisch Bay; and if our statesmen should attain to that, I say they will have done a good work. It has been my good fortune to meet people belonging to both sides of the House, and to hear their approval with regard to the development of the Northern territory. I am glad the Cape Colony will also share in the development of the country to the north. I feel assured that within my lifetime the limits of the Cape Colony will stretch as far as the Zambesi. Many of you are interested in the operations of the Chartered Company northwards; and it is a pleasure to me to announce that all risks of a collision are over, and that I believe there will be a peaceable occupation of Mashonaland. I have had the pleasure today to receive a telegram announcing the cession of the Barotse country, which I may tell you is over 200,000 square miles in extent. I think we are carrying out a practical object; we have at least sent five hundred of our citizens to occupy a new country.

'To show how great is the wish to go north, I may mention that a Dutch

Reformed minister at Colesberg has been called to Mossamedes, a place further even than the country we have annexed. I have often thought that if the people who originally took the Cape Colony had been told that the Colony would to-day extend to the Orange River, and a thousand miles beyond the Orange River, they would have laughed at the idea. I believe that people who live a hundred years hence will think that the present annexation is far too short.'

Not long after this Mr. Rhodes accompanied the High Commissioner in a journey to the north of Bechuanaland to visit the colonists and the native chiefs, and in the course of this journey the High Commissioner and the Premier were entertained at a banquet at Vryburg, to which the northern railroad had just been completed. Here Mr. Rhodes, amid loud laughter, alluded to the days when he saved Bechuanaland for the Empire, and yet was informed by a high Imperial officer (General Warren) that he was dangerous to the peace of the country. This was early in October 1890.

Mr. Rhodes, who was received with loud and prolonged cheering, said: 'Mr. Chairman, your Excellency and Gentlemen,—I have to thank you for the very cordial manner in which you have received my toast to-night. I cannot say I quite agree with the sanguine statements about my capacities which have been made by the gentleman who proposed my health, but I certainly feel the cordial way in which he has proposed it and you have received it. It is true that to-day memories of the past come back to me. I could not help thinking of five or six years ago, when I first came here, and when we had the Stella-land Bestuur, the party of loyals, and various sections, all working with one object—the good of the country—but each in their different way; so that, at certain periods, and on certain occasions, we had some unpleasant interviews. It seems almost impossible to think that five years ago this was a country that you might almost call barbarian. There was hardly a house in the place. It was a sort of "Tom Tiddler's ground," and every one was fighting for his own hand. When I think of the unpleasant terms which were used as to many individuals, I can only pardon the terms used as to myself, because I feel that it was a new ground we were each endeavouring to bring under civilisation here, and we rather differed as to the mode of doing it. When I think, Mr. Chairman, that the last time I left this country, I was informed by a high Imperial officer that I was dangerous to the peace of the country, and when I think I am here to-day and have brought you a gift, as the High Commissioner has kindly put it, a gift from the Cape Colony of a railway, a gift from the Cape Colony to Stellaland, I think I am entitled to say that I have wiped out that remark—that I was dangerous to the peace of the country; and I think, when I remind you that, owing to the cordial manner in which the High Commissioner has worked with the Government of Cape Colony and with the Government of the Free State, he has been enabled to arrange a Customs Union with those States, you need not have any distrust or fear that the Cape Colony is anxious to be too grasping with reference to your little State. Whenever the time may occur that you are anxious to join us, I think I may say we shall be only too willing to let you join. Do not think for one moment that with an octopus grasp we are trying to seize you against your will. We are simply trying in every way, by the railway, by the Customs Union,—we are simply trying to make you a part of the system of South Africa.

'I could not help hearing to-day the intense feeling that has been expressed as to what I think is a most ridiculous idea with regard to our neighbours in the Transvaal—with whom I may say the Cape Colony has been most cordially working—the idea that our neighbours are devising a scheme of a port of entry so remote that they would damage and would destroy the vested interests of this country. I cannot conceive that the Government of the country would, in a brutal manner, create a port of entry at Warrington, and deny any port of entry other than that along the border. I feel sure that such a suggestion is ridiculous, because I cannot help thinking that the late Convention entered into with the Transvaal is another indication of their intense desire to work in harmony, not only with the people of Cape Colony, but with Her Majesty's Government; and there could be no more cruel blow to the people of the Cape Colony and to Her Majesty's Government combined, than the suggestion said to be devised, that there should be only one port of entry for your goods, and that port so remote as to render the extension of the railway practically useless. Therefore I feel, Mr. Chairman and gentlemen, that it is a bugbear, and I have spoken strongly on it to-night, because I believe that there is not such a feeling on the part of the Transvaal Government, and I would like to give publicity to my belief that the Transvaal Government could not devise an unfriendly or unneighbourly act. Mr. Chairman and your Excellency, it was only the other day that I was informed on "the best authority" that as regards the territory we have lately occupied, and which has been guaranteed to us, the Government of the Transvaal was already devising the seizure and occupation of a part of it. I just mention this to show the fallacious rumours that go about. Could you believe it possible that a friendly and neighbourly State, when the ink was hardly dry, could enter on a scheme to seize a territory which was already guaranteed to a neighbouring and friendly power. But I mention this to show how fast these rumours come, and how groundless is their origin. Mr. Chairman, I do feel to-night it is a pleasing thing to see that these three great systems in this country are united systems, namely, a system governed by a Charter; a system of a Crown Colony; and, last but not least, a system of self-government as represented by the Cape of Good Hope. We have amongst us to-night two gentlemen who are members of Parliament for Cape Colony, and I wish to say to you it was due to the efforts of those two gentlemen, and the sections of the House with which they are connected, that this railway to Vryburg be-came an accomplished fact. They were thorough Afrikanders, but, whilst they had every regard to neighbouring States, they felt that Cape Colony should look after its own interests and its own trade, and it is due to their action that you at the present moment have the railway to Vryburg.

'I would point out to you, Mr. Chairman, that these three classes of Gov-ernment happen most fortunately at the present moment to be working in entire unity. You have the Chartered system on the North, dealing with pure barbarism; a Crown Colony lying between the Cape and the North, under the direction of his Excellency the High Commissioner; and you have at the base self-government. There has been a great deal said about the desire of the Cape Colony to annex and absorb you. I can assure you to-night, we shall never take that step until you are anxious to join with us, but you must all feel it is a matter of time—that the whole matter rests on the word "time." I know, in looking to the future, that the Charter must change first, perhaps to a system of Imperial Government, but finally to self-government; and I remind you that that period must also come to you in the course of time; and when your territory is developed, and when you possess the men who have a desire to deal with the government of the country, you must proceed from direct Imperial government to self-government. And I feel this too, that this is a desire and wish of Her Majesty's Government, based on the word "time," when the time arrives for it; and, when it does, I feel you will join with me in remembering and recognising the debt we owe Her Majesty's Government, who in the period of your infancy has spent its wealth for you, has con-ducted you through your boyhood, and who, when you are ready for self-government, will grant it you without one word, as freely as, year by year, it has given you its wealth to develop the resources of this country.

SOURCE: Chapters 12 and 9 in *The Speeches of Cecil Rhodes 1881–1900*, ed. Vindex. (London: Chapman and Hall, 1900), 361–96, 227–50. "Vindex" was the pseudonym for the editor and commentator of twenty years of speeches by Cecil Rhodes.

Excerpts from *Men, Mines, and Animals in South Africa*

LORD RANDOLPH S. CHURCHILL

[Randolph Churchill, husband of "Jennie" of New York and father of Winston Churchill, was a leader in the House of Commons and chancellor of the Exchequer in 1886. In 1891 he visited southern Africa, and the letters that he wrote at that time to the *Daily Graphic* were collected in the volume later published as *Men, Mines, and Animals in South Africa.*]

What is to be done with this country? Agriculture on a large scale, cattle-ranching or sheep-farming, except for the feeding of a large mining population, would be a wild and ruinous enterprise. The climate seems to be altogether adverse to colonization and settlement by small emigrants. Moreover, if this region of Africa so exceptionally favoured in some ways by nature is found to be of little value, how infinitely worthless for all European purposes must be the great district of the Central Lakes, the wide possessions of the East African Company, and the much-vaunted Congo State! Sometimes when thinking of Africa as a whole, of Egypt, Tunis, and Morocco, of the Soudan, and of Abyssinia, of the Congo and of the Zambesi, of the many fruitless attempts made by many nations to discover, conquer, and civilize, of the many hopes which have been raised and dashed, of the many expectations which have been formed and falsified, it occurs to me that there must be upon this great continent some awful curse, some withering blight, and that to delude and to mock at the explorer, the gold hunter, the merchant, the speculator, and even at ministers and monarchs, is its dark fortune and its desperate fate. It is possible, even probable, that these are views too gloomy, formed and set down as they occur to me under the influence of the disappointment occasioned by the discovery that, as in the Mazoe so in the Hartley Hill district, there are probably no gold reefs of value to be acquired.

The company sustains a considerable loss annually, estimated now at from 10 to 15 per cent., by diamonds being stolen from the mines. To check this loss, extraordinary precautions have been resorted to. The natives are engaged for a period of three months, during which time they are confined in a compound surrounded by a high wall. On returning from their day's work, they have to strip off all their clothes, which they hang on pegs in a shed. Stark naked, they then proceed to the searching room, where their mouths, their hair, their toes, their armpits, and every portion of their body are subjected to an elaborate examination. White men would never submit to such a process, but the native sustains the indignity with cheerful equanimity, considering only the high wages which he earns. After passing through the searching room, they pass, still in a state of nudity, to their apartments in the compound, where they find blankets in which to wrap themselves for the night. During the evening, the clothes which they have left behind them are carefully and minutely searched, and are restored to their owners in the morning. The precautions which are taken a few days before the natives leave the compound, their engagement being terminated, to recover diamonds which they may have swallowed, are more easily imagined than described. In addition to these arrangements, a law of exceptional rigour punishes illicit diamond buying, known in the slang of South Africa as I.D.B.ism. Under this statute, the ordinary presumption of law in favour of the accused disappears, and an accused person has to prove his innocence in the clearest manner, instead of the accuser having to prove his guilt. Sentences are constantly passed on persons convicted of this offence ranging from five to fifteen years. It must be admitted that this tremendous law is in thorough conformity with South African sentiment, which elevates I.D.B.ism almost to the level, if not above the level, of actual homicide. If a man walking in the streets or in the precincts of Kimberley were to find a diamond and were not immediately to take it to the registrar, restore it to him, and to have the fact of its restoration registered, he would be liable to a punishment of fifteen years' penal servitude. In order to prevent illicit traffic, the quantities of diamonds produced by the mines are reported to the detective department both by the producers and the exporters. All diamonds, except those which pass through illicit channels, are sent to England by registered post, the weekly shipments averaging from 40,000 to 50,000 carats. The greatest outlet for stolen diamonds is through the Transvaal to Natal, where they are shipped by respectable merchants, who turn a deaf ear to any information from the diamond fields to the effect that they are aiding the sale of stolen property. The most ingenious ruses are resorted to by the illicit dealers for conveying the stolen diamonds out of Kimberley. They are considerably assisted by the fact that the boundaries of the Transvaal and of the Free State approach within a few miles of Kimberley, and once across the border they are comparatively safe. Recently, so I was informed, a notorious diamond thief was seen leaving Kimberley on horseback for the Transvaal. Convinced of his iniquitous designs, he was seized by the police on the border and thoroughly searched. Nothing was found on him, and he was perforce allowed to proceed. No sooner was he well across the border, than he, under the eyes of the detective, deliberately shot and cut open his horse, extracting from its intestines a large parcel of diamonds which, previous to the journey, had been administered to the unfortunate animal in the form of a ball.

SOURCE: Lord Randolph S. Churchill, *Men, Mines, and Animals in South Africa* (London: Sampson Low, Marston, 1895), 273–74, 44–47.

Personal Reminiscences of Mr. Rhodes

DR. L. S. JAMESON

CHAPTER I

[Leander Starr Jameson was an intimate associate of Rhodes and his appointed administrator of Matabele. The raid that he led into the Transvaal in December 1895 ended in a fiasco, with most of his forces killed—and Rhodes obliged at the time to resign all his offices in South Africa. Nonetheless, Rhodes refused to denounce Jameson's action.]

I have been asked by the author of what is practically the first biography of Cecil Rhodes, who, at any rate, knows his subject, though I have not read his book, to supply what reminiscences I can give of Mr. Rhodes. Having lived with Mr. Rhodes so many years, and being one of his oldest friends, I have much pleasure in doing my best, though I am no penman. The best part of twenty years has passed since I first met Mr. Rhodes. It was at Kimberley, in 1878. I had come out and settled there to practice as a doctor. From the day of my arrival at Kimberley, when I fell in with him, we drew closely together, and quickly became great friends.

Rhodes was then steadily working at his great scheme for the amalgamation of the diamond mines. He had been at work at it for years, and had still nearly ten years of persevering effort before him, for the amalgamation was not completed till 1888. We were young men together then, and naturally saw a great deal of each other. We shared a quiet little bachelor establishment together, walked and rode out together, shared our meals, exchanged our views on men and things, and discussed his big schemes, which even then filled me with admiration. I soon admitted to myself that for sheer natural power I had never met a man to come near Cecil Rhodes; and I still retain my early impressions of him, which have been fully justified by experience.

Even at that early period, Cecil Rhodes, then a man of twenty-six or twenty-seven, had mapped out, in his clear brain, his whole policy just as it has since been developed. He had obtained his opinions from no book, and no other man. He had thought out everything for himself independently; his success when he put thoughts into action increased his confidence in himself. He has good reason for his self-confidence. Where are you to find so large a man of ideas combined with so big a man of action? The rare amalgamation of these two kinds of men in Cecil Rhodes results in a statesman compared with whom a mere parliamentary leader in England, however consummate his skill, looks very small indeed.

I remember his first big speech at Cape Town. He was living with me at Kimberley, and was down with fever. He had not written a note, or a line of the speech. In fact, he had not put it into shape at all. He thought the subject out the night before he got up from his sick bed, and, though still very shaky, travelled down to Cape Town. This was in 1884. The speech was a big success. It was the first statement made in the Cape House as to his Northern Expansion policy, and shows the continuity of that policy. That policy consisted of the occupation of the *hinterland* of the Cape, by which he proposed to effect the ultimate federation of South Africa. He used to talk over all his plans and schemes with me, and, looking back at them now, it surprises me to note how little change there is in his policy. It is substantially the same to-day as it was then. He had, for instance, even at that early date (1878−9) formed the idea of doing a great work for the over-crowded British public at home, by opening up fresh markets for their manufactures. He was deeply impressed with a belief in the ultimate destiny of the Anglo-Saxon race. He dwelt repeatedly on the fact that their great want was new territory fit for the overflow population to settle in permanently, and thus provide markets for the wares of the old country—the workshop of the world.

This purpose of occupying the interior and ultimately federating South Africa was always before his eyes. The means to that end were the conciliation, the winning of the Cape Dutch support. They were the majority in the country, he used to say, and they must be worked with. 'I recognise the conditions and I shall make all the concessions necessary to win them. I mean to have the whole unmarked country north of the colony for England, and I know I can only get it and develope it through the Cape Colony—that is, at present, through the Dutch majority.' This idea of the occupation of unoc-cupied Africa, both South and Central, for England's benefit, was always in Cecil Rhodes's mind, from the time I knew him; and how long before I cannot, of course, say. I only know he talked about it just as freely and frankly when I first knew him, and his schemes seemed all in the air, in 1878, as when they grew ripe for fulfilment ten years later, in 1888.

Next to his powerful mind, what most struck me in Cecil Rhodes was his independent attitude towards all questions that came up for discussion.

The speech which set forth his Northern policy, was the cause of the High Commissioner sending him to Bechuanaland, to deal with the Boer freebooters, in 1884. It had besides made his mark in the House. He was listened to, ever after, with attention. A thing I have noticed in Mr. Rhodes is the way he sticks to his ideas. The ideas he has in 1897 are the ideas he had in 1879, only he has, of course, matured them. In the same way his Northern policy to-day was his policy unknown then to any but intimate friends, eighteen years ago, before he had put up for a seat in in the Legislative Assembly.

People talk of him as an opportunist. No doubt he is on matters he thinks unimportant. On what seems important to him, he has always been absolutely independent. Take his relations to the Bond.

Sometime before he became Premier, when Sprigg's Ministry was in, Mr. Rhodes met Mr. Hofmeyr at a dinner. Mr. Hofmeyr thought Rhodes would be a more competent Premier than Sprigg, and offered him to come in as the nominee of the Bond. Rhodes refused. He was willing to work with the Bond, but refused to be their instrument.

It is perhaps not generally known that Mr. Rhodes has never joined the Bond. He was willing to lead them and to conciliate them, but he always kept his independence of action throughout. He wished to be fair to the Dutch, but the British was to be the governing race in South Africa, and the supreme flag the British flag. Mr. Hofmeyr, confident in himself, thought that he could manage and make use of Mr. Rhodes, but he has since found out he mistook his man.

Rhodes likes the Dutch individually: if he be asked to support their rights—Yes; but if he be asked to support the Dutch as a governing body—No. He has never changed from this attitude.

One of the facts that weighed with Mr. Rhodes in deciding to start the Chartered Company in order to occupy the Northern territories, was the fact that the Imperial Government, after they had spent about a million in Bechuanaland, had nothing to show—not a settler in the country—and progress and development not so much as attempted. I dwelt on this point in a speech at Cape Town at the end of 1894, when I compared what the British Government had left undone in Bechuanaland with what the Chartered Company had done in Rhodesia.

Mr. Rhodes considered that he would have done something more had he had the management of a company with the same amount of money to spend; and this he has practically proved in the general development of Rhodesia by the Chartered Company.

I have a very bad memory for stories, but here is one, characteristic of Mr. Rhodes's way of doing things, which is certainly never dull or commonplace. I was up at Victoria in 1893. The Matabele impis were close to the town, and kept attacking and killing our Mashona workmen. I remonstrated with them, and ordered them off in vain. I was besieged with complaints from the settlers, who threatened to trek out of the country if these marauders were not promptly brought to reason. I sent Lendy to drive them off, if they would not go quietly. They fired on him, and he charged and broke them, inflicting considerable loss. Thereupon other *impis* advanced and threatened Victoria.

Rhodes was down at the House at Cape Town. I wired to him from Victoria the exact situation, and said it was an absolute necessity to assume the offensive, and strike straight at Bulawayo at once. Rhodes, who does not waste words, wired back briefly, "Read Luke fourteen thirty-one." Of course, I had not a notion of what he meant.

This enigma could, no doubt, be made clear by reading the passage. I asked for a Bible and looked up the passage and read: "Or what king going to make war against another king, sitteth not down first and consulteth whether he be able with ten thousand to meet him that cometh against him with twenty thousand." Of course, I understood at once what Mr. Rhodes meant. The Matabele had an army of many thousands. I had nine hundred settlers available for action. Could I, after careful consideration, venture to face such unequal odds?

I decided at once in the affirmative, and immediately telegraphed back to Mr. Rhodes at Cape Town "All right. Have read Luke fourteen thirty-one." Five words from Mr. Rhodes and eight from myself decided the question of our action in the first Matabele war. This story I give to show what a man of action and not of words Mr. Rhodes is.

The decision had its difficulties, besides the smallness of the number of men. Mr. Rhodes knew the Chartered Company's coffers were empty, and that if it was to be war he would have to find the money out of his own private purse.

Observe, too, Mr. Rhodes left the decision to the man on the spot, myself, who might be supposed to be the best judge of the conditions. This is Mr. Rhodes's way. It is a pleasure to work with a man of his immense ability, and it doubles the pleasure when you find that, in the execution of his plans, he leaves all to you; although no doubt in the last instance of the Transvaal business he has suffered for this system, still in the long run the system pays.

As long as you reach the end he has in view he is not careful to lay down the means or methods you are to employ. He leaves a man to himself, and that is why he gets the best work they are capable of out of all his men.

I was forgetting one of Mr. Rhodes's most prominent characteristics, which from the first impressed me greatly. This characteristic is his great liking for, and sympathy with the black men, the natives of the country. He likes to be with them, he is fond of them and trusts them, and they admire and trust him. He had thousands of natives under him in the De Beers mines. He carefully provided for their comfort, recreation and health. He was always looking after their interests. He liked to be with them, and his favourite recreation every Sunday afternoon was to go into the De Beers native compound, where he had built them a fine swimming bath, and throw in shillings for natives to dive for. He knew enough of their languages to talk to them freely, and they looked up to him—indeed, fairly worshipped the great white man.

It was just the same at a later date. He likes to have the natives round him, and be a sort of father to them. In his house near Cape Town there are no white men or women servants; his servants are all native boys, Matebele, Mashonas, and boys from Inhambane.

At the native school, near Groote Schuur, he has two of Lobengula's sons, who have the run of the house and garden at Groote Schuur on Saturdays and whenever they have a holiday. I have often watched them feeding in the strawberry beds and the vineries at Groote Schuur. They never go back to school without going to have a personal talk with Mr. Rhodes.

They, in common with all the other natives, delight in their big, kindly, white friend. Mr. Rhodes, though perhaps he is not a perfect master of their language, always makes a point of talking to the natives in their own tongue.

I have had opportunities of observing all this because I have lived a good deal with Mr. Rhodes at Groote Schuur on my visits to Cape Town. His trusted body servant for twenty years is a coloured man. Need I say that Mr. Rhodes is absolutely free from contempt for the black man. He looks upon him and treats him as a fellow man, differing simply in his lower level of development.

He is really, by nature, strangely and deeply in sympathy with the natives. He regards them as children, with something of pity in his affection for them, and he treats them like children, affectionately but firmly. It is for this reason that the success of his great Indaba in the Matopos was no surprise to me. Besides, I have been with him at many Indabas in former years in Mashonaland and Matabeleland. We went together right through Mashonaland in 1891, and again went about among the natives there in 1893 and 1894. He always got on wonderfully well with the natives. He likes and trusts them, and does not conceal his feelings, which they are quick to perceive. They like and trust him in return. I have never seen any one else who had the same sympathy with them. If there is a man in South Africa who deserves the title of the black man's friend, it is Cecil Rhodes.

CHAPTER II

In his management of the Chartered Company's territory Mr. Rhodes was, of course, almost from the first, closely associated with myself, and I had continual opportunities of observing the methods of his supervision. I had already done a good deal of work in the country when I succeeded Mr. Colquhoun in his duties of Administrator in the end of 1891. From that date till the end of 1895 everything that Mr. Rhodes did in Rhodesia necessarily came under my observation.

He took the deepest interest in the work of developing the country, and made himself acquainted with everything of importance that occurred. He took care that the individual officials who represented him should be thoroughly acquainted with his views, and trusted them to carry out those views in his absence.

He did not, however, leave them to themselves for any length of time. He went up to the Chartered Company's territories at short intervals, and not only visited the towns but went through the whole country, making journeys in all directions in order to see for himself that his views were being carried out. He felt his responsibility as Managing Director not only to the Chartered Company's Board but also to the Shareholders, whose interests he did all he could to further. He also felt deeply his responsibility for the trust placed in him by the Imperial Government when they gave the Charter, and in the discharge of his duties as Managing Director, the consciousness of this twofold responsibility to the Company and to the Empire was continually present with him.

As regards extension and development his work speaks for itself. As regards the treatment of the natives, I may say a few words.

In introducing a civilized government into the country, the natives, Mr. Rhodes considered, could not be expected at once to understand the white man's civilized methods. Accordingly he desired that as far as it did not conflict with the safety of life and property, the natives should remain as much as possible under the native laws to which they were accustomed, administered through their chiefs, to whom their hereditary attitude was an absolutely feudal loyalty.

An important part of my work in Matabeleland in 1893 was to teach the native Indunas the change in the law, which was considered necessary in substituting the Chartered Company's rule for that of Lobengula. This change consisted mainly in the much more serious view we took of the prevalent crimes of rape, murder, and witchcraft leading to murder. On Mr. Rhodes's journeys through the country, following the conquest of Matabeleland, all the Indunas were summoned to meet him, and it was carefully explained to them in detail what the requirements of their new rulers would be. As far as possible the natives were to remain under their own tribal law; but the white man's laws for the protection of life and property, and also for the protection of the women from rape, were to be strictly enforced. Witchcraft, also, which led to murder, was to be severely punished.

This, of course, was also the method that had been carried out in Mashonaland, where the Chartered Company had been the rulers prior to their conquest of Matabeleland.

As regards the question whether or not crime was equally dealt with alike among whites and black men, one can safely appeal to the Magistrates' records of the cases tried in the various districts since the occupation of the country. The Magistrates' reports of their cases were all sent to, and carefully preserved in, the Crown Prosecutor's office. The laws of the Cape Colony were strictly enforced, and a record of anything beyond the mere petty cases, had, by law, to be sent to the Judge of the High Court before the sentence was confirmed.

I fearlessly appeal to the clergymen and missionaries of the various denominations in the country, to the four London Missionary Society missionaries, who had been years in the country, to the four Roman Catholic priests, to the four clergymen of the Church of England, the three Wesleyan missionaries, and the two clergymen of the Dutch Reformed Church, as to any real case which could be named, which the authorities have failed to investigate, and deal with in accordance with its merits, meting out the same equal justice to black man and white.

The prison system and prison accommodation in Rhodesia would compare favourably with that of any country town in England. Black men and white had exactly equal treatment in prison as when on trial; but of course were kept separate, though in the same prison. The Magistrates were not allowed to use the lash, which could only be inflicted by order of the Judge of the High Court in very serious cases, as in the Cape Colony and in England.

The question of the land and cattle of the natives was dealt with practically by the Imperial Government not by the Chartered Company.

A Commission was appointed for the purpose, consisting of one Imperial

Representative, Captain Lindsell, who was at that time Magistrate of the Tati district under the Imperial Government, one representative of the Chartered Company, approved by the Imperial Government, Captain Heyman, and the third member to act as Chairman of the Commission, Mr. Vincent, who was at the time Crown Prosecutor of British Bechuanaland, and who was appointed Judge by the Imperial Government, to take up his duties after serving on the Land and Cattle Commission.

The Imperial Government further provided that after the Land Commission was dissolved, its duties being finished as regards cattle and native locations, that the Judge himself should act on the Commission in case of any disputes subsequently arising on any of these subjects.

The general marking of the cattle was for the protection of the natives' cattle from the thefts of the low whites who came into the country, and from the thefts of the cattle-lifting Boers who came across the Limpopo from the northern Transvaal. The Boers of Zoutspanberg used to cross the river sometimes to lift cattle, sometimes to exchange the rifles they had been given by the Boer Government for Government cattle, knowing that they could always get a new rifle from Pretoria on the plea of having lost their own. This is the chief source of the supply of rifles and ammunition which the natives used in the recent Rebellion.

I have said enough, I think, to show to any fair-minded enquirer that Mr. Rhodes cannot justly be charged with any neglect of duty in his management of Rhodesia, or with any harshness to the natives. At all events the most sceptical will be convinced if he will take the trouble to investigate my statements and thoroughly test their truth.

L. S. Jameson

SOURCE: "Personal Reminiscences of Mr. Rhodes" [from James Rochfort Maguire, *Cecil Rhodes: Biography and Appreciation* by an Imperialist (pseud) (London: Chapman and Hall, 1897), 391–413].

The Last Will and Testament of Cecil John Rhodes

[W. T. Stead, founder and editor of the *Review of Reviews,* was a friend and confidant of Rhodes, and as such was entrusted with the execution of the magnate's "last will and testament." The volume, edited by Stead, in which the testamentary document was published, includes selections, with commentary by Stead, from Rhodes's speeches and correspondence.]

PART I
THE LAST WILL AND TESTAMENT

The sixth and last Will and Testament of Cecil John Rhodes is dated July 1st, 1899. To this are appended various codicils, the last of which was dated March, 1902, when he was on his deathbed.

The full text of the Will and its Codicils will only be published when the Will is proved in South Africa.

The following are the substantive passages of the Will so far as they have as yet been given to the public.

The Will begins:—

I am a natural-born British subject and I now declare that I have adopted and acquired and hereby adopt and acquire and intend to retain Rhodesia as my domicile.[1]

(1.) His Burial Place in the Matoppos.

I admire the grandeur and loneliness of the Matoppos in Rhodesia and therefore I desire to be buried in the Matoppos[2] on the hill which I used to visit and which I called the "View of the World" in a square to be cut in the rock on the top of the hill covered with a plain brass plate with these words thereon—"Here lie the remains of Cecil John Rhodes" and accordingly I direct my Executors at the expense of my estate to take all steps and do all things necessary or proper to give effect to this my desire and afterwards to

1. Being thus domiciled in Rhodesia his estate is not subject to the death duties levied on those domiciled in England.

2. Mr. Betram Mitford says:—"For grim, gloomy savagery of solitude it is probable that the stupendous rock wilderness known as the Matoppo Hills is unsurpassed throughout earth's surface. Strictly speaking, the term 'hills' scarcely applies to this marvellous range, which is rather an expanse of granite rocks extending some seventy or eighty miles by forty or fifty, piled in titanic proportions and bizarre confusion, over what would otherwise be a gently undulating surface, forming a kind of island as it were, surrounded by beautiful rolling country, green, smiling, and in parts thickly bushed. High on the outside ridge of this remarkable range, about twenty miles distant from Bulawayo, towards which it faces, there rises a pile of granite boulders, huge, solid, compact. It is a natural structure; an imposing and dominating one withal, and appropriately so, for this is the sepulchre of the warrior King Umzilikazi, founder and first monarch of the Matabele nation." *Rhodesia* says:—"It would appear, according to the discovery of a Native Commissioner, that the hill on the summit of which the remains of Cecil Rhodes have been laid is known in the vernacular as 'Malindidzimo.' The literal translation of this is given as 'The Home of the Spirit of My Forefathers,' or, without straining the meaning unduly, 'The Home of the Guardian Spirit.' It does not appear that Mr. Rhodes was aware of this rendering when he expressed a desire to be buried on that spot after his race was run."

keep my grave in order at the expense of the Matoppos and Bulawayo Fund hereinafter mentioned.

I direct my Trustees on the hill aforesaid to erect or complete the monument to the men who fell in the first Matabele War at Shangani in Rhodesia the bas-reliefs for which are being made by Mr. John Tweed and I desire the said hill to be preserved as a burial-place[3] but no person is to be buried there unless the Government for the time being of Rhodesia until the various states of South Africa or any of them shall have been federated and after such federation the Federal Government by a vote of two-thirds of its governing body says that he or she had deserved well of his or her country.

(2.) His Property in Rhodesia.

I give free of all duty whatsoever my landed property near Bulawayo on Matabeleland Rhodesia and my landed property at or near Inyanga near Salisbury in Mashonaland Rhodesia to my Trustees hereinbefore named Upon trust that my Trustees shall in such manner as in their uncontrolled discretion they shall think fit cultivate the same respectively for the instruction of the people of Rhodesia.

I give free of all duty whatsoever to my Trustees hereinbefore named such a sum of money as they shall carefully ascertain and in their uncontrolled discretion consider ample and sufficient by its investments to yield income amounting to the sum of £4,000 sterling per annum and not less and I direct my Trustees to invest the same sum and the said sum and the investments for the time being representing it I hereinafter refer to as "the Matoppos and Bulawayo fund" And I direct that my Trustees shall for ever apply in such manner as in their uncontrolled discretion they shall think fit the income of the Matoppos and Bulawayo Fund in preserving protecting maintaining adorning and beautifying the said burial-place and hill and their surroundings and shall for ever apply in such manner as in their uncontrolled discretion they shall think fit the balance of the income of the Matoppos and Bulawayo Fund and any rents and profits of my said landed properties near Bulawayo in

---

3. A lady writing over the initials "S. C. S." in the *Westminster Gazette* says:—"Very beautiful is a little story which I once heard told of Mr. Rhodes by Mr. G. Wyndham. Beautiful, because it contains the simple expression of a great thought, said quite simply, and without any desire to produce effect, in private to a friend. Mr. Wyndham told how, during his last visit to Africa, they rode together on to the summit of a hill in the Matoppos, which commanded a view of fifty miles in every direction. Circling his hands about the horizon, Mr. Rhodes said, 'Homes, more homes; that is what I work for.'"

the cultivation as aforesaid of such property And in particular I direct my Trustees that a portion of my Sauerdale property a part of my said landed property near Bulawayo be planted with every possible tree and be made and preserved and maintained as a Park for the people of Bulawayo and that they complete the dam[4] at my Westacre property if it is not completed at my death and make a short railway line from Bulawayo to Westacre so that the people of Bulawayo may enjoy the glory of the Matoppos from Saturday to Monday.

I give free of all duty whatsoever to my Trustees hereinbefore named such a sum of money as they shall carefully ascertain and in their uncontrolled discretion consider ample and sufficient by its investments to yield income amounting to the sum of £2,000 sterling per annum and not less and I direct my Trustees to invest the same sum and the said sum and the investments for the time being representing it I hereinafter refer to as "the Inyanga Fund." And I direct that my Trustees shall for ever apply in such manner as in their absolute discretion they shall think fit the income of the Inyanga Fund and any rents and profits of my said landed property at or near Inyanga[5] in the

---

4. A *Daily Telegraph* correspondent, writing from Bulawayo on Oct. 14, 1901, gives the following account of the dam referred to in the will:—"Mr. Rhodes's Matoppo Dam is to be used in connection with the irrigation of a portion of his farm near Bulawayo. This farm is situated on the northern edge of the Matoppos, eighteen miles from Bulawayo, and through it runs the valley of a tributary from the Malima River. This tributary is dry eight months in the year, and the land around consequently parched. Mr. Rhodes has built a huge earthwork wall to dam the tributary. The work was commenced in May, 1899. It will render possible the cultivation of some 2,000 to 3,000 acres of the most fertile soil. The total cost up to date has been something under £30,000. The total capacity of the reservoir is 900,000,000 gallons. A small body of water was conserved last season, and fifty acres of lucerne planted as a commencement. It is doing extremely well under irrigation. The site of the works, the northern edge of the Matoppos, is very picturesque. The green lucerne makes a delightful contrast against the dull and hazy browns of the surrounding country which prevail during the dry season. An hotel has been built on some rising ground overlooking the dam, and it is expected that it will be very popular as a holiday resort for the youth and beauty of Bulawayo—become, in fact, the African replica of the famous Star and Garter at Richmond."

5. Mr. Seymour Fort, writing in the *Empire Review* for May, 1902, says:—"Apart from his position as managing director of the British South Africa Company, Mr. Rhodes is one of the chief pioneer agriculturists in Rhodesia, and has spared neither brain nor capital in endeavouring to develop the resources of its soil. In Manicaland he owns a block of farms on the high Inyanga plateau, some 80,000 acres in extent, where on the open grass country he is breeding cattle and horses, while a certain portion is fenced and placed under cultivation. Great things are expected from these horse-breeding experiments, as the Inyanga hills are so far free from the horse-sickness so prevalent in other parts of South Africa. This plateau forms a succession of downs at an elevation of some 6,000 feet above the sea. The soil is alluvial, of rich red colour and capable

cultivation of such property and in particular I direct that with regard to such property irrigation should be the first object of my Trustees.

For the guidance of my Trustees I wish to record that in the cultivation of my said landed properties I include such things as experimental farming, forestry, market and other gardening and fruit farming, irrigation and the teaching of any of those things and establishing and maintaining an Agricultural College.

(3.) Groote Schuur.

I give my property following that is to say my residence known as "De Groote Schuur"[6] situate near Mowbray in the Cape Division in the said Colony together with all furniture plate and other articles contained therein at the time of my death and all other land belonging to me situated under Table Moun-

---

of growing every form of produce, and by merely scratching the surface the natives raise crops of mealies and other cereals superior to those grown elsewhere in Manicaland. It is an old saying in South Africa that you find no good veldt without finding Dutchmen, and several Transvaal Boers have settled in the neighbourhood. English fruit trees flourish, and Mr. Rhodes has laid out orchards in which the orange, apple, and pear trees (now five years old) have borne well. Very interesting also are the evidences of an old and practically unknown civilisation—the ancient ruins, the mathematically constructed water-courses and old gold workings which are to be seen side by side with the trans-African telegraph to Blantyre and Cairo which runs through the property, and connects Tete with the Zambesi."

6. Mr. Garrett, writing in the *Pall Mall Magazine* for May, 1902, says:—"If you would see Rhodes on his most winning side, you would seek it at Groote Schuur. It lies behind the Devil Peak, which is a flank buttressed by the great bastion of rock that is called Table Mountain. The house lies low, nestling cosily among oaks. It was built in accordance with Mr. Rhodes's orders to keep it simple—beams and whitewash. It was originally thatched, but it was burnt down at the end of 1896, and everything was gutted but one wing. From the deep-pillared window where Mr. Rhodes mostly sat, and the little formal garden, the view leads up to a grassy slope and over woodland away to the crest of the buttressed peak and the great purple precipices of Table Mountain. Through the open park land and wild wood koodoos, gnus, elands, and other African animals wander at will. Only the savage beasts are confined in enclosures. No place of the kind is so freely, so recklessly shared with the public. The estate became the holiday resort of the Cape Town masses; but it is to be regretted that some of the visitors abused their privileges— maimed and butchered rare and valuable beasts, and careless picknickers have caused great havoc in the woods by fire. Sometimes the visitors treat the house itself as a free museum, and are found wandering into Mr. Rhodes's own rooms or composedly reading in his library. Brown people from the slums of Cape Town fill the pinafores of their children with flowers plucked in his garden, and wander round the house as if it were their own. The favourite rendezvous in the ground was the lion-house, a classical lion-pit in which the tawny form of the king of beasts could be caught sight of between marble columns."

tain including my property known as "Mosterts" to my Trustees hereinbefore named upon and subject to the conditions following (that is to say):—

(i.) The said property (excepting any furniture or like articles which have become useless) shall not nor shall any portion thereof at any time be sold let or otherwise alienated.

(ii.) No buildings for suburban residences shall at any time be erected on the said property and any buildings which may be erected thereon shall be used exclusively for public purposes and shall be in a style of architecture similar to or in harmony with my said residence.

(iii.) The said residence and its gardens and grounds shall be retained for a residence for the Prime Minister for the time being of the said Federal Government of the States of South Africa to which I have referred in clause 6 hereof my intention being to provide a suitable official residence for the First Minister in that Government befitting the dignity of his position and until there shall be such a Federal Government may be used as a park for the people.[7]

---

7. Writing in the *Times* on the artistic side of Mr. Rhodes, Mr. Herbert Baker, his architect, says:—"Artistic problems first presented themselves to his mind when, as Premier of Cape Colony, he made his home in the Cape Peninsula. His intense and genuine love of the big and beautiful in natural scenery prompted him to buy as much as he could of the forest slopes of Table Mountain, so that it might be saved for ever from the hands of the builder, and the people, attracted to it by gardens, wild animals, and stately architecture, might be educated and ennobled by the contemplation of what he thought one of the finest views in the world. This love of mountain and distant view—the peaks of the South African plateaux are seen 100 miles away across the Cape flats—was deep-seated in his nature, and he would sit or ride silently for hours at a time, dreaming and looking at the views he loves—a political poet.

> But from these create he can
> Forms more real than living man,
> Nurslings of Immortality.

There are many stories of him telling worried and disputing politicians to turn from their "trouble of ants" to the Mountain for calm, and in the same spirit he placed the stone Phœnician hawk, found at Zimbabye, in the Cabinet Council-room, that the emblem of time might preside over their deliberations. The ennobling influence of natural scenery was present in his mind in connection with every site he chose and every building he contemplated; such as a cottage he built, where poets or artists could live and look across to the blue mountain distance; a University, where young men could be surrounded with the best of nature and of art; a lion-house, a feature of which was to have been a long open colonnade, where the people could at once see the king of beasts and the lordliest of mountains; the Kimberley "Bath," with its white marble colonnades embedded in a green oasis of orange grove and vine trellis, looking to the north over illimitable desert. Such things would perhaps occur to most men, but with him they were a (iv.) The grave of the late Jan Hendrik Hofmeyr upon the said property shall be protected and access be permitted thereto at all reasonable times by any member of the Hofmeyr family for the purpose of inspection or maintenance.

I give to my Trustees hereinbefore named such a sum of money as they shall carefully ascertain and in their uncontrolled discretion consider to be ample and sufficient to yield income amounting to the sum of one thousand pounds sterling per annum and not less upon trust that such income shall be applied and expended for the purposes following (that is to say)—

(i.) On and for keeping and maintaining for the use of the Prime Minister for the time being of the said Federal Government of at least two carriage horses one or more carriages and sufficient stable servants.

(ii.) On and for keeping and maintaining in good order the flower and kitchen gardens appertaining to the said residence.

(iii.) On and for the payment of the wages or earnings including board and lodging of two competent men servants to be housed kept and employed in domestic service in the said residence.

(iv.) On and for the improvement repair renewal and insurance of the said residence furniture plate and other articles.

I direct that subject to the conditions and trusts hereinbefore contained the said Federal Government shall from the time it shall be constituted have the management administration and control of the said devise and legacy and that my Trustees shall as soon as may be thereafter vest and pay the devise and legacy given by the two last preceding clauses hereof in and to such Government if a corporate body capable of accepting and holding the same or if not then in some suitable corporate body so capable named by such Government and that in the meantime my Trustees shall in their uncontrolled discretion manager administer and control the said devise and legacy.

---

passion, almost a religion. Of his more monumental architectural schemes few have been realised. For these his taste lay in the direction of the larger and simpler styles of Rome, Greece, and even Egypt, recognizing the similarity of the climate and natural scenery of South Africa to that of classic Southern Europe. He had the building ambition of a Pericles or a Hadrian, and in his untimely death architecture has the greatest cause to mourn."

(4.) Bequests to Oriel College, Oxford.

I give the sum of £100,000 free of all duty whatsoever to my old college Oriel College in the University of Oxford[8] and I direct that the receipt of the Bursar or other proper officer of the College shall be a complete discharge for that legacy and inasmuch as I gather that the erection of an extension to High Street of the College buildings would cost about £22,500 and that the loss to the College revenue caused by pulling down of houses to make room for the said new College buildings would be about £250 per annum I direct that the sum of £40,000 part of the said sum of £100,000 shall be applied in the first place in the erection of the said new College building[9] and that the remainder of such sum of £40,000 shall be held as a fund by the income whereof the aforesaid loss to the College revenue shall so far as possible be made good.

And inasmuch as I gather that there is a deficiency in the College revenue of some £1,500 per annum whereby the Fellowships are impoverished and the status of the College is lowered I direct that the sum of £40,000 further part of the said sum of £100,000 shall be held as a fund by the income whereof the

8. In the list of the Masters of Arts of Oriel College, in the year 1881, occurs this entry: "Rhodes, Cecil John," to which a note is added, "late Premier of the Cape Colony."

Tradition says that Oriel was first founded by Edward II., who vowed as he fled from Bannockburn he would found a religious house in the Virgin's honour if only Our Lady would save from the pursuing Scot. Edward III. gave the University the mansion called Le Oriole which stood on the present site of the College.

A portrait of Sir Walter Raleigh hangs on the walls of the College Hall.

The present income of the College is said to be not more than £7,500 per annum. The revenue of the twenty-one Colleges of Oxford is £206,102, or less than £10,000 each.

The present Provost of Oriel is David Binning Monro: he is also Vice-Chancellor of the University. Among the hon. Fellows are Mr. Goldwin Smith, Lord Goschen, and Mr. Bryce.

Among the famous names associated with Oriel besides those of Raleigh and Rhodes are the following:—Archbishop Arundel, Cardinal Allen, Bishop Butler, Prynne, Langland, author of "Piers Plowman"; Barclay, author of "The Ship of Fools"; Gilbert White, author of the "Natural History of Selborne"; Thomas Hughes, author of "Tom Brown's Schooldays"; Dr. Arnold, Bishop Wilberforce, Archbishop Whately, Cardinal Newman, Dr. Pusey, John Keble, Bishop Hampden.

9. The extension of Oriel College cannot at present take place. St. Mary Hall, which adjoins the College, belongs to the Principal (Dr. Chase), who was appointed to that position as far back as December, 1857. A statute made by the last Commission provided that upon his death St. Mary Hall shall be merged into Oriel College. The College has always contemplated, sooner or later, an extension of its buildings to High Street. The Hall runs close up to the houses facing the University Church, and the majority of these premises already belong to Oriel College. The northern side of the quadrangle of St. Mary Hall will ultimately be pulled down, together with the High Street shops, and the new buildings will face the main thoroughfare on the one hand and the quadrangle on the other.

income of such of the resident Fellows of the College as work for the honour
and dignity of the College shall be increased.[10]

And I further direct that the sum of £10,000 further part of the said sum of
£100,000 shall be held as a fund by the income whereof the dignity and
comfort of the High Table may be maintained by which means the dignity
and comfort of the resident Fellows may be increased.

And I further direct that the sum of £10,000 the remainder of the said sum
of £100,000 shall be held as a repair fund the income whereof shall be expended in maintaining and repairing the College buildings.

And finally as the College authorities live secluded from the world and so
are like children[11] as to commercial matters I would advise them to consult
my Trustees as to the investment of these various funds for they would receive
great help and assistance from the advice of my Trustees in such matters and I
direct that any investment made pursuant to such advice shall whatsoever it
may be be an authorized investment for the money applied in making it.

(5.) The Scholarships at Oxford.

Whereas I consider that the education of young Colonists at one of the
Universities in the United Kingdom is of great advantage to them for giving
breadth to their views for their instruction in life and manners[12] and for

---

10. A senior member of Oriel when interviewed on the subject of Mr. Rhodes's bequests said:—
"The College revenues do not admit at present of their paying the Fellows as much as the
Commission contemplated, and so far they had been at a disadvantage. Mr. Rhodes probably
became aware of this fact, and wished to enable the College to reach the limit set by the
Commission, £200 a year, as the maximum. The limit imposed by the Commissioners will not
apply to Mr. Rhodes's bequest, it being a new endowment, so that not only may the emoluments
of the Fellowships reach the figure specified by the Commissioners, but go beyond that. So far
Oriel College has not been able to rise to the level which the Commissioners considered a proper
amount. As to the amount set apart for the High Table, we do not want more comforts or
luxuries, we are quite happy as we are. We have enough to eat, but still, it was very kind of Mr.
Rhodes to think of us in that way."

11. Possibly Cecil Rhodes was thinking when he spoke of the childlike and secluded Don of a
story current in his day at Oriel—and current still—of John Keble, who was better at Christian
poetry than at worldly calculation. One day Keble, who was Bursar, discovered to his horror that
the College accounts came out nearly two thousand pounds on the wrong side. The learned and
pious men of Oriel tried to find the weak spot, but it was not until expert opinion was called that
they found that Keble, casting up a column, had added the date of the year to Oriel's debts.

12. Mr. Rhodes, speaking to Mr. Iwan Miller on the subject of his scholarships, said: "A lot of
young Colonials go to Oxford and Cambridge, and come back with a certain anti-English feeling,
imagining themselves to have been slighted because they were Colonials. That, of course, is all
nonsense. I was a Colonial, and I knew everybody I wanted to know, and everybody who wanted

instilling into their minds the advantage to the Colonies as well as to the United Kingdom of the retention of the unity of the Empire.

And whereas in the case of young Colonists studying at a University in the United Kingdom I attach very great importance to the University having a residential system such as is in force at the Universities of Oxford and Cambridge for without it those students are at the most critical period of their lives left without any supervision.

And whereas there are at the present time 50 or more students from South Africa studying at the university of Edinburgh many of whom are attracted there by its excellent medical school and I should like to establish some of the Scholarships hereinafter mentioned in that University but owing to its not having such a residential system as aforesaid I feel obliged to refrain from doing so. And whereas my own University the University of Oxford has such a system and I suggest that it should try and extend its scope so as if possible to make its medical school at least as good as that at the University of Edinburgh.[13]

---

to know me. The explanation is that most of these youngsters go there on the strength of scholarships, and insufficient allowances, and are therefore practically confined to one set; that of men as poor as themselves, who use the University naturally and quite properly only as a stepping-stone to something else. They are quite right, but they don't get what I call a University Education, which is the education of rubbing shoulders with every kind of individual and class on absolutely equal terms; therefore a very poor man can never get the full value of an Oxford training."

13. "Mr. Rhodes," says "A Senior Member of Oriel," "suggests that the University shall develop a medical school of the kind they have in Edinburgh. That might involve a considerable expense on the University which it is hardly in a position to bear, being very short of money as it is. The question of a medical school has been often discussed, and so far the conclusion arrived at has been adverse to the idea of the establishment of a medical school at Oxford. It has been considered that the infirmary at Oxford is not big enough, and the cases are not sufficiently numerous to provide practical experience for the students. The idea has been that they should get their general knowledge at Oxford, and then obtain practical hospital work elsewhere."

Commenting upon this, a distinguished Oxford Professor said:—"The opinion expressed by a senior member of Oriel College of the present position of the Medical School in Oxford is in the main correct, but contains one sentence which conveys an erroneous impression of the present attitude of the University in relation to medical teaching.

"A medical education comprises three kinds of study, each of which must be of first-rate quality. One of these is preliminary, and consists in the theoretical and practical study of general science. The second comprises anatomy, physiology, pathology, pharmacology, and hygiene. The third is purely professional, and corresponds to what used to be called walking the hospitals.

"The subject of the first, namely, inorganic and organic chemistry, natural philosophy, and biology are now amply provided for in the University. We have laboratories which are well equipped for present needs, though no doubt they may require extension at a future period; and very complete collections for illustrating the instruction given in zoology and botany.

"The subjects of the second part are those which constitute the science of medicine as

And whereas I also desire to encourage and foster an appreciation of the advantages which I implicitly believe will result from the union of the English-speaking peoples throughout the world and to encourage in the students from the United States of North America who will benefit from the American Scholarships to be established for the reason above given at the University of Oxford under this my Will an attachment to the country from which they have sprung but without I hope withdrawing them or their sympathies from the land of their adoption or birth.

Now therefore I direct my Trustees as soon as may be after my death and either simultaneously or gradually as they shall find convenient and if gradually then in such order as they shall think fit to establish for male students the Scholarships hereinafter directed to be established each of which shall be of the yearly value of £300 and be tenable at any College in the University of Oxford for three consecutive academical years.[14]

---

distinguished from its practice. A physiological department was established some fifteen years ago, the equipment of which will certainly bear comparison with any other in the country. More space is, however, required for the development of certain branches of the subject. The department of human anatomy has been completed for ten years.

"It has a museum, a commodious dissecting room with all modern improvements, and all other adjuncts that are required for the teaching of a subject so important to medicine. The pathological laboratory was opened by the Vice-Chancellor six months ago. It is more closely related to practical medicine than the others, and constitutes a common ground between the University and the Radcliffe Infirmary. As regards the building and the internal arrangements, it is all that could be desired, but the funds available for its complete equipment are inadequate, nor has the University as yet been able to provide sufficient remuneration for the teaching staff.

"The only branches of medical science, for the teaching of which special departments have not yet been established, are pharmacology (action of drugs) and public health.

"As regards the third part of the medical curriculum, viz., instruction in the practice of medicine, the University had adopted the principle that the two or three years which its students must devote to their purely professional studies must be spent where the existence of great hospitals affords opportunities for seeing medical and surgical practice in all its branches.

"As regards medicine, Oxford has been for the last dozen years providing what it considers the best possible education. The practical difficulty which prevents many from taking advantage of it is the long duration of the total period of study. The Oxford student of medicine must spend some six or seven years, reckoned from the date of matriculation to the completion of his hospital work. This time cannot be shortened with advantage. For those who come with the income to which Mr. Rhodes's munificent bequest affords this difficulty will scarcely exist. The scholarship will abundantly provide for the years spent in Oxford and enable its holders to compete with advantage for the Hospital Scholarships which have been already mentioned."

14. The Rev. W. Greswell, M.A., wrote to the *Times* on April 9th as follows:—"A scholarship foundation given during his lifetime by the Right Hon. C. J. Rhodes has already been in force at the Diocesan College, Rondebosch, near Cape Town. This year two members of the college—W. T. Yeoman and F. Reid—have been awarded £175 per annum and £125 per annum respectively

I direct my Trustees to establish certain Scholarships and these Scholarships I sometimes hereinafter refer to as "the Colonial Scholarships."[15]

The appropriation of the Colonial Scholarships and the numbers to be annually filled up shall be in accordance with the following table:—

---

in order to help them to go to one of the colleges at Oxford and continue the studies they have begun at the Cape. Originally the endowment was of £250 per annum for a single scholarship, tenable for three years at Oxford; but quite recently, by an additional act of generosity on the part of the donor, £50 per annum was added to the value of the scholarship, bringing it up to £300 per annum. At the same time a discretionary power was given to the Diocesan College to apportion the whole sum, *pro hac vice,* between the first two competitors, if it seemed expedient to do so and if the parents were willing and able to add something of their own. For Mr. Rhodes always thought that a student coming to Oxford should have a thoroughly sufficient, if not good, allowance, in order that he might enter into every phase of University life without the ever-present thought of the 'res angusta domi.' The scholars-elect are still continuing their studies at the college at Rondebosch until such time as they are ready to proceed to Oxford in 1903. Mr. Rhodes made, in the case of the Diocesan College, somewhat the same stipulation as to tests and proficiency as in his subsequent magnificent endowments.

The Bursar of Christ Church being questioned as to the point whether the £300 a year would close the gates of Christ Church to the Rhodes scholars, Mr. Skene pointed out that it all depended on the question whether the £300 a year was to keep the scholars the whole year through, both in term time at the University and in vacation elsewhere, or merely during the University years of six months. "If the latter," he said, "then £300 a year will keep them comfortably enough at Christ Church, and will enable them to enter into the social and varied life of the House. But if this amount is also to serve for vacation expenses, the balance left for the University will make it impossible, or, at any rate, inadvisable, for them to come to Christ Church."

A senior member of Oriel says Mr. Rhodes contemplated that the sum he provides shall be sufficient to maintain the recipients, together with their personal expenses, travelling, clothing, etc., and to enable them to mix freely in the society of the place and take a position amongst men who are well equipped in this world's goods. An ordinary young man at Oxford—I don't say at this college—would be comfortably off with an allowance of £250 a year, and many parents allow their sons that amount. Mr. Rhodes makes it £300—probably he took into consideration that people coming from abroad would have to face extra expenditure in the shape of travelling expenses.

15. Mr. Stevenson, of Exeter College, says there already exists in Oxford a small Colonial club for occasional meetings and dinners and the supply of friendly information. But the Colonials whom I have known very readily merge in the surrounding mass of undergraduates. There are several Colonials and Americans, for example, at Balliol, and Corpus, and Lincoln, and St. John's. Morally they are strong men, and they are popular. Then they are good athletes. We had two Americans in the boat this year. If Mr. Rhodes's trust should be the means of our getting some gigantic Colonials—or even Boers, for he exludes no race—who can do great things, say, at putting the weight, we may be able to wipe out Cambridge altogether! All Oxonians would agree that that would be a great achievement.

	Total No. Appropriated	To be tenable by Students of or from	No. of Scholarships to be Filled up in each Year.
South Africa 24	9	Rhodesia	3 and no more
	3	The South African College School in the Colony of the Cape of Good Hope.	1 and no more
	3	The Stellenbosch College School in the same Colony	1 and no more
	3	The Diocesan College School of Rondebosch in the same Colony	1 and no more
	3	St. Andrew's College School Grahamstown	1 and no more
	3	The Colony of Natal in the same Colony	1 and no more
Australasia 21	3	The Colony of New South Wales	1 and no more
	3	The Colony of Victoria	1 and no more
	3	The Colony of South Australia	1 and no more
	3	The Colony of Queensland	1 and no more
	3	The Colony of Western Australia	1 and no more
	3	The Colony of Tasmania	1 and no more
	3	The Colony of New Zealand	1 and no more
Canada 6	3	The Province of Ontario in the Dominion of Canada	1 and no more
	3	The Province of Quebec in the Dominion of Canada	1 and no more
Atlantic Islands 6	3	The Colony or Island of Newfoundland and its Dependencies	1 and no more
	3	The Colony or Islands of the Bermudas	1 and no more
West Indies 3	3	The Colony or Island of Jamaica	1 and no more
Total 60			20[16]

I further direct my Trustees to establish additional Scholarships sufficient in number for the appropriation in the next following clause hereof directed and those Scholarships I sometimes hereinafter refer to as "the American Scholarships."

16. The following is a list of Colonies to which no Scholarships have been appropriated:—

		POPULATION	
		White.	Coloured.
Canada	Nova Scotia	459,000	
	New Brunswick	331,000	
	Prince Edward Island	103,250	about
	Manitoba	246,500	100,000
	North-West Territories	220,000	
	British Columbia	190,000	
		1,549,750	100,000
West Indies	Bahamas	15,000	38,000
	Leeward Islands	5,000	122,500
	Windward Islands	5,000	92,500
	Barbados	15,000	180,000
	Trinidad and Tobago	10,000	262,000
		50,000	695,000
Mediterranian	Gibraltar	22,000	—
	Malta	5,000	179,000
	Cyprus	237,000	—
		264,000	179,000
Indian Ocean	Mauritius	10,000	360,000
	Ceylon	10,000	3,562,000
		20,000	3,922,000
Far East	Borneo	1,000	174,000
	New Guinea	250	350,000
	Hong Kong	2,500	97,500
		3,750	621,200
Indian Empire		150,000	295,000,000
Egypt		108,000	9,700,000
Soudan		—	10,000,000

The following is the population of the Colonies to which scholarships have been allotted:

		POPULATION		
		White.	Coloured.	Scholarships.
South Africa	Rhodesia	11,000	800,000	9
	Cape Colony	500,000	1,850,000	12
	Natal	64,000	865,000	3

I appropriate two of the American Scholarships to each of the present States and Territories of the United States of North America.[17] Provided that if any of the said Territories shall in my lifetime be admitted as a State the Scholarships appropriated to such Territory shall be appropriated to such State and that my Trustees may in their uncontrolled discretion with

Australasia	New South Wales	1,359,000	7,200	3
	Victoria	1,193,000	7,500	3
	South Australia	359,000	7,000	3
	Queensland	473,000	30,200	3
	Western Australia	152,500	30,000	3
	New Zealand	770,000	46,000	3
	Tasmania	173,000	—	3
Canada	Ontario	2,168,000	—	3
	Quebec	1,621,000	—	3
Atlantic Islands	Newfoundland	210,000	—	3
	Bermudas	6,500	11,200	3
West Indies	Jamaica	15,000	730,000	3
Total		9,075,900	4,384,100	60

Thus a population of 13,460,000 persons in the British Colonies is allotted 60 scholarships. A population of 76,000,000 in the United States is only allowed 100 scholarships. But a population of 7,405,000 persons, excluding India, Nigeria and Egypt, are allotted no scholarships at all. The average of scholarships to population is one in 760,000 in the United States, and one in 224,000 in the fifteen British Colonies to which they have been allotted. If the omitted British Colonies were dealt with on the same scale as the fifteen, 33 new scholarships would have to be founded. 17. The following is a list of the States and Territories of the United States, with their population at the time of the last census:—

Population—United States, 1900.

State.	Population.	State.	Population.
Alabama	1,828,697	Ohio	4,157,545
Arkansas	1,311,564	Oregon	413,536
California	1,485,053	Pennsylvania	6,302,115
Colorado	539,700	Rhode Island	428,556
Connecticut	908,355	South Carolina	1,340,316
Delaware	184,735	South Dakota	401,570
Florida	528,542	Tennessee	2,020,616
Georgia	2,216,331	Texas	3,048,710
Idaho	161,772	Utah	276,749
Illinois	4,821,550	Vermont	343,641
Indiana	2,516,462	Virginia	1,854,184

hold for such time as they shall think fit the appropriation of Scholarships to any Territory.

I direct that of the two Scholarships appropriated to a State or Territory not more than one shall be filled up in any year so that at no time shall more than two Scholarships be held for the same State or Territory.[18]

By Codicil executed in South Africa Mr. Rhodes after stating that the German Emperor had made instruction in English compulsory in German schools establishes fifteen Scholarships at Oxford (five in each of the first three years after his death) of £250 each tenable for three years for students of German birth to be nominated by the German Emperor for "a good understanding between England Germany and the United States of America

Iowa	2,231,853	Washington	518,103
Kansas	1,470,495	West Virginia	958,800
Kentucky	2,147,174	Wisconsin	2,069,042
Louisiana	1,381,625	Wyoming	92,531
Maine	694,466		
Maryland	1,190,050	45 States Total	74,610,523
Massachusetts	2,805,346		
Michigan	2,420,982	Territories, etc.	
Minnesota	1,751,394	Alaska	63,441
Mississippi	1,551,270	Arizona	122,931
Missouri	3,106,665	District of Columbia	278,718
Montana	243,329	Hawaii	154,001
Nebraska	1,068,539	Indian Territory	391,960
Nevada	42,335	New Mexico	195,310
New Hampshire	411,588	Oklahoma	398,245
New Jersey	1,883,669	Persons in Service	84,400
New York	7,268,012	Stationed Abroad.	
North Carolina	1,893,810	5 Territories.	
North Dakota	319,146	U.S. Total	76,299,529

18. Mr. Stevenson, of Exeter College, told an interviewer recently a good story of an American who came to Oxford without a scholarship or other aid. He was a wild Westerner, and unceremoniously walked into a college one day and asked to see the Head. He then asked to be admitted on the books. He had no particular references, but clearly was a strong man. After some time he was admitted. He read hard and played hard. In the long vacation he returned to America and worked for his living—at one time as a foreman of bricklayers—and brought back enough money to go on with. In the Christmas "vac." he went to America and lectured on Oxford and England, and again brought back more money. And so he gradually kept his terms and eventually took double honours. "He was very well read: most interesting: most enthusiastic. We could do with many like him."

will secure the peace of the world and educational relations form the strongest tie."[19]

My desire being that the students who shall be elected to the Scholarships shall not be merely bookworms I direct that in the election of a student to a Scholarship regard shall be had to

(i.) his literary and scholastic attainments

(ii.) his fondness of and success in manly outdoor sports such as cricket football and the like

(iii.) his qualities of manhood truth courage devotion to duty sympathy for the protection of the weak kindliness unselfishness and fellowship
and

(iv.) his exhibition during school days of moral force of character and of instincts to lead and to take an interest in his schoolmates for those latter attributes will be likely in after-life to guide him to esteem the performance of public duty as his highest aim.

As mere suggestions for the guidance of those who will have the choice of students for the Scholarships I record that (i.) my ideal qualified student would combine these four qualifications in the proportions of three-tenths for the first two-tenths for the second three-tenths for the third and two-tenths for the fourth qualification so that according to my ideas if the maximum number of marks for any Scholarship were 200 they would be apportioned as follows—60 to each of the first and third qualifications and 40 to each of the second and fourth qualifications (ii.) the marks for the several qualifications would be awarded independently as follows (that is to say) the marks for the first qualification by examination for the second and third qualifications respectively by ballot by the fellow-students of the candidates and for the fourth qualification by the head master of the candidate's school and (iii.) the results of the awards (that is to say the marks obtained by each candidate for each qualification) would be sent as soon as possible for consideration to the

19. I am assured, says the *Daily Telegraph* Berlin correspondent, that Kaiser Wilhelm himself was much struck by the donor's generosity, and by the motives which actuated him in thinking of Germany in this way. His Majesty was specially touched by the attention shown to himself, and forthwith signified his intention to comply with the stipulation that candidates for the scholarships should be nominated by himself. In due time they will be so selected by the Kaiser.

Mr. W. G. Black, of Glasgow, writes to the *Spectator:*—"Mr. Rhodes seems to have been impressed by the German Emperor's direction that English should be taught in the schools of Germany. It may not be uninteresting to note that his Majesty's first action on receiving Heligoland from Great Britain was to prohibit the teaching of English in the island schools. That was in 1890. The prohibition was bitterly resented by the people, who had since 1810 been subjects of the British Crown, but they were, of course, powerless."

Trustees or to some person or persons appointed to receive the same and the person or persons so appointed would ascertain by averaging the marks in blocks of 20 marks each of all candidates the best ideal qualified students.[20]

No student shall be qualified or disqualified for election to a Scholarship on account of his race or religious opinions.

20. The following account of the discussion which took place when the proportion of marks was finally settled is quoted from the *Review of Reviews*, May, 1902, p. 480. The discussion is reported by Mr. Stead, who was present with Mr. Rhodes and Mr. Hawksley:—

Then, later on, when Mr. Hawksley came in, we had a long discussion concerning the number of marks to be allotted under each of the heads.

Mr. Rhodes said: "I'll take a piece of paper. I have got my three things. You know the way I put them," he said laughing, as he wrote down the points. "First, there are the three qualities. You know I am all against letting the scholarships merely to people who swot over books, who have spent all their time over Latin and Greek. But you must allow for that element which I call 'smug,' and which means scholarship. That is to stand for four-tenths. Then there is 'brutality,' which stands for two-tenths. Then there is tact and leadership, again two-tenths, and then there is 'unctuous rectitude,' two-tenths. That makes up the whole. You see how it works."

Then Mr. Hawksley read the draft clause, the idea of which was suggested by Lord Rosebery, I think. The scheme as drafted ran somewhat in this way:—

A scholarship tenable at Oxford for three years at £300 a year is to be awarded to the scholars at some particular school in the Colony or State. The choice of the candidate ultimately rests with the trustees, who, on making their choice, must be governed by the following considerations. Taking one thousand marks as representing the total, four hundred should be allotted for an examination in scholarship, conducted in the ordinary manner on the ordinary subjects. Two hundred shall be awarded for proficiency in manly sports, for the purpose of securing physical excellence. Two hundred shall be awarded (and this is the most interesting clause of all) to those who, in their intercourse with their fellows, have displayed most of the qualities of tact and skill which go to the management of men, who have shown a public spirit in the affairs of their school or their class, who are foremost in the defence of the weak and the friendless, and who display those moral qualities which qualify them to be regarded as capable leaders of men. The remaining two hundred would be vested in the headmaster.

The marks in the first category would be awarded by competitive examination in the ordinary manner; in the second and third categories the candidate would be selected by the vote of his fellows in the school. The headmaster would of course vote alone. It is provided that the vote of the scholars should be taken by ballot; that the headmaster should nominate his candidate before the result of the competitive examination under (1), or of the ballot under (2) and (3) was known, and the ballot would take place before the result of the competitive examination was known, so that the trustees would have before them the names of the first scholar judged by competitive examination, the first selected for physical excellence and for moral qualities, and the choice of the headmaster. The candidate under each head would be selected without any knowledge as to who would come out on top in the other categories. To this Mr. Rhodes had objected on the ground that it gave "unctuous rectitude," a casting vote, and he said "unctuous rectitude" would always vote for "smug," and the physical and moral qualities would go by the board. To this I added the further objection that "smug" and "brutality" might tie, and "unctuous rectitude" might nominate a third person, who was selected neither by "smug" nor "unctuous rectitude,"

Except in the cases of the four schools hereinbefore mentioned the election to Scholarships shall be by the Trustees after such (if any) consultation as they shall think fit with the Minister having the control of education in such Colony, Province, State or Territory.

A qualified student who has been elected as aforesaid shall within six calendar months after his election or as soon thereafter as he can be admitted into residence or within such extended time as my Trustees shall allow commence residence as an undergraduate at some college in the University of Oxford.

---

with the result that there would be a tie, and the trustees would have to choose without any information upon which to base their judgment. So I insisted, illustrating it by an imaginary voting paper, that the only possible way to avoid these difficulties was for the trustees or the returning officer to be furnished not merely with the single name which heads each of the four categories, but with the result of the ballot to five or even ten down, and that the headmaster should nominate in order of preference the same number. The marks for the first five or ten in the competitive examination would of course also be recorded, and in that case the choice would be automatic. The scholar selected would be the one who had the majority of marks, and it might easily happen that the successful candidate was one who was not top in any one of the categories. Mr. Rhodes strongly supported this view, and Mr. Hawksley concurred, and a clause is to be prepared stating that all the votes rendered at any rate for the first five or ten should be notified to the trustees, and also the order of precedence for five or ten to the headmaster. Mr. Rhodes then said he did not see why the trustees need have any responsibility in the matter, except in case of dispute, when their decision should be final. This I strongly supported, saying that provided the headmaster had to prepare his list before the result in the balloting or competition was known, he might be constituted returning officer, or, if need be, one of the head boys might be empowered to act with him, and then the award of the scholarship would be a simple sum in arithmetic. There would be no delay, and nothing would be done to weaken the interest. As soon as the papers were all in the marks could be counted up, and the scholarship proclaimed.

First I raised the question as to whether the masters should be allowed to vote. Mr. Rhodes said it did not matter. There would only be fourteen in a school of six hundred boys, and their votes would not count. I said that they would have a weight far exceeding their numerical strength, for if they were excluded from any voice they would not take the same interest that they would if they had a vote, while their judgment would be a rallying point for the judgment of the scholars. I protested against making the masters Outlanders, depriving them of votes, and treating them like political helots, at which Rhodes laughed. But he was worse than Kruger, and would not give them the franchise on any terms.

Then Mr. Hawksley said he was chiefly interested in the third category—that is, moral qualities of leadership. I said yes, it was the best and the most distinctive character of Mr. Rhodes's school; that I was an outside barbarian, never having been to a university or a public school, and therefore I spoke with all deference; but speaking as an outside barbarian, and knowing Mr. Rhodes's strong feeling against giving too much preponderance to mere literary ability, I thought it would be much better to alter the proportion of marks to be awarded for "smug" and moral qualities respectively, that is to say, I would reduce the "smug" to 200 votes,

The scholarships shall be payable to him from the time when he shall commence such residence.

I desire that the Scholars holding the scholarships shall be distributed amongst the Colleges of the University of Oxford and not resort in undue numbers to one or more Colleges only.

Notwithstanding anything hereinbefore contained my Trustees may in their uncontrolled discretion suspend for such time as they shall think fit or remove any Scholar from his Scholarship.

In order that the Scholars past and present may have opportunities of meeting and discussing their experiences and prospects I desire that my Trustees shall annually give a dinner to the past and present Scholars able and willing to attend at which I hope my Trustees or some of them will be able to be present and to which they will I hope from time to time invite as guests persons who have shown sympathy with the views expressed by me in this my Will.

---

and put 400 on to moral qualities. Against this both Mr. Rhodes and Mr. Hawksley protested, Mr. Rhodes objecting that in that case the vote of the scholars would be the deciding factor, and the "smug" and "unctuous rectitude" would be outvoted. If brutality and moral qualities united their votes they would poll 600, as against 400.

It was further objected, both Mr. Rhodes and Mr. Hawksley drawing upon their own reminiscences of school-days, that hero-worship prevailed to such an extent among schoolboys that a popular idol, the captain of an eleven, or the first in his boat, might be voted in although he had no moral qualities at all. Mr. Hawksley especially insisted upon the importance of having a good share of culture in knowledge of Greek and Roman and English history. Then I proposed as a compromise that we should equalise "smug" and moral qualities. Mr. Rhodes accepted this, Mr. Hawksley rather reproaching him for being always ready to make a deal. But Mr. Rhodes pointed out that he had resisted the enfranchisement of the masters, who were to be helots, and he had also refused to reduce "smug" to 200, and thought 300 was a fair compromise. So accordingly it was fixed that it had to be 300—300 for "smug" and 300 for moral qualities, while "unctuous rectitude" and "brutality" are left with 200 each.

We all agreed that this should be done, half the marks are at the disposal of the voting of the scholars, the other half for competition and the headmaster. It also emphasises the importance of qualities entirely ignored in the ordinary competitive examinations, which was Mr. Rhodes's great idea. Mr Rhodes was evidently pleased with the change, for just as we were leaving the hotel he called Mr. Hawksley back and said, "Remember, three-tenths," so three-tenths it is to be.

(6.) The Dalham Hall Estate.

The Dalham Hall Estate[21] is by Codicil dated January 18th 1902 strictly settled on Colonel Francis Rhodes and his heirs male with remainder to Captain Ernest Frederick Rhodes and his heirs male.

The Codicil contains the following clause:—

Whereas I feel that it is the essence of a proper life that every man should during some substantial period thereof have some definite occupation and I object to an expectant heir developing into what I call a "loafer."

And whereas the rental of the Dalham Hall Estate is not more than sufficient for the maintenance of the estate and my experience is that one of the things making for the strength of England is the ownership of country estates which could maintain the dignity and comfort of the head of the family but that this position has been absolutely ruined by the practice of creating charges upon the estates either for younger children or for the payment of debts whereby the estates become insufficient to maintain the head of the family in dignity and comfort.

And whereas I humbly believe that one of the secrets of England's strength has been the existence of a class termed "the country landlords" who devote their efforts to the maintenance of those on their own property.[22] And whereas this is my own experience. Now therefore I direct that if any person

21. Dalham Hall Estate was purchased by Mr. Rhodes the year before his death. It is situate in Suffolk, not far from Newmarket, and is 3,475 acres in extent.

22. In the *Fortnightly Review* for May, 1902, Mr. Iwan-Müller gives the following account of the reasons which Mr. Rhodes gave him for preferring country landlords to manufacturers:—"He told me how during a recent visit to England he had stayed with an English country gentleman of very large estates.

" 'I went about with him,' he said in effect, although I do not profess to be able to recall the exact working of his sentences, 'and I discovered that he knew the history and personal circumstances of every man, woman, and child upon his property. He was as well instructed in their pedigrees as themselves, and could tell how long every tenant or even labourer had been connected with the estate, and what had happened to any of them in the course of their lives. From there I went on to a successful manufacturer, a man of high standing and benevolent disposition. He took me over his works, and explained the machinery and the different improvements that had been made, with perfect familiarity with his subject, but, except as to the heads of departments, foremen and the like, he absolutely knew nothing whatever about the lives and conditions of his "hands." Now,' he added, 'my manufacturing friend was a more progressive man, and probably a more capable man than my landlord friend. Yet the very necessities of the latter's position compelled him to discharge duties of the existence of which the other had no idea. The manufacturer built schools and endowed libraries, and received reports as to their management, but he never knew, or cared to know, what effect his philanthropy had upon the individual beneficiaries.' "

who under the limitations hereinbefore contained shall become entitled as tenant for life or as tenant in tail male by purchase to the possession or to the receipt of the rents and profits of the Dalham Hall Estate shall attempt to assign charge or incumber his interest in the Dalham Hall Estate or any part thereof or shall do or permit any act or thing or any event shall happen by or in consequence of which he would cease to be entitled to such interest if the same were given to him absolutely or if any such person as aforesaid (excepting in this case my said brothers Francis Rhodes and Ernest Frederick Rhodes) (i) shall not when he shall become so entitled as aforesaid have been for at least ten consecutive years engaged in some profession or business or (ii.) if not then engaged in some profession or business and (such profession or business not being that of the Army) not then also a member of some militia or volunteer corps shall not within one year after becoming so entitled as aforesaid or (being an infant) within one year after attaining the age of twenty-one years whichever shall last happen unless in any case prevented by death become engaged in some profession or business and (such profession or business not being that of the Army) also become a member of some militia or volunteer corps or (iii.) shall discontinue to be engaged in any profession or business before he shall have been engaged for ten consecutive years in some profession or business then and in every such case and forthwith if such person shall be tenant for life then his estate for life shall absolutely determine and if tenant in tail male then his estate in tail male shall absolutely determine and the Dalham Hall Estate shall but subject to estates if any prior to the estate of such person immediately go to the person next in remainder under the limitations hereinbefore contained in the same manner as if in the case of a person whose estate for life is so made to determine that person were dead or in the case of a person whose estate in tail male is so made to determine were dead and there were a general failure of issue of that person inheritable to the estate which is so made to determine.

Provided that the determination of an estate for life shall not prejudice or effect any contingent remainders expectant thereon and that after such determination the Dalham Hall Estate shall but subject to estates if any prior as aforesaid remain to the use of the Trustees appointed by my said Will and the Codicil thereto dated the 11th day of October 1901 during the residue of the life of the person whose estate for life so determines upon trust during the residue of the life of that person to pay the rents and profits of the Dalham Hall Estate to or present the same to be received by the person or persons for the time being entitled under the limitations hereinbefore contained to the first vested estate in remainder expectant on the death of that person.

After various private dispositions Mr. Rhodes in his original will left the residue of his real and personal estate to the Earl of Rosebery, Earl Grey, Alfred Beit, William Thomas Stead, Lewis Lloyd Michell and Bourchier Francis Hawksley absolutely as joint tenants.

The same persons were also appointed executors and trustees.

In a Codicil dated January, 1901, Mr. Rhodes directed that the name of W. T. Stead should be removed from the list of his executors.

In a second Codicil dated October, 1901, Mr. Rhodes added the name of Lord Milner to the list of joint tenants, executors and trustees.

In a third Codicil, dated March, 1902, Mr. Rhodes appointed Dr. Jameson as one of his trustees, with all the rights of other trustees.

SOURCE: In *The Last Will and Testament*, ed. W. T. Stead (London: Review of Reviews Office, 1902), 3–49.

The Burial

RUDYARD KIPLING

(C. J. Rhodes, buried in the Matoppos, 10 April 1902)

When that great Kings return to clay,
  Or Emperors in their pride,
Grief of a day shall fill a day,
  Because its creature died.
But we—we reckon not with those
  Whom the mere Fates ordain,
This Power that wrought on us and goes
  Back to the Power again.

Dreamer devout, by vision led
  Beyond our guess or reach,
The travail of his spirit bred
  Cities in place of speech.
So huge the all-mastering thought that drove—
  So brief the term allowed—
Nations, not words, he linked to prove
  His faith before the crowd.

It is his will that he look forth
 Across the world he won—
The granite of the ancient North—
 Great spaces washed with sun.
There shall he patient take his seat
 (As when the Death he dared),
And there await a people's feet
 In the paths that he prepared.

There, till the vision he foresaw
 Splendid and whole arise,
And unimagined Empires draw
 To council 'neath his skies
 Shall quicken and control.
Living he was the land, and dead,
 His soul shall be her soul!

SOURCE: In *The Works of Rudyard Kipling* (Hertfordshire: Wordsworth, 1994).

IV
CRISES OF EMPIRE

GORDON AT KHARTOUM

INTRODUCTION
Gordon at Khartoum: From Cavil to Catastrophe
BARBARA HARLOW

"At last!" was the title to the 7 February 1885 *Punch* cartoon that jubilantly anticipated the arrival of the relief expedition to General Gordon and his forces in the besieged city of Khartoum. A week later (14 February 1885), a bereaved Britannia, her sword thrust into the ground, bemoaned in the same magazine, "Too Late!" The caption to this next *Punch* cartoon read further, "Khartoum taken by the Mahdi. General Gordon's fate uncertain." General Gordon had in fact been beheaded and his head presented with all due ceremony to his opponent, Mohammed Ahmed, the "Mahdi" who lead the popular Sudanese insurrection against the Anglo-Egyptian occupation of that territory.

He had come to be known as "Chinese" Gordon for his famous role in England's earlier colonial exploits in China, first in the capture of Pekin and later during the Taiping rebellion. But he would be most commemorated after his death for his renowned defense of Khartoum in 1884–1885. All England, it seemed, awaited word of his fate in the early months of that year, from his sister Mary in whom he confided epistolarily both his belief in the will of God (or "D.V." as he invoked it in his letters to her) and his distrust in the intentions and policies of the English government, to Victoria herself, who wrote in condolence to Mary following the news of Gordon's demise. "To think of your dear, noble, heroic Brother," she penned, "who served his Country and his Queen so truly, not having been rescued." Before China even, however, Gordon had served in the Crimea, at the siege of Sebastopol, and in Turkey. He had participated in the exploration of the African continent, fought the Arab slave trade there, and conducted archeological research in Palestine. To Lord Cromer, administering English interests in Egypt, Gordon was "above all things a soldier, and, moreover, a very bellicose soldier" (Cromer, 563). In contrast, for Wilfred Scawen Blunt, a distinguished critic of England's colonial policies and practices in Egypt, India, and Ireland,

and an ardent supporter of the Egyptian nationalist Ahmed 'Urabi, Gordon was a "man of many contradictions and, singularly complex character," well "above the rank of the common soldier of fortune" (Blunt, 87). No less than had been the case during the Crimean War in 1854–1856 or following the Indian Mutiny in 1857, and much as would happen in the course of the Anglo-Boer War (1899–1902) or through the Congo controversy at the turn of the nineteenth century, public opinion and political positions would be divided over the integrity of England's imperial project as it foundered on the failed rescue of Gordon.

In late 1883, however, Gordon was about to enter King Leopold's service in the Congo when, abruptly, he was called on by his own country to embark on a mission to the Sudan. Whether Gordon was the most appropriate choice for such a task was much debated, as were the parameters of the mission itself. There was an uprising under way in the Sudan, led by the Mahdi; British interests were at stake; English and Egyptian lives were at risk. An earlier mission in 1883, led by Colonel Hicks, had met with devastating disaster and death. What was Gordon to do? According to Cromer (Evelyn Baring), Gordon was supposed to evacuate whomever he could from Khartoum and withdraw. But how did Gordon understand his orders? And just what were those orders? Evacuation of the city? Defense of the city? The establishment of an orderly government there? Or, as is imputed to Gordon by some of his critics, was he himself set on nothing less than to "smash the Mahdi"?

If there had been a question as to the sending of Gordon to Khartoum at all, there was even more difficult debate over the decision to rescue him, to send a relief expedition to his aid. For Gordon, it was the second such expedition, his mission, he maintained, having been the first sent in assistance to the city and its inhabitants. In any case, in August 1884, Lord Wolseley was given the orders to pursue such an endeavor of relief . . . "at last." But Wolseley and his forces arrived "too late." Khartoum fell to the Mahdist forces in early February 1885, and the Mahdi received the head of Gordon as evidence of his success and of England's catastrophic failure to pursue its imperial policy through the congested corridors of political cavil and public outcry.

The fall of Khartoum replayed variously thereafter: in the reminiscences of participants such as Slatin Pasha; in the scenarios of novelist John Buchan; in A. Conan Doyle's novelistic reprise in *The Tragedy of the Korosko* (1898); in A. E. W. Mason's *The Four Feathers* (1901), which resolves the disgraces of the Crimea through recoveries in Khartoum; and even on the cinema screen, with Basil Dearden's 1966 epic *Khartoum*, starring Laurence Olivier as the Mahdi and Charlton Heston as Gordon. The delivery of Gordon's head would become in turn an icon in the hall of heroes of empire, and his statues—like the one in Trafalgar Square—would memorialize the stand he took and the political cavil and colonial catastrophe that it enlivened. The Mahdi himself outlived Gordon by only a few months, but it would be more than a decade before England restored its prominence in the Sudan through General Kitchener's army's defeat of the Mahdist forces at Omdurman in 1898. From Omdurman, Kitchener, in pursuit of his own illustrious colonial career, would travel south—from Cairo to the Cape—to join the Anglo-Boer War in South Africa.

BIBLIOGRAPHY

Allen, B. M. *Gordon and the Sudan.* London: Macmillan, 1931.

Blunt, Wilfred S. *Gordon at Khartoum.* London: Stephen Swift and Co., 1911.

Cooper, Merian C., and Lothar Mendes, dirs. *The Four Feathers.* United States, 1929. Film.

Cromer, Lord (Evelyn Baring). *Modern Egypt.* Volume 1. London: Macmillan, 1908.

Dearden, Basil, and Eliot Eliotson, dirs. *Khartoum.* United States, 1966. Film.

Doyle, Arthur Conan. *The Tragedy of the Korosko.* London: Smith, Elder, 1898.

Farwell, Byron. "The Sudan I: Heroes in Distress" and "The Sudan II: Too Late!" In *Queen Victoria's Little Wars.* 1972. New York: W. W. Norton, 1985.

Farwell, Byron. *Prisoners of the Mahdi.* New York: Harper and Row, 1967.

Henty, G. A. *The Dash for Khartoum: A Tale of the Nile Expedition.* London: Blackie and Son, 1892.

Holt, P. M. *The Mahdist State in the Sudan.* Oxford: Clarenden Press, 1958.

Korda, Zoltan. *The Four Feathers.* United Kingdom, 1939. Film.

Mason, A. E. W. *The Four Feathers.* London: Smith, Elder, 1902.

Robson, Brian. *Fuzzy-Wuzzy: The Campaigns in the Eastern Sudan 1884–1885.* Tunbridge Wells, England: Spellmount, 1993.

Sharp, Don, dir. *The Four Feathers.* United Kingdom, 1978. Film.

Spiers, Edward M., ed. *Sudan: The Reconquest Reappraised.* London: Frank Cass, 1998.

Wingate, Francis Reginald. *Mahdism and the Egyptian Sudan.* London: Cass, 1968.

Wingate, Sir Ronald. *Wingate of the Sudan.* London: Murray, 1955.

Young, Terence, and Zoltan Korda, dirs. *Storm over the Nile.* United Kingdom, 1955. Film.

Zulfo, Ismat Hasan. *Karari: The Sudanese Account of the Battle of Omdurman.* London: Frederick Warne, 1980.

———

Chronology of Events

1881		Appearance of the Mahdi
1883		Mahdists destruction of Egyptian forces under English command
1884	18 January	General Gordon leaves London for Cairo
	28 January	Gordon leaves Cairo for Khartoum
	March	Khartoum besieged
	August	Gladstone announces plans for a relief expedition to Khartoum under Lord Wolseley
1885	26 January	Fall of Khartoum and death of Gordon
	5 February	London hears of the fall of Khartoum and the death of Gordon
	29 May	Death of the Mahdi
1898		Kitchener's defeat of the Mahdist forces at Omdurman

———

Excerpts from
The Journals of Major-General C. G. Gordon, C. B. at Kartoum
CHARLES G. GORDON

Vide note as to pruning down on outside.—C. G. G.

September 10.—Colonel Stewart, MM. Power and Herbin, left during the night for Dongola, *viâ* Berber.

Spy came in from south front, and one from Halfeyeh reports Arabs will not attack, but will continue the blockade.

Sent off two sets of telegrams by a spy, who will go to Shendy.

Yesterday, when the messenger went out to deliver my answer to the Arabs, in response to Mahdi's letter, though he had a white flag, they fired on him, and tried to capture him. They use the white flag, and find it respected by us, and that we let their men go back. They chain any men we send to them.

It is wonderful how the people of the town, who have every possible facility to leave the city, cling to it, and how, indeed, there are hundreds who flock in, though it is an open secret we have neither money nor food.[1] Somehow this makes me feel confident in the future, for it is seldom that an impulse such as this acts on each member of a disintegrated mass without there being some reason for it, which those who act have no idea of, but which is a sort of instinct. Truly I do not think one could inflict a greater punishment on an inhabitant of Kartoum than to force him to go to the Arabs.

Halfeyeh reports that Faki Mustapha, who was in command of the Arabs on the west or left bank of the White Nile, wishes to join the Government. He is informed we are glad of it, but wish him to remain quiet, and to take no active part till he sees how the scales of the balance go; if we rise, then he can act, if we fall he is not to compromise himself; but what we ask him is to send up our spies, which he can do without risk.[2] The same advice was given to the people of Shendy, who wished to issue out and attack Berber.

The runaways of Tuti[3] wish to come back, which is allowed.

The "matches" used for the mines are all finished, and we are obliged to go back to powder hose, and unite the mines in families of ten.

Rows on rows of wire entanglement are being placed around the lines. General Gordon's horse was captured by the Arabs in the defeat of El foun; the other staff horse got a cut on the head, but is now all right.

1. The military, civilians, Ulemas, inhabitants and settlers in Kartoum telegraphed on August 19th to the Khedive as follows: "Weakened and reduced to extremities, God in His mercy sent Gordon Pasha to us in the midst of our calamities of the siege, and we should all have perished of hunger and been destroyed. But we, sustained by his intelligence and great military skill, have been preserved in Kartoum until now."—*Egypt, No. 35,* p. 112;—ED

2. In this passage we have an example of the old and perfect fairness with which General Gordon dealt with others. Before allowing Mustapha Faki, the neutral, to join his ranks and aid him against the Mahdi, he must first himself be satisfied that such a step would not endanger Faki Mustapha's life. Success or failure was still doubtful. This, of course, he could not tell Mustapha, but would it be right and just to use him while such a doubt existed? Gordon was of opinion that it would not, and thus he bade Mustapha wait events, and do for him that only which involved no risks.—ED.

3. Tuti is an island at the junction of the White and Blue Nile.—ED.

The Mahdi is still at Rahad.[4] The answer to his letter (*vide* Colonel Stewart's journal) was sent open, so that the Arab leaders could read its contents.

With respect to letters written to the Mahdi and to the Arab chiefs, commenting on the apostacy of Europeans, they may, and are, no doubt, hard, but it is not a small thing for a European, for fear of death, to deny our faith; it was not so in old times, and it should not be regarded as if it was taking off one coat, and putting on another. If the Christian faith is a myth, then let men throw it off, but it is mean and dishonourable to do so merely to save one's life if one believes it is the true faith. What can be more strong than these words, "He who denies Me on earth I will deny in heaven." The old martyrs regarded men as their enemies, who tried to prevent them avowing their faith. In the time of Queens Mary and Elizabeth, what men we had, and then it was for less than here, for it was mainly the question of the Mass, while here it is the question of the denial of our Lord and of his passion. It is perhaps as well to omit this, if this journal is published, for no man has a right to judge another. Politically and morally, however, it is better for us not to have anything to do with the apostate Europeans in the Arab camp. Treachery never succeeds, and, however matters may end, it is better to fall with clean hands, than to be mixed up with dubious acts and dubious men. Maybe it is better for us to fall with honour, than to gain the victory with dishonour, and in this view the Ulemas of the town are agreed; they will have nought to do with the proposals of treachery.

No doubt the letters to the Arabs will make the Arab chiefs work on the Europeans with them, to take an active part against us, by saying to those Europeans, "You are cast out;" but the Arabs will never trust them really, so they can do little against us.

We had a regular gaol delivery to-day, letting out some fifty, and are sending to the Arabs about nine prisoners whom it is not advisable to keep in the town. A donkey quietly grazing near the north fort, exploded one of the mines there (an iron alembic which belonged to the time of Mahomet Ali, and had been used for the reduction of gold; it held some 10 lbs. of powder); the donkey, angry and surprised, walked off unhurt! These alembics are of this shape, braced by iron straps together. It is extraordinary that after a good deal of rain, and three months' exposure, the domestic matchbox should have retained its vitality.

4. Near El Obeyed and about 200 miles from Kartoum.—ED.

At Last! SOURCE: *Punch* 88 (7 February 1885): 67. [These two cartoons from *Punch*, which appeared in succeeding weeks, indicate the concern of the English populace in following the fate of General Gordon in Khartoum. The year before, the question had already been whether to send Gordon to the Sudan at all. But by the turn of the year 1884–1885, public attention and political opinion were focused instead on the consequences of that very mission. First, would there be a relief expedition? And if so, when? Once sent, would such an expedition succeed? It did not.]

"*Too Late!*" Telegram, Thursday Morning, Feb. 5.—
"Khartoum taken by the Mahdi. General Gordon's fate uncertain."
SOURCE: *Punch* 88 (14 February 1885): 79.

The school here is most interesting, as the scholars get a certain ration. It is always full, viz., two hundred. Each boy has a wooden board, on which his lesson is written, and on visiting it the object of each boy is to be called out to read his lesson, which they do with a swaying motion of body, and in a sing-song way, like the Jews do at the wailing place at Jerusalem and in their synagogues, from which we may infer this was the ancient way of worship, for the lessons are always from the Koran. Little black doves with no pretension to any nose, and not more than two feet high, push forward to say the first ten letters of the alphabet, which is all they know.

We have completed the census (*vide* Colonel Stewart's Journal), and have 34,000 people in the town.

THE RELIEF EXPEDITION

I altogether *decline* the imputation that the projected expedition has come to *relieve me. It* has *come to save our national honour in extricating the garrisons, &c., from a position our action in Egypt has placed these garrisons. I was relief expedition No. I.* They are *relief expedition No.* 2. As for myself I could make good my retreat at any moment if I wished. Now realise what would happen if this *first relief expedition* was to bolt and the steamers fell into the hands of the Mahdi: *this second relief expedition* (for the honour of England engaged in extricating garrisons) would be somewhat hampered. We the *first* and *second* expeditions are equally engaged for the honour of England. This is fair logic. *I came up to extricate the garrisons and failed. Earle comes up to extricate garrisons and (I hope) succeeds. Earle does not come to extricate me.* The extrication of the garrisons was supposed to affect our "national honour." If Earle succeeds the "national honour" thanks him and I hope rewards him, but it is altogether independent of me, who for failing incurs its blame. I am not the *rescued lamb,* and I will not be.

I hope the officers and men of Her Majesty's forces will be considerate to the Egyptian soldiers and sailors; *they do not understand English,* but as they have done some good service, I hope they will be kindly treated. They are a trying lot, as I well know, but if it were not for them, our soldiers would have to tramp many a weary sandy mile. It is one of my joys that I never have to see Great Britain again. I hope to get out of this affair, and either go to the Congo, *viâ* Equatorial Province, or by Brussels. At any rate I shall never have to undergo the worries I underwent during the week I was in England this year. I say this in order that those who may have to do with me may know how very determined a man's will must be who does not wish (and indeed *will not ever*) go back to England again, and to whom continuance in Her Majesty's Service, except for the honour of it, is a matter of indifference.

I am now going to be egotistic, but it will save a mint of trouble, and I may be pardoned, considering the circumstances. By being so I may save myself what I should much regret, a quarrel.

My idea is to induce Her Majesty's Government to undertake the extrication of all people or garrisons, now hemmed in or captive, and that if this is not their programme, then to resign my commission and do what I can to attain it (the object). As long as a man remains in Her Majesty's Service he is bound to obey the orders of his superiors, but if he resigns he cannot be held as insubordinate if he disobeys. Of course it may turn on the question of whether once having entered the service of Her Majesty's Army, one is free to leave it at one's will. But we officers are not like the private soldiers engaged for a term of years, and perhaps one may risk dismissal if the cause is worthy of it—which, I think, the question of abandoning the garrisons is.

I say this, because I should be sorry for Lord Wolseley to advance from Dongola without fully knowing my views. If Her Majesty's Government are going to abandon the garrisons, then do not advance. I say nothing of evacuating the country, I merely maintain that if we do so, every one in the Soudan, captive or hemmed in, ought to have the option and power of retreat. Having given them that option and power, I have nothing more to say, and I would not care whether the country is evacuated or not.

It is a miserable country, but it is joined to Egypt, and to my idea it would be difficult to divorce the two.

I will end these egotistical remarks by saying that no persuasion will induce me to change my views; and that as to force, it is out of the question, for I have the people with me—at any rate of the towns which hold out. Therefore, if Her Majesty's forces are not prepared to relieve the whole of the garrisons, the General should consider whether it is worth coming up—in his place, *if not so prepared,*[5] I would not do so. I do not dictate, but I say what every gentleman[6]

---

5. The position of the garrisons in Darfour, the Bahr-el-Gazelle and Equatorial provinces renders it impossible that you should take any action which would facilitate their retreat without extending your operations far beyond the sphere which Her Majesty's Government is prepared to sanction.

As regards the Sennaar garrison, Her Majesty's Government is not prepared to sanction the dispatch of an expedition of British troops up the Blue Nile in order to insure its retreat.

From the last telegrams received from General Gordon, there is reason to hope that he has already taken steps to withdraw the Egyptian portion of the Sennaar garrison.

You will use your best endeavours to insure the safe retreat of the Egyptian troops which in Her Majesty's Army would agree to—that it would be *mean* (*coûte que coûte*) to leave men who (though they may not come up to our ideas as heroes) have stuck to me, though a *Christian dog in their eyes,* through great difficulties, and thus force them to surrender to those who have not conquered them, and to do that at the bidding of a foreign Power, to save one's own skin. Why the black sluts would stone me if they thought I meditated such action. Stewart knows all this and used to groan over perversity.

September 30. The Arabs fired seven shells last night at 9 P.M. which fell inside the lines, but did no harm. To-day being Bairam, they fired four rounds in their camp—a salute I suppose.

The spy who came in yesterday, says the report is rife that Seyd Mahomet Osman's men have entered Katarif.

The three steamers will leave here to-day for Shendy at 4 P.M.

I believe that a good recruitment of blacks and Chinese would give England all the troops she wants for expeditions, mixed with one-sixth English. As for those wretched Sepoys, they are useless. I would garrison India with Chinese and blacks, with one-sixth English, and no army could stand against us. The Chinese in Shanghai had the greatest contempt for the Bombay Sepoys, and

---

constitute the Kartoum garrison, and of such of the civil employees of Kartoum, together with their families, as may wish to return to Egypt.

As regards the future government of the Soudan, and especially of Kartoum, Her Majesty's Government would be glad to see a Government at Kartoum which, so far as all matters connected with the internal administration of the country are concerned, would be wholly independent of Egypt.—*Lord Wolseley's Instructions, Egypt, No.* 35, 1884, *No.* 157.—ED.

6. "I am strongly against any permanent retention of the Soudan, but I think we ought to leave it with decency, and give the respectable people a man to lead them, around whom they can rally, and we ought to support that man by money and by opening road to Berber. Pray do not consider me in any way to advocate retention of Soudan; I am quite averse to it, but you must see that you could not recall me nor could I possibly obey until the Cairo employés get out from all the places. I have named men to different places, thus involving them with Mahdi; how could I look the world in the face if I abandoned them and fled? As a gentleman, could you advise this course? It may have been a mistake to send me up, but having been done I have no option but to see evacuation through, for even if I was mean enough to escape I have no power to do so. You can easily understand this; would you do so? If you were the people of Khartoum, you would, like they would, make terms with Mahdi by making me backsheesh Madhi."—*Gen. Gordon to Sir E. Baring, Kartoum, March* 3, 1884; *Egypt, No.* 12, 1884; *No.* 231. This telegram, forwarded by Sir E. Baring to Lord Granville, was received by H. M. Ministers on March 11, 1884. On April 3 Mr. Gladstone stated in the House of Commons that "General Gordon was under no orders and under no restraint to stay at Kartoum."—ED.

used to knock them about. Beloochees and Sikhs are a different class. I have the greatest contempt for the pure Indian Sepoys. Chinese, or blacks, or Goorkas, or Belochees are far better. The moment he (the pure Sepoy) is off parade, he puts off all uniform that connects him with Her Majesty's Government, and puts on his dish-clout. I hate these snake-like creatures. Any man accustomed to judge by faces sees that they hate us.

I would back the Mussulmans of India against the lot of those snakes. India, to me, is not an advantage; it accustoms our men to a style of life which they cannot keep up in England; it deteriorates our women. If we kept the sea-coast, it is all that we want. It is the centre of all petty intrigue, while if our energy were devoted elsewhere, it would produce tenfold. India sways all our policy to our detriment. Lord Cardwell replied (when I asked him the question as to the benefit we got from India), "*that we could not get out of it,*" and I suppose that is the answer that must be given.

October 13.—Cavalry sortie this morning from Bourré; captured fifteen slaves and killed thirteen men who resisted. This sortie was under Abdoul Hamid, the Sandjak of the Shaggyeh. We lost none.

The Arabs on Omdurman side have spread out their huts in a semicircle (but at a considerable distance) around Omdurman, on the left bank.

Shaggyeh from Halfeyeh will be in the North Fort to-day. The Arabs off South Front, near the White Nile, fired musketry against the lines, but did no harm.

Last night cavalry Shaggyeh captured three men who were going off to Sheikh el Obeyed from Halfeyeh; they had their arms with them. I have to let them go again.

No definite news yet of the arrival of the Mahdi at Omdurman. The Mahdi will be furious with this cavalry sortie; it will be disagreeable news to him on his arrival here.

A man from the Arabs has come in to Omdurman with two letters; it is too late to see them to-night. By telegraph I hear that the man brought two letters for the Commandant at Omdurman from Faki Mustapha, saying the Mahdi was coming the day after to-morrow, and inviting him to submit; so I have told them to send the man off again.

We are a wonderful people; it was never our Government which made us a great nation; our Government has been ever the drag on our wheels. It is, of course, on the cards that Kartoum is taken under the nose of the expeditionary force, which will be *just too late.*

The expeditionary force will perhaps think it necessary to retake it; but that will be of no use, and will cause loss of life uselessly on both sides. It had far better quietly return, with its tail between its legs; for once Kartoum is taken, it matters little if the Opposition say "You gave up Kartoum," or "You gave up Kartoum, Sennaar," &c., &c., the sun will have set, people will not care much for the satellites.

SOURCE: Charles G. Gordon, *The Journals of Major-General C.B. Gordon, C. G. at Kartoum* (London: K. Paul, Trenchand and Co., 1885), 3–7, 111–15, 189–91.

Letters to Mary Gordon
QUEEN VICTORIA

[Victoria was among those who lent their sympathy and support to Gordon and his mission, and she shared her condolences with Gordon's sister, Mary, on hearing the news of the general's death at the hands of the Mahdist forces.]

Osborne, 17 Feb. 1885.
Dear Miss Gordon,
    How shall I write to you, or how shall I attempt to express *what I feel!* To *think* of your dear, noble, heroic Brother, who served his Country and his Queen so truly, so heroically, with a self-sacrifice so edifying to the World, not having been rescued. That the promises of support were not fulfilled—which I so frequently and constantly pressed on those who asked him to go—is to me *grief inexpressible!* indeed, it has made me ill! My heart bleeds for you, his Sister, who have gone through so many anxieties on his account, and who loved the dear Brother as he deserved to be. You are all so good and trustful, and have such strong faith, that you will be sustained even now, when *real* absolute evidence of your dear Brother's death does not exist—but I fear there cannot be much doubt of it. Some day I hope to see you again, to tell you all I cannot express. My daughter Beatrice, who has felt quite as I do, wishes me to express her deepest sympathy with you. I hear so many expressions of sorrow and sympathy from *abroad:* from my eldest daughter, the Crown Princess, and from my Cousin, the King of the Belgians,—the very warmest. Would you express to your other Sisters and your elder Brother my true sympathy, and what I do so keenly feel, the *stain* left upon England for your dear Brother's cruel, though heroic, fate!

Ever,
Dear Miss Gordon,
Yours sincerely and sympathizingly
V. R. I.

Windsor Castle,
March 16, 1885.
Dear Miss Gordon,

It is most kind and good of you to give me this precious Bible,[1] and I only hope that you are not depriving yourself and family of such a treasure, if you have no other. May I ask you, during how many years your dear heroic Brother had it with him? I shall have a case made for it with an inscription, and place it in the Library here, with your letter and the touching extract from his last to you. I have ordered, as you know, a Marble Bust of your dear Brother to be placed in the Corridor here, where so many Busts and Pictures of our greatest Generals and Statesmen are, and hope that you will see it before it is finished, to give your opinion as to the likeness.

Believe me always, yours very sincerely,
Victoria R. I.

SOURCE: In *Letters of General C. G. Gordon* (London: Macmillan, 1890), xv–xvi.

1. The Bible here referred to was one used by my Brother for many years, and was his constant companion when at Gravesend, Galatz, and during his first sojourn in the Soudan; it was then so worn out that he gave it to me. Hearing that the Queen would like to see it, I forwarded it to Windsor Castle, and subsequently offered it to Her Majesty, who was graciously pleased to accept it. The Bible is now placed in the South Corridor in the private apartments, enclosed in an enamel and crystal case, called the "St. George's Casket," where it lies open on a white satin cushion, with a marble bust of General Gordon on a pedestal beside it.

The End of General Gordon

LYTTON STRACHEY

[For Lytton Strachey, General Gordon was another "eminent Victorian" (along with Florence Nightingale and Thomas Arnold). But the debate persisted for Strachey as it did for other observers: should Gordon have been sent on that mission? And should—could—Gordon have been rescued at the end of the day?]

Gordon's last great adventure, like his first, was occasioned by a religious revolt. At the very moment when, apparently for ever, he was shaking the dust of Egypt from his feet, Mohammed Ahmed was starting upon his extraordinary career in the Sudan. The time was propitious for revolutions. The effete Egyptian Empire was hovering upon the verge of collapse. The enormous territories of the Sudan were seething with discontent. Gordon's administration had, by its very vigour, only helped to precipitate the inevitable disaster. His attacks upon the slave-trade, his establishment of a government monopoly in ivory, his hostility to the Egyptian officials, had been so many shocks, shaking to its foundations the whole rickety machine. The result of all his efforts had been, on the one hand, to fill the most powerful classes in the community—the dealers in slaves and ivory—with a hatred of the government, and on the other to awaken among the mass of the inhabitants a new perception of the dishonesty and incompetence of their Egyptian masters. When, after Gordon's removal, the rule of the Pashas once more asserted itself over the Sudan, a general combustion became inevitable: the first spark would set off the blaze. Just then it happened that Mohammed Ahmed, the son of an insignificant priest in Dongola, having quarrelled with the Sheikh from whom he was receiving religious instruction, set up as an independent preacher, with his headquarters at Abba Island, on the Nile, a hundred and fifty miles above Khartoum. Like Hong-siu-tsuen, he began as a religious reformer, and ended as a rebel king. It was his mission, he declared, to purge the true Faith of its worldliness and corruptions, to lead the followers of the Prophet into the paths of chastity, simplicity, and holiness; with the puritanical zeal of a Calvin, he denounced junketings and merry-makings, songs and dances, lewd living and all the delights of the flesh. He fell into trances, he saw visions, he saw the Prophet and Jesus, and the Angel Izrail accompanying him and watching over him for ever. He prophesied, and performed miracles, and his fame spread through the land.

There is an ancient tradition in the Mohammedan world, telling of a mysterious being, the last in succession of the twelve holy Imams, who, untouched by death and withdrawn into the recesses of a mountain, was destined, at the appointed hour, to come forth again among men. His title was the Mahdi, the guide; some believed that he would be the forerunner of the Messiah; others that he would be Christ himself. Already various Mahdis had made their appearance; several had been highly successful, and two, in mediæval times, had founded dynasties in Egypt. But who could tell whether all these were not impostors? Might not the twelfth Imam be still waiting, in mystical concealment, ready to emerge, at any moment, at the bidding of God? There were signs by which the true Mahdi might be recognised—unmistakable signs, if one could but read them aright. He must be of the family of the prophet; he must possess miraculous powers of no common kind; and his person must be overflowing with a peculiar sanctity. The pious dwellers beside those distant waters, where holy men by dint of a constant repetition of one of the ninety-nine names of God, secured the protection of guardian angels, and where groups of devotees, shaking their heads with a violence which would unseat the reason of less athletic worshippers, attained to an extraordinary beatitude, heard with awe of the young preacher whose saintliness was almost more than mortal and whose miracles brought amazement to the mind. Was he not also of the family of the prophet? He himself had said so; and who would disbelieve the holy man? When he appeared in person, every doubt was swept away. There was a strange splendour in his presence, an overpowering passion in the torrent of his speech. Great was the wickedness of the people, and great was their punishment! Surely their miseries were a visible sign of the wrath of the Lord. They had sinned, and the cruel tax-gatherers had come among them, and the corrupt governors, and all the oppressions of the Egyptians. Yet these things, too, should have an end. The Lord would raise up his chosen deliverer: the hearts of the people would be purified, and their enemies would be laid low. The accursed Egyptians would be driven from the land. Let the faithful take heart and make ready. How soon might not the long-predestined hour strike, when the twelfth Imam, the guide, the Mahdi, would reveal himself to the World? In that hour, the righteous would triumph and the guilty be laid low for ever. Such was the teaching of Mohammed Ahmed. A band of enthusiastic disciples gathered round him, eagerly waiting for the revelation which would crown their hopes. At last, the moment came. One evening, at Abba Island, taking aside the foremost of his followers, the Master whispered the portentous news. He was the Mahdi.

That Mr. Gladstone's motives and ambitions were not merely those of a hunter after popularity was never shown more clearly than in that part of his career which, more than any other, has been emphasised by his enemies—his conduct towards General Gordon. He had been originally opposed to Gordon's appointment, but he had consented to it partly, perhaps, owing to the persuasion that its purpose did not extend beyond the making of a "report." Gordon once gone, events had taken their own course; the policy of the Government began to slide, automatically, down a slope at the bottom of which lay the conquest of the Sudan and the annexation of Egypt. Sir Gerald Graham's bloody victories awoke Mr. Gladstone to the true condition of affairs; he recognised the road he was on and its destination; but there was still time to turn back. It was he who had insisted upon the withdrawal of the English army from the Eastern Sudan. The imperialists were sadly disappointed. They had supposed that the old lion had gone to sleep, and suddenly he had come out of his lair, and was roaring. All their hopes now centred upon Khartoum. General Gordon was cut off; he was surrounded, he was in danger; he must be relieved. A British force must be sent to save him. But Mr. Gladstone was not to be caught napping a second time. When the agitation rose, when popular sentiment was deeply stirred, when the country, the Press, the sovereign herself, declared that the national honour was involved with the fate of General Gordon, Mr. Gladstone remained immovable. Others might picture the triumphant rescue of a Christian hero from the clutches of heathen savages; before *his* eyes was the vision of battle, murder, and sudden death, the horrors of defeat and victory, the slaughter and the anguish of thousands, the violence of military domination, the enslavement of a people. The invasion of the Sudan, he had flashed out in the House of Commons, would be a war of conquest against a people struggling to be free. "Yes, those people are struggling to be free, and they are rightly struggling to be free." Mr. Gladstone—it was one of his old-fashioned simplicities—believed in liberty. If, indeed, it should turn out to be the fact that General Gordon was in serious danger, then, no doubt, it would be necessary to send a relief expedition to Khartoum. But he could see no sufficient reason to believe that it was the fact. Communications, it was true, had been interrupted between Khartoum and Cairo but no news was not necessarily bad news, and the little information that had come through from General Gordon seemed to indicate that he could hold out for months. So his agile mind worked, spinning its familiar web of possibilities and contingencies and fine distinctions. General Gordon, he was convinced, might be hemmed in, but he was not surrounded. Surely, it was the duty of the Government to take no rash step, but to consider and to enquire and, when it acted, to act upon reasonable conviction. And then, there was another question. If it was true—and he believed it was true—that General Gordon's line of retreat was open, why did not General Gordon use it? Perhaps he might be unable to withdraw the Egyptian garrison, but it was not for the sake of the Egyptian garrison that the relief expedition was proposed; it was simply and solely to secure the personal safety of General Gordon. And General Gordon had it in his power to secure his personal safety himself; and he refused to do so; he lingered on in Khartoum, deliberately, wilfully, in defiance of the obvious wishes of his superiors. Oh! it was perfectly clear what General Gordon was doing: he was trying to force the hand of the English Government. He was hoping that if he remained long enough at Khartoum he would oblige the English Government to send an army into the Sudan which should smash up the Mahdi. That, then, was General Gordon's calculation! Well, General Gordon would learn that he had made a mistake. Who was he that he should dare to imagine that he could impose his will upon Mr. Gladstone? The old man's eyes glared. If it came to a struggle between them—well, they should see! As the weeks passed, the strange situation grew tenser. It was like some silent deadly game of bluff. And who knows what was passing in the obscure depths of that terrifying spirit? What mysterious mixture of remorse, rage and jealousy? Who was it that was ultimately responsible for sending General Gordon to Khartoum? But then, what did that matter? Why did not the man come back? He was a Christian hero, was he? Were there no other Christian heroes in the world? A Christian hero! Let him wait till the Mahdi's ring was really round him, till the Mahdi's spear was really about to fall! That would be the test of heroism! If he slipped back then, with his tail between his legs—! The world would judge.

SOURCE: In *Eminent Victorians* (1918) (New York: Harcourt, Brace and World, n.d.), 265–67, 301–4.

<hr />

Relief Expedition
LORD CROMER (EVELYN BARING)

The truth is that General Gordon was above all things a soldier, and, moreover, a very bellicose soldier.[1] His fighting instincts were too strong to admit of his working heartily in the interests of peace. The Arabs, he said, "must have one good defeat to wipe out Hicks's disasters and *my* defeats. . . . I do not care to wait to see the Mahdi walk in on your heels into Khartoum. One

1. Sir Samuel Baker, who knew General Gordon well, said to me, some years after the fall of Khartoum: "When I heard that Gordon was to go to the Soudan, I knew there would be a fight."

cannot think that . . . it is a satisfactory termination if, after extricating the garrisons and contenting ourselves with that, we let the Mahdi come down and boast of driving us out. It is a thousand pities to give up Khartoum to the Mahdi when there is a chance of keeping it under Zobeir.[2] So long as the Mahdi is alongside, no peace is possible."

In fact, General Gordon wished to "smash up" the Mahdi. This was the keynote of all his actions in the Soudan. "If," he wrote on November 7, "Zobeir had been sent to the Soudan, we would have beaten the Mahdi without any exterior help; it is sad, when the Mahdi is moribund, that we should by evacuation of Khartoum raise him again."

As to his instructions, he threw them to the winds.[3] Both the spirit and the text of his instructions were clear. "The main end to be pursued," he was told in the letter addressed to him on January 25, 1884, "is the evacuation of the Soudan." The policy of establishing some sort of settled government in the Soudan was approved, but this, though desirable, was considered a subsidiary point. It was specifically stated that it must "be fully understood that the Egyptian troops were not to be kept in the Soudan merely with a view to consolidate the power of the new rulers of the country." When it was decided not to employ Zobeir Pasha, General Gordon should have seen that all that remained for him to do was to concentrate his efforts on evacuation. He did nothing of the sort. He thought mainly of the subsidiary portion of his instructions and neglected the main issue.

But, it may be said, even if General Gordon had abandoned the idea of establishing an anti-Mahdist government in the Soudan, he would still have been unable to carry out his instructions, for the garrisons of the Soudan were scattered, and it was impossible to save all of them. General Gordon appears to have held that it was incumbent on him to save the whole of these garrisons. "I was named," he wrote, "for evacuation of Soudan (against which I have nothing to say), *not to run away from Khartoum and leave the garrisons elsewhere to their fate.*" He reverts to this subject over and over again in his Journal.[4] He held that it was "a palpable dishonour" to abandon the garrisons, and that "every one in the Soudan, captive or hemmed in, ought to have the option and power of retreat." On November 19, he wrote: "I declare *positively* and *once for all that I will not leave the Soudan until every one who wants to go*

---

2. This was written on September 24, 1884, that is to say, several months after the Zobeir policy had been rejected by the Government, and had, in fact, become quite impracticable.

3. On May 28, 1880, General Gordon wrote to his sister: "Having the views I hold, I could never curb myself sufficiently to remain in Her Majesty's service. Not one in ten million can agree with my motives, and it is no use expecting to change their views."—*Letters, etc.,* p. 158.

4. *Journal,* pp. 56, 72, 93, 112, 113, 125, 292, 298, 305, 307.

down is given the chance to do so, unless a government is established which relieves me of the charge; therefore, if any emissary or letter comes up here ordering me to come down, I will not obey it; but will stay here and fall with the town and run all risks."

All that can be said about arguments of this sort is that they bring to mind General Bosquet's famous remark on the Balaklava charge: "C'est magnifique, mais ce n'est pas la guerre."[5] We may admire, and for my own part, I do very much admire General Gordon's personal courage, his disinterestedness, and his chivalrous feeling in favour of the beleaguered garrisons, but admiration of these qualities is no sufficient plea against a condemnation of his conduct on the ground that it was quixotic. In his last letter to his sister, dated December 14, 1884, he wrote: "I am quite happy, thank God, and, like Lawrence, I have tried to do my duty." The phrase, which must have occurred to many a countryman of Sir Henry Lawrence when placed in a position of difficulty or danger, has become historical. The words, under the circumstances in which they were first used by Sir Henry Lawrence and afterwards repeated by General Gordon, are particularly touching. But, after all, when the emotions are somewhat quelled, and the highly dramatic incidents connected with the situation are set aside, reason demands answers to such questions as these: What was General Gordon's duty? Did he in reality try to do his duty?

A statesman in the responsible position which Mr. Gladstone then occupied, does well to pause before he calls upon a great nation to put forth its military strength. Can, however, the lengthened pause, which Mr. Gladstone made before he decided to send an expedition to Khartoum, be justified? I will endeavour to answer this question.

Mr. Gladstone's principal reply to his critics is contained in the following words, which he used in the House of Commons on February 23, 1885: "Our contention," he said, "was that we must be convinced that an expedition for the relief of General Gordon was necessary and practicable. We had no proof, as we believed, that General Gordon was in danger within the walls of Khartoum. We believed, and I think we had reason to believe from his own expressions, that it was in the power of General Gordon to remove himself and those immediately associated with him from Khartoum by going to the south. . . . General Gordon said himself, speaking of it as a thing distinctly

---

5. This remark is frequently attributed to Marshal Canrobert. According to Kinglake (*Invasion of the Crimea,* vol. iv. p. 269), it was made by General Bosquet to Mr. Layard in the field and at the time of the charge.

within his power, that he would in certain contingencies withdraw to the Equator." I proceed to analyse these remarks.

No one will be disposed to contest the statement that, before the Government decided on sending an expedition, it was incumbent on them to be convinced that the adoption of this measure was both "necessary and practicable." It only remains to be considered whether the evidence in respect to both the necessity and the practicability was not sufficient to justify action being taken before the month of August.

The practicability argument may be readily disposed of. It was conclusively answered by Lord Hartington at a later period (February 27) of the debate in which Mr. Gladstone used the words quoted above. With characteristic honesty, Lord Hartington said: "Although the difficulties of a military decision were great, and although there was a difference of opinion among military authorities, I have no hesitation in saying that the justification or, if you will, the excuse of the Government has rested mainly on the fact, which we have never attempted to conceal, that the Government were not, until a comparatively recent period, convinced of the absolute necessity of sending a military expedition to Khartoum." This frank statement, coming from the Minister who was then responsible for the administration of the War Office, effectually disposes of the argument in justification of delay based on the doubtful practicability of the military enterprise.

I turn, therefore, to the question of necessity. "We had no proof," Mr. Gladstone said, "as we believed, that General Gordon was in danger within the walls of Khartoum." The gist of the Government case is contained in these words. The same idea was embodied in all the messages, which Mr. Egerton was instructed to send to General Gordon during the summer of 1884, and which I find it difficult, even after the lapse of many years, to read without indignation. Not only does reason condemn them, but their whole tone runs, without doubt unconsciously, counter to those feelings of generous sympathy, which the position of General Gordon and his companions was so well calculated to inspire. Before General Gordon left London, I had warned the Government that, if he were sent to Khartoum, he would "undertake a service of great difficulty and danger." General Gordon, it is true, had, *more suo*, been inconsistent in his utterances on this subject. He had, in the first place, greatly underrated the difficulties of his task. So late as February 20, 1884, he had spoken of Khartoum being "as safe as Kensington Park." But the last messages, which he sent before telegraphic communication between Cairo and Khartoum was interrupted, breathed a very different spirit. He spoke, on March 8, of "the storm which was likely to break," of the probability of his being "hemmed in," and he added, with something of prophetic instinct, "I feel a conviction that I shall be caught in Khartoum." Lord Wolseley, myself, and others had dwelt on the dangers of General Gordon's position, and even if no such warnings had been given, the facts spoke for themselves. General Gordon and Colonel Stewart were beleaguered in a remote African town by hordes of warlike savages, who were half mad with fanaticism and elated at their recent successes. Yet Mr. Gladstone wanted further proof that they were in danger. If the proofs which already existed in the early summer of 1884 were not sufficient, one is tempted to ask what evidence would have carried conviction to Mr. Gladstone's mind, and the only possible answer is that Mr. Gladstone was well-nigh determined not to believe a fact which was, naturally enough, most distasteful to him.[6] General Gordon, in a passage of his Journal, which would be humorous if it were not pathetic, has himself described what every one of common sense must think of Mr. Gladstone's attitude during this period. "It is," he wrote on September 28, "as if a man on the bank, having seen his friend in the river already bobbed down two or three times, hails: 'I say, old fellow, let us know when we are to throw you the life-buoy; I know you have bobbed down two or three times, but it is a pity to throw you the life-buoy until you are really *in extremis*, and I want to know *exactly*, for I am a man brought up in a school of exactitude.'"

Mr. Gladstone said that General Gordon spoke of withdrawing to the Equator "as a thing distinctly in his power." It is true that in two telegrams of March 9 and of April 7, General Gordon had spoken of the possibility of retiring toward the Equatorial Province, but I had informed Lord Granville, on March 26, that Colonel Coetlogon, who spoke with authority on this subject, ridiculed the idea, and although Colonel Stewart had said at the beginning of April: "I am inclined to think my retreat will be safer by the Equator," the context clearly showed that he only used these words because he considered retreat *via* Berber so difficult, unless a British expedition were sent to open the road, that he preferred the desperate risk of a retreat in a southerly direction. It was, in fact, only necessary to look at a map, to glance at the accounts given by General Gordon himself and by Sir Samuel Baker of the physical difficulties to be overcome in moving up the White Nile, and to remember that both banks of that river for a long distance above Khartoum

---

6. There is a close analogy between Mr. Gladstone's attitude at this time and that of Lord Aberdeen before the Crimean War. Both practised the art of self-deception. "Almost to the last," Mr. Kinglake says (*Invasion of the Crimea*, vol. i. p. 307), "Lord Aberdeen misguided himself. His loathing for war took such a shape that he could not and would not believe in it; and when at last the spectre was close upon him, he covered his eyes and refused to see."

were in the hands of the Dervishes, to appreciate the fact that retreat in the direction of Gondokoro was little better than a forlorn hope.

For these reasons, the arguments adduced by Mr. Gladstone do not appear to afford any sufficient justification for the long delay which ensued before it was decided to send an expedition to Khartoum.

A different class of argument may, however, be advanced in favour of the course adopted by the Government at this time. It may be said that General Gordon never attempted to carry out the policy of the Government, that he was sent to evacuate the Soudan, that he turned his peaceful mission into an endeavour to "smash the Mahdi," and that he could have retreated from Khartoum, but that he never attempted to do so. Little was said about this aspect of the question at the time, for this line of argument necessarily involved reflections on General Gordon's conduct, which, under all the circumstances of the case, would have been considered ungenerous, and which, moreover, would have produced little effect, for the public were in no humour to listen to them. General Gordon, in Mr. Gladstone's words, was considered a "hero of heroes," and, at the time, a defence based on any faults he might have committed would, for all Parliamentary purposes, have been worse than none at all. At the same time, the order of ideas embodied in these arguments did to a certain extent find expression. Whilst Sir Stafford Northcote invited the House of Commons to assert the principle that it was incumbent on England to secure "a good and stable government for those portions of the Soudan which were necessary to the security of Egypt," Mr. John Morley, in a powerful speech, moved an amendment which was hostile alike to the Government and to the Opposition. He invited the House to express its regret that "the forces of the Crown were to be employed for the overthrow of the power of the Mahdi."[7] Moreover, although Mr. Gladstone's parliamentary position obliged him to oppose Mr. Morley's amendment, it is perhaps no very far-fetched conjecture to imagine that this amendment embodied an opinion, which did not differ widely from the views which Mr. Gladstone personally entertained. Mr. Gladstone had formerly spoken of the Soudanese as a "people rightly struggling to be free." The phrase had become historical. It was indiscreet in the mouth of an English Prime Minister, but at one time it contained a certain element of truth.[8] Moreover, I often heard at the time that Mr. Gladstone reasoned somewhat after this fashion: "The Soudanese wish to get rid of the Egyptians. The Egyptians, under pressure from England, are

7. Mr. Morley's amendment was rejected by 455 to 112 votes.
8. I mean that the Mahdist revolt would never have taken place if the people of the Soudan had not wished to throw off the Egyptian yoke.

prepared to leave the Soudan. It is inconceivable that, if the matter were properly explained to the Mahdi, he would not agree to facilitate the peaceful retreat of the Egyptian garrisons." To the logical European mind this position appears unassailable, but Mr. Gladstone never realised the fact that he was dealing with a race of savage fanatics to whom European processes of reasoning were wholly incomprehensible. The Mahdist movement was not only a revolt against misgovernment. It was also, in the eyes of its followers, a religious movement having for its object the forced conversion of the whole world to Mahdiism. There can be little doubt that it would have been practically impossible to treat with the Mahdi on the basis of a peaceful withdrawal of the Egyptian troops.

The line of argument to which allusion is made above, would appear more worthy of attention than that actually adopted by the Government. It has been already shown that General Gordon paid little heed to his instructions, that he was consumed with a desire to "smash the Mahdi," and that the view that he was constrained to withdraw every one who wished to leave from the most distant parts of the Soudan was, to say the least, quixotic. The conclusion to be drawn from these facts is that it was a mistake to send General Gordon to the Soudan. But do they afford any justification for the delay in preparing and in despatching the relief expedition? I cannot think that they do so. Whatever errors of judgment General Gordon may have committed, the broad facts, as they existed in the early summer of 1884, were that he was sent to Khartoum by the British Government, who never denied their responsibility for his safety, that he was beleaguered, and that he was, therefore, unable to get away. It is just possible that he could have effected his retreat if, having abandoned the southern posts, he had moved northwards with the Khartoum garrison in April or early in May. As time went on and nothing was heard of him, it became more and more clear that he either could not or would not,—probably that he could not,—move. The most indulgent critic would scarcely extend beyond June 27 the date at which the Government should have decided on the question of whether a relief expedition should or should not be despatched. On that day, the news that Berber had been captured on May 26 by the Dervishes was finally confirmed. Yet it was not till six weeks later that the Government obtained from Parliament the funds necessary to prepare for an expedition.

I began the examination of this branch of the subject by asking whether the errors of judgment committed by Mr. Gladstone's Government in the summer of 1884 were excusable. The points, which have been previously discussed, such as the tacit permission given to the Hicks expedition, the despatch of General Gordon to Khartoum, the rejection of Zobeir Pasha's services, and the refusal to make a dash to Berber in March, are questions as to which it may be said, either that the fact of any error having been committed may be contested, or that any condemnatory conclusion must in some degree be based upon an after-knowledge of events, which was not obtainable when the decisive step had to be taken. The same cannot be said of the point now under discussion. The facts were at the time sufficiently clear to any one who wished to understand them, and the conclusions to be drawn from them were obvious. Those conclusions were (1) that unless a military expedition was sent to Khartoum, General Gordon and his companions must sooner or later fall into the hands of the Mahdi; and (2) that prompt action was needed, all the more so because it was only during the short period while the Nile was high that rapidity of movement was possible. If Mr. Gladstone had said that the expenditure of blood and money which would be involved in an expedition to Khartoum was incommensurate with the objects to be attained, the argument would, in my opinion at all events, have been unworthy of the leader of a great nation, and to none of Mr. Gladstone's arguments does a censure of this description in any degree apply. Moreover, the adoption of this attitude would have probably sealed the fate of the Ministry in forty-eight hours. But such a statement would have had the merit of being comprehensible. The argument that no expedition was necessary because General Gordon was not proved to be in danger was so totally at variance with facts, which were patent to all the world, as to be well-nigh incomprehensible.

On these grounds, I maintain that of all the mistakes committed at this period in connection with Egyptian and Soudanese affairs, the delay in sending an expedition to the relief of Khartoum was the least excusable.[9] The House of Commons practically condemned the conduct of the Government. In a full House, the Government only escaped censure by a majority of 14. "If," General Gordon wrote on November 8, "it is right to send up an expedition now, why was it not right to send it up before?" The fact that General Gordon's pathetic question admits of no satisfactory answer must for ever stand as a blot on Mr. Gladstone's political escutcheon.

SOURCE: Chapter 27 in volume 1 of *Modern Egypt* (London: Macmillan, 1908), 562–65, 584–92.

9. Lord Northbrook wrote to me subsequently (January 13, 1886): "You gave us very distinct warnings in time that if Gordon was to be rescued an expedition would have to be sent, and no one regrets more than I do that the preparations were delayed from May to August." I may add that, some ten years later, I sent to Lord Northbrook a typewritten copy of the portion of this work which deals with the Soudan. He wrote the following words on the margin opposite the passage to which this note is attached: "I am afraid that all this is quite true. . . . As I had the misfortune to be a member of Mr. Gladstone's Government, I have to bear the blame with the rest. But I resolved never to serve under him again!"

Excerpts from *Gordon at Khartoum*
WILFRED S. BLUNT

And here, before I go further, it will, I think, make matters still clearer in regard to the history of the next twelve months in Egypt, including, as it must, Gordon's heroic defence of Khartoum, if I break off my personal narrative and devote a chapter or two to a critical examination of that truly wonderful man's character. I propose to do so not in the spirit of mere hero worship, though I hold him to have been by far the most chivalric figure among Englishmen of our generation; and still less of belittlement; but in the spirit of a sane historian, reconstructing from the many records we have of his inner spiritual life no less than of his public actions, and from some sources, too, of private knowledge and my own recollection of him, a picture of the living man he was.

To appreciate Gordon's character at all accurately, and thereby to judge his career at its true value, it is essential to recognize him as a man of many contradictions and a singularly complex character. He himself, in one of those intimate letters which through life he was in the habit of writing to his sister, and which form the most complete self-revelation made in any letters that have been published in our time, says: "Talk of two natures in one! I have a hundred, and none think alike and all want to rule"; and, again: "No man in the world is more changeable than I"—an exaggeration of the truth yet no less strictly true. Gordon had at least two distinctly antagonistic features in his nature—the one, that of a man of action, with an imperative need of strong practical work, the instinct of a soldier who saw the thing he had it in his mind to do with absolute clearness of vision, and as clearly the way to do it— the other, that of a religious mystic, occupied not with this world but with spiritual forces in a world unseen; perplexed perpetually, and perpetually in doubt as to the precise will of God with him, a fatalist, a disbeliever in his own free will, and consequently liable to sudden changes of plan; a seeker of omens and supernatural directions; at times (as he also himself says) a "religious fanatic," perhaps hardly on this one point sane. Not that Gordon was in the smallest degree a fanatic in the sense of one who hated another for his creed. His mind was large on this as on all other matters; but he was imbued with the belief in God's direct dealings with man and with his own interpretation of them, as suited to his own spiritual and temporal case, and with the nothingness of worldly affairs or of life and death for himself and others in view of a life to come.

Entering the army early he saw service for the first time at the siege of Sebastopol, and remained on in Turkey when the war was over as one of the officers on the Commission of frontier delimitation in Bessarabia and Armenia. This gave him his first experience of the Mohammedan East. In 1860 he joined the British forces in China, where he took part in the capture of Pekin, and again stayed on specially employed. Shanghai, one of the Treaty Ports, was just then threatened by the Taiping rebellion, and for its protection an Imperial Chinese force had been raised under European officers, and the command of it was given to Gordon. With the permission of his superiors he thus entered a foreign service, and found himself, at the early age of twenty-nine, commanding an army of Asiatics under the Chinese Emperor. His military authority was practically absolute, and by a display of strategy of the highest order and lavish personal courage he succeeded in breaking the Taiping rebellion, and restoring one of the richest provinces of China and some of its most populous cities to the Imperial Government. The Emperor, in gratitude for so great a service, loaded him with honours, and would have enriched him if Gordon had been willing. But with a fine contempt for wealth he would take nothing but his stipulated pay, and, the work done, returned to his ordinary duties in England without further remark or claim on his own Government.

This stamps him as a man entirely above the rank of the common soldier of fortune. That he was also a man of immense natural military genius cannot be doubted, with a power of exerting influence over the soldiers he commanded, and turning the rawest material into good fighting stuff, and in this he compares favourably with any of the great European leaders of Asiatics that can be named in history. It is by no means certain, however, to my mind that in this first brilliant episode of Gordon's life, any more than in his latest at Khartoum, he was fighting on what I should consider the right side, the side that is of those who had the better right in justice. Indeed the Taipings, though the methods of their insurrection were barbarous in the extreme, represented what was more probably the juster cause of the Chinese people than that of the Man Chu Emperors, in whose service Gordon was. Gordon, however, did not often stop to consider points like these when he accepted foreign employment, and only discovered his mistake when it was too late to retire from it. This was the case with him, as he found to his cost, when serving the Khedive Ismail, and so, too, he discovered and would have avowed it if he had survived his last campaign against the Mahdi. What is important about the Chinese episode is the strong effect it had upon his character. The terrible sights which he there witnessed in the lands laid waste by the Taipings, the appalling incidents of an Eastern civil war, the cruelties inflicted on the weak, the outraged women and the starving children, famine, pestilence, and death spread over immensely populous areas, joined with the almost miraculous victories achieved by the army he commanded, the huge personal risks daily run, and his unvarying success, bred in him a conviction that he was under immediate divine direction, and had for his special mission in life the redressing of wrongs and the protection of the helpless. His attitude thenceforth, though he made mistakes, was that of the Christian knight errant, seeking service through the world wherever there were dragons of iniquity to fight, or distressed persons to be rescued by feats of arms. It is necessary to remember this if we are to understand rightly the spirit of his early Egyptian service.

There are two ways of looking at this question. The slave raiding which prevailed along the whole border line between Equatorial Africa and the waterless northern deserts which extend from the White Nile to the Atlantic had for many centuries been a terrible scourge upon the indigenous black race. It was carried on by the Bedouin tribes, more or less Arab in their origin and Mohammedan in their religion, who had invaded and conquered North Africa in the early centuries of Islam. These considered the Pagan negroes their lawful booty wherever they could capture them, and made a trade of bringing them with other equatorial produce to the sea coasts of Morocco and the rest of the Mohammedan States bordering the Mediterranean and Red Seas. It was a yearly tithe of many thousands taken from the unwarlike agricultural villagers, and may justly be likened to the depredation inflicted on the antelope herds of the same borderland by lions living on the desert outskirts. At first sight, and from a humanitarian point of view, it would seem that the destruction of these human lions was the beneficent duty of any one who would undertake it, and the extirpation of the slave raiders by force of arms the surest way of bringing prosperity to the negro inhabitants. And such was the view taken by most of our European explorers of the nineteenth century, Schweinfurth, Baker, Stanley, and the rest, who were in correspondence with the anti-slavery association in London and were constantly urging the duty of the penetration and civilizing of Central Africa by the states of Europe. Africa once Europeanized, they argued, slave-raiding must necessarily be made to cease and the negroes be freed from an immemorial misfortune. The reasoning harmonized well with the commercial ideas of the day, which saw in Central Africa new fields for its enterprise; and the civilized occupation of the two lines of waterway by which the Soudan could most easily be reached, the Nile and the Congo, was pushed on by the societies as a duty of humanity. I remember attending a meeting of the Royal Geographical Society under Sir Roderick Murchison, to which I had just been elected in

1862, in which our then Consul Petherick at Khartoum was praised for his exploration of the White Nile, as yet an unknown region, on this very ground, that benefit must necessarily accrue to the negroes from the opening up of their country through Englishmen acting in conjunction with the Viceroy of Egypt. Yet this very exploration of Petherick's turned out to be the beginning of far worse evils to the negroes of the White Nile than any they had during all the centuries of their unexplored history experienced, even to the total destruction of some of their communities.

The truth is—and this Gordon came to understand at Khartoum, as we to-day are coming to understand it on the Congo—though European civilization is able to deal with certain evils incidental to uncivilized life, it brings with it other evils ten times more destructive than those it cures. It destroys the lions, but the antelopes are not found thereby to increase. On the contrary they become a prey, all of them, to the newcomer, their far more scientific and unsparing friend. And so it is also with the negroes who are ten times worse ruined by European conquest. Of the reality of this truth Gordon gained at least occasional glimpses during the years he served the Khedive Ismail in the Soudan. For myself I have never been in any doubt, since I have had an opinion at all on the matter, that the only true humanity towards the negroes of Equatorial Africa would have been to leave them unvisited, uncivilized, and severely alone with their own local troubles. The alternative policy to that of force applied to the slave raiders was that of the encouragement of Mohammedan reform in the Mediterranean Moslem states, and with it to secure the abolition of slavery as a legal institution and so the demand of slaves from the interior. This policy, however, was never one at all popular with the anti-slave-trade associations. Our professional humanitarians were no more anxious to abolish slavery altogether than masters of foxhounds are anxious to abolish foxes; and Mohammedan reformers were generally discouraged by the societies and reminded that slavery was recognized by the Koran, and so could not be legally condemned by any reformers professing themselves Moslems. This was certainly the case in 1882 when Sheykh Mohammed Abdu and Arabi included the complete abolition of slavery in their programme of national reform. Sir William Muir and Allen, the antislavery secretary, at once took up the cudgels against them in the "Times," and their anger knew no bounds. It was an unheard-of thing, they said, that a Mohammedan reformer should dare to strike at the roots of a time-honoured Oriental institution to which their English society owed its *raison d'être*.

Yet the Egyptian reformers of that day were perfectly sincere in their intention. They were poor men, representing a community too humble to be slave owning itself, arrayed against a wealthy ruling class possessed of slaves.

Their interests did not warp their judgement, and their judgement on this, as on other things, was humanitarian. The Khedive and the Turkish Pashas, however, were infinitely preferred by Allen and the agents of the society in Egypt, whose salaries would have ceased had slavery and slave dealing really disappeared from the Nile. As to our diplomatic representatives, at Cairo as elsewhere, they hated the worry of the whole slavery question and resented anything that raised its abolition in practical form. It meant for them the tiresome duty of presenting remonstrances to Mohammedan princes who all possessed slaves and who wished to keep them and not to be deprived of the means of getting new ones when required. I remember well the disgust with which dispatches from the Slave Trade department of the Foreign Office were regarded in our Chancelleries. All the same, the method of dealing with them as I have just indicated would have been the true line for our human-itarians to take if the interests of the raided black villagers of the Upper Nile had been alone in question. A pronouncement against slavery at Cairo by a Nationalist Sheykh el Islam, would have been worth more to them than a whole army of civilized protectors sent to guard their desert frontier against the *jellabat*.

The particular choice of Gordon for the mission Cromer had proposed, though as we have seen his name had been more than once talked of at the Foreign Office, would probably never have been actually made and insisted on but for a combination of chances closely connected with a Cabinet intrigue just then coming to a head in London. Down to the end of the year 1883 nobody was thinking at all of Gordon in connection with actual circum-stances in the Soudan, nor was anything known of Cromer's proposal. Gor-don had been away close on a year in Palestine, and had kept silence, an unusual thing with him, during the whole of it as far as the press was con-cerned. Not a dozen persons in England knew of his being on his way back to Europe, and his few friends at head-quarters looked upon him as being engaged to King Leopold for service on the Congo, and so out of the question for Khartoum—this although they knew also that the idea of the Soudan was once more present to his mind, since the defeat of Hicks, as a possibility and a temptation for his ambition. He had written to Wolseley to get him leave at the War Office to enter Leopold's service and on landing at Genoa had gone straight to Brussels, there to arrange terms with the King about the Congo. Except for a few reviews of Hake's book "Chinese Gordon," which had been published at Christmas time, I can find nothing about him in any of the London newspapers. And so things stood at the end of the year.

It would be a curious matter to speculate what might have been the respective fates of the Nile population and those of the Congo if Gordon's contract, then all but signed, with Leopold had been carried into effect. It would probably have been for the welfare, or, let us say, the lesser suffering of both. It is difficult to think of the Congo venture taking the inhuman shape it did had Gordon ever had personally to do with it, and had he been left alive to protest against a violation of human rights so monstrous, while, on the other hand, the Egyptian Soudan might have been spared the destruction of four-fifths of its inhabitants at the blundering hands of our government, and its present melancholy subjection to European rule. Chance, however, or whatever directs the destinies for good and evil in the world, ruled it otherwise, and Gordon, turned aside from the Congo, was to meet his fate, not there, but upon the Upper Nile, while the Congo was to become the scene of still greater horrors. Whose the hands were exactly that pulled the strings in the affair and sent him to his doom, and what was the relative amount of responsibility assignable to each of the chief actors, with the mystery of their secret motives, I have been at great pains to ascertain. This is how the thing, when carefully examined, appears to have come about.

SOURCE: Wilfred S. Blunt, *Gordon at Khartoum* (London: Stephen Swift and Co., 1911), 87–90, 96–100, 158–59.

The Desertion of General Gordon
RANDOLPH H. S. CHURCHILL

What was the mission of General Gordon? What was its nature? The mission, to my mind, was in theory and intention one of the noblest ever undertaken. The object of the mission was twofold. It was to rescue the garrisons in the Soudan, numbering something like 30,000, exclusive of women and children, and it was to restore freedom and tranquillity to harassed and oppressed tribes. The whole nation acquiesced in that mission, as, I believe, it acquiesced in the abandonment of the Soudan. I do not think it could be asserted for one moment that any person on the Opposition side of the House has ever advocated the re-conquest of the Soudan, and I may say that I have never heard anybody who is responsible on this side of the House censure the abandonment of the Soudan. But, although the nation and the Opposition acquiesced in the abandonment of the Soudan, the nation felt deeply the solemn and high duties which that abandonment imposed upon them, and the nation hailed with pleasure, and I may almost say with rapture, the mission of General Gordon, and was prepared to condone many an error because the Government had entrusted those duties to be discharged by so generous, so gallant, and so noble an officer as General Gordon. I do not believe that any mission which ever left this country had ever created so much interest; but the very intensity of the interest excited is the measure of the responsibility imposed upon the Government to do their part in assisting General Gordon to carry his dangerous mission to a successful conclusion. The Prime Minister said last night that the Government had discharged their responsibility to the utmost. I take leave to traverse the right honorable gentleman's statement, and say that the Government have not discharged one bit of that responsibility. I assert that, as it was the duty of the Government to have seconded to the very utmost the mission of General Gordon, they ought, at the outset, to have considerably increased their force in Egypt, and to have moved British troops up the Nile. The first appearance of General Gordon in Upper Egypt prevented disturbances. He found a state of semi-order, and he pacified it completely. There can be no doubt that if it had been known that the British force had been increased, and that British troops had been moved up the Nile, the first effect of the mission, instead of being transient, would have been permanent. More than that, the season was exceptionally favorable for the movement of troops, and that movement would have been perfectly consistent with the pacific character of the mission of General Gordon. Material support is not out of character with a mission which is essentially pacific; and if any supporter or member of the Government should deny that assertion, I have only to point to the conduct of the Government with respect to Suakin completely to make out my case. The conduct of the Government in that case was to give material support to the efforts to restore order in that part of the Soudan—and why should material support have been limited to Suakin? I submit that that was the first failure of the Government to recognize their responsibility to General Gordon. Then the Government had another warning. Soon after General Gordon arrived at Khartoum he made an urgent appeal to the Government to send him Zebehr Pacha. I have never been one of those who have been disposed to blame the Government for not acceding to that request. I think not only that Zebehr is a man with whom no British Government ought to have any connection, but I believe that he would have done his best to assassinate General Gordon when he got to Khartoum. But the Prime Minister, curiously enough, told the House last night that he thought General Gordon was right in asking for Zebehr, and said he had been disposed to go almost any length to meet the request, and gave an extraordinary reason for not doing what he said was right, and what he was prepared to go almost any length to do. He said, "I did not do what I thought I should do, because I feared I might be placed in a minority."

Let me compare the Government's treatment of Suakin with their treatment of General Gordon. What is Suakin? Suakin is a dirty, wretched, plague-stricken port on the Red Sea, of no value to Egypt, or to anyone but the Soudanese tribes. What is General Gordon? The Prime Minister told us last night that General Gordon is "a great personality"; more than that, he is the envoy of the Queen; more than that, Gordon's life is invaluable to his country, because a nation does not turn out Gordons by the dozen every day. The Prime Minister was angry with the right honorable gentleman last night because he said that the Government ought to have given material support to General Gordon. But why was it wrong to do that for General Gordon, a great personality, the envoy of the Queen, a man invaluable to his country, which you did so lavishly and so uselessly for this dirty port on the Red Sea? For this port the Government shed blood in torrents, they poured out money like water; but for Gordon they refused to advance one British soldier one single step, or to provide him with one single half-penny of money. In comparing the treatment of Suakin by the Government with the treatment of General Gordon, the logic of facts is hopelessly fatal to their position. As I listened to the Prime Minister last night a curious idea came into my head. I thought of the singularly different—the inexplicably different—manner in which different individuals appeal to his sympathies. I compared his efforts in the cause of General Gordon with his efforts in the cause of Mr. Bradlaugh. I remembered the courage, the perseverance, the eloquence, he displayed and the amount of time of the House of Commons which was consumed by the Government in their desperate adherence to that man. If the hundredth part of those invaluable moral qualities bestowed upon Mr. Bradlaugh had been given to the support of a Christian hero, the success of General Gordon's mission would have been at this time assured. And this struck me as most remarkable when the Prime Minister sat down—that the finest speech he ever delivered in the House of Commons was in support of Mr. Bradlaugh, and the worst speech he ever delivered, was, by common consent, in the cause of the Christian hero. That is an instructive historical contrast. The Prime Minister made a most extraordinary remark last night which reveals the incapacity of the present Government for dealing with those difficult commotions abroad. He said, in reply to the right honorable gentleman who questioned the wisdom of the Government in not sending troops to Berber, "What would be the use of sending a few British troops?" Well, for fifty years the Prime Minister has been more or less in the service of the Crown, and has been identified with some of the most glorious exploits of British valor, and after all that experience he gets up and asks the House of Commons what would be the value of a few hundred British soldiers? Surely, when he asked this question he must have been thinking, not of the early and military glories with which he was connected, but of the unfortunate events of Laing's Nek and Majuba Hill. For my part, I think the value of a few hundred soldiers at Berber would have been great. They would in the first place have opened up the road across the desert. Their very passing across the desert would have produced an effect; it would have confirmed the wavering, given hope to the fugitives, and saved the garrisons. It would have been very apparent to everyone in that part of the world that those British troops were merely the precursors of others, and it would have prevented the present isolation of General Gordon. The troops were ready and anxious to go; General Graham was anxious to go. I do not know whether the Prime Minister is aware of it, because in his exalted position he may be denied the knowledge open to humbler men—but the feeling of the troops coming away from Suakin was one of utter and intense disgust. Because those brave men, who whenever they perform deeds of fame are exposed to the jeers and jibes of honorable gentlemen opposite—these brave men were filled with the conviction that all their bravery had gone for nothing, and, more than that, that they had slaughtered brave and gallant foes for no purpose whatever. The whole of that force was only too anxious, too desirous, by opening up the road to Berber, to place something tangible on record as the result of their exertions. The Prime Minister argued in a most extraordinary manner that he and his colleagues had no longer any duties to perform toward the Soudan garrison. He sent General Gordon to get the garrisons out; General Gordon had failed; and, really, he and his colleagues cannot any further be bothered with the matter. That was the whole drift of his speech, because the House noticed how he descended upon the right honorable baronet, and asked which garrisons were to be rescued—that of Gondola, Bahr Gazette, or what others? Your duty is to recognize the claims of every one of them. They were recognized by a unanimous House of Commons when General Gordon was sent out. I adhere to that assertion. It was the duty of General Gordon to rescue them when you sent him out, and the duty of rescuing them lies heavily upon this country, that placed them in peril by abandoning the Soudan. At any rate, there is one duty, and that is the duty of England to support her envoy. The position of an envoy is sacred not so much to the country to which he is sent, because that may be an uncivilized country, but sacred to the country which sends him out, and essentially sacred when that envoy is placed in a position of peril in a distant land. The fear to go to war in support of an envoy is a certain indication of a decaying empire, and the abandonment of an envoy by a British Government, with the sanction of a British Parliament, is the sure sign of a falling state.

SOURCE: A speech delivered in the House of Commons, 13 May 1884. *Speeches of the Right Honourable Lord Randolph Churchill, M.P. 1880–1886* (London: Longmans, Green and Co., 1889), 420–26.

Excerpt from *In Relief of Gordon*
LORD WOLSELEY

[It was Lord Wolseley who was finally charged to lead the unsuccessful mission to relieve General Gordon under siege in Khartoum.]

Tuesday 24th Febry.

Gordon says in Vol. III of his journal at date of 6–10–84 'The appearance of one British Soldier or Officer here settles the question of relief vis-a-vis the towns people for then they know, I have not told them lies.'

At several places in his Journal he speaks very contemptuously of Artillery—under date of 24–9–84 he says—'I can say I owe three defeats in this country to having Artillery with me which delayed our march, & it was the Artillery with Hicks which in my opinion did for him.' Sent off another copy of my instructions to Brackenbury by special messenger from *Abu Dom* and have ordered Rundle at *Korosko* to send one through that desert to him. These Ababdehs show rather an indecision of purpose since the fall of *Khartoum* for the cure of which I must now look to a victory by Graham over Osman Digma. Had a grand function in the evening with the Mudir when I presented him with the Commission signed by the Queen for his Knighthood as K.C.M.G. He wore a most gorgeous uniform as a Pasha with epaulettes & aiguillet[te]s &c. Sheik Saleh was present looking cunning and cruel as usual. I have telegraphed to Baring saying that I think it would be better to make me Governor-General of the Soudan, as all my acts & proclamations would have much greater weight if emanating from the Governor-Genl., than simply from the General in command of H.M.'s Army: besides making me Governor-General would emphasize the inauguration of a new policy. I believe the approaching Soudan war to be a hideous mistake, the outcome of Mr. Gladstone's foolish policy in Egypt, beginning with that wicked, cruel and senseless bombardment of *Alexandria*. As a soldier I was very glad to go to Egypt in 1882 and simply as a soldier nothing could suit me better than this coming autumn campaign in the Soudan, but as an Englishman fully alive to our military weakness, to the almost impossibility of even carrying on the routine duties of peace with our existing Army establishments, I look upon this coming campaign with dislike. The civilian gentlemen who rule from Downing St. are prepared to rush into any war when by doing so they can retain office, and they do it with a light heart on account of their ignorance, but any soldier who knows our Army as I do can only view a serious war with dread, and this war in the Soudan is likely to be the most serious war we have undertaken since the idiotic cabinet of 1854 declared war against Russia. What makes me take this view is that I cannot foresee where this coming war is to end. If the Mahdi be wise he will retreat before we can tackle him seriously: we shall have spent ten millions & done nothing & when we begin to withdraw we shall very likely have a pack of yelping curs at our heels taking long shots at our retreating troops. The prospect is not a pleasing one to me. The relief of *Khartoum* was a definite, well-defined objective, and when it fell I confess if I had been at home I should have recommended the Cabinet to have withdrawn this Army to *Wady Halfa*. Indeed I think even now that would be the wisest course. I would tomorrow willingly say to France either consent to our terms as regards the debt &c. or take over the Govt. of the Country yourselves and send your troops there to relieve ours. As I have over and over told our Authorities, the Cape of Good Hope is a much more important place to us than Egypt. I argued this out with Northbrook last year, but he would not have my arguments. If you want to control the Suez Canal—the control of which I don't care much about if we hold the Cape strongly—you can do so from Cyprus. Make Famagusta a strong port, also Simondstown & clear out of the Soudan & of Egypt as soon as we can. I am sure this is our true policy having regard to the incompetence of our Army owing to its small numbers, and to the fact that we no longer rule any sea not even the English Channel much less the Mediterranean. Radicalism has reduced us to a second-rate power & we either accept the fact or have the courage to put our Army & Navy on a proper footing. This latter Mr. Chamberlain and all other screw-makers & carpet-makers from Birmingham will never consent to. Our effacement as a first-rate power is therefore a necessary and inevitable sequence. These are what the Tories would call unpatriotic sentiments. They look upon England as if [it?] were still the England that Pitt made it, proud of itself and self-confident. Faith had not died out in the Nation. There was a belief then in God and in the power

and future destiny of England. Now there is no faith except in money &
universal suffrage.

SOURCE: Lord Wolseley, *In Relief of Gordon: The Khartoum Relief Expedition 1884–1885* (1885;
London: Hutchinson, 1967), 152–54.

Excerpt from *Fire and Sword in the Sudan*
RUDOLF C. SLATIN PASHA

[Rudolf Slatin Pasha spent more than a decade as a captive of the Mahdi. *Fire
and Sword in the Sudan* recounts that captivity narrative, a signal part of which
was provided by the delivery of the head of Gordon to his conqueror at the fall
of Khartoum in 1885.]

When Gordon's head was brought to the Mahdi, he remarked he would have
been better pleased had they taken him alive; for it was his intention to
convert him, and then hand him over to the English Government in exchange for Ahmed Arabi Pasha, as he had hoped that the latter would have
been of assistance to him in helping him to conquer Egypt. My own opinion,
however, is that this regret on the part of the Mahdi was merely assumed; for
had he expressed any wish that Gordon's life should be spared, no one would
have dared to disobey his orders.

Gordon had done his utmost to save the lives of the Europeans who were
with him. Colonel Stewart, with some of the Consuls and many of the
Europeans, he had allowed to go to Dongola; but unfortunately the incapable
and disaffected crew of their steamer, the "Abbas," had run her on to a rock in
the cataracts, and had thus given up him and his companions to the treach-
erous death which had been prepared for them. On the pretext that the
Greeks were good men on boats, Gordon had offered them a steamer, on
which it was arranged they should make a visit of inspection on the White
Nile, thus intending to give them an opportunity to escape south to join
Emin Pasha; but they had refused to accept. Being much concerned as to
their safety, Gordon now made another proposal: he ordered all roads leading
toward the Blue Nile to be placed out of bounds after ten o'clock at night; and
he charged the Greeks with watching them, so that they might have a chance
of escaping to a steamer moored close by, in which it was arranged they
should escape; but, owing to a disagreement between themselves as to the
details of the plan, it fell through. I have little doubt in my own mind that

these Greeks did not really wish to leave the town. In their own homes and in Egypt most of them had been very poor, and had held merely subordinate positions; but here in the Sudan many had made their fortunes, and were therefore by no means anxious to quit a country from which they had reaped so great advantages.

Gordon seemed anxious about the safety of every one but himself. Why did he neglect to make a redoubt, or keep within the fortifications, the central point of which might well have been the Palace? From a military point of view I think this is a fair criticism; but probably Gordon did not do so, lest he should be suspected of being concerned for his own safety; and it was probably a similar idea which influenced him in his decision not to have a strong guard at the Palace. He might well have employed a company of soldiers for this purpose; and who would have thought of questioning the advantage of protecting himself? With a guard of this strength, he could easily have reached the steamer "Ismailia," which was lying close to the Palace, scarcely three hundred yards from the gate. Fagarli, the captain, saw the enemy rushing to the Palace. In vain he waited for Gordon; and it was only when the latter was killed, and he saw the Dervishes making for his boat, that he steamed off into midstream, and moved backwards and forwards along the front of the town until he received a message from the Mahdi offering him pardon. As his wife and family and some of his crew were in the city, he accepted the offer and landed; but how sadly had he been deluded. Rushing to his home, he found his son—a boy of ten years old—lying dead on the doorstep, whilst his wife, in her agony, had thrown herself on her child's body, and lay pierced with several lances.

SOURCE: Rudolf C. Slatin Pasha, *Fire and Sword in the Sudan: A Personal Narrative of Fighting and Serving the Dervishes 1879–1895* (London: E. Arnold, 1896), 344–45.

The Siege and Fall of Khartum
MAJOR F. R. WINGATE

[Captivity narratives were an important source for accounts of the Mahdi's role and rule in the Sudan. Father Ohrwalder, who spent ten years in the Mahdi's camp, from 1882 to 1892, was an Austrian priest and the first European to have escaped from the Mahdi after 1885. Major F. R. Wingate (1861–1953), who edited Ohrwalder's narrative, served in the Egyptian army from 1883 and later became director of Egyptian military intelligence, fighting in several battles against the Mahdi; he eventually served as governor-general of the Sudan.]

The surrender of Omdurman fort—Gordon's dispositions for defence—His great personal influence—The night before the assault—The attack and entry of the Dervishes—Gordon's death—The massacre in Khartum—How most of the Europeans died—Ruthless cruelty and bloodshed—The fate of the wives and daughters of Khartum—Ohrwalder's views on the situation in Khartum and the chances of relief by the British Expeditionary Force—His description of the town three months after the fall.

The Mahdi camped on the south side of Omdurman fort, and at once began to direct the siege. The command of his troops was vested in Abu Anga; but he did not dare to send his black troops, who had previously fought in the Egyptian service under Gordon, against Khartum, fearing that, owing to the influence which Gordon had formerly exercised over them, they might desert to him.

Omdurman Fort, which was then under the command of Faragallah Pasha, was soon reduced to great straits, and the Mahdiists threw up trenches, in which they were comparatively safe from the continuous fire. Eventually they succeeded in entrenching themselves between the fort and the river, thus cutting the communications, which Gordon was unable to restore. Consequently, the garrison soon began to starve; but they still fought courageously, and inflicted great loss on the Dervishes. Amongst the latter was a certain emir, named Mohammed Wad el Areik, who, while in the act of laying a gun at Omdurman, was struck in the back of the neck by a bullet. He was visited by the Khalifa Abdullah, who promised that he should recover; but, in spite of this promise, he died the following day.

Faragallah, having now no food left, was obliged to surrender, and thus the Mahdi was enabled to press the siege of Khartum more closely than ever.

The town itself was full of traitors; almost all the important townsmen had written to the Mahdi from time to time, to the effect that they wished to submit to him, and that they believed in him. Gordon was, so to speak, alone in the midst of enemies, but the expected arrival of the English kept the inhabitants from surrendering.

Every day Gordon invented some means of making the people believe that their deliverers were near; he frequently had the walls placarded with announcements that they were very near Khartum, but all his promises came to nothing.

Gordon was almost superhuman in his efforts to keep up hope. Every day, and many and many a time during the day, did he look towards the north from the roof of the palace for the relief which never arrived. He overcame the want of money by issuing paper bonds; but soon the people refused to accept them, and to enforce his order he sent fourteen merchants to the east bank, just in front of the enemy's guns; this he did to frighten them, and when they agreed to accept the bonds he had them brought back to the town. To further strengthen the belief of the people in the speedy arrival of the English, he hired all the best houses along the river bank, and had them prepared for their occupation. He was sure they would come—but when? The time was pressing. How eagerly he searched the distant horizon for the English flag he longed to see, but every day he was doomed to disappointment.

The troops were famine-stricken, and began to lose heart, whilst the enemy without the walls daily grew bolder in anticipation of the plunder they hoped so soon would be theirs. From Buri to Kalakala the Dervishes extended in one unbroken mass, whilst their hundreds of noggaras never ceased beating in Gordon's ears night and day.

The town was closely hemmed in on three sides. Wad Gubara on the north was near enough to shell his palace; and under the hole where the first shot struck the wall Gordon inscribed the date as a remembrance. None of us can realize how heavily his terrible responsibilities weighed upon him. Despair had seized upon the town. The unreliable nature of the Sudanese was a constant source of anxiety to him, and enhanced the critical situation. Those in charge of the biscuits and dhurra stole quantities of it on every possible occasion, and tried to deceive Gordon by assuring him that there were millions of okes in store, when in reality there was almost nothing. In their endeavours to enrich themselves they forgot that they were only preparing the way for their ultimate destruction.

The officer in charge of the dhurra store was arrested and brought before a Court of Inquiry; but Gordon had to point out to those who were making the investigation that they should not inquire too critically into the matter. He knew all that had taken place, but he was powerless to stop it. He won the people's hearts by his generosity; and even to this day all who knew him never cease speaking of his kindness. His endeavours to recompense the Greeks for their honesty are affecting in the extreme. He elaborated numerous plans for their escape. His first intention was to place a steamer at their disposal to convey them to Emin Pasha in Equatoria; and, to avoid ill-feeling and jealousy, he made known his plans to them at a public meeting, remarking that as most of them were natives of the Greek islands, they had necessarily considerable experience of boats and navigation, and that therefore it became their duty to patrol with the steamers on the Blue and White Niles, and watch the enemy's movements; but secretly he warned them that they should be in readiness, as soon as they saw Khartum was lost, to set off and join Emin Pasha.

This plan did not, however, please the Greeks, so Gordon proposed another, which was that, in case of great danger, they should proceed north; and for this purpose he kept a steamer moored off the palace, well stocked with biscuits and other necessaries. To enable them to get their families on board during the night without the other townspeople knowing about it, he gave orders that after 9 P.M. all traffic along the roads leading to the Blue Nile should be stopped, and that no persons were to be allowed out of their houses after that hour. In this way, should the Dervishes enter the town by night, the Greeks could easily escape to the steamer, start down stream, and meet the English. Some of them resolved that, should the Mahdiists effect an entrance, they would forcibly carry off Gordon and put him on board the steamer, for they felt sure he would not leave Khartum of his own accord. Everything was carefully prearranged and considered; and all would have been well but for a disagreement amongst the Greeks themselves, which mainly arose through the phlegmatic and short-sighted conduct of their consul Nicola Leontides.

On that fatal Sunday evening one of the principal Greeks came to the consul and begged him urgently to spend that night on the steamer. The consul refused, arguing that there was no imminent danger, and that he was sure the troops could hold out a few days longer. The Greek argued in vain, and at length left him; and that was the last time they saw each other.

That night proved to be the last night on earth for Gordon and thousands of others. While they were sleeping soundly, and dreaming perhaps of the arrival of the English, the Dervishes were creeping like snakes towards the parapets. It is hardly likely Gordon could have slept. For two days he had remarked considerable movement in the Mahdi's camp; he had observed numbers of boats passing to and fro on the White and Blue Niles. He could not have doubted that the Mahdi was preparing to strike the final blow. And so it proved, for he was planning the assault on Khartum. He had received news of the destruction of his troops at Abu Klea and Abu Kru, and of the advance of the English.

The Mahdi was convinced that if one Englishman reached Khartum his chance of success was gone, and that he must retire to Kordofan. That was his reason for attempting the assault. Gordon, on the other hand, expected the arrival of the English at any moment; and while he was counting the hours which might elapse ere they could reach him, his enemies were shaking their lances with which they should pierce him.

The moon had gone down, deep obscurity reigned; and now the Dervishes stealthily advanced in perfect silence towards that portion of the defence which had been destroyed during the high Nile, and which, as the river receded, had left an open space in which ditch and parapet had almost disappeared. Here there was little to impede their entry; and the Dervishes, shouting their wild battle-cry, dashed in wild disorder over this open ground.

Farag Pasha commanded the whole of this portion of the defences. Many people in the Sudan, more especially those who used to be in the Government service, say that Farag Pasha betrayed the town; but the fact that he was killed almost immediately after the fall points to his not having done so.

It is a well-known fact that many of the senior officers were wavering, and numbers of Khartum merchants were in correspondence with the Mahdi. It is possible that their action may have assisted the Dervishes. The latter naturally assert that Khartum was captured entirely by force of arms, for any acknowledgment on their part of treachery within the town would tend to detract from the effect of the Mahdi's success. The matter stands thus: the parapet which had been destroyed had never been repaired. This was not Gordon's fault; in his desperate position he could not be everywhere. It is a thousand pities that he had not a few trusty European officers with him. With the exception of this defective portion near the White Nile, the whole line of defence was almost impregnable; the ditch was so deep and the parapet so high that it would have been next to impossible to cross it.

On coming through the open space the Dervishes broke up into two parties. One party dashed along the parapet, breaking all resistance, and slaughtering the soldiers in all directions; the other party made for the town. The inhabitants, roused from their sleep by the shouts of the Arabs and the din of rifle-shots, hurried out, anticipating what had occurred. Like a pent-up stream suddenly released, over 50,000 wild Dervishes, with hideous yells, rushed upon the 40,000 inhabitants of Khartum, besides the 5,000 soldiers— all that was left of the 9,000 at the commencement of the siege. The only cry of these fanatical hordes was "Kenisa! Saraya!" ("To the church! the palace!")—*i.e.* the Austrian Mission Church and Gordon's palace, where they expected to find treasure stored up in the cellars, and priests and sisters.

The surging mass threw itself on the palace, overflowed into the lovely garden, and burst through the doors in wild search for their prey; but Gordon went alone to meet them. As they rushed up the stairs, he came towards them and tried to speak to them; but they could not or would not listen, and the first Arab plunged his huge spear into his body. He fell forward on his face, was dragged down the stairs, many stabbed him with their spears, and his head was cut off and sent to the Mahdi.

Such was the end of the brave defender of Khartum. When I came from El

Obeid to Omdurman I visited Khartum, and went to the palace, where I was shown some black spots on the stairs which they told me were the traces of Gordon's blood.

On Gordon's head being brought to the Mahdi, he appeared to have been much displeased at his death—not because he felt pity for him, but he believed that Gordon might join his army. Had he not done so, he would have imprisoned him and reduced him to slavery. It was much better that Gordon should have died when he did than have remained a captive in the hands of these cruel and fanatical Arabs. Gordon's head was hung on a tree in Omdurman, and the wild multitude rejoiced in heaping curses on it and insulting it.

After the palace, the Mission building was the next principal object on which the wild, plunder-seeking Arabs vented their fury. General Gordon had some time previously hired this building, which was of stone and bomb-proof, and turned it into a powder magazine and ammunition store. The Dervishes killed the guards mounted outside the garden, and then broke in, while others clambered over the high wall. A black who was employed in the Mission garden was lying on the point of death on his mattress in the garden; the Dervishes ended his life by ripping open his body.

The ruthless bloodshed and cruelty exercised by the Dervishes in Khartum is beyond description. I will briefly describe the deaths of the best-known people. Nicola Leontides, the Greek consul, who, on account of his amiable character, was much respected in Khartum, had his hands cut off first, and was then beheaded. Martin Hansal, the Austrian consul, who was the oldest member of the European colony, was alive up till 2 P.M., when some Arabs from Buri, led by his chief kavass, who was on bad terms with him, entered the courtyard of the house, and, on Hansal being summoned to come down, he was at once beheaded. At the same time Mulatte Skander, a carpenter who lived with him, was killed in the same way. His body, together with that of his dog and parrot, were then taken out, alcohol poured over them, and set fire to. After a time, when the body had become like a red-hot coal, it was thrown into the river.

Human blood and ruthless cruelty alone seemed to satisfy the Dervishes. The Austrian tailor, Klein, on making the sign of the cross, had his throat cut from ear to ear with a knife which was used to slaughter animals, and his life-blood was poured out before the eyes of his horror-stricken wife and children. Not satisfied with the death of the father, they seized his son, a youth of eighteen, and, burying their lances in his body, they stretched him out at his mother's feet, a corpse! They then took counsel as to how they should kill the next son, a lad of fifteen. But by this time the mother, a daughter of Cattarina Nobili, of Venice, was worked up into a state of mad despair. Seizing her son of five years old with her right hand, while she held her suckling babe to her breast with her left, she fought against these murderers like a tigress being robbed of her young, and they could not wrest her children from her; but they seized her daughter, a girl of eighteen, who became the wife of an Arab.

The son-in-law of Doctor Georges Bey (who had been killed in the Hicks's expedition) was roused from sleep by the noise of the Arabs breaking in. He rose from his bed, and, making the sign of the cross, rushed to the window, where he shouted "Aman" ("Security of life"); but a bullet struck him in the forehead, and he fell dead at the feet of his young wife. The Dervishes forced their way into the house, broke in the door of the room where the dead man lay stretched out on the bed, killed another Greek, and clove open the head of the little son, a boy of twelve years of age, with an axe, scattering his brains over his unfortunate mother, who was sitting beside him. She saved her little son of six months old by saying he was a girl. The mother herself was not killed, as she was with child, but she was reserved to become the wife of Abderrahman Wad en Nejumi.

Aser, the American consul, fell down dead on seeing his brother beheaded before his eyes. The males of most of the Coptic families were massacred, but the women were spared. I know several of these poor women who, from continuously weeping over the cruelties of that terrible 26th of January, have become quite blind.

Those men whose lives were spared have to thank Providence that either they fell into the hands of those less cruel than their comrades, or that they did not quit their houses for two days, at the end of which time the first wild passions of these murderers had cooled down.

The fate of seven Greeks was a sad one; these were all together in one house, for, through a merciful Providence, they had fallen into less cruel hands. It was past noon, and they were rejoicing at having escaped from the general massacre. Then a certain George Clementino entered. This Clementino had originally come from El Obeid, and had frequently been sent by the Mahdi with messages to Gordon, and when he returned from Khartum to the Mahdi, the latter treated him with much favour.

When the capture of Khartum was known in Omdurman, Clementino hastened to the town, with the intention of rescuing any compatriots he could find, and he soon heard of the seven surviving Greeks. Full of delight at their safety, he congratulated them, and advised them to make their way to the house of Manoli, the Greek who, with his wife and nephew, had escaped by concealing themselves in the dove-cot.

It was Clementino's intention to collect all the Greeks here, and then take them to Omdurman. The seven Greeks trusted to their compatriot's name and influence to protect them, but Dervishes were on the watch to stop them. As they were following Clementino to Manoli's house, which was only a short distance off—indeed, they had only gone a few steps—they were met by a party of Ahmed Sharfi's Danagla, who were searching the streets filled with the dead and wounded, with the object of giving the *coup de grâce* to any who might still be alive.

When these murderers espied the party of white men from a short distance, they shouted, "Look! Some of these dogs, these unbelievers, are still alive," and, full of anger, they rushed upon the unfortunate Greeks. Clementino begged and prayed that they might be spared, but they were beheaded before his eyes, and he himself barely escaped with his life. Pale, terror-stricken, and trembling, he fled to Omdurman, and for some months he lay on the point of death, so great had been the shock of witnessing the massacre of his fellow-countrymen.

Numbers even of women and little children were not spared, and the torture which the survivors had to undergo, to force them to produce their money, are scarcely credible. Ibrahim Pasha Fauzi (the favourite of Gordon) was tied for several days to a date-palm and flogged till he gave up all his money. The old widow of Mustafa Tiranis was flogged almost to death. She was a rich Circassian lady, and had supplied Gordon with money in donkey loads, and had been decorated by him with the Khartum medal.

Slaves were most cruelly tortured, beaten, and forced to disclose the hiding-places of their masters' money and treasures. The Shaigieh tribe in particular was most harshly dealt with; this was the only tribe which remained loyal to the Government, and even eight days after the fall of Khartum, if a Shaigi was seen, he was instantly killed; hence the Dervish proverb, "Esh Shaigi, Wad er Rif el Kelb ma yelga raha fil Mahadieh" ("The Shaigi, the Egyptian, *i.e.,* the white one, the dog, no rest shall he find in Mahdieh").[1]

Farag Pasha did not live long after the fall; some still said he had betrayed the town, and the Dervishes were furious with him because, some ten days before the assault, during one of the preliminary attacks, he had shot Abdullah Wad en Nur, an emir of great repute, and much beloved by the Ansar. Farag was summoned before Wad Suleiman, who ordered him to produce all the money he had. Incensed at his treatment and at the charge of treachery, he fell into a hot dispute with Wad Suleiman, who had him forthwith beheaded as an unbeliever and an obstinate man. If he was really a traitor, he richly deserved his fate; but if not, his death was that of a brave man.

---

1. According to the Mahdi doctrine, dogs, being considered impure animals, are destroyed; but this subject will be considered in another chapter.

When the massacre in Khartum was at an end, the Mahdi himself gave orders that the survivors should be spared, but the wild fury of these fanatical Arabs had been satiated at the cost of 10,000 lives; the streets were filled with headless corpses, which were left unburied until the plunder had been distributed.

The whole of Khartum was now divided up amongst hundreds of emirs and their mukuddums. Every emir planted his flag in the midst of the quarter captured by his men, and then the work of collecting the survivors was begun. Ahmed Wad Suleiman ordered all free women and slaves to be brought to the beit el mal; here the young and good-looking fair women were locked up in a separate enclosure, the good-looking, unmarried Sudanese girls in another zariba, and in a third were placed black slave girls, suitable as concubines.

It is deplorable to think that at such a time were found certain of the well-known townsmen of Khartum who assisted the Dervishes to lay hands on all the prettiest girls in Khartum; through their intermediary, many of the women who had cut off their hair, and in other ways concealed their beauty and sex by disguising themselves as men, fell into the hands of the Ansar.

May God's curse fall on those wicked traitors who delivered up these unfortunates in order to gain favour with the Mahdi! What sufferings these miserable creatures underwent when they lay huddled together like cattle in a pen, awaiting their cruel fate! Many of them were still in their silken robes, all bespattered with the blood of their husbands and children, and there they lay, awaiting their turn to become the wives of those who had murdered their husbands and their offspring!

The first selection was, of course, made for the Mahdi, who took for himself all girls of five years of age and upward, who, in a few years' time, he would take to his harem; then came the turn of the three Khalifas, whose selections were made especially under the direction of Wad Suleiman; then followed the emirs, each in the order of his rank, and one by one they made their choice of these wretched women. Those that were left were distributed amongst the Ansar. Then were openly enacted sights which would have melted hearts of stone. The weeping and lamentation of the white women, as they prayed and besought the pity of their masters, the rough jeering and foul replies of these monsters, it is all too horrible to relate.

The old unmarried women were given a few rags with which to partially cover themselves, and were sent to Nejumi's camp, where they were kept in captivity for a few days. All suffered the agonies of hunger and thirst, heat and cold. Little babies, not yet weaned, were left to die of hunger, and for weeks after the fall young widowed mothers could be seen wandering naked through the market at Omdurman, begging. Some poor woman brought forth children in the streets, and there they would lie, mother and child, naked and foodless, until death came as a happy release from their misery.

The Mahdi had directed that all gold and silver jewellery, precious stones and ornaments, should be collected in the beit el mal; but of course most of this had already found its way into the pockets of the emirs; and, in spite of the Mahdi's most stringent orders, and his threats that those who concealed the booty would be punished in hell-fire, still the Ansar kept the loot and risked the eternal flames.

Considerable quantities of treasure were, however, collected in the beit el mal, for Khartum was wealthy, and the women especially had quantities of gold and silver ornaments; but so much loot soon reduced the currency, and a sovereign was now valued at two and a half dollars. Every penny was extracted from the prisoners by the lash, and all were reduced to complete beggary. They were then sent to Nejumi's camp; and on their way thither they were again beaten and searched. They were kept a few days longer as prisoners in that camp, and then those who had the fortune to meet with relations or friends who had been released would weep together over their wretched state. The confusion was terrible. Women wandered through the camps in search of their children, children sought their parents; but how few ever found them!

After a time all the prisoners were permitted to live in Omdurman, where they eked out a miserable existence by begging; but hunger, disease, and all the sufferings they had undergone carried off hundreds. For days they remained naked, scorched under the burning sun by day, and perished with cold at night. How could people accustomed to ease and comfort bear up against such hardships?

When at length all the houses in Khartum had been evacuated, the furniture, &c., removed, and their owners robbed of all they possessed, the effects were sold from the beit el mal at a low price. The various coloured stuffs were cut up and utilised for making the patches on the jibbehs (Dervish uniform), gold brocades were purchased by those who knew their real value for a mere trifle, and the gold melted down and made into ornaments. Mirrors and looking-glasses were chopped in pieces with axes, and valuable china and pottery articles, which might have been sold for much, were smashed in pieces. The beautiful Khartum gardens were divided up amongst the chiefs; the Khalifa Abdullah became the possessor of Gordon's garden, Khalifa Sherif took that of the Roman Catholic Mission, and Khalifa Ali Wad Helu became owner of Albert Marquet's. Every emir selected the best house he could find, and there he installed himself with his wives and slaves; while the Ansar took the houses of the poorer Copts and Egyptians. But Omdurman, and not Khartum, was now considered the Dervish capital.

Intoxicated by their success, and insatiable in their desire for women and plunder, the Dervishes had forgotten altogether about the English, for whom Gordon had waited so long. How cruel is fate! Two days after the fall, on the 28th of January, 1885, two steamers were seen slowly making their way along the western shore of Tuti Island.

Khartum and Omdurman were electrified; a consultation was quickly held, and it was at once decided to prevent their landing. The English could be seen searching in all directions for some sign to show them that Gordon was still alive; but the only answer they got was the rain of thousands of bullets fired from thousands upon thousands of rifles and guns at Omdurman and Fort Mukrun. All rushed to the river bank. The women, seizing sticks and waving them over their heads, shrieked and yelled like hyenas, "Mót lil Inglez!" ("Death to the English!") and they were prepared to rush at them with their sticks if they attempted to land. When the English saw this, they could have had little doubt as to what had happened; they turned back and disappeared. The rage of the Dervishes at their departure was unbounded. They rained bullets and shell after them; but they were soon out of sight.

Let us now consider for a moment the chances of success of the English relief expedition. The defeat at Abu Klea struck terror into the Mahdiists gathered round Khartum; the arrival of some wounded men at Omdurman added to the general alarm. Had twenty redcoats arrived at Khartum, it would have been saved. Their presence would have given fresh courage to the inhabitants; and confident of their approaching deliverance, they would have striven might and main to hold out longer. General Gordon, assisted by the advice and energy of a few English officers, would have completely regained his influence. It is true, indeed, that the soldiers were weary of the long siege and continual fighting, and they had lost all faith in Gordon's repeated promises that the English were coming. They became heart-broken and in despair; but Khartum was not for long in the state of distress which prevailed in El Obeid before that town fell. In Khartum they had only been eating gum for a few days previous to the fall, while in El Obeid they had existed on it for months, and had practically nothing else to live upon.

Had the Khartum people but seen one Englishman with their own eyes, they would have taken fresh courage, and would in all probability have held out for another month, until the relief for which they had waited so long was a *fait accompli*. The Mahdi would not have dared to assault Khartum; and even if he had, it is most probable he would have been beaten back. Many survivors of Khartum often said to me, "Had we seen one Englishman, we should have been saved; but our doubt that the English were really coming, and the feeling that Gordon must be deceiving us, made us discouraged, and we felt that death would be preferable to the life of constant war and daily suffering we were leading during the siege."

The unaccountable delay of the English was the cause of the fall of Khartum, the death of Gordon, and the fate of the Sudan. The Mahdi only made up his mind to attack when he heard that they had delayed at Gubat. He did not begin to cross over his troops till the 24th of January, and it was not till Sunday night that the crossing was complete. He could not have attacked earlier than he did. When the first news of his defeat at Abu Klea reached him he wished to raise the siege and retire to Kordofan. If the English had appeared at any time before he delivered the attack he would have raised the siege and retired. Indeed, it was always his intention to revisit El Obeid before he made his attack.

Even to the present day people in the Sudan cannot understand the reason for the delay. Some say that the English general was wounded at Abu Klea, and was lying insensible, and that those who were acting for him did not dare to undertake any operations until he was sufficiently recovered to be able to give his own orders.

The Sudanese wondered why Europeans, who generally take precautions for every eventuality, should not have done so in this case. Others thought that Kashm el Mus Pasha must have urged the English to attack the Arabs about Metemmeh and Shendi, in revenge for the persistency with which they had attacked and harassed the steamers. The above are only some of the many reasons by which the Sudanese seek to explain the delay after the battle of Abu Klea.

When the English were convinced that Khartum had fallen, they retreated north. Once the town had fallen, the little English fighting force was in the gravest peril; the Mahdi had now his entire force at his disposal to combat them. He at once despatched Nejumi and a large number of his best emirs with a large force; and had not the English already retreated before he reached Metemmeh, they could not have escaped.

The Mahdi was furious when he heard that the English, who had killed such numbers of his best troops, had retired; and, though the latter failed in their object, still their bold attempt to snatch the prey from the lion's mouth must remain for ever a grand exploit. The bravery of the English in advancing on Khartum with such a small number of men is always a source of wonder to the Sudanese. But, alas, what a useless sacrifice of blood and money! The relief came too late.

The memory of Gordon, the heroic defender of Khartum, is still held in respectful remembrance in the Sudan. His bravery, generosity, and voluntary self-sacrifice have won the admiration of his bitterest enemies. It is the common saying amongst Moslems, "Had Gordon been one of us, he would have been a perfect man." I will now give a slight sketch of the events subsequent to the fall, and the fate of the town.

After the retreat of the English, the new masters of Khartum settled down and made themselves comfortable. The Ashraf, *i.e.* the Mahdi's relatives, especially made themselves at home in the best houses and gardens, the best dancers entertained them by night, and they lived a life of ease and luxury. After the death of the Mahdi, which occurred on the 22nd of June, 1885, his successor, the Khalifa Abdullah, looked on the prosperity of Khartum with jealous eyes.

When I arrived in Khartum from El Obeid in April 1886, I visited every part of the town, and examined it most carefully; very few houses had been destroyed, and the town was thickly populated. I also visited the lines of defence between the Blue and White Niles, they extended about six kilometres. The impression I gathered from the appearance of the ditch, which at that time had been much damaged by the heavy rains, was that it could not have been crossed, except near the White Nile where it was quite choked up with mud and sand. At various points along the line there were strongly-built forts manned with guns, and a little in rear of the parapets were high structures which commanded the ditch; behind every loophole were small mud shelters, evidently made by the troops to protect themselves from the cold and strong winds.

The Messalamieh gate was built of burnt bricks and cement and was then in a good state, but the iron gate lay unopened against the side of the ditch. I counted about 150 bodies along the parapet; there they lay, shrivelled up like mummies, while rats and mice had made their homes in them. In one place I saw two bodies tied together by the feet, they had evidently been killed in this position. It was impossible to distinguish the Egyptians from the blacks, for the sun had burnt up and shrivelled the skin into one black colour. Here, where there had been such bustling activity, now only the stillness of the tomb prevailed. As one walked along, lizards and other reptiles would creep from beneath the skeletons and dart off to take refuge under others.

I strolled on from the Messalamieh gate to the European cemetery. Here what desolation and desecration met my eyes! The crosses had been smashed to pieces and lay strewn about in little bits. Graves had been dug up and the bodies pulled out. I recognised from their clothes three who had died in January 1881. The grave of Bishop Comboni, who had died on the 11th of October, 1881, and had been buried in the Mission garden, had also been opened, but the obelisk erected to his memory by the townspeople of Khartum had not been destroyed. The church bells had been pulled down, but lay there in the garden undamaged.

Shortly after my visit, Khartum was reduced to ruins. The Khalifa Abdullah, jealous of the Ashraf, who had completely established themselves in the town, and whose actions he could not therefore sufficiently supervise, determined to order its evacuation. In August the command was given to all to quit the town within three days; it was carried out at once, and on the fourth day the destruction of Khartum began. Houses were pulled down, the wood of the windows, balconies, and doors was transported to Omdurman, and within a very short time the whole place was in ruins; the burnt bricks were for the most part brought to Omdurman; the only buildings which were spared were the Arsenal, in which work still continues to be done, Gordon's palace, and the Mission house. In fact, Khartum is now nothing but a heap of mud ruins, here and there a wall is left standing, everywhere large prickly thorn bushes have sprung up and cover as with a veil the sad remnants of the once thriving and populous metropolis of the Sudan.

SOURCE: Chapter 8 in *Ten Years' Captivity in the Mahdi's Camp*, from the original manuscripts of Father Joseph Ohrwalder (London: Sampson Low, Marston, 1892), 148–72.

Act the Fifth: The End

JOHN BUCHAN

[John Buchan was a chronicler and novelist of the turn-of-the-century years of the British Empire. His novels, such as *The Thirty-Nine Steps* and *Greenmantle,* anticipate the spy/thriller narrative that was inaugurated around that time. In *Gordon at Khartoum* he provides a generically tragic account of Gordon's end in the Sudan.]

Abu Klea was fought on January 17, and the news of it brought consternation to the Mahdi's camp. The sword of the infidel had proved more potent than the sword of the Prophet. A salute of 101 guns was ordered on January 20 to proclaim a victory, but this was only to delude the people of Khartoum, for in the camp itself there was lamentation. Gordon on that day saw through his telescope a multitude of weeping women and guessed the truth, and presently a spy confirmed it. Mohammed Ahmed called a council of his emirs, and all but one urged a retreat to El Obeid and the raising of the siege. 'If one Englishman,' they argued, 'has kept us at bay for a year, how much more will these thousands of English, who have defeated our bravest men at Abu Klea, be able to crush us and drive away.' Only Abd-el-Kerim stood out; let them attack Khartoum at once, he said, and there would still be time to fall back if they failed.

For a day or two the dervish council hesitated. News came of another victory of the English and their advance to the Nile bank. The sight of a dozen redcoats would have sent the whole army westward into the desert. But the 21st passed and the Mahdi's scouts reported no British movement, nor on the 22nd or the 23rd. The courage of the dervishes revived and their temper hardened. When at last on the 24th news came that the British were advancing, Abd-el-Kerim's views had prevailed, and it was resolved forthwith to attack the city. Abu Klea had been misrepresented; the infidels were in doubt and fear, for if they had been victorious they would long before have reached Khartoum.

On January 15 Omdurman had capitulated to the enemy, and he was now able to plant guns on the west bank of the White Nile and double the fury of his bombardment. More serious, the river was falling fast, and the trenches and ramparts on the west side of the lines, abutting on the stream, had to be pushed further into the drying mud. But with the loss of Omdurman this became impossible. The river was ceasing to be a defence, and presently it had receded so far that a sand ridge appeared some 300 yards from the east bank. If the enemy landed on this he had only to wade through a shallow lagoon to be inside the lines. A spy carried this news to the Mahdi's camp.

When Gordon wrote the last words in his journal on December 14 he closed his account with the outer world. After that date we have only the fragmentary evidence of the survivors of the garrison, and of prisoners in the dervish camp. By the end of the year the state of the city was desperate indeed. There was no food ration left to issue at the close of the second week of January. Gum was served out and the pith of date-trees, and for the rest the food was lean donkeys and dogs and rats. Dysentery was rife, and the soldiers on the ramparts were almost too weak to stand, their legs swollen, and their bodies distended by gum and water. The spirit had gone out of the stoutest, and even Faragh Pasha advised surrender. But Gordon was adamant. He suffered those civilians who desired it to go to the Mahdi, and many went, but he would permit no weakening in his council of notables. Resistance must be maintained to the end. The news of Abu Klea had for a moment given hope, and he issued daily announcements that the British were coming, would arrive any hour. But when no smoke appeared on the northern horizon the last dregs of resolution were drained from the sick and starving people. 'They will no longer believe me,' he told Bordeini. 'I can do nothing more.' But he did not relax his efforts. Day and night he was on the ramparts, in the streets, in the hospitals, the one vital thing in a place of death and despair.

We have no journal to tell us his thoughts, but we can guess them from the nature of the man. He had become two beings—one ceaselessly busy in his hopeless duties, scanning the distances anxiously for the smoke which would mean relief; the other calm and at ease. On the palace roof at night with the vault of stars above him he found that union with the Eternal which was peace. His life had always hung as loosely about him as an outworn garment, and now the world of space and time had become only a shadow. 'I would,' he had once written to his sister, 'that all could look on death as a cheerful friend, who takes us from a world of trial to our true home.' The communion with the unseen which had been the purpose of all his days was now as much a part of him as the breath he drew. Like the ancient votaries of the Great Mother, he had passed through the bath of blood and was *renatus in aeternum*. His soul was already with the congregation of the first-born.

The letters which Gordon's steamers brought to Gubat on the 21st were dated December 14 and their tone was sufficiently grave. Ten days' time was given as the extreme limit of resistance. There was another message on a scrap of paper: 'Khartoum all right. Could hold out for years'; but this was clearly meant as a device to deceive the enemy, should it fall into his hands. Sir Charles Wilson had no illusions about the need for haste, but his experience had not lain in the leading of men, and his was not the character for bold and decisive action.

Stewart's instructions from Wolseley had been to take Metemmah, which would serve as a base later for the River Column, and to send Wilson on to Khartoum in Gordon's steamers, accompanied by Lord Charles Beresford and part of the Naval Brigade. Wilson now found himself in command of the whole force, and he hesitated about his next duty. When he received Gordon's papers it is clear that he should at once have gone himself, or sent someone, to Khartoum. As it was, he delayed three days in spite of the protests of Gordon's Arab emissaries. The reason is obscure, but it is probable that Beresford was the cause. He was ill at the moment, suffering from desert boils, and he was eager to accompany the relief force, as he had been instructed. News came of an enemy advance from the south, and then of another from the north, and he induced Wilson to use the steamers to make reconnaissances in both directions, in the hope, doubtless, that he would presently be fit for duty. Two and a half days were wasted in a meaningless task.

This delay was the last and the most tragic of the tricks of fate. Had Burnaby lived it is certain that a steamer would have set out for Khartoum on the afternoon of the 21st. Had that been done, it is as certain as such things can be that Gordon would have been saved. It was not till the 24th that the Mahdi decided upon an assault, and it was not till the evening of the 25th that the details were agreed upon. Allowing for the difficulties of the journey, the steamers, had they left on the 21st, would have been in time to convince the hesitating dervishes, and turn them against Abd-el-Kerim's plan; they might even have been in time had they left on the 22nd. This was the view of the Europeans in the Mahdi's camp who were in the best position to know—of Slatin and of Father Ohrwalder. 'Had twenty redcoats arrived in Khartoum,' the latter has written, 'it would have been saved. . . . If the English had appeared any time before he delivered the attack, he would have raised the siege and retired. . . . Many survivors have said to me "Had we seen one Englishman, we should have been saved.'" By such a narrow margin did a great enterprise fail.

Wilson eventually set out on the morning of Saturday the 24th, in two steamers with twenty British soldiers and a few bluejackets—all the troops, at Gordon's request, being clad in scarlet tunics. Misfortune dogged his path. On the evening of the 25th the *Bordein* struck a rock in the Sixth Cataract, which caused a delay of twenty-four hours. Early on the 27th the Shablukah gorge was passed, and that day the voyage continued under heavy rifle fire from both banks. There were Arab cries from the shore that Khartoum had fallen, but they were not believed. Early on Wednesday the 28th, the expedition came in sight of Khartoum beyond the trees on Tuti island, and ran the gauntlet of the batteries at Halfaya. Then they opened the palace and saw through glasses that no flag was flying. The channel at Tuti was one long alley of rifle fire. As they rounded the corner they beheld a wrecked city, with the Mahdi's banners flaunting under the walls, and knew that all was over. They were sixty hours too late.

Wilson could only turn and retreat. The little gimcrack steamers had a perilous journey. Both were wrecked and in danger of capture, and a young officer of the 60th, Stuart-Wortley, set out alone in a boat for Gubat to bring help. On February 1 at dawn Beresford was hailed by a voice from the river, which could only stammer, 'Gordon is killed . . . Khartoum has fallen.' From Gubat the news crossed the desert, and was flashed to a world which for months had drawn its breath in suspense. Queen Victoria at this, as at most times, was the voice of her people. 'She went to my cottage, a quarter of a mile off,' her private secretary wrote to Baring, 'walked into the room, pale and trembling, and said to my wife, who was terrified at her appearance, "Too late!"'

All day on Sunday the 25th there was a movement of Arab troops to the east bank of the White Nile. Wad-el-Nejumi, the commander of the storm-troops, had his camp at Kalakala, a mile south of the defences. That evening, as twilight fell, a boat put off from the western shore, and four figures joined him and his emirs; it was Mohammed Ahmed himself with his three khalifas. The Mahdi blessed the troops and gave them his orders. In the name of God and the Prophet he bade them attack Khartoum in the dark of the night; let them have no fear, for those who fell would go straight to Paradise. The four returned as silently as they had come, and Wad-el-Nejumi unfolded his plans.

One part of the force should attack the western half of the defences, breaking through the gap which the falling river had left on the shore side. The second division should attack on the east between the Messalamieh Gate and Buri, but if the western assault succeeded this section was to hold its hand, side-step to the left, and follow the first division. In front would go the skirmishers, then the main force of spears and swords, and then further riflemen, with the cavalry in reserve on the rear flanks. Bedsteads and bundles of straw were carried to fill up the trenches, if necessary. The Mahdi had left no precautions untaken, for he was nervous about a direct assault, though his emirs had assured him that God had made their path easy and plain.

As soon as the moon set the movement began. In silence the left division crept towards the defences. Now they were at the ramparts, and at that moment a fierce bombardment broke out from every Arab gun around the city. Under this cover it was easy for the left flank of the attack to break through the gap at the river bank, which only three armed barges defended. In a few minutes they were inside the lines, sweeping to the east, and taking the rest of the defences in rear. Swiftly they crossed the space between the lines and Khartoum, a space dotted with cemeteries, magazines and slaughter-houses, and bore down on the helpless city. The post at the Messalamieh Gate, finding its position turned, was compelled to fall back, and through that gate poured the contingent destined for the Buri attack. By four o'clock Khartoum had fallen, and the siege of three hundred and seventeen days was over. Most of the attackers made for the streets and the business of plunder and massacre. But one body, with whom there were no emirs, rushed to the palace, and swarmed in at the garden entrance.

Of Gordon's last doings our accounts are few and bare. It appears that he had spent the day indoors, striving to put resolution into his notables, but in the evening he had examined part of the defences. From the palace roof he had his last search for the steamers that never came. He had seen the Arabs crossing the White Nile and may have guessed what was afoot, for he did not go to bed. The sound of musketry and guns after midnight told him of the attack, but he could do nothing. The end had come, and he was in the hands of God.

The firing drew nearer, and then he heard that dreadful sound which strikes terror into the boldest heart, savage men baying like hounds for lust and blood. Presently there came a tumult in the garden, and the death-cries of his black sentries. He walked to the head of the staircase, dressed in a white uniform, with a sword at his belt, and a revolver in his right hand. The darkness was passing, and the first crimson of dawn was in the sky.

He saw a mob of dark faces and bright spears, and with them no high officer. That he knew meant instant death. Not for him to be taken prisoner and confronted with the Mahdi, with the choice before him of recusancy or martyrdom. He must have welcomed the knowledge. He stood, his left hand resting on his sword-hilt, peering forward as was his fashion. An Arab— Mohammed Nebawi was his name; he fell at the battle of Omdurman— rushed on him, crying 'O cursed one, your time has come,' and struck at him with his spear. Gordon did not defend himself. He turned away with a gesture of contempt, and in a second a dozen spears were in his body, and men were slashing at him with their swords. The hour of his death was about 5:30, when it was almost full dawn.

His slayers cut off his head, and brought it in triumph to the Mahdi's camp. Mohammed Ahmed had wished him to be taken alive, but he bowed to the will of Allah. It was now broad day, and the captive Slatin, sick and anxious, crawled to his tent door. He found a group of shouting slaves, carrying something wrapped in a bloody cloth. They undid the cloth and revealed the head of Gordon, his blue eyes half opened and his hair as white as wool.

'Is not this,' cried one, 'the head of your uncle the unbeliever?'

'What of it?' said Slatin. 'A brave soldier who fell at his post. Happy is he to have fallen; his sufferings are over.'

SOURCE: Chapter 8 in *Gordon at Khartoum* (London: Peter Davies, 1934), 146–59.

―――――

"Fuzzy-Wuzzy"

RUDYARD KIPLING

(Soudan Expeditionary Force. Early Campaigns)

We've fought with many men acrost the seas,
   An' some of 'em was brave an' some was not:
The Paythan an' the Zulu an' Burmese;
   But the Fuzzy was the finest o' the lot.
We never get a ha'porth's change of 'im:
   'E squatted in the scrub an' 'ocked our 'orses,
'E cut our sentries up at Sua*kim*,
   An' 'e played the cat an' banjo with our forces.
      So 'ere's *to* you, Fuzzy-Wuzzy, at your 'ome in the
         Soudan;
      You're a pore benighted 'eathen but a first-class fightin'
         man;
      We gives you your certificate, an' if you want it signed
      We'll come an' 'ave a romp with you whenever you're
         inclined.

We took our chanst among the Kyber 'ills,
   The Boers knocked us silly at a mile,
The Burman give us Irriwaddy chills,
   An' a Zulu *impi* dished us up in style:
But all we ever got from such as they
   Was pop to what the Fuzzy made us swaller;
We 'eld our bloomin' own, the papers say,
   But man for man the Fuzzy knocked us 'oller.
      Then 'ere's *to* you, Fuzzy-Wuzzy, an' the missis and the
         kid;
      Our orders was to break you, an' of course we went an'
         did.
      We sloshed you with Martinis, an' it wasn't 'ardly
         fair;
      But for all the odds agin' you, Fuzzy-Wuz, you broke
         the square.

'E 'asn't got no papers of 'is own,
    'E 'asn't got no medals nor rewards,
So *we* must certify the skill 'e's shown
    In usin' of 'is long two-'anded swords:
When 'e's 'oppin' in an' out among the bush
    With 'is coffin-'eaded shield an' shovel-spear,
An 'appy day with Fuzzy on the rush
    Will last an 'ealthy Tommy for a year.
        So 'ere's *to* you,
Fuzzy-Wuzzy, an' your friends which
           are no more,
    If we 'adn't lost some messmates we would 'elp you to
        deplore.
But give an' take's the gospel, an' we'll call the bargain
        fair,
    For if you 'ave lost more than us, you crumpled up the
        square!

'E rushes at the smoke when we let drive,
    An', before we know, 'e's 'ackin' at our 'ead;
'E's all 'ot sand an' ginger when alive,
    An' 'e's generally shammin' when 'e's dead.
'E's a daisy, 'e's a ducky, 'e's a lamb!
    'E's a injia-rubber idiot on the spree,
'E's the on'y thing that doesn't give a damn
    For a Regiment o' British Infantree!
        So 'ere's *to* you, Fuzzy-Wuzzy, at your 'ome in the
           Soudan;
        You're a pore benighted 'eathen but a first-class fightin'
           man;
An' 'ere's *to* you, Fuzzy-Wuzzy, with your 'ayrick 'ead
           of 'air—
        You big black boundin' beggar—for you broke a British
        square!

SOURCE: In *The Works of Rudyard Kipling* (Hertfordshire: Wordsworth Editions, 1994), 400–401.

─────────

The Graphic Christmas Number, 1887

"True greatness has little, if anything, to do
with rank or power."—*Sir John Lubbock, F.R.S.*

"His life was gentle; and the elements so mixed in him, that
Nature might stand up
and say to all the world, 'This was a man!'"—*Shakespeare.*

"Throughout those 319 days when he held Khartoum by his matchless bravery, we may suppose ourselves present in that chamber of the citadel where, by
rare and fitful snatches, exhausted Nature gained a brief respite from the
terrific strain of the siege. The strong, serene face seems to shine with that
pure peace which breathes through every word of the last postscript written to
his sister, when all hope of succour had fled:—'I am quite happy, thank God;
and, like Lawrence, I have tried to do my DUTY.' Without a comrade, with no
one upon whom he could rely, obliged to see to every department of his
Government himself, compelled to spend most of the day and night on the
roof of the palace, telescope at eye, watching lest the very sentries should
go home to bed, combating at once the enemy at the gates and the enemy
within—what parallel is there for this lonely figure in the history of great
sieges? What endurance, faith, energy, patience can be compared to this?"
—*The Athenæum.*

Amongst the many pithy remarks of this Great Man—perhaps one of the
most unselfish and fearless APOSTLES of DUTY in ancient or modern times—
there is one which should never be forgotten in our daily life. Here are the
grand words of the Christian soldier:—*"There is now not one thing I value in
the world—its honours, they are false: its knick-knacks, they are perishable and
useless. Whilst I live I value God's blessing*—Health, and if you have that, as far
as this world goes, you are rich."

He rests with the little Bible in his hand, the book which was his daily
companion. We see the poor Chinaman, a type of the vast multitude saved
from the cruel "Tae-pings" by Gordon's "Ever Victorious Army." There is the
quiet country church—a reminiscence of his Hampshire home; there are the
boys of Gravesend gutters whom he rescued, clothed, whom he called his
"Kings," and transformed into gallant seamen; there are the wretched Egyptian slaves for whom he toiled; there is the vision of the long-expected aid—
the British soldiers who cut their perilous way through the hordes of the

Gordon's Dream.—The Martyr-Hero of Khartoum.
SOURCE: *The Graphic* (Christmas Number, 1887): 17.

Mahdi, only to arrive too late! there is the figure of the widowed Queen whom he served so well; above all, there is the Saviour in Whom he trusted, and Whose Cross he strove to bear. In this strange, tangled, shadowy background we obtain a glimpse of the troubled panorama which must have flashed through the anxious and weary, worn commander.

THE ANGLO-BOER WAR

INTRODUCTION
The Boer War: Accusations and Apologias
BARBARA HARLOW

FOUGHT FOR NEARLY three years, from October 1899 to May 1902, the Anglo-Boer War was perhaps the last of the major imperial wars. As the nineteenth century turned into the twentieth, global powers would prepare instead for world war. In the meantime, the Boer War—variously known as the Anglo-Boer War, the South African War, a "white man's war," or the second War of [Boer] Independence—cost more than £200 million, and the lives of some 22,000 British, 25,000 Boers, and 12,000 Africans. While prosecuted in the name of British empire in southern Africa, the war effort served no less the interests of international capital and monopoly trade. The war provided as well an extended occasion for discussion of the controversial concomitants of imperialism, domestic support, foreign interventions, and the settlement of scores, both topographic and demographic. From parliamentary speeches to poetic renditions, political cartoons, popular reviews in journals, and music hall revues, the archive of debate was voluminous and involved such literary luminaries as Rudyard Kipling, Arthur Conan Doyle, and Olive Schreiner, and popularizers like H. Rider Haggard and G. A. Henty.

Professional careers—financial, diplomatic, and military—that had developed across the stretches of British imperium were further consolidated in the course and consequences of the war, specifically the careers of Cecil John Rhodes, Sir Alfred Milner, and Major General Horatio Herbert Kitchener. W. T. Stead, influential editor of the *Review of Reviews* and publisher of the Rhodes's *Last Will and Testament* (1902), described his subject as a "very Colossus, [one who] stood astride a continent which was all too small a pedestal for the imperial dimensions of the man" (*Review of Reviews* 13 [1896]). Rhodes himself, in his 1894 speech on "The Native Question," described himself as "responsible for about two millions of human beings." Kitchener, on the other hand, had only recently arrived in South Africa, newly triumphant following his defeat of the Sudanese Mahdist forces at Omdurman in 1898. Milner, in turn, provided the diplomatic back-up for these imperial colleagues. Their critics, however, were no less distinguished and numbered in their ranks South African feminist Olive Schreiner and political economist J. A. Hobson. Schreiner, who knew Rhodes well, described the "political situation" in South Africa in 1896 thus: the "kafir's back and the poor men's enhanced outlay on the necessities of life pay the Monopolist's bribe" (Schreiner and Schreiner, *The Political Situation*, 41). Three years later, she presented *An English–South African's View of the Situation* (1899), in which she "fell to considering, who gains by war?" and concluded that it was neither England nor Africa nor the "great woman" (Victoria), and certainly not the "brave English soldier." J. A. Hobson was just as adamant in his challenge to the policies of the "new Imperialism": "Aggressive Imperialism," he wrote, "which costs the taxpayer so dear, which is of so little value to the manufacturer and trader, which is fraught with such grave incalculable peril to the citizen, is a source of great gain to the investor who cannot find at home the profitable use he seeks for his capital, and insists that his Government should help him to profitable and secure investments abroad" (*Imperialism*, 55).

In other words, the British war effort in southern Africa required support at home, both for the economic outlay and the soldiery that were required. Similar contests had long characterized the propagation of the imperial project—from debates over the East India Company's role in the Indian subcontinent to the proprieties and improprieties of the Crimean War (1854–1856), reports of atrocities in the Belgian Congo, and the vexed rescue mission to General Gordon beleaguered in Khartoum in 1884–1885. The policy debates, expressions of public opinion, and popular protest that marked these imperial crises provide important evidence and documentation of the complex of issues that accompanied the continuation of empire and its discontinuous departures and oppositional practices. The very personnel of empire building and maintenance functioned as well—even alternatively—as prototypes of the public intellectual. Debate was vituperative in autumn 1899, with the buildup to the outbreak of the war. "Shall We Let Hell Loose in South Africa?" was the banner headline of the *Review of Reviews*'s "Topic of the Month" in September 1899. The article questioned priorities: where did the question of the Transvaal, for example, stand relative to the Dreyfus trial in France or with respect to the overcrowded condition of London's poor? In other words, how do politicians secure popular support for an imperial war? "Impressions and Opinions," in the December 1899 issue of the *Anglo-Saxon Review*, compared the South African crisis with those of the Crimean War and the 1857 Mutiny in India, and reminded the policymakers of the disastrous consequences of their previous miscalculations and mistake of underrating the power of the "enemy." Stephen Wheeler, in the same issue, drew a further analogy with the Sikh War of 1845–1846, specifying the "bewilderment of the public mind, the dubious wisdom of people in power, the equivocal victory of troops attacked or attacking at a disadvantage" (221). Empire had now a history, one that posed as much of a threat as it might be said to hold promise—and to hold out promises. Arthur Waugh, the author the following year of "The Poetry of the South African Campaign" (42), also in the *Anglo-Saxon Review*, identified—and castigated—what had become a literary history as well. Pointing to the role of poetry in time of war, he lamented the lost "opportunities of the present campaign." Where once Tennyson had ennobled the Crimean War with "Maud," Rudyard Kipling, the critic complained, had commercialized the South African campaign with "The Absent-Minded Beggar," a poem that was popular from streetcorner to music hall and had indeed served to collect the pennies needed to support the families of the soldiers—"each of 'em doing his country's work"—fighting the Boer.

But what had become of that "country's work"? And for whose country was "Tommy" fighting an imperial war? In Kipling's story "A Sahib's War," the protagonist, an Indian in colonial service in South Africa, it was just that—a Sahib's war. "Do not herd me with these black Kaffirs. I am a Sikh—a trooper of the State," he says, and continues, "It is for Hind that the Sahibs are fighting this war. Ye cannot in one place rule and in another bear service. Either ye must everywhere rule or everywhere obey. God does not make the nations ringstraked. True—true—true!" (*War Stories and Poems*, 163–80). Breaker Morant, of the Australian Bushveldt Carbineers assigned to South Africa, saw it differently still, scapegoated as he was by the empire he fought for. Morant and several of his fellow Australians were court-martialled for shooting prisoners—under orders, they claimed at their trial, from above, from Kitchener himself. Morant was hung for his deeds, but Lieutenant George Witton was released. His account, *Scapegoats of the Empire* (1907), is a narrative of the progressive loss of faith in the imperial mission expressed in the story's opening paragraphs: "When war was declared between the British and Boers, I like many of my fellow-countrymen, became imbued with a warlike spirit, and when reverses had occurred among the British troops, and volunteers for the front were called for in Australia, I could not rest content until I had offered the assistance one man could give to our beloved Queen and the great nation to which I belong" (1). But if the Australians had entered the fray on behalf of Empire, there were Irish volunteers, like John MacBride of the Irish Republican Brotherhood, who saw the South African War as a challenge to Britain's imperial sway. On his return from the Natal front and the siege at Ladysmith, he met Maud Gonne, whom he would eventually marry. Gonne, in *A Servant of the Queen* (1938), remembers the tales that MacBride first told.

> It was so late that it was not worth while for MacBride to go to his lodgings, so he shared Griffiths's bed. Next morning, seated at my writing table he wrote the lecture, supplementing the sparse notes from MacBride's memory. I sat in an armchair, smoking cigarettes and listening. It was great to hear of Irishmen actually fighting England. The capture of General Buller's guns near Tugela was thrilling; the capture of English officers delighted me; the English have imprisoned so many Irishmen that it was good at last to have it the other way around.
>
> "I hope you treated your prisoners decently to give them a good example and show how much more civilised we are than they?" (308–9).

The issue of the treatment of the prisoners was central to public discussion of the war and crucial in mobilizing domestic opposition to its prosecution. Emily Hobhouse, for example, found herself forbidden re-admittance to South Africa as a consequence of her earlier *Report of a Visit to the Camps of Women and Children in the Cape and Orange River Colonies* (1901) and her appeals on behalf of the South Africa Conciliation Committee and the Ladies' Commission on the Concentration Camps. "Will you try," she had pleaded to the addressees of the report, "to make the British public understand the position, and force it to ask itself what is going to be done with these people? . . . If only the English would try to exercise a little imagination—picture the whole miserable scene" (4). Hobhouse's pamphleteering and public speaking were effective in enlisting outrage and indignation in England toward the atrocities committed in the name of war in South Africa, so effective that Millicent Fawcett, best known for her suffragist activism, was sent with an official women's delegation to counter the charges that Hobhouse had leveled. For Fawcett, the assignment was an "interruption" to her work for the enfranchisement of women, but she too had to acknowledge the abuses to the civilian population, Boer women and children, carried out by her countrymen. Fawcett nonetheless argued that the Boer women bore some culpability in the struggle, indicating that the very items with which they had been charitably supplied were put to use in the strife: "We did hear, however, that the Boer women were very expert in using candles as a means of signalling to their friends on commando in the quiet hours of the night." But she goes on, "I for one could not blame them if they did; if we had been in their position, should we not have done the same thing" (157)?

Arthur Conan Doyle, meanwhile, had come to the defense of the British military offensive—including executions, train hijackings, hostage taking, farm burnings, and the use of expansive and explosive (dum dum) bullets (outlawed by the Hague Convention in 1899). *The War in South Africa: Its Cause and Conduct* (1902) claimed to be a full-length representation of the British case: "In view of the persistent slanders to which our politicians and our soldiers have been equally exposed, it becomes a duty which we owe to our national honour to lay the facts before the world" (n.p.). Conan Doyle's research in this project was perhaps not without a certain resemblance to the detective work of his sleuth, Sherlock Holmes, in defense of "national honour" and the protection of a particular rule of law and order—and against the human-rights reporting of Emily Hobhouse and other members of her committees.

And when the war ended, in 1902, the question still remained of whether South Africa would be joined by a "closer union"—or bound together through federated allegiances.

BIBLIOGRAPHY

Amery, L. S., ed. *The Times History of the War in South Africa.* 7 vols. London: Low, Marston and Co., 1900–1909.

Balme, Jennifer Hobhouse. *To Love One's Enemies: The Work and Life of Emily Hobhouse.* British Columbia, Canada: Hobhouse Trust, 1994.

Beresford, Bruce, dir. *Breaker Morant.* Australian, 1980. Film.

Boehmer, Elleke, ed. *South African War?* Special issue of *Kunapipi* 21, no. 3 (1999).

—. *Bloodlines.* Claremont, South Africa: David Philip, 2000.

Churchill, Winston. *London to Ladysmith via Pretoria.* London: Longmans, Green and Co., 1900.

Dickson, W. K-L. *The Biograph in Battle: Its Story in the South African War.* 1901. Wiltshire, England: Flicks Books, 1995.

Doyle, Arthur Conan. *The Great Boer War.* London: Smith, Elder and Co., 1900.

Durbach, Renee. *Kipling's South Africa.* Diep River, South Africa: Chameleon, 1988.

Fawcett, Millicent Garrett. *What I Remember.* London: T. F. Unwin, 1924.

First, Ruth, and Ann Scott. *Olive Schreiner.* London: Andre Deutsch, 1980.

Foden, Giles. *Ladysmith.* London: Faber and Faber, 1999.

Greenwall, Ryno. *Artists and Illustrators of the Anglo-Boer War.* Vlaeberg, South Africa: Fernwood Press, 1992.

Hobhouse, Emily. *Boer War Letters.* Edited by Rykie Van Reenen. Cape Town: Human and Rousseau, 1984.

—. *Report of a Visit to the Camps of Women and Children in the Cape and Orange River Colonies.* London: Friars Printing Association, 1901.

Hobson, J. A. *Imperialism*. London: George Allen and Unwin, 1902; reprint, Ann Arbor: University of Michigan Press, 1965.

Hopkins, Pat, and Heather Dugmore. *The Boy: Baden-Powell and the Siege of Mafeking*. Rivonia, South Africa: Zebra Press, 1999.

"Impressions and Opinions." *Anglo-Saxon Review* 3 (1899): 248–56.

Kipling, Rudyard. *War Stories and Poems*. Oxford: Oxford University Press, 1990.

Koss, Stephen. *The Pro-Boers: The Anatomy of an Antiwar Movement*. Chicago: University of Chicago Press, 1973.

MacBride, Maud Gonne. *A Servant of the Queen*. 1938. Gerrards Cross: Colin Smythe, 1994.

Nasson, Bill. *Abraham Esau's War: A Black South African War in the Cape 1899–1902*. Cambridge: Cambridge University Press, 1991.

Pakenham, Thomas. *The Boer War*. 1979. New York: Avon Books, 1992.

Plaatje, Sol. *Mafeking Diary: A Black Man's View of a White Man's War*. Edited by John Comaroff. London: James Currey, 1990.

Pretorius, Fransjohan. *The Anglo-Boer War 1899–1902*. Cape Town: Struik Publishers, 1998.

Reitz, Deneys. *Commando: A Boer Journal of the Anglo-Boer War*. 1929. Johannesburg: Jonathan Ball, 1998.

Roberts, Brian. *Those Bloody Women: Three Heroines of the Boer War*. London: Murray, 1991.

Sandys, Celia. *Churchill Wanted Dead or Alive: Winston Churchill in the Boer War*. London: Harper Collins, 1999.

Schreiner, Olive. *The Story of an African Farm*. 1883. Parklands, South Africa: AD Donker, 1986.

——. *Thoughts on South Africa*. London: Hodder and Stoughton, 1901.

Schreiner, Olive, and C. S. Cronwright Schreiner. *The Political Situation*. London: T. Fisher Unwin, 1896.

Sibbald, Raymond. *The War Correspondents of the Boer War*. Johannesburg: Jonathan Ball, 1993.

Smith, M. Van Wyck. *Drummer Hodge: The Poetry of the Anglo-Boer War (1899–1902)*. Oxford: Clarendon Press, 1978.

South African Conciliation Committee. *Salient Facts from the Camps' Blue Books: The Official Report on the Concentration Camps*. London: South African Conciliation Committee, n.d.

Spies, S. B. *Methods of Barbarism? Roberts and Kitchener and Civilians in the Boer Republics, January 1900–May 1902*. Cape Town: Human and Rousseau, 1977.

Waugh, Arthur. "The Poetry of the South African Campaign." *Anglo-Saxon Review* 7 (1900): 42–58.

Wheeler, Stephen. "Sikhs and Boers: A Parallel." *Anglo-Saxon Review* 3 (1899): 221–30.

Witton, Lieut. George. *Scapegoats of the Empire: The True Story of Breaker Morant's Bushveldt Carbineers*. 1907. London: Angus and Robertson, 1982.

————

Excerpt from *An English–South African's*
View of the Situation

OLIVE SCHREINER

[Olive Schreiner (1855–1920) is perhaps best known for her novel *The Story of an African Farm* (1883) and her essay "Woman and Labour" (1911), as well as her association with Havelock Ellis in London. She was an ardent critic of British designs on her native South Africa, as a result of which she broke off her friendship with Cecil J. Rhodes. With her husband, C. S. Cronwright, she also wrote *The Political Situation* (1896), which anticipated the outbreak of the Anglo-Boer War in 1899.]

If it be asked, why at this especial moment we feel it incumbent on us not to maintain silence, and what that is which compels our action and speech, the answer may be given in one word—WAR!

The air of South Africa is

Heavy with Rumours;

inconceivable, improbable, we refuse to believe them; yet again and again they return.

There are some things the mind refuses seriously to entertain, as the man who has long loved and revered his mother would refuse to accept the assertion of the first passer-by that there was any possibility of her raising up her hand to strike his wife or destroy his child. But much repetition may at last awaken doubt, and the man may begin to look out anxiously for further evidence.

We English South Africans are stunned; we are amazed; we say there can be no truth in it. Yet we begin to ask ourselves, "What means this unwonted tread of armed and hired soldiers on South African soil? Why are they here?"

"Across the Dark Continent." Gippy. "Bravo, Cape!" Tommy. "Bravo, Cairo!" SOURCE: *Punch* (6 December 1899). [In September 1898 Major General Horatio Kitchener defeated the Khalifa's army at the Battle of Omdurman (Sudan) and retook Khartoum. In December 1899, following the decisive confrontation with the French at Fashoda, Kitchener was appointed chief of staff of the British army in South Africa.]

And the only answer that comes back to us, however remote and seemingly impossible, is—WAR!

To-night we laugh at it, and to-morrow when we rise up it stands before us again, the ghastly doubt—war—! War, and in South Africa! War—between white men and white! *War!*—Why?—Whence is the cause?—For whom?—For what?—And the question gains no answer.

We fall to considering, who gains by war?

Has our race in Africa and our race in England interests so diverse that any calamity so cataclysmic can fall upon us as war! Is any position possible that could make necessary that mother and daughter must rise up in one horrible embrace, and rend, if it be possible, each other's vitals? . . . Believing it impossible we fall to considering who is it gains by war?

There is peace to-day in the land; the two great white races, day by day, hour by hour, are blending their blood, and both are mixing with the stranger. No day passes but from the veins of some Dutch South African woman the English South African man's child is being fed; not a week passes but the birth cry of the English South African woman's child gives voice to the Dutchman's offspring; not an hour passes but on farm and in town and village Dutch hearts are winding about English,

And English about Dutch.

If the Angel of Death should spread his wings across the land and strike dead in one night every man and woman and child of either the Dutch or the English blood, leaving the other alive, the land would be a land of mourning. There would be not one household nor the heart of an African born man or woman that would not be weary with grief. We should weep the friends of our childhood, the companions of our early life, our grandchildren, our kindred, the souls who have loved us and whom we have loved. In destroying the one race he would have isolated the other. Time, the great healer of all differences, is blending us into a great mutual people, and love is moving faster than time. It is no growing hatred between Dutch and English South African born men and women that calls for war. On the lips of our babes we salute both races daily.

Then we look round through the political world, and we ask ourselves what great and terrible and sudden crime has been committed, what reckless slaughter and torture of the innocents that blood can alone wash out blood? And we find the blood.

And still we look, asking what great and terrible difference has suddenly arisen, so mighty that the human intellect cannot solve it by means of peace, that the highest and noblest diplomacy falls powerless before it, and the wisdom and justice of humanity cannot reach it, save by the mother's drawing a sword and planting it in the heart of the daughter.

We can find none. And again, we ask ourselves,

Who Gains by War?

What is it for? Who is there that desires it? Do men shed streams of human blood as children cut off poppy heads to see the white juice flow?

Not England! She has a great young nation's heart to lose. She has a cable of fellowship which stretches across the seas to rupture. She has treaties to violate. She has the great traditions of her past to part with. Whoever plays to win, she loses.

Not Africa! The great young nation, quickening to-day to its first consciousness of life, to be torn and rent, and bear upon its limbs into its fully ripened manhood the marks of the wounds—wounds from a mother's hands?

Not the great woman whose eighty years tonight,[1] who would carry with her to her grave the remembrance of the longest reign and the purest; who would have that when the nations gather round her bier the whisper should go round, "That was a mother's hand; it struck no child."

Not the brave English soldier; there are no laurels for him here. The dying lad with hands fresh from the plough; the old man tottering to the grave, who seizes up the gun to die with it; the simple farmer who as he falls hears yet his wife's last whisper, "For freedom and our land!" and dies hearing it—these men can bind no laurels on a soldier's brow! They may be shot, not conquered—fame rests with men. Go, gallant soldiers, and defend the shores of that small island that we love; there are no laurels for you here!

Who Gains by War?

Not we the Africans, whose hearts are knit to England. We love all. Each hired soldier's bullet that strikes down a South African does more; it finds a billet here in our hearts. It takes one African's life—in another it kills that which will never live again.

Who Gains by War?

There are some who *think* they gain! In the background we catch sight of misty figures; we know the old tread; we hear the rustle of paper passing from hand to hand, and we know the fall of gold; it is an old familiar sound in Africa; we know it now! There are some who *think* they gain! Will they gain?

But it may be said, "What matter who goads England on, or in whose cause she undertakes war against Africans; this at least is certain that she can win. We have the ships, we have the men, we have the money."

We answer, "Yes, might generally conquers—for a time at least." The greatest empire upon earth, on which the sun never sets, with its five hundred million subjects may rise up in its full majesty of power and glory, and crush those thirty thousand farmers. It may not be a victory, but at least it will be a slaughter. We ought to win. We have the ships, we have the men, and we have the money. May there not be something else we need? The Swiss had it when they fought with Austria; the three hundred had it at Thermopylæ though not a man was saved; it goes to make a victory. Is it worth fighting if we have not got it?

I suppose there is no man who to-day loves his country who has not perceived that in the life of the nation, as in the life of the individual, the hour

---

1. Written on the 24th May, 1899.

of external success may be the hour of irrevocable failure, and that the hour of death, whether to nations or individuals, is often the hour of immortality. When William the Silent, with his little band of Dutchmen, rose up to face the whole empire of Spain, I think there is no man who does not recognise that the hour of their greatest victory was not when they had conquered Spain, and hurled backward the greatest empire of the world to meet its slow, imperial death; it was the hour when that little band stood alone with the waters over their homes,

Facing Death and Despair,

and stood facing it. It is that hour that has made Holland immortal, and her history the property of all human hearts.

It may be said, "But what has England to fear in a campaign with a country like Africa? Can she not send out a hundred thousand or a hundred and fifty thousand men and walk over the land? She can sweep it by mere numbers." We answer yes—she might do it. Might generally conquers; not always. I have seen a little *meer-kat* attacked by a mastiff, the first joint of whose leg it did not reach. I have seen it taken in the dog's mouth, so that hardly any part of it was visible, and thought the creature was dead. But it fastened its tiny teeth inside the dog's throat, and the mastiff dropped it, and mauled and wounded and covered with gore and saliva, I saw it creep back to its hole in the red African earth. But might generally conquers, and there is no doubt that England might send out sixty or a hundred thousand hired soldiers to South Africa, and they could bombard our towns and destroy our villages; they could shoot down men in the prime of life, and old men and boys, till there was hardly a kopje in the country without its stain of blood, and the Karoo bushes grew up greener on the spot where men from the midlands who had come to help their fellows fell, never to go home. I suppose it would be quite possible for the soldiers to shoot all male South Africans who appeared in arms against them. It might not be easy, a great many might fall, but a great Empire could always import more to take their places; *we* could not import more, because it would be our husbands and sons and fathers who were falling, and when they were done we could not produce more. Then the war would be over. There would not be a house in Africa—where African-born men and women lived—without its mourners, from Sea Point to the Limpopo; but South Africa would be pacified—as Cromwell pacified Ireland three centuries ago, and she has been being pacified ever since! As Virginia was pacified in 1677: its handful of men and women in defence of their freedom were soon silenced by hired soldiers. "I care that for the power of England," said "a notorious and wicked rebel" called Sarah Drummond, as she took a small stick and broke it and lay it on the ground. A few months later her husband and all the men with him were made prisoners, and the war was over. "I am glad to see you," said Berkeley, the English Governor, "I have long wished to meet you; you will be hanged in half an hour!" and he was hanged and twenty-one others with him, and Virginia was pacified. But a few generations later in that State of Virginia was born George Washington, and on the 19th of April, 1775, was fought the battle of Lexington—"Where once the embattled farmers stood, and fired a shot, heard round the world,"—and the greatest crime and the greatest folly of England's career was completed. England acknowledges it now. A hundred or a hundred and fifty thousand imported soldiers might walk over South Africa: it would not be an easy walk, but it could be done. Then from east and west and north and south would come men of pure English blood to stand beside the boys they had played with at school and the friends they had loved; and a great despairing cry would rise from the heart of Africa. But we are still few. When the war was over the imported soldiers might leave the land—not all. Some must be left to keep the remaining people down. There would be quiet in the land. South Africa would rise up silently, and count her dead, and bury them. She would know the places where she found them. South Africa would be peaceful. There would be silence, the silence of a long exhaustion—but not peace! Have the dead no voices? In a thousand farmhouses black-robed women would hold memory of the count, and outside under African stones would lie the African men to whom South African women gave birth under our blue sky. There would be a silence, but no peace.

You say that all the fighting men in arms might have been shot. Yes, but what of the women? If there were left but five thousand pregnant South African born women, and all the rest of their people destroyed, those women would breed up again a race like to the first.

Oh, Lion Heart of the North,

do you not recognise your own lineage in these whelps of the South, who cannot live if they are not free?

The grandchildren and great-grandchildren of the men who lay under the stones (who will not be English then nor Dutch, but only Africans), will say as they pass those heaps, "There lie our fathers, or great-grandfathers, who died in the first great war of independence," and the descendants of the men who lay there will be the aristocracy of Africa. Men will count back to them and say: My father or my great-grandfather lay in one of those graves. We shall know no more of Dutch or English then; we shall know only the great African people. And *we?* We, the South Africans of to-day, who are still

English, who have been proud to do the smallest good so that it might bring honour to England, who have vowed our vows on the honour of Englishmen, and by the faith of Englishmen, What of us?

What of us? We, too, have had our vision of Empire. We have seen as in a dream the Empire of England as a great banyan tree; silently with the falling of the dew and the dropping of the rain it has extended itself; its branches have drooped down and rooted themselves in the earth; in it all the fowl of heaven have taken refuge, and under its shade all the beast of the field have lain down to rest. Can we change it for an upas tree, whose leaves distil poison and which spells death to those who have lain down in peace under its shadow?

You have no right to take our dream from us; you have no right to kill our faith! Of all the sins England will sin if she makes war on South Africa, the greatest will be towards us.

Of what importance is honour and faith we have given her? You say, we are but few! Yes, we are few; but all the gold of Witwatersrand would not buy one throb of that love and devotion we have given her.

Do not think that when imported soldiers walk across South African plains to take the lives of South African men and women that it is only African sand and African bushes that are cracking beneath their tread; at each step they are breaking the fibres, invisible as air but strong as steel, which bind the hearts of South Africans to England. Once broken they can never be made whole again; they are living things; broken they will be dead. Each bullet which a soldier sends to the heart of a South African to take his life wakes up another who did not know he was an African. You will not kill us with your Lee-Metfords; you will make us. There are men who do not know they love a Dutchman, but the first three hundred that fall, they will know it.

Do not say, "But you are English, you have nothing to fear; we have no war with you!" There are hundreds of us, men and women who have loved England; we would have given our lives for her; but rather than strike down one South African man fighting for freedom, we would take this right hand and hold it in the fire, till nothing was left of it but a charred and blackened bone.

I know of no more graphic image in the history of the world than

The Figure of Franklin

when he stood before the Lords of Council in England, giving evidence, striving, fighting to save America for England. Browbeaten, flouted, jeered at by the courtiers, his words hurled back at him, as lies, he stood there fighting for England. England recognises now that it was he who tried to save an empire for her, and that the men who flouted and browbeat him lost it. There is nothing more pathetic than the way in which Americans who loved England, Washington and Franklin, strove to keep the maiden vessel moored close to the mother's side, bound by the bonds of love and sympathy, that alone could bind them. Their hands were beaten down, bruised and bleeding, wounded by the very men they came to save till they let go the mother ship and drifted away on their own great imperial course across the seas of time.

England knows now what those men strove to do for her, and the names of Washington and Franklin will ever stand high in honour where the English tongue is spoken; the names of Hutchinson, and North, and Grafton are not forgotten also; it might be well for them if they were!

Do not say to us: "You Englishmen, when the war is over, you can wrap the mantle of our imperial glory round you and walk about boasting that the victory is yours."

We could never wrap that mantle round us again. We have worn it with pride. We could never wear it then. There would be blood upon it, and the blood would be our brothers'.

We put it to the men of England. In that day where should we be found— we who have to maintain English honour in the South? Judge for us, and by your judgment we will abide. Remember, we are Englishmen!

Looking around to-day along the somewhat over-clouded horizon of South African life, one figure strikes the eye, new to the circle of our existence here; and we eye it with something of that hope and sympathy with which a man is bound to view the new and unknown, which may be of vast possible good and beauty. What have we in this man, who represents English honour and English wisdom in South Africa? To a certain extent we know.

We have a man honourable in the relations of personal life, loyal to friend, and above all charm of gold; wise with the knowledge of books and men; a man who could not violate a promise or strike in the dark. This we know we have, and it is much to know this; but what have we more?

The man of whom South Africa has need to-day to sustain England's honour and her empire of the future is a man who must possess more than the knowledge and wisdom of the intellect.

When a woman rules the household with none but the children of her own body in it, her task is easy; let her obey nature, and she will not fail. But the woman who finds herself in a large, strange household, where children and stepchildren are blended, and where all have passed the stage of childhood and have entered on that stage of adolescence where coercion can no more avail, but where sympathy and comprehension are the more needed, that woman has need of large and rare qualities springing more from the heart than from the head. She who can win the love of her strange household in its adolescence will keep its loyalty and sympathy when adult years are reached, and will be rich indeed.

There have been Englishmen in Africa who had those qualities. Will

This New Englishman of Ours

evince them and save an empire for England and heal South Africa's wounds? Are we asking too much when we turn our eyes with hope to him?

Further off also, across the sea, we look with hope. The last of the race of great statesmen was not put into the ground with the old man of Hawarden; the great breed of Chatham and Burke is not extinct; the hour must surely bring forth the man.

We look further, yet with confidence, from the individual to the great heart of England, the people. The great fierce freedom-loving heart of England is not dead yet. Under a thin veneer of gold we still hear it beat. Behind the shrivelled and puny English Hyde, who cries only "gold," rises the great English Jekyll, who cries louder yet "Justice and honour." We appeal to him; history shall not repeat itself.

Nearer home, we turn to one whom all South Africa are proud of, and we would say to Paul Kruger, "Great old man, first but not last of South Africa's great line of rulers, you have shown us you can win peace. On the foot of that great statue which in the future the men and women of South Africa will raise to you let this stand written, 'This man loved freedom, and fought for it; but his heart was large; he could forget injuries and deal generously.'"

And to our fellow Dutch South Africans, whom we have learnt to love so much during the time of stress and danger, we would say: "Brothers, you have shown the world that you know how to fight, show it you know how to govern; forget the past; in that Great Book which you have taken for your guide in life, turn to Leviticus, and read there in the 19th chapter, 34th verse: Be strong, be fearless, be patient. We would say to you in the words of the wise dead President of the Free State which have become the symbol of South Africa, 'Wacht een bietje, alles zal recht kom.'" (Wait a little, all will come right.)

On our great African flag let us emblazon these words, never to take them down, "FREEDOM, JUSTICE, LOVE"; great are the two first, but without the last they are not complete.

SOURCE: Olive Schreiner, *An English-South African's View of the Situation* (London: Hasell, Watson, and Viney, 1899), 75–96.

Excerpt from *A History of the Transvaal*

H. RIDER HAGGARD

[H. Rider Haggard (1856–1925) spent time in South Africa in the 1870s as secretary to the governor of Natal. Haggard, who hoisted the flag at the annexation of the Transvaal in 1877, is perhaps best known for his African adventure novels *King Solomon's Mines* (1885), *She* (1887), and *Allan Quatermain* (1887).]

Difficult as it is to make the fact understood among a proportion of the home electorate and publicists, it cannot be stated too often or too clearly that this war, which is to come, is a war that was forced upon us by the Boers in their blind ignorance and conceit. The mass of them believe, because they defeated our troops in various small affairs in 1881, that they are a match for the British Empire. Their leaders are better instructed. They trust not so much, perhaps, to the rifles of their compatriots as to the prowess of certain party captains in England, and to the enthusiasm of their advocates among the English Press and public. They remember that the activity of these forces eighteen years ago was followed by a miserable surrender on the part of the English Government, and not understanding how greatly opinion has changed in this country, they hope that history may repeat itself, and that England, wearying of an unpopular struggle, will soon cede to them all they ask. They are mistaken, but such is their faith. They hope also, perchance with better reason, that other complications may force us to stay our hand. If no more telegrams can be extracted from the German Emperor, still there is a German regiment fighting on their side who will take with them the sympathies of the Fatherland, and they know that the hearts of the great Powers of Europe will go out towards any people who try to strike a blow at the root of the ever-growing tree of the might of the British Empire. Buoyed up by bubbles such as these they have determined to tempt the stern arbitrament of battle.[1]

Can it still be avoided? It would seem that except by our surrender, which is out of the question, for that means the loss not only of South Africa, but of our prestige throughout the world, this is not in any way possible. Already acts of war have taken place, such as the seizure of the gold from the mines, and the commandeering of goods belonging to British subjects, and perhaps

---

1. See the very remarkable letter of the Boer "P. S." to the *Times* of October 14th.

days before these lines can appear in print the guns will have begun their reasoning.[2]

After the rebellion of 1881 a Boer jury, to whom the case was committed by the tender mercies of Mr. Gladstone's Government, with the murdered man's bullet-riddled skull lying before them upon the table of the Court, acquitted the brutal slaughterers of Captain Elliot, not because they had not done the deed with every circumstance of horrible treachery and premeditation, but because to find them guilty was against their brethren's wish. In much the same way, with all the facts staring them in the face, there are men in England, some of them of high position and character, who urge the righteousness of the Boer cause, and with tongue and pen paint our national iniquity in hues black as ink and red as blood. They write of the "Objects of the War," which they do not hesitate to describe as self-seeking and infamous, so far of course as the English people are concerned, for according to the same authorities, the Boer objects are uniformly pure and noble. Would it not be better if they looked back a little and tried to discover the causes of the war? I think that if they could have witnessed a certain scene upon the market-square at Newcastle, at which it was my misfortune to be present, on that night of the year 1881 when the news of the base betrayal of the loyalists by England became known, they would win a better understanding of the question. In the spectacle of that maddened crowd of three or four thousand ruined and deserted men, English, Boer, and Kaffir, raving, weeping, and blaspheming in the despair of their shame and bitterness, they might have found enlightenment. Even now a study of the following forgotten letter written by Mr. White, the chairman of the Committee of Loyal Inhabitants, to Mr. Gladstone, might give to some a food for thought:—

"If, sir, you had seen, as I have seen, promising young citizens of Pretoria dying of wounds received for their country, and if you had had the painful duty, as I have had, of bringing to their friends at home the last mementoes of the departed; if you had seen the privations and discomforts which delicate women and children bore without murmuring for upward of three months; if you had seen strong men crying like children at the cruel and undeserved desertion of England; if you had seen the long strings of half-desperate loyalists, shaking the dust off their feet as they left the country, as I saw on my

2. Since the above was written, in the swift march of events, the Transvaal has despatched its "ultimatum," perhaps the most egregious document ever addressed to a great Power by a petty State. In effect it is a declaration of war, and hostilities have now commenced with the destruction by the Boers of an armoured train at Kraipan, and the capture or slaying of its escort. *14th October 1899.* H. R. H.

way to Newcastle; and if you yourself had invested your all on the strength of the word of England, and now saw yourself in a fair way of being beggared by the acts of the country in whom you trusted, you would, sir, I think, be 'pronounced,' and England would ring with eloquent entreaties and threats which would compel a hearing. . . . We claim, sir, at least as much justice as the Boers. We are faithful subjects of England, and have suffered and are suffering for our fidelity. Surely we, the friends of our country, who stood by her in the time of trial, have as much right to consideration as rebels who fought against her. We rely on her word. We rely on the frequently repeated pledges and promises of her ministers in which we have trusted. We rely on her sense of moral right not to do us the grievous wrong which this miserable peace contemplates. We rely on her fidelity to obligations, and on her ancient reputation for honour and honesty. We rely on the material consequences which will follow on a breach of faith to us. England cannot afford to desert us after having solemnly pledged herself to us."

"England cannot afford to desert us!" but England, or her rulers, could and did afford itself this luxury. In vain did such men as the late Lord Beaconsfield, the late Lord Cairns, and Lord Salisbury protest and point out dangers. In vain did agonised loyalists flourish their own words and promises in the face of her Majesty's Government; the spirit of party, or the promptings of a newly acquired conscience proved too strong. Her Majesty's loyal subjects were sneered at, insulted, and abandoned, and the Boer, who had butchered them, was bid to go on and prosper.

Now, nearly twenty years afterwards, England is called upon to pay the bill of what is in effect, whatever may have been its motives, one of the most infamous acts that stains the pages of her history. From the moment that the Convention of 1881 was signed it became as certain as anything human can be, that one of two things would happen—either that the Imperial Power must in practice be driven out of South Africa, or that a time would come when it must be forced to assert its dominion even at the price of war.

Now that miserable hour is with us, and we are called upon to suppress by arms a small, but sullen and obstinate people, whom we have taught to believe themselves our equals, if not our superiors. Unless they will yield at the last moment, which seems impossible seeing that the war is of their own choosing, the new settlement of South Africa must be celebrated by a mighty sacrifice of their blood and our blood. Not to dwell upon other griefs and dangers, when, I ask, will the smoke and the smell of it depart from the eyes and nostrils of the dwellers in that unhappy land? As they troop back merrily to their mines and workshops the money-spinners of Johannesburg may forget a past of which, in many instances at least, their chief impression will be that it was unpleasant and unprofitable. But after the Rand is worked out, when the stamps cease to fall heavily by day and night, when the great heaps of tailings no longer increase from month to month, when the broker's voice is quiet in the Exchange, and the promoter inhabits some new city, still the Boer women in the farmhouses will tell their children how the "damned English soldiers" shot their grandfathers and took the land. In South Africa new Irelands will arise, and from the dragon's teeth that we are forced to sow the harvest of hate will spring, and spring again. Thus must we eat of the bitter bread which we have baked, and thus the ill fowl that we reared have come home to roost, bringing their broods with them.

Again and again we have blundered in our treatment of the Dutch. For instance, with kinder and fairer management they would never have trekked from the Cape sixty years ago. Also, had the promises which were made to them at the annexation in 1877 been kept, and had not Sir Theophilus Shepstone, who grew up amongst them and to whom they were attached, been removed in favour of a military martinet, there would have been no rebellion, let the Cape wire-pullers working under a cloak of loyalty to the Crown strive as they might. But the rebellion came and the defeats, and after these that surrender whereof this country is called upon to pluck the fruit to-day, which, by the Boers, is attributed to those defeats with the fear of their prowess and to nothing else.

And now, in due season, the war comes; an inevitable war which cannot be escaped, and must be fought out to the end. There is only room for one paramount power in Southern Africa!

SOURCE: H. Rider Haggard, *A History of the Transvaal* (London: K. Paul, Trench, Trubner, and Co., 1900), xix–xxv.

Political Position in Cape Colony

J. A. HOBSON

[J. A. Hobson (1858–1940) was a political economist distinguished for his aggressive critique of expansionist–or "jingoist"–imperialism.]

South Africa is proverbially a land of surprises, and for a sojourner to express any confident judgment upon the delicate relations between the Colonial Government and the Imperial policy during the recent crisis of public affairs would be the pinnacle of folly. But having occupied myself at Cape Town chiefly in canvassing opinion on this matter, and having got, in conversation with different members of the Ministry and other political leaders, clear and outspoken judgments, I venture to present a fairly representative summary of a situation which is not unlikely to mark the beginning of a serious constitutional struggle. Whether the Colonial Secretary and the High Commissioner were justified or not in their espousal of the cause of the Outlander, and in the use of him to urge upon the Transvaal a sort of suzerainty neither set forth nor, in my judgment, implied in the Conventions, is not a point to be argued here. But it is of urgent importance that Englishmen should understand how sternly and strongly the policy of Downing Street was resented by the elective Assembly of what has hitherto been held to be, and distinctly holds itself to be by right, a substantially self-governing colony. The Home Government and the High Commissioner are felt to have ignored and overridden the judgment of a strong Ministry, representing a people whose commercial and political interests and experience entitle them to paramount consideration in the settlement of this Transvaal issue. The press and the voice of a British minority must not be allowed to conceal the essential facts of the situation. Here is a very strong Colonial Government, commanding a majority of twelve in an Assembly of ninety-five (thus corresponding to a majority of over eighty in the English House of Commons), and likely to be returned with fresh reinforcements if, as is rashly suggested in some quarters, the Governor dissolves the Assembly and appeals to the country. Nor is this likely to be a merely transient condition of affairs. A clear race cleavage, such as the present Imperial policy promotes, is likely to mean a permanent majority of Dutch Afrikanders in the Assembly, for it is unlikely that any new scheme of redistribution can be adopted enabling the British Afrikanders to triumph over the higher natural increase of the Dutch population and the greater influence which their broader dispersion rightly gives them in the country.

At the head of this majority, with seven exceptions entirely Dutch, sits a Ministry of experienced politicians (chiefly British and with but two Dutch Afrikanders), under a Premier (Mr. Schreiner) whose ability and force of character are admitted even by his adversaries. Men like Mr. Merriman, Mr. Sauer, and Mr. Solomon are no raw carpetbaggers hoisted into power by some sudden swell in the stream of party politics; they are men thoroughly conversant with the life and needs of the people and trained in the arts of administration. Such men feel that they know a hundred times more about the really salient points of the situation—the character of the Boer, the possible union of South African States, the native question—than the Colonial Office and a brand-new High Commissioner from Egypt. Their general diagnosis of the Transvaal situation and its bearing on the larger questions of

South African politics has been firm and consistent. They have been freely accused by the Jingo press of inciting the Transvaal Government to an obstinate refusal of British claims. So far is this from being true, that, when history comes to displace journalistic fabrication, it will be known that friendly representations from Cape Colony have been far more effectual to wring concessions and reforms from Mr. Kruger than the threats of the British Government. Mr. Schreiner and his Ministers were absolutely united in recognising the reality of grievances and the necessity of reforms along the lines proposed, but they regarded the grievances as gravely exaggerated and the forceful methods of reform adopted as foolish, unjust, and fraught with dangerous reactions on the peace and progress of South Africa. The concluding words of General Butler's speech at Grahamstown a year ago, generally held to have occasioned his recall, concisely express their judgment: "What South Africa needs is rest, and not a surgical operation." Holding that the Outlanders were not seriously threatened in life, liberty, or property, they deprecated alike the violence and the precipitancy of the present policy. Though progress in reform was slower than they would desire, there had been progress. The economic and other influences of the Rand had already acted as solvents of the old Boer conservatism. A few more years and the death of Mr. Kruger would, they argued, in all probability, work a fairly rapid and peaceful transformation in the politics of the Transvaal. One and all held that in the more distant future England would and must, in the natural course of events, control the Transvaal politically as well as economically, and that to force the pace by abrupt and artificial interference was injurious. Mr. Schreiner, Mr. Merriman, and their colleagues, were as firmly convinced as the most pronounced Jingo that England must in effect control the destinies of the whole of South Africa, but they deprecated the doctrine of force as the midwife of progress, seeing—what the Imperial Government fails to see—the moral and political reactions of menace and war upon the race questions which underlie the political future of the country.

Upon the immediate policy of the Transvaal I found no absolute agreement. Several of the leading politicians were convinced that the proposal of a joint inquiry was deliberately conceived in order to force on Mr. Kruger an admission of the suzerainty he has always denied. The Premier thought otherwise, holding that no such implication was involved, even if it were intended. His view was that Mr. Kruger might accept the inquiry as a step in the friendly intercourse entered upon at Bloemfontein, and that, as a first result of the report of such inquiry, the conference might be resumed between Sir A. Milner and the President with a view to final settlement.

It was impossible to go far in such a political inquiry as that which I undertook without perceiving that the most serious obstacle to an amicable settlement was the profound distrust of one another's motives entertained by the negotiating parties. Sir A. Milner did not hesitate to pronounce duplicity to be the distinctive trait of the Boer Government. When I reached Pretoria, I found that the same word contained the essence of Boer criticism upon British diplomacy. How could a real and lasting understanding be reached between such controversialists? The Cape Ministers, divided in their estimate of Mr. Kruger's policy, were united in denouncing the tactlessness of the Chamberlain-Milner method. Sir A. Milner, they held, utterly failed to understand the Boer character, and could not get at any point into sympathetic touch with it. This was made manifest by the proceedings at Bloemfontein. "How differently," one of them put it to me, "would Rhodes have handled the business in the days before the Raid had made him an impossible negotiator! Instead of bombarding the old man with a display of officialism, and seeking to wrest from him admissions by dint of academic argument, Rhodes would have said to his attachés, 'Now all you fellows, clear out,' and then he would have sat down by the fire, lighting cigarettes, while the old man smoked his long pipe; and they would have talked over things for a couple of days, so as to get to really understand one another before entering on any formal attempt at settlement." Sir A. Milner's method was to treat Kruger as a nineteenth-century up-to-date European diplomatist, instead of a slow-thinking, suspicious, seventeenth-century Puritan farmer, and a conference upon these lines was foredoomed to failure. The Dutch Afrikanders were, indeed, convinced that a peaceful conference was not intended to succeed; that Mr. Rhodes had got a clear understanding with Mr. Chamberlain after the Raid, whereby the latter undertook to direct the next attack upon the independence of the Republic; and that in Sir A. Milner there had been found an apt and sympathetic agent of this plan of campaign.

Although Cape Ministers did not in so many words commit themselves to this interpretation, it indubitably expressed their underlying conviction. The real aim, as they saw it, was not redress of grievances on the Rand, but the application of the new Imperialism to the affairs of South Africa. The optimist notion that a few months must see a final settlement; that, by the display or the actual use of arms, we should drive the Boers to a recognition of our power, and that after this moral or physical drubbing they would at once get to "know their place," was rejected by them as utterly fantastic. The dogs of war, once let loose, could not be so easily leashed again; force applied as a remedy to the stubborn Boers could not be soon replaced by sympathetic and enlightened democratic institutions; annexation would be inevitable, and could only be sustained by permanent militarism and the autocracy which pertains to it. What Cape Ministers first and chiefly dreaded was the effect of this upon the general governmental policy of South Africa. Government from Downing Street has ever been the bane of colonial statesmen of every party. Intensely loyal to the British flag, they constantly chafe against the bit of the Colonial Office when employed to drive them along roads which they know far better than Imperial Ministers can know them. The real unity of South Africa—a mere sounding phrase in the mouths of party politicians in England—is brought home to them by concrete facts, and gives them a clear right to exercise a prevailing voice in affairs which so vitally affect their interests. The Transvaal is a plain case in point. The Imperial Government in the early stages of the controversy, treated the issue as if it only affected Outlanders. But the Jameson Raid, and the policy which was its sequel, had already exercised most disastrous influences upon colonial trade. The proposals of taxation, which were hotly dividing parties in Cape Colony last summer, were directly due to the necessities arising from damage to commercial confidence and that diversion of railway traffic from the Cape Colony lines which has been a chief object of Transvaal endeavour during recent years. The colony suffered more than it was possible to compute from this policy of menace, and a catastrophic solution of the problem, attended by a *régime* of militarism and a close Imperial control over matters of vital domestic import, was dreaded by all who understood what it signified in the development of colonial life and institutions.

SOURCE: Chapter 1 in *The War in South Africa* (London: Macmillan, 1900), 3–9.

The Absent-Minded Beggar
RUDYARD KIPLING

[Kipling's poem was popular in music halls and other public venues during the Boer War.]

> When you've shouted "Rule Britannia," when you've sung
> "God save the Queen,"
>   When you've finished killing Kruger with your mouth,
> Will you kindly drop a shilling in my little tambourine
>   For a gentleman in khaki ordered South?
> He's an absent-minded beggar, and his weaknesses are great—
>   But we and Paul must take him as we find him—

He is out on active service, wiping something off a slate—
    And he's left a lot of little things behind him!
Duke's son—cook's son—son of a hundred kings—
    (Fifty thousand horse and foot going to Table Bay!)
Each of 'em doing his country's work
    (and who's to look after their things?)
Pass the hat for your credit's sake,
        and pay—pay—pay!

These are girls he married secret, asking no permission to,
    For he knew he wouldn't get it if he did.
There is gas and coals and vittles, and the house-rent falling due,
    And it's more than rather likely there's a kid,
There are girls he walked with casual. They'll be sorry now he's gone,
    For an absent-minded beggar they will find him,
But it ain't the time for sermons with the winter coming on.
    We must help the girl that Tommy's left behind him!
Cook's son—Duke's son—son of a belted Earl—
    Son of a Lambeth publican—it's all the same to-day!
Each of 'em doing his country's work
    (and who's to look after the girl?)
Pass the hat for your credit's sake,
        and pay—pay—pay!

There are families by thousands, far too proud to beg or speak,
    And they'll put their sticks and bedding up the spout,
And they'll live on half o' nothing, paid 'em punctual once a week,
    'Cause the man that earns the wage is ordered out.
He's an absent-minded beggar, but he heard his country call,
    And his reg'ment didn't need to send to find him!
He chucked his job and joined it—so the job before us all
    Is to help the home that Tommy's left behind him!
Duke's job—cook's job—gardener, baronet, groom,
    Mews or palace or paper-shop, there's someone gone away!
Each of 'em doing his country's work
    (and who's to look after the room?)
Pass the hat for your credit's sake,
        and pay—pay—pay!

Let us manage so as, later, we can look him in the face,
    And tell him—what he'd very much prefer—

That, while he saved the Empire, his employer saved his place,
  And his mates (that's you and me) looked after *her.*
He's an absent-minded beggar and he may forget it all,
  But we do not want his kiddies to remind him
That we sent 'em to the workhouse while their daddy hammered Paul,
  So we'll help the homes that Tommy left behind him!
Cook's home—Duke's home—home of a millionaire
  (Fifty thousand horse and foot going to Table Bay!)
Each of 'em doing his country's work
  (and what have you got to spare?)
Pass the hat for your credit's sake,
      and pay—pay—pay!

SOURCE: *The Works of Rudyard Kipling* (Hertfordshire: Wordsworth Editions, 1994), 459–60.

<hr />

Mr Thomas Atkins

E. J. HARDY

[E. J. Hardy was a chaplain to the British forces in South Africa. His account of British soldiers who fought in the Boer War is dedicated to the "officers, non-commissioned officers, and privates, from whom I learned what I know of the British army, and from whom I have received help and kindness which can never be forgotten." "Tommy Atkins," which became the epithet for ordinary British soldiers, was much popularized in the Rudyard Kipling poem of that nickname and might well be contrasted to "Tom Brown," which referred to the public-school elite, who fared rather differently in Britain's imperial wars.]

The origin of the name "Tommy Atkins" may be found in the soldier's small book. There, until lately, was given an imaginary clothing account as a model between the Government and Thomas Atkins.

Another derivation of the phrase is, perhaps, truer, and is certainly more flattering. In 1857, when rebellion broke out at Lucknow, all the Europeans fled to the Residency. On their way they met a private of the 32nd Regiment (Duke of Cornwall's Light Infantry) on sentry at an outpost. They told him to make his escape with them, but he would not do so, and was killed. His name happened to be Thomas Atkins, and so, throughout the mutiny campaign, when a daring deed was done, the doer was said to be "a regular

Tommy Atkins." There is no room, then, for the condescension or pity which sometimes seems to be suggested by the phrase when used by civilians.

People often write and speak of soldiers as if they were different from other men, but putting a man into a red coat does not alter his nature, and under the present system of short service Tommy Atkins has not time to change much from what he was when he enlisted. Still the environment of his life does develop certain humours and eccentricities which are interesting to study.

The first tendency we notice of the military profession is that it makes a soldier more or less a machine.

> "His not to reason why,
> His but to do and die."

To be "lord of himself" is often, as Lord Byron found to his cost, a "heritage of woe" to a man, and it is not a bad thing for him to be wound up like a clock and made to go right; but this winding up process converts him into, it may be a noble machine, but a machine still. Nearly everything which a soldier does he is ordered to do. He is put down for a new pair of boots or tunic without being asked whether he wants them or not. His dinner comes to him as though it were manna from Heaven. He is told when to get his hair cut, and when to put on or take off the several parts of his outfit. At length he ceases almost entirely to think for himself, and puts child-like trust in the "Queen's Regulations."

Soldiers are, as a rule, very well-mannered men. This may be because they come more into contact with their social superiors than do country bumpkins. They are frequently spoken to by their officers; a few are servants in the family of officers or in the mess; or they learn politeness from those of their companions who have had better opportunities than themselves. You may always suspect that a man in civilian life has been a soldier when he begins to address you with "Beg pardon, sir."

Faraday understood and made use of the habit of unquestioning obedience which a man acquires in the army. When he was preparing to lecture in natural science at the Royal Institution, he advertised for a retired sergeant to help him with his experiments. Being asked why he sought for a military man, he explained that some of the materials that would be used were dangerous, and that, therefore, he wanted for an assistant, not one who would follow his own ignorant judgment, and blow up himself, the professor, and the audience, but one who would do exactly what he would be told, and nothing else.

It cannot be said with truth that British soldiers never grumble or "grouce," as they call it, for they do make use of this privilege, as do the rest of their countrymen; but when they have by "groucing" "eased their chests," they will go anywhere and do anything. "I often say," writes "General" Booth, "if we could only get Christians to have one-half of the practical devotion and sense of duty that animate even the commonest Tommy Atkins, what a change would be brought about in the world!"

In their way soldiers are very philosophical. If anything in their work annoys them they say, "It's all in the seven," *i.e.* the seven years for which they join the army. This means the same thing as civilians mean when they say, "It's all in the day's work."

A pleasant trait in soldiers is their affection for children. You see them continually playing with the "kids," as they always call them, of the married men. Indeed, the wife of many an impecunious officer gets more than half her nursing done for her by her husband's soldier servant. About nine years ago I was stationed at Malta, with a battalion of the Welsh Regiment. They had as a sort of regimental pet a little Soudanese boy, whom some of their members who were on active service in the Soudan had picked up after the battle of Toski. The boy was almost starved, and was lying between his father and mother, both of whom had been shot by English bullets. The mounted infantry drummer who picked up the child, aged at the time about four years, rode a great distance to get milk for him, which the medical officers said was the only thing that would make him well. "Jimmy Welsh" became such a fine boy that my Roman Catholic colleague and myself each tried to get him for our respective Communions.

And children seem to trust and take to soldiers. A corporal told me lately with pride that a little girl about six years of age came up to him and caught hold of his coat. She seemed to be much frightened, and the soldier asked her what she feared. "A dog," she replied, "that lives near here, and I have been waiting for a soldier to come along."

Here is part of a letter which shows how tender is the heart of the British warrior. It was written from South Africa by a man of the Royal Medical Staff Corps:—

"We were out looking after the wounded at night when the fight was over, when I came across an old white-bearded Boer. He was lying behind a bit of rock supporting himself on his elbows. I was a bit wary of the old fellow at first. Some of these wounded Boers we've found are snakes in the grass. You go up to them with the best intentions, and the next thing you know is that the man you were going to succour is blazing at you with his gun. So I kept my eye on the old chap. But when I got nearer I saw that he was too far gone to raise his rifle. He was gasping hard for breath, and I saw he was not long for this world. He motioned to me that he wanted to speak, and I bent over him. He asked me to go and find his son—a boy of thirteen, who had been fighting by his side when he fell. Well I did as he asked me, and under a heap of wounded I found the poor lad, stone dead, and I carried him back to his father. Well, you know I'm not a chicken-hearted sort of a fellow. I've seen a bit of fighting in my time, and that sort of thing knocks all the soft out of a chap. But I had to turn away when that old Boer saw his dead lad. He hugged the body to him and moaned over it, and carried on in a way that fetched a big lump in my throat—until that very moment I never thought how horrible war is. I never wanted to see another shot fired. And when I looked round again the old Boer was dead, clasping the cold hand of his dead boy."

The observant powers of soldiers show themselves in the apt nicknames they give. Of these every officer has one or more. Some of the men can read their officers like a book. A strict officer is by no means disliked so long as he is fair, while one who is slack and easy-going, in order to become popular, misses his aim, and only gains contempt. It seems to Tommy that he is, as it were, defrauded when he deserves a scolding or a punishment and does not get one. He speaks of punishment as being due to him, as, for example, "I am indebted ten days C.B." (confinement to barracks) "for so-and-so." "If I get my rights I'll have a court-martial over this."

One cannot have much dealings with soldiers without discovering that they are very suspicious. When any social amusement, or indeed anything to benefit them, is got up, they immediately suspect that some one is going to make something out of them. If it be organised by a chaplain Tommy thinks that it is some device for getting hold of him in order to preach to him. Allow him to go into an entertainment without paying and he will not care to do so, suspecting that what is offered for nothing is not worth more. Even if it be worth going to he is proud, and prefers to pay his way.

Talk of the vanity of women, in my opinion that of men is quite as great. Certainly a large number of soldiers enlist simply for the sake of "the clothes." Not long since a soldier complained to me about the "cruelty" of his commanding officer, who was trying to prevent the men in his regiment from wearing a little curl of hair on each side of the forehead. "I would rather," he said, most solemnly, "lose an arm than have my front hair cut too short."

As an illustration of the kindness of soldiers to each other, I give the following instance:—A man was in the habit of drinking, neglecting his work, and keeping himself very dirty; yet he was a good-natured fellow, and the occupants of his barrack-room were sorry when they saw him getting into trouble every day with his officers. They determined to take him in hand, and try if they could not keep him straight. Accordingly, on the next pay-day they induced him, instead of spending his money in the canteen, to hand it over, all but one shilling, which he was to have for pocket-money, to one of their number, to be deposited for him in a savings bank. This soon mounted up to a respectable little sum. The man's nerves, which used to cause him to tremble when on parade, grew stronger, and in all ways the improvement of his character was so marked that he was made a lance-corporal. Alas, for the virtue that depends on man only! One of the many changes of military life removed from the poor fellow his kind friends. In the absence of their advice and interest in him he fell back into his old carelessness, and proceeded to dissipate himself and his money worse than before. Here was kindness shown, not in ministering to low desires, but in trying to eradicate them, which is surely the most friendly thing that one man can do for another.

Another instance of this sort of kindness came under my notice lately. A man was confined in a military prison, and his chum went to see him. "Ah, Jim," said the prisoner to his visitor, "if you had not been moved out of my room I would never have come here." As long as he had a friend to look after him he behaved well. When the friend was removed he broke away, so to speak, from his moorings.

Not long ago we saw it stated in a newspaper that some young gentlemen who were trying to get commissions through the ranks of the army were in the habit of wearing plain clothes, with the permission of their commanding officers, when off duty and away from barracks.

We doubt whether even commissioned officers should be allowed to do this, and we are quite sure that, except in very special cases, non-commissioned officers and privates should not. If a man is ashamed of Her Majesty's uniform, the sooner he ceases to wear it altogether the better.

Why should it be considered a privilege to get out of military uniform; and is it true that even the most respectable non-commissioned officers are sometimes made to feel uncomfortable in restaurants, theatres, and other public places?

There may be a morbid sensitiveness in this matter, and it is not unlikely that soldiers fancy their uniform is despised on many occasions when nothing of the kind is the case. At the same time, there does seem to be some reason for thinking that the social position of a British soldier is not what it ought to be. Certainly it is not what it is on the Continent, where officers and men travel on the railways and attend places of public entertainment at reduced prices, and have every consideration shown to them.

In time of war every one is ready to admire those who sacrifice ease and comfort and life itself for the supposed good of their country; but with the return of peace Tommy Atkins is subjected to the old social inconveniences because he is "only a soldier."

> "While it's Tommy this, an' Tommy that, an' 'Tommy,
>   fall be'ind,'
> But it's 'Please to walk in front, Sir, when there's
>   trouble in the wind.'"

At Netley Hospital the surgeons on probation used to ask me how in my opinion a medical officer should rank. I replied that he should have the rank of field marshal beside the bedside of his patient, and everywhere else as he behaved himself. In the same way, we should respect a soldier on the field of battle for his courage, and everywhere else as he behaves himself.

"He that is truly dedicated to war hath no self love," and if we do not honour a profession whose ideal is self-sacrifice what will we honour? Surely sacrifice for the sake of duty is what is meant by the cross of Christ.

Whence, then, this prejudice against a profession the ideal of which is so noble? It may, we think, in part be accounted for as follows: Napoleon called England a nation of shopkeepers, and though she was able to put down this European bully and hold her own against all comers by her arms, it was not by these, but by the arts of peace, that Britain became "Great."

She is a commercial and not a military nation, and as such cannot be expected to "dote on the military." We consider a standing army an evil, though a necessary one, and the fiction is kept up that it is only a temporary measure, for a new lease of life has to be given to it every year in Parliament by the passing of what is known as the Army Act.

Free Britons have a horror of even the thought of a military dictator riding at the head of an army over their individual rights and liberties. But besides this jealousy of the army there is another circumstance which has given it a traditional bad name, and that is the way recruits used to be obtained.

During the war with France, at the commencement of the century, when it was difficult to get enough soldiers, men who deserved to go to prison were frequently allowed to enter the army instead.

The character of our soldiers then was not unlike that of those whom Falstaff commanded, and thus described: "Nay, and the villains march wide betwixt the legs, as if they had gyves" (fetters) "on; for, indeed, I had the most of them out of prison."

It is not so long ago that parents spoke of a young hopeful "going for a soldier" in much the same tone of despair as would have been used if they had announced his incarceration.

Those who know soldiers are well aware that their conduct is, generally speaking, quite as good, or, perhaps, owing to discipline, rather better than that of civilians of the same class; but those who are bad are far more conspicuous on account of their uniform, and these acquire for all a bad reputation.

The social status of a soldier will not be what it ought to be until at least half as much care is taken to exclude from the army the morally bad as there now is to keep out the physically weak; until unworthy characters are dismissed more freely, and until some means is devised by which they can be prevented from rejoining, as they now do.

We gladly admit that the prejudice against soldiers in Britain, the origin of which we have tried to trace, has greatly lessened, especially in the last few years. Short service and the volunteer movement have made soldiering more popular. Citizen soldiers have connected the army with civilian life, and even the regulars are not now separated from it as they once were. They leave it for only a few years and then go back to it again, and this in such numbers that almost every family in the country is interested in the respectability and general well-being of the service.

SOURCE: Chapter 1 in *Mr Thomas Atkins* (London: T. Fisher Unwin, 1900), 1–15.

<hr />

D. F. Advertiser.
KIMBERLEY, FRIDAY, FEBRUARY 16, 1900.

[Like other sieges—Mafeking and Ladysmith, for example—the months-long assault on Kimberley was devastating for the town's besieged and besieging alike, no less than for the observers of war. C. J. Rhodes was in Kimberley for the duration, and the relief that eventually came was part of the transformation of the war from its traditional procedures into a guerrilla/counter-guerrilla set of strategies, from raids on railroads on the one hand to farm burnings on the other.]

Special Edition.   **Price 3d.**

D. F. ADVERTISER.

KIMBERLEY, FRIDAY, FEBRUARY 16, 1900.

RELIEF OF KIMBERLEY

BY FRENCH'S FLYING COLUMN.

GREAT CAVALRY MARCH.

ENTHUSIASM IN TOWN.

About 2.30 p.m. yesterday a large body of horsemen were observed riding towards Dutoitspan from the south-east, and shortly afterwards a heliograph message conveyed the welcome intelligence that General French's flying column had marched that morning from Modder River, and was now on the point of entering Kimberley. The news spread as quickly as good news always does, and soon the debris heaps at Beaconsfield, and the housetops of double-storied buildings, were alive with curious spectators, who could hardly believe that relief was so near at hand. The troops spread out in magnificent order, and, keeping well in the centre of the flat, advanced at a great pace, and by about 5 o'clock men from the relief column were riding into Beaconsfield. The honour of being the first man to enter Kimberley belongs, we believe, to Mr Beresford, a special correspondent of the London "Daily Telegraph," who, feeling that all was safe, struck into the town, by the nearest route, and proceeded to the Sanatorium, where he gave the first news of the column to Mr Rhodes. He was quickly followed by Captain Gale, of the Royal Engineers, attached to Rimington's Scouts, who galloped in with two of the native guides, and was greeted by Colonel Harris, who had the honour of being the first to shake hands with the first British officer entering Kimberley after the siege. "I suppose we're only just in time," remarked the gallant officer, "we must have that big gun," upon which, with a laugh, he put spurs to his horse, and rode off. About 5 o'clock Colonel Kekewich, accompanied by Major O'Meara, R.E. (Intelligence Officer), and Major Lorimer, of the Cape Police, rode out in the direction of Wesselton, with the object of meeting General French and staff, but unfortunately missed them, the General coming in by way of the Premier Mine. Passing through Beaconsfield to the accompaniment of ringing cheers from the inhabitants lining the streets, General French was met at the boundary between Beaconsfield and Kimberley by the Mayor of Kimberley (Councillor H A Oliver) who, in a few appropriate sentences, expressed the great pleasure he felt at thus being able to welcome the officer commanding the Kimberley relief force. The circumstances of the arrival (the Mayor added) precluded any formal official welcome, but he hoped that might be arranged later. General French briefly replied, remarking that he was as pleased to see the people of Kimberley as, he believed, they were to welcome him. The General then rode into Kimberley, which was reached shortly before 7 o'clock, and paid a brief visit to Kimberley Club. A large crowd assembled in the street, and cheered lustily as the General and staff entered and left the building, the General proceeding to the Sanatorium. The men bivouaced for the night just outside the town.

We are indebted to the courtesy of Mr Beresford, of the London "Daily Telegraph," for the following details of the operations of the column on the march to Kimberley:—

The column, consisting of about 8,000 men, all mounted, is composed of three brigades and 42 guns. The first brigade, under Brigadier-General Porter, consists of portions of the 2nd Scots Greys, 6th Dragoon Guards (Carabineers), the Inniskilling Dragoons, the New South Wales Lancers, and the New Zealanders. The second brigade, under Brigadier-General Broadwood, is made up of the Household Cavalry (1st and 2nd Life Guards and the "Blues"), the 10th Hussars, and the 12th Lancers. The third brigade, under Brigadier-General Barton, includes the 9th and 16th Lancers, and a large number of mounted infantry. The artillery consists of seven batteries of Royal Horse Artillery, splendidly horsed, and able to move over the ground with the speed of cavalry. The cavalry left Modder River on Sunday at 2 p.m., and proceeded to Randam, south-east of Honey Nest Kloof, where they found a large force of infantry, who had been brought down by train, arriving. All night long trains laden with troops were running between Modder River and the nearest point of the line. The flying column received orders to push into Kimberley with the greatest possible speed, arriving not later than Friday night. Leaving the infantry still massing in enormous force at Randam, they pushed on at 1.40 on Monday morning, marched for about an hour, and then halted till daylight. About 5.15 the march was resumed, and the next halting place was at the Riet River, where they encamped. Here there was a slight engagement. At about 6 o'clock in the evening the enemy brought a 9-pounder on to the flat, and commenced shelling General French and his staff, the advance scouts having already been fired upon. The range was only about 3,000 yards, and few shells were placed in most unpleasant proximity to the party. Our guns quickly came into action, and the Boer gun limbered up and disappeared. Our artillery then devoted its attention to the kopjes, which the Boers were known to occupy, on the Kimberley side of the Riet River. Here the enemy unmasked two guns, one a 9-pounder, and the other a 14-pounder. Four batteries were brought into action against these two guns, which were completely knocked out in a few minutes, but got away. The enemy, dismayed at the rapid movements of our troops, and the unexpected mobility, fled in all directions, and the column crossed at Kuil's Drift without any further opposition at that point. The troops marched forward in magnificent order right across the flat country, and, spread out in squadron columns, made a most imposing sight. On Tuesday the troops moved on to Modder River, passing Jacobsdal about five miles to the east, and crossing at Klip Drift after a long day's march of 27 miles. The crossing of the river was expected to be a most difficult performance, but although about 2,000 Boers were seen in the neighbourhood, they fled in a state of panic, leaving many wagons and a large quantity of stores, forage, food, &c, to fall into our hands. General French rested his men at Modder River on Wednesday. During the day a tremendous lot of "sniping" went on, and the Boers harassed the camp with a long-range gun, which, however, did no harm. Our patrols cut off a convoy of four Boer wagons. During the night the infantry arrived at Modder River with six batteries of Field Artillery, and on Thursday morning the flying column, which had been detained awaiting the infantry, proceeded on their march. The Boers now made some show of opposition. Artillery fire commenced at 10 o'clock, and was very heavy, the Boers having six or seven guns in action. Our infantry took up a position on the hills to the east of the camp at Klip Drift, and were heavily shelled by the enemy, who were about 2,000 strong, and appeared to have the range to an inch. The Boers also burnt shrapnel over the guns, wounding several artillerymen. Two naval '2-pounders then came on the scene, and one of these long-range weapons was mounted on the kopje due north of the camp, and the most dangerous Boer gun was speedily brought to silence. The cavalry then advanced on the right and, galloping hard for five miles, executed a most rapid turning movement, which completely demoralised the enemy, who fled in all directions. The cavalry charged among the fugitives, and killed about 20, but the majority were off on their ponies, and were difficult to catch. Those who could not get away fired until our men were within 10 yards of them, then went down on their knees and cried for quarter. Several Boers were found lying on the ground who had been killed by rifle fire, but the majority succumbed to cold steel. About noon the troops halted on a farm where there was some water for the men, but little for the horses, which practically got nothing from about 9 a.m. until 6 in the evening. At 3.30 the troops came in sight of Kimberley, and could see the guns firing and the heliograph working. There was no serious opposition on the part of the enemy. A few shots were fired by the Boer gun posted on Cannon Kopje (between Susannah and Alexandersfontein), and the weapon was then moved on to the ridge behind, whence it fired a few more shots, to which our artillery replied by bursting shrapnel shells in rapid succession exactly over the spot where the gun appeared to be firing. The enemy were evidently completely astonished at the sudden advent of so vast a body of mounted troops, and could be clearly seen from the lookout station at Beaconsfield galloping away across the Free State border. The troops reached Beaconsfield about 6 o'clock, having completed a journey of about 100 miles in four days, and arriving 24 hours before they were due.

We understand that a large British force is still in the neighbourhood of Modder River station, and that fighting took place while General French's column was still on the line of march, the result of which is not yet known. The absence of any serious opposition on the part of the Boers to General French's advance was, we understand a great surprise, but the column had orders to fight their way through at all costs, Lord Roberts having decided that the immediate relief of Kimberley was imperative. The column pushed on without transport, carrying their whole supplies on horseback.

OCCUPATION OF ALEXANDERSFONTEIN

FOOD SUPPLIES CAPTURED.

On Wednesday morning, acting on information brought in by native women to the effect that the Boers were evacuating Alexandersfontein owing to the reported advance of British troops, Major Fraser ordered out a number of the Beaconsfield Town Guard, and made a reconnaissance of the position. Finding that there was little or no sign of Boer activity, Major Fraser, on his own responsibility, and without waiting to communicate with Colonel Kekewich, at once occupied the enemy's trenches. Reinforcements were sent for, and Major Fraser having reported what he had done, orders were given for the place to be held. Companies of the Lancashire Regiment, Kimberley Light Horse, and Diamond Fields Horse were sent out for this purpose, under Major Peakman, Major Fraser returning to his post. Three wagons and spans of oxen were captured, and about 20 head of fine, fat slaughter oxen (making about 40 head of cattle in all), together with a number of horses, mules, and donkeys, and large quantities of vegetables, fresh butter, &c. Six prisoners were taken, and one or two Boers were shot. Further details will be given in to-morrow's paper. The credit of the capture is chiefly due to Major Fraser for his promptitude and resourcefulness, while the Beaconsfield Town Guard may also be deservedly congratulated on having been first on the field at this successful operation.

RELIEF OF KIMBERLEY

By French's Flying Column.
Great Cavalry March.
Enthusiasm in Town.

About 2.30 P.M. yesterday a large body of horsemen were observed riding towards Dutoitspan from the south-east, and shortly afterwards a heliograph message conveyed the welcome intelligence that General French's flying column had marched that morning from Modder River, and was now on the point of entering Kimberley. The news spread as quickly as good news always does, and soon the debris heaps at Beaconsfield, and the housetops of doublestoried buildings, were alive with curious spectators, who could hardly believe that relief was so near at hand. The troops spread out in magnificent order, and, keeping well in the centre of the flat, advanced at a great pace, and by about 5 o'clock men from the relief column were riding into Beaconsfield. The honour of being the first man to enter Kimberley belongs, we believe, to Mr Beresford, a special correspondent of the London "Daily Telegraph," who, feeling that all was safe, struck into the town, by the nearest route, and proceeded to the Sanatorium, where he gave the first news of the column to Mr Rhodes. He was quickly followed by Captain Gale, of the Royal Engineers, attached to Rimington's Scouts, who galloped in with two of the native guides, and was greeted by Colonel Harris, who had the honour of being the first to shake hands with the first British officer entering Kimberley after the siege. "I suppose we're only just in time," remarked the gallant officer, "we must have that big gun," upon which, with a laugh, he put spurs to his horse, and rode off. About 5 o'clock Colonel Kekewich, accompanied by Major O'Meara, R.E. (Intelligence Officer), and Major Lorimer, of the Cape Police, rode out in the direction of Wesselton, with the object of meeting General French and staff, but unfortunately missed them, the General coming in by way of the Premier Mine. Passing through Beaconsfield to the accompaniment of ringing cheers from the inhabitants lining the streets, General French was met at the boundary between Beaconsfield and Kimberley by the Mayor of Kimberley (Councillor H. A. Oliver) who, in a few appropriate sentences, expressed the great pleasure he felt at thus being able to welcome the officer commanding the Kimberley relief force. The circumstances of the arrival (the Mayor added) precluded any formal official welcome, but be hoped that might be arranged later. General French briefly replied, remarking that he was as pleased to see the people of Kimberley as, he believed, they were to welcome him. The General then rode into Kimberley, which was reached shortly before 7 o'clock, and paid a brief visit to Kimberley Club. A large crowd assembled in the street, and cheered lustily as the General and staff entered and left the building, the General proceeding to the Sanatorium. The men bivouaced for the night just outside the town.

We are indebted to the courtesy of Mr Beresford, of the London "Daily Telegraph," for the following details of the operations of the column on the march to Kimberley:—

The column, consisting of about 8,000 men, all mounted, is composed of three brigades and 42 guns. The first brigade, under Brigadier-General Porter, consists of portions of the 2nd Scots Greys, 6th Dragoon Guards (Carabineers), the Inniskilling Dragoons, the New South Wales Labours, and the New Zealanders. The second brigade, under Brigadier-General Broadwood, is made up of the Household Cavalry (1st and 2nd Life Guards and the "Blues"), the 10th Hussars, and the 12th Lancers. The third brigade, under Brigadier-General Barton, includes the 9th and 16th Lancers, and a large number of mounted infantry. The artillery consists of seven batteries of Royal Horse Artillery, splendidly horsed, and able to move over the ground with the speed of cavalry. The cavalry left Modder River on Sunday at 2 P.M., and proceeded to Randam, south-east of Honey Nest Kloof, where they found a large force of infantry, who had been brought down by train, arriving. All night long trains laden with troops were running between Modder River and the nearest point of the line. The flying column received orders to push into Kimberley with the greatest possible speed, arriving not later than Friday night. Leaving the infantry still massing in enormous force at Randam, they pushed on at 1.40 on Monday morning, marched for about an hour, and then halted till daylight. About 5.15 the march was resumed, and the next halting place was at the Riet River, where they encamped. Here there was a slight engagement. At about 6 o'clock in the evening the enemy brought a 9-pounder on to the flat, and commenced shelling General French and his staff, the advance scouts having already been fired upon. The range was only about 3,000 yards, and five shells were placed in most unpleasant proximity to the party. Our guns quickly came into action, the Boer gun limbered up and disappeared. Our artillery then devoted its attention to the kopjes, which the Boers were known to occupy, on the Kimberley side of the Riet River. Here the enemy unmasked two guns, one a 9-pounder, and the other a 14-pounder. Four batteries were brought into action against these two guns, which were completely knocked out in a few minutes, but got away. The enemy, dismayed at the rapid movements of our troops, and the unexpected mobility, fled in all directions, and the column crossed at Kuil's Drift without any further opposition at that point. The troops marched forward in magnificent order right across the flat country, and, spread out in squadron columns, made a most imposing sight. On Tuesday the troops moved on to Modder River, passing Jacobedal about five miles to the east, and crossing at Klip Drift after a long day's march of 27 miles. The crossing of the river was expected to be a most difficult performance, but although about 2,000 Boers were seen in the neighbourhood, they fled in a state of panic, leaving many wagons and a large quantity of stores, forage, food, &c, to fall into our hands. General French rested his men at Modder River on Wednesday. During the day a tremendous lot of "sniping" went on, and the Boers harassed the camp with a long-range gun, which, however, did no harm. Our patrols cut off a convoy of four Boer wagons. During the night the infantry arrived at Modder River with six batteries of Field Artillery, and on Thursday morning the flying column, which had been detained awaiting the infantry, proceeded on their march. The Boers now made some show of opposition. Artillery fire commenced at 10 o'clock, and was very heavy, the Boers having six or seven guns in action. Our infantry took up a position on the hills to the east of the camp at Klip Drift, and were heavily shelled by the enemy, who were about 2,000 strong, and appeared to have the range to an inch. The Boers also burst shrapnel over the guns, wounding several artillerymen. Two naval 12-pounders then came on the scene, and one of these long-range weapons was mounted on the kopje due north of the camp, and the most dangerous Boer gun was speedily brought to silence. The cavalry then advanced on the right, and, galloping hard for five miles, executed a most rapid turning movement, which completely demoralised the enemy, who fled in all directions. The cavalry charged among the fugitives, and killed about 20 but the majority were off on their ponies, and were difficult to catch. Those who could not get away fired until our men were within 10 yards of them, then went down on their knees and cried for quarter. Several Boers were found lying on the ground who had been killed by rifle fire, but the majority succumbed to cold steel. About noon the troops halted on a farm where there was some water for the men, but little for the horses, which practically got nothing from about 9 A.M. until 6 in the evening. At 3.30 the troops came in sight of Kimberley, and could see the guns firing and the heliograph working. There was no serious opposition on the part of the enemy. A few shots were fired by the Boer gun posted on Cannon Kopje (between Susannah and Alexandersfontain), and the weapon was then moved on to the ridge behind, whence it fired a few more shots, to which our artillery replied by bursting shrapnel shells in rapid succession exactly over the spot where the gun appeared to be firing. The enemy were evidently completely astonished at the sudden advent of so vast a body of mounted troops, and could be clearly seen from the lookout-station at Beaconsfield galloping away across the Free State border. The troops reached Beaconsfield about 6 o'clock, having completed a journey of about 100 miles in four days, and arriving 24 hours before they were due.

We understand that a large British force is still in the neighbourhood of Modder River station, and that fighting took place while General French's column was still on the line of march, the result of which is not yet known.

The absence of any serious opposition on the part of the Boers to General French's advance was, we understand a great surprise, but the column had orders to fight their way through at all costs, Lord Roberts having decided that the immediate relief of Kimberley was imperative. The column pushed on without transport, carrying their whole supplies on horseback.

OCCUPATION OF ALEXANDERSFONTEIN

Food Supplies Captured.

On Wednesday morning, acting on information brought in by native women to the effect that the Boers were evacuating Alexandersfontein owing to the reported advance of British troops, Major Fraser ordered out a number of the Beaconsfield Town Guard, and made a reconnaissance of the position. Finding that there was little or no sign of Boer activity, Major Fraser, on his own responsibility, and without waiting to communicate with Colonel Kekewich, at once occupied the enemy's trenches. Reinforcements were sent for, and Major Fraser having reported what he had done, orders were given for the place to be held. Companies of the Lancashire Regiment, Kimberley Light Horse, and Diamond Fields Horse were sent out for this purpose, under Major Peakman, Major Fraser returning to his post. Three wagons and spans of oxen were captured, and about 20 head of fine, fat slaughter oxen (making about 40 head of cattle in all), together with a number of horses, mules, and donkeys, and large quantities of vegetables, fresh butter, &c. Six prisoners were taken, and one or two Boers were shot. Further details will be given in to-morrow's paper. The credit of the capture is chiefly due to Major Fraser for his promptitude and resourcefulness, while the Beaconsfield Town Guard may also be deservedly congratulated on having been first on the field at this successful operation.

Excerpt from *Report of a Visit to the
Camps of Women and Children in the Cape
and Orange River Colonies*

EMILY HOBHOUSE

[Emily Hobhouse (1860–1926) was secretary to the South African Conciliation Committee (formed in November 1899). She visited South Africa in
1900 and reported on the atrocities against the Boers held in British concentration camps. Having outraged political opinion in England by her writing and public speaking, she was forcibly prevented from entering South
Africa when she attempted to visit again in 1901.]

*To the Committee of the Distress Fund
for South African Women and Children.*

I.—REPORT AND EXTRACTS FROM LETTERS.

As I have been acting as your delegate in South Africa I am anxious to submit
to you without delay some account of the Camps in which the women and
children are concentrated, and to put before you the need for further effort on
their behalf. By the kind permission of Lord Milner and Lord Kitchener I
have been enabled to visit a certain number of these Camps, investigate the
needs of the people and arrange for the partial administration of the Fund
with which you entrusted me.

Considering the changing condition of the Camps, it is hardly possible to
draw up an ordinary conventional report. It would seem better to place before
you what was written down day by day, as it was seen and as it happened. Here
and there foot-notes point out alterations or improvements of later date. By
this means some faint picture may be presented to your minds of what is being
undergone by the weaker members of two whole countries. Some suggestions
are appended which, if adopted, would go far, in my opinion, to alleviate the
conditions of life in the Camps during the months or years they may be
maintained.—I have, etc.,

E. Hobhouse.

January 22nd.

"I had a splendid truck given me at Capetown, through the kind co-operation
of Sir Alfred Milner—a large double-covered one, capable of holding 12 tons.

I took £200 worth of groceries, besides all the bales of clothing I could muster. The truck left Capetown the day before myself, was hitched on to my train at De Aar, and so arrived when I did. The first thing next day was to go down to the goods station, claim the truck, and arrange for its unloading. This morning I have spent arranging all my stores—unpacking and sorting them. It is very hot. I think the essence of delightful work is when you quite forget you have a body, but here the heat keeps you in constant recollection that you are still in the flesh, and it's a great hindrance. I did not have a bad journey from Capetown, though it was rather a lonely one. Going through the Karoo it was very hot, and the second day there were horrible dust-storms, varied by thunderstorms. The sand penetrated through closed windows and doors, filled eyes and ears, turned my hair red and covered everything like a table-cloth. As far as extent and sweep of land and sky go the Karoo is delightful, but it's a vast solitude, and in many parts the very plants grow two or three yards apart, as if they shunned society. From Colesberg on it was a desolate outlook. The land seemed dead and silent as far as eye could reach, absolutely without life, only carcases of horses, mules, and cattle, with a sort of acute anguish in their look, and bleached bones and refuse of many kinds. I saw a few burnt farms, but those unburnt seemed still and lifeless also, and no work is going on in the fields. Really, the line the whole way up is a string of Tommies, yawning at their posts, and these always crowded to the carriage windows to beg for newspapers, or anything, they said, to pass the time. I gave them all I had, and all my novels. . . . But I must pass on to tell you about the Women's Camp, which, after all, is the central point of interest."

The Bloemfontein Camp.

January 26th.

The exile camp here is a good two miles from the town, dumped down on the southern slope of a kopje, right out on to the bare brown veldt, not a vestige of a tree in any direction, nor shade of any description. It was about four o'clock of a scorching afternoon when I set foot in the camp, and I can't tell you what I felt like, so I won't try.

I began by finding a woman whose sister I had met in Capetown. It is such a puzzle to find your way in a village of bell tents, no streets or names or numbers. There are nearly 2,000 people in this one camp, of which some few are men—they call them "hands up" men—and over 900[1] children.

Imagine the heat outside the tents, and the suffocation inside! We sat on

1. Those numbers are now nearly doubled.

their khaki blankets, rolled up, inside Mrs. B.'s tent; and the sun blazed through the single canvas, and the flies lay thick and black on everything; no chair, no table, nor any room for such; only a deal box, standing on its end, served as a wee pantry. In this tiny tent live Mrs. B.'s five children (three quite grown up) and a little Kaffir servant girl. Many tents have more occupants. Mrs. P. came in, and Mrs. R. and others, and they told me their stories, and we cried together, and even laughed together, and chatted bad Dutch and bad English all the afternoon. On wet nights the water streams down through the canvas and comes flowing in, as it knows how to do in this country, under the flap of the tent, and wets their blanket as they lie on the ground. While we sat there a snake came in. They said it was a puff adder, very poisonous, so they all ran out, and I attacked the creature with my parasol. I could not bear to think the thing should be at large in a community mostly sleeping on the ground. After a struggle I wounded it, and then a man came with a mallet and finished it off.

Mrs. P. is very brave and calm. She has six children, ranging from fifteen down to two years, and she does not know where any one of them is.[2] She was taken right away from them; her husband is in detention of some kind at Bloemfontein, but not allowed to see her. She expects her confinement in about three weeks, and yet has to lie on the bare ground till she is stiff and sore, and she has had nothing to sit on for over two months, but must squat on a rolled-up blanket. I felt quite sure you would like her to have a mattress, and I asked her if she would accept one. She did so very gratefully, and I did not rest yesterday till I got one out to her. All her baby linen was in readiness at home, but all is lost. This is but one case, quite ordinary, among hundreds and hundreds. The women are wonderful. They cry very little and never complain. The very magnitude of their sufferings, indignities, loss and anxiety seems to lift them beyond tears. These people, who have had comfortable, even luxurious homes, just set themselves to quiet endurance and to make the best of their bare and terrible lot; only when it cuts afresh at them through their children do their feelings flash out. Mrs. M., for instance. She has six children in camp, all ill, two in the tin hospital with typhoid, and four sick in the tent. She also expects her confinement soon. Her husband is in Ceylon. She has means, and would gladly provide for herself either in town or in the Colony, where she has relations, or by going back to her farm. It was not burnt, only the furniture was destroyed; yet here she has to stay, watching her children droop and sicken. For their sakes she did plead with tears that she might go and fend for herself.

2. Three months later—Mrs. P. has been rejoined to all her children, except two.

I call this camp system a wholesale cruelty. It can never be wiped out of the memories of the people. It presses hardest on the children. They droop in the terrible heat, and with the insufficient, unsuitable food; whatever you do, whatever the authorities do, and they are, I believe, doing their best with very limited means, it is all only a miserable patch upon a great ill. Thousands, physically unfit, are placed in conditions of life which they have not strength to endure. In front of them is blank ruin. There are cases, too, in which whole families are severed and scattered, they don't know where.

Will you try, somehow, to make the British public understand the position, and force it to ask itself what is going to be done with these people? There must be full 15,000[3] of them; I should not wonder if there are not more. Some few have means, but more are ruined, and have not a present penny. In one of two ways must the British public support them, either by taxation through the authorities, or else by voluntary charity.

If the people at home want to save their purses (you see, I appeal to low motives), why not allow those who can maintain themselves to go to friends and relatives in the Colony? Many wish ardently to do so. That would be some relief. If only the English people would try to exercise a little imagination—picture the whole miserable scene. Entire villages and districts rooted up and dumped in a strange, bare place.

To keep these Camps going is murder to the children. Still, of course, by more judicious management they could be improved; but, do what you will, you can't undo the thing itself.

To-day is Sunday; and all the day I have been toiling and moiling over the bales of clothes—unpacking, sorting, and putting up in bundles. We were so glad of such odd things, such as stays and little boys' braces! I found some baby linen for Mrs. P. I do not think that there is a single superfluous article. But what a family to clothe!

Now I must tell you their rations:—

Daily—
  Meat, ½ lb (with bone and fat).
  Coffee, 2 oz.
  Wholemeal, ¾ lb.
  Condensed milk, one-twelfth of tin.
  Sugar, 2 oz.
  Salt, ½ oz.

3. Of course the numbers are now largely increased; over 20,000 on the Orange River Colony alone; 25,000 in Transvaal Camps, besides the Colony and Natal.

That is all, nothing else to fill in. Once they sometimes had potatoes, seven potatoes for seven people, but that has long been impossible. Soap also has been unattainable, and none given in the rations.[4] Some people have money, and may add to the above by purchasing certain things at some little retail shops allowed in the Camp, which charge exorbitant prices,[5] for instance, 6d. for a reel of cotton. But they are, naturally, terribly afraid of parting with their money, feeling it is all they will have to begin life on again, for every one's income is stopped, nothing is coming in. It is, indeed, a dreary prospect. Some few of those who had cash in hand buried it out on their farms for safety, and now, of course, cannot reach it. All say, if released, they would make a living somehow, and shelter beneath the ruined home would be as good as these often rotten tents. It is hard enough that, but countless children's lives would be saved thereby.

We have much typhoid, and are dreading an outbreak, so I am directing my energies to getting the water of the Modder River boiled. As well swallow typhoid germs whole as drink that water—so say doctors. Yet they cannot boil it all; for—first, fuel is very scarce; that which is supplied weekly would not cook a meal a day, and they have to search the already bare kopjes for a supply. There is hardly a bit to be had. Second, they have no extra utensil to hold the water when boiled. I propose, therefore, to give each tent another pail or crock, and get a proclamation issued that all drinking water must be boiled. It will cost nearly £50 to do this, even if utensils are procurable.

In spite of small water supply, and it is very spare, all the tents I have been in are exquisitely neat and clean, except two, and they were ordinary, and such limitations!

January 31st.

I suggested a big railway boiler[6] to boil every drop of water before it is served out. This would economise fuel, and be cheaper in the long run, besides ensuring the end desired, for many could not be trusted to boil their own. Next we want forage for the cows. Fifty have been secured, but they only

---

4. With much persuasion, and weeks after requisitioning, soap is now given in occasionally in very minute quantities—certainly not enough for clothes and personal washing.

5. In some camps steps are now taken to prevent exorbitant charges in these shops in certain articles.

6. None could be had, so the Government built furnaces and tanks. When the camp doubled this would not supply sufficient, so I left money to put up another.

get four buckets of milk out of the poor starved things.[7] What is needed is a wash-house with water laid on from the town, but I see no chance of it. Some people in town still assert that the Camp is a haven of bliss. Well, there are eyes and no eyes. I was at the camp to-day, and just in one little corner this is the sort of thing I found. The nurse, underfed and overworked, just sinking on to her bed, hardly able to hold herself up, after coping with some thirty typhoid and other patients, with only the untrained help of two Boer girls—cooking as well as nursing to do herself.

Next, I was called to see a woman panting in the heat, just sickening for her confinement. Fortunately, I had a night-dress in my bundle to give her, and two tiny baby gowns.

Next tent, a six months' baby gasping its life out on its mother's knee. The doctor had given it powders in the morning, but it had taken nothing since. Two or three others drooping and sick in that tent.

Next, child recovering from measles, sent back from hospital before it could walk, stretched on the ground, white and wan; three or four others lying about.

Next, a girl of twenty-one lay dying on a stretcher. The father, a big, gentle Boer, kneeling beside her; while, next tent, his wife was watching a child of six, also dying, and one of about five drooping. Already this couple had lost three children in the hospital and so would not let these go, though I begged hard to take them out of the hot tent. "We must watch these ourselves," he said. I sent ——— to find brandy, and got some down the girl's throat, but for the most part you must stand and look on, helpless to do anything, because there is nothing to do anything with.

Then a man came up and said: "Sister" (they call me "Sister," or "Di Meisie van England"), "come and see my child, sick for nearly three months." It was a dear little chap of four, and nothing left of him but his great brown eyes and white teeth, from which the lips were drawn back, too thin to close. His body was emaciated. The little fellow had craved for fresh milk; but, of course, there had been none till these last two days, and now the fifty cows only give four buckets, so you can imagine what feed there is for them. I sent ——— for some of this, and made him lay the child outside on a pillow to get the breeze that comes up at sunset. I can't describe what it is to see these children lying about in a state of collapse. It's just exactly like faded flowers thrown away. And one has to stand and look on at such misery, and be able to do almost nothing.

SOURCE: Emily Hobhouse, *Report of a Visit to the Camps of Women and Children in the Cape and Orange River Colonies* (London: Friars Printing Association, 1901), 3–5.

7. Forage was refused, being too precious. After the rains the milk supply was better.

Excerpt from *What I Remember*
DAME MILLICENT GARRETT FAWCETT

[For fifty years Dame Millicent Fawcett (1847–1929) campaigned ardently for women's suffrage in England. In 1901 she was asked by the government to lead a women's delegation to South Africa to investigate the allegations of atrocities in the British concentration camps. Depending on the political perspective, her report either vindicated—or whitewashed—the administration of the camps.]

All through the camps we found almost without exception that the schools were a great success. There had been no attempt whatever by the Boer Government in the Transvaal to provide organized education for their people, and they availed themselves eagerly and in considerable numbers of the facilities for education which the camp schools afforded. It was rather touching to see grown-up young men and women sitting among the children and learning with them; the most popular subjects with these adults were English and arithmetic. Dutch teachers were in many instances appointed in the schools. It interested us on one occasion to hear a Dutch schoolmaster instructing his class how to grapple with the pronunciation of the English G. He wrote on the blackboard the letters D, T, Z, and then ended with a half-suppressed sneeze, which he could not express by letters of the alphabet. We had never realized before that our poor English G presented such difficulties to foreigners, though we knew how curiously difficult the Dutch G was to us.

In this journey through the concentration camps I first came to know and value the extraordinary lovable qualities of the British Tommy. He was kindness and gentleness itself to every child and woman among the refugees; he was also generous to a fault. He would give thoughtlessly and profusely to those he came across, and although he was a good grumbler on his own account when things were going smoothly, his spirits always seemed to rise when he was in acute discomfort and misery himself. I have seen our Tommies bivouacking in a station in the pouring rain, and have heard no grousing from them under what must have been physical misery. A lady with whom we made friends at De Aar told us of recent floods there owing to the rapid rising of the river after torrential rain. The men were ordered to save the forage supplies, and were working for hours up to their waists in water, shouting at the top of their voices some soldiers' chanty, such as, "Oh why did I leave my nice little 'ome in Bloomsberree? Where for three and six a week I lived in Luxuree."

What we saw in the camps and especially the eagerness of the people in them to get education, led my daughter to apply to the Government at home for leave to go back and take part in the setting up of permanent educational machinery in the Transvaal, then under the control of Mr. E. B. Sargant, and later of Mr. (now General Sir) Fabian Ware. She returned to Newnham in 1901, but came out again in 1902 to share in the interesting work of establishing public elementary education in the Transvaal. I went to see her there in 1903, and revisited many of the places I had seen on my first visit, my dear friend Katherine Brereton bearing me company. On this second visit, the war being over, I saw something of the gradual recovery of the country from its devastating effects; railway and other bridges were repaired, houses rebuilt; animals, sheep, and oxen looking less like concertinas; the horrid flocks of vultures had vanished and the great veldt was less thickly strewn with dead animals. But I also saw something of the crowd of orphans which every war leaves behind it. The new Transvaal Government had assembled many of these poor children at Irene, where they were under the care and guidance of a most gentle and kindly lady, Miss Frances Taylor, sister of Mrs. George Cadbury. She and I made the forty-eight hours' journey from Johannesburg to Cape Town together, and had the carriage to ourselves; we therefore had many opportunities for conversation, of which we thoroughly availed ourselves. One thing which Miss Taylor said stuck in my memory. It was this: "Do tell my brother-in-law, Mr. George Cadbury, that the concentration camps were not in the least like what he imagined them to be." I replied by asking her if she had told him that herself. She said that she had, and I naturally rejoined, "If he did not believe you, what reason have I to hope that he will believe me?"

On this second visit I was much interested in seeing something of the process of reconstruction going on to repair the ravages of the war: schools, orphanages, training colleges for nurses and teachers, all doing good work. At one place where a training college had been established I was particularly interested to find that the Dutch board of management had applied to a well-known institution in London to supply them with an English teacher of Domestic Economy. I hoped it looked as if the iron of hatred had not entered very deeply into their souls. My cousin Edmund, mentioned in an earlier chapter, had taken a very active part in the events which led up to the war; but he never lost his appreciation of the fine qualities of the Boers. For one of the British and Boer cemeteries, I think at Wagon Hill, he wrote the following epitaph:

> Together, sundered once by blood and speech,
> Joined here in equal muster of the brave,

Lie Boer and Briton, foes each worthy each.
    May Peace strike root into their common grave,
    And blossoming where the fathers fought and died,
    Bear fruit for sons that labour side by side.

To return to our first visit: we saw all the concentration camps except the one at Fort Elizabeth, of which even the pro-Boer ladies at Cape Town had no complaint to make; some of the camps—for instance, Mafeking, Vryburg, and Kimberley—we saw twice, with a considerable interval between our two visits. We went back to Mafeking because of the renewal of a severe epidemic. On 15th August, just before our first visit, a number of Boer refugees had been brought in, and these had among them the following diseases: measles of a malignant type, enteric, malaria, fever, cerebrospinal meningitis, whooping cough, and chicken-pox. The new-comers were neither examined nor isolated, and the various diseases which they had brought with them spread and flourished to an appalling degree. Our recommendations had been neglected, and therefore on our second visit we urged the removal of the Superintendent, and that adequate support should be given to Dr. Morrow, who was working loyally and faithfully to supply his place. We also put on record our opinion that the Superintendent and the former medical officer had been grossly to blame for the bad condition and the high death-rate in this camp. We felt more and more how great was the need of the people for fresh vegetables. "Bully beef and bread," we said in our report, "are quite unsuitable diet for young children," and we urged that if suitable food could not be provided for a camp of 4,000 at Mafeking the camp should be removed elsewhere. Lord Methuen, who was then in military command of the district, did everything he could to help the poor people in the camp, giving up to them his own special E.P. tents to provide additional hospital accommodation.

Our experience of our two visits to Kimberley was instructive. On our first visit on 26th and 27th August 1901, we found two English ladies, Miss A. and Miss B., sent by a committee sitting in London. We called on them; it was quite easy to see which was their tent because of the baths outside put upside down to dry. We told them of our desire to see everything that we ought to see in the camp and to make recommendations calculated to help the people and reduce the death-rate. The deaths in August up to the 26th had been 141, of which 93 had been of children of from 1 to 3 years. We begged the ladies to put the knowledge they must have acquired during their residence, so far as it was possible, at our disposal; but they were very uncommunicative, and obviously hostile to us. Miss A., who had resided for five weeks in the camp, hardly told us anything. She said she wished to remove to some other camp "where the need was greater," and gave us no practical suggestions of any kind. We thought the death-rate just quoted showed as great a "need" as the most zealous philanthropist could desire. We were sorry they were so uncommunicative, because we felt that if they had chosen to do so they could have helped us very much. When we revisited the Kimberley camp on 6th and 7th November we found the whole condition immensely improved. The hospital accommodation was adequate, the medical and nursing staff had been reinforced; four trained nurses, who were helped by nine Boer probationers, were doing their work well. A camp matron who had been furnished by the Victoria League with four 10-gallon Soyer stoves was now looking after the convalescent children and supplying about 200 of them with a pint of good soup daily, and the excellent camp matron was just beginning to induce some of the Boer girls in the camp to act for her as visiting sisters. I believe she eventually got a staff of 12 of these girls. Miss A. and Miss B. were still in residence, but they had entirely changed in their demeanour towards us. From having been extremely cold and distant, they had become helpful and friendly; and they told us frankly some of their recent experiences. Like ourselves they had been impressed by the great need in the camp of fresh vegetables, and had urged that practically the only way of getting them was to grow them on the spot. They had encouraged families to make little gardens of their own round their tents, offering prizes varying from £2 for an adult to 10s, for a child for the best garden; but the supply thus promoted was inadequate. By co-operation with the authorities the Misses A. and B. had secured a promise of a grant of land in the immediate neighbourhood suitable for a large garden; one of the ladies, on behalf of her committee in London, had promised £70 for fencing it in; the Government promised water, an all-important and expensive item, besides seeds and implements, if the able-bodied men, of whom there were over 200 in the camp, would give the labour: these men called a meeting to consider whether they would do this or not, and they decided to refuse. Their line of argument was that the British had brought them there and were therefore responsible for providing them and the whole camp with everything that was necessary for their health. Both the ladies were very angry and disappointed. Our colleague, Dr. Jane Waterston, who had lived in Cape Colony for about half a century, was not at all surprised. It is one of the curses of having manual labour done by what most people consider an inferior race that labour itself is despised, the people who work being considered for that very reason inferior to those who overlook or do nothing. Miss B. said the people in the camp ought to be compelled to work, and told us, moreover, that in her opinion giving relief in the form of clothes did more harm than good; both ladies had their doubts whether the gifts of clothing had not been taken down into the town of Kimberley and sold. Miss A. was also indignant at the alleged maladministration at Cape Town in reference to £600 worth of goods sent out to her by her committee in London. Instead of forwarding them to her, the goods had been consigned to the Dutch clergyman resident in the camp, who had given them away without any reference to her or to the source from which they had been provided. We expressed sympathy, but did not feel we had any authority to take action in the matter.

We were decidedly pleased by the improvement which had taken place in the camp since our first visit. One woman with whom we had a good deal of conversation began rather bitterly that she did not know why she should be interned there, although her husband was on commando. She gradually became more friendly and said that she had nothing to complain of, that the food was good and sufficient, but that she would like the opportunity of earning a little pocket-money. Finally, looking round her tent, which was orderly and clean, she said, "It is beginning to be a little home to me."

We visited an orphanage in Kimberley of over 50 children, some of whom had been sent from the camp. Their ages varied from 1 ½ to 15 years. They looked healthy and were very bright and cheerful. They all spoke and understood English perfectly, and were learning their lessons, from Dutch teachers, out of English books.

When we were wending our way northwards again towards Pretoria, we sought an interview with General Kitchener. We had already had the advantage of several conversations with Sir A. Milner (now Lord Milner) and had told him our views about the necessity of a more varied dietary for the camps. He said he would support our application, but that the final decision must rest with Lord Kitchener, the allocation of extra trucks for the supply of the camps being a military matter. We therefore wrote and asked Lord Kitchener to see us. He agreed to do so, and sent his letter by General Sir John Maxwell, who had the camps especially under his charge. We had heard a good deal of Lord Kitchener's general opinion of the female sex, and rather smiled when we read his letter, for he expressed a wish that of the six of us only two should come on the deputation to see him. Our colleagues decided that these should be Lady Knox and myself. At the appointed hour General Maxwell arrived with a carriage to take us to Lord Kitchener's house. It was a charming and attractive building standing in a garden. We entered a large square hall, where we were asked to be seated while General Maxwell went into the room where Lord Kitchener was working. He left the door wide open, and we could not help hearing what he said. Again we smiled when we heard Lord Kitchener's voice inquire anxiously, "How many are there of them?" In another minute we were shown into his room, and thereupon there ensued the most satisfactory and businesslike interview that I, at any rate, had ever had of an approximately similar nature. We set forth our views as to the necessity of providing greater variety in the dietary of the camps, and suggested the addition of rice to the rations on account of the number of ways in which, with even the simplest appliances, it could be cooked: stewed in milk for children, made appetizing for adults by adding a little curry powder, and so on. He listened, and then said, "It is a question of trucks. What you propose would mean an extra truck every week." We said we had recognized that, but still urged that the extra truck should be provided. He replied, "I allow 30 trucks per week for the food supply of the whole civil population of the Free State; of these 30, 16 go to the camps and 14 to the rest of the civil population. Do you wish me to give 17 to the camps and only 13 to the other civilians?" We exclaimed, "Certainly not. We have been in these people's houses and know that already they are on very short commons before the end of each week. We don't want to take an ounce from them; we want an extra truck." And an extra truck was agreed to, so that we felt that our talk with the great man had been very satisfactory. Not an unnecessary word had been spoken, and therefore no time had been wasted. I liked him far better than any of the politicians I had gone to on deputations in London. I always say that Lady Knox and I, after this interview with Lord Kitchener, received the compliment of our lives, for, after sampling two of us, he invited the whole six of us to dinner! We did not all go; but I think there were four of us. Lord Kitchener took me in to dinner and I had much interesting conversation with him. Later we had many talks about him with men of his staff and others. We were told that on his journeys up and down the line or on horseback his keen eye saw everything and everybody, noting which men were doing their work well and which were slack or indifferent; the first were promoted, the latter were, in the phrase of the day, "Stellenbosched," i.e. sent where they could do no harm. Previous to our conversation with Lord Kitchener, we had had experience of subordinate officials of the type which believed that as soon as a thing was written down on a piece of paper, it was done. One man had read out to us a list of groceries and asked us if we did not think it admirable English: another, when we emphasized the urgency of the fuel question, replied that he had indented for further supplies six weeks ago, and seemed quite hurt when we said that it had not actually arrived. These were the sort of people who ought to be "Stellenbosched," especially in a life-and-death business like war.

As soon as our work of inspection was over we repaired to Durban to draw up our final report. We stayed there over a week and worked daily at our report. It was signed by the whole six of us without reservations. The rest and excellent food of our good hotel were very welcome to us. We took a German ship, the *Herzog,* from Durban to Naples, and had a most interesting journey, putting in at Beira, Mozambique, Zanzibar, Dar-es-Salaam, Lamu, Aden, etc. At Lamu our ship was visited by a health officer, who turned out to be Dr. Alfred Paget, son of our old friend Sir George Paget, of Cambridge. He knew the place well, and was very good to us in helping us to see some of its curious manners and customs. A well-born native lady at Lamu is not content with being veiled; when she walks abroad she is enclosed in a little movable tent, which is carried by a female attendant who precedes her mistress. I got a "snap" of this example of female modesty, but Dr. Paget was very careful not to allow this to be discovered. Our ship proceeded very leisurely up the East Coast of Africa. Zanzibar, we found a most entrancing place; the architecture was very attractive, the immensely thick walls giving deep recesses to all windows and doors, and making an admirable effect. What I most remember of Zanzibar, however, is the wonderful beauty of the gold mohur-tree: it was in full blossom when we were there. The tree itself is as big as an English forest tree, and it was crowned by great trusses of scarlet flowers, glowing like fire against the dark blue sky. Sir Harry Johnston made a beautiful drawing of it, and used it as a sort of wall-paper design for a lining to one of his books on Africa. It was worth going to Africa just to see it in all its glory. We were also taken to Sir John Kirk's garden, a few miles out of Durban, full of all kinds of botanical treasures. The frangipani-tree is what I best remember there: very lovely and very sweet-scented, but not equal to the gold mohur-tree.

There was a Boer lady on board the *Herzog* with whom we made friends. She told us that at the same time as the terrible infant mortality was raging in the concentration camps Mrs. Kruger, whom she knew intimately, had had six of her grandchildren to stay with her. The virulent form of measles which had swept the camps carried away four of these children in their grandmother's house, notwithstanding all the care which they received from the outset of the illness.

After we had returned home, and when our report had appeared as a Blue Book and had been circulated to both Houses of Parliament, I received the following letter from Mr. Brodrick, now Lord Midleton:

War Office, *March 6,* 1902.
Dear Mrs. Fawcett,

Now that with the publication of the Blue Book your task may be said to be at an end, I cannot let time pass without expressing to you, and your colleagues, who worked with you on the Concentration Camps Commission, my very sincere thanks for the able way in which you carried out the work which we asked you to undertake. The difficulties of it are well known to you who had to surmount them and did so with great success. The importance of it is patent to all who know what a great mass of questions were involved, and I hope you will kindly convey to your colleagues, both here and in South Africa, the thanks which are due to them and to yourself from me, on behalf of His Majesty's Government, for the very zealous and able way in which their arduous work was brought to a conclusion, which is, I think, universally recognized to have been satisfactory.

Yours very truly,
St. John Brodrick.

To this I replied:

2, Gower Street, *March* 8, 1902.
Dear Mr. Brodrick,

Your kind letter received last night gave me very great pleasure, and I am sure my colleagues, both here and in South Africa, will be equally gratified by it. We also feel grateful for the kind and generous terms in which you and Mr. Chamberlain alluded to the work of our Commission, in the House of Commons, on Tuesday last. I am sure I may speak for my colleagues as well as for myself when I say it was a real satisfaction to us to be allowed to do some special work for our country in South Africa during the present crisis. I will not say that visiting and reporting on the camps was not fatiguing; but it was very interesting and quite straightforward and easy, for, as we said in reply to inquiries from the camp people at Aliwal North, all we had to do was "to see and hear all we could and to tell the truth."

Believe me, yours very truly,
Millicent G. Fawcett.

SOURCE: Millicent Garrett Fawcett, *What I Remember* (London: T. F. Unwin, 1924), 163–74.

Prisoners of War

WINSTON CHURCHILL

[Winston Churchill was a newspaper correspondent in South Africa during the early part of the Anglo-Boer War. His account includes stories of train hijackings, Boer imprisonment, the battle of Spion Koop, and the siege of Ladysmith.]

Pretoria: November 24, 1899.

The position of a prisoner of war is painful and humiliating. A man tries his best to kill another, and finding that he cannot succeed asks his enemy for mercy. The laws of war demand that this should be accorded, but it is impossible not to feel a sense of humbling obligation to the captor from whose hand we take our lives. All military pride, all independence of spirit must be put aside. These may be carried to the grave, but not into captivity. We must prepare ourselves to submit, to obey, to endure. Certain things—sufficient food and water and protection during good behaviour—the victor must supply or be a savage, but beyond these all else is favour. Favours must be accepted from those with whom we have a long and bitter quarrel, from those who feel fiercely that we seek to do them cruel injustice. The dog who has been whipped must be thankful for the bone that is flung to him.

When the prisoners captured after the destruction of the armoured train had been disarmed and collected in a group we found that there were fifty-six unwounded or slightly wounded men, besides the more serious cases lying on the scene of the fight. The Boers crowded round, looking curiously at their prize, and we ate a little chocolate that by good fortune—for we had had no breakfast—was in our pockets, and sat down on the muddy ground to think. The rain streamed down from a dark leaden sky, and the coats of the horses steamed in the damp. 'Voorwärts,' said a voice, and, forming in a miserable procession, two wretched officers, a bare-headed, tattered Correspondent, four sailors with straw hats and 'H.M.S. Tartar' in gold letters on the ribbons—ill-timed jauntiness—some fifty soldiers and volunteers, and two or three railwaymen, we started, surrounded by the active Boer horsemen. Yet, as we climbed the low hills that surrounded the place of combat I looked back and saw the engine steaming swiftly away beyond Frere Station. Something at least was saved from the ruin; information would be carried to the troops at Estcourt, a good many of the troops and some of the wounded would escape, the locomotive was itself of value, and perhaps in saving all these things some little honour had been saved as well.

'You need not walk fast,' said a Boer in excellent English; 'take your time.' Then another, seeing me hatless in the downpour, threw me a soldier's cap—one of the Irish Fusilier caps, taken, probably, near Ladysmith. So they were not cruel men, these enemy. That was a great surprise to me, for I had read much of the literature of this land of lies, and fully expected every hardship and indignity. At length we reached the guns which had played on us for so many minutes—two strangely long barrels sitting very low on carriages of four wheels, like a break in which horses are exercised. They looked offensively modern, and I wondered why our Army had not got field artillery with fixed ammunition and 8,000 yards range. Some officers and men of the Staats Artillerie, dressed in a drab uniform with blue facings, approached us. The commander, Adjutant Roos—as he introduced himself—made a polite salute. He regretted the unfortunate circumstances of our meeting; he complimented the officers on their defence—of course, it was hopeless from the first; he trusted his fire had not annoyed us; we should, he thought, understand the necessity for them to continue; above all he wanted to know how the engine had been able to get away, and how the line could have been cleared of wreckage under his guns. In fact, he behaved as a good professional soldier should, and his manner impressed me.

We waited here near the guns for half an hour, and meanwhile the Boers searched amid the wreckage for dead and wounded. A few of the wounded were brought to where we were, and laid on the ground, but most of them were placed in the shelter of one of the overturned trucks. As I write I do not know with any certainty what the total losses were, but the Boers say that they buried five dead, sent ten seriously wounded into Ladysmith, and kept three severely wounded in their field ambulances. Besides this, we are told that sixteen severely wounded escaped on the engine, and we have with the prisoners seven men, including myself, slightly wounded by splinters or injured in the derailment. If this be approximately correct, it seems that the casualties in the hour and a half of fighting were between thirty-five and forty: not many, perhaps, considering the fire, but out of 120 enough at least.

After a while we were ordered to march on, and looking over the crest of the hill a strange and impressive sight met the eye. Only about 300 men had attacked the train, and I had thought that this was the enterprise of a separate detachment, but as the view extended I saw that this was only a small part of a large, powerful force marching south, under the personal direction of General Joubert, to attack Estcourt. Behind every hill, thinly veiled by the driving rain, masses of mounted men, arranged in an orderly disorder, were halted, and from the rear long columns of horsemen rode steadily forward. Certainly I did not see less than 3,000, and I did not see nearly all. Evidently an important operation was in progress, and a collision either at Estcourt or Mooi River impended. This was the long expected advance: worse late than never.

Our captors conducted us to a rough tent which had been set up in a hollow in one of the hills, and which we concluded was General Joubert's headquarters. Here we were formed in a line, and soon surrounded by a bearded crowd of Boers cloaked in mackintosh. I explained that I was a Special Correspondent, and asked to see General Joubert. But in the throng it was impossible to tell who were the superiors. My credentials were taken from me by a man who said he was a Field Cornet, and who promised that they should be laid before the General forthwith. Meanwhile we waited in the rain, and the Boers questioned us. My certificate as a correspondent bore a name better known than liked in the Transvaal. Moreover, some of the private soldiers had been talking. 'You are the son of Lord Randolph Churchill?' said a Scottish Boer, abruptly. I did not deny the fact. Immediately there was much talking, and all crowded round me, looking and pointing, while I heard my name repeated on every side. 'I am a newspaper correspondent,' I said, 'and you ought not to hold me prisoner.' The Scottish Boer laughed. 'Oh,' he said, 'we do not catch lords' sons every day.' Whereat they all chuckled, and began to explain that I should be allowed to play football at Pretoria.

All this time I was expecting to be brought before General Joubert, from whom I had some hopes I should obtain assurances that my character as a press correspondent would be respected. But suddenly a mounted man rode up and ordered the prisoners to march away towards Colenso. The escort, twenty horsemen, closed round us. I addressed their leader, and demanded either that I should be taken before the General, or that my credentials should be given back. But the so-called Field Cornet was not to be seen. The only response was, 'Voorwärts,' and as it seemed useless, undignified, and even dangerous to discuss the matter further with these people, I turned and marched off with the rest.

We tramped for six hours across sloppy fields and along tracks deep and slippery with mud, while the rain fell in a steady downpour and soaked everyone to the skin. The Boer escort told us several times not to hurry and to go our own pace, and once they allowed us to halt for a few moments. But we had had neither food nor water, and it was with a feeling of utter weariness that I saw the tin roofs of Colenso rise in the distance. We were put into a corrugated iron shed near the station, the floors of which were four inches deep with torn railway forms and account books. Here we flung ourselves down exhausted, and what with the shame, the disappointment, the excitement of the morning, the misery of the present, and physical weakness, it seemed that love of life was gone, and I thought almost with envy of a soldier I had seen during the fight lying quite still on the embankment, secure in the calm philosophy of death from 'the slings and arrows of outrageous fortune.'

After the Boers had lit two fires they opened one of the doors of the shed and told us we might come forth and dry ourselves. A newly slaughtered ox lay on the ground, and strips of his flesh were given to us. These we toasted on sticks over the fire and ate greedily, though since the animal had been alive five minutes before one felt a kind of cannibal. Other Boers not of our escort who were occupying Colenso came to look at us. With two of these who were brothers, English by race, Afrikanders by birth, Boers by choice, I had some conversation. The war, they said, was going well. Of course, it was a great matter to face the power and might of the British Empire, still they were resolved. They would drive the English out of South Africa for ever, or else fight to the last man. I said:

'You attempt the impossible. Pretoria will be taken by the middle of March. What hope have you of withstanding a hundred thousand soldiers?'

'If I thought,' said the younger of the two brothers vehemently, 'that the Dutchmen would give in because Pretoria was taken, I would smash my rifle on those metals this very moment. We will fight for ever.' I could only reply:

'Wait and see how you feel when the tide is running the other way. It does not seem so easy to die when death is near.' The man said,

'I will wait.'

Then we made friends. I told him that I hoped he would come safely through the war, and live to see a happier and a nobler South Africa under the flag which had been good enough for his forefathers; and he took off his blanket—which he was wearing with a hole in the middle like a cloak—and gave it to me to sleep in. So we parted, and presently, as night fell, the Field Cornet who had us in charge bade us carry a little forage into the shed to sleep on, and then locked us up in the dark, soldiers, sailors, officers, and Correspondent—a broken-spirited jumble.

I could not sleep. Vexation of spirit, a cold night, and wet clothes withheld sweet oblivion. The rights and wrongs of the quarrel, the fortunes and chances of the war, forced themselves on the mind. What men they were, these Boers! I thought of them as I had seen them in the morning riding forward through the rain—thousands of independent riflemen, thinking for themselves, possessed of beautiful weapons, led with skill, living as they rode without commissariat or transport or ammunition column, moving like the wind, and supported by iron constitutions and a stern, hard Old Testament God who should surely smite the Amalekites hip and thigh. And then, above the rain storm that beat loudly on the corrugated iron, I heard the sound of a chaunt. The Boers were singing their evening psalm, and the menacing notes—more full of indignant war than love and mercy—struck a chill into my heart, so that I thought after all that the war was unjust, that the Boers were better men than we, that Heaven was against us, that Ladysmith, Mafeking, and Kimberley would fall, that the Estcourt garrison would perish, that foreign Powers would intervene, that we should lose South Africa, and that that would be the beginning of the end. So for the time I despaired of the Empire, nor was it till the morning sun—all the brighter after the rain storms, all the warmer after the chills—struck in through the windows that things reassumed their true colours and proportions.

SOURCE: Chapter 8 in *London to Ladysmith via Pretoria* (London: Longman, Green, 1900), 98–109.

Methods of Barbarism

[Many were the reports on the "methods of barbarisms" attributed to the British army in South Africa, as reflected in the following excerpts from various sources.]

Farm burning goes merrily on, and our course through the country is marked, as in prehistoric ages, by pillars of smoke by day and fire by night. We usually burn from six to a dozen farms a day; these being about all that in this sparsely inhabited country we encounter. I do not gather that any special reason or cause is alleged or proven against the farms burnt. If Boers have used the farm; if the owner is on commando; if the line within a certain distance has been blown up; or even if there are Boers in the neighbourhood who persist in fighting—these are some of the reasons. Of course the people living in the farms have no say in these matters, and are quite powerless to interfere with the plans of the fighting Boers. Anyway we find that one reason or other generally covers nearly every farm we come to, and so to save trouble we burn the lot without inquiry; unless, indeed, which sometimes happens, some names are given in before marching in the morning of farms to be spared. (Captain L. March Philips. *With Rimington* [London: Arnold, 1901], 41)

'Then why did you burn the farms?' 'By the General's orders. We used to have plenty of fun. All the rooms were ransacked. You can't imagine what beautiful things there were there—copper kettles, handsome chairs and couches, lovely chests of drawers, and all sort of books. I've smashed dozens of pianos. Half a dozen of us would go up to as fine a grand piano as ever I've seen. Some would commence playing on the keys with the butts of their rifles. Others would smash off the legs and panels, and, finally, completely wreck it. Pictures would be turned into targets, and the piano panels would be taken outside and used as fuel to boil our tea or coffee. And then we could enjoy ourselves if it was cold; but,' he added ruefully, 'it was generally hot—boiling hot. After this we would set the building on fire, and as we left, riding together or detached over the sandy waste, we would see the flames rising up, and soon there would be nothing left but black smouldering embers. We would do the same with the next farm we came across.' (Soldier from the Warwickshire Regiment, quoted in the *Warwickshire Advertiser* 22, no. 6 [1901])

No doubt instances of violence and cruelty have often disgraced the military operations of all European Powers, but whenever they have occurred they have taken place in violation of the laws of international warfare. In times past British generals have earned an honourable repute for moderation and humanity in their dealings with the people of the country in which they have had to operate, and the history of our nation tells us that war can be carried on with safety to the troops and with brilliant success without resorting to methods of oppression, and the more especially against the families of the combatants and non-combatants. Even in the dark days of the Indian Mutiny, when there was an ever-present sense of the inhumanities practised by the mutineers and others who abetted them, there never existed the idea that the horrors of war were to be indiscriminately carried into the homes of the population. Happily the representative of the Crown then in India was a nobleman of calm, humane instincts and history now lauds the part played by the man who at the time was railed against as 'Clemency Canning.' (Field Marshal Sir Neville Chamberlain, veteran of the Indian campaign, in a letter to the *Manchester Guardian*, 5 August 1901)

Mind you—I am all for the most forbearing and generous treatment of the Boers when they are once completely beaten—if only because that is the sole means of absorbing and ultimately getting rid of them as a separate, exclusive caste. But complete victory is the first condition of successful advances. And our victory is far from complete. Of course, we have absolutely smashed up the armies of the enemy and his political organization. A more highly organized and advanced political entity would be annihilated by the loss of its capital, treasury, archives, and the whole machinery of Government. But, with their primitive social and political conditions, the Boers can go on merrily for a long time without any of these (which only seem to embarrass them), just as low types of animal organisms will long survive injuries which would kill organisms of a higher type outright. (Sir A. Milner to R. B. Haldane, 21 January 1901, marked "very confidential," in *The Milner Papers: South Africa 1899–1905*, volume 2, edited by Cecil Headlam [London: Cassell and Company, 1933], 205–6.)

———

Suggestions for a New Departure
W. T. STEAD

[Much of the controversy over the prosecution of the British war in South Africa derived from the problematic methods and strategies deployed on both sides—from Boer guerrilla raids on railroad and telegraph connections to retaliatory farm burnings and a generalized "scorched earth" policy on the part of the British. W. T. Stead, editor of the *Review of Reviews* and an ardent antiwar activist, published many pamphlets, editorials, and books criticizing Britain's actions throughout the war. In many of those publications he included citations from other media sources, such as soldiers' reports on their participation in the atrocities.]

The question as to how to make peace is being discussed anxiously, even in the highest quarters. How not to make peace we have seen. How to make peace is a much more difficult question. Personally, I do not think that it is possible to make peace after all that has passed on any terms short of the repentance of the British nation, the confession of its sins, and the bringing forth of fruits meet for repentance. Our duty is to stand in sackcloth with ashes on our heads, before the world, and humbly to crave for permission to use our imperial resources for the purpose of making restitution to the burghers, whom we have injured, and of effacing, so far as it is possible, the memory of this year of crime. I am, however, well aware that at present we have not suffered enough tribulation to bring us to the stool of penitence. We have suffered, but not enough, and we shall go forward from tribulation to tribulation until at last the righteous retribution which will overtake us for our sins, compels us, like Israel of old, to turn from our evil ways, and cry unto the Lord, if haply He may hear our supplications, and deliver us from the consequences of our manifold sins and iniquities.

But it is no use discussing now a catastrophe which appears to me much more inevitable than the war ever was, and for the moment our statesmen are casting about for a New Departure. It may, therefore, be worth while to reproduce here the suggestions for an altered policy which appeared under the signature of "A Rhodesian" in the *Westminster Gazette*.

The situation in South Africa has arrived at a point when, in the interests of both combatants, in the interest of South Africa, and above all in the interest of the Empire, we should ask ourselves whether the time has not come for readjusting our policy to the altered position of affairs. In the suggestions which I hope you will permit me to lay before your readers, I wish to disclaim all party feeling, or any desire to revive old controversies. I take it that we are all anxiously desirous of securing the pacification and future prosperity of South Africa, and that any suggestions that may be offered, based upon a close study of the situation, would not be unwelcome to those who hold the decision of our future policy in their hands.

It may clear the ground somewhat if we attempt to survey the situation as we find it to-day. We have now been at war nearly fourteen months. We have put forth our imperial strength, concentrated an army of over 200,000 men in our South African colonies, and have used this force with such effect, that at the present moment we have destroyed all authority other than our own in the two Republics. President Kruger is an exile in Europe; the Boer Executive Government has ceased to exist; Mr. Steyn's whereabouts are not known; and we are officially informed that the war, since the suspension of regular military operations, is at an end. Nevertheless, although we occupied Bloemfontein and Pretoria, and have formally annexed both the South African Republic and the Orange Free State, there is not at present one square yard of territory in either of the Republics outside the range of our sentries on which an Englishman can pass without peril of being shot. There is not a train passes along any of the railways that reaches its destination without having been under fire. Every day the rails are displaced and the permanent way injured; and although these injuries are rapidly repaired, each accident of the kind emphasises the fact that our authority is strictly confined to the area within the range of our rifles. Within the Republics it is not too much to say that universal anarchy prevails up to the very suburbs of Pretoria and Johannesburg. Industry is impossible; the resumption of operations on the Rand is out of the question; and every day brings us news of collisions with the hostile bands of Boers, the majority of which may be mere bushranging marauders, who prey impartially upon both Boer and Briton; but a nucleus remains, variously estimated at from 1000 to 3000 men, who constitute what may be described as the Old Guard of the Republic, Dopper Boers, who are regularly organised for war under the supreme control of the commander-in-chief, who directs their operations in accordance with a regular plan of campaign, and whose commandos are usually accompanied by artillery.

Outside the Republic we are maintaining day by day as prisoners of war, in St. Helena, Ceylon, and Cape Colony, a force of from fifteen thousand to twenty thousand male Boers. In the Transvaal, under the protection of our camps, and at Port Elizabeth we have great numbers of women and children also held as prisoners of war, but of whose numbers no full return has yet been received.

In Northern Natal the hostile bands of Boers show sufficient activity to render the railway communications unsafe; and in the northern parts of Cape Colony great apprehension is expressed concerning a sudden descent of General De Wet for the purpose of war into the enemy's territory. Throughout the whole of Cape Colony there is universal agreement that the hostility of the Dutch Colonists to the Imperial Government has never before been so intense; and although no active outbreak is apprehended, every one agrees that we may safely calculate upon our Dutch fellow-subjects adopting every method which the wit of man can devise for embarrasing, weakening, and paralysing the Imperial authorities. The situation is declared by some to be worse than it has ever been since the war broke out—that is to say, it is more perilous to the Empire and fraught with less hope for the future.

On the other side, we have an army of two hundred thousand men, of whom the majority may be described as war-seasoned veterans, but who contain a minority of what may be described as war-sodden men, who have lost the go, the elasticity, and the energy with which they entered upon the campaign; and as they cannot be relied upon for efficient service in the field, demands are being made for their immediate replacement by fresh troops from home. The cost of the war in actual money outlay, without reckoning any expenditure for wear and tear and the replacing of material and the preparations necessary for increasing the standing army, is £1,250,000 per week, or close upon £180,000 a day—a sum which those interested in statistics have ciphered out to amount to £125 a minute from week's end to week's end. However great this expenditure may be, however severe and continuous the drain upon our reserves of men, the Empire is rich, our population is increasing, and no argument that in any way suggests the exhaustion of either money or men would be listened to for a moment. The only question for discussion among practical men who have to face the situation as it stands to-day is whether this expenditure of £125 a minute brings us any nearer the goal which we have in view. I am expressing the opinion of many of those who have studied the subject closely for months past at the seat of war when I say that instead of nearing our goal it is at this moment receding farther into the distance; and there is no reason to believe, if we go steadily on on our present lines, that the situation will be any less serious twelve months hence than it is to-day.

This is, indeed, universally admitted; but while every one agrees that something further must be tried, there is no such agreement as to what that something should be. There are, roughly speaking, two alternatives. The first is that of resorting to increased severity. This finds favour chiefly with the military, and with journalists who have no stake in the country, and whose one idea of dealing with a difficult situation is to cry out for more and more rigour. Now, that the rule "Whenever you see a head, hit it," may be sound policy in some cases is not denied; but it is essential for the success of such a scheme that the head should stop in one place long enough to receive your blow. But that is precisely what it will not do. The more the country is denuded the greater the difficulty of transport, and the greater the advantage of the more mobile and lightly equipped force. At present we fail to catch De Wet or to lay hands upon the Boer bushrangers, for the simple reason that we are chasing a horse with an ox. The Boer travels light, and, like the moss-trooper of the Border, has no impedimenta beyond those which he carries at his saddle-bow; while the British column is tied by the leg to the ox-waggons which carry its supplies. But even if this were not the case it should never be forgotten that we have gone into the country to stay there. A policy of scuttle is repudiated on all hands. Hence, while we may make a solitude and call it peace, it is not in our interest to have a desert on our hands when we begin the work of reconstruction. This, however, might be a possible policy if we could exterminate the whole race—men, women, and children. To make thorough short work by reducing the *personnel* of the Boers to a vanishing point by the prolonged process of attrition recommended early in the war by Winston Churchill is not a policy likely to commend itself to any party in this country at the present time. We came very near carrying it out in Ireland in the days of Elizabeth; but even there we left a remant in the land sufficiently numerous to make the Irish question a perennial source of difficulty to the Empire. What Elizabeth's generals failed to do Lord Kitchener is not likely to accomplish, even if he were given *carte blanche* to massacre the population and devastate the country. However attractive the policy of increased severity may appear to the unthinking, it will be found on examination to aggravate every evil from which we are at present suffering, while at the same time it will dangerously excite against us the opinion of the civilised world.

If, therefore, we cannot adopt a policy of atrocity with any hope of permanent or even temporary access, we are shut up to consider the other alternative; and it is in this direction that I wish to submit to you some suggestions, in doing which I am merely the mouthpiece of others who are much better qualified to form an opinion than myself.

I now come to deal with the practical suggestions as to what might be done within the lines of the Government policy to improve the present difficult and dangerous position in South Africa. I assume that it is taken for granted, by all those in whose hands the decision of the question lies, that the policy of annexation is irrevocable, and that never again shall we allow an independent authority to be established between Cape Colony and the Zambesi. That being postulated, the next question is, How can we best secure the acceptance of this irrevocable decision by the Boers who are at present in arms, and by their sympathisers in the Cape and Natal, from whom they receive unlimited moral support, and who may be tempted, if the struggle lasts much longer, to afford them support of a more material description? The first suggestion which I venture to lay before your readers I submit with the more confidence because it is one to which the *Westminster Gazette* has repeatedly alluded in its discussion of the question. I refer to the impolicy of confounding a determination to annex the Republics with a demand for the unconditional surrender of the Boers now in arms against us. Unconditional surrender sounds well in melodrama; but what practical advantage does it give us? Its disadvantage is obvious enough. A demand for unconditional surrender can be represented as involving a liability on the part of those who surrender to be sent across the sea to St. Helena or to Ceylon; but no one in this country would wish to maintain the whole Dutch population of the two Republics permanently at the expense of the British taxpayer. To board, feed, and clothe 250,000 persons in perpetuity at the Imperial expense is not a consummation desired by any one. If, therefore, we do not intend to transport the Boers, why should we not say so? When the great American Civil War was fought to a finish, and General Grant summoned General Lee to surrender, he was met by a demand on the part of the Confederates for terms. Did he insist upon unconditional surrender? Nothing of the kind. General Grant at once responded to General Lee's appeal by writing out the terms upon which he was willing to receive the submission of the army of Northern Virginia. He demanded the surrender of all arms, artillery, and public property in the possession of the army; and then he assured all the officers and soldiers in the enemy's camp of their personal freedom and unmolested return to their own homes. On receiving these terms their surrender at Appomattox Courthouse followed, and the War of Secession came to an end. Why should we insist upon standing more stiffly upon our dignity than the Commander-in-Chief of the Northern Army? Is not, therefore, the first thing to be done to waive immediately that impolitic demand for unconditional surrender; and to proclaim our readiness to grant honourable terms to all those who are in the field against us?

The second suggestion follows on the same lines. It may be said that there will be no objection to offer such terms to the rank and file of the Boers, but that we must insist upon exempting from any such offer the members of the late Government of the Free State and Transvaal, and those who have taken a prominent part in the war and its disastrous prolongation.

Of course if this is insisted upon, the value of the first suggestion falls to the ground. It is extremely difficult to deal with, or even to reach, the rank and file of the Boers now on commando. Our only chance of securing their acceptance of our offer, or even of making them aware that such an offer has been made, lies through their commanding officers; but if we insist, as an inviolable condition that, while terms may be offered to the privates of the Boer army, their political and military chiefs have to be abandoned to our mercy, nothing can be done. Mr. Gould's admirable cartoon satirising the absurdity of the appeal of the European Powers to Prince Tuan to "come and be killed," would apply equally to any overtures of pacification which were based upon the abandonment of the Boer chiefs to the uncovenanted mercies of General Kitchener and Mr. Chamberlain. May it not, therefore, be admitted that this impolitic stipulation or reservation be withdrawn?

Having established these two preliminary points, I now come to the third—viz., whether we can honourably and consistently offer to the Boers a general amnesty if they lay down their arms, including in its provisions their restoration to their farms and the repudiation of any schemes of confiscation. It may be alleged by some that the Boers are rebels, and that it is not for the Government against which they are in revolt to demean itself by offering an amnesty. But,

First, the Boers can only be held to be rebels on the assumption that the proclamation of annexation in a territory which is not in our effective occupation causes such a change in their status, from the point of view of international law, as would convert legitimate belligerents into rebels; and

Secondly, the policy of granting a complete amnesty to rebels is by no means unprecedented, and has been held on more than one occasion to be the soundest policy to be pursued by a sovereign Power embarrassed by the persistent opposition of its own subjects to the restoration of its authority. Those who protest against the granting of such an amnesty will do well to read the despatch which Lord John Russell sent to the British Ambassador in St. Petersburg embodying the convictions of the British Government as to the best method of coping with the Polish rebellion. Lord John Russell in that despatch (which reads somewhat strangely nowadays) informed the Russian

Emperor that, in the opinion her Majesty's advisers, the first thing which he ought to do in Poland to secure the pacification of the country was to grant a complete amnesty to all the insurgents. The course which the British Government ventured to press upon the Russian Czar in 1863 might reasonably be adopted by her Majesty's Ministers in dealing with the quasi-rebels of South Africa.

If this be admitted, the repudiation of confiscation follows as a matter of course, for it is indeed the corollary of the amnesty. To a landed Boer his estate is his country. To offer him an amnesty with one hand and to confiscate his farm with the other is to tempt him with the shadow and deprive him of the substance. Proceeding with my suggestions, I venture to submit that, if we decide to waive the demand for unconditional surrender, and are willing to proclaim a general amnesty and repudiate confiscation, it will be expedient to go a step further and, in the interest of the general pacification of the country, to proclaim that, animated by a sincere desire to induce both sides to agree that bygones shall be bygones, compensation should be made in full to all those who have suffered in the war, whether British or Dutch. No doubt many objections can be raised to this by political pendants: but we are dealing with a grave problem which appears to be almost insoluble, and if we are to allow pedantic sticklers to interpose their veto we may as well give up the whole business. Let us look at the matter from a practical point of view. Along the frontiers of the British Colonies, and over the whole area of the South African Republics, the war has resulted in widespread devastation. Dwelling-houses have been looted, the farming stock has been lifted, crops have been destroyed, and within the Republics a great number of farms have been given to the flames. Whether or not in every case such destruction of property was justified by the rules of war or by the hard necessities of military operations need not be here discussed. Rightly or wrongly, this work of devastation has gone on unchecked on both sides for twelve months and more. What we have now to do is to try to heal the wound. Why should we not propose, as part of our great pacificatory scheme, that all sufferers from the war shall be compensated; that every British colonist whose house has been looted by the Boer commandos or by the Kaffirs, who took advantage of the opportunities of war to possess themselves of the white man's goods, shall be re-established in his home, and that the same measure shall be dealt out to all the Boers who have suffered by the punitive operations of our armies?

I can well imagine the horror which will possess the souls of Treasury officials and of the high-flying loyalists at the proposal to compensate the Boers equally with our own colonists who suffered at the hands of the Boers. But it cannot be denied that, whatever guilt or criminality may attach to the misguided rulers of the Republics, the rank and file of the population had no act or part in the decision that precipitated the war. But even if this is denied, we are sitting as God Almighty on the judgment-seat meting our rewards and punishments according to the deserts of either party. We are face to face with a situation which tends every day to become worse, and which entails upon the British taxpayer an infinitely greater expense than would rebuild and refurnish every ruined homestead in South Africa. If the principle be once admitted, the question of cost will be seen to be comparatively insignificant. No precise information is accessible as to the number of farms that have been destroyed within the Republics; but, judging from the information which has been permitted to leak out, it may be assumed that at least 1000 farmsteads have been burnt. This wholesale burning of property has occurred solely in the Free State and in the southern part of the Transvaal. General Buller appears to have succeeded in carrying his operations through to a successful issue without having found it necessary in a single case to resort to a policy of wholesale terrorism. Here and there a farmstead used as a fort, or misused for the purposes of treachery, may have suffered the penalties of war. But in the area of General Buller's operations it is not even alleged that any serious destruction of property has taken place. We may, therefore, take it that 1000 farms in the area of Lord Roberts's command represent all those which have been destroyed; while live stock and produce of about two or three times that number, have been commandeered without payment, on one pretext or another, by the invading armies.

It is, of course, impossible to deal with this question of values, except on the broadest possible basis; but South Africans who have studied the subject have made an estimate that the average stock on a farm might be replaced for £2000, while the farmstead and the buildings might be put up for half that sum. This would give us a total expenditure, for restoring ruined homesteads of our unwilling subjects of £3,000,000 sterling. Add another million for compensation for injuries inflicted upon our own colonists in the border districts, and we have a sum of £4,000,000 sterling, which, it is estimated, would go far to heal the scars inflicted by the war and render it possible for the populations on both sides of the frontier to live and thrive on their own holdings.

Suppose that, instead of £4,000,000 it was twice that sum. What is £8,000,000 compared with the necessity of carrying on military operations on the present scale? In less than two months the whole of this £8,000,000 will be swallowed in futile chasings after De Wet and in punitive operations, every one of which tends to increase the number of desperate and homeless men who swell the commandos against whom we are fighting.

I have only one more suggestion to make in the present stage of affairs, because the first thing to do is to increase the number of those who are willing to lay down their arms, and to offer the greatest possible inducement to those who are fighting to reconcile themselves to the inevitable. But in addition to those practical, material inducements, it will be necessary to go to the uttermost in the way of political reconciliation. It is not necessary to go one hair's breadth beyond the pledges which we gave to the world as to our intentions when we entered upon this war. We stand pledged to concede to our unwilling subjects the liberty and privileges of self-governing British Colonies. To the majority of the Boers these are mere phrases. The majority of them have not the faintest idea of what a self-governing British colony is. If, instead of sending them to Ceylon and St. Helena, we could have shipped them to Australia or New Zealand, and allowed their leaders opportunity for studying in Melbourne, in Sydney, or in Wellington the full, unlimited liberty of independent, self-governing British colonists, something might be done in the way of dispelling the prejudices which make the average Boer regard the term "British subject" as the political equivalent of a Russian serf. What is necessary to do is, not to extend our offers in the least, but to make it plain and clear to the understanding of the average Boer, that, under the British flag, in South Africa he will be as free to govern himself or misgovern himself—if he so pleases—as if he were still a citizen of an independent Republic. How this can best be done is a matter upon which I have my ideas; but it is not necessary to enter into the question at present. What ought to be done, however, is to call to our counsel as speedily as possible all the leaders of the Boers whom we can induce to enter into a conference with our representatives, for the purpose of explaining to them exactly the kind of government which we propose to set up in their country, and to explain to them how much or how little it will differ from the government which we have overthrown. The experiment might fail, but it would at least enable them to understand what we meant to be at. It would also in any case be an indispensable preliminary to any system of pacification. For a time, no doubt, while the homesteads are being rebuilt and the prisoners of war are returning from Ceylon to St. Helena, it will be necessary to have some form of military government; but it should be made plain to the Boers that this is a temporary expedient, and that as soon as the burghers and the refugees have returned to their homesteads they will be allowed to frame their own government on their own lines, subject always to the undisputed supremacy of Great Britain. Those who regard the substance as more important than the names of things which I take it to be the mark of a practical statesman—would endeavour to soften to the uttermost the demand that the Boers should regard themselves as British subjects, being content to recognise them as fellow-colonists. The word carries with it no such sense of political servitude as is involved in the word "subject." The federation of South Africa might then be undertaken, and each of the five States in the federation could be freely allowed the same liberty of hoisting its own flag which is already possessed by Western Australia, to mention only one instance, of which there may be several.

These, however, are matters of detail. The supreme object which we have in view is to secure the pacification of the country, with a view to the ultimate federation of South Africa. It is quite clear we cannot get there by muddling on our present lines. The situation is one which calls for a display of bold and generous statesmanship; and in the hope that these suggestions may commend themselves to our Colonial Secretary, I venture to submit them to the consideration of your readers.

To these suggestions of "A Rhodesian" I may venture to add some few further suggestions.

Even when all this is done, it is probable that the stalwarts and irreconcilables would remain in arms against us. Still, it must not be forgotten that De Wet has twice offered to surrender on terms which might have been conceded without any detriment to the policy of "Never again!" Further, it must be remembered that the leaders of the Boers have never had any opportunity of realising the kind of liberty to which they would be entitled if the two Republics were converted into self-governing Colonies upon the Australian model. A very significant conversation is reported by a Canadian officer, who while in hospital took the opportunity of explaining to De Wet the liberties enjoyed by the citizens of the Dominion. What is wanted is a clearly stated, broadly liberal political programme, which we could pledge ourselves to carry out. In doing this, we should not go a step beyond the pledges with which we entered upon the war. We repudiated indignantly the accusation that we were going into the Transvaal in order to subdue the burghers to an alien yoke. On the contrary, we declared before high heaven, that our one object was to establish liberal institutions in the Transvaal, and to secure to men of all races these equal rights which the Boers had denied to the Outlanders. Yet at present, all that we have done is to abolish all political rights of every kind, whether belonging to the Outlanders or to the burghers, and in the immediate future we hold out nothing before them beyond a military despotism resting upon the rifles of an enormous standing army, which is to be maintained for an indefinite period in South Africa. The burghers would be unworthy of the name of Republicans if they did not carry on a struggle against such a destiny to their last cartridge.

Why should not some such settlement be proposed as that of allowing the

Johannesburghers to have an Inferno of their own, within a ring fence, including the whole of the Rand, and all the minerals, as their own particular province, while we leave the rest of the Transvaal and the Orange Free State to be governed by the burghers according to their sweet will and pleasure? They would, of course, give up their artillery, they would have no foreign policy, and they would be integral portions of the British Empire; but, subject to those restrictions, why should they not, both in the Free State and in the Transvaal, be left to govern themselves, just as the Australasians and the Canadians are left to govern themselves? Heaven knows, we do not wish to have the trouble of governing South Africa added to the burdens of the over-wearied Titan. Then we could further hold out the prospect of a Federal Union, which would practically result in a Dutch South Africa. The majority of the electors of the Cape Colony are at this moment Dutch, and are likely to remain Dutch. Both the Transvaal and the Orange Free State would be Dutch States, and Rhodesia and Natal would be the only two Colonies in which there would be a British majority. Free federation on democratic principles, which prevails in every other Colony, would result in giving a Dutch majority liberty to run the South African federation upon its own lines. This, of course, is very abhorrent to those high-flyers who think that the great gain of the war is to establish the ascendency of the English-speaking race; but the British Empire has never rested upon race ascendency. The attempt to enforce race ascendency in Canada kept Canada in constant hot water, and the same and much worse results would follow in South Africa, where the bloody memories of this disastrous war are still fresh in the minds of the people.

We are face to face with very clear alternatives in South Africa. Either we are going to leave the white races to govern themselves on the basis of equal rights and free representative government, or we are not. If we are, then the Dutch ascendency in South Africa is certain; but if we can use the present moment in order to convince the Boers that we are honest in our professions, there is no reason why the Dutch ascendency in the African Federation should not be as beneficial to the Empire as French ascendency is in the province of Quebec. If, on the other hand, we are determined to trample under foot all the principles of Colonial government on which we have been acting for the last sixty years, and if we insist upon governing South Africa in perpetuity under martial law, enforced by a hundred thousand bayonets, well and good. In that case there will be no peace in South Africa, and British authority throughout the whole country will extend just so far as the bullets of our garrisons reach, and no further.

I do not put forward this alternative policy as certain to secure success. I only say that it has an off-chance of securing the acquiescence of the Dutch population in their inclusion within the limits of the British Empire. The policy at present in vogue has not even an off-chance. Every day the war lasts, it increases and it intensifies the bitter animosity between the white races, which, horrible anywhere, is unspeakably horrible when the feud is prosecuted in the presence of an overwhelming majority of Kaffirs. The suggested policy may possibly, nay even probably, fail. Personally I have no faith in anything short of an uncompromising confession of sin and making of restitution. There are those who do not believe that England is great enough and strong enough to dare to make such a frank acknowledgement of error. As for me, I have not so learned to despise my country. I do not see anything to be proud of in the greatness of an Empire, if its very magnitude makes it afraid to act justly. But I admit that at present the conversion of our people is far from being complete. They are still in the gall of bitterness and the bonds of iniquity: their pride will not brook the suggestion of humble confession of sin, and the making of compensation to their victims. But in that way and in that way alone do I see any chance of saving the Empire in South Africa. The policy of Devastation now in full swing spells blank ruin. For the alternative policy which I have ventured to sketch, it may be too late, but so long as it has even one chance of success, it is better worth while trying than persisting in the present policy which appears to be modelled upon the conduct of the swine of Gadara.

SOURCE: Chapter 3 in *How Not to Make Peace* (London: Stop the War Committee, 1900), 90–104.

Further Charges against British Troops
SIR ARTHUR CONAN DOYLE

[Best known for his Sherlock Holmes stories, Arthur Conan Doyle (1855–1930) was also an eager apologist for British involvement in South Africa, which he visited in 1900 as an unofficial supervisor in support of British forces. For all this support for the British efforts in South Africa, however, he was also a vociferous critic of Belgian oppression in the Congo.]

EXPANSIVE AND EXPLOSIVE BULLETS

When Mr. Stead indulges in vague rhetoric it is difficult to corner him, but when he commits himself to a definite statement he is more open to attack. Thus, in his 'Methods of Barbarism' he roundly asserts that 'England sent several million rounds of expanding bullets to South Africa, and in the North of the Transvaal and at Mafeking for the first three months of the war no other bullets were used.' Mr. Methuen, on the authority of a letter of Lieutenant de Montmorency, R.A., states also that from October 12, 1899, up to January 15, 1900, the British forces north of Mafeking used nothing but Mark IV. ammunition, which is not a dum-dum but is an expansive bullet.

Mr. Methuen's statement differs, as will be seen, very widely from Mr. Stead's; for Mr. Stead says Mafeking, and Mr. Methuen says north of Mafeking. There was a very great deal of fighting at Mafeking, and comparatively little north of Mafeking during that time, so that the difference is an essential one. To test Mr. Stead's assertion about Mafeking, I communicated with General Baden-Powell, the gentleman who is most qualified to speak as to what occurred there, and his answer lies before me: 'We had no expanding bullets in our supply at Mafeking, unless you call the ordinary Martini-Henry an expanding bullet. I would not have used them on humane principles, and moreover, an Army order had been issued against the use of dum-dum bullets in this campaign. On the other hand, explosive bullets are expressly forbidden in the Convention, and these the Boers used freely against us in Mafeking, especially on May 12.'

I have endeavoured also to test the statement as it concerns the troops to the north of Mafeking. The same high authority says: 'With regard to the northern force, it is just possible that a few sportsmen in the Rhodesian column may have had some sporting bullets, but I certainly never heard of them.' A friend of mine who was in Lobatsi during the first week of the war assures me that he never saw anything but the solid bullet. It must be remembered that the state of things was very exceptional with the Rhodesian force. Their communications to the south were cut on the second day of the war, and for seven months they were dependent upon the long and circuitous Beira route for any supplies which reached them. One could imagine that under such circumstances uniformity of armament would be more difficult to maintain than in the case of an army with an assured base.

The expansive bullet is not, as a matter of fact, contrary to the Conventions of The Hague. It was expressly held from being so by the representatives of the United States and of Great Britain. In taking this view I cannot but think that these two enlightened and humanitarian powers were ill-advised. Those Conventions were of course only binding on those who signed them, and therefore in fighting desperate savages the man-stopping bullet could still have been used. Whatever our motives in taking the view that we did, a swift retribution has come upon us, for it has prevented us from exacting any retribution, or even complaining, when the Boers have used these weapons against us. Explosive bullets are, however, as my distinguished correspondent points out, upon a different footing, and if the Boers claim the advantages of the Conventions of The Hague, then every burgher found with these weapons in his bandolier is liable to punishment.

Our soldiers have been more merciful than our Hague diplomatists, for in spite of the reservation of the right to use this ammunition, every effort has been made to exclude it from the firing line. An unfortunate incident early in the campaign gave our enemies some reason to suspect us. The facts are these.

At the end of the spring of 1899 some hundreds of thousands of hollow-headed bullets, made in England, were condemned as unsatisfactory, not being true to gauge, &c., and were sent to South Africa for target practice only. A quantity of this ammunition, known as 'Metford Mark IV.,' was sent up to Dundee by order of General Symons for practice in field firing. As Mark IV. was not for use in a war with white races all these cartridges were called in as soon as Kruger declared war, and the officers responsible thought they were every one returned. By some blundering in the packing at home, however, some of this Mark IV. must have got mixed up with the ordinary, or Mark II., ammunition, and was found on our men by the Boers on October 30. Accordingly a very careful inspection was ordered, and a few Mark IV. bullets were found in our men's pouches, and at once removed. Their presence was purely accidental, and undoubtedly caused by a blunder in the Ordnance Department long before the war, and it was in consequence of this that some hollow-headed bullets were fired by the English early in the war without their knowledge.

What is usually known as the dum-dum bullet is a 'soft-nosed' one: but the regulation Mark II. is also made at the dum-dum factory, and the Boers, seeing the dum-dum label on boxes containing the latter, naturally thought the contents were the soft-nosed, which they were not.

It must be admitted that there was some carelessness in permitting sporting ammunition ever to get to the front at all. When the Derbyshire Militia were taken by De Wet at Roodeval, a number of cases of sporting cartridges were captured by the Boers (the officers had used them for shooting springbok). My friend, Mr. Langman, who was present, saw the Boers, in some instances, filling their bandoliers from these cases on the plausible excuse that they were only using our own ammunition. Such cartridges should never have been permitted to go up. But in spite of instances of bungling, the evidence shows that every effort has been made to keep the war as humane as possible. I am inclined to hope that a fuller knowledge will show that the same holds good for our enemies, and that in spite of individual exceptions, they have never systematically used anything except what one of their number described as a 'gentlemanly' bullet.

CONDUCT TO PRISONERS ON THE FIELD

On this count, also, the British soldiers have been exposed to attacks, both at home and abroad, which are as unfounded and as shameful as most of those which have been already treated.

The first occasion upon which Boer prisoners fell into our hands was at the Battle of Elandslaagte, on October 21, 1899. That night was spent by the victorious troops in a pouring rain, round such fires as they were able to light. It has been recorded by several witnesses that the warmest corner by the fire was reserved for the Boer prisoners. It has been asserted, and is again asserted, that when the Lancers charged a small body of the enemy after the action, they gave no quarter—'too well substantiated and too familiar,' says one critic of this assertion. I believe, as a matter of fact, that the myth arose from a sensational picture in an illustrated paper. The charge was delivered late in the evening, in uncertain light. Under such circumstances it is always possible, amid so wild and confused a scene, that a man who would have surrendered has been cut down or ridden over. But the cavalry brought back twenty prisoners, and the number whom they killed or wounded has not been placed higher than that, so that it is certain there was no indiscriminate slaying. I have read a letter from the officer who commanded the cavalry and who directed the charge, in which he tells the whole story confidentially to a brother officer. He speaks of his prisoners, but there is no reference to any brutality upon the part of the troopers.

Mr. Stead makes a great deal of some extracts from the letters of private soldiers at the front who talk of bayoneting their enemies. Such expressions should be accepted with considerable caution, for it may amuse the soldier to depict himself as rather a terrible fellow to his home-staying friends. Even if isolated instances could be corroborated, it would merely show that men of fiery temperament in the flush of battle are occasionally not to be restrained, either by the power of discipline or by the example and exhortations of their officers. Such instances, I do not doubt, could be found among all troops in all wars. But to found upon it a general charge of brutality or cruelty is unjust in the case of a foreigner, and unnatural in the case of our own people.

There is one final and complete answer to all such charges. It is that we have now in our hands 42,000 males of the Boer nations. They assert, and we cannot deny, that their losses in killed have been extraordinarily light during two years of warfare. How are these admitted and certain facts compatible with any general refusal of quarter? To anyone who, like myself, has seen the British soldiers jesting and smoking cigarettes with their captives within five minutes of their being taken, such a charge is ludicrous, but surely even to the most biassed mind the fact stated above must be conclusive.

In some ways I fear that the Conventions of The Hague will prove, when tested on a large scale, to be a counsel of perfection. It will certainly be the extreme test of self-restraint and discipline—a test successfully endured by the British troops at Elandslaagte, Bergendal, and many other places—to carry a position by assault and then to give quarter to those defenders who only surrender at the last instant. It seems almost too much to ask. The assailants have been terribly punished; they have lost their friends and their officers, in the frenzy of battle they storm the position, and then at the last instant the men who have done all the mischief stand up unscathed from behind their rocks and claim their own personal safety. Only at that moment has the soldier seen his antagonist or been on equal terms with him. He must give quarter, but it must be confessed that this is trying human nature rather high.

But if this holds good of an organised force defending a position, how about the solitary sniper? The position of such a man has never been defined by the Conventions of The Hague, and no rules are laid down for his treatment. It is not wonderful if the troops who have been annoyed by him should on occasion take the law into their own hands and treat him in a summary fashion.

The very first article of the Conventions of The Hague states that a belligerent must (1) Be commanded by some responsible person; (2) Have a distinctive emblem visible at a distance; (3) Carry arms openly. Now it is evident that the Boer sniper who draws his Mauser from its hiding-place in order to have a shot at the Rooineks from a safe kopje does not comply with any one of these conditions. In the letter of the law, then, he is undoubtedly outside the rules of warfare.

In the spirit he is even more so. Prowling among the rocks and shooting those who cannot tell whence the bullet comes, there is no wide gap between him and the assassin. His victims never see him, and in the ordinary course he incurs no personal danger. I believe such cases to have been very rare, but if the soldiers have occasionally shot such a man without reference to the officers, can it be said that it was an inexcusable action, or even that it was outside the strict rules of warfare?

I find in the 'Gazette de Lausanne' a returned Swiss soldier named Pache, who had fought for the Boers, expresses his amazement at the way in which the British troops after their losses in the storming of a position gave quarter to those who had inflicted those losses upon them.

'Only once,' he says, 'at the fight at Tabaksberg, have I seen the Boers hold on to their position to the very end. At the last rush of the enemy they opened a fruitless magazine fire, and then threw down their rifles and lifted their hands, imploring quarter from those whom they had been firing at at short range. I was astounded at the clemency of the soldiers, who allowed them to live. For my part I should have put them to death.'

Of prisoners after capture there is hardly need to speak. There is a universal consensus of opinion from all, British or foreign, who have had an opportunity of forming an opinion, that the prisoners have been treated with humanity and generosity. The same report has come from Green Point, St. Helena, Bermuda, Ceylon, Ahmednager, and all other camps. An outcry was raised when Ahmednager in India was chosen for a prison station, and it was asserted, with that recklessness with which so many other charges have been hurled against the authorities, that it was a hot-bed of disease. Experience has shown that there was no grain of truth in these statements, and the camp has been a very healthy one. As it remains the only one which has ever been subjected to harsh criticism, it may be of use to append the conclusions of Mr. Jesse Collings during a visit to it last month:

'The Boer officers said, speaking for ourselves and men, we have nothing at all to complain of. As prisoners of war we could not be better treated, and Major Dickenson (this they wished specially to be inserted), is as kind and considerate as it is possible to be.'

Some sensational statements were also made in America as to the condition of the Bermuda Camps, but a newspaper investigation has shown that there is no charge to be brought against them.

Mr. John J. O'Rorke writes to the 'New York Times,' saying, 'That in view of the many misrepresentations regarding the treatment of the Boer prisoners in Bermuda, he recently obtained a trustworthy opinion from one of his correspondents there.' . . . The correspondent's name is Musson Wainwright, and Mr. O'Rorke describes him 'as one of the influential residents in the island.' He says, 'That the Boers in Bermuda are better off than many residents in New York. They have plenty of beef, plenty of bread, plenty of everything except liberty. There are good hospitals and good doctors. It is true that some of the Boers are short of clothing, but these are very few, and the Government is issuing clothing to them. On the whole,' says Mr. Wainwright, 'Great Britain is treating the Boers far better than most people would.'

Compare this record with the undoubted privations, many of them unnecessary, which our soldiers endured at Waterval near Pretoria, the callous neglect of the enteric patients there, and the really barbarous treatment of British Colonial prisoners who were confined in cells on the absurd plea that in fighting for their flag they were traitors to the Africander cause.

EXECUTIONS

The number of executions of Boers as distinguished from the execution of Cape rebels, has been remarkably few in a war which has already lasted twenty-six months. So far as I have been able to follow them, they have been limited to the execution of Cordua for broken parole and conspiracy upon August 24, 1900, at Pretoria, the shooting of one or two horse-poisoners in Natal, and the shooting of three men after the action of October 27, 1900, near Fredericstad. These men, after throwing down their arms and receiving quarter, picked them up again and fired at the soldiers from behind. No doubt there have been other cases, scattered up and down the vast scene of warfare, but I can find no record of them, and if they exist at all they must be few in number. Since the beginning of 1901 four men have been shot in the Transvaal, three in Pretoria as spies and breakers of parole, one in Johannesburg as an aggravated case of breaking neutrality by inciting Boers to resist.

At the beginning of the war 90 per cent. of the farmers in the northern district of Cape Colony joined the invaders. Upon the expulsion of the Boers these men for the most part surrendered. The British Government, recognising that pressure had been put upon them and that their position had been a difficult one, inflicted no penalty upon the rank-and-file beyond depriving them of the franchise for a few years. A few who, like the Douglas rebels, were taken red-handed upon the field of battle, were condemned to periods of imprisonment which varied from one to five years.

This was in the year 1900. In 1901 there was an invasion of the Colony by Boers which differed very much from the former one. In the first case the country had actually been occupied by the Boer forces, who were able to exert real pressure upon the inhabitants. In the second the invaders were merely raiding bands, who traversed many places but occupied none. A British subject who joined on the first occasion might plead compulsion, on the second it was undoubtedly of his own free will.

These Boer bands being very mobile, and never fighting save when they were at an overwhelming advantage, penetrated all parts of the Colony and seduced a number of British subjects from their allegiance. The attacking of small posts and the derailing of trains, military or civilian, were their chief employment. To cover their tracks they continually murdered natives whose information might betray them. Their presence kept the Colony in confusion and threatened the communications of the Army.

The situation may be brought home to a continental reader by a fairly exact parallel. Suppose that an Austrian army had invaded Germany, and that while it was deep in German territory bands of Austrian subjects who were of German extraction began to tear up the railway lines and harass the communications. That was our situation in South Africa. Would the Austrians under these circumstances show much mercy to those rebel bands, especially if they added cold-blooded murder to their treason? Is it likely that they would?

The British, however, were very long-suffering. Many hundreds of these rebels passed into their hands, and most of them escaped with fine and imprisonment. The ringleaders, and those who were convicted of capital penal offences, were put to death. I have been at some pains to make a list of the executions in 1901, including those already mentioned. It is at least approximately correct:

Number	Place	Date	Reason
		1901	
2	De Aar	March 19	Train wrecking.
2	Pretoria	June 11	Boers breaking oath of neutrality.
1	Middelburg	July 10	Fighting.
1	Cape Town	July 13	Fighting.
1	Cradock	July 13	Fighting.
2	Middelburg	July 24	Fighting.
2	Kenhardt	July 25	Fighting.
1	Pretoria	Aug. 22	Boer spy.
3	Colesburg	Sept. 4	Fighting.
1	Middelburg	Oct. 10	Fighting.
1	Middelburg	Oct. 11	Fighting.
1	Vryburg (hanged)	Oct. 12	Fighting.
Several	Tarkastad	Oct. 12	Fighting.
1	Tarkastad	Oct. 14	Fighting.
1	Middelburg	Oct. 15	Fighting.
2	Cradock (1 hanged, 1 shot)	Oct. 17	Train-wrecking and murdering native.
2	Vryburg	Oct. 29	Fighting.
1	Mafeking	Nov. 11	Shooting a native.
1	Colesburg	Nov. 12	Fighting, marauding, and assaulting, etc.
1	Johannesburg	Nov. 23	Persuading surrendered burghers to break oath.
1	Aliwal North	Nov. 26	Cape Police deserter.
1	Krugersdorp	Dec. 26	Shooting wounded.
2	Mafeking	Dec. 27	Kaffir murder.

Allowing 3 for the 'several' at Tarkastad on October 12, that makes a total of 34. Many will undoubtedly be added in the future, for the continual murder of inoffensive natives, some of them children, calls for stern justice. In this list 4 were train-wreckers (aggravated cases by rebels), 1 was a spy, 4 were murderers of natives, 1 a deserter who took twenty horses from the Cape Police, and the remaining 23 were British subjects taken fighting and bearing arms against their own country.

HOSTAGES UPON RAILWAY TRAINS

Here the military authorities are open, as it seems to me, to a serious charge, not of inhumanity to the enemy but of neglecting those steps which it was their duty to take in order to safeguard their own troops. If all the victims of derailings and railway cuttings were added together it is not an exaggeration to say that it would furnish as many killed and wounded as a considerable battle. On at least five occasions between twenty and thirty men were incapacitated, and there are very numerous cases where smaller numbers were badly hurt.

Let it be said at once that we have no grievance in this. To derail a train is legitimate warfare, with many precedents to support it. But to checkmate it by putting hostages upon the trains is likewise legitimate warfare, with many precedents to support it also. The Germans habitually did it in France, and the result justified them as the result has justified us. From the time (October 1901) that it was adopted in South Africa we have not heard of a single case of derailing, and there can be no doubt that the lives of many soldiers, and possibly of some civilians, have been saved by the measure.

I will conclude this chapter by two extracts chosen out of many from the diary of the Austrian, Count Sternberg. In the first he describes his capture:

'Three hours passed thus without our succeeding in finding our object. The sergeant then ordered that we should take a rest. We sat down on the ground, and chatted good-humouredly with the soldiers. They were fine fellows, without the least sign of brutality—in fact, full of sympathy. They had every right to be angry with us, for we had spoiled their sleep after they had gone through a trying day; yet they did not visit it on us in any way, and were most kind. They even shared their drinking-water with us. I cannot describe what my feelings were that night. A prisoner!'

He adds: 'I can only repeat that the English officers and the English soldiers have shown in this war that the profession of arms does not debase, but rather ennobles man.'

SOURCE: Chapter 9 in *The War in South Africa: Its Cause and Conduct* (New York: McClure, Phillips and Co., 1902), 108–16.

Excerpt from Hague Convention (II) with Respect to the Laws and Customs of War on Land, 29 July 1899

[Great Britain was a signatory to the Hague Conventions on international rules of war in 1899.]

SECTION II. ON HOSTILITIES

Chapter I. On means of injuring the Enemy, Sieges, and Bombardments

ARTICLE 22

The right of belligerents to adopt means of injuring the enemy is not unlimited.

ARTICLE 23

Besides the prohibitions provided by special Conventions, it is especially prohibited:

(a.) To employ poison or poisoned arms;

(b.) To kill or wound treacherously individuals belonging to the hostile nation or army;

(c.) To kill or wound an enemy who, having laid down arms, or having no longer means of defence, has surrendered at discretion;

(d.) To declare that no quarter will be given;

(e.) To employ arms, projectiles, or material of a nature to cause superfluous injury;

(f.) To make improper use of a flag of truce, the national flag, or military ensigns and the enemy's uniform, as well as the distinctive badges of the Geneva Convention;

(g.) To destroy or seize the enemy's property, unless such destruction or seizure be imperatively demanded by the necessities of war.

ARTICLE 24

Ruses of war and the employment of methods necessary to obtain information about the enemy and the country, are considered allowable.

ARTICLE 25

The attack or bombardment of towns, villages, habitations or buildings which are not defended, is prohibited.

ARTICLE 26

The Commander of an attacking force, before commencing a bombardment, except in the case of an assault, should do all he can to warn the authorities.

ARTICLE 27

In sieges and bombardments all necessary steps should be taken to spare as far as possible edifices devoted to religion, art, science, and charity, hospitals, and places where the sick and wounded are collected, provided they are not used at the same time for military purposes.

The besieged should indicate these buildings or places by some particular and visible signs, which should previously be notified to the assailants.

ARTICLE 28

The pillage of a town or place, even when taken by assault, is prohibited.

SOURCE: University of Minnesota Human Rights Library: http://www1.umn.edu/humanarts/instree/1899b.htm.

————

Treaty of Vereeniging, 31 May 1902

[Peace was finally concluded in May 1902 in the peace treaty signed in Vereeniging, with severe conditions imposed on the Boer antagonists, but anticipating—in other clauses on reparations and culture—the union that would come in 1910.]

His Excellency General Lord Kitchener and his Excellency Lord Milner, on behalf of the British Government, and Messrs. M. T. Steyn, J. Brebner, General C. R. De Wet, General C. Olivier, and Judge J. B. M. Hertzog, acting as the Government of the Orange Free State, and Messrs. S. W. Burger, F. W. Reitz, Generals Louis Botha, J. H. Delarey, Lucas Meyer, and

Krogh, acting as the Government of the South African Republic, on behalf of their respective burghers desirous to terminate the present hostilities, agree on the following Articles:—

1. The burgher forces in the field will forthwith lay down their arms, handing over all guns, rifles, and munitions of war in their possession or under their control, and desist from any further resistance to the authority of his Majesty King Edward VII., whom they recognise as their lawful Sovereign. The manner and details of this surrender will be arranged between Lord Kitchener and Commandant-General Botha, Assistant Commandant-General Delarey, and Chief Commandant De Wet.

2. All burghers in the field outside the limits of the Transvaal or Orange River Colony and all prisoners of war at present outside South Africa who are burghers will, on duly declaring their acceptance of the position of subjects of his Majesty King Edward VII., be gradually brought back to their homes as soon as transport can be provided and their means of subsistence ensured.

3. The burghers so surrendering or so returning will not be deprived of their personal liberty or their property.

4. No proceedings, civil or criminal, will be taken against any of the burghers surrendering or so returning for any acts in connection with the prosecution of the war. The benefit of this clause will not extend to certain acts, contrary to usages of war, which have been notified by Commander-in-chief to the Boer Generals, and which shall be tried by court-martial immediately after the close of hostilities.

5. The Dutch language will be taught in public schools in the Transvaal and Orange River Colony where the parents of the children desire it, and will be allowed in courts of law when necessary for the better and more effectual administration of justice.

6. The possession of rifles will be allowed in the Transvaal and Orange River Colony to persons requiring them for their protection on taking out a licence according to the law.

7. Military administration in the Transvaal and Orange River Colony will, at the earliest possible date, succeeded by Civil Government, and, as soon as circumstances permit, by representative institutions, leading up to self-government, be introduced.

8. The question of granting the franchise to natives will not be decided until after the introduction of self-government.

9. No special tax will be imposed on landed property in the Transvaal and Orange River Colony to defray the expenses of the war.

10. As soon as conditions permit, a Commission, on which the local inhab-

itants will be represented, will be appointed in each district of the Transvaal and Orange River Colony, under the presidency of a Magistrate or other official, for the purpose of assisting the restoration of the people to their homes and supplying those who, owing to war losses, are unable to provide themselves with food, shelter, and the necessary amount of seed, stock, implements, etc., indispensable to the resumption of their normal occupations.

His Majesty's Government will place at the disposal of these Commissions a sum of £3,000,000 for the above purposes, and will allow all notes issued under Law 1 of 1900 of the South African Republic and all receipts given by officers in the field of the late Republics, or under their orders, to be presented to a Judicial Commission, which will be appointed by the Government, and if such notes and receipts are found by this Commission to have been duly issued in return for valuable considerations, they will be received by the first-named Commissions as evidence of war losses suffered by the persons to whom they were originally given.

In addition to the above-named free grant of £3,000,000, his Majesty's Government will be prepared to make advances on loan for the same purposes free of interest for two years, and afterwards repayable over a period of years with 3 per cent. interest. No foreigner or rebel will be entitled to the benefit of this clause.

SOURCE: William T. Stead, *The Best or the Worst of Empires: Which?* (London: Review of Reviews Office, 1906), 196–97.

THE CONGO

INTRODUCTION
The Congo: Abominations and Denunciations
BARBARA HARLOW

ALL EUROPE. CONRAD'S MARLOW aboard the *Nellie* told his audience of company director, lawyer, and accountant, "All Europe contributed to the making of Kurtz" (*Heart of Darkness*, 50). The Berlin Conference (1884–1885), which had convened the nations of Europe and the United States in order to distribute parcels of Africa among the participating countries, had excepted the Congo, which was given to Belgian King Leopold II as his own personal prize and was recognized as the Congo Free State, which had had its beginnings in Leopold's Association Internationale du Congo (AIC) established in 1876. The United States had been the first to recognize the AIC as a state in 1884, followed by Germany and Britain, and continuing with the acknowledgments of France, Russia, Portugal, and Belgium that were confirmed at the end of the Berlin Conference in February 1885. The Congo Free State was formally proclaimed in July of that year. Leopold had made his case for suzerainty in a rhetorical announcement of the benefits of improvement, delivery, development, and humanitarian assistance to be provided to the natives that would ensue from his rule. Slavery and the slave trade, he asserted, would be forthwith abolished. But Leopold's rhetoric and the atrocities it concealed had yet to be exposed. Such exposure, however, was itself an arduous process, involving committed individuals and the movements that they represented, across several continents. It engaged the work of men such as the political activists Roger Casement and E. D. Morel, and was complemented by the polemical writings of literati like Mark Twain and Sir Arthur Conan Doyle. Joseph Conrad, his own travels and observations in the Congo notwithstanding and for all of Marlow's dislike for the "lie," would be less forthcoming in support of the work. As Conrad wrote to Casement in 1903, "it is an extraordinary thing that the conscience of Europe, which seventy years ago has put down the slave trade on humanitarian grounds, tolerates the Congo State today. It is as if the moral clock had been put back many hours. And yet nowadays if I were to overwork my horse so as to destroy its happiness and physical well-being, I should be hauled before a magistrate. . . . In the old days, England had in her keeping the conscience of Europe. The initiative came from her. But I suppose we are busy with other things—too much involved in great affairs to take up the cudgels for humanity, decency and justice" (Hawkins, 69–70). Conrad, apologizing that he was "only a wretched novelist," declined the request from Casement to assist in the public protests against Leopold (Inglis, *Roger Casement,* 96–97).

Despite early, if sporadic, reports from missionaries and traders, the various accounts of the inhumanity of Leopold's sway over the Congo and its indigenous inhabitants were largely dismissed in European political circles and dispelled by Leopold's own protestations to the benevolence of his African regime and its select representatives. Then, in 1903, Roger Casement submitted his *Congo Report* to the British Parliament. Casement, from an Irish Protestant family in Antrim, had acquired significant experience in West Africa in the employ of a Liverpool trading firm with interests there. In 1903, following up on the mercantile concern at Leopold's monopolization of commerce in the region and the obstructions to the "free trade" of other European enterprises, Casement was commissioned by the British Foreign Office to carry out a fact-finding trip up the Congo River. The report that he eventually presented was perhaps more than even his contractors had anticipated, containing as it did appalling narratives and eye-witness accounts of abuse and atrocity rampant in the Congo Free State. Not just an obstruction to the interests of "free trade," Leopold's rule was an abomination to humanitarian ideals. Casement's immediate audience, however, was not ready to hear the story that he had to tell. The British Foreign Office was torn between the need to placate Leopold (a relative of Victoria) and assure his support for their own European designs on the one hand and to respond to the demands of Liverpool merchants on the other. Humanitarian objectives were almost incidental to the immediate political agenda, overriding as the incidents of the abuse of humanity might have been in Casement's *Congo Report.*

In 1904 Casement and E. D. Morel formed the Congo Reform Association. Morel, a Frenchman resident in England, had long been involved in the efforts to right the wrongs being perpetrated in the Congo Free State, working in significant part with H. R. Fox Bourne and the Aborigines Protection Society. Morel's account of *King Leopold's Rule in Africa* (1904) is a passionate denunciation of the state of affairs in the Congo at the time and expresses as well the frustration of reformers at the persistent recalcitrance of politicians and public opinion alike to recognize the "horrors" being committed there. "How much longer," Morel wrote, "would the civilised world tolerate these things?" Part of the problem, he goes on, is that it is "only by accident [that] we ever hear of those deeds of darkness." It was necessary, he determined, to organize a movement that would systematically appeal to and mobilize public indignation, and political action. *The History of the Congo Reform Movement,* a work that Morel began in 1910, tells the story of that movement, its strategies of information gathering, modes of presentation, and tactics of appeal that were undertaken in order to challenge Leopold's hold over the territory and peoples of the Congo Free State, a hold that Sir Arthur Conan Doyle decried in 1905 as nothing less than the "crime of the Congo." Such a crime, argued Conan Doyle, should not be just exposed but also punished at an international tribunal that would additionally award reparations to the victims of the Belgian king's brutality and concupiscence. Leopold, though, would not submit without a retort of his own—and a massive counter-campaign from Europe to the United States of disinformation and rhetorical defamation of his denouncers—a retort that Mark Twain caricatured in his essay "King Leopold's Soliloquy" (1905). "They spy and spy and run into print with every foolish trifle," Twain has Leopold complain. But Leopold's complaints and counter-campaign notwithstanding, the Congo Free State was abolished in 1908, when it became the Belgian Congo. Roger Casement, for his part, would go on to denounce abuses similar to those he had uncovered in the Congo on the rubber plantations in South America in *The Putumayo Report.* And in 1916 Casement was tried and hung for treason after being caught running guns to the Irish republican movement on the eve of the Easter Rising. According to Casement, "in those lonely Congo forests where I found Leopold, I found also myself, the incorrigible Irishman" (quoted in Inglis, *Roger Casement,* 159).

BIBLIOGRAPHY

Anstey, Roger. *King Leopold's Legacy: The Congo under Belgian Rule 1908–1960.* London: Oxford University Press, 1966.

Cardiff, Jack, dir. *Dark of the Sun/The Mercenaries.* United States, 1968. Film.

Casement, Roger. *The Black Diaries.* Edited by Peter Singleton-Gates and Maurice Girodias. London: Sidgwick and Jackson, 1959.

Cocks, F. Seymour. *E. D. Morel: The Man and His Work.* London: n.p., 1920.

Conrad, Joseph. *Heart of Darkness.* 1898–1899. 3rd edition, edited by Robert Kimbrough. New York: W. W. Norton, 1988.

Coppola, Frances Ford, dir. *Apocalypse Now.* United States, 1979. Film.

Fabian, Johannes. *Remembering the Present: Painting and Popular History in Zaire.* Berkeley: University of California Press, 1996.

Gast, Leon, dir. *When We Were Kings.* United States, 1996. Film.

Gide, André. *Travels in the Congo.* Translated by Dorothy Bussy. Harmondsworth: Penguin, 1986.

Guevara, Ernesto "Che." *The African Dream: The Diaries of the Revolutionary War in the Congo.* Translated by Patrick Camiller. London: Harvill Press, 2000.

Hawkins, Hunt. "Joseph Conrad, Roger Casement, and the Congo Reform Movement." *Journal of Modern Literature* 9 (1981): 65–80.

Hochschild, Adam. *King Leopold's Ghost.* Boston: Houghton Mifflin, 1998.

Inglis, Brian. *Roger Casement.* 1973. Belfast: Blackstone Press, 1993.

Keith, A. Berriedale. *The Belgian Congo and the Berlin Act.* Oxford: Clarendon Press, 1919.

Marshall, Frank, dir. *Congo.* United States, 1995. Film.

Morel, E. D. *Great Britain and the Congo.* London: Smith, Elder and Co., 1909.

Peck, Raoul, dir. *Lumumba.* France/Belgium/Germany/Haiti, 2001. Film.

Wrong, Michela. *In the Footsteps of Mr Kurtz: Living on the Brink of Disaster in the Congo.* London: Fourth Estate, 2000.

The Congo State
ANONYMOUS

The Congo State
Is a thriving speculation
For the happy Belgian nation
The receipts are great
And getting yearly bigger
—But I'm glad I'm not a nigger
In the Congo State

SOURCE: In *Punch* 124 (6 May 1903): 313.

The Congo Report
ROGER CASEMENT

[Roger Casement (1864–1916) lived a third of his life in West Africa, both as representative for a trading company and in the service of the British government. In 1903 he presented his controversial report on the state of affairs in Leopold's Congo to Parliament. He also kept meticulous diaries during his journey up the river. Later, in "The Putumayo Report" (1910), he would similarly investigate abuses on the rubber plantations in South America. He was executed for treason in 1916 for his role in running guns from Germany to the Irish rebels at the time of the Easter Rising. His writings, collected as *The Black Diaries*, were long suppressed and only published in a limited edition in 1959.]

Mr. Casement to the Marquess of Lansdowne

London, December 11, 1903.

My Lord,

I have the honour to submit my Report on my recent journey on the Upper Congo.

I left Matadi on the 5th of June, and arriving at Leopoldville on the 6th, remained in the neighbourhood of Stanley Pool until the 2nd of July, when I set out for the Upper Congo. My return to Leopoldville was on the 15th of September, so that the period spent in the Upper River was one of only two and a half months, during which time I visited several points on the Congo River itself, up to the junction of the Lolongo River, ascended that river and its principal feeder, the Lopori, as far as Bongandanga, and went round Lake Mantumba.

Although my visit was of such short duration, and the points touched at nowhere lay far off the beaten tracks of communication, the region visited was one of the most central in the Congo State, and the district in which most of my time was spent, that of the Equator, is probably the most productive. Moreover, I was enabled, by visiting this district, to contrast its present day state with the condition in which I had known it some sixteen years ago. Then (in 1887) I had visited most of the places I now revisited, and I was thus able to institute a comparison between a state of affairs I had myself seen when the natives lived their own savage lives in anarchic and disorderly communities, uncontrolled by Europeans, and that created by more than a decade of very energetic European intervention. That very much of this intervention has been called for no one who formerly knew the Upper Congo could doubt, and there are today widespread proofs of the great energy displayed by Belgian officials in introducing their methods of rule over one of the most savage regions of Africa.

Admirably built and admirably kept stations greet the traveller at many points; a fleet of river steamers, numbering, I believe, forty-eight, the property of the Congo Government, navigate the main river and its principal affluents at fixed intervals. Regular means of communication are thus afforded to some of the most inaccessible parts of Central Africa.

A railway, excellently constructed in view of the difficulties to be encountered, now connects the ocean ports with Stanley Pool, over a tract of difficult country, which formerly offered to the weary traveller on foot many obstacles to be overcome and many days of great bodily fatigue. The cataract region, through which the railway passes, is a generally unproductive and even sterile tract of some 220 miles in breadth. This region is, I believe, the home, or birthplace of the sleeping sickness—a terrible disease, which is, all too rapidly, eating its way into the heart of Africa, and has even traversed the entire continent to well-nigh the shores of the Indian Ocean. The population of the Lower Congo has been gradually reduced by the unchecked ravages of this, as yet, undiagnosed and incurable disease, and as one cause of the seemingly wholesale diminution of human life which I everywhere observed in the regions visited, a prominent place must be assigned to this malady. The natives certainly attribute their alarming death rate to this as one of the inducing causes, although they attribute, and I think principally, their rapid decrease in numbers to other causes as well. Perhaps the most striking change observed during my journey into the interior was the great reduction observable everywhere in native life. Communities I had formerly known as large and flourishing centres of population are today entirely gone, or now exist in such diminished numbers as to be no longer recognizable. The southern shores of Stanley Pool had formerly a population of fully 5,000 Batekes, distributed through the three towns of Ngaliema's (Leopoldville), Kinchasa and Ndolo, lying within a few miles of each other. These people, some two years ago, decided to abandon their homes, and in one night the great majority of them crossed over into the French territory on the north shores of Stanley Pool. Where formerly had stretched these populous native African villages, I saw today a few scattered European houses, belonging either to Government officials or local traders. In Leopoldville today there are not, I should estimate, 100 of the original natives or their descendants now residing.

A hospital for Europeans and an establishment designed as a native hospital are in charge of a European doctor. Another doctor also resides in the Government station whose bacteriological studies are unremitting and worthy of much praise. When I visited the three mud huts which serve the purpose of the native hospital, all of them dilapidated, and two with the thatched roofs almost gone, I found seventeen sleeping sickness patients, male and female, lying about in the utmost dirt. Most of them were lying on the bare ground—several out on the pathway in front of the houses, and one, a woman, had fallen into the fire just prior to my arrival (while in the final, insensible stage of the disease) and had burned herself very badly. She had since been well bandaged, but was still lying out on the ground with her head almost in the fire, and while I sought to speak to her, in turning she upset a pot of scalding water over her shoulder. All the seventeen people I saw were near their end, and on my second visit two days later, the 19th June, I found one of them lying dead in the open.

In somewhat striking contrast to the neglected state of these people, I found, within a couple of hundred yards of them, the Government workshop for repairing and fitting the steamers. Here all was brightness, care, order, and activity, and it was impossible not to admire and commend the industry which had created and maintained in constant working order this useful establishment. In conjunction with a local missionary, some effort was made during my stay at Leopoldville to obtain an amelioration of the condition of the sleeping sickness people in the native hospital, but it was stated, in answer to my friend's representations, that nothing could be done in the way of building a proper hospital until plans now under consideration had been matured elsewhere. The structures I had visited, which the local medical staff greatly deplored, had endured for several years as the only form of hospital accommodation provided for the numerous native staff of the district.

The Government stores at Leopoldville are large and well built, and contain not only the goods the Government itself sends up river in its fleet of steamers, but also the goods of the various Concession Companies. As a rule, the produce brought down river by the Government steamers is transshipped direct into the railway trucks which run alongside the wharf, and is carried by train to Matadi for shipment to Europe. The various Companies carrying on operations on the Upper Congo, and who hold concessions from the Congo Government, are bound, I was told, by Conventions to abstain from carrying, save within the limits of their Concessions, either goods or passengers. This interdiction extends to their own merchandise and their own agents. Should they carry, by reason of imperative need outside these limits any of their own goods or their own people, they are bound to pay to the Congo Government either the freight or passage money according to the Government tariff, just as though the goods or passengers had been conveyed on one of the Government vessels. The tariff upon goods and passengers carried along the interior waterways is a fairly high one, not perhaps excessive under the circumstances, but still one that, by reason of this virtual monopoly, can produce a yearly revenue which must go far toward maintaining the Government flotilla [...]. That this restriction of public conveyance by Government vessel alone is not altogether a public gain my own experience demonstrated. I had wished to leave Stanley Pool for the Upper Congo at an early date after my arrival in Leopoldville, but as the Government vessels were mostly crowded, I could not proceed with any comfort by one of these. The steamship 'Flandre', one of the largest of these vessels, which left Leopoldville for Stanley Falls on the 22nd of June, and by which I had, at first, intended to proceed, quitted port with more than twenty European passengers over her complement, all of whom, I was informed, would have to sleep on deck.

I accordingly was forced to seek other means of travelling, and through the kindness of the Director of one of the largest commercial companies (the

Société Anonyme Belge du Haut-Congo) I found excellent accommodation, as a guest, on one of his steamers. Although thus an invited guest and not paying any passage money, special permission had to be sought from the Congo Government before this act of courtesy could be shown to me, and I saw the telegram from the local authority, authorizing my conveyance to Chumbiri.

At F... I spent four days. I had visited this place in August 1887 when the line of villages comprising the settlement contained from 4,000 to 5,000 people. Most of these villages today are completely deserted, the forest having grown over the abandoned sites, and the entire community at the present date cannot number more than 500 souls. There is no Government station at F... but the Government telegraph line which connects Leopoldville with Co-quilhatville, the headquarters of the Equator district, runs through the once townlands of the F... villages close to the river bank. The people of the riverside towns, and from 20 miles inland, have to keep the line clear of undergrowth, and in many places the telegraph road serves as a useful public path between neighbouring villages. Some of the natives of the neighbour-hood complained that for this compulsory utilitarian service they had received no remuneration of any kind; and those at a distance that they found it hard to feed themselves when far from their homes they were engaged upon this task. Inquiry in the neighbourhood established that no payment for this work had seemingly been made for fully a year.

Men are also required to work at the neighbouring wood-cutting post for the Government steamers, which is in charge of a native Headman or Kapita, who is under the surveillance of a European 'Chef de Poste' at Bolobo, the nearest Government station, which lies about forty miles upstream. These wood-cutters, though required compulsorily to serve and sometimes irregularly detained, are adequately paid for their services.

In most parts of the Upper Congo the recognised currency consists of lengths varying according to the district. At one period the recognised length of a brass rod was 18 inches, but today the average length of a rod cannot be more than 8 or 9 inches. The nominal value of one of these rods is ½d, twenty of them being reckoned to the franc; but the intrinsic value, or actual cost of a rod to any importer of the brass wire direct from Europe, would come to less than a ¼d, I should say. Such as it is, clumsy and dirty, this is the principal form of currency known on the Upper Congo, where, saving some parts of the French Congo I visited, European money is still unknown.

The reasons for the decrease of population at F... given me, both by the natives and others, point to sleeping-sickness as probably one of the principal factors. There has also been emigration to the opposite side of the river, to the

French shore, but this course, has never, I gather, been popular. The people have not easily accommodated themselves to the altered conditions of life brought about by European Government in their midst. Where formerly they were accustomed to take long voyages down to Stanley Pool to sell slaves, ivory, dried fish, or other local products against such European merchandise as the Bateke middlemen around the Pool had to offer in exchange, they find themselves today debarred from all such forms of activity.

The open selling of slaves and the canoe convoys, which once navigated the Upper Congo, have everywhere disappeared. No act of the Congo State Government has perhaps produced more laudable results than the vigorous suppression of this widespread evil. In the 160 miles journey from Leopold-ville to F... I did not see one large native canoe in midstream, and only a few small canoes creeping along the shore near to native villages. While the suppression of an open form of slave dealing has been an undoubted gain, much that was not reprehensible in native life has disappeared along with it. The trade in ivory today has entirely passed from the hands of the natives of the Upper Congo, and neither fish nor any other outcome of local industry now changes hands on an extensive scale or at any distance from home.

So far as I could observe in the limited time at my disposal the people at F... rarely leave their homes save when required by the local Government official at Bolobo to serve as soldiers, or woodcutters at one of the Government posts, or to convey the weekly supplies of food required of them to the nearest Government station. These demands for foodstuffs comprise fowls and goats for the consumption of the European members of the Government staff at Leopoldville, or for passengers on the Government steamers. They emanate from the Chief of the Staff at Bolobo, who, I understand, is required in so far as he can to keep up this supply. In order to obtain this provision he is forced to exercise continuous pressure on the local population, and within recent times that pressure has not always taken the form of mere requisition. Armed expeditions has been necessary and a more forcible method of levying supplies has been adopted than the law either contemplated or justifies. Very specific statements as to the harm one of these recent expeditions worked in the country around F... were made to me during my stay there. The officer in command of G... district, at the head of a band of soldiers passed through a portion of the district wherein the natives, unaccustomed to the duties expected of them, had been backward in sending both goats and fowls.

The results of this expedition, which took place towards the end of 1900, was that in fourteen small villages traversed seventeen persons disappeared. Sixteen of these whose names were given to me were killed by the soldiers, and their bodies recovered by their friends, and one was reported as missing.

Of those killed, eleven were men, three women and one a boy child of five years. Ten persons were tied up and taken away as prisoners, but were released on payment of sixteen goats by their friends, except one, a child, who died at Bolobo. In addition 48 goats were taken away and 225 fowls; several houses were burned and a quantity of their owner's property either pillaged or destroyed. Representations on behalf of the injured villagers were made to the Inspecteur d'Etat at Leopoldville, who greatly deplored the excesses of his subordinates, and for the livestock or goods destroyed or taken away. The local estimate of the damage done amounted to 71,730 brass rods (3,586 Fr) which included 20,500 brass rods (1,025 Fr) assessed as compensation for the seventeen people. Three of these were Chiefs, and the amount asked for would have worked out at about 1,000 brass rods (50 Fr) per head, not probably an extravagant estimate for human life, seeing that the goats were valued at 400 rods each (20 Fr). A total sum, I was told, of 18,000 brass rods (950 Fr) was actually paid to the injured villagers by the Government Commissioner who came from Stanley Pool; and this sum, it was said, was levied as a fine for his misconduct on the officer responsible for the raid. I could not learn what other form of punishment, if any, was inflicted on this officer. He remained as the Government representative for some time afterwards, was then transferred to another post in the immediate neighbourhood, and finally went home at the expiration of his service.

At Bolobo, where I spent ten days waiting for a steamer to continue my journey, a similar state of affairs prevails to that existing at F... Bolobo used to be one of the most important native settlements along the south bank of the Upper Congo, and the population in the early days of civilised rule numbered fully 40,000 people, chiefly of the Bobangi tribe. Today the population is believed to be not more than 7,000 to 8,000 souls. The Bolobo tribes were famous in their former days for their voyages to Stanley Pool and their keen trading ability. All of their large canoes have today disappeared, and while some of them still hunt hippopotami—which are still numerous in the adjacent waters—I did not observe anything like industry among them.

Indeed, it would be hard to say how the people now live or how they occupy their own time. They did not complain so much of the weekly enforced food supplies required of them, which would, indeed, seem to be an unavoidable necessity of the situation, as to the unexpected calls frequently made upon them. Neither ivory nor rubber is obtained in this neighbourhood. The food supply and a certain amount of local labour is all that is enforced. As wood-cutters, station hands in the Government post, canoe paddlers, workers on the telegraph route or in some other public capacity, they are liable to frequent requisition.

The labour required did not seem to be excessive, but it would seem to be irregularly called for, unequally distributed, or only poorly remunerated, or sometimes not remunerated at all.

Complaints as to the manner of exacting service are much more frequent than complaints as to the fact of service being required. If the local official has to go on a sudden journey men are summoned on the instant to paddle his canoe, and a refusal entails imprisonment or a beating. If the Government plantation or the kitchen garden require weeding, a soldier will be sent to call in the women from some of the neighbouring towns. To the official this is a necessary public duty which he cannot but impose, but to the women suddenly forced to leave their household tasks and to tramp off, hoe in hand, baby on back, with possibly a hungry and angry husband at home, the task is not a welcome one.

I learned at Bolobo that a large influx from the I... district which comprises the 'Domaine de la Couronne' had lately taken place into the country behind G... The nearest settlement of these emigrants was said to be about 20 to 25 miles from G... and I determined to visit the place. I spent three days on this journey, visited two large villages in the interior belonging to the K... tribe, wherein I found that fully half the population now consisted of refugees belonging to the L... tribe who had formerly dwelt near I... I saw and questioned several groups of these people, whom I found to be industrial blacksmiths and brassworkers. These people consisted of old and young men, women and children. They had fled from their country and sought asylum with their friends the K... during the last four years. The distance they had travelled in their flight they put at about six or seven days' march—which I should estimate at from 120 to 150 miles of walking. They went on to declare, when asked why they had fled, that they had endured such ill-treatment at the hands of the Government officials and the Government soldiers in their own country that life had become intolerable, that nothing had remained for them at home but to be killed for failure to bring in a certain amount of rubber or to die from starvation or exposure in their attempts to satisfy the demands made upon them. The statements made to me by these people were of such a nature that I could not believe them to be true. The fact remained, however, that they had certainly abandoned their homes and all that they possessed, had travelled a long distance and now preferred a species of mild servitude among the K... to remaining in their own country. I took careful notes of the statements made to me by these people.

(Here Casement refers to Enclosure I, which is printed in the Blue Book. Extracts from this enclosure follow:)

The town of N... consists approximately of seventy-one K... houses and seventy-three occupied by L... These latter seemed industrious, simple folk, many weaving palm fibre into mats or native cloth; others had smithies, working brass wire into bracelets, chains and anklets; some iron workers making knives. Sitting down in one of these blacksmith's sheds, the five men at work ceased and came over to talk to us. I counted ten women, six grown up men and eight lads and women in this shed of L... I then asked them to tell me why they had left their homes. Three of the men sat down in front of me, and told a tale which I cannot think can be true, but it seemed to come straight from their hearts. I repeatedly asked certain parts to be gone over again while I wrote in my notebook. The fact of my writing down and asking for names, etc., seemed to impress them, and they spoke with what certainly impressed me as being great sincerity.

I asked, first, why they had left their homes, and had come to live in a strange, far-off country among the K... where they owned nothing, and were little better than servitors. All, when this was put, women as well, shouted out: 'On account of the rubber tax levied by the Government posts.'

I asked, then, how this tax was imposed. One of them, who had been hammering out an iron collar on my arrival, spoke first:

'I am N.N. These two beside me are O.O. and P.P. all of us Y... From our country each village had to take twenty loads of rubber. These loads were big; they were as big as this...' (producing an empty basket which came nearly up to the handle of my walking stick). 'That was the first size. We had to fill that up, but as rubber got scarcer the white man reduced the amount. We had to take these loads in four times a month.'

Question: 'How much pay do you get for this?'

Answer (entire audience): 'We got no pay. We got nothing.'

And then, N.N., whom I asked again, said:

'Our village got cloth and a little salt, but not the people who did the work. Our Chief ate up the cloth; the workers got nothing. The pay was a fathom of cloth and a little salt for every basket full, but it was given to the Chief, never to the men. It used to take ten days to get the twenty baskets of rubber—we were always in the forest to find the rubber vines, to go without food, and our women had to give up cultivating the fields and gardens. Then we starved. Wild beasts—the leopards killed some of us while we were working away in the forest and others got lost or died from exposure and starvation and we begged the white men to leave us alone, saying we could get no more rubber, but the white men and their soldiers said: "Go. You are only beasts yourselves, you are only nyama (meat)." We tried, always going further into the forest, and when we failed and our rubber was short, the soldiers came to our towns and killed us. Many were shot, some had their ears cut off; others were tied up with ropes round their necks and bodies and taken away. The white men sometimes at the post did not know of the bad things the soldiers did to us, but it was the white men who sent the soldiers to punish us for not bringing in enough rubber.'

Another native took up the story: 'We said to the white man: "We are not enough people now to do what you want of us. Our country has not many people in it and we are dying fast. We are killed by the work you make us do, by the stoppage of our plantations, and the breaking up of our homes." The white man looked at us and said: "There are lots of people in Mputu" (Europe, the white man's country). "If there are many people in the white man's country there must be many people in the black man's country." The white man who said this was the chief white man at F.F... His name was A.B. He was a very bad man. Other white men at Bula Matadi had been bad and wicked. These had killed us often and killed us by their own hands as well as by their soldiers. Some white men were good. These ones told them to stay in their homes and did not hunt and chase them as the others had done, but after what they had suffered they did not trust more anyone's word and they had fled from their country and were now going to stay here, far from their homes, in this country where there was no rubber.'

Question: 'How long is it since you left your homes, since the big trouble you speak of?'

Answer: 'It lasted three full seasons, and it is now four seasons since we fled and came into this country.'

Question: 'How many days is it to your own country?'

Answer: 'Six days of quick marching. We fled because we could not endure the things done to us. Our Chiefs were hanged and we were killed and starved and worked beyond endurance to get rubber.'

Question: 'How do you know it was the white men themselves who ordered these cruel things to be done to you? These things must have been done without the white men's knowledge by the black soldiers.'

Answer: 'The white men told their soldiers: "You kill only women; you cannot kill men." So then the soldiers when they killed us' (here P.P. who was answering stopped and hesitated, and then pointing to the private parts of my bulldog—it was lying asleep at my feet) 'then they cut off those things and took them to the white men, who said: "It is true, you have killed men.'"

Question: 'You mean to tell me that any white man ordered your bodies to be mutilated like that and those parts of you carried to him?'

Answer (all shouting out): 'Yes, any white man. D.E. did it.'

There is no doubt that these people were not inventing. Their vehemence, their flashing eyes, their excitement was not simulated. Doubtless they exaggerated the numbers, but they were clearly telling me what they knew and loathed.

Went on about fifteen minutes to another L... group of houses in the midst of the K... town. Found here an old Chief sitting in the open village Council house with two lads. An old woman soon came and joined, and another man. The woman began talking with much earnestness. She said the Government had worked them so hard that they had no time to tend their fields and gardens and they had starved to death. Her children had died; her two sons had been killed. The old Chief said:

'We used to hunt elephants long ago and there were plenty in our forests, and we got much meat; but Bula Matadi killed the elephant hunters because they could not get rubber, and so we starved. We were sent out to get rubber, and when we came back with little rubber we were shot.'

Question: 'Who shot you?'

Answer: 'The white men sent their soldiers out to kill us.'

Question: 'How do you know it was the white men sent the soldiers? It might be only these savage soldiers themselves?'

Answer: 'No, no, sometimes we brought rubber into the white men's stations. We took rubber to D.E...'s station, E.E... and to F.F... When it was not enough rubber the white men would put some of us in lines, one behind the other and would shoot through all our bodies. Sometimes he would shoot us like that with his own hand; sometimes his soldiers would do it.'

Question: 'You mean to say that you were killed in the Government posts by the Government white men themselves or under their very eyes?'

Answer (emphatically): 'We were killed in the stations of the white men themselves. We were killed by the white man himself. We were shot before his eyes.'

The foregoing entries made at the time in my notebook seemed to me, if not false, greatly exaggerated, although the statements were made with every air of conviction and sincerity. A few days afterwards when I was at Stanley Pool, I received further evidence in a letter of which the following is an extract:

'I was sorry not to see you as you passed down and so missed the opportunity of conveying to you personally a lot of evidence as to the terrible maladministration practised in the past in this district. I saw the official at the post of E.E... He is the successor of the infamous wretch D.E. of whom you heard so much yourself from the refugees at N... This D.E. was in this district and he it was that depopulated the country. His successor M.N. is very vehement in his denunciation of him and declares that he will leave nothing undone that he can do to bring him to justice. M.N. told me that when he took over the station at E.E... from D.E., he visited the prison and almost fainted, so horrible was the condition of the place and the poor wretches in it. He told me of many things he had heard from the soldiers. Of D.E. shooting with his own hand man after man who had come in with an insufficient quantity of rubber. Of his putting one behind the other and shooting them all with one cartridge. Those who accompanied me also heard from the soldiers many frightful stories and abundant confirmation of what was told us at N... about the taking to D.E. of the organs of the men slain by the sentries of the various posts. I saw a letter from the present officer at R.F... to M.N. in which he upbraids him for not using more vigorous means, telling him to talk less and shoot more, and reprimanding him for not killing more than one in a district under his care where there was a little trouble.'

From a separate communication I extract the following:

'After a few hours we came to a State rubber post. In nearly every instance these posts are most imposing, some of them giving rise to the supposition that several white men were residing in them. But in only one did we find a white man—the successor of D.E. At one place I saw lying about in the grass surrounding the post, which is built on the site of several large towns, human bones, skulls and in some cases complete skeletons. On enquiring the reason for this unusual sight: "Oh," said my informant, "when the bambote (soldiers) were sent to make us cut rubber there were so many killed we got tired of burying, and sometimes when we wanted to bury we were not allowed to."

' "But why did they kill you so?"

' "Oh, sometimes we were ordered to go and the sentry would find us preparing food to eat while in the forest, and he would shoot two or three to hurry us along. Sometimes we would try and do a little work on our plantations, so that when the harvest time came we should have something to eat, and the sentry would shoot some of us to teach us that our business was not to plant but to get rubber. Sometimes we were driven off to live for a fortnight in the forest without any food and without anything to make a fire with, and many died of cold and hunger. Sometimes the quantity brought was not sufficient, and then several would be killed to frighten us to bring more. Some tried to run away, and died of hunger and privation in the forest in trying to avoid the State posts."

' "But," said I, "if the sentries killed you like that, what was the use? You could not bring more rubber when there were fewer people."

' "Oh, as to that, we do not understand it. These are the facts."

'And looking around on the scene of desolation, on the untended farms and neglected palms, one could not but believe that in the main the story was true.

From State sentries came confirmation and particulars even more horrifying, and the evidence of a white man as to the state of the country—the unspeakable condition of the prisons at the State posts—all combined to convince me over and over again that, during the last seven years, this "Domaine Privé" of King Leopold has been a veritable hell on earth.'

Leaving Bolobo on the 23rd of July, I passed on up river in a small steam launch I had been fortunate enough to secure for my own private use. We touched at several points on the French shore, and on the 25th July reached Lukolela, where I spent two days. This district had, when I visited it in 1887, numbered fully 5,000 people; today the population is given, after a careful enumeration, at less than 600. The reasons given me for their decline in numbers were similar to those furnished elsewhere, viz., sleeping sickness, general ill-health, insufficiency of food and the methods employed to obtain labour from them by local officials and the exactions levied upon them...

Several reasons for the increase of sickness and the great falling off in the population of the district were stated by the local missionary, who has resided for many years at Lukolela, in two letters which he recently addressed to the Governor General of the Congo State. A copy of these letters was handed to me by the writer—the Rev. John Whitehead—on my calling on him at Lukolela on my way down river on the 12th September.

I had no opportunity of verifying, by personal observation, the statements made by Mr. Whitehead in his letter, for my stay at Lukolela was only of a few hours. I have, however, no right to doubt Mr. Whitehead's veracity and he declared himself to accept full responsibility for the statements his letters contained.

The 1903 Diary
ROGER CASEMENT

This is a faithful reproduction of a diary for the year 1903, alleged to have been written by Roger Casement, as it appears in a typewritten copy bearing on the front sheet the following inscription: 'New Scotland Yard, August 1916. REX v. CASEMENT. Copies of entries in Lett's diary for the year 1903 and part of 1904.' Although we are aware of many mistakes made by the copyist, we have only corrected the most obvious, in order to avoid any possible misinterpretation of the original author's writings.

COPY OF ENTRIES IN ROGER CASEMENT'S
DIARY FOR THE YEAR 1903

Helene Hofmeister, Munchen, Zahnstrasse, 15/1st floor, Bavaria 1520–1620.
Books to get.
   'Tennyson', Sir Alfred Lyall, K.C.B., Macmillan.
   'Today and Tomorrow in Ireland', by Stephen Gwynn. 7½×5, 223 pp.,
Hodges and Figgis, 5/-net.
   Ed. M. wrote H.W. on 13th. Mch., '03: 'Did you see Stephen Gwynn's
article in Fortnightly Review?' This à propos of Congo Affairs.

> There is some act, design—some holy strife
> that leads us to a larger life.

Name for Novel: 'The Far from Maddening Crowd', by R. McAsmunde.
Serene enclosings of a mightier self.

21.25	2.38.35
1.20.	1.41.25
1.41.25	4.20.00

Leo. to Bolobo : 101 miles.
Voyage up Congo 1903.   Steamed 23.35.

		Miles		
Left Kiri	2.30, 2 July	15	H. 4.	
Left Camp	6.45, 3 July	15	3.50	
Left Camp	7.00, 4 July	30	8.30	Kwam.
Left Camp	7.15, 5 July	30	7.15	5.45
Left Camp	6.58, 6 July	25	5.17	17.05
	Chumbiri		H.28.52	
	Kiri to Chumbiri.			

Morgan wrote 1.7. '03 about hire of Pioneer if C.P.M., at Lulanga agree
  —'Accepted—number of months time of possible arrival.'
  He lent me two pillows and four pillow slips for my bed.

Bwamba	s. Lat.	2°	30'	35"
Bolobo	do.	2	10'	08"
Leo.	do.	4	20'	00"
		1	51'	25"

Congo State. D. P. Revenue.
  Taxation.
  Decree 6 Oct., 1891. Completed by decree of 5 Dec., 1902. Giving Sec. of
State power to take such steps as he thinks necessary 'to assure the exploita-

tion of the wealth of the D. Privé' (in which may be included the payments in kind by the natives).

The decree of 6 Oct., 1891, states:

Art. 1. The Chief to be recognised by Gov. General within certain regions.

2. The investiture to be carried out by a public document and to be given to the Chief—the others kept in local archives. Each investiture to be accompanied by the bestowal of a medal or sign decided on by G.G.

3. At each investiture a table must be drawn up giving the name of the village and its exact situation, the name of the headman, the number of houses and the number of inhabitants—men, women and children.

4. At the same time the Com. de District will draw up a table of the annual payments in kind to be furnished by each village—and in 'corvées,' workmen or soldiers. This table must also indicate the lands which the natives must clear and help planted, or develop in the general interest. 'These tables must be first approved by the Gov. General.'

5. The Chiefs to exercise their authority in accordance with established usage and custom when in harmony with the law. The Chiefs are placed under the 'surveillance' of the Com. de District.

6. The Gov. Gen. regulates when necessary the relations of Chiefs with Chiefs, Chiefs with natives under their authority, and Chiefs with the local authorities.

Decree of 28 Nov., 1893. Prescribes system of payments in kind and forced labour in the Macuaya.

Arrêté of 30 April, 1897. Sec. of State. Establishing plantations of cocoa and coffee. Chiefs recognised by Govt. must establish and keep up on the vacant lands belonging to the State in the districts under their authority those plantations.

Art. 2. The extent of these plantations to be decided by Com. de District or his delegate on the basis of the density of population and a 20th. of the amount of work that this population must annually furnish.

Art. 3. The plantations are put under control of a [undecipherable].

Art. 4. 10 cub. to be granted each Chief for each coffee and cocoa tree transplanted in good condition.

Art. 5 and 6. Provide for the rendering to the State of the product of these plantations at a price to be fixed on, and confer the ownership of the plantations to the Chiefs and their lawful successors. This decree, insofar as Arts. 4, 5 and 6 are concerned, has no application to any of the State plantations I know of. R.C.

For treatment of the natives on general lines and their right to judicial protection see p. 537: 'Texte coordonné des diverses instructions valorim aux rapports des agents de l'Etat avec les indigènes' (B.O. 1896, p. 255).

See also 'Infractions non punies de peines spéciales', p. 285, punished by from 1 to 7 days imprisonment and a fine of not more than 200 francs.

Art. 2. The fines must be imposed by the Tribunals of the State in conformity with the laws in force. B. O. 1896, p. 141. Decree of 11 Aug., 1886.

See also 'Réquisitions militaires', Decree of 16 July, 1890 (B.O. 1890, p. 93).

Art. 12 and 13. (Which have no application to the 'Prestations à fournir par les indigènes'—but which possibly will be invoked as authority for the fining and arbitrary imprisonment of villages and individuals.)

For India Rubber Exploitation see 'Domaine Privé'—Decree of 5 Dec., 1892. Decree (India Rubber) 30 Oct., 1892. Also 'Instructions Générales pour l'exploitation des forêts domaniales', B.O. 1896, p. 272 (page 187 of Code).

See p. 194. Code. India Rubber exploitation.

The Lady Ffrench, St. Josephs, 29, Ailesbury Road, Merrion, Dublin.

[February 14th.] Writing in morning. Labelling G.B.'s heads for Club. Then to 53 Chester Square to lunch. Mortens there, with them to Paddington 3.35. Then to Nina to tea, then to studio (H. W. gone). Then to Club. H. W. Collins, [undeciph.] and I. Then to Collins' to dinner. Did not wire Dick Morton as agreed. Home early on bus. 10.15 to Nina. She still sadly. To bed at 11.10, slept very long, no letters. Very interesting articles in 'West Africa' about Burrows book.

[February 15th.] Bought at Stores £4.1/6. Up 9.40. Dressed quick. Wrote long Congo Concessions Memo for Farnall—sent it in at 4 p.m. with private line. Went Princess for an instant then on to 53, not in. Up to 30, Henstall Road—saw all. Brought Bertie back to Nina, still seedy. Went supper with Cui (and Mrs. Cui) at Carlton, home at 11. Walked home via Oxford Street. Goodbye to Cui and Collins y'day.

[February 16th.] Wired Dick. Went 53 bid Mrs W. goodbye at 10 o'clock, then to Stores bought things for Congo, then to Host's and back at 4. Out to Dick's with Darkie Heod, very tired after and mine fell asleep. Miss Lathbury there. Turned in at Dick's. No letter from States, mail possibly delayed.

[February 17th.] Left Denham 9, Uxbridge, 9.32. Saw in paper 'Saxonia' arrived Queenstown 16th and proceeded immediately. Back to pack at Aubrey, lovely weather, sharp frost but at 11 bright glorious sunshine. Lunch with Nina, then both of us to Park, saw troops from Parliament and then to H.W. studio and then home. Letter from S. and Mr. Tyrrell with it at 8. Then club, dinner with H.W., then walk, papers (saw enormous—youthful). Home letter from G.B. of 6 File at New York, and from Parkins about 'rags'.

[February 18th.] Beautiful frosty morning, busy writing all day, intended leaving 'Bonny' today, too late for her, Nina went Kings. Drew 250 and cheque book for 50. Sent clothes 'two packages, hat box and trunk' to 55 Ebury Street, E. Peacock. Went to 'Alladin' with Nina, awfully stupid piece. Wrote G.B. to New York, Hartford Hotel, 309 Pearl Street, NY.

[February 19th.] Went City, got ticket from E.D. & Co., self and Charlie to Cape Palmas. Lunch Oxford Street, wired H.W., Bertie, and Miss H. to come dinner. Found card from Nisco at G. Central, all dined there, and met there before dinner. 'La Boheme' after, home—saw Miss H. home, back tired after walk. Last day in London.

[February 20th]. Went Euston with Nina and Charlie, Bertie, Nisco, H.W., and Miss Hivel there to see me off by 12.14 train, Lime Street, 4.50., went with porter, went Auntie's. She Lizzie and [undecipherable] well. Back by Frederick St. at Sailor's Home, H. Abrahams from Demerara, 'Arthur' 11/6. Drove to Park home, supper and to bed. Paid all bills and at 2 Aubrey Walk. Medium, butmu ami, monene, monene, beh! beh!

[February 21st.] Auntie and Lizzie to breakfast. Went stage at 10 a.m., luggage by hotel porters to 'Jebba' got off about 11 a.m., good cabin, beastly ship. Egerton again purser, bad weather outside, lay down in afternoon trying to sleep, weather getting worse, turned in at 12.

[February 22nd.] Beastly weather, 'Jebba' a tub, and rolling fearfully, past south of Tuskar at noon going worse in evening, food very bad, Charlie sick in bed, poor little beggar. Ran 184 miles.

[February 23rd.] Sea bad—wind s.s.w. Ran 184 miles at noon, ship rolling fearfully, in evening sea somewhat better, as night went on it got quieter.

[February 24th.] Sea got worse at 7 a.m., wind became gale. Ran 187 miles. Arrived 8.40 from Madeira, gale freshened in afternoon, sea very bad. Ship doing about 5 knots now, awful tub, very uncomfortable indeed.

[February 25th.] Ran 157 miles only. Gale in our teeth. She is a tub and horror.

[February 26th.] Wind abated. Ran 239 miles. Madeira 448 distant. Weather warmer, to get in Saturday morning.

[February 27th.] Weather better. Ship going well. Wrote 7 letters home. Ran 257 miles. Wrote F.O. in evening, also for Burrows book on Congo to Farnall and Spicer, Nina, H.W., Kings, Roger Dennett, to go by 'Jebba'. Beautiful day.

[February 28th.] At 6 a.m., past Ford Island. In to Funchal at 7:30. Perestrello as in September 1897, on 'Scott' with photos. Grown tall, eyes beautiful, down on lip, curls. On shore with Reid to Careno. At cafe in square, and coffee and Carro offered. Lunched with Hon. A. Bailey, they off at 3. 'Jebba' 3.30. Walked Alameda, types, dark, distressful, then gardens at 4. Band of Majestic—Prowse, R.N., of 'Jupiter' came up and spoke. Squadron goes on

Monday, dinner very stupid. Hotel Careno bad. Out at 8 to Old Town, same place as in Feb. 1885, 18 years ago, then to square. Two offers, one doubtful, the other got cigarettes, same I think as in Alameda in afternoon. Whisky drunk by waiters, 8/−both: 16/−; a day at Careno far too dear. Went Casino at 5, one milreis on roulette, lost.

[March 1st.] Lovely morning. Slept very badly. Bed too short and Carreo up to 3 a.m. Returning from ball at Palace. Manoel to Paseo do Pico. Went up till past Santa Clara Hotel, met Dr. Connelly. $1,250. Saw evening on square. West Casino, Called on Spence, not in.

[March 2nd.] Went up to Marte with the Jones. Laura, Lady Wilton there. Delightful, beautiful creature coming down by stream at tramlines. Called on Spence, not in—on Hogue. 19—cigarettes—clubfoot. Went Casino, lost about 3$. Connelly to dinner. Then cafe, same in square, turned in early.

[March 3rd.] Went to Perestrello's, bought 12/6 photos. Lunched with Connelly, Spence and Mrs. Spence. On to Mr. Fletcher till 5 at Casino. Won four times, about £4. To dinner and then again to Casino at 10 till midnight. Did not play at night. American won about £600. Cape Liner arrived. Home Mail steamer will take our letters. Qui Ser Senhor $3.80. Went quay to steamer.

[March 4th.] Smoked too much y'day. Walked up hill to Mount Church. Beautiful there. John Hughes, an Irishman, at Hotel. Beautiful types at Carro and Belmonte. Stayed all day there, lunching at Reids, nice waiters. 'Kildorin' arrived from England, very bad weather reported. Back on Carro $1. Dinner and then to Casino, lost £2.10/-, home early and turned in 11.

[March 5th.] Stayed in garden and reading papers, no news of interest. After lunch to Mount by train, beautiful not there. Hughes down by train at 6. Dinner, lovely evening, to Casino at 10. Played, won on 33 $7,500, on 200 reis. Back at 10.30 in Badock Carro. Tired turned in at 11. Slept better.

[March 6th.] Lovely morning as usual. Walked up to First station, then train. Young P. in cab Belmonte Hotel. Looked camera, took photo asked, White said Homas de Arminestreda Veirra de Machicos. Walked about all day. Beautiful there. Josiah 115, Carreiro de Monte. Lunch at Belmonte and dinner at Reids. Down by 8 train. Lost cigarette case. Walked a bit, home at 10.

[March 7th.] Went Perestrello's with roll of films for developing to try and get V. de Machicos done, asked his address. Told out by Groves Hotel, so walked there. Quinta Nures. Lovely spot; but Jones told me it belonged to Blandy. Ordered dinner at Casino, invited Connelly. Back to lunch and to Perestrello's again. Developed asked prints and Machicos address in Funchal. Saw very beautiful near Casino at shop door and again at bridge when going back to lunch. Casino in afternoon with friends. Band very good, Spence there. Played and lost about 27/-. Back to dress for dinner and then with Connelly there. To Grove at 9. Many people there, dancing and playing, including Spences. I lost about £2. They went and Connelly at 10 or so. Lieut. of 'Dom Carlos' there, splendid. Then suivant in gardens with Senhora— Quinta? Bestante there. Miente frio, many times $4,000. Tomorrow and Agostinho about 17½, segunda feira.

[March 8th.] 'Cameron' came and left. Up Mount with photos for Veirra, then to Spences for lunch, then on board 'Dom Carlos' to dance. To English rooms and back to Casino. Music good, not played. To dinner thro' gardens all Madeira there, listening to band. To Casino at 9. Lost 2,500, smoked too much at Bar. Back walking lovely night. No sign of Agostinho. Waited long. Slept fairly well. Played, won £6 and then lost it and £2.

[March 9th.] Beautiful morning, waited all morning for Veirra de Machicos but no visit. Went Casino in afternoon to music—played and lost. After dinner, walked there, played and lost again. Many types, two Ruada Carreira up to S. Pedro and there in [undeciph.] sailor to sea. Walked home stranded and strong. Lovely night. No Agostinho. Lost about £3.

[March 10th.] 'Norman' arr. at 10. Joe McV. on shore at noon. Went with Miss Roland to snapshot him, and to club. Many beauties there, exquisite eyes. Joe and others after lunch to Mount. In Square most of day with Miss Rolland. Bought dog for Boorers. Went Casino at 8.30. Won £3 nearly and lost but came away with 30/- clear and all expenses paid. Home met Alvaro and £2,000, poor boy, 19, is a clerk in an office. Mother a seamstress.

[March 11th.] Cold night. 'Saxon' in at up getting. Went up Mount with Miss Rolland. At Reids with Hughes. At Belmonte, waiter said had given letter to Veirra who would come to Careno to thank me. Down in Carro with Miss R. lunch, noisy as usual. At 4 to Mrs. Spence and then to Casino together with black pup, after dinner to Casino, and lost 30/-; at one point had lost £2.10/-, and then got it back with about 3 dollars over, but played too late. Home at 12 on foot.

[March 12th.] Better day at 7 a.m. Sun out again but cold. Went up Mount to Belmonte. Left four photos for Veirra with waiter and noon and card. Walked down. Slept after lunch, very tired. To Casino at 4.45, many people there. Band good. Played and lost about £2. Introduced to Mrs. Stanford and Lady Edgecumbe. Invited to lunch tomorrow. Spence to dinner in Carro. Dined in private room. To Casino after. Spence went early. I played hard. Won pleno on 19 and side—20. Then lost a lot and then won again pleno and on 19 and on 9. Total gain after all losses about £3. Home in rain—very heavy.

[March 13th.] Stayed in bed till 12. Then to lunch at Quit. Stanford, Duke of Montrose there too. Then to Mrs. Fletcher. All day rain. Then to Spence. Long yarn, and to Casino. I won about £8 on 27 pleno and on 9 pleno—55 dollars. Dinner—to Theatre—only a minute. Then to Casino and back to Theatre. Agostinho kissed many times. 4 dollars. To Casino, lost £3.

[March 14th.] Stayed in bed till 12. After lunch to Convent at Rua dos Cruzes, then to Cemetery and then to Casino. Lost £3.10. Home to dinner. Dressed and to Casino again. Lost £3. Total losses today nearly £7. Plenty of dancing, but nearly all English. Portuguese beauties there. Augur not there, walked about, talked to Lady Edgecumbe and then home at 11 walked in rain. No good today. Have finished all my money but 20 dollars. Heavy rain since Thursday 7 p.m. almost without intermission night and day. One is more sure of not getting wet.

[March 15th.] Still raining. Agostinho and whiskers. Have left exactly $17,000 at 5,610: £3.0/6 out of £29 a fortnight ago. Have spent £26 in 15 days.

Today: Boots	$8,000.
Carro to Reids. 1,700 & down 2,000	3,700.
Perestrello for 3 dozen photos	2,500.
Lost at Casino	2,500.
To Club foot.	1,000.
	8,700.
To Agostinho	5,000.
	2,500.
Have left	16,200.

Went Reids with Connelly. Then to Brescia. Then after dinner Agostinho, splendid. Casino, lost, home 10.30. Boas nata up sidewalk with cape.

[March 16th.] Stayed in all day, not feeling well. Lay down in afternoon with 3 overcoats on—cold. After dinner to Casino with Somersets. Took £3. Won plenos on 31, 27 and 19, and came away after much play with £4.6/- to good. Mrs. Raglan Somerset gave me a Hymn book. Came back with Somersets 10.30 walking and turned in at once. Slept nearly all day, feeling seedy.

[March 17th.] Since y'day £5.9/- won. Got Shamrock. Stayed in all morning, went Stanford's call at 4. Mrs. S. ill. To Casino to meet Duke of Montrose, played with Lady Edgecumbe and lost about 25 dollars, then won it back and 10 dollars to good. In evening again with $26,800 to Casino, lost it all. Borrowed £3 and lost it, altho' once I got 18 dollars on 31 plenos on small table. Home with Nelson Ward at 11.45. Strong book. Having lost $43,600. Club foot a traitor.

[March 18th.] Beautiful morning. Went to club, read papers and after lunch to Spences'. Duke of Montrose there. Charming again. After lunch to Casino. Lost £3.10/-, $43,000. Then won [undeciph.] times on 3 dozen, close on $60,000 but blew it again in 4 or 5 coups. 'Teneriffe' arrived. After dinner to Casino, and lost $3, bid Lady Edgecumbe and on board at 10.20. Vile. Left at 11.30.

[March 19th.] Going to Grand Canary on the worst ship I've been on yet. Vile Germans on board. Reading 'Daily Mail' lent me by Mrs. Sexton.

[March 20th.] Arr. at Las Palmas 7.30. To S. Catalina, charming. Old waiters' faces just same, all welcome one, Swanston at door. To town by tram, many beautiful, out with Swanston and to lunch with him and Mrs. S. Loafed in garden. In to town at 6.5. by tram, dinner (vile) at Union Restaurant in Old Square. To Cathedral Square. Beautiful and then on bridge followed. No offers. Saw one, that one. Home at 10.15 on foot.

[March 21st.] Juan 20. Left in 'Vierga y Clarige' at 10.30. Teneriffe at 4. p.m. Letters at Consulate. 2 from George Brown with photo, and two from Nina, three from Tom with wretched story of deception and mystery again unfolding. To Pino de Oro, poor shore, stayed with Olsen on way up. Some types at pier head on landing. Did not see M. Violetta. After bad dinner at Pino and learning that my big basket of official papers is lost by Charlie, went downtown. Filled with Spaniards on Square. Home by Plaza di Constitucion at 10.30. Sat down and then to waste ground. Came X..., not shaved, about 21 or 22, gave pesetas 13 about, to meet tomorrow. Slept many mosquitoes in bed. Got Burrows book by post.

[March 22nd.] Went to Laguna by tram. Broke down. Innocencio there. Lunched at Aguerre. Then to Crokers and saw them all there, 'John' in great form. Down by 6 tram. Many most beautiful in the day. In evening to Square, to Band. Beautiful in white, exquisite. Home at 12 after music and stood. Wired to Reid for basket and to Catalina again.

[March 23rd.] Fair hair, blue eyes, brown clothes, round about 17. Reading Burrows book and wrote to Spence about basket and to Davie at W.O. Wired again to Las Palmas about basket. Enormous at 10 o'clock in Square. Lunched with Cambrelyn at Paris Rest. Then to Camachos where met Sir. McDonel with Croker. Home to lie down. Dined with Olsens, nice waiters. After to Plaza. Wayles and Whip in hand to Avidiva by new road. X... mu mua ami. Mal umi maudi matuvia brambit, gidkili. 25 note and 13 pesetas.

[March 24th.] Slept badly. Lovely weather. Not well. Went Paco's house at 11 breakfast, back lay down, then to Laguna, feeling very seedy, got 'John', dined with Croker and Mrs. C. at Teneriffe. Drove back in carriage at 9 p.m.

arriving at 10. To bed. To W.C. 11 times awfully bad attack, half dysentery, 'John' barked all night. Charlie's fault leaving him out. Feeling very ill, lots of blood passing.

[March 25th.] X... 'Mucho amigo' X... Not at all well. Very bad night between 'John' and dysentery, lying down nearly all day. Dr. Otto advised going to bed and not leaving for Congo, in afternoon slightly better so decided to go. 'Philippeville' in all day, sailed for home at 5 p.m., after dinner went to Olsens to pay for dinner of Monday, 3/5 to waiter. In street and to Avenida. Juan mua mu ami diaka N. sono 18 p. 20 years. Back to Olsens. Pepe, 17, bought cigarettes mucho dueno, dia tidiaka moko mavabela mu muami mucho mucho bueno fiba, fiba, X..., p. 16.

[March 26th.] Lauro his name. 'Anversville' in when got up. August says Captain is giving me the best room on board No. 14. Went aboard 10.30 after leaving card on Dom Paco. Photograph boys there. Bought £1 same as last year but grown most exquisite. M. Violetta at Las Palmas, but this one on 'Anversville' too last year. Smiled often. Gave 2.00 p. in copper. Left Santa Cruz at 11.15 about. Steamed splendidly. Bloom and Vourland on board, also Wilson and Madame Weber. Thought of Pepe X and his pellos of y'day. Saw Crokers' son at E. D.and Co.'s office, got letter from George.

[March 27th.] 'Anversville' steaming splendidly, 312 miles at noon. Got up at noon. Read 'Le Temps' lent by Blom and lay down most of the day. George wrote from New York—will send him £20 from S. Leone, cannot spare more. Trade winds, but not too strong. 'John' behaving very well, but poor 'Jack' catching it.

[March 28th.] Manuel Violetta at Jordao Perestrello. No breakfast, stayed in bed till 9.30. dressed slowly, read papers, Rye has followed Woolwich giving Liberal huge majority. Now Chertsey has to Poll. North Fermanagh too may give Russellite and then Camborn where Caine has died—his majority was only 108, so the Torys have a chance there. A.C. seat. N. Fermanagh polled Sat. 21st. Craig (U) Mitchell (L). A.C. seat by big majority. Chertsey polled 26 Thursday. Fyler (C). Longman (L). Ship ran 321 miles today, only 197 from Cape Verde, should be in S. Leone by 5 p.m. on Monday. The voyage like all on this Coast is very wearisome.

[March 29th.] Lauro of Santa Cruz. Manuel Violetta gone to Las Palmas. Pepe and Juan again. Stayed in cabin. Feeling very seedy. Bleeding badly aft as in Santa Cruz. Ran 312 miles from S. Leone 393. Will not get in until about 7 p.m. tomorrow. So will probably be kept all night there. I rather hope so as it will give more time to make enquiry for basket. Hope to find it or hear of it. Feeling very seedy indeed. Turned in 10.30 after talk with Blom.

[March 30th.] Much hotter today. Busy writing in cabin in morning.

Wrote many letters. Borrowed £20 from ship for G.B. Ran 327 miles, S. Leone 66 off. Arr. there about 5.15. 'Teneriffe' in. No sign of basket. Wrote G.B. with £15 to go by 'Jebba' tomorrow and other letters about basket. On shore to agents with Captain. Left at 8.35 p.m.

[March 31st.] Pepe of Guimar at Teneriffe 17. Ran 201 miles to noon, splendid, 288 left to Cape Palmas and total from S. Leone to Axim 840. Read Loti's 'Mon Frère Yves'. B. boy on board. Read 'Smart Set', very hot indeed. 'Mon Frère Yves' is peculiar. 'John' is not very well, poor old soul, with the heat.

[April 1st.] Very hot, only did 286; 2 miles short of Cape Palmas, and passed along near it, a steamer there, 344 to Axim. Passed Cavally and Tabu and then to sea. Read 'Les Carnets du Roi', stupid exposition of a beast king.

[April 2nd.] Ship ran better owing to current with us, Captain says. Young Stuart Wortley on board going to Nigeria. Ran to noon 311 miles. Axim 33. Send life certificate home from Sekondi. We got to Axim at 1.50 so that we either made 33 miles in 1 hour 50 minutes or (more likely) our true distance at noon was about 320. Left Axim 2.30 at Sekondi at 6. Landed Stuart Wortley and others and after repairing feed pump left S. at 8.30. Lovely clear soft weather, blue delicious sea, steamed 197 miles in 15½ hours. Left to Banana 879.

[April 3rd.] Reading Henri de Régnier's 'La Double Maîtresse'—Pauvre M. de Galandat. We should be in Banana by noon on Monday with luck, but Skipper Lovejoy says he cannot enter after 1.30 p.m. and the current may make us lose the tide and so—mardi matin. Alas.

[April 4th.] Ran 307 miles by log. Tornado prevented sights. Left to Banana 572 miles. Captain says we have really only done about 280. Toward 6 p.m. sighted Aunobom a good 30 miles off or more. Not a beam till 10 p.m. Log reset, strong current against us. Very tired of ship, got only dinner (outline of Aunobom).

[April 5th.] Another strong tornado this morning. Captain says we now cannot possibly make Congo till Tuesday morning. Ran 232 miles. To Banana 340. A second worse tornado, ship going poorly. Read M. Corelli's 'The Soul of Lilith'.

[April 6th.] XX 'Accra' enormous in. Beautiful morning. Congo water. At noon 296 miles. At 12.30 saw the tree-top by Red Point or Cabinda, only 44 miles to Banana. Captain says will try to go in. Monrovian... Down and oh! oh!, quick, about 18. Arrived Banana 4.30 on shore to Wright. Back to dinner at 7. Plenty people, and bad noise all night.

[April 7th.] Did not sleep last night. Left Banana at 8.30 for Boma, struck twice on sand, last time badly. Did not see 'Accra' again. Invited for tonight Underwood and Borrow at 2.30 on board went to Chiquengue, dinner awful as of old. Slept better. Kenboys of Cape Palmas, only a few there. Walked a bit. Boat boy talked of 'Doctor'. 'John' and Charlie together. Lots of letters.

[April 8th.] Up at 8. Letters from 'Anvusich' were interesting. Blom called. 'Tarquati' down at 8.30. Went on board at 10.30. Left for Malella at 11.30, called there and Banana and off for Loanda at 5 p.m. Walked with 'John' on board—played with him. Captain Harry good sort.

[April 9th.] Arr. Loanda at 11 p.m. on shore to N.T. Dined at Julius Caesar's with him and Dr. Ansorgi. Waiters clean, in an Angolesi lad. 'John' ate good dinner. Nothing interesting. Home to bed with N. at 11.

[April 10th.] Wrote F.O. and sent duplicate life certificate by 'Ambaca'. Took passage by her to leave tonight for Ambriz and Cabinda. Went on board after dinner. Lots of people there as usual. Left about 11. No sleep all night. Had to sit up with 'John.'

[April 11th.] At Ambriz at 6.30. Left Ambriz at 12 noon. At Ambrizette at 4 p.m. Left Ambrizette at 8.30 p.m. No food all day, beastly dirty boat, 'Ambaca' and a rotten lot on board. A. Nightingale and I squared up; he paid me £5.15. for Saidu Kabu and charged me £3.15. for another S.Leone man he repatriated, named Movella or some such name. Gave him cheque for £21.13/8. To send £20 to G. Brown from Lisbon by notes or postal order.

[April 12th.] Arr. Cabinda at 7.45. On shore at 8.30 with A. N. Bought things for Davis and for A.N. He off after breakfast. 'Ambaca' sailed at 3. Young Martens, 'John' and Ite seasick. 'John' got sick with salt water, poor old soul. Jones sick, Royle all right. Standing. Turned in at 9.30 in old room on top. Cabinda quite dead like Loanda and Boma too. Jones not lively. Mosquitoes are lively.

[April 13th.] Beautiful morning, getting rooms ready. In hand, gold frs. 130, silver 22.50, silver 2/-: 2.40. Frs. 154.90. Spent quiet day. 'John' got better after y'day's debauch of salt water. This day last year I arrived at Lisbon, and curls and.... in Avenida.

[April 14th.] This day last year. Another beautiful morning sun and clear. Weather cool and agreeable, got very hot. Royle sick. Walked with 'John' to Obras Publicas and back. Heavy rain and lightning.

[April 15th.] Last night's rain tremendous. It rained from 12.15 to 8 a.m. and most of it very heavy. 'Wall' arr. from Congo at 1 p.m. with letters for me—one from Rlwy. Co., and one from home and from Underwood. Bouvier and then to dinner. Talked till 10 p.m. Then to bed. Read Conan Doyle's 'Mystery of Cloomber,' rather good. Walked to Mission with Gibson and 'John.' Latter pigged.

[April 16th.] 'Nigeria' at Teneriffe. 'Wall' left. Wrote to F.O. by her Africa 3. Also to Cowan and to Wilkes, C.B.M., and under 'Tarquati' in at 7.30. Got

6 Irish whisky. She left for London at 12 p.m. No news! Wrote official letters and fixed up registers to find out missing corres. in basket lost at Canary. In rain in evening. Two fights between 'John' and 'Snip' and later with Jack. Both fled. 'John' with both eyes bunged up Master of Ceremonies. Turned in tired.

SOURCE: In *The Black Diaries: An Account of Roger Casement's Life and Times with a Collection of His Diaries and Public Writings*, ed. Peter Singleton-Gates and Maurice Girodias (London: Sidgwick and Jackson, 1959).

An Open Letter to Roger Casement
JOSEPH CONRAD

[In 1903 British Consul Roger Casement conducted the first official investigation of conditions in the Congo Free State. He returned to England at the end of the year ready to use his report to start a movement for reform in the Congo. Afraid that the British government might suppress his report, Casement contacted Joseph Conrad immediately on his return to England to solicit his support for the reform movement. They had met in the Congo thirteen years earlier, and Casement obviously thought that the author of *Heart of Darkness* could become a powerful ally in the cause. Although Conrad declined to become an active participant, he provided the following open letter to be used as Casement saw fit. Most of the letter was published in E. D. Morel's *King Leopold's Rule in Africa* (1904), and it was probably circulated through other Congo Reform Association publications. In 1905 a short quote from the letter was used as the caption for an illustration of a mutilated boy in the American Congo Reform Association's publication of Mark Twain's "King Leopold's Soliloquy."]

21 December 1903

My dear Casement,

You cannot doubt that I form the warmest wishes for your success. A king, wealthy and unscrupulous, is certainly no mean adversary; for if the personality in this case be a rather discredited one, the wealth, alas, has never a bad odour—or this wealth in particular would tell its own suffocating tale.

It is an extraordinary thing that the conscience of Europe which seventy years ago put down the slave trade on humanitarian grounds tolerates the Congo State to-day. It is as if the moral clock had been put back many hours. And yet nowadays if I were to overwork my horse so as to destroy its happiness or physical well-being I should be hauled before a magistrate. It seems to me that the black man—say, of Upoto—is deserving of as much humanitarian regard as any animal since he has nerves, feels pain, can be made physically miserable. But as a matter of fact his happiness and misery are much more complex than the misery or happiness of animals and deserving of greater regard. He shares with us the consciousness of the universe in which we live—no small burden. Barbarism per se is no crime deserving of a heavy visitation; and the Belgians are worse than the seven plagues of Egypt insomuch that in that case it was a punishment sent for a definite transgression; but in this the Upoto man is not aware of any transgression, and therefore can see no end to the infliction. It must appear to him very awful and mysterious; and I confess that it appears so to me too. The slave trade has been abolished—and the Congo State exists to-day. This is very remarkable. What makes it more remarkable is this: the slave trade was an old established form of commercial activity; it was not the monopoly of one small country established to the disadvantage of the rest of the civilized world in defiance of international treaties and in brazen disregard of humanitarian declarations. But the Congo State created yesterday is all that and yet it exists. It is very mysterious. One is tempted to exclaim (as poor Thiers did in 1871), "Il n'y a plus d'Europe." But as a matter of fact in the old days England had in her keeping the conscience of Europe. The initiative came from here. But now I suppose we are busy with other things; too much involved in great affairs to take up cudgels for humanity, decency and justice. But what about our commercial interests? These suffer greatly as Morel has very clearly demonstrated in his book. There can be no serious attempt to controvert his facts. Or it is impossible to controvert them for the hardest of lying wont do it. That precious pair of African witch-men seem to have cast a spell upon the world of whites—I mean Leopold and Thys of course. This is very funny.

And the fact remains that in 1903, seventy five years or so after the abolition of the slave trade (because it was cruel) there exists in Africa a Congo State, created by the act of European powers where ruthless, systematic cruelty towards the blacks is the basis of administration, and bad faith towards all the other States the basis of commercial policy.

I do hope we shall meet before you leave. Once more my best wishes go with you in your crusade. Of course you may make any use you like of what I write to you.

Cordially yours Jph Conrad.

SOURCE: In Hunt Hawkins, "Joseph Conrad, Roger Casement, and the Congo Reform Movement," *Journal of Modern Literature* 9 (1981): 65–80.

Native Life under Congo State Rule

E. D. MOREL

[E. D. Morel (1873–1924) was a British journalist and reformer who left his job as a shipping clerk at the firm of Elder Dempster to edit the *African Mail* and later his own *West African Mail.* In 1904 he founded the Congo Reform Association and served as its honorary secretary until 1913.]

But depopulation, after all, is only an outward and visible sign of inward causes. What a sum total of human wretchedness does not lie behind that bald word "depopulation"! To my mind, the horror of this curse which has come upon the Congo peoples reaches its maximum of intensity when we force ourselves to consider its everyday concomitants; the crushing weight of perpetual, remorseless oppression; the gradual elimination of everything in the daily life of the natives which makes that life worth living. Under the prevailing system, every village is a penal settlement. Armed soldiers are quartered in every hamlet; the men pass nearly the whole of their lives in satisfying the ceaseless demands of the "Administration," or its affiliates the Trusts; whether it be in the collection of rubber, of gum-copal, of food-stuffs, or forced labour in Government plantations, or in the construction of those "fine brick houses" on which the apologists of the State are for ever harping. Women and children do not enjoy as much protection as a dog in this country. They are imprisoned, flogged, left at the mercy of the soldiery, taxed beyond endurance, regarded as lower than the beasts. Native industries die out. Intercommunication between native communities ceases. The people who are taxed in what may be termed sedentary taxation can never leave their homes, where they reside under the vigilant eye of a sentry, loaded rifle or cap-gun in hand, the real king of the village, omnipotent and insolent. Monstrous fines are inflicted for the slightest shortage in taxes, and punishments varying in degree from murder and mutilation to the chain-gang, the "house of hostages," and the *chicotte.* If the taxation involves long journeys, such as the fish tax, the natives' whole time is taken up in journeyings to and fro from the fishing grounds and the State stations. "It would be hard to say how the people live," says Consul Casement of the Bolobo tribe, famous in the old days for their trading abilities. Floggings are perpetual; for insufficient supplies of rubber; for inadequate supplies of food; as a punishment for lack of activity or ability in forced labour; on the most trivial pretexts, sparing neither age nor sex. *La chicotte,* like the *collier national,* otherwise the "chains," is regarded as an indispensable adjunct in production—a sort of trading asset.[1] It is one unending, heartrending story of odious brutality from first to last.

Chiefs are shamelessly degraded in the eyes of their people; made to fetch and carry for the soldiers; cast in the chains, and flogged for remissness in village taxes; flung into the "prisons" often to die of neglect, ill-treatment, and starvation; forced to the commitment of unspeakable bestialities[2] by their "moral and material" regenerators. Mr. Whitehead[3] mentions the case of a Chief—Mabungikindo from Bokobo—who was actually wearing his "State Chief's medal" when Mr. Whitehead (who knew him) met him "returning from the chains in which he had been detained to get three more baskets of rubber." He had also been beaten. He took his medal in his hand and asked Mr. Whitehead to look at it, remarking bitterly upon his treatment. "I cringed with shame," says Mr. Whitehead. And no wonder! Such things are an ineffaceable blot upon the white race in Africa; and every white man who has a soul, whether brought into contact with them on the spot, or acquainted with them from a distance, cannot but "cringe with shame" for his race. I have before me the translation of a pathetic statement[4] drawn up by the people of Monsembe concerning the death of their Chief "in the chain" which took place a few months ago. It is worthy, it seems to me, of reproduction:

> "Afterwards, M—— (native name of the local Congo State official) called Mangumbe (that was the name of the Chief of Monsembe) and said to him, 'Your tax is very good; however, because you do not come with the tax every time, you must go to prison for eight days.' Mangumbe said to him, 'I did not come because I went to seek a goat (goats are part of the tax levied, and being now very scarce, have to be fetched at long distances) at Malele.' When M—— heard that, he called soldiers to tie the Chief up, and to put him in prison. And the soldiers seized him, and beat him with the butt end of their guns on his chest and side and loins, because M—— himself spoke to them thus, 'It does not matter, if

1. Mr. Whitehead, in his letter to the Governor-General (Lukolela, Sept. 7, 1903), mentions the case of a Chief who had been so frightfully flogged and cut about the feet "that he despaired of walking again, and those who had seen him last said he got along by dragging himself along on his buttocks."

   Mr. Casement refers to men "so severely flogged, in one of the *maison des ôtages*, that they were seen being carried away by their friends."

2. The Chief Lisanginya, of Mbenga, was compelled to drink from the white man's latrine. —Whitehead to Governor-General, Africa, No. 1, 1904, *op. cit.*

3. Letter to Governor-General, *op. cit.*

4. For which I am indebted to Mr. Charles Dodds. Mr. Weeks writes me the wretched man was only 20 days in the chains.

he dies, no palaver.' And the soldiers cast him into prison. And on account of this persecution and beating, Mangumba suffered in his back, chest, and sides. When the time appointed by M——, eight days, was passed, we went up river to embark Mangumbe. On arrival at Nouvelle Anvers, we went to L—— (another State official), and we said to him that the time appointed by them for our father (the natives call their Chiefs 'our father') having ended, we had come to fetch him away. Then L—— said, 'But he will not be released just now, because he does not understand tax collecting. He constantly delays, and does not bring his tax quickly, he despises me. He will not be released until 22 days are over. At present I shall punish him, and if he does not obey them afterwards I shall hang him.' And we replied, 'Commissaire, if hitherto he has not been energetic (cunning) enough, how dare he do so again? As regards the tax, he will bring you, everything you want he will give you. When is there anything he has refused you? You say he despises you.' We besought him passionately again and again, but he would not hear, until at last we grew weary, and returned to our town. We had been home just over a week, when we saw some men coming with our father's corpse. We asked them if they had brought his body. They said, 'He died in prison, and we begged his body from the Commissaire, just as we bring it to you.' We received the body and buried it."

Of the treatment of women and children by King Leopold's "agents of civilisation" it is difficult to write calmly. You will find nothing worse in the pages of Motley. And the agents of Phillip of Spain had this much in their favour that, in their eyes, every woman killed meant the elimination of un-born or unconceived heretics. It was clearly the Lord's work from their point of view, if we saturate our minds so far as we can with the spirit of those distant days. But on the Congo, in the twentieth century, where is the ghost of an excuse to be found? Talk of the exploits of the Arab! The exploits of the Arabs pale beside these, and Civilisation, stirred to its depths by Livingstone's revelations, still hearkens to the blasphemies and hypocrisies of Brussels. Civilisation, which held up its hands in horror at the thought of Tippu-Tib, is content to do no more than look somewhat askance at Leopold II. The former was a rough, uneducated Arab half-breed; the latter is a product of Christian culture, and wears a crown.

The European defenders of the conception of tropical African "develop-ment" which the Sovereign of the Congo State has so logically and ruthlessly carried out, allege that in his natural condition, the native of tropical Africa is content to smoke and drink all day, while his wife labours. It is either grossly exaggerated, or totally untrue; but even were it true to the very letter, then the male African is an angel of light by comparison with those who, on the Congo, profess (in Europe) to lead him into better ways. Under the aboriginal African system women are not flogged to death, and there are no "prisons"—*maisons des ôtages*—for the detention of women for faults, or alleged faults committed by their husbands, where such things, as these are the habitual accompaniments thereof:

"Women, often big with child, or with babies at their breast, tied neck by neck, in long files, are imprisoned at the 'factory' until redeemed by a large quantity of rubber. In the 'prisons' can always be seen men and children, and women in all stages of pregnancy, all herded together."[5]

"Men are first applied for, and if they do not present themselves, a soldier, or soldiers are sent, who tie up the women or the chiefs until the workmen are forthcoming."[6]

"I have seen men and women chained together by the neck, being driven by an armed soldier."[7]

"They also seized Balua, the wife of Botanga, and M. F—— had her flogged, giving her 200 *chicotte*.[8] So severely was she dealt with that urine and blood flowed from her. Just as they were dragging her away to the prison, her husband appeared with 20 fowls to redeem her. He took her home, but she died shortly after from the effect of the punishment she received."[9]

"On July 8, 1899, M——, after making inquiries, went to the factory, and released 106 prisoners. We saw them pass our stations—living skeletons . . . among them grey-headed old men and women. Many children were born in prison. One poor woman was working in the sun three days after the child was born."[10]

"Imprisoning 60 women and putting them in the chain, where all but five died of starvation."[11]

"This man himself, when I visited him in Boma goal, in March 1901, said that more than 100 women and children had died of starvation at his

5. Report from a missionary on the spot. Equateurville District, 1903. In a letter communicated to the author.

6. Rev. A. Billington, Bwanbu, 1903. American Memorial, *op. cit.*

7. Rev. Joseph Clark, Ikoko, 1903. Ibid.

8. 200 blows this means.

9. Mr. Ruskin's evidence before Judge Rossi in 1903. Incident in 1899.

10. Ibid.

11. One of the counts in the indictment drawn up against the agents of the *Anversoise* in the Mongalla massacres of 1900.

hands, but that the responsibility for both their arrest and his own lack of food to give them was due to his superiors' orders and neglect."[12]

"That, above all, the facts that the arrest of women and their detention, to compel the villages to furnish both produce and workmen, was tolerated and admitted even by certain of the Administrative Authorities of the region."[13]

"Upon the least resistance the men were shot down, and the women were captured as slaves and made to work. It was a sad sight to behold these poor creatures, driven like dogs here and there, and kept hard at their toil from morning to night."[14]

"At the different Congo Government stations, women are kept for the following purposes. In the daytime they do all the usual station work . . . at night they are obliged to be at the disposal of the soldiers. . . . The women are slaves captured by the Government soldiers when raiding the country."[15]

"Here the soldiers have taken away women as prisoners all because these people have no rubber for the Lufoi station."[16]

"Long strings of captives, mostly women and children," brought in after raids by State troops, "made to serve seven years as prisoners of war."[17]

"On —— removing from the station, his successor almost fainted on attempting to enter the station prison, in which were numbers of poor wretches so reduced by starvation and the awful stench from weeks of accumulation of filth, that they were not able to stand."[18]

"The accused detained arbitrarily a large number of men and women, many of whom died owing to the insanitary condition of the prison where the accused incarcerated them, and through the fearful misery in which he left them."[19]

12. Cyrus Smith to Consul Casement. Incident in the Mongalla atrocities of 1900 (Africa, No. 1, 1904).

13. Findings of the Boma Court in the above case. Arguments for "extenuating circumstances" towards Cyrus Smith.

14. Semliki region. Lloyd, 1899.

15. Katanga region. Affidavit. March 1903.

16. Johnston Falls neighbourhood. Diary.

17. Katanga region. Missionary evidence received by Mr. H. R. Fox Bourne in 1903—covering period from 1894 to 1903.

18. Domaine de la Couronne region. Scrivener.

19. Rubi-Welle region. M. de Favereau reading out to Belgian House charges against Tilkens. Tilkens' defence is that "these hostages were inscribed each month on the reports sent to my

"In an open shed I found two sentries of the La Lulanga Company guarding fifteen women, five of whom had infants at the breast, and three of whom were about to become mothers. . . . The remaining eleven women, whom he indicated, he said he had caught, and was detaining as prisoners to compel their husbands to bring in the right amount of indiarubber required of them on the next market day. When I asked if it was a woman's work to collect indiarubber, he said 'No;[20] that of course it was man's work.' 'Then why do you catch the women and not the men?' I asked. 'Don't you see,' was the answer, 'if I caught and kept the men, who would work the rubber? But if I catch their wives, the husbands are anxious to have them home again, and so the rubber is brought in quickly and quite up to the mark.' When I asked what would become of these women if their husbands failed to bring in the right quantity of rubber on the next market day, he said at once that then they would be kept there until their husbands had redeemed them.' . . . At nightfall the fifteen women in the shed were tied together, either neck to neck, or ankle to ankle, to secure them for the night, and in this posture I saw them twice during the evening. They were then trying to huddle around a fire."[21]

"Later in the day . . . two armed soldiers came up to the agent as we walked, guarding sixteen natives, five men tied neck to neck, with five untied women and six young children. This somewhat embarrassing situation, it was explained to me, was due to the persistent failure of the people of the village these persons came from to supply its proper quota of food. . . . I asked if the children also were held responsible for food supplies, and they, along with an elderly woman, were released. . . . The remaining five men and four women were led off to the *maison des ôtages* under guard of the sentry. The agent explained that he was forced to catch women in preference to the men, as then supplies were brought in quicker; but he did not explain how the children deprived of their parents obtained their own food supplies."[22]

"I met, when walking in the Abir grounds with the subordinate agent of the factory, a file of fifteen women, under the guard of three unarmed

---

Chiefs. If there was mortality amongst them my Chiefs knew it, and never made of the fact a cause of complaint against me."—*Annales parlimentaires*, Part V.

20. Mr. Scrivener writes me that he hears that women are also about to be compelled to collect indiarubber in his district. He does not mention it as a fact, but as a rumour.

21. Lulonga district. Consul Casement, 1903. Africa, White Book, No. 1, 1904.

22. Lopori-Maringa District. Consul Casement, 1903. Ibid.

sentries, who were being brought in from the adjoining villages, and were led past me. These women, who were evidently wives and mothers, it was explained in answer to my inquiry, had been seized in order to compel their husbands to bring in antelope or other meat which was overdue."[23]

"The Commissaire had visited P—— and had ordered the people of that town to work daily at Q—— for the La Lulonga factory. W—— had replied that it was too far for the women of P—— to go daily to Q—— as was required; but the Commissaire in reply had taken fifty women and carried them away with him."[24]

"In addition fifty women are required each morning to go to the factory and work there all day. They complained that the remuneration given for these services was most inadequate, and that they were continually beaten."[25]

"A considerable number of children necessarily engaged in this work, and, moreover, were often held by the State as 'hostages' because of delinquencies or defects."[26]

If this is not the slave trade, what is it? How much longer will the civilised world tolerate these things?[27]

It would need a volume in itself to deal in a thorough manner with the exotic abominations introduced into the Congo territories under King Leopold's sway. One labours under the weight of well-nigh overpowering testimony. These short extracts I have quoted can give no adequate account of the full misery upon the people which such measures entail.

The cumulative effects of depopulation and infantile mortality by dragging women away from their homes for forced labour requisitions—seizing them as "hostages," and "tying them up," whether virgins, wives, mothers, or those about to become mothers, in order to bring pressure to bear upon brothers, husbands, and fathers for the adequate supply of rubber or food taxes; flinging them into "prison," together with their children, often to die of starvation and neglect; flogging them, sometimes even unto death; leaving them at the mercy of the soldiers; distributing them after punitive raids among hangers-on— must be enormous. There we have depopulation through the infamous torture

23. Lopori-Maringa District. Consul Casement, 1903. Africa, White Book, No. 1, 1904.
24. Lulonga District. Consul Casement, 1903. Ibid.
25. Lulonga District. Consul Casement, 1903. Ibid.
26. E. A. Layton. Coquilhatville District. American Memorial, *op. cit.*
27. It will be observed that I have left out of account all records of a similar character, of ancient date, such as Glave's, Sjöblom, Murphy, etc.

of women—often enough shot outright or mutilated[28]—and the neglect and the mutilation of young children and boys; most of whom, it may be presumed, when so mutilated do not survive the operation, in order to have "the bad taste to show their stumps to the missionaries," as one of the Belgian deputies said in the course of the Congo debate in the Belgian House last year.

What has come over the civilised people of the globe that they can allow their Governments to remain inactive and apathetic in the face of incidents which recall in aggravated form the worst horrors of the over-sea slave trade, which surpass the exploits of Arab slave catchers? What could be worse than scenes such as these, which can be culled by the dozen from Consul Casement's report, and from the testimony of a score of independent, non-official resident observers, scattered throughout the country:

> "Then the soldiers came again to fight us. We ran into the bush. . . .
> After that they saw a little of my mother's head, and the soldiers ran
> quickly towards the place where we were, and caught my grandmother,
> my mother, my sister, and another little one younger than us. Several of
> the soldiers argued about my mother, because each wanted her for a wife,
> so they finally decided to kill her. They killed her with a gun, they shot
> her through the stomach and she fell, and when I saw that I cried very
> much, because they killed my grandmother and my mother, and I was
> left alone. My mother was near her confinement at the time. And they
> killed my grandmother too, and I saw it all done . . . "

Offence: villages slow in the production of rubber!

> "While they were both standing outside the soldiers came upon them
> and took them both. One of the soldiers said, 'We might keep them
> both, the little one is not bad looking.' But the others said, 'No, we are
> not going to carry her all the way; we must kill the younger girl.' So they
> put a knife through the child's stomach, and left the body lying there
> where they had killed it. . . . "

Merely an incident in a rubber war!

Take the case of the twenty poor wretches belonging to the villages of Bokongo and Bongondo, murdered for being behindhand in their supply of

---

28. Referring to the depopulation of the Lake Mantumba towns, Consul Casement says: "War in which children and women were killed as well as men. Women and children were killed, not in all cases by stray bullets, but were taken as prisoners and killed. Sad to say, these horrible cases were not always the acts of some black soldier. Proof was laid against one officer who shot one woman and one man, when they were before him as prisoners with their hands tied, and no attempt was made by the accused to deny the truth of the statement."—Africa, No. 1, 1904, p. 70.

goats. Eleven of the victims of this outrage, which occured last May twelve-month, were women, and one was a girl. The crime has gone unpunished, although I have published the full list of names.[29] That is a recent case. The massacre of 120 natives in "cold blood" in the raids against the Banza (Caudron case) is another recent case. How many of the victims were women and children, I wonder? Let the reader never fail to bear in mind that it is only by accident we ever hear of any of these deeds of darkness which, as I pen these lines, are going on all over the Congo unchecked and unpunished, a necessary and endemic effect of the new slave trade which has replaced the milder one of the Arabs.

The Congo Government boasts that, in stopping intertribal warfare, it has stopped the selling of tribal prisoners of war into domestic slavery. The condition of the domestic slave under the African system is blissful beyond words, if you compare his lot with that of the degraded serf under the Leopoldian system.[30]

But, in point of fact, the State, having violently reduced free communities to agglomerations of broken-spirited bondsmen, is deliberately encouraging the slave traffic in another form. Individuals in a village are frequently compelled to sell themselves, and each other, to neighbouring tribes, in order that the village as a whole may not suffer from one or other of the fearful punishments inflicted for non-compliance in that filling of a bottomless sack which the Congo Executive describes as "taxation"—the light, extremely light, "taxation" of "40 hours per month"! We have reports of this from various widely removed parts of the Congo.

> "A close acquaintance with the conditions," writes Dr. Lyon,[31] "shows the cogency of the natives' contentions that they are no less than slaves to

29. This atrocity was brought to my notice by Mr. Weeks, who denounced it to the authorities on November 30, 1903. See *West African Mail*, January 22, 1904; also Congo issue, June. The crimes were perpetrated by State soldiers under a Government officer, who, if not actually present, was in the neighbourhood, and who has been allowed to return with this charge hanging over his head. Several weeks after he was allowed to leave, a judicial officer was sent to investigate and found the statements fully proved!

30. If it be objected that in certain instances the lot of the domestic slave was apt to be cut short for culinary purposes in the pre-regenerating days, it may with equal point be retorted that, after 20 years of "regeneration," Government soldiers and auxiliaries are found in the plentitude of their civilising mission, and under the eyes of Government officials, disembowelling and cutting up the recently slaughtered bodies of recalcitrant native taxpayers for similar purpose.—*Vide* Yandjali massacre, 1903. And further, that instances of cannibalism by soldiers in the Abir territory have been openly committed—the facts clearly established—many times during the last few months.

31. American Memorial, *op. cit.*

the State. And as slaves, I have observed they must sometimes 'make bricks without straw,' as when one must furnish fish nearly the year round, and he can catch fish only at certain seasons. Then one is forced to buy in other parts, paying in this way ten to forty times what will be received in return at the State post. To meet these obligations A——, of W——, one of the remaining few of a once large family, had to pawn, *i.e.* sell into slavery, a younger member of his family."

Mr. Weeks gives me the names of twenty-one persons, with their villages, whom their relatives were compelled to sell into slavery, in his district last year in order to supply the goats required as part of the food tax levied upon their villages.[32] In his letter to the Commissaire-General of the Bangala District (November 30, 1903) protesting against this occurrence, which letter was published in the *West African Mail* of January 22, 1904, Mr. Weeks says: "Thus to supply your table at Bangala the life of these people is being slowly crushed out, and many sold into slavery."

Mr. Gilchrist, in his letter to the Governor-General (July, 1903), explains how in order to meet an exorbitant fine levied for shortness in the supply of food-stuffs: "Some of the men had to sell their wives and children into slavery, and some sold themselves to the river people."

Consul Casement reports similar incidents. A village near Coquilhatville, for instance, is fined 55,000 rods (£110) for failure in supplying food-stuffs in sufficient quantities:

"This sum they had been forced to pay, and as they had no other means of raising so large a sum, they had, many of them, been compelled to sell their children and their wives."

And again:

"A father and mother stepped out and said that they had been forced to sell their son, a little boy called F——, for 1000 rods to meet their share of the fine. A widow came and declared she had been forced, in order to meet her share of the fine, to sell her daughter, G——, a little girl, whom I judged from her description to be about ten years of age."

---

32. A few years ago every village in the Congo had its goats. Now very few villages, which are not too remote from the State posts to be got at, have any left. But the natives are still expected to provide the officials with these animals, as part and parcel of the food tax. The result is that the price of goats has reached a phenomenal figure. These particular twenty-one poor people were sold to other tribes—29,000 rods, for thirty-one goats!

Our Consul remarks that he was not able to verify all these statements, but the one he was able to do turned out correct. It was the case of two little children. One of them was, by his intervention, restored to her parents, but the other had "again changed hands, and was promised in sale to a town on the north bank of the Congo named Iberi, whose people are still said to be open cannibals." Charming picture of moral and material regeneration!

Again, I ask, if this is not the slave trade, what is it?

Pages could be given to the evidence available proving that workmen and soldiers are obtained by methods differing in very little, if at all, from open slave-raiding, but it will be sufficient to give a translation of the following order for Government workmen drawn up by "Le Capitaine-Commandant Sarrazyn,"[33] a former Commissaire of the Equateur District, surnamed by the natives "Widjima," or "Darkness":

> "The Chief Ngula of Wangasa is sent into the Maringa to buy slaves for me. The agents of the Abir are instructed to be good enough to let me know of the ill-deeds (*les méfaits*) which he may commit on the road."

Comment is needless.[34]

Once more—if this is not the slave trade, what is it?

We have many sad glimpses of the inward effect produced upon the people by this system of organised murder, robbery, and oppression. The women, Consul Casement tells us, are deliberately practising abortion, because, as they say, "If war should come, a woman big with child, or with a baby to carry, cannot well run away and hide from the soldiers." The Rev. Joseph Clark has the same tale to tell:

> "The native mind is not at rest. He has no desire for the improvement of his surroundings. He will not make a good house or large gardens, because that will give the State a greater hold on him. His wife refuses to become a mother because she will not be able to run away in case of an attack. Twice this week the people of Ikoko have been rushing off to the 'bush' to hide on the approach of a large canoe with soldiers."[35]

33. White Book, Africa, No. 1, 1904.

34. "I have had several cases brought to my knowledge lately of the mode of slavery adopted at the post. Briefly it is as follows: a man for some reason . . . commences work at the post. He completes his term, and he is told he cannot have his pay unless he engages himself another term or brings another in his place. I know of those who have left their earnings in the hands of the Chef de Poste rather than begin again. Such compulsion is contrary to civilised law, and is rightly termed slavery, and is utterly illegal."—Whitehead to Governor-General, Sept., 1903.

35. American Memorial, *op. cit.*

Weeks, writing of the effect of a yearly taxation of £1605 16s. 8d. on a miserable population of 820 persons, of both sexes, says:

"I need scarcely point out that young children, very old people, and invalids cannot earn a wage, or even farm or fish; consequently the burden falls heavier on those who can, and the vision before them is one of unceasing toil in order to comply with the demands of the State. Is it any wonder the natives die under the burden? The wonder to me is that so many are alive after these seven years of oppression and taxation. Were this tax a yearly, or even a half-yearly one, it would not be so bad; but it is a fortnightly one, and consequently an ever-present nightmare. No sooner is one tax sent off in canoes than they have to worry about collecting materials for the next. Thus it is a constant grind, grind, grind, that is sapping the spirit and strength of these people, and causing them to succumb. Death is kinder than this kind of living."[36]

"Death and decay in all around I see," was the impression of a colleague of my friend Mr. Weeks in returning last December from a visit to the Ndobo towns, whose inhabitants live on the banks of streamlets and lakelets about twenty miles from Monsembe and the main river. "A policy"—to quote Weeks once more—"that is impoverishing these people, sapping their strength, and sending them to the grave."[37] "Surely this is slavery," writes Mr. Frame, describing the usual tale of brutal oppression, and adds: "The slavery of the people on this side of Stanley Pool to the Nkissi River is fairly complete, with no hope of improvement."[38] "Oppressive measures under which the people are groaning and dying," writes Mr. Gilchrist.[39]

"The people are regarded as the property of the State for any purpose for which they may be needed. That they have any desires of their own, or any plans worth carrying out in connection with their own lives, would create a smile among the officials."[40]

"The poor people of this section" (Bolengi near Coquilhatville, one of the most important State stations on the Upper River) "are broken-spirited and poverty-stricken by an arbitrary and oppressive system of taxation."[41]

36. Weeks to Author, Dec. 24, 1903.
37. Weeks to Author, Dec. 23, 1903.
38. W. B. Frame to Author, March 16, 1904.
39. S. Gilchrist to Governor-General, Sept. 1903.
40. Scrivener to Author, Oct., 1903.
41. Dr. Lyon, 1903 or 1904, American Memorial, *op. cit.*

"In the village of W———," writes Consul Casement, "extortionately fined for being in arrears, one of the natives, a strong, indeed a splendid-looking man, broke down and wept, saying that their lives were useless to them, and that they knew of no means of escape from the troubles which were gathering round them."[42]

Our Consul's report abounds in incidents showing the utter misery and demoralisation of the people. Some persons seem to think that rubber falls off the trees in Africa like apples in autumn, and all that the "lazy native" has to do is to pick it up. In point of fact, rubber collecting is, even under normal conditions, dangerous to health—any one acquainted with the South American rubber business will bear me out. What must it be under the compulsory conditions prevalent in the Congo? Hundreds, if not thousands, of natives on the Congo must die every year merely through fatigue, exposure, chills, ill-health, engendered by working in fœtid swamps, the attacks of wild animals, and privations of all kinds. Rubber collecting in the tropical African forests is the most ultimately exhausting of all forms of labour voluntarily undertaken by the African; but he knows the product is of value, and that he will get many more goods for a couple of pounds of pure rubber than for most other things that the white man requires. On the Congo, however, the native is *driven* into the forest. He is not a trader, but a beast. If he brings in the stipulated quantity after days of absence from his family, he gets a few teaspoonfuls of salt, or a handful of beads, and immediately he must begin again, and so on, until he dies or manages to escape to remoter regions.

Here is a typical insight into native life in a rubber district, under the gloriously humanitarian system beneath the "blue banner with the golden star," so dear to the severely impartial hearts of Sir Hugh Gilzean Reid, Mr. Demetrius C. Boulger, Sir Alfred Jones, and his crowd of obedient followers:

"I went to the homes of these men, some miles away, and found out their circumstances. To get the rubber they had first to go fully a two days' journey from their homes, leaving their wives, and being absent for from five to six days. They were seen to the forest limits under guard, and, if not back by the sixth day, trouble was likely to ensue. To get the rubber in the forests, which, generally speaking, are very swampy, involves much fatigue, and often fruitless searching for a well-flowing vine. As the area of supply diminishes, moreover, the demand for rubber constantly increases. Some little time back I learned the Bongandanga District supplied seven tons of rubber a month, a quantity which it was

42. Africa, No. 1, 1904, *op. cit.*

hoped would shortly be increased to ten tons. . . . In addition to these formal payments, they are liable at times to be dealt with in another manner, for should their work, which might have been just as hard, have proved less profitable in its yield of rubber, the local prison would have seen them. The people everywhere assured me that they were not happy under this system, and it was apparent to a callous eye that in this they spoke the strict truth."

"They were not happy." Mr. Casement has never forgotten in the course of his report that he was a machine sent to record in a spirit of calm, judicial impartiality the sights he witnessed, and he performed his task with marvellous self-restraint; for, though an official, he may be presumed to have the feelings of an ordinary mortal, and his "they were not happy" conveys, under the circumstances, a story of abject and unspeakable wretchedness. Enough has been said to show that under this system of "moral and material regeneration," constituting a monstrous invasion of primitive rights which has no parallel in the whole world, the family life and social ties of the people are utterly destroyed. Another horrible aspect of Congo State rule is touched upon by Mr. Dugald Campbell in the letter which will be found in the Appendix, viz. the spread of syphilis through promiscuous "forcing into lives of shame" of women and young girls to pander to the lusts of the ceaselessly shifting and enormous army. Under native conditions, he says, strict measures are taken to circumscribe the area of this disease, but under the Congo Government system it is everywhere extending and infecting whole districts.

Within the last few weeks detailed and specific accounts, clearly established, have come to hand from Messrs. Stannard, Harris, and Frost, all in the Baringa district of the *Abir* concession, painting a picture of native misery at the hands of the servants of that insatiable rubber-hunting corporation which would touch a heart of stone. They will be found in full in the Appendix. What is the reply which King Leopold flings to the world?[43] It consists in the appointment to the Board of Administration of Count John d'Oultremont, Grand Marshal to the Belgian Court, and Baron Dhanis, an ex-Governor-General of the Congo State! This measure is accompanied by a statement from the worthy Senator who nominally presides over the destinies of this Trust, to the effect that its rubber-producing capacities have not nearly attained their zenith, for the labour of the natives may be easily requisitioned to produce one hundred and twenty tons of that article a month, whereas the present output is only sixty tons!

I will conclude with an extract of a letter I have recently received from my

---

43. The Congo Government, as already shown, holds half the shares of the *Abir*.

friend Mr. Weeks, who has rendered such invaluable service during the past year, in helping the cause of these oppressed people. The letter is dated Monsembe, Dec. 26, 1903.

"What does the native receive in return for all this taxation? I know of absolutely no way in which he is benefited. Some point to the telegraph. In what way does that benefit a native? Those who live near the line have to keep the road clear for nothing, and in tropical Africa that is not an easy task. Others point to the scores of steamers running on the Upper Congo. In what way do they benefit the native? Here and there along the river, natives are forced to supply large quantities of firewood for an inadequate remuneration. Others, again, point to well-built State stations. In what way do they benefit the native? They are largely built, and are now largely maintained, by forced labour. Then others point to the railway. It is a splendid achievement of engineering skill, and is paying large dividends to shareholders, but in what way does it benefit the thousands of natives on the Upper Congo? It certainly takes the rubber they are forced to supply so cheaply, more rapidly than otherwise possible, to the European markets. Is there more security for life now than under the old *régime?* It does not appear so when a white officer of the State allowed his soldiers last May to shoot down 22 men and women for the paltry offence of owing a paternal State a few groats. Is there more security for property now than under the old *régime?* No, for then men defended his goods by his spear; now their goods are open to the depredations of State messengers and soldiers. And there is no redress."

If Gladstone had been alive he would perhaps have found a phrase adequate to describe the revival of the slave trade under the ægis of a European Sovereign in Equatorial Africa, and the forms which that revival takes. But I doubt if even he could have found one more fittingly characterising it than that he so truly applied to other quarters. The "Negation of God" erected with a system—yes, indeed!

Why are these people allowed to suffer thus cruelly? What crime have they collectively committed in past ages that they should undergo to-day so terrible an expiation? Are they "groaning and dying" under this murderous system as a great object-lesson to Europe? What price, then, will Europe later on have to pay for the teaching? Inscrutable are the decrees of Providence. One wonders whether the deepening horror of this colossal crime will end by a reaction so violent that an era of justice will, for the first time in the history of Caucasian relationship with the Dark Continent, arise, never to be eradicated, for the peoples of Africa. Or that some day tropical Africa may breed brains as she breeds muscles, and then . . . ? But it bodes little to dwell among the mists of conjecture. The future is closed to us. We grope in the dark, puzzled, incensed, impatient. The future is with God. To the past man may look and gather consolation in the knowledge that evils such as these bring their own Nemesis upon the nation whose moral guilt is primarily involved. Belgium, technically unconcerned, is morally responsible, and Belgium will suffer. Strange that it should be the seceded Southern Provinces of those very Netherlands, so terribly served five hundred years ago, which are allowing another foreign Monarch of theirs to plagiarise in Africa, exploits formerly visited upon themselves. Strange too, perhaps, that a descendant of one of the victims of Philip II. should have been driven by Fate to participate in the movement directed against his latter-day prototype, in all respects save re-ligious fanaticism. We are powerless as to the future, and if in past history we may find a partial solace, it is the present that concerns us. And here we are neither blindfolded nor impotent for action. Action it is we claim; action there must be.

If the policy of the Congo State were a national policy; if the Congo tribes were being systematically bled to death either through distorted zeal, as the population of the Netherlands were harried with fire and sword by Philip and his lieutenants, or through lust of conquest; if the Congo Basin were capable of being colonised by the Caucasian race, the policy we condemn and repro-bate would still be a crime against humanity, an outrage upon civilisation. But the Congo territories can never be a white man's country; the "Congo State" is naught but a collection of individuals—with one supreme above them all—working for their own selfish ends, caring nothing for posterity, callous of the present, indifferent of the future, as of the past, animated by no fanaticism other than the fanaticism of dividends—and so upon the wickedness of this thing is grafted the fatuous stupidity and inhumanity of the Powers in allow-ing the extermination of the Congo races to go on unchecked, barely, if at all, reproved.

Surely the time has come to cease the usage of kid gloves and rose-water in dealing with this Congo question? For eight years that process has been adopted, and it has yielded nothing—absolutely nothing. Things are infinitely worse to-day than they were eight years ago. Anyhow, it is time some one called a spade a spade in this infernal business, even if the tender suscep-tibilities of certain estimable people are hurt by so unfashionable a method.

SOURCE: In *King Leopold's Rule in Africa* (1904; Westport, Conn.: Negro Universities Press, 1970), 242–56.

Excerpts from *History of the
Congo Reform Movement*

E. D. MOREL

[A work that Morel did not complete, the *History of the Congo Reform Movement* is his quasi-autobiographical account of the establishment of the Congo Reform Association and the difficulties and challenges that accompanied that movement.]

CHAPTER 7
ORIGINS OF THE CONGO CONTROVERSY

Over the Congo itself there hung a dense fog of mystery. Now and again a corner of it would lift. When that happened, scenes of apparently purposeless carnage and delirious chaos were sometimes, and for an instant, visible. On other occasions one had the fleeting impression of a prosperous population and a benign rule. At other times military revolts and military expeditions commanded by Belgian officers and operating far beyond the international confines of the State were momentarily observable. Then the fog would settle down again as impenetrable as ever. The conflict of evidence may be estimated from the fact that one year—1898—had seen the appearance of a British Consular Report containing some moderate criticisms of certain features of Congo Free State rule: a book by Captain Guy Burrows, a British officer in the State's employ, dedicated by permission to King Leopold and containing a letter from the King in which he declared that 'our only programme is the work of material and moral regeneration': a book by another English writer, Mr. Demetrius C. Boulger, effusively praising the magnificent work accomplished by King Leopold and his officials; and a book by a Belgian Professor containing both criticism and praise. The next year had witnessed a further protest and denunciation from Morrison, the chief representative of the American missions in the Kasai, and one or two brief condemnatory remarks by a British lay missionary in Uganda who had returned to Europe via the Congo. On the other hand, three volumes had appeared from the pens of a Belgian Senator and two French gentlemen respectively, who had visited the Lower Congo (on the occasion of the opening of the railway connecting the lower and the upper reaches of the river) which, while they contained some criticisms were, in the main, highly complimentary to the Congo administration. In 1900 Mr. E. S. Grogan published contemptuous and outspoken allu-

sions concerning the conditions of the eastern border-region of the Congo
Free State, condemning the State as a 'vampire growth.'

Towards the end of the same year the curtain had been dramatically lifted
from the territory exploited by the *Anversoise* Company, the first *Belgian*
disclosure of Belgian deeds on the Congo. In these days King Leopold's Press
Bureau had not been invented, the corruption of Belgian Editors with Congo
gold, and Congo decorations, had not been systematised, and the atrocious
self-confessed crimes perpetrated by certain subordinate Belgian agents of
the Company, as they averred, under orders, had shocked Belgian Public
Opinion. But alas the effect had been fleeting. The outcry was quickly stifled.
A powerful and subtle machinery was set immediately to work to discount the
emotion produced. Only two men in the Belgian Chamber—Emile Vandervelde and Georges Lorand—had had the courage to protest in the name of
Belgian honour. As already noted the President of the *Anversoise* was himself
a Member of the Senate, the Guardian of the King's privy purse sat on its
board and the Congo Government held half the shares. Even Lorand's reading from the Parliamentary tribune of a letter from a Belgian in another part
of the Congo casually mentioning that his soldiers had brought him 1,300
severed hands as testimony to their prowess in punishing recalcitrant rubber
collectors, was insufficient to move Belgian Ministers and their solid majority.
To Lorand's and Vandervelde's passionate denunciation of a policy of 'pillage,
devastation and assassination', all that Belgium's Premier had seen fit to reply
was that the Congo Free State as a sovereign independent State was its own
master in its own house and for the rest, that the 'disinterestedness of its
creators will find its reward in the gratitude of the country'. The entire Min-
isterial Press and most of the Liberal papers—notably the *Indépendance
Belge* and the *Étoile Belge*—had denounced the two courageous Deputies as
personal enemies of the King and 'unpatriotic'. And so the incident was
dismissed.

Looking back now it may appear strange at first sight that Public Opinion
in Britain was not more deeply stirred by these successive, if sporadic, revelations spread over nearly five years. But the reasons were many. From the close
of 1899 to the period I am writing of (i.e. early in 1901) the Boer War had
absorbed the national mind. The Congo was far away. Official circles were
averse from stirring up the Congo mud from motives of traditional policy
with regard to Belgium. The Foreign Office had a lively dread of King Leopold's power of intrigue. Moreover, the late Queen was opposed to a strong
line of action being taken against the son of the man for whom she had
entertained such strong affection. I have been assured on good authority that
Lord Salisbury was only deterred from acting as vigorously towards Belgium's

King over the Stokes affair as he did towards Portugal over Major Serpa Pinto's African promenades, by the Queen's opposition. To similar influence was probably due the fact that Mr. Chamberlain had been unable in 1895–6 to get his colleagues to agree to the setting up of British Consular jurisdiction in the Congo in connection with the ill-treatment of British coloured subjects who had taken service in various capacities under King Leopold's Government. The Liberals had for their part committed themselves deeply and disastrously with King Leopold over the ill-starred Bahr-el-Ghazal agreement of 1894, although it is fair to add that at the time the Cabinet had no knowledge of the outrages of which the Congo was the scene. Indeed, Lord Morley—the Right Honourable John Morley as he was then—frankly admitted three years later at Fox Bourne's meeting called to hear Sjöblom, that in the light of what he then knew, the 1894 agreement was a 'great mistake'. All the reports received by the Foreign Office from its Consuls in the Congo, from the Governors of the West African possessions, and from British officers or officials in neighbouring British territory between 1896 to the end of 1900, had been suppressed, with the sole exception of the very much abridged and innocuous Pickersgill report of 1898, to which allusion has already been made. Naturally all this only became known to me later, but a reference at this stage of the narrative seemed necessary in order to explain what the British official attitude was when the year 1901 opened. That social influences were quietly exerted in favour of King Leopold is not, I think, doubtful. Stanley, who was still in some measure connected with the Congo Free State, had the *entrée* everywhere in any question affecting that part of the world, and he could never, apparently, bring himself to believe in any of the charges against an enterprise he had so largely contributed in creating. As for any real Public Opinion on the subject, it is no disloyalty to Fox Bourne's memory to say that it did not exist. Fox Bourne was an honest, sincere and genuine philanthropist. His efforts were persistent, protracted and beyond praise. He was perfectly disinterested. He worked for pure zeal on behalf of oppressed peoples all over the world, and, although hampered by failing health, his efforts never relaxed. But the very catholicity of his sympathies was a source of popular weakness in a case of superlative wrongdoing of this kind, and the Aborigines Protection Society of which he was the life and soul, was notorious for criticising every European Government (often quite justly) in its dealings with subject races. Fox Bourne himself was no faddist, although he was prone to think European interference with coloured peoples had no redeeming features, and that the Congo horror was merely the inevitable result, in specially aggravated form, of contact between the White and Black races on African soil. With the assistance of Sir Charles Dilke—that most loyal and generous of public men—he did splendid work, and exposed many an abuse in widely distant lands. But, although he had succeeded in arousing a certain amount of interest in the Congo, it was very restricted and it had no driving force. He and I had our occasional differences of opinion as to tactics. But our co-operation was close and our interchange of letters continuous for nearly nine years, during which our relationship was uniformly friendly. Either had complete confidence in the other and placed his knowledge and information unreservedly at the other's disposal.

I have indicated in a previous chapter some of the doubts which assailed my own mind when I first began to look into the question. Similar doubts, even after the Belgian revelations of the latter part of 1900, must have been uppermost in the minds of men capable of influencing public opinion, who were more or less familiar with the subject and who might have been expected to take an intelligent interest in it, such as Newspaper Editors, politicians and leaders of religious thought. Indeed how those doubts persisted I was soon to learn by my own experience. Nor is it possible to feel real surprise that such should have been the case. Collectively the actual evidence of misgovernment from the Congo was very grave. But it was scattered over a number of years: not accessible in any summarised form. There seemed no connecting link between the various accounts and there was no apparent motive for the crimes reported. There was rebutting evidence—not much, then, at least from the Congo itself, but still some. The periodical denials of King Leopold's Secretaries of State in Brussels had been absolute and conceived in a tone of virtuous indignation. Their protestations of philanthropic intent were so earnest, their profession of a desire to investigate and remedy any abuses which might be found to exist, apparently so sincere, their appeal for fair play towards a poor little struggling 'State' hampered by lack of funds and endeavouring to carry out a great civilising work, so eloquently worded that any tendency to harshness of criticism was mitigated. The cloak of philanthropy in which the Congo Free State had been nurtured was not yet worn wholly threadbare: the shreds still clung about it and predisposed people in its favour. Then, had not the King given a most signal proof of the purity of his motives by creating four years previously a permanent Commission 'charged with the protection of natives throughout the territory of the State'? Was this Commission not composed of the Godliest men in the Congo, the Superior of the Jesuit Mission, the Revs. George Grenfell and Holman Bentley, of the Baptist Missionary Society; Father de Cleene of the Congregation de Scheut, Dr. Sims of the American Baptist Union, with the Vicar-Apostolic of the Congo, as President? Was it conceivable that if these accusations contained a particle of truth, these holy men would reserve silence? What Editor could resist such arguments, presented in the mellifluent tones of the Consul-General for the Congo Free State in London; promulgated from Brussels in periods of outraged righteousness?

These representations notwithstanding, the embarrassing Belgian revelations of the latter end of 1900, reviving memories of and confirming Glave's and Sjöblom's disclosures of an earlier date, might conceivably have made things awkward for King Leopold, had the Belgian Government adopted for its part a less pronounced attitude. But in identifying itself so wholly with the defence of the Congo Free State Government, in supporting that defence so uncompromisingly, the Belgian Government had adopted a course of action which English public men could with difficulty bring themselves to believe was not due to knowledge of the true state of the case. Vandervelde's indictment was in large measure set down to his socialist views and the personal antagonism he was alleged to bear to the King.

Such, in brief, then, was the position which, I hope and think to have faithfully portrayed, when my own turn came to enter the lists.

PLANNING THE CAMPAIGN

From this survey, one central fact of capital importance stood out—in bold relief. Public Opinion had not grasped that the occurrences reported from the Congo were the inevitable results of a fixed policy, carefully thought out, deliberately planned, immovable as the Pyramids. The Public was not aware that any such policy existed. It was not realised that reports from the spot were immaterial to the formation of a reasoned judgement of the true situation in which the Congo was plunged. It was not understood that rebutting or merely negative evidence was worthless, indicating at most that the circumstances either ethnologic or physiological of particular parts of the Congo made the application of the policy impracticable or undesirable. This capital feature in the case was not, and could not be apprehended because the material was lacking. That material, it seemed, I alone possessed. The problem for me then was simply this. Had I the necessary qualifications to so present the case in writing and in speech as to bring conviction to men's minds: and what was the best way to set about it?

I felt intimately assured that it was impossible to rouse anything in the nature of an agitation which would be more than ephemeral, by concentrating solely upon the scattered reports of atrocities perpetrated upon the native population. Moreover these were merely incidental. The central wrong was the reduction of millions of men to a condition of absolute slavery, by a system of legalised robbery enforced by violence. The appeal must be to the mind as well as to the heart. Assume an overwhelming case made out as to the atrocities even on a scale of unparalleled magnitude. However strong, it would be met by promises and protestations of reforms: by the punishment of a few scapegoats; by the promulgation of new laws breathing the quintessence of philanthropy. The Official Bulletins were full of such laws already. The Congo native having been reduced to eternal servitude, it was decided that he should be treated with humanity. His land having been converted into the private property of the King, it was decreed that no one should interfere with his liberty. The only articles in which he could trade with the European having been appropriated by the King and his financial friends, it was decreed that he could trade in anything which was legitimate. Moreover, an element of doubt would always linger as to the thorough reliability of a case built upon statements unverifiable by ordinary processes and made by individuals suspect to many. It should be remembered that there was a complete absence of reports from the consular representatives of the Powers. These resided at Boma, south in the Lower Congo where the policy did not apply. They did not travel in the interior. Or, at any rate if they did, or if reports reached them from the north, nothing transpired outside the Chancelleries. Apart from the observations of chance travellers what were the human elements through whom evidence was procurable? There were only four classes of White men permanently resident in the Congo Free State: the officials (officials were rewarded proportionately to the amount of rubber they succeeded in squeezing out of their districts: but it was decreed that any official guilty of cruel treatment should be severely punished. And the 'Magistrates' were the high officials!), the agents of the Thys group of Companies, the agents of the concessionnaire, or privileged companies, and the Missionaries. Of independent European traders or residents there were none. The summary execution of Stokes, and the impossibility of trading in a country where the raw material of trade had been seized by its Government *by law,* had scared away all international-commercial enterprise properly so called. Two or three trading firms lingered on in the Lower Congo doing a retail business. That was all.

Now it was obvious that any disclosures from officials or ex-officials, as from agents or ex-agents of the Concessionnaire Companies would be largely discounted on the ground that they emanated from men who were participating in, or had been participators of, the very conditions which they condemned. Moreover the Congo Free State authorities could be trusted to trump up any kind of charge against such people, true or false, and it was at least probable that tactics of that sort would nine times out of ten be successful. The prejudice in the public mind would persist. It would be extremely difficult to make the average man believe the statements of an official with a grievance, and in most cases the average man's judgement would be sound. But not in all. The conditions of the Congo were peculiar. The newcomer, honest or dishonest, with a clean heart or an evil one, was swept into a maelstrom from which there was no escape, save by a miracle. A raw European, with decent instincts might find himself caught in the meshes of a system which compelled him at least to connive at acts of habitual violence and oppression. But in terms of his contract he would be unable to free himself before his three years' contract was over, however desirous he might be of relinquishing his employment, or of indicating the character of his employers. And by that time, save under exceptionally favourable circumstances, he would either have sunk to the level of the system, or have committed suicide, or died. We shall never know a tithe of the individual White tragedies on the Congo, although a chapter might be written on specific cases familiar to some of us.

Once in the Congo, the new arrival was bound in fetters of steel to a system as pitiless in its way to the Whites as it was to the Blacks. If his past life in Europe contained some blemish he sank into the grip of a system like a stone sinks in water. The Government was itself the hourly violator of the elaborately humane laws published in Brussels for European consumption. The Concessionnaire Companies were the Government's partners in crime and in the profits wrung from 'Red Rubber'. But the Government took care to maintain a judicial machinery which could be invoked against recalcitrant subordinates. It could be swiftly galvanised into aggressive activity towards subordinates in the event of unlooked-for contumacy. It could be set into operation against subordinates if and when disclosures filtered through to Europe by some means or another. And rare, indeed, under such circumstances would be the occasion when connivance in an act, illegal according to the law, could not be brought home to the wretched scapegoat. His defence would never be published. No one would plead his cause. Thus the Congo 'tenderfoot' was absolutely at the mercy of his employers from the moment he stepped out on to the banks of the River. But they surrounded themselves with additional safeguards against his indiscretion. Half of his salary—which was scandalously low—was retained in Brussels to be paid over to him on his return: or withheld. He was bound down strictly in his articles not to communicate any knowledge he might have acquired during his employment. If he made himself a nuisance, his medical and other stores would be unaccountably delayed, and he would be lucky if he suffered no worse inconvenience. He might seek to leave the country. This was peculiarly difficult. The Ocean passage to Europe was £24, and the chances of a subordinate in the Congo service having this amount of money in his possession was remote. Unless he was given a passage on a Missionary steamer out of compassion, the only craft he could travel in on the rivers belonged to the Government. And the Captain of the Government steamer could, of course, refuse to take him. Consulting his own interest he would probably do so; or if he did not he could compel his unwelcome passenger to forage for himself, and what this incurs in Central Africa even under normal conditions some African travellers know to their cost. But if, triumphing over all these and other obstacles too numerous to mention, he had succeeded in actually boarding a boat going down river, he was liable upon arrival at Leopoldville or (had he secured a passage on the railway) at Boma, to be arrested for 'desertion,' or to see himself detained and under surveillance pending 'judicial enquiry' into some alleged breach of 'legality'. This experience was almost inevitable, for his superior officer would be morally certain to have telegraphed his 'dossier' to headquarters. In my experience I never came across but one case of a Belgian subordinate official or agent getting out of the river before the expiration of his period of service, except through illness. As already remarked, after three years' service, the man became identified with the system he worked for, and even if he had kept himself clean—a well-nigh physical and moral impossibility in the rubber districts—such evidence as he then might give was immediately stigmatised by the Congo Authorities in Brussels as that of a dissatisfied ex-servant against whose character much would be hinted if not positively asserted. Nor would the trouble of the unfortunate individual end with his arrival home. Wherever he turned for employment he would find a mysterious influence blocking his chances. If he had spoken out, he was literally hunted down and driven to destitution or emigration. I have known of several such cases. The King's reach was a long one, his attention to detail was marvellous and he never forgave. But no one would have believed all this at the time of which I am writing. And I had only a very faint perception of it myself.

Missionary evidence, on the other hand, is always suspect of a certain class of opinion in Britain. It is not, or used not to be, evidence which commanded public acceptance, although the magnificent manner in which the statements of such of the Protestant missionaries as testified to the truth was eventually vindicated has probably modified that attitude. The Catholic missionaries were mainly Belgians, and it is antagonistic to the Roman system for individual Priests engaged in missionary enterprise to make public declarations on matters affecting the Government under which they live.

Considerations such as these, though not so fully apparent to me then as they have afterwards become, were, nevertheless sufficiently obvious to convince me of the impracticability of leading a crusade against the Congo Free State by invoking humanitarian sentiment alone. After all, the atrocities were merely the effect of a root cause. While that root cause continued to exist, they would continue fatally, inexorably. It was the root cause which needed to be laid bare. It was the policy itself, the whole infernal system, its legal bases, its monstrous claims, its fraudulent accounts and fraudulent statistics, its gross and enormous profits, which required to be dragged into the daylight and pilloried. If one could only make men who counted and the public generally realise that the 'Congo Free State' was neither State nor Protectorate, but a personal enterprise thriving upon pillage, whose aims necessitated the servitude and destruction of innumerable human beings, which began and ended with rubber wrung from the bowels of a helpless people then, surely, the fight would be half won, and the American and the European Governments, guarantors of the Congo Free State, trustees for the natives, above all the Government of Great Britain, with its peculiar and special historical liabilities, would be speedily galvanised into action. Thus I thought in my inexperience. And I still think, looking backwards over a long vista of years that King Leopold would have been summoned to the bar of an international conference with the Congo peoples freed from the human vultures fattening on their agony, in a comparatively short time, if a public man of influence possessing a strong moral character had made the question his own and devoted his whole leisure to it. How often in the days that were to come, did I curse my inability to find such a man and lament my own miserable insufficiency.

Such then was the main task: to convince the world that this Congo horror was not only and unquestionably a fact; but that it was not accidental or temporary, or capable of internal cure. To show conclusively that it was deliberate, and that the consequences would be identical in any part of the tropics where similar conceptions might be introduced. To demonstrate that it was at once a survival and a revival of the slave-mind at work, of the slave-trade in being.

Now it was quite evident that this evil, if it were not struck down, would contaminate the whole tropical region of Africa as it had already contaminated a neighbouring region. And if it were to be struck down the appeal must be varied and widened in character, and forces other than humanitarian must be brought into play. There must be the appeal to national honour, which meant that the Public, and especially the philanthropic and religious Public, whose aid Stanley had enlisted with such effect in the early eighties in securing British adhesion to King Leopold's enterprise, must be vividly reminded of the very special national responsibility which rested upon England and Englishmen in the matter. There must be appeal to the Imperial side, the side which would resent King Leopold's filibustering expeditions beyond the

Congo Free State's international confines; which would appreciate the danger of perpetual uprisings and unrest on the Congo to the peace and good government of contiguous British territory; which would be affected by the knowledge that arms and ammunition were being poured into the Congo both for the use of hordes of undisciplined soldiery, for the arming of friendly tribes to raid other tribes, for ivory-loot, and for sale or presentation to powerful Chiefs.

There must be appeal to the commercial side. At bottom, the problem in one sense, was economic. The basis of the Congo Free State's policy constituted a complete revolution of accepted economics. The material factor governing the relationship of peoples is the exchange of commodities—in other words, trade. In so far as the scramble for tropical Africa had been inspired by economic considerations (and these played a large part) the latter involved two inter-connected factors. These factors were the creation [of markets] in tropical Africa for the sale to the natives of European merchandise on the one part and the collection and cultivation by the native, in exchange for that merchandise, of the tropical produce increasingly required by European industrialism. Indeed, one of the main arguments advanced in favour of conferring a definite status upon King Leopold's so-called 'International Association' had been that it would promote trade, and trade unrestricted by differential tariffs. The support given by the British Chambers of Commerce to Stanley when he conducted his famous pilgrimage through England on the King's behalf, was acquired by the explicitness of the pledges that under the new dispensation trade would be encouraged and untrammeled. The Opposition of the Chambers to the Anglo-Portuguese Treaty for the settlement of the Congo drawn up by Lord Fitzmaurice and Sir Charles Dilke in 1883–4 was due to legitimate dislike of the fiscal policy adopted by Portugal in her dependencies. This opposition was fanned to a flame by Stanley's campaign. 'We made a great mistake. But we relied upon the word of a King'. Thus wrote to me in 1901 a member of one of the British Chambers of Commerce which took a prominent part in opposing the Anglo-Portuguese Treaty. When Continental jealousy, provoked by Leopold II, and philanthropic, religious and commercial agitation in England promoted by Stanley, Sir John Kennaway, Lady Burdett-Coutts, the Baptist Union and the Chambers of Commerce had between them succeeded in—as Sir Charles Dilke once put it—'kicking the Treaty out of the House of Commons', the British Government was driven to support King Leopold's enterprise as the only hope 'of preventing a practical monopoly of the interior of Africa being obtained by France'. But as neither Lord Granville, the Foreign Minister, nor his assistants at the Foreign Office, apparently entertained any belief in King

Leopold's philanthropy, 'it was decided to bind down the new State by conditions as stringent as those in the defunct Anglo-Portuguese Treaty, to secure freedom of trade and the protection of the natives'. These conditions were subsequently embodied in the Congo Free State's international Charter drawn up at Berlin in 1884 and in the Protocols attached to it.

But not only had freedom of trade been destroyed. Trade itself had been declared illegal over three-fifths of the Congo. An embargo had been laid upon the products of the soil which was the raw material of trade. It had been declared the property of the 'State' demesne. The land which yielded it had by law been converted into a 'Private demesne' (*Domaine Privé*) of Europe's trustee. Portions of it had been hired out to Concessionnaire Companies. The whole of the land and everything within it had become not a monopoly merely, involving a monopoly of trade: but a gigantic preserve the like of which the world had never seen, exploitable by the sovereign and his financial associates.

The appeal to international commerce to assert its rights was justified in itself because the policy of the Congo Free State was a cynical and outrageous violation of the world's trading rights, as solemnly inscribed in the Congo Free State's international charter of existence, with an enormous region rich in natural products and inhabited by races in which the trading instinct was a second nature. But if the appeal was justified from the point of view of international commerce, it was absolutely vital to the purpose of succouring the native peoples of the Congo from their intolerable position. To denounce the cruelties inflicted upon the native population was a mere beating of the air, while the basic cause of the cruelties remained unchallenged. So long as King Leopold's claim to dispossess his African subjects of the natural wealth of the country on the ground that it was his, was not contested, the foundations of his system could weather every assault. So long as King Leopold's claim to call upon his African subjects to gather that natural wealth for himself, his government and his financial associates was undisputed, public discussion of the affairs of the Congo could never advance beyond the stage of charge and counter-charge affecting specific acts of cruelty. So long as Public Opinion acquiesced through lack of appreciation of the facts, in King Leopold converting by simple decree the raw material of Afro-European trade on the Congo into the raw material of taxation, the situation could undergo no real change. This was the key-note of the whole matter. From that wholesale appropriation everything sprang: while that claim persisted as the working basis of the Congo Free State's administrative machinery, the Congo natives were doomed to perpetual slavery and perennial outrage. What in its external aspect appeared at first sight to be a trade question, a question of the way in which the rights of international trade were treated by King Leopold, a question—reduced to its simplest form—of whether John Bull, brother Jonathan, Jacques Bonhomme and Hans Schneider were to be excluded from selling goods to and buying produce from the Bayanzis, Bangalas and Bakubas of the Congo, was something immeasurably greater. In its solution the lives and liberties not of the present generation of Congo natives only, but of millions of Congo natives yet unborn; not of Congo natives alone but of the inhabitants of the African tropics as a whole were inseparably bound up.

It will be instructive to note as the story proceeds, how this simple and irrefutable economic argument, upon which I insisted, in season and out of season for years, and the truth of which is now universally recognised, was represented by the Congo Free State as proof that the Congo reform movement, and myself in particular, were inspired by base, 'commercial' motives. It was an inevitable and obvious move, of course. Not less instructive will it be to observe how Belgian Ministers, prominent Belgian Senators, Deputies, and writers, cosmopolitan jurists and continental Editors; the leaders of the French Colonial Party, and the Belgian, French and part of the German Colonial Press, derided and denounced my conclusion as the emendation of an arm-chair theorist. Even here at home, the presentation of the economic case which I had fondly imagined would command immediate acceptance and carry instant conviction, was long misunderstood, and even raised prejudice against me in many quarters, prejudices which lasted a considerable time, and were overcome in some instances only with the greatest difficulty. Again and again I found when referring to the natives' right to trade, in conversation with men I sought to interest in the Congo cause, that they became at once suspicious and aloof. Even Sir Charles Dilke and Mr. Fox Bourne queried the wisdom of my insistence upon this fundamental issue. The former, while he never doubted my bona fides, took occasion more than once to dissociate himself publicly and pointedly from what he called the 'commercial' side of the case. But he ultimately came round to my way of thinking (as did Fox Bourne) and with his usual loyalty he publicly testified to the fact in a letter published in 1908. I may, perhaps, be pardoned for giving the passage:

> Your own chief contribution to the movement, of which you are now properly the head, was that you brought to those of us who originally raised the matter, a firm grasp of a great principle really constituting the spirit of the Berlin Act. You showed us that all depended upon the right of the original black inhabitants of the soil to own their property and carry on trade.

Such, then, was the plan of campaign which commended itself to my judgement if Public Opinion as a whole was to be captured and the eman-

cipation of the Congo natives secured. As the main object of assault and
exposure, the 'Congo Free State' *itself:* not its officials in Africa and their
actions, but its constitution, its claims, its laws and its Sovereign. That attack
to be driven home by an appeal addressed to four principles: human pity the
world over: British honour: British Imperial responsibilities in Africa: international commercial rights *co-incident with and inseparable from native economic and personal liberties.*

To these ends I laboured to the best of my ability with pen and voice for
two years, making a few precious and enduring friendships, and a host of
bitter enemies. I worked in close association with Sir Charles Dilke and Mr.
Fox Bourne, gaining much help and guidance from their ripe experience of
men and things; and from the encouragement and good counsel of my old
friend Mr. John Holt and Mrs. John Richard Green, who about that time
began to honour me with a regard which I have been fortunate in retaining
and from which I have derived immeasurable advantage. [During this period,
the cause advanced with, as it seemed to me, desperate slowness, but so
steadily and surely that in 1903 Mr. Herbert Samuel's resolution was accepted
by the Unionist Government, after a debate, in which the strong feeling
which animated all Parties was remarkably exemplified, and voted by the
House of Commons without a dissentient voice.

By this first and most signal victory, to which I shall refer in detail later on,
Great Britain, through its Government, and on the strength of a mandate
proceeding from the manifestation of the will of the entire House of Commons,
became pledged to the cause of Congo emancipation. And it was with poignant if pardonable emotion that my Wife and I in our modest little home at
Hawarden, together with kind messages from Sir Charles Dilke, Mr. Herbert
Samuel, Mr. Alfred Emmott, and one or two others, read the following lines
from a friend who was present on the occasion:

> I do not think you were at the debate on the Congo. The reports do not
> do you justice and you may like to know that your name was referred to
> in the highest terms by Samuel, Dilke and Emmott, and the reference
> was warmly cheered. You were referred to as the man who knew more of
> the subject than anyone else and to whom we should all be grateful.

The story of the progress and development of the movement up to the
moment of the debate in the Commons contains many features of interest
which may now be dealt with.

SOURCE: Chapters 7 and 8 in *History of the Congo Reform Movement.* 1910–1914, edited by
William Roger Louis and Jean Stengers (Oxford: Clarendon Press, 1968), 52–69.

———

An Open Letter to
His Serene Majesty Leopold II

GEORGE WASHINGTON WILLIAMS

[George Washington Williams (1849–1891) began his career in the United States as a soldier, later becoming a minister and journalist, as well as a lawyer and politician. His career as a soldier ended on his return from Africa in 1891, but his investigations into the Belgian king's aggressions in the Congo Free State were an important part of his legacy.]

Good and Great Friend,

I have the honour to submit for your Majesty's consideration some reflections respecting the Independent State of Congo, based upon a careful study and inspection of the country and character of the personal Government you have established upon the African Continent.

In order that you may know the truth, the whole truth, and nothing but the truth, I implore your most gracious permission to address you without restraint, and with the frankness of a man who feels that he has a duty to perform to *History, Humanity, Civilization* and to the *Supreme Being,* who is himself the "King of Kings."

Your Majesty will testify to my affection for your person and friendship for your African State, of which you have had ample practical proofs for nearly six years. My friendship and service for the State of Congo were inspired by and based upon your publicly declared motives and aims, and your personal statement to your humble subscriber:—humane sentiments and work of Christian civilization for Africa. Thus I was led to regard your enterprise as the rising of the Star of Hope for the Dark Continent, so long the habitation of cruelties; and I journeyed in its light and laboured in its hope. All the praisefull things I have spoken and written of the Congo country, State and Sovereign, was inspired by the firm belief that your Government was built upon the enduring foundation of *Truth, Liberty, Humanity* and *Justice.*

It afforded me great pleasure to avail myself of the opportunity afforded me last year, of visiting your State in Africa; and how thoroughly I have been disenchanted, disappointed and disheartened, it is now my painfull duty to make known to your Majesty in plain but respectful language. Every charge which I am about to bring against your Majesty's personal Government in the Congo has been carefully investigated; a list of competent and veracious witnesses, documents, letters, official records and data has been faithfully prepared, which will be deposited with Her Brittanic Majesty's Secretary of State for Foreign Affairs, until such time as an International Commission can be created with power to send for persons and papers, to administer oaths, and attest the truth or falsity of these charges.

I crave your Majesty's indulgence while I make a few preliminary remarks before entering upon the specifications and charges.

Your Majesty's title to the territory of the State of Congo is badly clouded, while many of the treaties made with the natives by the "Association Internationale du Congo," of which you were Director and Banker, were tainted by frauds of the grossest character. The world may not be surprised to learn that your flag floats over territory to which your Majesty has no legal or just claim, since other European Powers have doubtful claims to the territory which they occupy upon the African Continent; but all honest people will be shocked to know by what grovelling means this fraud was consummated.

There were instances in which Mr. Henry M. Stanley sent one white man, with four or five Zanzibar soldiers, to make treaties with native chiefs. The staple argument was that the white man's heart had grown sick of the wars and rumours of war between one chief and another, between one village and another; that the white man was at peace with his black brother, and desired to "confederate all African tribes" for the general defense and public welfare. All the sleight-of-hand tricks had been carefully rehearsed, and he was now ready for his work. A number of electric batteries had been purchased in London, and when attached to the arm under the coat, communicated with a band of ribbon which passed over the palm of the white brother's hand, and when he gave the black brother a cordial grasp of the hand the black brother was greatly surprised to find his white brother so strong, that he nearly knocked him off his feet in giving him the hand of fellowship. When the native inquired about the disparity of strength between himself and his white brother, he was told that the white man could pull up trees and perform the most prodigious feats of strength. Next came the lens act. The white brother took from his pocket a cigar, carelessly bit off the end, held up his glass to the sun and complaisantly smoked his cigar to the great amazement and terror of his black brother. The white man explained his intimate relation to the sun, and declared that if he were to request him to burn up his black brother's village it would be done. The third act was the gun trick. The white man took a percussion cap gun, tore the end of the paper which held the powder to the bullet, and poured the powder and paper into the gun, at the same time slipping the bullet into the sleeve of the left arm. A cap was placed upon the nipple of the gun, and the black brother was implored to step off ten yards and shoot at his white brother to demonstrate his statement that he was a spirit, and, therefore, could not be killed. After much begging the black brother aims the gun at his white brother, pulls the trigger, the gun is discharged, the white man stoops. . . . and takes the bullet from his shoe!

By such means as these, too silly and disgusting to mention, and a few boxes of gin, whole villages have been signed away to your Majesty.

In your personal letter to the President of the Republic of the United States of America, bearing date of August 1st, 1885, you said that the possessions of the International Association of the Congo will hereafter form the Independent State of the Congo. "I have at the same time the honour to inform you and the Government of the Republic of the United States of America that, authorised by the Belgian Legislative Chambers to become the Chief of the new State, I have taken, in accord with the Association, the title of Sovereign of the Independent State of Congo." Thus you assumed the headship of the State of Congo, and at once organised a personal Government. You have named its officers, created its laws, furnished its finances, and every act of the Government has been clothed with the majesty of your authority.

On the 25th of February 1884, a gentleman, who has sustained an intimate relation to your Majesty for many years, and who then wrote as expressing your sentiments, addressed a letter to the United States in which the following language occurs:—"It may be safely asserted that no barbarous people have ever so readily adopted the fostering care of benevolent enterprise, as have the tribes of the Congo, and never was there a more honest and practical effort made to increase their knowledge and secure their welfare." The letter, from which the above is an excerpt, was written for the purpose of securing the friendly action of the Committee on Foreign Relations, which had under consideration a Senate Resolution in which the United States recognised the flag of the "Association Internationale du Congo" as the flag of a friendly Government. The letter was influential, because it was supposed to contain the truth respecting the natives, and the programme, not only of the Association, but of the new State, its legitimate successor, and of your Majesty.

When I arrived in the Congo, I naturally sought for the results of the brilliant programme:—"*fostering care,*" "*benevolent enterprise,*" an "*honest and practical effort*" to increase the knowledge of the natives "*and secure their welfare.*" I had never been able to conceive of Europeans, establishing a government in a tropical country, without building a hospital; and yet from the mouth of the Congo River to its head-waters, here at the seventh cataract, a distance of 1,448 miles, there is not a solitary hospital for Europeans, and only three sheds for sick Africans in the service of the State, not fit to be occupied by a horse. Sick sailors frequently die on board their vessels at Banana Point; and if it were not for the humanity of the Dutch Trading

Company at that place—who have often opened their private hospital to the sick of other countries—many more might die. There is not a single chaplain in the employ of your Majesty's Government to console the sick or bury the dead. Your white men sicken and die in their quarters or on the caravan road, and seldom have christian burial. With few exceptions, the surgeons of your Majesty's government have been gentlemen of professional ability, devoted to duty, but usually left with few medical stores and no quarters in which to treat their patients. The African soldiers and labourers of your Majesty's Government fare worse than the whites, because they have poorer quarters, quite as bad as those of the natives; and in the sheds, called hospitals, they languish upon a bed of bamboo poles without blankets, pillows or any food different from that served to them when well, rice and fish.

I was anxious to see to what extent the natives had *"adopted the fostering care"* of your Majesty's "benevolent enterprise" (?), and I was doomed to bitter disappointment. Instead of the natives of the Congo "adopting the fostering care" of your Majesty's Government, they everywhere complain that their land has been taken from them by force; that the Government is cruel and arbitrary, and declare that they neither love nor respect t[h]e Government and its flag. Your Majesty's Government has sequestered their land, burned their towns, stolen their property, enslaved their women and children, and committed other crimes too numerous to mention in detail. It is natural that they everywhere shrink from *"the fostering care"* your Majesty's Government so eagerly proffers them.

There has been, to my absolute knowledge, no *"honest and practical effort made to increase their knowledge and secure their welfare."* Your Majesty's Government has never spent one franc for educational purposes, nor institu[t]ed any practical system of industrialism. Indeed the most unpractical measures have been adopted *against* the natives in nearly every respect; and in the capital of your Majesty's Government at Boma there is not a native employed. The labour system is radically unpractical; the soldiers and labourers of your Majesty's Government are very largely imported from Zanzibar at a cost of £10 *per capita*, and from Sierre Leone, Liberia, Accra and Lagos at from £1 to £1/10.-*per capita*. These recruits are transported under circumstances more cruel than cattle in European countries. They eat their rice twice a day by the use of their fingers; they often thirst for water when the season is dry; they are exposed to the heat and rain, and sleep upon the damp and filthy decks of the vessels often so closely crowded as to lie in human ordure. And, of course, many die.

Upon the arrival of the survivors in the Congo they are set to work as labourers at one shilling a day; as soldiers they are promised sixteen shillings per month, in English money, but are usually paid off in cheap handkerchiefs and poisonous gin. The cruel and unjust treatment to which these people are subjected breaks the spirits of many of them, makes them distrust and despise your Majesty's Government. They are enemies, not patriots.

There are from sixty to seventy officers of the Belgian army in the service of your Majesty's Government in the Congo of whom only about thirty are at their post; the other half are in Belgium on furlough. These officers draw double pay,—as soldiers and as civilians. It is not my duty to criticise the unlawful and unconstitutional use of these officers coming into the service of this African State. Such criticism will come with more grace from some Belgian statesman, who may remember that there is no constitutional or organic relation subsisting between his Government and the purely personal and absolute monarchy your Majesty has established in Africa. But I take the liberty to say that many of these officers are too young and inexperienced to be entrusted with the difficult work of dealing with native races. They are ignorant of native character, lack wisdom, justice, fortitude and patience. They have estranged the natives from your Majesty's Government, have sown the seed of discord between tribes and villages, and some of them have stained the uniform of the Belgian officer with murder, arson and robbery. Other officers have served the State faithfully, and deserve well of their Royal Master.

Of the unwise, complicated and stupid dual Government of the State of Congo I cannot say much in this letter, reserving space for a careful examination of it in another place. I may say that the usefullness of many a Congo official is neutralised by having to keep a useless set of books. For example: an officer is in command of a station and he wishes to buy two eggs. He makes this entry in a ruled and printed book: "For nourishment bought two eggs for two Ntaka." In another book he must make this entry: "Two Ntaka gone out of the store." And in another book he must enter this purchase *seven times!* Comment upon such supreme folly is unnecessary. We need only feel compassion for the mental condition of the man in Brussels who invented this system, and deep sympathy with its victims in the Congo.

From these general observations I wish now to pass to specific charges against your Majesty's Government.

First.—Your Majesty's Government is deficient in the moral, military and financial strength, necessary to govern a territory of 1,508,000 square miles, 7,251 miles of navigation, and 31,694 square miles of lake surface. In the Lower Congo river there is but one post, in the cataract region one. From Leopoldville to N'Gombe, a distance of more than 300 miles, there is not a single soldier or civilian. Not one out of every twenty State-officials know the language of the natives, although they are constantly issuing laws, difficult even for Europeans, and expect the natives to comprehend and obey them. Cruelties of the most astounding character are practised by the natives, such as burying slaves alive in the grave of a dead chief, cutting off the heads of captured warriors in native combats, and no effort is put forth by your Majesty's Government to prevent them. Between 800 and 1,000 slaves are sold to be eaten by the natives of the Congo State annually; and slave raids, accomplished by the most cruel and murderous agencies, are carried on within the territorial limits of your Majesty's Government which is impotent. There are only 2,300 soldiers in the Congo.

Second.—Your Majesty's Government has established nearly fifty posts, consisting of from two to eight mercenary slave-soldiers from the East Coast. There is no white commissioned officer at these posts; they are in charge of the black Zanzibar soldiers, and the State expects them not only to sustain themselves, but to raid enough to feed the garrisons where the white men are stationed. These piratical, buccaneering posts compel the natives to furnish them with fish, goats, fowls, and vegetables at the mouths of their muskets; and whenever the natives refuse to feed these vampires, they report to the main station and white officers come with an expeditionary force and burn away the homes of the natives. These black soldiers, many of whom are slaves, exercise the power of life and death. They are ignorant and cruel, *because* they do not comprehend the natives; they are imposed upon them by the State. They make no reports as to the number of robberies they commit, or the number of lives they take; they are only required to subsist upon the natives and thus relieve your Majesty's Government of the cost of feeding them. They are the greatest curse the country suffers now.

Third.—Your Majesty's Government is guilty of violating its contracts made with its soldiers, mechanics and workmen, many of whom are subjects of other Governments. Their letters never reach home.

Fourth.—The Courts of your Majesty's Government are abortive, unjust, partial and delinquent. I have personally witnessed and examined their clumsy operations. The laws printed and circulated in Europe "for the protection of the blacks" in the Congo, are a dead letter and a fraud. I have heard an officer of the Belgian Army pleading the cause of a white man of low degree who had been guilty of beating and stabbing a black man, and urging race distinctions and prejudices as good and sufficient reasons why his client should be adjudged innocent. I know of prisoners remaining in custody for six and ten months because they were not judged. I saw the white servant of the Governor-General, Camille Janssen, detected in stealing a bottle of wine from a hotel table. A few hours later the Procurer-General searched his room and found many more stolen bottles of wine and other things, not the property of servants. No one can be prosecuted in the State of Congo without an order of the Governor-General, and as he refused to allow his servant to be arrested, nothing could be done. The black servants in the hotel, where the wine had been stolen, had been often accused and beaten for these thefts, and now they were glad to be vindicated. But to the surprise of every honest man, the thief was sheltered by the Governor-General of your Majesty's Government.

Fifth.—Your Majesty's Government is excessively cruel to its prisoners, condemning them, for the slightest offences, to the chain gang, the like of which cannot be seen in any other Government in the civilised or uncivilised world. Often these ox-chains eat into the necks of the prisoners and produce sores about which the flies circle, aggravating the running wound; so the prisoner is constantly worried. These poor creatures are frequently beaten with a dried piece of hippopotamus skin, called a "chicote," and usually the blood flows at every stroke when well laid on. But the cruelties visited upon soldiers and workmen are not to be compared with the sufferings of the poor natives who, upon the slightest pretext, are thrust into the wretched prisons here in the Upper River. I cannot deal with the dimensions of these prisons in this letter, but will do so in my report to my Government.

Sixth.—Women are imported into your Majesty's Government for immoral purposes. They are introduced by two methods, viz, black men are dispatched to the Portuguese coast where they engage these women as mistresses of white men, who pay to the procurer a monthly sum. The other method is by capturing native women and condemning them to seven years' servitude for some imaginary crime against the State with which the villages of these women are charged. The State then hires these women out to the highest bidder, the officers having the first choice and then the men. Whenever children are born of such relations, the State maintains that the woman being its property the child belongs to it also. Not long ago a Belgian trader had a child by a slave-woman of the State, and he tried to secure possession of it that he might educate it, but the Chief of the Station where he resided, refused to be moved by his entreaties. At length he appealed to the Governor-General, and he gave him the woman and thus the trader obtained the child also. This was, however, an unusual case of generosity and clemency; and there is only one post that I know of where there is not to be found children of the civil and military officers of your Majesty's Government abandoned to degradation; white men bringing their own flesh and blood under the lash of a most cruel master, the State of Congo.

Seventh.—Your Majesty's Government is engaged in trade and commerce, competing with the organised trade companies of Belgium, England, France, Portugal and Holland. It taxes all trading companies and exempts its own goods from export-duty, and makes many of its officers ivory-traders, with the promise of a liberal commission upon all they can buy or get for the State. State soldiers patrol many villages forbidding the natives to trade with any person but a State official, and when the natives refuse to accept the price of the State, their goods are seized by the Government that promised them "protection." When natives have persisted in trading with the trade-companies the State has punished their independence by burning the villages in the vicinity of the trading houses and driving the natives away.

Eighth.—Your Majesty's Government has violated the General Act of the Conference of Berlin by firing upon native canoes; by confiscating the property of natives; by intimidating native traders, and preventing them from trading with white trading companies; by quartering troops in native villages when there is no war; by causing vessels bound from "Stanley-Pool" to "Stanley-Falls," to break their journey and leave the Congo, ascend the Aruhwimi river to Basoko, to be visited and show their papers; by forbidding a mission steamer to fly its national flag without permission from a local government; by permitting the natives to carry on the slave-trade, and by engaging in the wholesale and retail slave-trade itself.

Ninth.—Your Majesty's Government has been, and is now, guilty of waging unjust and cruel wars against natives, with the hope of securing slaves and women, to minister to the behests of the officers of your Government. In such slave-hunting raids one village is armed by the State against the other, and the force thus secured is incorporated with the regular troops. I have no adequate terms with which to depict to your Majesty the brutal acts of your soldiers upon such raids as these. The soldiers who open the combat are usually the bloodthirsty cannibalistic Bangalas, who give no quarter to the aged grandmother or nursing child at the breast of its mother. There are instances in which they have brought the heads of their victims to their white officers on the expeditionary steamers, and afterwards eaten the bodies of slain children. In one war two Belgian Army officers saw, from the deck of their steamer, a native in a canoe some distance away. He was not a combatant and was ignorant of the conflict in progress upon the shore, some distance away. The officers made a wager of £5 that they could hit the native with their rifles. Three shots were fired and the native fell dead, pierced through the head, and the trade canoe was transformed into a funeral barge and floated silently down the river.

In another war, waged without just cause, the Belgian Army officer in command of your Majesty's forces placed the men in two or three lines on the steamers and instructed them to commence firing when the whistles blew. The steamers approached the fated town, and, as was usual with them, the people came to the shore to look at the boats and sell different articles of food. There was a large crowd of men, women and children, laughing, talking and exposing their goods for sale. At once the shrill whistles of the steamers were heard, the soldiers levelled their guns and fired, and the people fell dead, and wounded, and groaning, and pleading for mercy. Many prisoners were made, and among them four comely looking young women. And now ensued a most revolting scene: your Majesty's officers quarreling over the selection of these women. The commander of this murderous expedition, with his garments stained with innocent blood, declared, that his rank entitled him to the first choice! Under the direction of this same officer the prisoners were reduced to servitude, and I saw them working upon the plantation of one of the stations of the State.

Tenth.—Your Majesty's Government is engaged in the slave-trade, wholesale and retail. It buys and sells and steals slaves. Your Majesty's Government gives £3 per head for able-bodied slaves for military service. Officers at the chief stations get the men and receive the money when they are transferred to the State; but there are some middle-men who only get from twenty to twenty-five francs per head. Three hundred and sixteen slaves were sent down the river recently, and others are to follow. These poor natives are sent hundreds of miles away from their villages, to serve among other natives whose language they do not know. When these men run away a reward of 1,000 N'taka is offered. Not long ago such a re-captured slave was given one hundred "chikote" each day until he died. Three hundred N'taka-brassrod is the price the State pays for a slave, when bought from a native. The labour force at the stations of your Majesty's Government in the Upper River is composed of slaves of all ages and both sexes.

Eleventh.—Your Majesty's Government has concluded a contract with the Arab Governor at this place for the establishment of a line of military posts from the Seventh Cataract to Lake Tanganyika, territory to which your Majesty has no more legal claim, than I have to be Commander-in-Chief of the Belgian army. For this work the Arab Governor is to receive five hundred stands of arms, five thousands kegs of powder, and £20,000 sterling, to be paid in several installments. As I write, the news reaches me that these much-treasured and long-looked for materials of war are to be discharged at Basoko, and the Resident here is to be given the discretion as to the distribution of them. There is a feeling of deep discontent among the Arabs here, and they seem to feel that they are being trifled with. As to the significance of this move Europe and America can judge without any comment from me, especially England.

Twelfth.—The agents of your Majesty's Government have misrepresented the Congo country and the Congo railway. Mr. H. M. Stanley, the man who was your chief agent in setting up your authority in this country, has grossly misrepresented the character of the country. Instead of it being fertile and productive it is sterile and unproductive. The natives can scarcely subsist upon the vegetable life produced in some parts of the country. Nor will this condition of affairs change until the native shall have been taught by the European the dignity, utility and blessing of labour. There is no improvement among the natives, because there is an impassable gulf between them and your Majesty's Government, a gulf which can never be bridged. Henry M. Stanley's name produces a shudder among this simple folk when mentioned; they remember his broken promises, his copious profanity, his hot temper, his heavy blows, his severe and rigorous measures, by which they were mulcted of their lands. His last appearance in the Congo produced a profound sensation among them, when he led 500 Zanzibar soldiers with 300 campfollowers on his way to relieve Emin Pasha. They thought it meant complete subjugation, and they fled in confusion. But the only thing they found in the wake of his march was misery. No white man commanded his rear column, and his troops were allowed to straggle, sicken and die; and their bones were scattered over more than two hundred miles of territory.

Emigration cannot be invited to this country for many years. The trade of the Upper Congo consists only of ivory and rubber. The first is very old and the latter very poor. If the railway were completed now, it would not be able to earn a dividend for ten or twelve years; and as I have carefully inspected the line of the proposed road, I give it as my honest judgment that it cannot be completed for eight years. This is due to the stock-holders; they should be undeceived. I am writing a report on the Congo Railway, and will not present any data in this letter upon that subject.

CONCLUSIONS

Against the deceit, fraud, robberies, arson, murder, slave-raiding, and general policy of cruelty of your Majesty's Government to the natives, stands their record of unexampled patience, long-suffering and forgiving spirit, which put the boasted civilisation and professed religion of your Majesty's Government to the blush. During thirteen years only one white man has lost his life by the hands of the natives, and only two white men have been killed in the Congo. Major Barttelot was shot by a Zanzibar soldier, and the captain of a Belgian trading-boat was the victim of his own rash and unjust treatment of a native chief.

All the crimes perpetrated in the Congo have been done in *your* name, and *you* must answer at the bar of Public Sentiment for the misgovernment of a people, whose lives and fortunes were entrusted to you by the august Conference of Berlin, 1884–1885. I now appeal to the Powers, which committed this infant State to your Majesty's charge, and to the great States which gave it international being; and whose majestic law you have scorned and trampled upon, to call and create an International Commission to investigate the charges herein preferred in the name of Humanity, Commerce, Constitutional Government and Christian Civilisation.

I base this appeal upon the terms of Article 36 of Chapter VII of the General Act of the Conference of Berlin, in which that august assembly of Sovereign States reserved to themselves the right "to introduce into it later and by common accord the modifications or ameliorations, the utility of which may be demonstrated experience."

I appeal to the Belgian people and to their Constitutional Government, so proud of its traditions, replete with the song and story of its champions of human liberty, and so jealous of its present position in the sisterhood of European States,—to cleanse itself from the imputation of the crimes with which your Majesty's personal State of Congo is polluted.

I appeal to Anti-Slavery Societies in all parts of Christendom, to Philanthropists, Christians, Statesmen, and to the great mass of people everywhere, to call upon the Governments of Europe, to hasten the close of the tragedy your Majesty's unlimited Monarchy is enacting in the Congo.

I appeal to our Heavenly Father, whose service is perfect love, in witness of the purity of my motives and the integrity of my aims; and to history and mankind I appeal for the demonstration and vindication of the truthfulness of the charges I have herein briefly outlined.

And all this upon the word of honour of a gentleman, I subscribe myself your Majesty's humble and obedient servant.

Geo. W. Williams.
Stanley Falls, Central Africa,
July 18th, 1890.

SOURCE: Appendix 1 in John Hope Franklin, *George Washington Williams: A Biography* (Durham, N.C.: Duke University Press, 1998), 242–54.

King Leopold's Soliloquy

MARK TWAIN

A Defense of His Congo Rule

[*Throws down pamphlets which he has been reading. Excitedly combs his flowing spread of whiskers with his fingers; pounds the table with his fists; lets off brisk volleys of unsanctified language at brief intervals, repentantly drooping his head, between volleys, and kissing the Louis XI crucifix hanging from his neck, accompanying the kisses with mumbled apologies; presently rises, flushed and perspiring, and walks the floor, gesticulating*]

—— —— !! —— —— !! If I had them by the throat! [*Hastily kisses the crucifix, and mumbles*] In these twenty years I have spent millions to keep the press of the two hemispheres quiet, and still these leaks keep on occurring. I have spent other millions on religion and art, and what do I get for it? Nothing. Not a compliment. These generosities are studiedly ignored, in print. In print I get nothing but slanders—and slanders again—and still slanders, and slanders on top of slanders! Grant them true, what of it? They are slanders all the same, when uttered against a king.

Miscreants—they are telling *everything!* Oh, everything: how I went pilgriming among the Powers in tears, with my mouth full of Bible and my pelt oozing piety at every pore, and implored them to place the vast and rich and populous Congo Free State in trust in my hands as their agent, so that I might root out slavery and stop the slave raids, and lift up those twenty-five millions of gentle and harmless blacks out of darkness into light, the light of our blessed Redeemer, the light that streams from his holy Word, the light that makes glorious our noble civilization—lift them up and dry their tears and fill their bruised hearts with joy and gratitude—lift them up and make them comprehend that they were no longer outcasts and forsaken, but our very brothers in Christ; how America and thirteen great European states wept in sympathy with me, and were persuaded; how their representatives met in convention in Berlin and made me Head Foreman and Superintendent of the Congo State, and drafted out my powers and limitations, carefully guarding the persons and liberties and properties of the natives against hurt and harm; forbidding whisky traffic and gun traffic; providing courts of justice; making commerce free and fetterless to the merchants and traders of all nations, and welcoming and safe-guarding all missionaries of all creeds and denominations. They have told how I planned and prepared my establishment and selected my horde of officials—"pals" and "pimps" of mine, "unspeakable Belgians" every one—and hoisted my flag, and "took in" a President of the United States, and got him to be the first to recognize it and salute it. Oh, well, let them blackguard me if they like; it is a deep satisfaction to me to remember that I was a shade too smart for that nation that thinks itself so smart. Yes, I certainly did bunco a Yankee—as those people phrase it. Pirate flag? Let them call it so—perhaps it is. All the same, *they were the first to salute it.*

These meddlesome American missionaries! these frank British consuls! these blabbing Belgian-born traitor officials!—those tiresome parrots are always talking, always telling. They have told how for twenty years I have ruled the Congo State not as a trustee of the Powers, an agent, a subordinate, a foreman, but as a sovereign—sovereign over a fruitful domain four times as large as the German Empire—sovereign absolute, irresponsible, above all law; trampling the Berlin-made Congo charter underfoot; barring out all foreign traders but myself; restricting commerce to myself, through concessionaires who are my creatures and confederates; seizing and holding the State as my personal property, the whole of its vast revenues as my private "swag"—mine, solely mine—claiming and holding its millions of people as my private property, my serfs, my slaves; their labor mine, with or without wage; the food they raise not their property but mine; the rubber, the ivory and all the other riches of the land mine—mine solely—and gathered for me by the men, the women and the little children under compulsion of lash and bullet, fire, starvation, mutilation and the halter.

These pests!—it is as I say, they have kept back nothing! They have revealed these and yet other details which shame should have kept them silent about, since they were exposures of a king, a sacred personage and immune from reproach, by right of his selection and appointment to his great office by God himself; a king whose acts cannot be criticized without blasphemy, since God has observed them from the beginning and has manifested no dissatisfaction with them, nor shown disapproval of them, nor hampered nor interrupted them in any way. By this sign I recognize his approval of what I have done; his cordial and glad approval, I am sure I may say. Blest, crowned, beatified with this great reward, this golden reward, this unspeakably precious reward, why should I care for men's cursings and revilings of me? [*With a sudden outburst of feeling*] May they roast a million aeons in—[*Catches his breath and effusively kisses the crucifix; sorrowfully murmurs, "I shall get myself damned yet, with these indiscretions of speech."*]

Yes, they go on telling everything, these chatterers! They tell how I levy incredibly burdensome taxes upon the natives—taxes which are a pure theft;

taxes which they must satisfy by gathering rubber under hard and constantly harder conditions, and by raising and furnishing food supplies gratis—and it all comes out that, when they fall short of their tasks through hunger, sickness, despair, and ceaseless and exhausting labor without rest, and forsake their homes and flee to the woods to escape punishment, my black soldiers, drawn from unfriendly tribes, and instigated and directed by my Belgians, hunt them down and butcher them and burn their villages—reserving some of the girls. They tell it all: how I am wiping a nation of friendless creatures out of existence by every form of murder, for my private pocket's sake. But they never say, although they know it, that I have labored in the cause of religion at the same time and all the time, and have sent missionaries there (of a "convenient stripe," as they phrase it), to teach them the error of their ways and bring them to Him who is all mercy and love, and who is the sleepless guardian and friend of all who suffer. They tell only what is against me, they will not tell what is in my favor.

They tell how England required of me a Commission of Inquiry into Congo atrocities, and how, to quiet that meddling country, with its disagreeable Congo Reform Association, made up of earls and bishops and John Morleys and university grandees and other dudes, more interested in other people's business than in their own, I appointed it. Did it stop their mouths? No, they merely pointed out that it was a commission composed wholly of my "Congo butchers," "the very men whose acts were to be inquired into." They said it was equivalent to appointing a commission of wolves to inquire into depredations committed upon a sheepfold. *Nothing* can satisfy a cursed Englishman![1]

---

1. Recent information is to the effect that the resident missionaries found the commission as a whole apparently interested to promote reforms. One of its members was a leading Congo official, another an official of the government in Belgium, the third a Swiss jurist. The commission's report will reach the public only through the king, and will be whatever he consents to make it; it is not yet forthcoming, though six months have passed since the investigation was made. There is, however, abundant evidence that horrible abuses were found and conceded, the testimony of missionaries, which had been scouted by the king's defenders, being amply vindicated. One who was present at one hearing of the commission writes: "Men of stone would be moved by the stories that are being unfolded as the commission probes into the awful history of rubber collection." Certain reforms were ordered in the one section visited, but the latest word is that after the commission's departure, conditions soon became worse than before its coming. Very well, then, the king has investigated himself. One stage is achieved. The next one in order is the investigation of conditions in the Congo State *by the Powers responsible for the creation of the Congo State.* The United States is one of these. Such an investigation is advocated by Lyman Abbott, Henry Van Dyke, David Starr Jordan and other prominent citizens in petitions to the President and Congress.—M.T.

And are the fault-finders frank with my private character? They could not be more so if I were a plebian, a peasant, a mechanic. They remind the world that from the earliest days my house has been chapel and brothel combined, and both industries working full time; that I practised cruelties upon my queen and my daughters, and supplemented them with daily shame and humiliations; that, when my queen lay in the happy refuge of her coffin, and a daughter implored me on her knees to let her look for the last time upon her mother's face, I refused; and that, three years ago, not being satisfied with the stolen spoils of a whole alien nation, I robbed my own child of her property and appeared by proxy in court, a spectacle to the civilized world, to defend the act and complete the crime. It is as I have said: they are unfair, unjust; they will resurrect and give new currency to such things as those, or to any other things that count against me, but they will not mention any act of mine that is in my favor. I have spent more money on art than any other monarch of my time, and they know it. Do they speak of it, do they tell about it? No, they do not. They prefer to work up what they call "ghastly statistics" into offensive kindergarten object lessons, whose purpose is to make sentimental people shudder, and prejudice them against me. They remark that "if the innocent blood shed in the Congo State by King Leopold were put in buckets and the buckets placed side by side, the line would stretch 2000 miles; if the skeletons of his ten millions of starved and butchered dead could rise up and march in single file, it would take them seven months and four days to pass a given point; if compacted together in a body, they would occupy more ground than St. Louis covers, World's Fair and all; if they should all clap their bony hands at once, the grisly crash would be heard at a distance of—" Damnation, it makes me tired! And they do similar miracles with the money I have distilled from that blood and put into my pocket. They pile it into Egyptian pyramids; they carpet Saharas with it; they spread it across the sky, and the shadow it casts makes twilight in the earth. And the tears I have caused, the hearts I have broken—oh, nothing can persuade them to let *them* alone!

[*Meditative pause*] Well . . . no matter, I *did* beat the Yankees, anyway! there's comfort in that. [*Reads with mocking smile, the President's Order of Recognition of April 22, 1884*]

". . . the government of the United States announces its sympathy with and approval of the humane and benevolent purposes of (my Congo scheme,) and will order the officers of the United States, both on land and sea, to recognize its flag as the flag of a friendly government."

Possibly the Yankees would like to take that back, now, but they will find that my agents are not over there in America for nothing. But there is no danger; neither nations nor governments can afford to confess a blunder. [*With a contented smile, begins to read from "Report by Rev. W. M. Morrison, American missionary in the Congo Free State"*]

"I furnish herewith some of the many atrocious incidents which have come under my own personal observation; they reveal the *organized system* of plunder and outrage which has been perpetrated and is now being carried on in that unfortunate country by King Leopold of Belgium. I say King Leopold, because he and he *alone* is now responsible, since he is the *absolute sovereign. He styles himself such.* When our government in 1884 laid the foundation of the Congo Free State, by recognizing its flag, little did it know that this concern, parading under the guise of philanthropy, was really King Leopold of Belgium, one of the shrewdest, most heartless and most conscienceless rulers that ever sat on a throne. This is apart from his known corrupt morals, which have made his name and his family a byword in two continents. Our government would most certainly not have recognized that flag had it known that it was really King Leopold individually who was asking for recognition; had it known that it was setting up in the heart of Africa an *absolute monarchy;* had it known that, having put down African slavery in our own country at great cost of blood and money, it was *establishing a worse form of slavery right in Africa.*"

[*With evil joy*] Yes, I certainly was a shade too clever for the Yankees. It hurts; it gravels them. They can't get over it! Puts a shame upon them in another way, too, and a graver way; for they never can rid their records of the reproachful fact that their vain Republic, self-appointed Champion and Promoter of the Liberties of the World, is the only democracy in history that has lent its power and influence to the establishing of an *absolute monarchy!*

[*Contemplating, with an unfriendly eye, a stately pile of pamphlets*] Blister the meddlesome missionaries! They write tons of these things. They seem to be always around, always spying, always eye-witnessing the happenings; and everything they see they commit to paper. They are always prowling from place to place; the natives consider them their only friends; they go to them with their sorrows; they show them their scars and their wounds, inflicted by my soldier police; they hold up the stumps of their arms and lament because their hands have been chopped off, as punishment for not bringing in enough rubber, and as proof to be laid before my officers that the required punishment was well and truly carried out. One of these missionaries saw eighty-one of these hands drying over a fire for transmission to my officials—and of course he must go and set it down and print it. They travel and travel, they spy and spy! And nothing is too trivial for them to print. [*Takes up a pamphlet. Reads a passage from Report of a "Journey made in July, August and September, 1903, by Rev. A. E. Scrivener, a British missionary"*]

". . . . Soon we began talking, and without any encouragement on my part the natives began the tales I had become so accustomed to. They were living in peace and quietness when the white men came in from the lake with all sorts of requests to do this and that, and they thought it meant slavery. So they attempted to keep the white men out of their country but without avail. The rifles were too much for them. So they submitted and made up their minds to do the best they could under the altered circumstances. First came the command to build houses for the soldiers, and this was done without a murmur. Then they had to feed the soldiers and all the men and women—hangers on—who accompanied them. Then they were told to bring in rubber. This was quite a new thing for them to do. There was rubber in the forest several days away from their home, but that it was worth anything was news to them. A small reward was offered and a rush was made for the rubber. 'What strange white men, to give us cloth and beads for the sap of a wild vine.' They rejoiced in what they thought their good fortune. But soon the reward was reduced until at last they were told to bring in the rubber for nothing. To this they tried to demur; but to their great surprise several were shot by the soldiers, and the rest were told, with many curses and blows, to go at once or more would be killed. Terrified, they began to prepare their food for the fortnight's absence from the village which the collection of rubber entailed. The soldiers discovered them sitting about. 'What, not gone yet?' Bang! bang! bang! and down fell one and another, dead, in the midst of wives and companions. There is a terrible wail and an attempt made to prepare the dead for burial, but this is not allowed. All must go at once to the forest. Without food? Yes, without food. And off the poor wretches had to go without even their tinder boxes to make fires. Many died in the forests of hunger and exposure, and still more from the rifles of the ferocious soldiers in charge of the post. In spite of all their efforts the amount fell off and more and more were killed. I was shown around the place, and the sites of former big chiefs' settlements were pointed out. A careful estimate made the population of, say, seven years ago, to be 2,000 people in and about the post, within a radius of, say, a quarter of a mile. All told, they would not muster 200 now, and there is so much sadness and gloom about them that they are fast decreasing."

"We stayed there all day on Monday and had many talks with the people. On the Sunday some of the boys had told me of some bones which they had seen, so on the Monday I asked to be shown these bones. Lying about on the grass, within a few yards of the house I was occupying, were numbers of human skulls, bones, in some cases complete skeletons. I counted thirty-six skulls, and saw many sets of bones from which the skulls were missing. I called one of the men and asked the meaning of it. 'When the rubber palaver began,' said he, 'the soldiers shot so many we grew tired of burying, and very often we were not allowed to bury; and so just dragged the bodies out into the grass and left them. There are hundreds all around if you would like to see them.' But I had seen more than enough, and was sickened by the stories that came from men and women alike of the awful time they had passed through. The Bulgarian atrocities might be considered as mildness itself when compared with what was done here. How the people submitted I don't know, and even now I wonder as I think of their patience. That some of them managed to run away is some cause for thankfulness. I stayed there two days and the one thing that impressed itself upon me was the collection of rubber. I saw long files of men come in, as at Bongo, with their little baskets under their arms; saw them paid their milk tin full of salt, and the two yards of calico flung to the headmen; saw their trembling timidity, and in fact a great deal that all went to prove the state of terrorism that exists and the virtual slavery in which the people are held."

That is their way; they spy and spy, and run into print with every foolish trifle. And that British consul, Mr. Casement, is just like them. He gets hold of a *diary which had been kept by one of my government officers*, and, although it is a private diary and intended for no eye but its owner's, Mr. Casement is so lacking in delicacy and refinement as to print passages from it. [*Reads a passage from the diary*]

"Each time the corporal goes out to get rubber, cartridges are given him. He must bring back all not used, and for every one used he must bring back a right hand. M.P. told me that sometimes they shot a cartridge at an animal in hunting; they then cut off a hand from a living man. As to the extent to which this is carried on, he informed me that in six months the State on the Mambogo River had used 6,000 cartridges, which means that 6,000 people are killed or mutilated. It means more than 6,000, for the people have told me repeatedly that the soldiers kill the children with the butt of their guns."

When the subtle consul thinks silence will be more effective than words, he employs it. Here he leaves it to be recognized that a thousand killings and mutilations a month is a large output for so small a region as the Mambogo River concession, silently indicating the dimensions of it by accompanying his report with a map of the prodigious Congo State, in which there is not room for so small an object as that river. That silence is intended to say, "If it is a thousand a month in this little corner, imagine the output of the whole vast State!" A gentleman would not descend to these furtivenesses.

Now as to the mutilations. You can't head off a Congo critic and make him stay headed-off; he dodges, and straightway comes back at you from another direction. They are full of slippery arts. When the mutilations (severing hands, unsexing men, etc.) began to stir Europe, we hit upon the idea of excusing them with a retort which we judged would knock them dizzy on that subject for good and all, and leave them nothing more to say; to wit, we boldly laid the custom on the natives, and said we did not invent it, but only followed it. Did it knock them dizzy? did it shut their mouths? Not for an hour. They dodged, and came straight back at us with the remark that "if a Christian king can perceive a saving moral difference between inventing bloody barbarities, and *imitating them from savages,* for charity's sake let him get what comfort he can out of his confession!"

It is most amazing, the way that that consul acts—that spy, that busy-body. [*Takes up pamphlet "Treatment of Women and Children in the Congo State; what Mr. Casement Saw in 1903"*] Hardly two years ago! *Intruding* that date upon the public was a piece of cold malice. It was intended to weaken the force of my press syndicate's assurances to the public that my severities in the Congo *ceased,* and ceased utterly, *years and years ago.* This man is fond of trifles— revels in them, gloats over them, pets them, fondles them, sets them all down. One doesn't need to drowse through his monotonous report to see that; the mere sub-headings of its chapters prove it. [*Reads*]

"Two hundred and forty persons, *men, women and children,* compelled to supply government with *one ton* of carefully prepared foodstuffs *per week,* receiving in remuneration, all told, the princely sum of 15s. 10d!"

Very well, it was liberal. It was not much short of a penny a week for each nigger. It suits this consul to belittle it, yet he knows very well that I could have had both the food and the labor for nothing. I can prove it by a thousand instances. [*Reads*]

"Expedition against a village behindhand in its (compulsory) supplies; result, slaughter of sixteen persons; among them three women and a boy of five years. Ten carried off, to be prisoners till ransomed; among them a child, who died during the march."

But he is careful not to explain that we are *obliged* to resort to ransom to collect debts, where the people have nothing to pay with. Families that escape to the woods sell some of their members into slavery and thus provide the ransom. He knows that I would stop this if I could find a less objectionable way to collect their debts. . . . Mm—here is some more of the consul's delicacy! He reports a conversation he had with some natives:

Q. "How do you know it was the *white* men themselves who ordered these cruel things to be done to you? These things must have been done without the white man's knowledge by the black soldiers."

A. "The white men told their soldiers: 'You only kill *women;* you cannot kill men. You must prove that you kill men.' So then the soldiers when they killed us" (here he stopped and hesitated and then pointing to . . . he said:) "then they . . . and took them to the white men, who said: 'It is true, you have killed *men.*'"

Q. "You say this is true? Were many of you so treated after being shot?"

All [*shouting out*]: "*Nkoto! Nkoto!*" ("Very many! Very many!")

There was no doubt that these people were not inventing. Their vehemence, their flashing eyes, their excitement, were not simulated."

Of course the critic had to divulge that; he has no self-respect. All his kind reproach me, although they know quite well that I took no pleasure in punishing the men in that particular way, but only did it as a warning to other delinquents. Ordinary punishments are no good with ignorant savages; they make no impression. [*Reads more sub-heads*]

"Devasted region; population reduced from 40,000 to 8,000."

He does not take the trouble to say how it happened. He is fertile in concealments. He hopes his readers and his Congo reformers, of the Lord-Aberdeen-Norbury-John-Morley-Sir Gilbert-Parker stripe, will think they were all killed. They were not. The great majority of them escaped. They fled to the bush with their families because of the rubber raids, and it was there they died of hunger. Could we help that?

One of my sorrowing critics observes: "Other Christian rulers tax their people, but furnish schools, courts of law, roads, light, water and protection to life and limb in return; King Leopold taxes his stolen nation, but provides *nothing in return but hunger, terror, grief, shame, captivity, mutilation and massacre.*" That is their style! I furnish "nothing!" I send the gospel to the survivors; these censure-mongers know it, but they would rather have their tongues cut out than mention it. I have several times required my raiders to give the dying an opportunity to kiss the sacred emblem; and if they obeyed me I have without doubt been the humble means of saving many souls. None of my traducers have had the fairness to mention this; but let it pass; there is One who has not overlooked it, and that is my solace, that is my consolation.

[*Puts down the Report, takes up a pamphlet, glances along the middle of it*]

This is where the "death-trap" comes in. Meddlesome missionary spying around—Rev. W. H. Sheppard. Talks with a black raider of mine after a raid; cozens him into giving away some particulars. The raider remarks:

"I demanded 30 slaves from this side of the stream and 30 from the other side; 2 points of ivory, 2,500 balls of rubber, 13 goats, 10 fowls and 6 dogs, some corn chumy, etc.

'How did the fight come up?' I asked.

'I sent for all their chiefs, sub-chiefs, men and women, to come on a certain day, saying that I was going to finish all the palaver. When they entered these small gates (the walls being made of fences brought from other villages, the high native ones) I demanded all my pay or I would kill them; so they refused to pay me, and I ordered the fence to be closed so they couldn't run away; then we killed them here inside the fence. The panels of the fence fell down and some escaped.'

'How many did you kill?' I asked.

'We killed plenty, will you see some of them?'

That was just what I wanted.

He said: 'I think we have killed between eighty and ninety, and those in the other villages I don't know, I did not go out but sent my people.'

He and I walked out on the plain just near the camp. There were three dead bodies with the flesh carved off from the waist down.

'Why are they carved so, only leaving the bones?' I asked.

'My people ate them,' he answered promptly. He then explained, 'The men who have young children do not eat people, but all the rest ate them.' On the left was a big man, shot in the back and without a head. (All these corpses were nude.)

'Where is the man's head?' I asked.

'Oh, they made a bowl of the forehead to rub up tobacco and diamba in.'

We continued to walk and examine until late in the afternoon, and counted forty-one bodies. The rest had been eaten up by the people.

On returning to the camp, we crossed a young woman, shot in the back of the head, one hand was cut away. I asked why, and Mulunba N'Cusa explained that they always cut off the right hand to give to the State on their return.

'Can you not show me some of the hands?' I asked.

So he conducted us to a framework of sticks, under which was burning a slow fire, and there they were, the right hands—I counted them, eighty-one in all.

There were not less than sixty women (Bena Pianga) prisoners. I saw them.

We all say that we have as fully as possible investigated the whole outrage, and find it was a plan previously made to get all the stuff possible and to catch and kill the poor people in the 'death-trap.'"

Another detail, as we see!—cannibalism. They report cases of it with a most offensive frequency. My traducers do not forget to remark that, inasmuch as I am absolute and with a word can prevent in the Congo anything I choose to prevent, then whatsoever is done there by my permission is my act, my *personal* act; that *I* do it; that the hand of my agent is as truly *my* hand as if it were attached to my own arm; and so they picture me in my robes of state, with my crown on my head, munching human flesh, saying grace, mumbling thanks to Him from whom all good things come. Dear, dear, when the soft-hearts get hold of a thing like that missionary's contribution they quite lose their tranquility over it. They speak out profanely and reproach Heaven for allowing such a fiend to live. Meaning me. They think it irregular. They go shuddering around, brooding over the reduction of that Congo population from 25,000,000 to 15,000,000 in the twenty years of my administration; then they burst out and call me "the King with Ten Million Murders on his Soul." They call me a "record." The most of them do not stop with charging merely the 10,000,000 against me. No, they reflect that but for me the population, by natural increase, would now be 30,000,000, so they charge another 5,000,000 against me and make my total death-harvest 15,000,000. They remark that the man who killed the goose that laid the golden egg was responsible for the eggs she would subsequently have laid if she had been let alone. Oh, yes, they call me a "record." They remark that twice in a generation, in India, the Great Famine destroys 2,000,000 out of a population of 320,000,000, and the whole world holds up its hands in pity and horror; then they fall to wondering where the world would find room for its emotions if I had a chance to trade places with the Great Famine for twenty years! The idea fires their fancy, and they go on and imagine the Famine coming in state at the end of the twenty years and prostrating itself before me, saying: "Teach me, Lord, I perceive that I am but an apprentice." And next they imagine Death coming, with his scythe and hour-glass, and begging me to marry his daughter and reorganize his plant and run the business. For the whole world, you see! By this time their diseased minds are under full steam, and they get down their books and expand their labors, with me for text. They hunt through all biography for my match, working Attila, Torquemada, Ghengis Khan, Ivan the Terrible, and the rest of that crowd for all they are worth, and evilly exulting when they cannot find it. Then they examine the historical earthquakes and cyclones and blizzards and cataclysms and volcanic eruptions: verdict, none of them "in it" with me. At last they do really hit it (as they think), and they close their labors with conceding—reluctantly—that I have *one* match in history, but only one—the *Flood*. This is intemperate.

But they are always that, when they think of me. They can no more keep quiet when my name is mentioned than can a glass of water control its feelings with a seidlitz powder in its bowels. The bizarre things they can imagine, with me for an inspiration! One Englishman offers to give me the odds of three to one and bet me anything I like, up to 20,000 guineas, that for 2,000,000 years I am going to be the most conspicuous foreigner in hell. The man is so beside himself with anger that he does not perceive that the idea is foolish. Foolish and unbusinesslike: you see, there could be no winner; both of us would be losers, on account of the loss of interest on the stakes; at four or five per cent, compounded, this would amount to—I do not know how much, exactly, but, by the time the term was up and the bet payable, a person could buy hell itself with the accumulation.

Another madman wants to construct a memorial for the perpetuation of my name, out of my 15,000,000 skulls and skeletons, and is full of vindictive enthusiasm over his strange project. He has it all ciphered out and drawn to scale. Out of the skulls he will build a combined monument and mausoleum to me which shall exactly duplicate the Great Pyramid of Cheops, whose base covers thirteen acres, and whose apex is 451 feet above ground. He desires to stuff me and stand me up in the sky on that apex, robed and crowned, with my "pirate flag" in one hand and a butcher-knife and pendant handcuffs in the other. He will build the pyramid in the centre of a depopulated tract, a brooding solitude covered with weeds and the mouldering ruins of burned villages, where the spirits of the starved and murdered dead will voice their laments forever in the whispers of the wandering winds. Radiating from the pyramid, like the spokes of a wheel, there are to be forty grand avenues of approach, each thirty-five miles long, and each fenced on both sides by skul-less skeletons standing a yard and a half apart and festooned together in line by short chains stretching from wrist to wrist and attached to tried and true old handcuffs stamped with my private trade-mark, a crucifix and butcher-knife crossed, with motto, "by this sign we prosper"; each osseous fence to consist of 200,000 skeletons on a side, which is 400,000 to each avenue. It is remarked with satisfaction that it aggregates three or four thousand miles (single-ranked) of skeletons—15,000,000 all told—and would stretch across America from New York to San Francisco. It is remarked further, in the hopeful tone of a railroad company forecasting showy extensions of its mile-age, that my output is 500,000 corpses a year when my plant is running full time, and that therefore if I am spared ten years longer there will be fresh skulls enough to add 175 feet to the pyramid, making it by a long way the loftiest architectural construction on the earth, and fresh skeletons enough to continue the transcontinental file (on piles) a thousand miles into the Pacific. The cost of gathering the materials from my "widely scattered and innumer-able private graveyards," and transporting them, and building the monument and the radiating grand avenues, is duly ciphered out, running into an aggre-gate of millions of guineas, and then—why then, (— —!!— —!!) this idiot asks me *to furnish the money!* [*Sudden and effusive application of the crucifix*] He reminds me that my yearly income from the Congo is millions of guineas, and that "*only*" 5,000,000 would be required for his enterprise. Every day wild attempts are made upon my purse; they do not affect me, they cost me not a thought. But *this one*—this one troubles me, makes me nervous; for there is no telling what an unhinged creature like this may think of next. . . . *If he should think of Carnegie*—but I must banish that thought out of my mind! it worries my days; it troubles my sleep. That way lies madness. [*After a pause*] There is no other way—I have got to buy Carnegie.

[*Harassed and muttering, walks the floor a while, then takes to the Consul's chapter-headings again. Reads*]

"Government starved a woman's children to death and killed her sons."

"Butchery of women and children."

"*The native has been converted into a being without ambition because without hope.*"

"Women chained by the neck by rubber sentries."

"Women refuse to bear children because, with a baby to carry, they cannot well run away and hide from the soldiers."

"Statement of a child. 'I, my mother, my grandmother and my sister, we ran away into the bush. A great number of our people were killed by the soldiers. . . . After that they saw a little bit of my mother's head, and the soldiers ran quickly to where we were and caught my grandmother, my mother, my sister and another little one younger than us. Each wanted my mother for a wife, and argued about it, so they finally decided to kill her. They shot her through the stomach with a gun and she fell, and when I saw that I cried very much, because they killed my grandmother and mother and I was left alone. I saw it all done!'"

It has a sort of pitiful sound, although they are only blacks. It carries me back and back into the past, to when my children were little, and would fly— to the bush, so to speak—when they saw me coming. . . . [*Resumes the reading of chapter-headings of the Consul's report*]

"They put a knife through a child's stomach."
  "They cut off the hands and brought them to C.D. (white officer) and spread them out in a row for him to see."
  "Captured children left in the bush to die, by the soldiers."
  "Friends came to ransom a captured girl; but sentry refused, saying the white man wanted her because she was young."
  "Extract from a native girl's testimony. 'On our way the soldiers saw a little child, and when they went to kill it the child laughed, so the soldier took the butt of his gun and struck the child with it and then cut off its head. One day they killed my half-sister and cut off her head, hands and feet, because she had bangles on. Then they caught another sister, and sold her to the W.W. people, and now she is a slave there.'"

The little child laughed! [*A long pause. Musing*] That innocent creature. Somehow—I wish it had not laughed. [*Reads*]

"Mutilated children."
  "Government encouragement of inter-tribal slave-traffic. The monstrous fines levied upon villages tardy in their supplies of foodstuffs compel the native to sell their fellows—and children—to other tribes in order to meet the fine."
  "A father and mother forced to sell their little boy."
  "Widow forced to sell her little girl."

[*Irritated*] Hang the monotonous grumbler, what would he have me do! Let a widow off merely because she is a widow? He knows quite well that there is nothing much left, now, *but* widows. I have nothing against widows, as a class, but business is business, and I've got to live, haven't I, even if it does cause inconvenience to somebody here and there? [*Reads*]

"Men intimidated by the torture of their wives and daughters. (To make the men furnish rubber and supplies and so get their captured women released from chains and detention.) The sentry explained to me that he caught the women and brought them in (chained together neck to neck) by direction of his employer."

"An agent explained that he was forced to catch women in preference to men, as then the men brought in supplies quicker; but he did not explain how the children deprived of their parents obtained their own food supplies."

"A file of 15 (captured) women."

"Allowing women and children to die of starvation in prison."

[*Musing*] Death from *hunger*. A lingering, long misery that must be. Days and days, and still days and days, the forces of the body failing, dribbling away, little by little—yes, it must be the hardest death of all. And to see food carried by, every day, and you can have none of it! Of course the little children cry for it, and that wrings the mother's heart. . . . [*A sigh*] Ah, well, it cannot be helped; circumstances make this discipline necessary. [*Reads*]

"The crucifying of sixty women!"

How stupid, how tactless! Christendom's goose flesh will rise with horror at the news. "Profanation of the sacred emblem!" That is what Christendom will shout. Yes, Christendom will buzz. It can hear me charged with half a million murders a year for twenty years and keep its composure, but to profane the Symbol is quite another matter. It will regard this as serious. It will wake up and want to look into my record. Buzz? Indeed it will; I seem to hear the distant hum already. . . . It was wrong to crucify the women, clearly wrong, manifestly wrong, I can see it now, myself, and am sorry it happened, sincerely sorry. I believe it would have answered just as well to skin them. . . . [*With a sigh*] But none of us thought of that; one cannot think of everything; and after all it is but human to err.

It will make a stir, it surely will, these crucifixions. Persons will begin to ask again, as now and then in times past, how I can hope to win and keep the respect of the human race if I continue to give up my life to murder and pillage. [*Scornfully*] When have they heard me say I wanted the respect of the human race? Do they confuse me with the common herd? do they forget that I am a king? What king has valued the respect of the human race? I mean deep down in his private heart. If they would reflect, they would know that it is impossible that a king should value the respect of the human race. He stands upon an eminence and looks out over the world and sees multitudes of meek human things worshipping the persons, and submitting to the oppressions and exactions, of a dozen human things who are in no way better or finer than themselves—made on just their own pattern, in fact, and out of the same quality of mud. When it *talks*, it is a race of whales; but a king knows it for a race of tadpoles. Its history gives it away. If men were really *men*, how could a Czar be possible? and how could I be possible? But we *are* possible; we are quite safe; and with God's help we shall continue the business at the old stand. It will be found that the race will put up with us, in its docile immemorial way. It may pull a wry face now and then, and make large talk, but it will stay on its knees all the same.

Making large talk is one of its specialties. It works itself up, and froths at the mouth, and just when you think it is going to throw a brick—it heaves a poem! Lord, what a race it is! [*Reads*]

A Czar—1905

"A pasteboard autocrat; a despot out of date;
   A fading planet in the glare of day;
   A flickering candle in the bright sun's ray,
Burnt to the socket; fruit left too late,
   High on a blighted bough, ripe till it's rotten.

By God forsaken and by time forgotten,
Watching the crumbling edges of his lands,
   A spineless god to whom dumb millions pray,
   From Finland in the West to far Cathay,
Lord of a frost-bound continent he stands,
   Her seeming ruin his dim mind appalls,
And in the frozen stupor of his sleep
   He hears dull thunders, pealing as she falls,
   And mighty fragments dropping in the deep."[2]

It is fine, one is obliged to concede it; it is a great picture, and impressive. The mongrel handles his pen well. Still, with opportunity, I would cruci—flay him. . . . "A spineless god." It is the Czar to a dot—a god, and spineless; a royal invertebrate, poor lad; soft-hearted and out of place. "A spineless god to *whom dumb millions pray.*" Remorselessly correct; concise, too, and compact—the soul and spirit of the human race compressed into half a sentence. On their knees—140,000,000. On their knees to a little tin deity. Massed together, they would stretch away, and away, and away, across the plains, fading and dimming and failing in a measureless perspective—why, even the telescope's vision could not reach to the final frontier of that continental

2. B. H. Nadal, in *New York Times.*

spread of human servility. Now *why* should a king value the respect of the human race? It is quite unreasonable to expect it. A curious race, certainly! It finds fault with me and with my occupations, and forgets that neither of us could exist an hour without its sanction. It is our confederate and all-powerful protector. It is our bulwark, our friend, our fortress. For this it has our gratitude, our deep and honest gratitude—but not our respect. Let it snivel and fret and grumble if it likes; that is all right; we do not mind that.

[*Turns over leaves of a scrapbook, pausing now and then to read a clipping and make a comment*] The poets—how they do hunt that poor Czar! French, Germans, English, Americans—they all have a bark at him. The finest and capablest of the pack, and the fiercest, are Swinburne (English, I think), and a pair of Americans, Thomas Bailey Eldridge and Colonel Richard Waterson Gilder, of the sentimental periodical called *Century Magazine* and *Louisville Courier-Journal*. They certainly have uttered some very strong yelps. I can't seem to find them—I must have mislaid them. . . . If a poet's bite were as terrible as his bark, why dear me—but it isn't. A wise king minds neither of them; but the poet doesn't know it. It's a case of little dog and lightning express. When the Czar goes thundering by, the poet skips out and rages alongside for a little distance, then returns to his kennel wagging his head with satisfaction, and thinks he has inflicted a memorable scare, whereas nothing has really happened—the Czar didn't know he was around. They never bark at me; I wonder why that is. I suppose my Corruption-Department buys them. That must be it, for certainly I ought to inspire a bark or two; I'm rather choice material, I should say. Why—here *is* a yelp at me. [*Mumbling a poem*]

> ". . . What gives the holy right to murder hope
> And water ignorance with human blood?
>
> .   .   .
>
> From what high universe-dividing power
> Draws't thou thy wondrous, ripe brutality?
>
> .   .   .
>
> O horrible . . . Thou God who seest these things
> Help us to blot this terror from the earth."

. . . No, I see it is "To the Czar,"[3] after all. But there are those who would say it fits me—and rather snugly, too. "Ripe brutality." They would say the Czar's isn't ripe yet, but that mine is; and not merely *ripe* but rotten. Nothing could keep them from saying that; they would think it smart. "This terror." Let the Czar keep that name; I am supplied. This long time I have been "the

3. Louise Morgan Sill, in *Harper's Weekly*.

monster"; that was their favorite—the monster of crime. But now I have a
new one. They have found a fossil Dinosaur fifty-seven feet long and sixteen
feet high, and set it up in the museum in New York and labeled it "Leopold
II." But it is no matter, one does not look for manners in a republic. Um . . .
that reminds me; I have never been caricatured. Could it be that the corsairs
of the pencil could not find an offensive symbol that was big enough and ugly
enough to do my reputation justice? [*After reflection*] There is no other way—I
will buy the Dinosaur. And suppress it. [*Rests himself with some more chapter-
headings. Reads*]

"More mutilation of children." (Hands cut off.)
"Testimony of American Missionaries."
"Evidence of British Missionaries."

It is all the same old thing—tedious repetitions and duplications of shop-
worn episodes; mutilations, murders, massacres, and so on, and so on, till one
gets drowsy over it. Mr. Morel intrudes at this point, and contributes a
comment which he could just as well have kept to himself—and throws in
some italics, of course; these people can never get along without italics:

"It is one heartrending story of human misery from beginning to end,
and *it is all recent.*"

Meaning 1904 and 1905. I do not see how a person can act so. This Morel is
a king's subject, and reverence for monarchy should have restrained him from
reflecting upon me with that exposure. This Morel is a reformer; a Congo
reformer. That sizes *him* up. He publishes a sheet in Liverpool called "The
West African Mail," which is supported by the voluntary contributions of the
sap-headed and the soft-hearted; and every week it steams and reeks and
festers with up-to-date "Congo atrocities" of the sort detailed in this pile of
pamphlets here. I will suppress it. I suppressed a Congo atrocity book there,
after it was actually in print; it should not be difficult for me to suppress a
newspaper.

[*Studies some photographs of mutilated negroes—throws them down. Sighs*]
The kodak has been a sore calamity to us. The most powerful enemy that has
confronted us, indeed. In the early years we had no trouble in getting the press
to "expose" the tales of the mutilations as slanders, lies, inventions of busy-
body American missionaries and exasperated foreigners who had found the
"open door" of the Berlin-Congo charter closed against them when they
innocently went out there to trade; and by the press's help we got the Christian nations everywhere to turn an irritated and unbelieving ear to those tales
and say hard things about the tellers of them. Yes, all things went harmo-

niously and pleasantly in those good days, and I was looked up to as the benefactor of a down-trodden and friendless people. Then all of a sudden came the crash! That is to say, the incorruptible *kodak*—and all the harmony went to hell! The only witness I have encountered in my long experience that I couldn't bribe. Every Yankee missionary and every interrupted trader sent home and got one; and now—oh, well, the pictures get sneaked around everywhere, in spite of all we can do to ferret them out and suppress them. Ten thousand pulpits and ten thousand presses are saying the good word for me all the time and placidly and convincingly denying the mutilations. Then that trivial little kodak, that a child can carry in its pocket, gets up, uttering never a word, and knocks them dumb!

. . . . What is this fragment? [*Reads*]

"But enough of trying to tally off his crimes! His list is interminable, we should never get to the end of it. His awful shadow lies across his Congo Free State, and under it an unoffending nation of 15,000,000 is withering away and swiftly succumbing to their miseries. It is a land of graves; it is *The* Land of Graves; it is the Congo Free Graveyard. It is a majestic thought: that is, this ghastliest episode in all human history is the work of *one man alone;* one solitary man; just a single individual—Leopold, King of the Belgians. He is personally and solely responsible for all the myriad crimes that have blackened the history of the Congo State. He is *sole* master there; he is absolute. He could have prevented the crimes by his mere command; he could stop them today with a word. He withholds the word. For his pocket's sake.

It seems strange to see a king destroying a nation and laying waste a country for mere sordid money's sake, and solely and only for that. Lust of conquest is royal; kings have always exercised that stately vice; we are used to it, by old habit we condone it, perceiving a certain dignity in it; but *lust of money—lust of shillings—lust of nickels—lust of dirty coin,* not for the nation's enrichment but for *the king's alone*—this is new. It distinctly revolts us, we cannot seem to reconcile ourselves to it, we resent it, we despise it, we say it is shabby, unkingly, out of character. Being democrats we ought to jeer and jest, we ought to rejoice to see the purple dragged in the dirt, but—well, account for it as we may, we don't. We see this awful king, this pitiless and blood-drenched king, this money-crazy king towering toward the sky in a world-solitude of sordid crime, unfellowed and apart from the human race, sole butcher for personal gain findable in all his caste, ancient or modern, pagan or Christian, proper and legitimate target for the scorn of the lowest and the highest, and the execrations of all who hold in cold esteem the oppressor and the coward; and—well, it is a mystery, but *we do not wish to look;* for he is a king, and it hurts us, it troubles us, by ancient and inherited instinct it shames us to see a king degraded to this aspect, and we shrink from hearing the particulars of how it happened. We *shudder* and *turn away* when we come upon them in print."

Why, certainly—*that* is my protection. And you will continue to do it. I know the human race.

SOURCE: [1905] In *Life As I Find It*, ed. Charles Neider (Garden City, N.J.: Hanover House, 1961), 275–95.

Excerpts from *The Crime of the Congo*
SIR ARTHUR CONAN DOYLE

CHAPTER 6
VOICES FROM THE DARKNESS

I will now return to the witnesses of the shocking treatment of the natives. Rev. Joseph Clark was an American missionary living at Ikoko in the Crown Domain, which was King Leopold's own special private preserve. These letters cover the space between 1893 and 1899.

This is Ikoko as he found it in 1893:

"Irebo contains say 2,000 people. Ikoko has at least 4,000, and there are other towns within easy reach, several as large as Irebo, and two probably as large as Ikoko. The people are fine-looking, bold and active."

In 1903 there were 600 people surviving.

In 1894 Ikoko in the Crown Domain began to feel the effects of King Leopold's system. On May 30th of that year Mr. Clark writes:

"Owing to trouble with the State the Irebo people fled and left their homes. Yesterday the State soldiers shot a sick man who had not attempted to run away, and others have been killed by the State (native) soldiers, who, in the absence of a white man, do as they please."

In November, 1894:

"At Ikoko quite a number of people have been killed by the soldiers, and most of the others are living in the bush."

In the same month he complained officially to Commissaire Fievez:

"If you do not come soon and stop the present trouble the towns will be empty. . . . I entreat you to help us to have peace on the Lake. . . . It seems so hard to see the dead bodies in the creek and on the beach, and to know why they are killed. . . . People living in the bush like wild beasts without shelter or proper food; and afraid to make fires. Many died in this way. One woman ran away with three children—they all died in the forest, and the woman herself came back a wreck and died before long—ruined by exposure and starvation. We knew her well. My hope was to get the facts put before King Leopold, as I was sure he knew nothing of the awful conditions of the collection of the so-called 'rubber tax.' "

On November 28th he writes:

"The State soldiers brought in seven hands, and reported having shot the people in the act of running away to the French side. . . . We found all that the soldiers had reported was untrue, and that the statements made by the natives to me were true. We saw only six bodies; a seventh had evidently fallen into the water, and we learned in a day or two that an eighth body had floated into the landing-place above us—a woman that had either been thrown or had fallen into the water after being shot."

On December 5th he says:

"A year ago we passed or visited between here and Ikoko the following villages:

Probable population	
Lobwaka	250
Boboko	250
Bosungu	100
Kenzie	150
Bokaka	200
Mosenge	150
Ituta	80
Ngero	2,000
Total	3,180

"A week ago I went up, and only at Ngero were there any people: there we found ten. Ikoko did not contain over twelve people other than those employed by Frank. Beyond Ikoko the case is the same."

April 12th, 1895, he writes:

"I am sorry that rubber palavers continue. Every week we hear of some fighting, and there are frequent 'rows,' even in our village, with the armed and unruly soldiers. . . . During the past twelve months it has cost more lives than native wars and superstition would have sacrificed in three to five years. The people make this comparison among themselves. . . . It seems incredible and awful to think of these savage men armed with rifles and let loose to hunt and kill people, because they do not get rubber to sell at a mere nothing to the State, and it is blood-curdling to see them returning with hands of the slain and to find the hands of young children, among bigger ones, evidencing their 'bravery.'"

The following was written on May 3rd, 1895:

"The war is on account of rubber. The State demands that the natives shall make rubber and sell same to its agents at a very low price. The natives do not like it. It is hard work and very poor pay, and takes them away from their homes into the forest, where they feel very unsafe, as there are always feuds among them. . . . The rubber from this district has cost hundreds of lives, and the scenes I have witnessed while unable to help the oppressed have been almost enough to make me wish I were dead. The soldiers are themselves savages, some even cannibals, trained to use rifles, and in many cases they are sent away without supervision, and they do as they please. When they come to any town no man's property or wife is safe, and when they are at war they are like devils.

"Imagine them returning from fighting some 'rebels'; see, on the bow of the canoe is a pole and a bundle of something on it. . . . These are the hands (right hands) of sixteen warriors they have slain. 'Warriors!' Don't you see among them the hands of little children and girls? I have seen them. I have seen where even the trophy has been cut off while yet the poor heart beat strongly enough to shoot the blood from the cut arteries to a distance of fully four feet.

"A young baby was brought here one time; its mother was taken prisoner, and before her eyes they threw the infant in the water to drown it. The soldiers coolly told me and my wife that their white man did not want them to bring infants to their place. They dragged the woman off and left the infant beside us, but we sent the child to its mother, and said we would report the matter to the chief of the post. We did so, but the men were not punished. The principal offender was told before me he would get fifty lashes, but I heard the same mouth send a message to say he would not be flogged."

Compare with this the following extracts from King Leopold's Bulletin Officiel, referring to this very tract of country:

"The exploitation of the rubber vines of this district was undertaken barely three years ago by M. Fievez. The results he obtained have been unequalled. The district produced in 1895 more than 650 tons of rubber, bought (sic) for ½d. (European price), and sold at Antwerp for 5s.5d. per kilo (2 lbs.)."

A later bulletin adds:

"With this development of general order is combined an inevitable amelioration in the native's condition of existence wherever he comes into contact with the European element."

"Such is, in fact, one of the ends of the general policy of the State, to promote the regeneration of the race by instilling into him a higher idea of the necessity of labour."

Truly, I know nothing in history to match such documents as these—pirates and bandits have never descended to that last odious abyss of hypocrisy. It stands alone, colossal in its horror, colossal, too, in its effrontery.

A few more anecdotes from the worthy Mr. Clark. This is an extract from a letter to Mueller, the Chief of the District:

"There is a matter I want to report to you regarding the Nkake sentries. You remember some time ago they took eleven canoes and shot some Ikoko people. As a proof they went to you with some hands, of which three were the hands of little children. We heard from one of their paddlers that one child was not dead when its hand was cut off, but did not believe the story. Three days after we were told the child was still alive in the bush. I sent four of my men to see, and they brought back a little girl whose right hand had been cut off, and she left to die from the wound. The child had no other wound. As I was going to see Dr. Reusens about my own sickness I took the child to him, and he has cut the arm and made it right, and I think she will live. But I think such awful cruelty should be punished."

Mr. Clark still clung to the vain hope that King Leopold did not know of the results of his own system. On March 25th, 1896, he writes:

"This rubber traffic is steeped in blood, and if the natives were to rise and sweep every white person on the Upper Congo into eternity there would still be left a fearful balance to their credit. Is it not possible for some American of influence to see the King of the Belgians, and let him know what is being done in his name? The Lake is reserved for the King—no traders allowed—and to collect rubber for him hundreds of men, women and children have been shot."

At last the natives, goaded beyond endurance, rose against their oppressors. Who can help rejoicing that they seem to have had some success:

Extracts from letter-book, commencing 29th January, 1897:

"The native uprising.—This was brought about at last by sentries robbing and badly treating an important chief. In my presence he laid his complaint before M. Mueller, reporting the seizure of his wives and goods and the personal violence he had suffered at the hands of M. Mueller's soldiers stationed in his town. I saw M. Mueller kick him off his verandah. Within forty-eight hours there were no 'sentries' or their followers left in that chief's town—they were killed and utilized—and soon after M. Mueller, with another white officer and many soldiers, were killed, and the revolt began."

Such is some of the evidence, a very small portion of the whole narrative furnished by Mr. Clark. Remember that it is extracted from a long series of letters written to various people during a succession of years. One could conceive a single statement being a concoction, but the most ingenious apologist for the Congo methods could not explain how such a document as this could be other than true.

So much for Mr. Clark, the American. The evidence of Mr. Scrivener, the Englishman, covering roughly the same place and date, will follow. But lest the view should seem too Anglo-Saxon, let me interpolate a paragraph from the travels of a Frenchman, M. Leon Berthier, whose diary was published by the Colonial Institute of Marseilles in 1902:

"Belgian post of Imesse well constructed. The Chef de Poste is absent. He has gone to punish the village of M'Batchi, guilty of being a little late in paying the rubber tax. . . . A canoe full of Congo State soldiers returns from the pillage of M'Batchi. . . . Thirty killed, fifty wounded. . . . At three o'clock arrive at M'Batchi, the scene of the bloody punishment of the Chef de Poste at Imesse. Poor village! The debris of miserable huts. . . . One goes away humiliated and saddened from these scenes of desolation, filled with indescribable feelings."

In showing the continuity of the Congo horror and the extent of its duration (an extent which is the shame of the great Powers who acquiesced in it by their silence), I have marshalled witnesses in their successive order. Messrs. Glave, Murphy and Sjoblom have covered the time from 1894 to 1897, Mr. Clark has carried it on to 1900; we have had the deeds of 1901–4 as revealed in the Boma Law Courts. I shall now give the experience of Rev. Mr. Scrivener, an English missionary, who in July, August and September, 1903, traversed a section of the Crown Domain, that same region specially assigned to King Leopold in person, in which Mr. Clark had spent such nightmare years. We shall see how far the independent testimony of the Englishman and the American, the one extracted from a diary, the other from a succession of letters, corroborate each other.

"At six in the morning woke up to find it still raining. It kept on till nine, and we managed to get off by eleven. All the cassava bread was finished the day previous, so a little rice was cooked, but it was a hungry crowd that left the little village. I tried to find out something about them. They said they were runaways from a district a little distance away, where rubber was being collected. They told us some horrible tales of murder and starvation, and when we heard all we wondered that men so maltreated should be able to live without retaliation. The boys and girls were naked, and I gave them each a strip of calico, much to their wonderment.

"Four hours and a half brought us to a place called Sa. . . . On the way we passed two villages with more people than we had seen for days. There may have been 120. Close to the post was another small village. We decided to stay there the rest of the day. Three chiefs came in with all the adult members of their people, and altogether there were not 300. And this where, not more than six or seven years ago, there were at least 3,000! It made one's heart heavy to listen to the tales of bloodshed and cruelty. And it all seemed so foolish. To kill the people off in the wholesale way in which it has been done in this Lake district, because they would not bring in a sufficient quantity of rubber to satisfy the white men—and now here is an empty country and a very much diminished output of rubber as the inevitable consequence."

Finally Mr. Scrivener emerged in the neighbourhood of a large State station. He was hospitably received, and had many chats with his host, who seems to have been a good-hearted man, doing his best under very trying circumstances. His predecessor had worked incalculable havoc in the country; and the present occupant of the post was endeavouring to carry out the duties assigned to him (those duties consisting, as usual, in orders to get all the rubber possible out of the people) with as much humanity as the nature of the task permitted. In this he, no doubt, did what was possible. But he had only succeeded in getting himself into trouble with the district commander in consequence. He showed Mr. Scrivener a letter from the latter upbraiding him for not using more vigorous means, telling him to talk less and shoot more, and reprimanding him for not killing more than one man in a district under his care where there was a little trouble.

Mr. Scrivener had the opportunity while at this State post under the rule of a man who was endeavouring to be as humane as his instructions allowed, to actually see the process whereby the secret revenues of the "Crown Domain," are obtained. He says:

"Everything was on a military basis, but, so far as I could see, the one and only reason for it all was rubber. It was the theme of every conversation, and it was evident that the only way to please one's superiors was to increase the output somehow. I saw a few men come in, and the frightened look even now on their faces tells only too eloquently of the awful time they have passed through. As I saw it brought in, each man had a little basket, containing, say, four or five pounds of rubber. This was emptied into a larger basket and weighed, and being found sufficient, each man was given a cupful of coarse salt and to some of the headmen a fathom of calico. . . . I heard from the white men and some of the soldiers some most gruesome stories. The former white man (I feel ashamed of my colour every time I think of him) would stand at the door of the store to receive the rubber from the poor trembling wretches who after, in some cases, weeks of privation in the forest, had ventured in with what they had been able to collect. A man bringing rather under the proper amount, the white man flies into a rage, and seizing a rifle from one of the guards, shoots him dead on the spot. Very rarely did rubber come in but one or more were shot in that way at the door of the store—'to make the survivors bring more next time.' Men who had tried to run from the country and had been caught, were brought to the station and made to stand one behind the other, and an Albini bullet sent through them. 'A pity to waste cartridges on such wretches.' Only the roads to and fro from the various posts are kept open, and large tracts of country are abandoned to the wild beasts. The white man himself told me that you could walk for five days in one direction, and not see a single village or a single human being. And this where formerly there was a big tribe!

"As one by one the surviving relatives of my men arrived, some affecting scenes were enacted. There was no falling on necks and weeping, but very genuine joy was shown and tears were shed as the losses death had made were told. How they shook hands and snapped their fingers! What expressions of surprise—the wide-opened mouth covered with the open hand to make its evidence of wonder the more apparent. . . . So far as the State post was concerned, it was in a very dilapidated condition. . . . On three sides of the usual huge quadrangle there were abundant signs of a former population, but we only found three villages—bigger, indeed, than any we had seen before, but sadly diminished from what had been but recently the condition of the place. . . . Soon we began talking, and, without any encouragement on my part, they began the tales I had become so accustomed to. They were living in peace and quietness when the white men came in from the Lake with all sorts of requests to do this and to do that, and they thought it meant slavery. So they attempted to keep the white men out of their country, but without avail. The rifles were too much for them. So they submitted, and made up their minds to do the best they could under the altered circumstances. First came the command to build houses for the soldiers, and this was done without a murmur. Then they had to feed the soldiers, and all the men and women— hangers-on—who accompanied them.

"Then they were told to bring in rubber. This was quite a new thing for them to do. There was rubber in the forest several days away from their home, but that it was worth anything was news to them. A small reward was offered, and a rush was made for the rubber; 'What strange white men, to give us cloth and beads for the sap of a wild vine.' They rejoiced in what they thought was their good fortune. But soon the reward was reduced until they were told to bring in the rubber for nothing. To this they tried to demur, but to their great surprise several were shot by the soldiers, and the rest were told, with many curses and blows, to go at once or more would be killed. Terrified, they began to prepare their food for the fortnight's absence from the village, which the collection of the rubber entailed. The soldiers discovered them sitting about. 'What, not gone yet!' Bang! bang! bang! bang! And down fell one and another, dead, in the midst of wives and companions. There is a terrible wail, and an attempt made to prepare the dead for burial, but this is not allowed. All must go at once to the forest. And off the poor wretches had to go, without even their tinder-boxes to make fires. Many died in the forests from exposure and hunger, and still more from the rifles of the ferocious soldiers in charge of the post. In spite of all their efforts, the amount fell off, and more and more were killed.

"I was shown round the place, and the sites of former big chiefs' settlements were pointed out. A careful estimate made the population, of say, seven years ago, to be 2,000 people in and about the post, within a radius of, say, a quarter of a mile. All told, they would not muster 200 now, and there is so much sadness and gloom that they are fast decreasing. . . . Lying about in the grass, within a few yards of the house I was occupying, were numbers of human bones, in some cases complete skeletons. I counted thirty-six skulls, and saw many sets of bones from which the skulls were missing. I called one of the men, and asked the meaning of it. 'When the rubber palaver began,' said he, 'the soldiers shot so many we grew tired of burying, and very often we were not allowed to bury, and so just dragged the bodies out into the grass and left them. There are hundreds all round if you would like to see them.' But I had seen more than enough, and was sickened by the stories that came from men and women alike of the awful time they had passed through. The Bulgarian atrocities might be considered as mildness itself when compared with what has been done here.

"In due course we reached Ibali. There was hardly a sound building in the place. . . . Why such dilapidation? The Commandant away for a trip likely to extend into three months, the sub-lieutenant away in another direction on a punitive expedition. In other words the station must be neglected, and rubber-hunting carried out with all vigour. I stayed here two days, and the one thing that impressed itself upon me was the collection of rubber. I saw long files of men come, as at Mbongo, with their little baskets under their arms,

saw them paid their milk-tin full of salt, and the two yards of calico flung
to the headmen; saw their trembling timidity, and a great deal more, to prove
the state of terrorism that exists, and the virtual slavery in which the people
are held.

"So much for the journey to the Lake. It has enlarged my knowledge of the
country, and also, alas! my knowledge of the awful deeds enacted in the mad
haste of men to get rich. So far as I know, I am the first white man to go into
the Domaine Privé of the King, other than the employees of the State. I
expect there will be wrath in some quarters, but that cannot be helped."

So far Mr. Scrivener. But perhaps the reader may think that there really was
a missionary plot to decry the Free State. Let us have some travellers, then.
Here is Mr. Grogan from his "Cape to Cairo":

"The people were terrorized and were living in marshes." This was on the
British frontier. "The Belgians have crossed the frontier, descended into
the valley, shot down large numbers of natives, British subjects, driven off the
young women and cattle, and actually tied up and burned the old women. I do
not make these statements without having gone into the matter. I remarked
on the absence of women and the reason was given. It was on further inquiry
that I was assured by the natives that white men had been present when the
old women had been burned. . . . They even described to me the personal
appearance of the white officers with the troops. . . . The wretched people
came to me and asked me why the British had deserted them."

Further on he says:

"Every village had been burned to the ground, and as I fled from the
country I saw skeletons, skeletons everywhere. And such postures! What tales
of horror they told."

Just a word in conclusion from another witness, Mr. Herbert Frost:

"The power of an armed soldier among these enslaved people is absolutely
paramount. By chief or child, every command, wish, or whim of the soldier
must be obeyed or gratified. At his command with rifle ready a man will. . . .
outrage his own sister, give to his persecutor the wife he loves most of all, say
or do anything, indeed, to save his life. The woes and sorrows of the race
whom King Leopold has enslaved have not decreased, for his Commissaires,
officers and agents have introduced and maintain a system of devilry hitherto
undreamed of by his victims."

Does this all seem horrible? But in the face of it is there not something
more horrible in a sentence of this king?—

"Our only programme, I am anxious to repeat, is the work of moral and
material regeneration, and we must do this among a population whose degen-
eration in its inherited conditions it is difficult to measure. The many horrors

and atrocities which disgrace humanity give away little by little before our intervention."

It is King Leopold who speaks.

CHAPTER 7
CONSUL ROGER CASEMENT'S REPORT

Up to this time the published reports as to the black doings of King Leopold and his men were, with the exception of a guarded document from Consul Pickersgill, in 1898, entirely from private individuals. No doubt there were official letters, but the Government withheld them. In 1904, this policy of reticence was abandoned, and the historic report of Consul Roger Casement confirmed, and in some ways amplified, all that had reached Europe from other sources.

A word or two as to Mr. Casement's own personality and qualifications may not be amiss, since both were attacked by his Belgian detractors. He is a tried and experienced public servant, who has had exceptional opportunities of knowing Africa and the natives. He entered the Consular service in 1892, served on the Niger till 1895, was Consul at Delagoa Bay to 1898, and was finally transferred to the Congo. Personally, he is a man of the highest character, truthful, unselfish—one who is deeply respected by all who know him. His experience which deals with the Crown Domain districts in the year 1903, covers some sixty-two pages, to be read in full in "White Book Africa, No. 1, 1904." I will not apologize for the length of the extracts, as this, the first official exposure, was a historical document, and from its publication we mark the first step in that train of events which is surely destined to remove the Congo State from hands which have proved so unworthy, and to place it in conditions which shall no longer be a disgrace to European civilization. It may be remarked before beginning that at some of these conversations with the natives Mr. Scrivener was present, and that he corroborates the account given by the Consul.

The beginning of Mr. Casement's report shows how willing he was to give praise where praise was possible, and to say all that could be said for the Administration. He talks of "energetic European intervention," and adds, "that very much of this intervention has been called for no one who formerly knew the Upper Congo could doubt." "Admirably built and admirably kept stations greet the traveller at many points." "To-day the railway works most efficiently." He attributes sleeping sickness as "one cause of the seemingly wholesale diminution of human life which I everywhere observed in the regions revisited. The natives certainly attribute their alarming death-rate to this as one of the inducing causes, although they attribute, and I think principally, their rapid decrease in numbers to other causes as well."

The Government workshop "showed brightness, care, order, and activity, and it was impossible not to admire and commend the industry which had created and maintained in constant working order this useful establishment."

These are not the words of a critic who has started with a prejudiced mind or the desire to make out a case.

In the lower reaches of the river above Stanley Pool Casement found no gross ill-usage. The natives were hopeless and listless, being debarred from trade and heavily taxed in food, fish and other produce. It was not until he began to approach the cursed rubber zones that terrible things began to dawn upon him. Casement had travelled in 1887 in the Congo; and was surprised to note the timidity of the natives. Soon he had his explanation.

"At one of these villages, after confidence had been restored and the fugitives had been induced to come in from the surrounding forest, where they had hidden themselves, I saw women coming back carrying their babies, their household utensils, and even the food they had hastily snatched up, up to a late hour of the evening. Meeting some of these returning women in one of the fields I asked them why they had run away at my approach, and they said, smiling, 'We thought you were Bula Matadi' (i.e., 'men of the Government'). Fear of this kind was formerly unknown on the Upper Congo; and in much more out-of-the-way places visited many years ago the people flocked from all sides to greet a white stranger. But today the apparition of a white man's steamer evidently gave the signal for instant flight.'

"Men, he said, still came to him whose hands had been cut off by the Government soldiers during those evil days, and he said there were still many victims of this species of mutilation in the surrounding country. Two cases of the kind came to my actual notice while I was on the lake. One, a young man, both of whose hands had been beaten off with the butt-ends of rifles against a tree, the other a young lad of eleven or twelve years of age, whose right hand was cut off at the wrist. This boy described the circumstances of his mutilation, and, in answer to my inquiry, said that although wounded at the time he was perfectly sensible of the severing of his wrist, but lay still fearing that if he moved he would be killed. In both these cases the Government soldiers had been accompanied by white officers whose names were given to me. Of six natives (one a girl, three little boys, one youth, and one old woman) who had been mutilated in this way during the rubber regime, all except one were dead at the date of my visit. The old woman had died at the beginning of this year, and her niece described to me how the act of mutilation in her case had been accomplished."

The fines inflicted upon villages for trifling offences were such as to produce the results here described:

"The officer had then imposed as further punishment a fine of 55,000 brass rods (2,750 fr.)—£110. This sum they had been forced to pay, and as they had no other means of raising so large a sum they had, many of them, been compelled to sell their children and their wives. I saw no live-stock of any kind in W— save a very few fowls—possibly under a dozen—and it seemed, indeed, not unlikely that, as these people asserted, they had great difficulty in always getting their supplies ready. A father and mother stepped out and said that they had been forced to sell their son for 1,000 rods to meet their share of the fine. A widow came and declared that she had been forced, in order to meet her share of the fine, to sell her daughter, a little girl whom I judged from her description to be about ten years of age. She had been sold to a man in Y—, who was named, for 1,000 rods, which had then gone to make up the fine."

The natives were broken in spins by the treatment.

"One of them—a strong, indeed, a splendid-looking man broke down and wept, saying that their lives were useless to them, and that they knew of no means of escape from the troubles which were gathering around them. I could only assure these people that their obvious course to obtain relief was by appeal to their own constituted authorities, and that if their circumstances were clearly understood by those responsible for these fines, I trusted and believed some satisfaction would be forthcoming."

These fines, it may be added, were absolutely illegal. It was the officer, not the poor harried natives, who had broken the law.

"These fines, it should be borne in mind, are illegally imposed; they are not 'fines of Court'; are not pronounced after any judicial hearing, or for any proved offence against the law, but are quite arbitrarily levied according to the whim or ill-will of the executive officers of the district, and their collection, as well as their imposition, involves continuous breaches of the Congolese laws. They do not, moreover, figure in the account of public revenues in the Congo 'Budgets'; they are not paid into the public purse of the country, but are spent on the needs of the station or military camp of the officer imposing them, just as seems good to this official."

Here is an illustrative anecdote:

"One of the largest Congo Concession Companies had, when I was on the Upper River, addressed a request to its Directors in Europe for a further supply of ball-cartridge. The Directors had met this demand by asking what had become of the 72,000 cartridges shipped some three years ago, to which a reply was sent to the effect that these had all been used in the production of india-rubber. I did not see this correspondence, and cannot vouch for the truth of the statement; but the officer who informed me that it had passed before his own eyes was one of the highest standing in the interior."

Another witness showed the exact ratio between cartridges and rubber:

"The S. A. B. on the Bussira, with 150 guns, get only ten tons (rubber) a month; we, the State, at Momboyo, with 130 guns, get thirteen tons per month.' 'So you count by guns?' I asked him. 'Partout,' M. P. said. 'Each time the corporal goes out to get rubber cartridges are given to him. He must bring back all not used; and for every one used, he must bring back a right hand.' M. P. told me that sometimes they shot a cartridge at an animal in hunting, they then cut off a hand from a living man. As to the extent to which this is carried on, he informed me that in six months they, the State, on the Momboyo River, had used 6,000 cartridges, which means that 6,000 people are killed or mutilated. It means more than 6,000, for the people have told me repeatedly that the soldiers kill children with the butt of their guns."

That the statement about the cutting off of living hands is correct is amply proved by the Kodak. I have photographs of at least twenty such mutilated negroes in my own possession.

Here is a copy of a dispatch from an official quoted in its naked frankness:

"Le Chef Ngulu de Wangata est envoyé dans la Maringa, pour m'y acheter des esclaves. Prière à MM. les agents de A.B.I.R. de bien vouloir me signaler les méfaits que celui-ci pourrait commettre en route.

"Le Capitaine-Commandant,
(Signé) "SARRAZZYN."
"Colquilhaiville, le 1er Mai, 1896."

Pretty good for the State which boasts that it has put down the slave trade.

There is a passage showing the working of the rubber system which is so clear and authoritative that I transcribe it in full:

"I went to the homes of these men some miles away and found out their circumstances. To get the rubber they had first to go fully a two days' journey from their homes, leaving their wives, and being absent for from five to six days. They were seen to the forest limits under guard, and if not back by the sixth day trouble was likely to ensue. To get the rubber in the forests—which, generally speaking, are very swampy—involves much fatigue and often fruitless searching for a well-flowing vine. As the area of supply diminishes, moreover, the demand for rubber constantly increases. Some little time back I learned the Bongandanga district supplied seven tons of rubber a month, a quantity which it was hoped would shortly be increased to ten tons. The quantity of rubber brought by the three men in question would have represented, probably, for the three of them certainly not less than seven kilog. of pure rubber. That would be a very safe estimate, and at an average of 7fr. per kilog. they might be said to have brought in £2 worth of rubber. In return for this labour, or imposition, they had received goods which cost certainly under 1s., and whose local valuation came to 45 rods (1s. 10d.). As this process repeats itself twenty-six times a year, it will be seen that they would have yielded £52 in kind at the end of the year to the local factory, and would have received in return some 24s. or 25s. worth of goods, which had a market value on the spot of £2 7s. 8d. In addition to these formal payments they were liable at times to be dealt with in another manner, for should their work, which might have been just as hard, have proved less profitable in its yield of rubber, the local prison would have seen them. The people everywhere assured me that they were not happy under this system, and it was apparent to a callous eye that in this they spoke the strict truth."

Again I insert a passage to show that Casement was by no means an ill-natured critic:

"It is only right to say that the present agent of the A.B.I.R. Society I met at Bongandanga seemed to me to try, in very difficult and embarrassing circumstances, to minimize as far as possible, and within the limits of his duties, the evils of the system I there observed at work."

Speaking of the Mongalla massacres—those in which Lothaire was implicated—he quotes from the judgment of the Court of Appeal:

"That it is just to take into account that, by the correspondence produced in the case, the chiefs of the Concession Company have, if not by formal orders, at least by their example and their tolerance, induced their agents to take no account whatever of the rights, property, and lives of the natives; to use the arms and the soldiers which should have served for their defence and the maintenance of order to force the natives to furnish them with produce and to work for the Company, as also to pursue as rebels and outlaws those who sought to escape from the requisitions imposed upon them. . . . That, above all, the fact that the arrest of women and their detention, to compel the villages to furnish both produce and workmen, was tolerated and admitted even by certain of the administrative authorities of the region."

Yet another example of the workings of the system:

"In the morning, when about to start for K—, many people from the surrounding country came in to see me. They brought with them three individuals who had been shockingly wounded by gun fire, two men and a very small boy, not more than six years of age, and a fourth—a boy child of six or seven—whose right hand was cut off at the wrist. One of the men, who had been shot through the arm, declared that he was Y of L—, a village situated some miles away. He declared that he had been shot as I saw under the following circumstances: the soldiers had entered his town, he alleged, to enforce the due fulfilment of the rubber tax due by the community. These men had tied him up and said that unless he paid 1,000 brass rods to them they would shoot him. Having no rods to give them they had shot him through the arms and had left him."

I may say that among my photographs are several with shattered arms who have been treated in this fashion.

This is how the natives were treated when they complained to the white man:

"In addition, fifty women are required each morning to go to the factory and work there all day. They complained that the remuneration given for these services was most inadequate, and that they were continually beaten. When I asked the Chief W. why he had not gone to D F to complain if the sentries beat him or his people, opening his mouth he pointed to one of the teeth which was just dropping out, and said: 'That is what I got from D F four days ago when I went to tell him what I now say to you.' He added that he was frequently beaten along with others of his people, by the white man."

One sentry was taken almost red-handed by Mr. Casement.

"After some little delay a boy of about fifteen years of age appeared, whose left arm was wrapped up in a dirty rag. Removing this, I found the left hand had been hacked off by the wrist, and that a shot hole appeared in the fleshy part of the forearm. The boy, who gave his name as II, in answer to my inquiry, said that a sentry of the Lulanga Company now in town had cut off his hand. I proceeded to look for this man, who at first could not be found, the natives to a considerable number gathering behind me as I walked through the town. After some delay the sentry appeared, carrying a cap-gun. The boy, whom I placed before him, then accused him to his face of having mutilated him. The men of the town, who were questioned in succession, corroborated the boy's statement. The sentry, who gave his name as KK, could make no answer to the charge. He met it by vaguely saying some other sentry of the Company had mutilated II; his predecessor, he said, had cut off several hands, and probably this was one of the victims. The natives around said that there were two other sentries at present in town, who were not so bad as KK, but that he was a villain. As the evidence against him was perfectly clear, man after man standing out and declaring he had seen the act committed, I informed him and the people present that I should appeal to the local authorities for his immediate arrest and trial."

Such is the story—or a very small portion of it—which His Majesty's Consul conveyed to His Majesty's Government as to the condition of those

"*The Guilt of Delay.*" Congo Slave-Driver.
"I'm all right. They're still talking."
SOURCE: *Punch* 313 (24 November 1909): 137.

natives, whom, "in the name of Almighty God," we had pledged ourselves to defend!

The same damning White Book contained a brief account of Lord Cromer's experience upon the Upper Nile in the Lado district. He notes that for eighty miles the side of the river which is British territory was crowded with native villages, the inhabitants of which ran along the bank calling to the steamer. The other bank (Congolese territory), was a deserted wilderness. The "Tu quoque" argument which King Leopold's henchmen are so fond of advancing will find it hard to reconcile the difference. Lord Cromer ends his report:

"It appears to me that the facts which I have stated above afford amply sufficient evidence of the spirit which animates the Belgian Administration, if, indeed, Administration it can be called. The Government so far as I could judge, is conducted almost exclusively on commercial principles, and, even judged by that standard, it would appear that those principles are somewhat short-sighted."

In the same White Book which contains these documents there is printed the Congolese defence drawn up by M. de Cuvelier. The defence consists in simply ignoring all the definite facts laid before the public, and in making such statements as that the British have themselves made war upon natives, as if there were no distinction between war and massacre, and that the British have put a poll-tax upon natives, which, if it be reasonable in amount, is a perfectly just proceeding adopted by all Colonial nations. Let the possessors of the Free State use this system, and at the same time restore the freedom of trade by throwing open the country to all, and returning to the natives that land and produce which has been taken from them. When they have done this—and punished the guilty—there will be an end of anti-Congo agitation. Beyond this, a large part (nearly half) of the Congo Reply (notes sur le rapport de Mr. Casement, de Dec. 11, 1903) is taken up by trying to show that in one case of mutilation the injuries were, in truth, inflicted by a wild boar. A glance at the photographs which preface this book will show that there must be many wild boars in Congoland, and that their habits are of a singular nature. It is not in the Congo that these boars are bred.

source: Chapters 6 and 7 in *The Crime of the Congo* (London: Hutchinson, 1909), 46–67.

INDEX

BARBARA HARLOW is the Louann and Larry Temple
Centennial Professor of English at the University of Texas, Austin.
MIA CARTER is an associate professor of English at the
University of Texas, Austin. They are coeditors of *Imperialism
and Orientalism: A Documentary Sourcebook.*

Library of Congress Cataloging-in-Publication Data
Archives of Empire: volume II. the scramble for
Africa / edited by Barbara Harlow and Mia Carter.
Includes bibliographical references and index.
ISBN 0-8223-3176-4 (cloth : alk. paper : v. 1)
ISBN 0-8223-3164-0 (pbk. : alk. paper : v. 1)
1. Great Britain—Colonies—History—Sources. I. Harlow,
Barbara. II. Carter, Mia.
DA16.A73 2003   909'.0971241—dc21   2003010580